GREGG

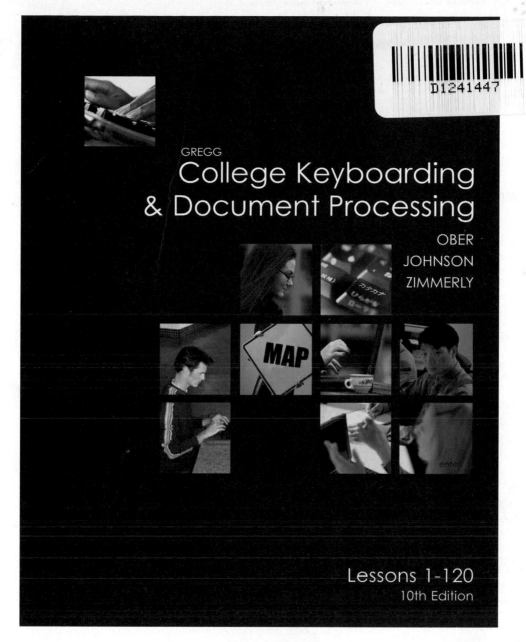

College Keyboarding & Document Processing

OBER
JOHNSON
ZIMMERLY

MAP

Lessons 1-120
10th Edition

Scot Ober
Ball State University

Jack E. Johnson
State University of West Georgia

Arlene Zimmerly
Los Angeles City College

Visit the *College Keyboarding* Web site at **www.mhhe.com/gdp**

Boston Burr Ridge, IL Dubuque, IA Madison, WI New York San Francisco St. Louis
Bangkok Bogotá Caracas Kuala Lumpur Lisbon London Madrid Mexico City
Milan Montreal New Delhi Santiago Seoul Singapore Sydney Taipei Toronto

The McGraw·Hill Companies

GREGG COLLEGE KEYBOARDING & DOCUMENT PROCESSING, LESSONS 1-120
Published by McGraw-Hill/Irwin, a business unit of The McGraw-Hill Companies, Inc., 1221 Avenue of the Americas, New York, NY, 10020.

Some ancillaries, including electronic and print components, may not be available to customers outside the United States.

This book is printed on acid-free paper.

Printed in China

5 6 7 8 9 0 SDB/SDB 0 9 8 7

ISBN-13: 978-0-07-296338-0
ISBN-10: 0-07-296338-7

Editorial director: *John E. Biernat*
Publisher: *Linda Schreiber*
Sponsoring editor: *Doug Hughes*
Developmental editor: *Tammy Higham*
Developmental editor: *Megan Gates*
Marketing manager: *Keari Bedford*
Lead producer, Media technology: *Victoria Bryant*
Lead project manager: *Pat Frederickson*
Freelance project manager: *Rich Wright*
Senior production supervisor: *Michael R. McCormick*
Lead designer: *Matthew Baldwin*
Photo research coordinator: *Lori Kramer*
Senior supplement producer: *Susan Lombardi*
Senior digital content specialist: *Brian Nacik*
Cover design: *Subtle Intensity*
Interior design: *Matthew Baldwin*
Typeface: *11/12 Times Roman*
Compositor: *Seven Worldwide Publishing Solutions*
Printer: *Shenzhen Donnelley Printing Co., Ltd.*

www.mhhe.com

CONTENTS

PART ONE: The Alphabet, Number, and Symbol Keys

PART TWO Basic Business Documents

PART THREE: Reports, Correspondence, and Employment Documents

PART FOUR: Advanced Formatting

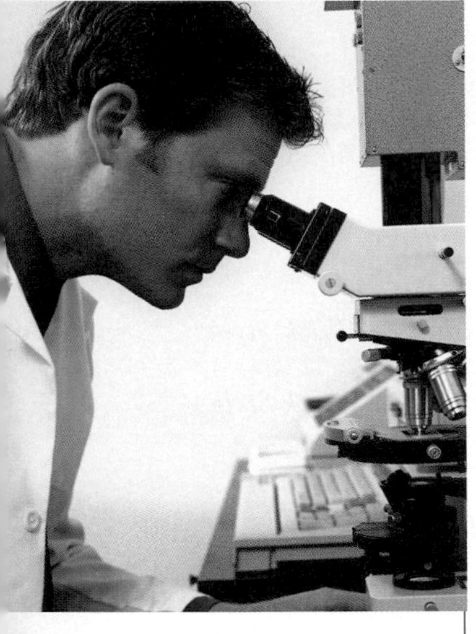

PART FIVE: Specialized Applications

PART SIX: Using and Designing Business Documents

ABOUT KEYBOARDING

Each day the world becomes more and more technologically advanced. As a result, learning new skills for the world of work is even more important.

One such skill that can prepare you for virtually any job in the world is keyboarding. From accountants to zoologists and every occupation in between, the ability to quickly and accurately type information is an essential skill that can increase your chances of being hired (or getting your dream job).

Formerly referred to as "typing," keyboarding is the act of entering data by means of designated computer keys. Today, as we rely more and more on computers to handle everyday work and leisure activities, the ability to accurately convey information is a necessity. So, whether you are e-mailing a relative, developing a class presentation, or downloading map directions, keyboarding knowledge can make the job easier.

PREFACE

Gregg College Keyboarding & Document Processing Lessons 1–120, 10th Edition, is a multi-component instructional program designed to give the student and the instructor a high degree of flexibility and a high degree of success in meeting their respective goals. For student and instructor convenience, the core components of this instructional system are available in either a kit format or a book format. *Gregg College Keyboarding Lessons 1–20, 10th Edition,* is also available for the development of touch-typing skills for use in shorter computer keyboarding classes.

The Kit Format

Gregg College Keyboarding & Document Processing Lessons 1–120, 10th Edition, provides a complete kit of materials for both courses in the keyboarding curriculum generally offered by colleges. Each kit, which is briefly described below, contains a softcover textbook and a student word processing manual.

Kit 1: Lessons 1–60. This kit provides the text and word processing manual for the first course. Since this kit is designed for the beginning student, its major objectives are to develop touch control of the keyboard and proper typing techniques, to build basic speed and accuracy, and to provide practice in applying those basic skills to the formatting of reports, letters, memos, tables, and other kinds of personal and business communications.

Kit 2: Lessons 61–120. This kit provides the text and word processing manual for the second course. This course continues developing of basic typing skills and emphasizes the formatting of various kinds of business correspondence, reports, tables, electronic forms, and desktop publishing projects from arranged, unarranged, and rough-draft sources.

The Book Format

For the convenience of those who wish to obtain the core instructional materials in separate volumes, *Gregg College Keyboarding & Document Processing Lessons 1–120, 10th Edition,* offers textbooks for the first course: *Gregg College Keyboarding & Document Processing Lessons 1–60, 10th Edition,* or *Gregg College Keyboarding Lessons 1–20, 10th Edition.* For the second course, *Gregg College Document Processing Lessons 61–120* is offered, and for the two-semester course, *Gregg College Keyboarding & Document Processing Lessons 1–120* is available. In each instance, the content of the textbooks is identical to that of the corresponding textbooks in kit format. Third semester instruction is available in *Gregg College Document Processing Lessons 121–180.*

Supporting Materials

Gregg College Keyboarding & Document Processing Lessons 1–120, 10th Edition, includes the following additional components:

Instructional Materials. Supporting materials are provided for instructor use with either the kits or the textbooks. The special Instructor Wraparound Edition (IWE) offers lesson plans and reduced-size student pages to enhance classroom instruction. Distance-learning tips, instructional methodology, adult learner strategies, and special needs features are also included in this wraparound edition. Solution keys for all of the formatting exercises in Lessons 1–180 are contained in separate booklets used with this program. Finally, test booklets are available with the objective tests and alternative document processing tests for each part.

Computer Software. PC-compatible computer software is available for the entire program. The computer software provides complete lesson-by-lesson instruction for the entire 120 lessons.

Structure

Gregg College Keyboarding & Document Processing, 10th Edition, opens with a two-page part opener that introduces students to the focus of the instruction. Objectives are presented, and opportunities within career clusters are highlighted. The unit opener familiarizes students with the lesson content to be presented in the five lessons in the unit.

Every lesson begins with a Warmup that should be typed as soon as students are settled at the keyboard. In the New Keys Section, all alphabet, number, and symbol keys are introduced in the first 20 lessons. Drill lines in this section provide the practice necessary to achieve keyboarding skills.

An easily identifiable Skillbuilding section can be found in every lesson. Each drill presents to the student a variety of different activities designed to improve speed and accuracy. Skillbuilding exercises include Technique Timings, Diagnostic Practice, Paced Practice, Progressive Practice, MAP (Misstroke Analysis and Prescription), and Timed Writings, which progress from 1 to 5 minutes in length.

Many of the Skillbuilding sections also include a Pretest/Practice/Posttest routine. This routine is designed to build speed and accuracy skills as well as confidence. The Pretest helps identify speed and accuracy needs. The Practice activities consist of a variety of intensive enrichment drills. Finally, the Posttest measures improvement.

Part 1

The Alphabet, Number, and Symbol Keys

Keyboarding in Arts, Audio, Video Technology, and Communications Services

Occupations in this cluster deal with organizing and communicating information to the public in various forms and media. This cluster includes jobs in radio and television broadcasting, journalism, motion pictures, the recording industry, the performing arts, multimedia publishing, and the entertainment services. Book editors, computer artists, technical writers, radio announcers, news correspondents, and camera operators are just a few jobs within this cluster.

Qualifications and Skills

Strong oral and written communication skills and technical skills are necessary for anyone in communications and media. Without a doubt, competent keyboarding skill is extremely advantageous.

Working in the media requires creativity, talent, and accurate use of language. In journalism, being observant, thinking clearly, and seeing the significance of events are all of utmost importance. Announcers must have exceptional voices, excellent speaking skills, and a unique style. The ability to work under pressure is important in all areas of media.

Objectives

KEYBOARDING

- Operate by touch the letter, number, and symbol keys.
- Demonstrate proper typing technique.
- Use the correct spacing with punctuation.
- Type at least 28 words per minute on a 2-minute timed writing with no more than 5 errors.

TECHNICAL

- Answer correctly at least 90 percent of the questions on an objective test.

1

Goals

- Type at least 30wpm/3'/5e
- Format one-page business reports

Starting a Lesson

Each lesson begins with the goals for that lesson. Read the goals carefully so that you understand the purpose of your practice. In the example at the left (from Lesson 26), the goals for the lesson are to type 30wpm (words per minute) on a 3-minute timed writing with no more than 5 errors and to format one-page business reports.

Building Straight-Copy Skill

Warmups. Each lesson begins with a Warmup that reinforces learned alphabet, number, and/or symbol keys.

Skillbuilding. The Skillbuilding portion of each lesson includes a variety of drills to individualize your keyboarding speed and accuracy development. Instructions for completing the drills are always provided beside each activity.

Additional Skillbuilding drills are included in the back of the textbook. These drills are intended to help you meet your individual goals.

Measuring Straight-Copy Skill

Straight-copy skill is measured in wpm. All timed writings are the exact length needed to meet the speed goal for the lesson. If you finish a timed writing before time is up, you have automatically reached your speed goal for the lesson.

Counting Errors. Specific criteria are used for counting errors. Count an error when:

1. Any stroke is incorrect.
2. Any punctuation after a word is incorrect or omitted. Count the word before the punctuation as incorrect.
3. The spacing after a word or after its punctuation is incorrect. Count the word as incorrect.
4. A letter or word is omitted.
5. A letter or word is repeated.
6. A direction about spacing, indenting, and so on, is violated.
7. Words are transposed.

(**Note:** Only one error is counted for each word, no matter how many errors it may contain.)

Determining Speed. Typing speed is measured in wpm. To compute wpm, count every 5 strokes, including spaces, as 1 "word." Horizontal word scales below an activity divide lines into 5-stroke words. Vertical word scales beside an activity show the number of words in each line cumulatively totaled. For example, in the illustration below, if you complete a line, you have typed 8 words. If you complete 2 lines, you have typed 16 words. Use the bottom word scale to determine the word count of a partial line. Add that number to the cumulative total for the last complete line.

```
23 Ada lost her letter; Dee lost her card.          8
24 Dave sold some of the food to a market.         16
25 Alva asked Walt for three more matches.         24
26 Dale asked Seth to watch the last show.         32
   | 1 | 2 | 3 | 4 | 5 | 6 | 7 | 8 |
```

Correcting Errors

As you learn to type, you will probably make some errors. To correct an error, press BACKSPACE (shown as ← on some keyboards) to delete the incorrect character. Then type the correct character.

If you notice an error on a different line, use the up, down, left, or right arrows to move the insertion point immediately to the left or right of the error. Press BACKSPACE to delete a character to the left of the insertion point, or DELETE to delete a character to the right of the insertion point. Error-correction settings in the GDP software determine whether you can correct errors in timed writings and drills. Consult your instructor for error-correction guidelines.

Typing Technique

Correct position at the keyboard enables you to type with greater speed and accuracy and with less fatigue. When typing for a long period, rest your eyes occasionally by looking away from the screen. Change position, walk around, or stretch when your muscles feel tired. Making such movements and adjustments may help prevent your body from becoming too tired. In addition, long-term bodily damage, such as carpal tunnel syndrome, can be prevented.

If possible, adjust your workstation as follows:

Chair. Adjust the height so that your upper and lower legs form a 90-degree angle and your lower back is supported by the back of the chair.
Keyboard. Center your body opposite the J key, and lean forward slightly. Keep your forearms horizontal to the keyboard.
Screen. Position the monitor so that the top of the screen is just below eye level and about 18 to 26 inches away.
Text. Position your textbook or other copy on either side of the monitor as close to it as vertically and horizontally possible to minimize head and eye movement and to avoid neck strain.

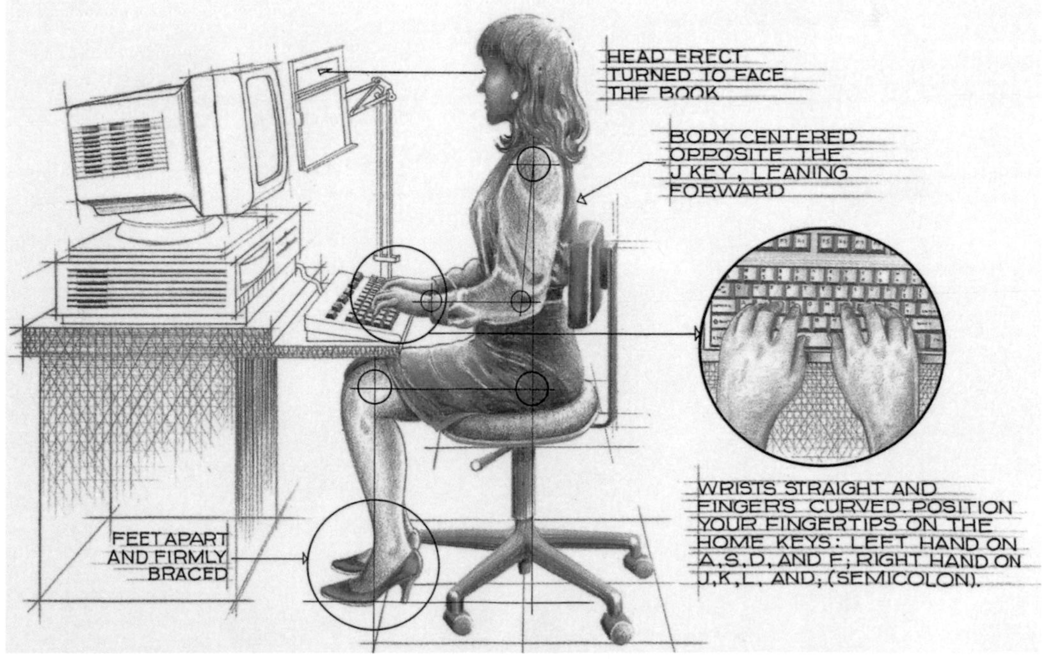
HEAD ERECT TURNED TO FACE THE BOOK
BODY CENTERED OPPOSITE THE J KEY, LEANING FORWARD
WRISTS STRAIGHT AND FINGERS CURVED. POSITION YOUR FINGERTIPS ON THE HOME KEYS: LEFT HAND ON A,S,D, AND F; RIGHT HAND ON J,K,L, AND ; (SEMICOLON).
FEET APART AND FIRMLY BRACED

BEFORE YOU BEGIN

Using Microsoft Windows

If you are using *Gregg College Keyboarding & Document Processing Lessons 1–120, 10th Edition,* you must know how to use a mouse, and you must know some basic information about Microsoft Windows.

Before you begin Lesson 1, turn to the Getting Started section in your word processing manual and read the information presented there. **Note:** If you are using the book for Lessons 1-20, use the Help feature in Windows to familiarize yourself with Windows.

Starting Your Program

Once you have completed the Getting Started section in your word processing manual, you are ready to begin Lesson 1. If you are using the *Gregg College Keyboarding & Document Processing Lessons 1–120, 10th Edition* software (hereafter referred to as GDP), begin by starting Windows.

Next, start GDP by locating and clicking the Irwin Keyboarding group icon in your Windows program list to open the program group. (**Note:** If you are saving data to a data disk, you should insert it now.) If you are working at your school on a network, click the GDP Classes icon, click your class and then your name for the class list. If you are a new student, follow the directions on the screen to add yourself as a new student. Then follow the directions to log on and begin using GDP.

If you see any other icons or are working on a different installation of GDP, consult your instructor for help in logging on.

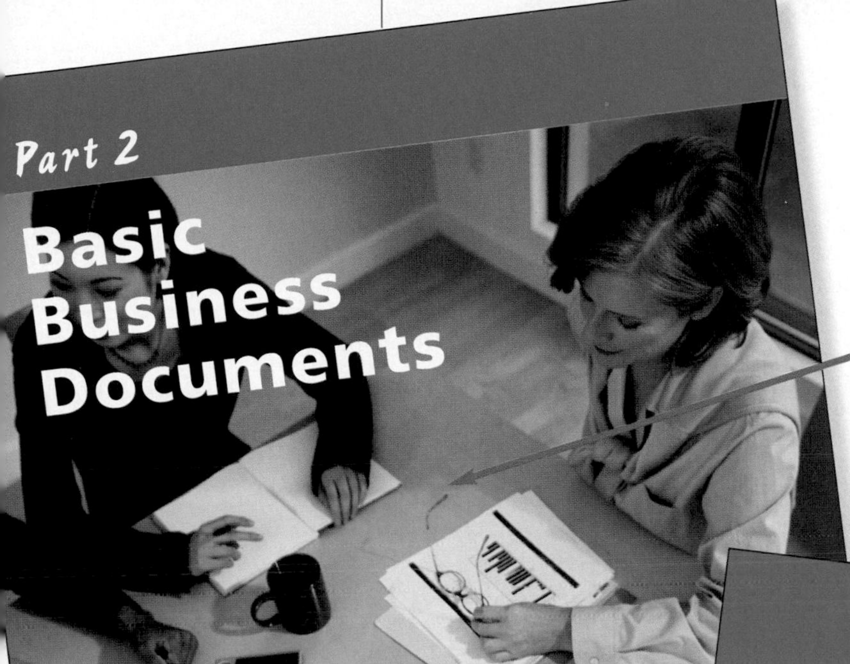

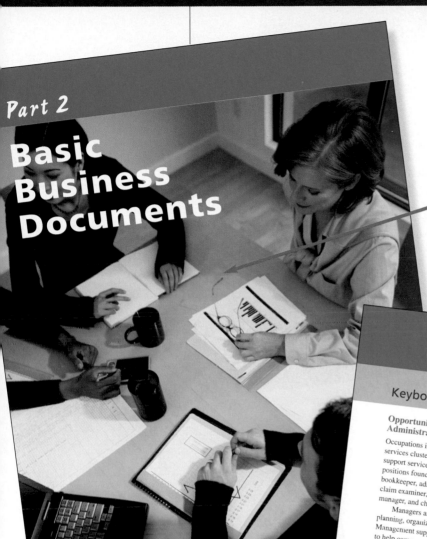

Each **Part Opener** is a two-page spread that provides a list of the part objectives and a special feature that focuses on the use of your keyboarding skills in various career clusters.

Keyboarding in Business and Administrative Services

Opportunities in Business and Administrative Careers

Occupations in the business and administrative services cluster focus on providing management and support services for various companies. The many positions found in this cluster include receptionist, bookkeeper, administrative professional or assistant, claim examiner, accountant, word processor, office manager, and chief executive officer.

Managers and administrators are in charge of planning, organizing, and controlling businesses. Management support workers gather and analyze data to help company executives make decisions. Administrative support workers perform a variety of tasks, such as recordkeeping, operating office equipment, managing their own projects and assignments, and developing high-level integrated software skills as well as Internet research skills. Ideally, everyone in business should be patient, detail-oriented, and cooperative. Excellent written and oral communication skills are definitely an asset as well.

Many companies have been revolutionized by advances in computer technology. As a result, keyboarding skill provides a definite advantage for those who work in business and administrative services. Now, more than ever, success in the business world is dependent upon adaptability and education.

Objectives

KEYBOARDING

- Operate the keyboard by touch.
- Type at least 36 words per minute on a 3-minute timed writing with no more than 4 errors.

LANGUAGE ARTS

- Develop proofreading skills and correctly use proofreaders' marks.
- Use capitals, commas, and apostrophes correctly.
- Develop composing and spelling skills.

WORD PROCESSING

- Use the word processing commands necessary to complete the document processing activities.

DOCUMENT PROCESSING

- Format e-mail, business and academic reports, business letters in block style, envelopes, memos, and tables.

TECHNICAL

- Answer at least 90 percent of the questions correctly on an objective test.

49

The **Unit Opener** helps you organize your study of unit concepts. The listing of the lessons clearly previews what will be taught in the unit.

Color Coding is used in the early lessons to help you differentiate which finger is used. On the keyboard chart shown at the beginning of each new-key lesson, new keys are highlighted, previously learned keys are labeled but not highlighted, and unlearned keys are blank. You will have a sense of progress as you move through the 20 new-key lessons.

Handwritten examples are used to make lessons more realistic since many letters, reports, and so on, are originally prepared with pen and paper. Including handwritten manuscript also enhances your ability to accurately read and type at the same time.

Timed Writings are used to improve both accuracy and speed. Timed Writings measure how well you are progressing in keyboarding skill development. In addition, timed writings bolster your self-confidence and ability.

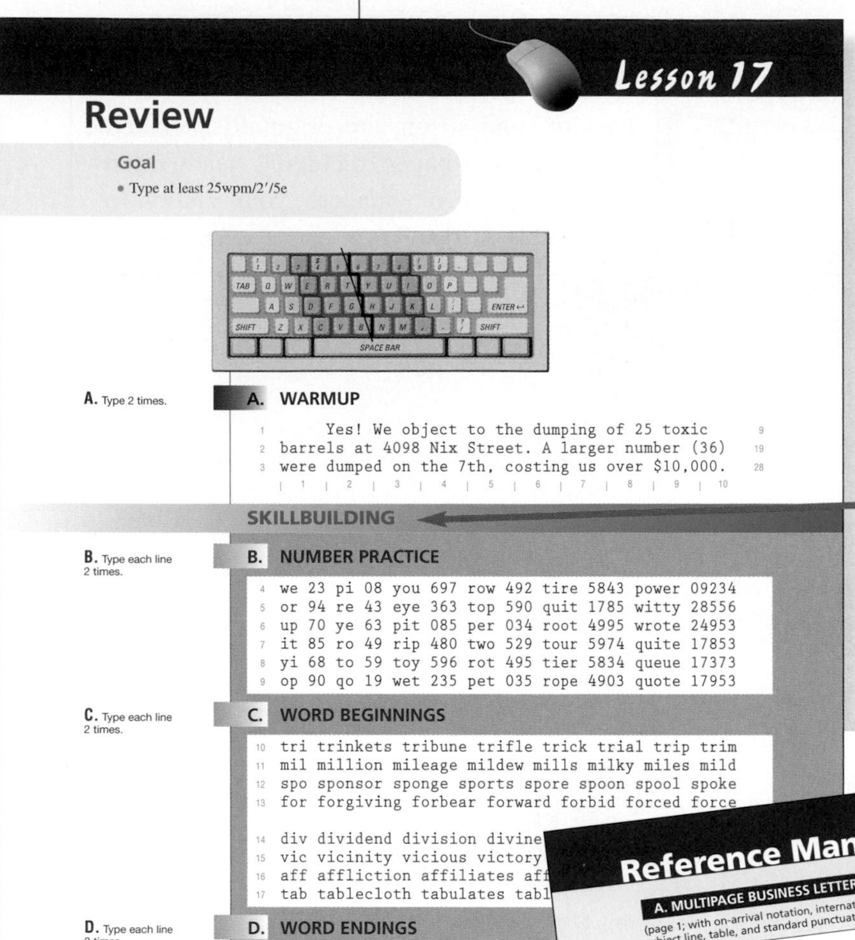

Lesson 17

Review

Goal
• Type at least 25wpm/2′/5e

A. Type 2 times.

A. WARMUP

```
    Yes! We object to the dumping of 25 toxic      9
barrels at 4098 Nix Street. A larger number (36)  19
were dumped on the 7th, costing us over $10,000.  28
  | 1 | 2 | 3 | 4 | 5 | 6 | 7 | 8 | 9 | 10
```

SKILLBUILDING

B. Type each line 2 times.

B. NUMBER PRACTICE

```
we 23 pi 08 you 697 row 492 tire 5843 power 09234
or 94 re 43 eye 363 top 590 quit 1785 witty 28556
up 70 ye 63 pit 085 per 034 root 4995 wrote 24953
it 85 ro 49 rip 480 two 529 tour 5974 quite 17853
yi 68 to 59 toy 596 rot 495 tier 5834 queue 17373
op 90 qo 19 wet 235 pet 035 rope 4903 quote 17953
```

C. Type each line 2 times.

C. WORD BEGINNINGS

```
tri trinkets tribune trifle trick trial trip trim
mil million mileage mildew mills milky miles mild
spo sponsor sponge sports spore spoon spool spoke
for forgiving forbear forward forbid forced force

div dividend division divine
vic vicinity vicious victory
aff affliction affiliates aff
tab tablecloth tabulates tabl
```

D. Type each line 2 times.

D. WORD ENDINGS

```
ive repulsive explosive alive
est nearest invest attest wise
ply supply simply deeply damply
ver whenever forever whoever qu
```

Skillbuilding practice in every lesson offers an individualized plan for speed and accuracy development. A variety of skill-building exercises, including Technique Practice, Pretest/Practice/Posttest, Sustained Practice, 12-Second Speed Sprints, Diagnostic Practice, Progressive Practice, Paced Practice, and Number Practice, provide the foundation for progress in your skill development.

Reference Manual

A. MULTIPAGE BUSINESS LETTER
(page 1; with on-arrival notation, international address, subject line, table, and standard punctuation)

B. MULTIPAGE BUSINESS LETTER
(page 2; with company name; multiline list; enclosure, delivery, copy, postscript, blind copy notations; and standard punctuation)

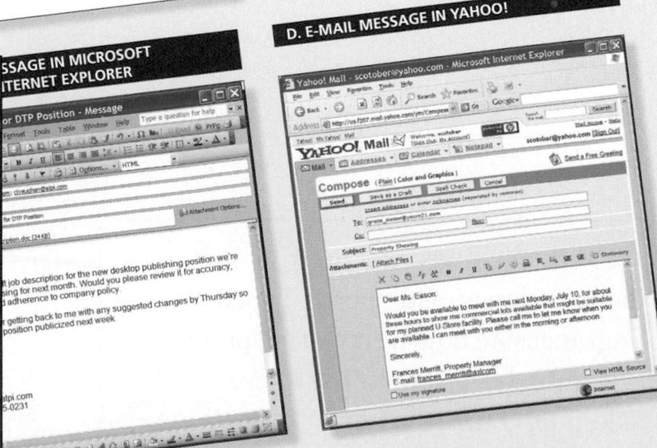

The Reference Manual material found in the front of the book and in the Word manual enables you to easily locate information regarding the proper way to format business letters, reports, e-mail messages, memoranda, and other forms of written communication. Elements such as line spacing and the placement of letterhead and body text are all illustrated in detail for your instructional support. In addition, 50 "must-know" rules for language arts in business contexts are included with examples in the Reference Manual to help improve writing skills.

R-5 Reference Manual

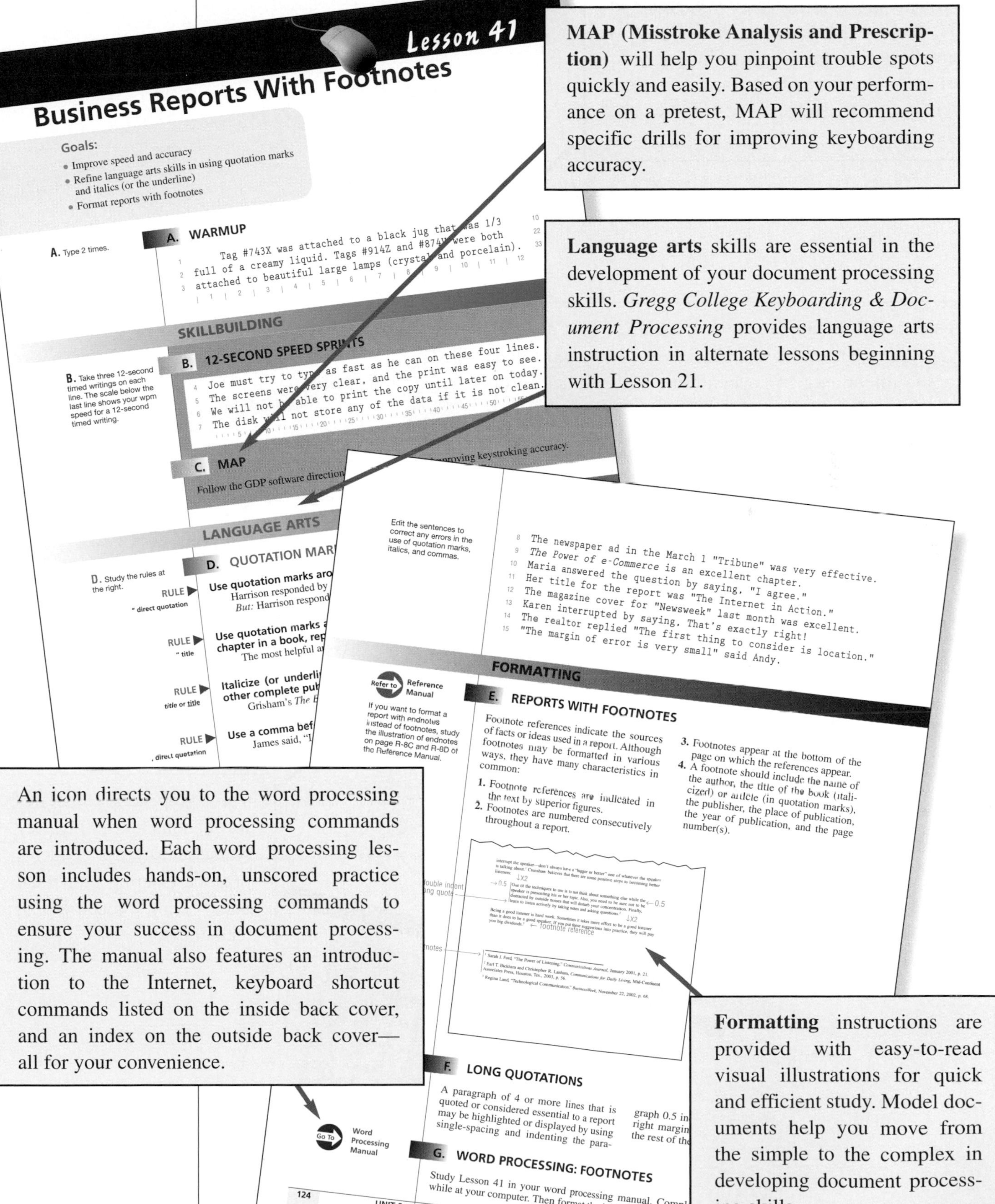
MAP (Misstroke Analysis and Prescription) will help you pinpoint trouble spots quickly and easily. Based on your performance on a pretest, MAP will recommend specific drills for improving keyboarding accuracy.
Language arts skills are essential in the development of your document processing skills. *Gregg College Keyboarding & Document Processing* provides language arts instruction in alternate lessons beginning with Lesson 21.
An icon directs you to the word processing manual when word processing commands are introduced. Each word processing lesson includes hands-on, unscored practice using the word processing commands to ensure your success in document processing. The manual also features an introduction to the Internet, keyboard shortcut commands listed on the inside back cover, and an index on the outside back cover—all for your convenience.
Formatting instructions are provided with easy-to-read visual illustrations for quick and efficient study. Model documents help you move from the simple to the complex in developing document processing skills.
Lesson 41
Business Reports With Footnotes
Goals:
Improve speed and accuracy
Refine language arts skills in using quotation marks and italics (or the underline)
Format reports with footnotes
A. WARMUP
SKILLBUILDING
B. 12-SECOND SPEED SPRINTS
C. MAP
LANGUAGE ARTS
D. QUOTATION MARKS
FORMATTING
E. REPORTS WITH FOOTNOTES
F. LONG QUOTATIONS
G. WORD PROCESSING: FOOTNOTES

The last document processing exercise in most units is designated as a Progress Check/Proofreading Check. Make it your goal is to have zero typographical errors when the GDP software first scores the document.

Special features are designed to enhance your study of keyboarding. The *Keyboarding Connection* features illustrate the importance of keyboarding skills outside of the classroom. The *Strategies for Career Success* features offer an employment-related narrative, including useful hints for succeeding in any career.

The Appendix contains instructions for the Ten-Key Numeric Keypad. Students practice entering numerical data using touch-typing techniques.

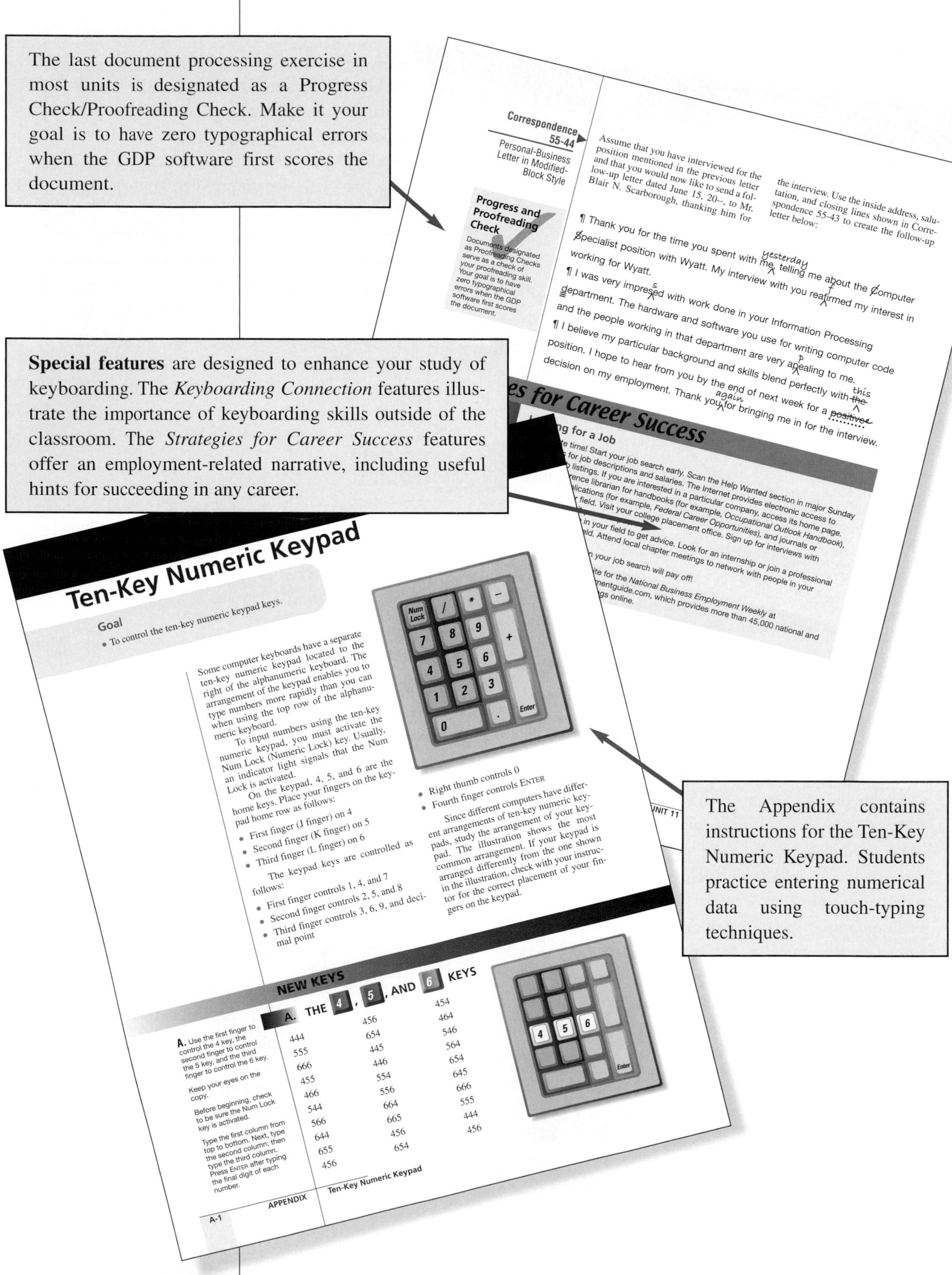

Correspondence 55-44
Personal-Business Letter in Modified-Block Style
Progress and Proofreading Check
Documents designated as Proofreading Checks serve as a check of your proofreading skill. Your goal is to have zero typographical errors when the GDP software first scores the document.
Assume that you have interviewed for the position mentioned in the previous letter and that you would now like to send a follow-up letter dated June 15, 20--, to Mr. Blair N. Scarborough, thanking him for the interview. Use the inside address, salutation, and closing lines shown in Correspondence 55-43 to create the follow-up letter below:
Ten-Key Numeric Keypad
Goal
• To control the ten-key numeric keypad keys.
Some computer keyboards have a separate ten-key numeric keypad located to the right of the alphanumeric keyboard. The arrangement of the keypad enables you to type numbers more rapidly than you can when using the top row of the alphanumeric keyboard.
NEW KEYS
A. THE 4, 5, AND 6 KEYS
APPENDIX
Ten-Key Numeric Keypad
A-1

The back-of-the book skillbuilding routines are designed with YOU in mind. The Paced Practice skillbuilding paragraphs use an upbeat, motivational storyline with guidance in career choices. The Supplementary Timed Writings relate critical thinking skills to careers.

SKILLBUILDING

70wpm Indexing is the ability of a word processor to accumulate a list of words that appear in a document, including page numbers, and then print a revised list in alphabetic order.

72wpm When a program needs information from you, a dialog box will appear on the desktop. Once the dialog box appears, you must identify the option you desire and then choose that option.

74wpm A facsimile is an exact copy of a document, and it is also a process by which images, such as typed letters, graphs, and signatures, are scanned, transmitted, and then printed on paper.

76wpm Compatibility refers to the ability of a computer to share information with another computer or to communicate with some other apparatus. It can be accomplished by using hardware or software.

78wpm Some operators like to personalize their desktops when they use Windows by making various changes. For example, they can change their screen colors and the pointer so that they will have more fun.

80wpm Wraparound is the ability of a word processor to move words from one line to another line and from one page to the next page as a result of inserting and deleting text or changing the size of margins.

82wpm It is possible when using Windows to evaluate the contents of different directories o... screen at the very same time. You can then choose to ... particular file from one directory to anoth...

84wpm List processing is a ... lists of data that c... numeric order. A li... is stored in one's ...

86wpm A computer is a wo... input and then pr... computer performs... programs, which ...

88wpm The configurati... processing sys... used for enter... one disk driv...

SB-9 SKILLBUILDING Progressive Pr...

SKILLBUILDING

Supplementary Timed Writing 3

Office employees perform a variety of tasks during 10
their workday. These tasks vary from handling telephone 21
calls to forwarding personal messages, from sending short 33
e-mail messages to compiling complex office reports, and 44
from writing simple letters to assembling detailed letters 56
with tables, graphics, and imported data. Office workers 67
are a fundamental part of a company's structure. 77
The office worker uses critical thinking in order to 88
accomplish a wide array of daily tasks. Some of the tasks 100
are more urgent than other tasks and should be completed 111
first. Some tasks take only a short time, while others take 123
a lot more time. Some tasks demand a quick response, while 135
others may be taken up as time permits or even postponed 147
until the future. Some of the tasks require input from 158
coworkers or managers. Whether a job is simple or complex, 170
big or small, the office worker must decide what is to be 182
tackled first by determining the priority of each task. 193
When setting priorities, critical thinking skills are 204
essential. The office worker evaluates each aspect of the 216
task. It is a good idea to identify the size of the task, 228
determine its complexity, estimate its effort, judge its 239
importance, and set its deadline. Once the office worker 250
assesses each task that is to be finished within a certain 262
period of time, then the priority for completing all tasks 274
can be set. Critical thinking skills, if applied well, 285
can save the employer money or, if executed poorly, can 296
cost the employer. 300

| 1 | 2 | 3 | 4 | 5 | 6 | 7 | 8 | 9 | 10 | 11 | 12 |

SKILLBUILDING Supplementary Timed Writings SB-30

Reference Manual

COMPUTER SYSTEM

CORRESPONDENCE

EMPLOYMENT DOCUMENTS

FORMS

LANGUAGE ARTS

PROOFREADERS' MARKS

REPORTS

TABLES

U.S. POSTAL SERVICE STATE ABBREVIATIONS

Reference Manual

A. MAJOR PARTS OF A MICROCOMPUTER SYSTEM

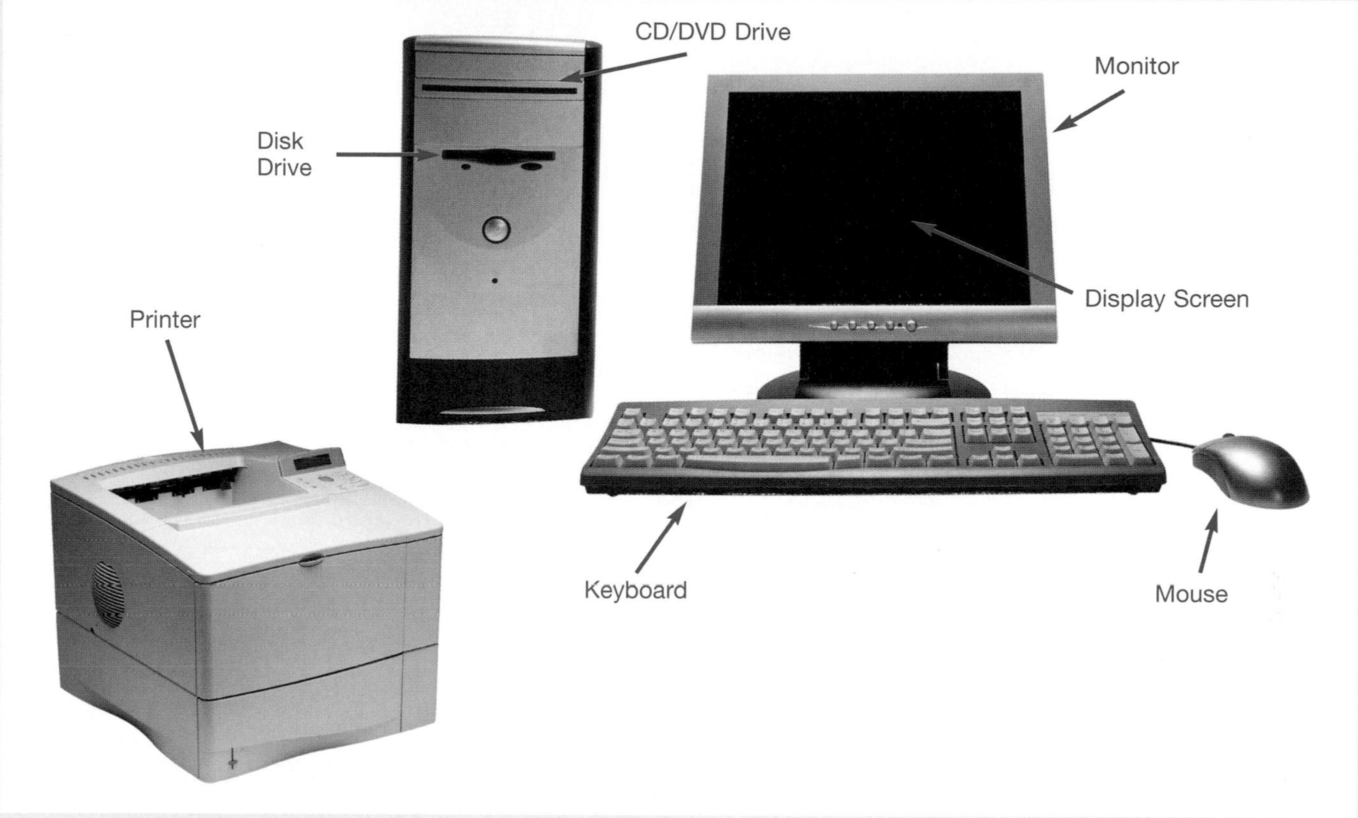

CD/DVD Drive
Monitor
Disk Drive
Display Screen
Printer
Keyboard
Mouse

B. THE COMPUTER KEYBOARD

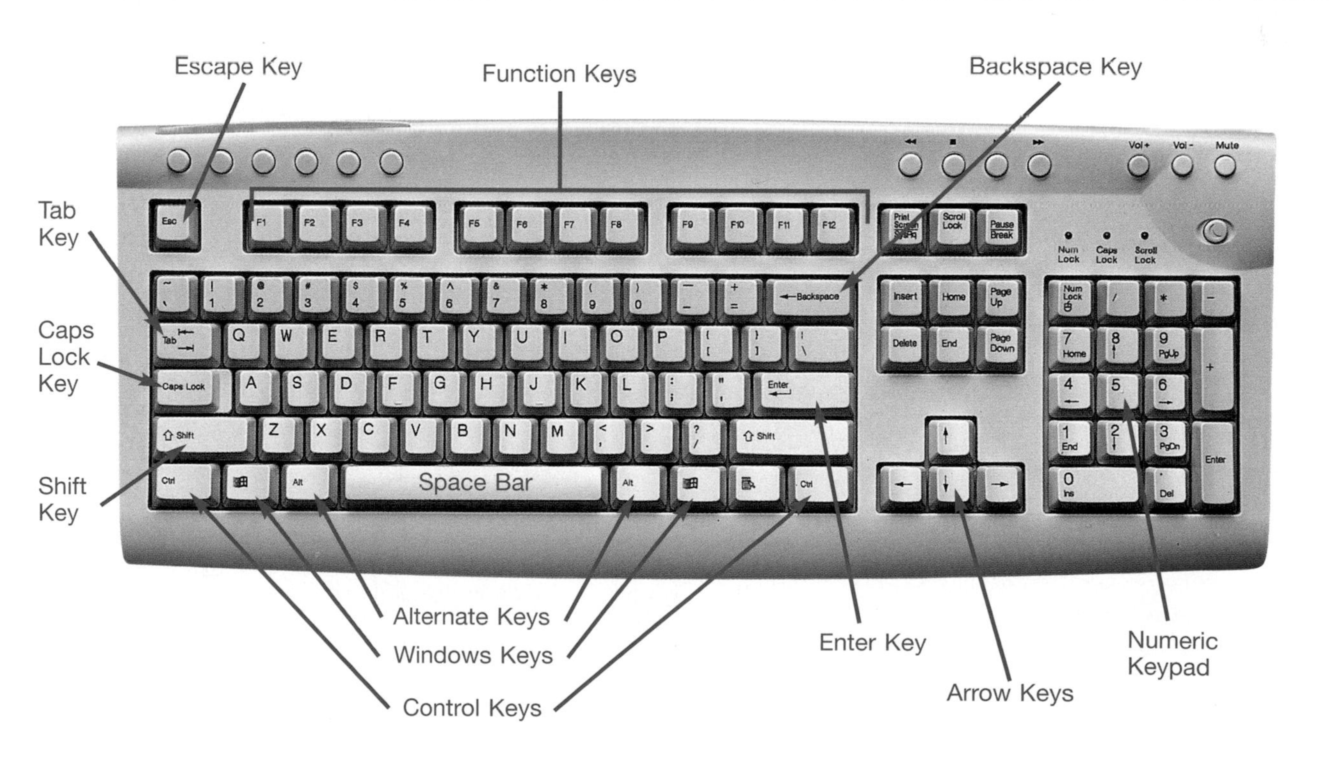

A. BUSINESS LETTER IN BLOCK STYLE

(with standard punctuation)

↓6X

Date line September 5, 20-- ↓4X

Inside address Ms. Joan R. Hunter
Bolwater Associates
One Parklands Drive
Darien, CT 06820 ↓2X

Salutation Dear Ms. Hunter: ↓2X

Body You will soon receive the signed contract to have your organization conduct a one-day workshop for our employees on eliminating repetitive-motion injuries in the workplace. As we agreed, this workshop will apply to both our office and factory workers and you will conduct separate sessions for each group.

We revised Paragraph 4b to require the instructor of this workshop to be a full-time employee of Bolwater Associates. In addition, we made changes to Paragraph 10-c to require our prior approval of the agenda for the workshop.

If these revisions are satisfactory, please sign and return one copy of the contract for our files. We look forward to this opportunity to enhance the health of our employees. I know that all of us will enjoy this workshop. ↓2X

Complimentary closing Sincerely, ↓4X

John L. Merritt

Writer's identification John L. Merritt, Director ↓2X

Reference initials fej

B. BUSINESS LETTER IN MODIFIED-BLOCK STYLE

(with open punctuation, multiline list, and enclosure notation)

Left tab: 3"
↓6X
→tab to centerpoint May 15, 20-- ↓4X

Mr. Ichiro Xie
Bolwater Associates
One Parklands Drive
Darien, CT 06820 ↓2X

Dear Mr. Xie ↓2X

I am returning a signed contract to have your organization conduct a one-day workshop for our employees on eliminating repetitive-motion injuries in the workplace. We have made the following changes to the contract:

Multiline list

1. We revised Paragraph 4b to require the instructor of this workshop to be a full-time employee of Bolwater Associates.

2. We made changes to Paragraph 10-c to require our prior approval of the agenda for the workshop.

If these revisions are satisfactory, please sign and return one copy of the contract for our files. We look forward to this opportunity to enhance the health of our employees. I know that all of us will enjoy this workshop. ↓2X

→tab to centerpoint Sincerely ↓4X

Reinalda Guerrero

Reinalda Guerrero, Director ↓2X

pec

Enclosure notation Enclosure

C. BUSINESS LETTER IN SIMPLIFIED STYLE

(with single-line list, enclosure notation, and copy notation)

↓6X

October 5, 20-- ↓4X

Mr. Dale P. Griffin
Bolwater Associates
One Parklands Drive
Darien, CT 06820 ↓3X

Subject line WORKSHOP CONTRACT ↓3X

I am returning the signed contract, Ms. Hunter, to have your organization conduct a one-day workshop for our employees on eliminating repetitive-motion injuries in the workplace. We have amended the following sections of the contract:

Single-line list

- Paragraph 4b
- Table 3
- Attachment 2

If these revisions are satisfactory, please sign and return one copy of the contract for our files. We look forward to this opportunity to enhance the health of our employees. I know that all of us will enjoy this workshop. ↓4X

Kachina Haddad

KACHINA HADDAD, DIRECTOR ↓2X

iww
Enclosure

Copy notation c: Legal Department

D. PERSONAL-BUSINESS LETTER IN MODIFIED-BLOCK STYLE

(with international address and standard punctuation)

Left tab: 3"
↓6X
→tab to centerpoint July 15, 20-- ↓4X

Mr. Luis Fernandez, President
Arvon Industries, Inc.
21 St. Claire Avenue East
International Address Toronto, ON M4T IL9
CANADA ↓2X

Dear Mr. Fernandez: ↓2X

As a former employee and present stockholder of Arvon Industries, I wish to protest the planned sale of the Consumer Products Division.

According to published reports, consumer products accounted for 19 percent of last year's corporate profits, and they are expected to account for even more this year. In addition, Dun & Bradstreet predicts that consumer products nationwide will outpace the general economy for the next five years.

I am concerned about the effect that this planned sale will have on overall corporate profits, on cash dividends for investors, and on the economy of Melbourne, where the two consumer-products plants are located. Please ask your board of directors to reconsider this matter. ↓2X

→tab to centerpoint Sincerely, ↓4X

Roger J. Michaelson

Return address Roger J. Michaelson
901 East Benson, Apt. 3
Fort Lauderdale, FL 33301

A. BUSINESS LETTER ON EXECUTIVE STATIONERY

(7.25" x 10.5"; 1" side margins; with delivery notation and standard punctuation.)

↓6X

July 18, 20-- ↓4X

Mr. Rodney Eastwood
BBL Resources
52A Northern Ridge
Fayetteville, PA 17222 ↓2X

Dear Rodney: ↓2X

I see no reason why we should continue to consider the locality around Geraldton for our new plant. Even though the desirability of this site from an economic view is undeniable, there is insufficient housing readily available for our workers.

In trying to control urban growth, the city has been turning down the building permits for new housing or placing so many restrictions on foreign investment as to make it too expensive.

Please continue to seek out other areas of exploration where we might form a joint partnership. ↓2X

Sincerely, ↓4X

Dalit Chande

Dalit Chande
Vice President for Operations ↓2X

mme
Delivery notation By Fax

B. BUSINESS LETTER ON HALF-PAGE STATIONERY

(5.5" x 8.5"; 0.75" side margins and standard punctuation)

↓4X

July 18, 20-- ↓4X

Mr. Aristeo Olivas
BBL Resources
52A Northern Ridge
Fayetteville, PA 17222 ↓2X

Dear Aristeo: ↓2X

We should continue considering Geraldton for our new plant. Even though the desirability of this site from an economic view is undeniable, there is insufficient housing readily available.

Please continue to search out other areas of new exploration where we might someday form a joint partnership. ↓2X

Sincerely, ↓4X

Mieko Nakamura

Mieko Nakamura
Vice President for Operations ↓2X

adk

C. BUSINESS LETTER FORMATTED FOR A WINDOW ENVELOPE

(with standard punctuation)

↓6X

July 18, 20-- ↓3X

Ms. Reinalda Guerrero
BBL Resources
52A Northern Ridge
Fayetteville, PA 17222 ↓3X

Dear Ms. Guerrero: ↓2X

I see no reason why we should continue to consider the locality around Geraldton for our new plant. Even though the desirability of this site from an economic view is undeniable, there is insufficient housing readily available for our workers.

In trying to control urban growth, the city has been turning down the building permits for new housing or placing so many restrictions on foreign investment as to make it too expensive.

Please continue to seek out other areas of exploration where we might form a joint partnership. ↓2X

Sincerely, ↓4X

Arlyn J. Bunch

Arlyn J. Bunch
Vice President for Operations ↓2X

woc

D. MEMO

(with table and attachment notation)

↓6X →tab

MEMO TO: Nancy Price, Executive Vice President ↓2X

FROM: Arlyn J. Bunch, Operations *ajb* ↓2X

DATE: July 18, 20-- ↓2X

SUBJECT: New Plant Site ↓2X

As you can see from the attached letter, I've informed BBL Resources that I see no reason why we should continue to consider the locality around Geraldton for our new plant. Even though the desirability of this site from an economic standpoint is undeniable, there is insufficient housing available. In fact, as of June 25, the number of appropriate single-family houses listed for sale within a 25-mile radius of Geraldton was as follows: ↓2X

Agent	Units
Belle Real Estate	123
Castleton Homes	11
Red Carpet	9
Geraldton Homes	5

↓1X

In addition, in trying to control urban growth, Geraldton has been either turning down building permits for new housing or placing excessive restrictions on them.

Because of this deficiency of housing for our employees, we have no choice but to look elsewhere. ↓2X

woc
Attachment notation Attachment

Reference Manual

A. MULTIPAGE BUSINESS LETTER

(page 1; with on-arrival notation, international address, subject line, table, and standard punctuation)

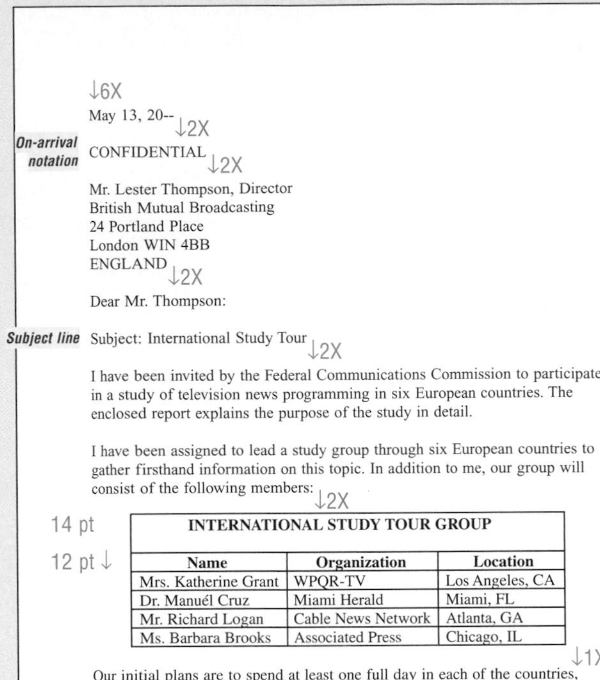

May 13, 20--

CONFIDENTIAL

Mr. Lester Thompson, Director
British Mutual Broadcasting
24 Portland Place
London WIN 4BB
ENGLAND

Dear Mr. Thompson:

Subject: International Study Tour

I have been invited by the Federal Communications Commission to participate in a study of television news programming in six European countries. The enclosed report explains the purpose of the study in detail.

I have been assigned to lead a study group through six European countries to gather firsthand information on this topic. In addition to me, our group will consist of the following members:

INTERNATIONAL STUDY TOUR GROUP		
Name	**Organization**	**Location**
Mrs. Katherine Grant	WPQR-TV	Los Angeles, CA
Dr. Manuél Cruz	Miami Herald	Miami, FL
Mr. Richard Logan	Cable News Network	Atlanta, GA
Ms. Barbara Brooks	Associated Press	Chicago, IL

Our initial plans are to spend at least one full day in each of the countries, meeting with the news programming staff of one or two of the major networks,

B. MULTIPAGE BUSINESS LETTER

(page 2; with company name; multiline list; enclosure, delivery, copy, postscript, blind copy notations; and standard punctuation)

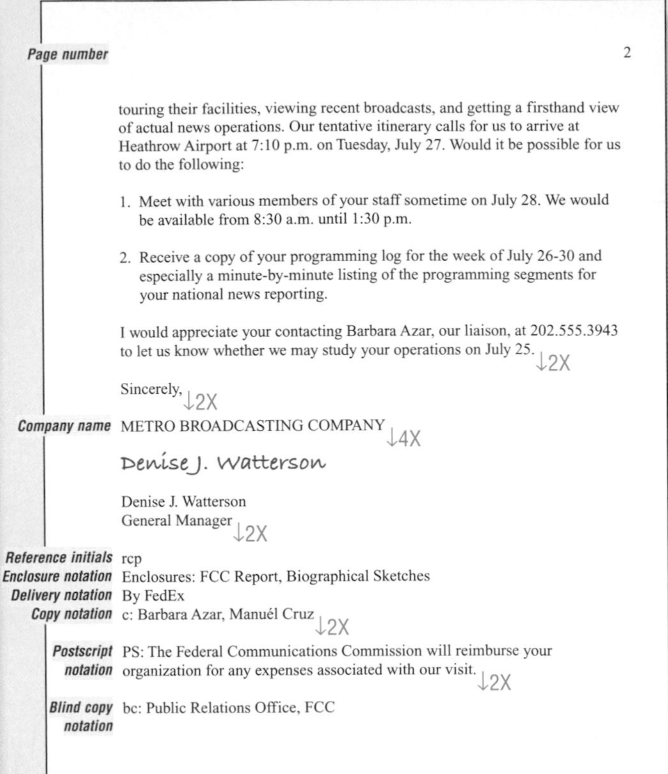

2

touring their facilities, viewing recent broadcasts, and getting a firsthand view of actual news operations. Our tentative itinerary calls for us to arrive at Heathrow Airport at 7:10 p.m. on Tuesday, July 27. Would it be possible for us to do the following:

1. Meet with various members of your staff sometime on July 28. We would be available from 8:30 a.m. until 1:30 p.m.

2. Receive a copy of your programming log for the week of July 26-30 and especially a minute-by-minute listing of the programming segments for your national news reporting.

I would appreciate your contacting Barbara Azar, our liaison, at 202.555.3943 to let us know whether we may study your operations on July 25.

Sincerely,

METRO BROADCASTING COMPANY

Denise J. Watterson

Denise J. Watterson
General Manager

rcp
Enclosures: FCC Report, Biographical Sketches
By FedEx
c: Barbara Azar, Manuél Cruz

PS: The Federal Communications Commission will reimburse your organization for any expenses associated with our visit.

bc: Public Relations Office, FCC

C. E-MAIL MESSAGE IN MICROSOFT OUTLOOK/ INTERNET EXPLORER

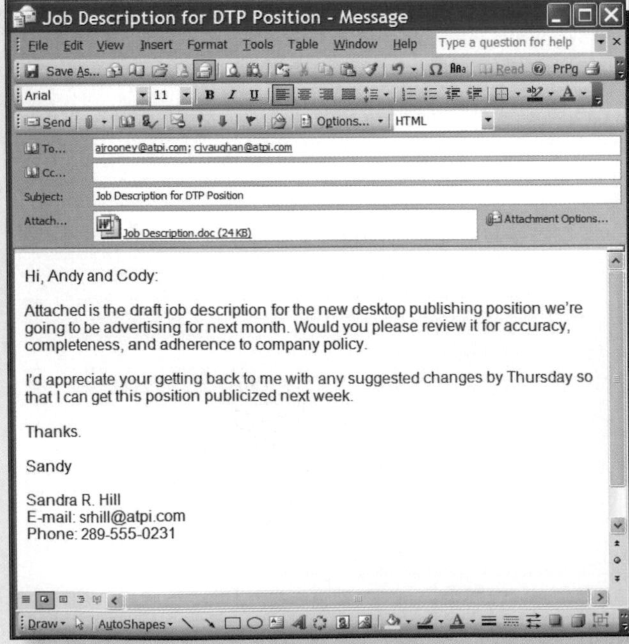

Hi, Andy and Cody:

Attached is the draft job description for the new desktop publishing position we're going to be advertising for next month. Would you please review it for accuracy, completeness, and adherence to company policy.

I'd appreciate your getting back to me with any suggested changes by Thursday so that I can get this position publicized next week.

Thanks.

Sandy

Sandra R. Hill
E-mail: srhill@atpi.com
Phone: 289-555-0231

D. E-MAIL MESSAGE IN YAHOO!

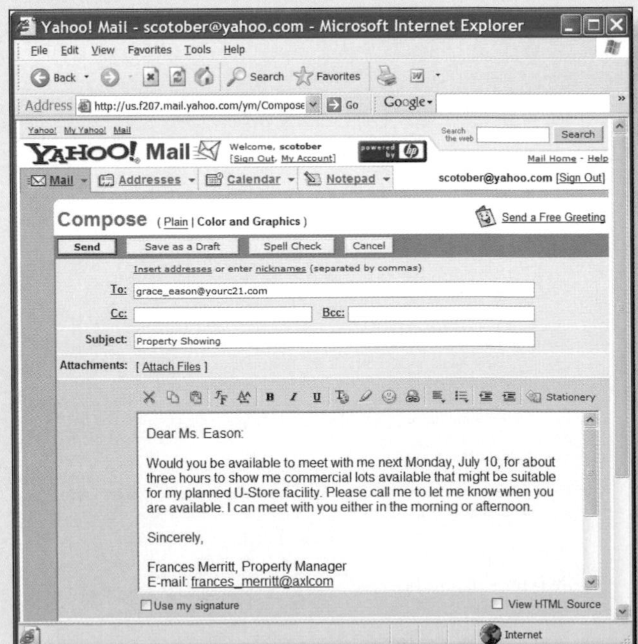

Dear Ms. Eason:

Would you be available to meet with me next Monday, July 10, for about three hours to show me commercial lots available that might be suitable for my planned U-Store facility. Please call me to let me know when you are available. I can meet with you either in the morning or afternoon.

Sincerely,

Frances Merritt, Property Manager
E-mail: frances_merritt@axlcom

A. FORMATTING ENVELOPES

A standard large (No. 10) envelope is 9.5 by 4.125 inches. A standard small (No. 6¼) envelope is 6.5 by 3.625 inches. Although either address format shown below is acceptable, the format shown for the large envelope (all caps and no punctuation) is recommended by the U.S. Postal Service for mail that will be sorted by an electronic scanning device.

Window envelopes are often used in a word processing environment because of the difficulty of aligning envelopes correctly in some printers. A window envelope requires no formatting, since the letter is formatted and folded so that the inside address is visible through the window.

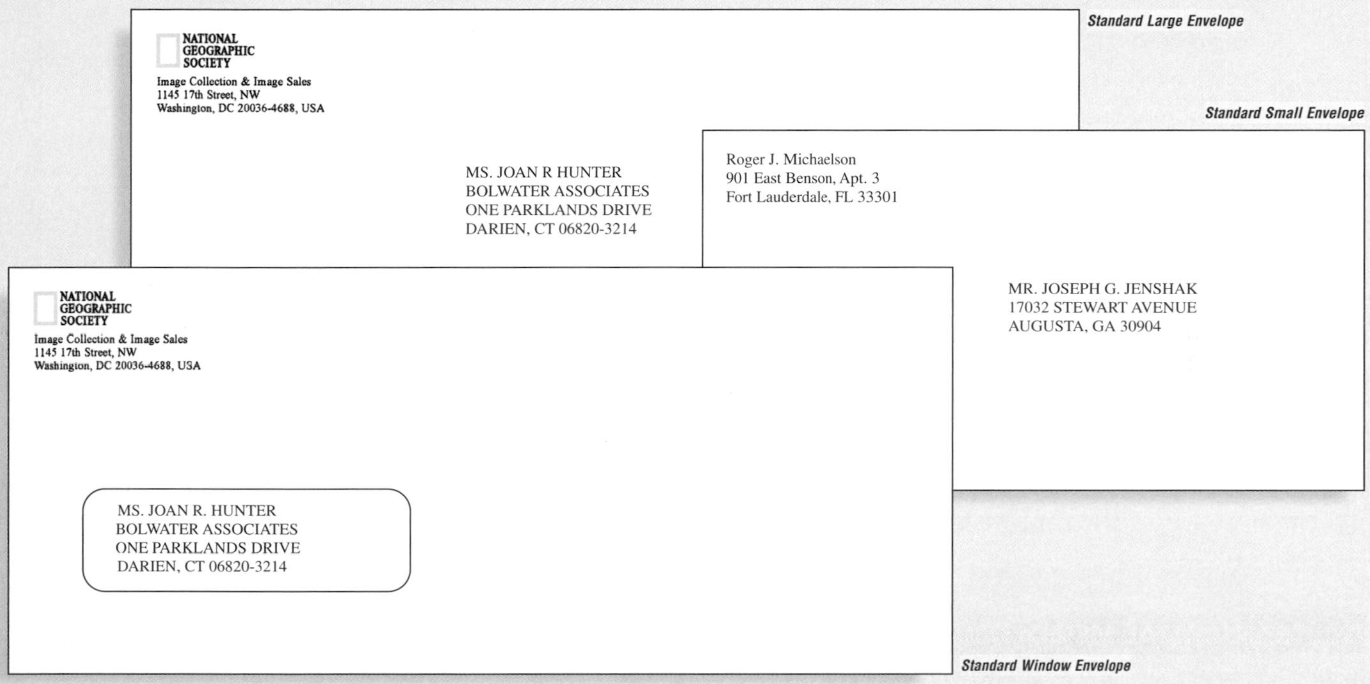

B. FOLDING LETTERS

To fold a letter for a large envelope:

1. Place the letter *face up* and fold up the bottom third.
2. Fold the top third down to 0.5 inch from the bottom edge.
3. Insert the last crease into the envelope first, with the flap facing up.

To fold a letter for a small envelope:

1. Place the letter *face up* and fold up the bottom half to 0.5 inch from the top.
2. Fold the right third over to the left.
3. Fold the left third over to 0.5 inch from the right edge.
4. Insert the last crease into the envelope first, with the flap facing up.

To fold a letter for a window envelope:

1. Place the letter *face down* with the letterhead at the top and fold the bottom third of the letter up.
2. Fold the top third down so that the address shows.
3. Insert the letter into the envelope so that the address shows through the window.

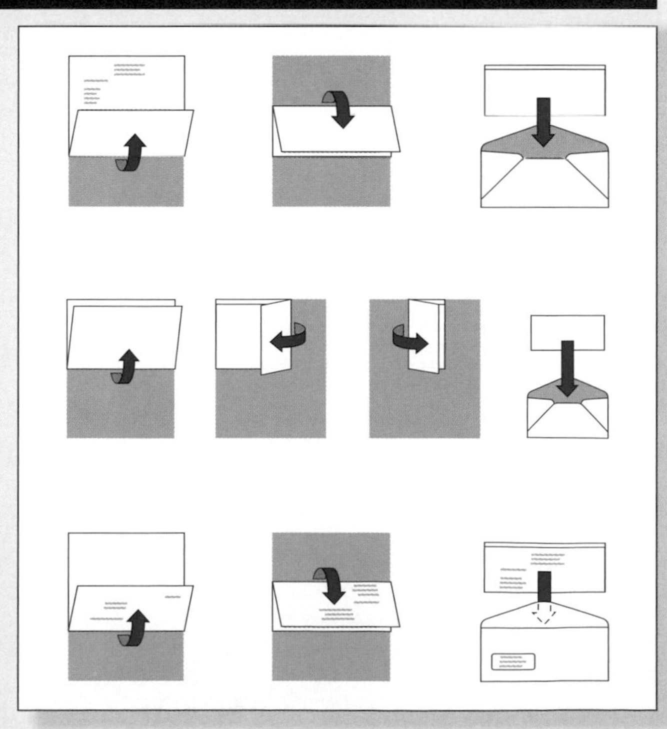

A. OUTLINE

Right tab: 0.3"; left tabs: 0.4", 0.7"

↓6X

14 pt **AN ANALYSIS OF THE SCOPE AND EFFECTIVENESS OF ONLINE ADVERTISING** ↓2X

12 pt↓ **The Status of Point-and-Click Selling** ↓2X

tab

Jonathan R. Evans ↓2X

January 19, 20-- ↓2X

I. INTRODUCTION ↓2X

II. SCOPE AND TRENDS IN INTERNET ADVERTISING
A. Internet Advertising
B. Major Online Advertisers
C. Positioning and Pricing
D. Types of Advertising ↓2X

III. ADVERTISING EFFECTIVENESS
A. The Banner Debate
B. Increasing Advertising Effectiveness
C. Measuring ROI ↓2X

IV. CONCLUSION

B. TITLE PAGE

center page↓

14 pt **AN ANALYSIS OF THE SCOPE AND EFFECTIVENESS OF ONLINE ADVERTISING** ↓2X

12 pt↓ **The Status of Point-and-Click Selling** ↓12X

Submitted to ↓2X

Luis Torres
General Manager
ViaWorld, International ↓12X

Prepared by ↓2X

Jonathan R. Evans
Assistant Marketing Manager
ViaWorld, International ↓2X

January 19, 20--

C. TRANSMITTAL MEMO

(with 2-line subject line and attachment notation)

↓6X

→ tab

MEMO TO: Luis Torres, General Manager ↓2X

FROM: Jonathan R. Evans, Assistant Marketing Manager *jre* ↓2X

DATE: January 19, 20-- ↓2X

SUBJECT: An Analysis of the Scope and Effectiveness of Online Advertising ↓2X

Here is the report analyzing the scope and effectiveness of Internet advertising that you requested on January 5, 20--.

The report predicts that the total value of the business-to-business e-commerce market will reach $1.3 trillion by 2003, up from $190 billion in 1999. New technologies aimed at increasing Internet ad interactivity and the adoption of standards for advertising response measurement and tracking will contribute to this increase. Unfortunately, as discussed in this report, the use of "rich media" and interactivity in Web advertising will create its own set of problems.

I enjoyed working on this assignment, Luis, and learned quite a bit from my analysis of the situation. Please let me know if you have any questions about the report. ↓2X

plw
Attachment

D. TABLE OF CONTENTS

Left tab: 0.5"; right dot-leader tab: 6".

↓6X

14 pt **CONTENTS** ↓2X

A. BUSINESS REPORT

(page 1; with footnotes and multiline list)

↓6X

Title 14 pt **AN ANALYSIS OF THE SCOPE AND EFFECTIVENESS OF ONLINE ADVERTISING** ↓2X

Subtitle 12 pt↓ **The Status of Point-and-Click Selling** ↓2X

Byline **Jonathan R. Evans** ↓2X

Date **January 19, 20--** ↓2X

Over the past three years, the number of American households online has tripled, from an estimated 15 million in 1996 to 45 million in 1999. Jupiter Communications, predicts that by the year 2003, 70 million households, representing about 62 percent of all U.S. households, will be online. ↓2X

Side head **GROWTH FACTORS** ↓2X

Online business has grown in tandem with the expanding number of Internet users. Forrester Research Inc. predicts that the total value of business-to-business e-commerce will reach $109 billion in 1999 and is likely to reach $1.3 trillion by 2003.[1] ↓2X

Paragraph head **Uncertainty**. The uncertainties surrounding advertising on the Internet remain one of the major impediments to the expansion. The Internet advertising industry is today in a state of flux. ↓2X

Reasons for Not Advertising Online. A recent Association of National Advertisers survey found two main reasons cited for not advertising online:[2] ↓2X

1. The difficulty of determining return on investment, especially in terms of repeat business

2. The lack of reliable tracking and measurement data

Footnotes

[1] George Anders, "Buying Frenzy," *The Wall Street Journal*, July 12, 1999, p. R6.
[2] "eStats: Advertising Revenues and Trends," *eMarketer*, August 11, 1999, <http:www.emarketer.com/estats/ad>, accessed on January 7, 2000.

B. BUSINESS REPORT

(page 3; with long quotation and table)

3

who argue that banners have a strong potential for advertising effectiveness point out that it is not the banner format itself which presents a problem to advertising effectiveness, but rather the quality of the banner and the attention to its placement. According to Mike Windsor, president of Ogilvy Interactive: ↓2X

indent 0.5"→ ←indent 0.5"

Long quotation

> It's more a case of bad banner ads, just like there are bad TV ads. The space itself has huge potential. As important as using the space within the banner creatively is to aim it effectively. Unlike broadcast media, the Web offers advertisers the opportunity to reach a specific audience based on data gathered about who is surfing at a site and what their interests are[1]

Thus, while some analysts continue to argue that the banner advertisement is passé, there is little evidence of its abandonment. Instead, ad agencies are focusing on increasing the banner's effectiveness. ↓2X

SCOPE AND TRENDS IN ONLINE ADVERTISING ↓2X

Starting from zero in 1994, analysts agree that the volume of Internet advertising spending has risen rapidly. However, as indicated in Table 3, analysts provide a wide range of the exact amount of such advertising. ↓2X

14 pt **TABLE 3. INTERNET ADVERTISING**
12 pt ↓ **1998 Estimates**

Source	Estimate
Internet Advertising Board	$1.92 billion
Forester	1.30 billion
IDC	1.20 billion
Burst! Media	560 million

Table source: Source: "Advertising Age Teams with eMarketer for Research Report," *Advertising Age*, May 3, 1999, p. 24. ↓1X

The differences in estimates of total Web advertising spending is generally attributed to the different methodologies used by the research agencies to

[1] Lisa Napoli, "Banner Ads Are Under the Gun—And On the Move," *The New York Times*, June 17, 1999, p. D1.

C. ACADEMIC REPORT

(page 1; with endnotes and multiline list)

↓3DS

14 pt **AN ANALYSIS OF THE SCOPE AND EFFECTIVENESS** ↓1DS **OF ONLINE ADVERTISING** ↓1DS

12 pt↓ **The Status of Point-and-Click Selling** ↓1DS

Jonathan R. Evans ↓1DS

January 19, 20-- ↓1DS

Over the past three years, the number of American households online has tripled, from an estimated 15 million in 1996 to 45 million in 1999. Jupiter Communications, predicts that by the year 2003, 70 million households, representing about 62 percent of all U.S. households, will be online. ↓1DS

GROWTH FACTORS ↓1DS

Online business has grown in tandem with the expanding number of Internet users. Forrester Research Inc. predicts that the total value of business-to-business e-commerce will reach $109 billion in 1999.[i]

Reasons for Not Advertising Online. A recent Association of National Advertisers survey found two main reasons cited for not advertising online:[ii]

1. The difficulty of determining return on investment, especially in terms of repeat business.
2. The lack of reliable tracking and measurement data.

Some analysts argue that advertising on the Internet can and should follow the same principles as advertising on television.[iii] Other visual media

D. ACADEMIC REPORT

(last page; with long quotation and endnotes)

14

advertising effectiveness, but rather the quality of the banner and the attention to its placement. According to Mike Windsor, president of Ogilvy Interactive: ↓1DS

indent 0.5"→ ←indent 0.5"

Long quotation

> It's more a case of bad banner ads, just like there are bad TV ads. The space itself has huge potential. As important as using the space within the banner creatively is to aim it effectively. Unlike broadcast media, the Web offers advertisers the opportunity to reach a specific audience based on data gathered about who is surfing at a site and what their interests are.[vii] ↓1SS

From the advertiser's perspective, the most effective Internet ads do more than just deliver information to the consumer and grab the consumer's attention—they also gather information about consumers (e.g., through "cookies" and other methodologies). From the consumer's perspective, this type of interactivity may represent an intrusion and an invasion of privacy. There appears to be a shift away from the ad-supported model and toward the transaction model, wherein users pay for the content they want and the specific transactions they perform.

Endnotes

i George Anders, "Buying Frenzy," *The Wall Street Journal*, July 12, 1999, p. R6.
ii "eStats: Advertising Revenues and Trends," *eMarketer*, August 11, 1999, <http:www.emarketer.com/estats/ad>, accessed on August 11, 1999.
iii Bradley Johnson, "Nielsen/NetRatings Index Shows 4% Rise in Web Ads," *Advertising Age*, July 19, 2003, p. 18.
iv Tom Hyland, "Web Advertising: A Year of Growth," *Internet Advertising Board*, November 13, 1999, <http:www.iab.net/advertise>, accessed on January 8, 2000.
v Adrian Mand, "Click Here: Free Ride Doles Out Freebies to Ad Surfers," *Brandweek*, March 8, 1999, p. 30.
vi Andrea Petersen, "High Price of Internet Banner Ads Slips Amid Increase in Web Sites," *The Wall Street Journal*, March 2, 1999, p. B20.
vii Lisa Napoli, "Banner Ads Are Under the Gun—And On the Move," *The New York Times*, June 17, 1999, p. D1.

A. LEFT-BOUND BUSINESS REPORT

(page 1; with endnotes and single-line list)

Left margin: 1.75″ Right margin: *default* (1.25″)

↓6X

14 pt **AN ANALYSIS OF THE SCOPE AND EFFECTIVENESS OF ONLINE ADVERTISING** ↓2X

12 pt↓ **The Status of Point-and-Click Selling** ↓2X

Jonathan R. Evans ↓2X

January 19, 20-- ↓2X

Over the past three years, the number of American households online has tripled, from an estimated 15 million in 1996 to 45 million in 1999. Jupiter Communications predicts that by the year 2003, 70 million households will be online. ↓2X

GROWTH FACTORS ↓2X

Online business has grown in tandem with the expanding number of Internet users. Forrester Research Inc. predicts that the total value of business-to-business e-commerce will reach $109 billion in 1999 and is likely to reach $1.3 trillion by 2003.[i] ↓2X

Uncertainty. The uncertainties surrounding advertising on the Internet remain one of the major impediments to the expansion. Dating from just 1994, when the first banner ads appeared on the Hotwired home page, the Internet advertising industry is today in a state of flux. ↓2X

Some analysts argue that advertising on the Internet can and should follow the same principles as advertising on television and other visual media. Others contend that advertising on the Internet should reflect the unique characteristics of this new medium. ↓2X

Reasons for Not Advertising Online. A recent Association of National Advertisers survey found two main reasons cited for not advertising online:[ii] ↓2X

1. The difficulty of determining return on investment
2. The lack of reliable tracking and measurement data

B. BIBLIOGRAPHY

(for business or academic style using either endnotes or footnotes)

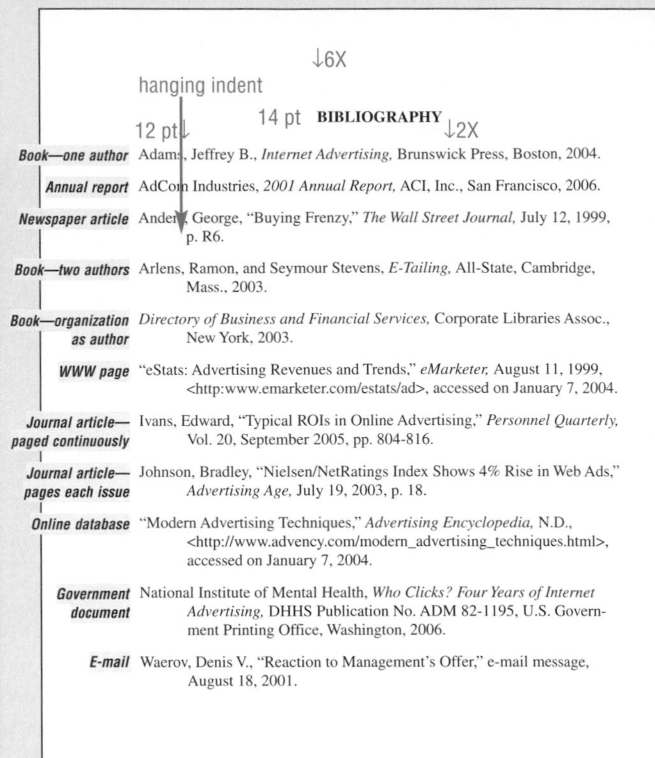

↓6X

hanging indent

14 pt **BIBLIOGRAPHY** ↓2X

12 pt↓

Book—one author	Adams, Jeffrey B., *Internet Advertising,* Brunswick Press, Boston, 2004.
Annual report	AdCom Industries, *2001 Annual Report,* ACI, Inc., San Francisco, 2006.
Newspaper article	Anders, George, "Buying Frenzy," *The Wall Street Journal,* July 12, 1999, p. R6.
Book—two authors	Arlens, Ramon, and Seymour Stevens, *E-Tailing,* All-State, Cambridge, Mass., 2003.
Book—organization as author	*Directory of Business and Financial Services,* Corporate Libraries Assoc., New York, 2003.
WWW page	"eStats: Advertising Revenues and Trends," *eMarketer,* August 11, 1999, <http:www.emarketer.com/estats/ad>, accessed on January 7, 2004.
Journal article—paged continuously	Ivans, Edward, "Typical ROIs in Online Advertising," *Personnel Quarterly,* Vol. 20, September 2005, pp. 804-816.
Journal article—pages each issue	Johnson, Bradley, "Nielsen/NetRatings Index Shows 4% Rise in Web Ads," *Advertising Age,* July 19, 2003, p. 18.
Online database	"Modern Advertising Techniques," *Advertising Encyclopedia,* N.D., <http://www.advency.com/modern_advertising_techniques.html>, accessed on January 7, 2004.
Government document	National Institute of Mental Health, *Who Clicks? Four Years of Internet Advertising,* DHHS Publication No. ADM 82-1195, U.S. Government Printing Office, Washington, 2006.
E-mail	Waerov, Denis V., "Reaction to Management's Offer," e-mail message, August 18, 2001.

C. MEMO REPORT

(page 1, with single-line list)

↓6X

→tab

MEMO TO: Luis Torres, General Manager ↓2X

FROM: Jonathan R. Evans, Assistant Marketing Manager *jre* ↓2X

DATE: January 19, 20-- ↓2X

SUBJECT: An Analysis of the Scope and Effectiveness of Online Advertising ↓2X

According to a July 12, 1999, Wall Street Journal article, over the past three years, the number of American households online has tripled, from an estimated 15 million in 1996 to 45 million in 1999. Jupiter Communications, predicts that by the year 2003, 70 million households, representing 62 percent of all U.S. households, will be online. Online business has grown in tandem with the expanding number of Internet users. Forrester Research Inc. predicts that the total value of business-to-business e-commerce will reach $109 billion in 1999 and is likely to reach $1.3 trillion by 2003. ↓2X

UNCERTAINTY ↓2X

The uncertainties surrounding advertising on the Internet remain one of the major impediments to the expansion. Dating from just 1994, when the first banner ads appeared on the Hotwired home page, the Internet advertising industry is today in a state of flux.

Some analysts argue that advertising on the Internet can and should follow the same principles as advertising on television and other visual media. Others contend that all of the advertising on the Internet should reflect the unique characteristics of this new medium.

A recent Association of National Advertisers survey found two main reasons cited for not advertising online:

1. The difficulty of determining return on investment
2. The lack of reliable tracking and measurement data

D. REPORTS: SPECIAL FEATURES

Margins and Spacing. Use a 2-inch top margin for the first page of each section of a report (for example, the table of contents, first page of the body, and bibliography page) and a 1-inch top margin for other pages. Use default side margins (1.25 inches) and bottom margins (1 inch) for all pages. If the report is going to be bound on the left, add 0.5 inch to the left margin. Single-space business reports and double-space academic reports.

Headings. Center the report title in 14-point font (press ENTER to space down before switching to 12-point font). Single-space multiline report titles in a single-spaced report and double-space multiline titles in a double-spaced report. Insert 1 blank line before and after all parts of a heading block (consisting of the title, subtitle, author, and/or date) and format all lines in bold.

Insert 1 blank line before and after side headings and format in bold, beginning at the left margin. Format paragraph headings in bold; begin at the left margin for single-spaced reports and indent for double-spaced reports. The text follows on the same line, preceded by a period and 1 space.

Citations. For business and academic reports, format citations using your word processor's footnote (or endnote) feature. For reports formatted in APA or MLA style, use the format shown on page R-10.

A. REPORT IN APA STYLE

(page 1; with author/year citations)

Top, bottom, and side margins: 1″

Online Advertising 3 **header**

An Analysis of the Scope and Effectiveness

of Online Advertising

Jonathan R. Evans

Over the past three years, the number of American households online has tripled, from an estimated 15 million in 1996 to 45 million in 1999. Jupiter Communications predicts that by the year 2003, 70 million households, which represent 62 percent of all U.S. households, will be online (Napoli, 2003).

main head Growth Factors

Online business has grown in tandem with the expanding number of Internet users. Forrester Research Inc. predicts that the total value of business-to-business e-commerce will reach $109 billion in 2003 (Arlens & Stevens, 2003).

subhead *Uncertainty*

The uncertainties surrounding advertising on the Internet remain one of the major impediments to the expansion. Dating from just 1994. when the first banner ads appeared on the Hotwired home page, the Internet advertising ındustry is today in a state of flux.

Some analysts argue that advertısing on the Internet can and should follow the same principles as advertising on television and other visual media ("eStats," 2004). Others contend that advertising on the Internet should reflect

B. REFERENCES IN APA STYLE

Top, bottom, and side margins: 1″

Double-space throughout.

Online Advertising 14 **header**

hanging indent

References

Book—one author Adams, J. B. (2004). *Internet advertising.* Boston: Brunswick Press.

Annual report AdCom Industries. (2006). 2005 *annual report.* San Francisco: ACI, Inc.

Newspaper article Anders, G. (2003, July 12). Buying frenzy. *The Wall Street Journal,* p. R6.

Book—two authors Arlens, R., & Stevens, S. (2003). *E-tailing.* Cambridge, MA: All-State.

Book—organization as author *Directory of business and financial services.* (2003). New York: Corporate Libraries Association.

WWW page eStats: Advertising revenues and trends. (n.d.). New York: eMarketer. Retrieved August 11, 2004, from the World Wide Web: http://www.emarketer.com/estats/ad

Journal article—paged continuously Ivans, E. (2005). Typical ROIs in online advertising. *Personnel Quarterly,* 20, 804-816.

Journal article—paged each issue Johnson, B. (2003, July 19). Nielsen/NetRatings Index shows 4% rise in Web ads. Advertising Age, 39, 18.

Online database *Modern advertising techniques.* (1998, January). *Advertising Encyclopedia.* Retrieved January 7, 2004, from http://www.advency.com/ads.html

Government document National Institute of Mental Health *Who clicks? Four years of Internet advertising* (DHHS Publication No. ADM 82-1195). Washington, DC. (2006).

C. REPORT IN MLA STYLE

(page 1; with author/page citations)

Top, bottom, and side margins: 1″

Double-space throughout.

Evans 1 **header**

Jonathan R. Evans

Professor Inman

Management 302

19 January 20--

An Analysis of the Scope and Effectiveness

of Online Advertising

Over the past three years, the number of American households online has tripled, from an estimated 15 million in 1996 to 45 million in 1999. Jupiter Communications predicts that by the year 2003, 70 million households, representing about 62% of all U.S. households, will be online (Napoli D1). Online business has grown in tandem with the expanding number of Internet users. Forrester Research Inc. predicts that the total value of business-to-business e-commerce will reach $109 billion in 1999 and is likely to reach $1.3 trillion by 2003 (Arlens & Stevens 376-379).

The uncertainties surrounding advertising on the Internet remain one of the major impediments to the expansion. Dating from just 1994, when the first banner ads appeared on the Hotwired home page, the Internet advertising industry is today in a state of flux.

Some analysts argue that advertising on the Internet can and should follow the same principles as advertising on television and other visual media (“eStats”). Others contend that advertising on the Internet should reflect the

D. WORKS CITED IN MLA STYLE

Top, bottom, and side margins: 1″

Double-space throughout.

Evans 13 **header**

hanging indent

Works Cited

Book—one author Adams, Jeffrey B. *Internet Advertising.* Boston: Brunswick Press, 2004.

Annual report AdCom Industries. *2006 Annual Report.* San Francisco: ACI, Inc., 2005.

Newspaper article Anders, George. “Buying Frenzy,” *Wall Street Journal,* July 12, 2003, p. R6.

Book—two authors Arlens, Ramon, and Seymour Stevens. *E-Tailing.* Cambridge, MA: All-State, 2003.

Book—organization as author Corporate Libraries Association. *Directory of Business and Financial Services.* New York: Corporate Libraries Association, 2003.

WWW page “eStats: Advertising Revenues and Trends.” *eMarketer,* 11 Aug. 1999. 7 Jan. 2004. <http:www.emarketer.com/estats/ad>.

Journal article—paged continuously Ivans, Edward. “Typical ROIs in Online Advertising.” *Personnel Quarterly* Sep. 2005: 804-816.

Journal article—paged each issue Johnson, Bradley. “Nielsen/NetRatings Index Shows 4% Rise in Web Ads.” *Advertising Age* 19 July 2003: 18.

Online database *Modern Advertising Techniques.* 2003. Advertising Encyclopedia. 7 Jan. 2004 <http://www.advency.com/modern_advertising_techniques.html>.

Government document National Institute of Mental Health. *Who Clicks? Four Years of Internet Advertising.* DHHS Publication No. ADM 82-1195. Washington, DC: GPO, 2006.

E-mail Richards, Denis V. E-mail to the author. 18 Dec. 2005.

A. MEETING AGENDA

↓6X

14 pt **MILES HARDWARE EXECUTIVE COMMITTEE** ↓2X

12 pt↓ **Meeting Agenda** ↓2X

June 7, 20--, 3 p.m. ↓2X

1. Call to order ↓2X
2. Approval of minutes of May 5 meeting
3. Progress report on building addition and parking lot restrictions (Norman Hodges and Anthony Pascarelli)
4. May 15 draft of Five-Year Plan
5. Review of National Hardware Association annual convention
6. Employee grievance filed by Ellen Burrows (John Landstrom)
7. New expense-report forms (Anne Richards)
8. Announcements
9. Adjournment

B. MINUTES OF A MEETING

↓6X

14 pt **RESOURCE COMMITTEE** ↓2X 12 pt↓ **Minutes of the Meeting** ↓2X **March 13, 20--** ↓1X	
ATTENDANCE	The Resource Committee met on March 13, 20--, at the Airport Sheraton in Portland, Oregon, with all members present. Michael Davis, chairperson, called the meeting to order at 2:30 p.m. ↓1X
APPROVAL OF MINUTES	The minutes of the January 27 meeting were read and approved. ↓1X
OLD BUSINESS	The members of the committee reviewed the sales brochure on electronic copyboards and agreed to purchase one for the conference room. Cynthia Giovanni will secure quotations from at least two suppliers. ↓1X
NEW BUSINESS	The committee reviewed a request from the Purchasing Department for three new computers. After extensive discussion regarding the appropriate use of the computers and software to be purchased, the committee approved the request. ↓1X
ADJOURNMENT	The meeting was adjourned at 4:45 p.m. ↓2X Respectfully submitted, ↓4X *D. S. Madsen* D. S. Madsen, Secretary

(Note: Table shown with "Show Gridlines" active.)

C. ITINERARY

↓6X

14 pt **ITINERARY** ↓2X 12 pt↓ **For Arlene Gilsdorf** ↓2X **March 12-15, 20--** ↓1X	
THURSDAY, MARCH 12	↓1X
5:10 p.m.-7:06 p.m.	Flight from Detroit to Portland; Northwest 83 (Phone: 800-555-1212); e-ticket; Seat 8D; nonstop; dinner ↓2X Jack Weatherford (Home: 503-555-8029; Office: 503-555-7631) will meet your flight on Thursday, provide transportation during your visit, and return you to the airport on Saturday morning. ↓2X Airport Sheraton (503-555-4032) King-sized bed, nonsmoking room; late arrival guaranteed (Reservation No. 30ZM6-02) ↓1X
FRIDAY, MARCH 13	
9 a.m.-5:30 p.m.	Portland Sales Meeting 1931 Executive Way, Suite 10 Portland (503-555-7631)
Evening	On your own
SATURDAY, MARCH 14	
7:30 a.m.-2:47 p.m.	Flight from Portland to Detroit; Northwest 360; e-ticket; Seat 9a; nonstop; breakfast

(Note: Table shown with "Show Gridlines" active.)

D. LEGAL DOCUMENT

Left tabs: 1″, 3″

↓6X

12 pt↓ POWER OF ATTORNEY ↓2X

KNOW ALL MEN BY THESE PRESENTS that I, ATTORNEY LEE FERNANDEZ, of the City of Tulia, County of Swisher, State of Texas, do hereby appoint my son, Robert Fernandez, of this City, County, and State as my attorney-in-fact to act in my name, place, and stead as my agent in the management of my business operating transactions.

I give and grant unto my said attorney full power and authority to do and perform every act and thing requisite and necessary to be done in the said management as fully, to all intents and purposes, as I might or could do if personally present, with full power of revocation, hereby ratifying all that my said attorney shall lawfully do.

IN WITNESS WHEREOF, I have hereunto set my hand and seal this _____ day of ____________________, 20--. ↓2X

5 underscores ↑ 20 underscores ↑

→tab to centerpoint ____________________ ↓2X

SIGNED and affirmed in the presence of: ↓4X

____________________ ↓4X

____

Reference Manual

A. RESUME

↓6X

14 pt **TERRY M. MARTINA** ↓2X

12 pt ↓ **250 Maxwell Avenue, Boulder, CO 80305**
Phone: 303-555-9311; e-mail: tmartina@ecc.edu ↓1X

↓1X

OBJECTIVE	Position in resort management anywhere in Colorado or the Southwest. ↓1X
EDUCATION	A.A. in hotel management to be awarded May 2005 Edgewood Community College, Boulder, Colorado. ↓1X
EXPERIENCE	*Assistant Manager, Burger King Restaurant* Boulder, Colorado: 2003-Present • Achieved grade point average of 3.1 (on 4.0 scale). • Received Board of Regents tuition scholarship. • Financed all college expenses. ↓2X *Student Intern, Ski Valley Haven* Aspen, Colorado: September-December 2004 • Worked as an assistant to the night manager. • Gained experience in operating First-Guest software. • Was in charge of producing daily occupancy reports. • Received Employee-of-the-Month award. ↓1X
PERSONAL	• Speak and write fluent Spanish. • Competent in Microsoft Office 2003. • Secretary of ECC Hospitality Services Association. • Special Olympics volunteer: Summer 2004. ↓1X
REFERENCES	Available upon request

(Note: Table shown with "Show Gridlines" active.)

B. APPLICATION LETTER IN BLOCK STYLE

(with standard punctuation)

↓6X

March 1, 20-- ↓4X

Mr. Lou Mansfield, Director
Human Resources Department
Rocky Resorts International
P.O. Box 1412
Denver, CO 80214 ↓2X

Dear Mr. Mansfield: ↓2X

Please consider me an applicant for the position of concierge for Suite Retreat, as advertised in last Sunday's *Denver Times.*

I will receive my A.A. degree in hotel administration from Edgewood Community College in May and will be available for full-time employment immediately. In addition to my extensive coursework in hospitality services and business, I've had experience in working for a ski lodge similar to Suite Retreats in Aspen. As a lifelong resident of Colorado and an avid skier, I would be able to provide your guests with any information they request.

After you've reviewed my enclosed resume, I would appreciate having an opportunity to discuss with you why I believe I have the right qualifications and personality to serve as your concierge. I can be reached at 303-555-9311. ↓2X

Sincerely, ↓4X

Terry M. Martina

Terry M. Martina
250 Maxwell Avenue, Apt. 8
Boulder, CO 80305 ↓2X

Enclosure

C. FORMATTING LISTS

Numbers or bullets may be used in letters, memos, and reports to call attention to items in a list. If the sequence of the items is important, use numbers rather than bullets.

- ❑ Begin the number or bullet at the paragraph point, that is, at the left margin for blocked paragraphs and indented 0.5 inch for indented paragraphs.
- ❑ Insert 1 blank line before and after the list.
- ❑ Within the list, use the same spacing (single or double) as is used in the rest of the document.
- ❑ For single-spaced documents, if all items require no more than 1 line, single-space the items in the list. If any item requires more than 1 line, single-space each item and insert 1 blank line between each item.

To format a list:

1. Type the list unformatted.
2. Select the items in the list.
3. Apply the number or bullet feature.
4. If necessary, use the Decrease Indent or Increase Indent button in Microsoft Word to adjust the position of the list.

The three bulleted and numbered lists shown at the right are all formatted correctly.

D. EXAMPLES OF DIFFERENT TYPES OF LISTS

According to PricewaterhouseCoopers and the Internet Advertising Bureau, the following are the most common types of advertising on the Internet.

- Banner ads that feature some type of animation to attract the viewer's attention.

- Sponsorship, in which an advertiser sponsors a content-based Web site.

- Interstitials, ads that flash up while a page downloads.

There is now considerable controversy about the effectiveness of banner ads. As previously noted, a central goal of banner advertisements is to increase the

***

According to PricewaterhouseCoopers, the following are the most common types of advertising on the Internet, shown in order of popularity:

1. Banner ads
2. Sponsorship
3. Interstitials

There is now considerable controversy about the effectiveness of banner ads. As previously noted, a central goal of banner advertisements is to increase the

***

According to PricewaterhouseCoopers, the following are the most common types of advertising on the Internet:

- Banner ads that feature some type of animation to attract the viewer's attention.
- Sponsorship, in which an advertiser sponsors a Web site.
- Interstitials, ads that flash up while a page downloads.

There is now considerable controversy about the effectiveness of banner advertising. As previously noted, a central goal of banner advertisements is to

Reference Manual

A. BOXED TABLE (DEFAULT STYLE)

(with subtitle, braced headings, total line, and table note.)

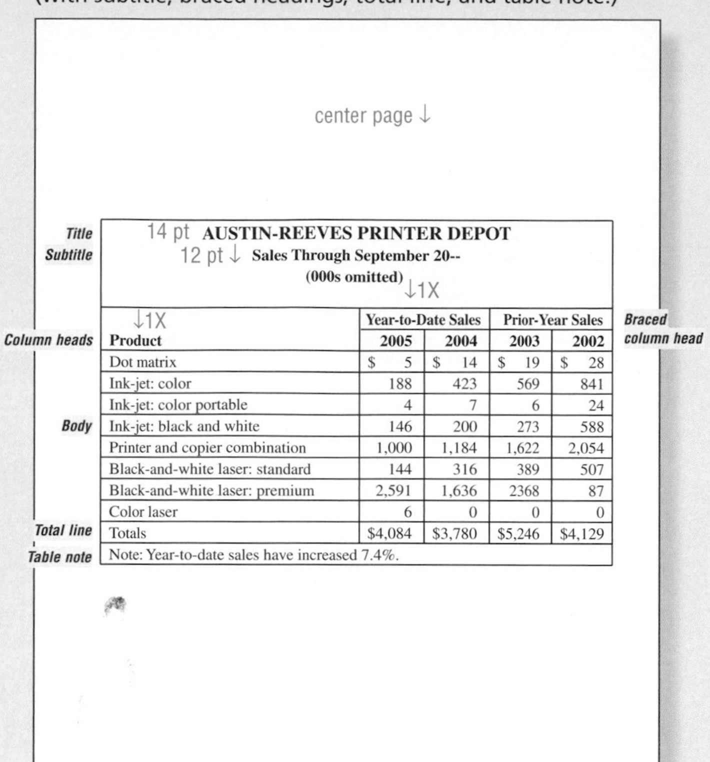

center page ↓

Title: 14 pt **AUSTIN-REEVES PRINTER DEPOT**

Subtitle: 12 pt ↓ **Sales Through September 20--**

(000s omitted) ↓1X

Column heads / Braced column head:

↓1X Product	Year-to-Date Sales		Prior-Year Sales	
	2005	**2004**	**2003**	**2002**
Dot matrix	$ 5	$ 14	$ 19	$ 28
Ink-jet: color	188	423	569	841
Ink-jet: color portable	4	7	6	24
Ink-jet: black and white	146	200	273	588
Printer and copier combination	1,000	1,184	1,622	2,054
Black-and-white laser: standard	144	316	389	507
Black-and-white laser: premium	2,591	1,636	2368	87
Color laser	6	0	0	0
Totals	$4,084	$3,780	$5,246	$4,129
Note: Year-to-date sales have increased 7.4%.				

Body — Total line — Table note

B. OPEN TABLE

(with subtitle, blocked column headings, and 2-line heading)

center page ↓

14 pt **SUITE RETREAT**

12 pt ↓ **New Lodging Rates** ↓1X

↓1X **Location**	**Rack Rate**	**Discount Rate**	↓1X **Saving**
Bozeman, Montana	$ 95.75	$ 91.50	4.4%
Chicago, Illinois	159.00	139.50	12.3%
Dallas, Texas	249.50	219.00	12.2%
Las Vegas, Nevada	98.50	89.95	8.7%
Los Angeles, California	179.00	139.00	22.3%
Minneapolis, Minnesota	115.00	95.00	17.4%
New York, New York	227.50	175.00	23.1%
Orlando, Florida	105.75	98.50	6.3%
Portland, Maine	93.50	93.50	0.0%
Seattle, Washington	143.75	125.75	12.5%

C. RULED TABLE

(with table number and centered column headings)

2

an effort to reduce errors and provide increased customer support, we have recently added numerous additional telephone support services, some of which are available 24 hours a day and others available during the workday. These are shown in Table 2. ↓2X

14 pt **Table 2. COMPUTER SUPPLIES SUPPORT SERVICES** ↓1X

12 pt↓

Support Service	**Telephone**	**Hours**
Product literature	800-555-3867	6 a.m. to 5 p.m.
Replacement parts	303-555-3388	24 hours a day
Technical documentation	408-555-3309	24 hours a day
Troubleshooting	800-555-8277	10 a.m. to 5 p.m.
Printer drivers	800-555-2377	6 a.m. to 5 p.m.
Software notes	800-555-3496	24 hours a day
Technical support	800-555-1205	24 hours a day
Hardware information	303-555-4289	6 a.m. to 5 p.m.

↓1X

We hope you will take advantage of these additional services to ensure that the computer hardware and software you purchase from Computer Supplies continues to provide you the quality and service you have come to expect from our company.

Sincerely,

Douglas Pullis

Douglas Pullis
General Manager

cds

D. TABLES: SPECIAL FEATURES

Vertical Placement. Vertically center a table that appears on a page by itself. Insert 1 blank line before and after a table appearing with other text.

Heading Block. Center and bold all lines of the heading, typing the title in all caps and 14-point font and the subtitle in upper- and lowercase and in 12-point font. If a table has a number, type the word *Table* in upper- and lowercase. Follow the table number with a period and 1 space.

Column Headings. If *all* columns in the table consist of text (such as words, phone numbers, or years), center all column headings and left-align all column entries. In all other situations, left-align all text column headings and text column entries and right-align all quantity column headings and quantity column entries. Regardless of the type of column, center braced headings. Use bold upper- and lowercase.

Column Capitalization. Capitalize only the first word and proper nouns in column entries.

Percentages and Dollars. Repeat the % sign for each number in a column (unless the heading identifies the data as percentages). Insert the $ sign only before the first amount and before a total amount. Align the $ sign with the longest amount in the column, inserting spaces after the $ sign as needed (leaving 2 spaces for each digit and 1 space for each comma).

Total Line. Add a border above a total line. Use the word *Total* or *Totals* as appropriate.

A. FORMATTING BUSINESS FORMS

Many business forms can be created and filled in by using templates that are provided within commercial word processing software. Template forms can be used "as is" or they can be edited. Templates can also be used to create customized forms for any business.

When a template is opened, the form is displayed on screen. The user can then fill in the necessary information, including personalized company information. Data are entered into cells or fields, and you can move quickly from field to field with a single keystroke—usually by pressing TAB or ENTER.

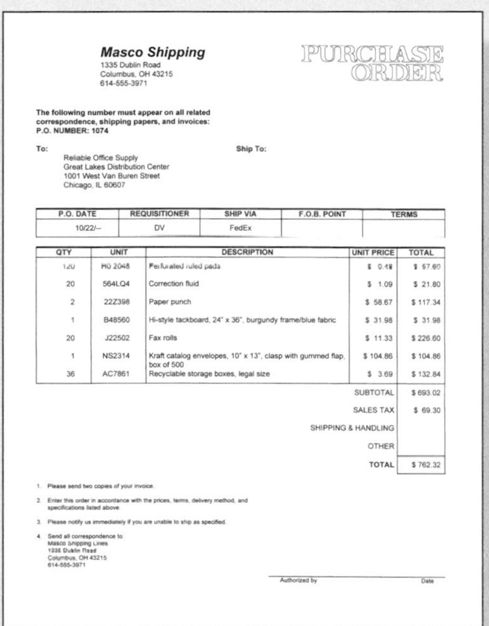

Masco Shipping
1335 Dublin Road
Columbus, OH 43215
614-555-3971

PURCHASE ORDER

The following number must appear on all related correspondence, shipping papers, and invoices:
P.O. NUMBER: 1074

To:
Reliable Office Supply
Great Lakes Distribution Center
1001 West Van Buren Street
Chicago, IL 60607

Ship To:

P.O. DATE	REQUISITIONER	SHIP VIA	F.O.B. POINT	TERMS
10/22/--	DV	FedEx		

QTY	UNIT	DESCRIPTION	UNIT PRICE	TOTAL
120	H0 2048	Perforated ruled pads	$ 0.48	$ 57.60
20	564LQ4	Correction fluid	$ 1.09	$ 21.80
2	22Z398	Paper punch	$ 58.67	$ 117.34
1	B48560	Hi-style tackboard, 24" x 36", burgundy frame/blue fabric	$ 31.98	$ 31.98
20	J22502	Fax rolls	$ 11.33	$ 226.60
1	NS2314	Kraft catalog envelopes, 10" x 13", clasp with gummed flap, box of 500	$ 104.86	$ 104.86
36	AC7861	Recyclable storage boxes, legal size	$ 3.69	$ 132.84
			SUBTOTAL	$ 693.02
			SALES TAX	$ 69.30
			SHIPPING & HANDLING	
			OTHER	
			TOTAL	$ 762.32

1. Please send two copies of your invoice.
2. Enter this order in accordance with the prices, terms, delivery method, and specifications listed above.
3. Please notify us immediately if you are unable to ship as specified.
4. Send all correspondence to:
   Masco Shipping Lines
   1335 Dublin Road
   Columbus, OH 43215
   614-555-3971

Authorized by Date

B. U.S. POSTAL SERVICE ABBREVIATIONS

(for States, Territories, and Canadian Provinces)

States and Territories

Alabama	AL
Alaska	AK
Arizona	AZ
Arkansas	AR
California	CA
Colorado	CO
Connecticut	CT
Delaware	DE
District of Columbia	DC
Florida	FL
Georgia	GA
Guam	GU
Hawaii	HI
Idaho	ID
Illinois	IL
Indiana	IN
Iowa	IA
Kansas	KS
Kentucky	KY
Louisiana	LA
Maine	ME
Maryland	MD
Massachusetts	MA
Michigan	MI
Minnesota	MN
Mississippi	MS
Missouri	MO
Montana	MT
Nebraska	NE
Nevada	NV
New Hampshire	NH
New Jersey	NJ
New Mexico	NM
New York	NY
North Carolina	NC
North Dakota	ND
Ohio	OH
Oklahoma	OK
Oregon	OR
Pennsylvania	PA
Puerto Rico	PR
Rhode Island	RI
South Carolina	SC
South Dakota	SD
Tennessee	TN
Texas	TX
Utah	UT
Vermont	VT
Virgin Islands	VI
Virginia	VA
Washington	WA
West Virginia	WV
Wisconsin	WI
Wyoming	WY

Canadian Provinces

Alberta	AB
British Columbia	BC
Labrador	LB
Manitoba	MB
New Brunswick	NB
Newfoundland	NF
Northwest Territories	NT
Nova Scotia	NS
Ontario	ON
Prince Edward Island	PE
Quebec	PQ
Saskatchewan	SK
Yukon Territory	YT

C. PROOFREADERS' MARKS

Proofreaders' Marks		Draft	Final Copy
⌢	Omit space	data base	database
v or ∧	Insert	if he's going (not)	if he's not going,
≡	Capitalize	Maple street	Maple Street
⸿	Delete	a final draft	a draft
#	Insert space	allready to	all ready to
when / ~~if~~	Change word	and ~~if~~ you (when)	and when you
/	Use lowercase letter	our President	our president
¶	Paragraph	… to use it.¶We can	… to use it. We can
• • •	Don't delete	a ~~true~~ story	a true story
○	Spell out	the only 1	the only one
∽	Transpose	they all see	they see all
SS	Single-space	ss [first line second line	first line second line
ds	Double-space	ds [first line second line	first line second line
⊐	Move right	Please send	Please send
⊏	Move left	May I	May I
∿∿	Bold	Column Heading	**Column Heading**
ital	Italic	*ital* Time magazine	*Time* magazine
u/l	Underline	u/l Time magazine	Time magazine
♂	Move as shown	readers will see	will see readers

Language Arts for Business

(50 "must-know" rules)

PUNCTUATION

COMMAS

RULE 1 , direct address (L. 21)

Use commas before and after a name used in direct address.

Thank you, John, for responding to my e-mail so quickly.

Ladies and gentlemen, the program has been canceled.

RULE 2 , independent clause (L. 27)

Use a comma between independent clauses joined by a coordinate conjunction (unless both clauses are short).

Ellen left her job with IBM, and she and her sister went to Paris.

But: Ellen left her job with IBM and went to Paris with her sister.

But: John drove and I navigated.

Note: An independent clause is one that can stand alone as a complete sentence. The most common coordinate conjunctions are *and, but, or,* and *nor.*

RULE 3 , introductory expression (L. 27)

Use a comma after an introductory expression (unless it is a short prepositional phrase).

Before we can make a decision, we must have all the facts.

But: In 2004 our nation elected a new president.

Note: An introductory expression is a group of words that come before the subject and verb of the independent clause. Common prepositions are *to, in, on, of, at, by, for,* and *with.*

RULE 4 , direct quotation (L. 41)

Use a comma before and after a direct quotation.

James said, "I shall return," and then left.

RULE 5 , date (L. 57)

Use a comma before and after the year in a complete date.

We will arrive on June 2, 2006, for the conference.

But: We will arrive on June 2 for the conference.

RULE 6 , place (L. 57)

Use a comma before and after a state or country that follows a city (but not before a ZIP Code).

Joan moved to Vancouver, British Columbia, in May.

Send the package to Douglasville, GA 30135, by Express Mail.

But: Send the package to Georgia by Express Mail.

RULE 7 ▶ , series (L. 61)

Use a comma between each item in a series of three or more.

We need to order paper, toner, and font cartridges_ for the printer.

They saved their work, exited their program, and turned off their computers_ when they finished.

Note: Do not use a comma after the last item in a series.

RULE 8 ▶ , transitional expression (L. 61)

Use a comma before and after a transitional expression or independent comment.

It is critical, therefore, that we finish the project on time.

Our present projections, you must admit, are inadequate.

But: You must admit_ our present projections are inadequate.

Note: Examples of transitional expressions and independent comments are *in addition to, therefore, however, on the other hand, as a matter of fact,* and *unfortunately.*

RULE 9 ▶ , nonessential expression (L. 71)

Use a comma before and after a nonessential expression.

Andre, who was there, can verify the statement.

But: Anyone_ who was there_ can verify the statement.

Van's first book, *Crisis of Management,* was not discussed.

Van's book_ *Crisis of Management*_ was not discussed.

Note: A nonessential expression is a group of words that may be omitted without changing the basic meaning of the sentence. Always examine the noun or pronoun that comes before the expression to determine whether the noun needs the expression to complete its meaning. If it does, the expression is *essential* and does *not* take a comma.

RULE 10 ▶ , adjacent adjectives (L. 71)

Use a comma between two adjacent adjectives that modify the same noun.

We need an intelligent, enthusiastic_ individual for this job.

But: Please order a new_ bulletin board for our main_ conference room.

Note: Do not use a comma after the second adjective. Also, do not use a comma if the first adjective modifies the combined idea of the second adjective and the noun (for example, *bulletin board* and *conference room* in the second example above).

SEMICOLONS

RULE 11 ▶ ; no conjunction (L. 97)

Use a semicolon to separate two closely related independent clauses that are *not* joined by a conjunction (such as *and, but, or,* or *nor*).

Management favored the vote; stockholders did not.

But: Management favored the vote, but stockholders did not.

RULE 12 ▶ ; series (L. 97)

Use a semicolon to separate three or more items in a series if any of the items already contain commas.

Staff meetings were held on Thursday, May 7; Monday, June 7; and Friday, June 12.

Note: Be sure to insert the semicolon *between* (not within) the items in a series.

HYPHENS

RULE 13 ▶ - number (L. 57)

Hyphenate compound numbers between twenty-one and ninety-nine and fractions that are expressed as words.

Twenty-nine recommendations were approved by at least three-fourths of the members.

RULE 14 ▶ - compound adjective (L. 67)

Hyphenate compound adjectives that come before a noun (unless the first word is an adverb ending in *-ly*).

We reviewed an up-to-date report on Wednesday.

But: The report was up to date.

But: We reviewed the highly rated report.

Note: A compound adjective is two or more words that function as a unit to describe a noun.

APOSTROPHES

RULE 15 ▶ ' singular noun (L. 37)

Use *'s* to form the possessive of singular nouns.

The hurricane's force caused major damage to North Carolina's coastline.

RULE 16 ▶ ' plural noun (L. 37)

Use only an apostrophe to form the possessive of plural nouns that end in *s*.

The investors' goals were outlined in the stockholders' report.

But: The investors outlined their goals in the report to the stockholders.

But: The women's and children's clothing was on sale.

RULE 17 ▶ ' pronoun (L. 37)

Use *'s* to form the possessive of indefinite pronouns (such as *someone's* or *anybody's*); do not use an apostrophe with personal pronouns (such as *hers, his, its, ours, theirs,* and *yours*).

She could select anybody's paper for a sample.

It's time to put the file back into its cabinet.

COLONS

RULE 18 ▶
: explanatory material
(L. 91)

Use a colon to introduce explanatory material that follows an independent clause.

The computer satisfies three criteria: speed, cost, and power.

But: The computer satisfies the three criteria of speed, cost, and power.

Remember this: only one coupon is allowed per customer.

Note: An independent clause can stand alone as a complete sentence. Do not capitalize the word following the colon.

PERIODS

RULE 19 ▶
. polite request
(L. 91)

Use a period to end a sentence that is a polite request.

Will you please call me if I can be of further assistance.

Note: Consider a sentence a polite request if you expect the reader to respond by doing as you ask rather than by giving a yes-or-no answer.

QUOTATION MARKS

RULE 20 ▶
" quotation
(L. 41)

Use quotation marks around a direct quotation.

Harrison responded by saying, "Their decision does not affect us."

But: Harrison responded by saying that their decision does not affect us.

RULE 21 ▶
" title
(L. 41)

Use quotation marks around the title of a newspaper or magazine article, chapter in a book, report, and similar terms.

The most helpful article I found was "Multimedia for All."

ITALICS (OR UNDERLINE)

RULE 22 ▶
title
(L. 41)

Italicize (or underline) the titles of books, magazines, newspapers, and other complete published works.

Grisham's *The Brethren* was reviewed in a recent *USA Today* article.

GRAMMAR

SENTENCES

RULE 23 ▶ fragment (L. 21)

Avoid sentence fragments.

Not: She had always wanted to be a financial manager. But had not had the needed education.

But: She had always wanted to be a financial manager but had not had the needed education.

Note: A fragment is a part of a sentence that is incorrectly punctuated as a complete sentence. In the first example above, "but had not had the needed education" is not a complete sentence because it does not contain a subject.

RULE 24 ▶ run-on (L. 21)

Avoid run-on sentences.

Not: Mohamed is a competent worker he has even passed the MOS exam.

Not: Mohamed is a competent worker, he has even passed the MOS exam.

But: Mohamed is a competent worker; he has even passed the MOS exam.

Or: Mohamed is a competent worker. He has even passed the MOS exam.

Note: A run-on sentence is two independent clauses that run together without any punctuation between them or with only a comma between them.

AGREEMENT

RULE 25 ▶ agreement singular, agreement plural (L. 67)

Use singular verbs and pronouns with singular subjects; use plural verbs and pronouns with plural subjects.

I was happy with my performance.

Janet and Phoenix were happy with their performance.

Among the items discussed were our raises and benefits.

RULE 26 ▶ agreement pronoun (L. 81)

Some pronouns *(anybody, each, either, everybody, everyone, much, neither, no one, nobody,* and *one)* are always singular and take a singular verb. Other pronouns *(all, any, more, most, none,* and *some)* may be singular or plural, depending on the noun to which they refer.

Each of the employees has finished his or her task.

Much remains to be done.

Most of the pie was eaten, but most of the cookies were left.

RULE 27 ▶ agreement intervening words (L. 81)

Disregard any intervening words that come between the subject and verb when establishing agreement.

The box containing the books and pencils has not been found.

Alex, accompanied by Tricia, is attending the conference and taking his computer.

RULE 28 ▶ agreement nearer noun (L. 101)

If two subjects are joined by *or, either/or, neither/nor,* or *not only/but also,* make the verb agree with the subject nearer to the verb.

Neither the coach nor the players are at home.

Not only the coach but also the referee is at home.

But: Both the coach and the referee are at home.

PRONOUNS

RULE 29 nominative pronoun (L. 107)

Use nominative pronouns (such as *I, he, she, we, they,* and *who)* as subjects of a sentence or clause.

The programmer and he are reviewing the code.

Barb is a person who can do the job.

RULE 30 objective pronoun (L. 107)

Use objective pronouns (such as *me, him, her, us, them,* and *whom)* as objects of a verb, preposition, or infinitive.

The code was reviewed by the programmer and him.

Barb is the type of person whom we can trust.

ADJECTIVES AND ADVERBS

RULE 31 adjective/adverb (L. 101)

Use comparative adjectives and adverbs (*-er, more,* and *less)* when referring to two nouns or pronouns; use superlative adjectives and adverbs *(-est, most,* and *least)* when referring to more than two.

The shorter of the two training sessions is the more helpful one.

The longest of the three training sessions is the least helpful one.

WORD USAGE

RULE 32 accept/except (L. 117)

***Accept* means "to agree to"; *except* means "to leave out."**

All employees except the maintenance staff should accept the agreement.

RULE 33 affect/effect (L. 117)

***Affect* is most often used as a verb meaning "to influence"; *effect* is most often used as a noun meaning "result."**

The ruling will affect our domestic operations but will have no effect on our Asian operations.

RULE 34 farther/further (L. 117)

***Farther* refers to distance; *further* refers to extent or degree.**

The farther we drove, the further agitated he became.

RULE 35 personal/personnel (L. 117)

***Personal* means "private"; *personnel* means "employees."**

All personnel agreed not to use e-mail for personal business.

RULE 36 principal/principle (L. 117)

***Principal* means "primary"; *principle* means "rule."**

The principle of fairness is our principal means of dealing with customers.

MECHANICS

CAPITALIZATION

RULE 37 ≡ sentence (L. 31)

Capitalize the first word of a sentence.

Please prepare a summary of your activities.

RULE 38 ≡ proper noun (L. 31)

Capitalize proper nouns and adjectives derived from proper nouns.

Judy Hendrix drove to Albuquerque in her new Pontiac convertible.

Note: A proper noun is the official name of a particular person, place, or thing.

RULE 39 ≡ time (L. 31)

Capitalize the names of the days of the week, months, holidays, and religious days (but do not capitalize the names of the seasons).

On Thursday, November 25, we will celebrate Thanksgiving, the most popular holiday in the fall.

RULE 40 ≡ noun # (L. 77)

Capitalize nouns followed by a number or letter (except for the nouns *line, note, page, paragraph,* and *size).*

Please read Chapter 5, which begins on page 94.

RULE 41 ≡ compass point (L. 77)

Capitalize compass points (such as *north, south,* or *northeast)* only when they designate definite regions.

From Montana we drove south to reach the Southwest.

RULE 42 ≡ organization (L. 111)

Capitalize common organizational terms (such as *advertising department* and *finance committee)* only when they are the actual names of the units in the writer's own organization and when they are preceded by the word *the.*

The report from the Advertising Department is due today.

But: Our advertising department will submit its report today.

RULE 43 ≡ course (L. 111)

Capitalize the names of specific course titles but not the names of subjects or areas of study.

I have enrolled in Accounting 201 and will also take a marketing course.

NUMBER EXPRESSION

RULE 44 # general (L. 41)

In general, spell out numbers zero through ten, and use figures for numbers above ten.

We rented two movies for tonight.

The decision was reached after 27 precincts sent in their results.

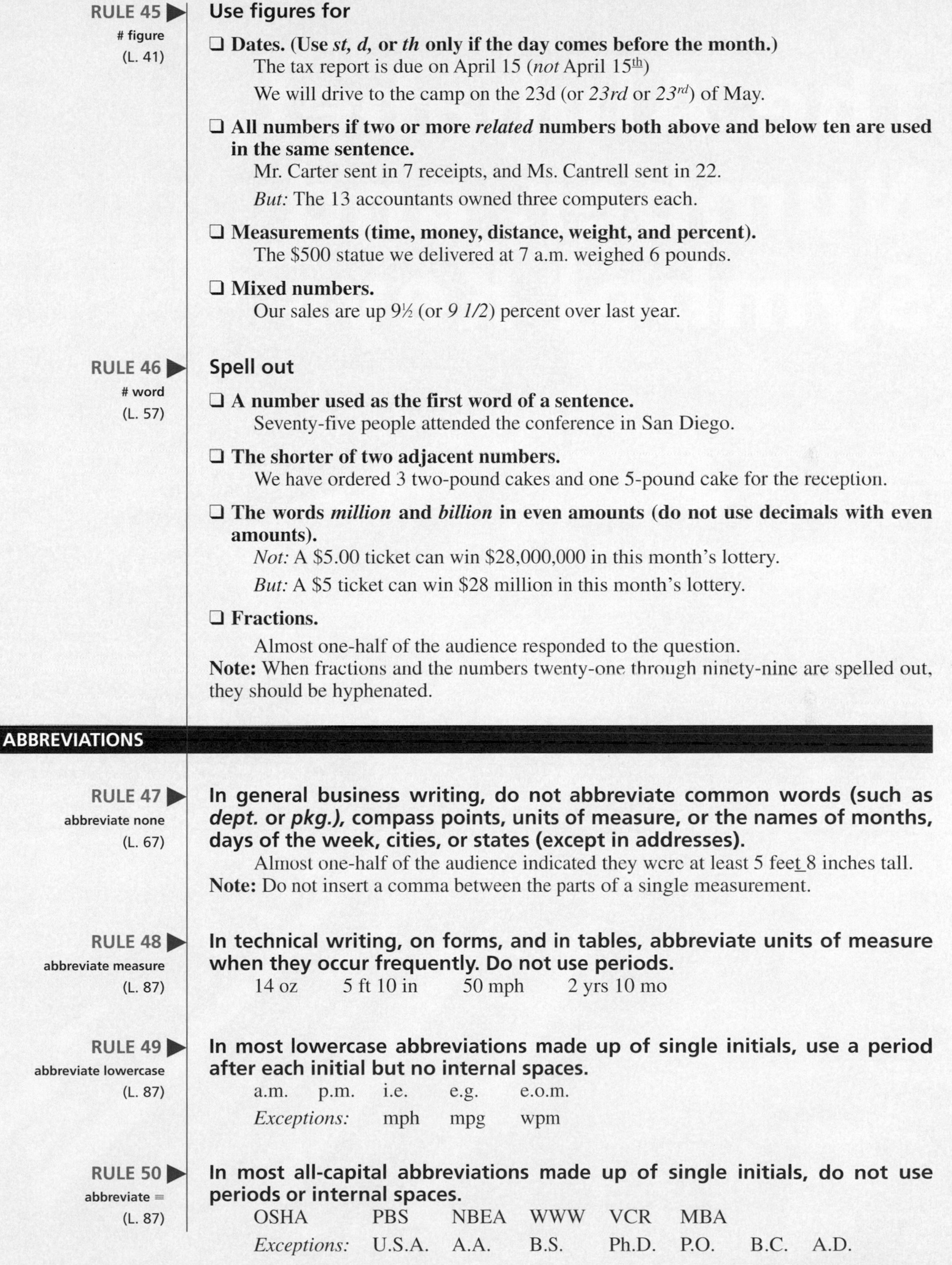

RULE 45 ▶ # figure (L. 41)

Use figures for

❑ **Dates. (Use *st, d,* or *th* only if the day comes before the month.)**
The tax report is due on April 15 (*not* April 15th)
We will drive to the camp on the 23d (or *23rd* or *23rd*) of May.

❑ **All numbers if two or more *related* numbers both above and below ten are used in the same sentence.**
Mr. Carter sent in 7 receipts, and Ms. Cantrell sent in 22.
But: The 13 accountants owned three computers each.

❑ **Measurements (time, money, distance, weight, and percent).**
The $500 statue we delivered at 7 a.m. weighed 6 pounds.

❑ **Mixed numbers.**
Our sales are up 9½ (or *9 1/2*) percent over last year.

RULE 46 ▶ # word (L. 57)

Spell out

❑ **A number used as the first word of a sentence.**
Seventy-five people attended the conference in San Diego.

❑ **The shorter of two adjacent numbers.**
We have ordered 3 two-pound cakes and one 5-pound cake for the reception.

❑ **The words *million* and *billion* in even amounts (do not use decimals with even amounts).**
Not: A $5.00 ticket can win $28,000,000 in this month's lottery.
But: A $5 ticket can win $28 million in this month's lottery.

❑ **Fractions.**
Almost one-half of the audience responded to the question.

Note: When fractions and the numbers twenty-one through ninety-nine are spelled out, they should be hyphenated.

ABBREVIATIONS

RULE 47 ▶ abbreviate none (L. 67)

In general business writing, do not abbreviate common words (such as *dept.* or *pkg.*), compass points, units of measure, or the names of months, days of the week, cities, or states (except in addresses).
Almost one-half of the audience indicated they were at least 5 feet_8 inches tall.

Note: Do not insert a comma between the parts of a single measurement.

RULE 48 ▶ abbreviate measure (L. 87)

In technical writing, on forms, and in tables, abbreviate units of measure when they occur frequently. Do not use periods.
14 oz   5 ft 10 in   50 mph   2 yrs 10 mo

RULE 49 ▶ abbreviate lowercase (L. 87)

In most lowercase abbreviations made up of single initials, use a period after each initial but no internal spaces.
a.m.   p.m.   i.e.   e.g.   e.o.m.
Exceptions: mph   mpg   wpm

RULE 50 ▶ abbreviate ≡ (L. 87)

In most all-capital abbreviations made up of single initials, do not use periods or internal spaces.
OSHA   PBS   NBEA   WWW   VCR   MBA
Exceptions: U.S.A.   A.A.   B.S.   Ph.D.   P.O.   B.C.   A.D.

Part 1

The Alphabet, Number, and Symbol Keys

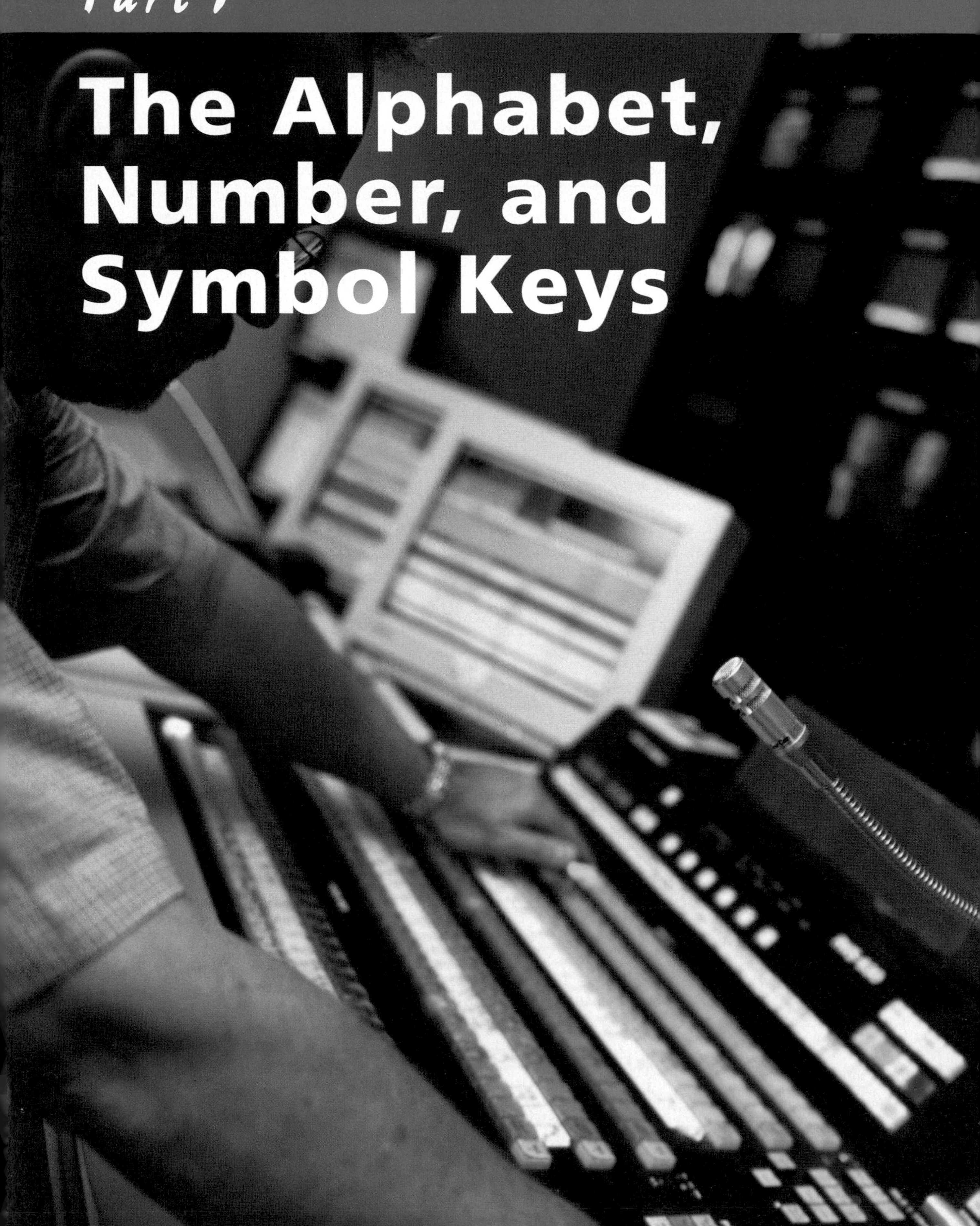

Keyboarding in Arts, Audio, Video Technology, and Communications Services

Occupations in this cluster deal with organizing and communicating information to the public in various forms and media. This cluster includes jobs in radio and television broadcasting, journalism, motion pictures, the recording industry, the performing arts, multimedia publishing, and the entertainment services. Book editors, computer artists, technical writers, radio announcers, news correspondents, and camera operators are just a few jobs within this cluster.

Qualifications and Skills

Strong oral and written communication skills and technical skills are necessary for anyone in communications and media. Without a doubt, competent keyboarding skill is extremely advantageous.

Working in the media requires creativity, talent, and accurate use of language. In journalism, being observant, thinking clearly, and seeing the significance of events are all of utmost importance. Announcers must have exceptional voices, excellent speaking skills, and a unique style. The ability to work under pressure is important in all areas of media.

Objectives

KEYBOARDING

- Operate by touch the letter, number, and symbol keys.
- Demonstrate proper typing technique.
- Use the correct spacing with punctuation.
- Type at least 28 words per minute on a 2-minute timed writing with no more than 5 errors.

TECHNICAL

- Answer correctly at least 90 percent of the questions on an objective test.

Unit 1

Keyboarding: The Alphabet

LESSON 1
A S D F J K L ;
ENTER SPACE BAR

LESSON 2
H E O R

LESSON 3
M T P C

LESSON 4
RIGHT SHIFT V . W

LESSON 5
Review

Home Keys

Goals

- Touch-type the home keys (A S D F J K L ;)
- Touch-type the SPACE BAR
- Touch-type the ENTER key
- Type at least 10wpm/1′/3e

LEFT HAND	
First Finger	F
Second Finger	D
Third Finger	S
Fourth Finger	A

	RIGHT HAND
J	First Finger
K	Second Finger
L	Third Finger
;	Fourth Finger
SPACE BAR	Thumb

NEW KEYS

A. Follow the directions to become familiar with the home keys.

The semicolon (;) is commonly called the semi key.

A. THE HOME KEYS

The **A S D F J K L ;** keys are known as the home keys.

1. Place the fingers of your left hand on the home keys as follows: first finger on **F**; second finger on **D**; third finger on **S**; fourth finger on **A**.
2. Place the fingers of your right hand on the home keys as follows: first finger on **J**; second finger on **K**; third finger on **L**; and fourth finger on **;**.
3. Curve your fingers.
4. Using the correct fingers, type each character as you say it to yourself: `a s d f j k l ;`.
5. Remove your fingers from the keyboard and replace them on the home keys.
6. Press each home key again as you say each character: `a s d f j k l ;`.

B. THE SPACE BAR

The SPACE BAR, located beneath the letter keys, is used to space between words and after marks of punctuation.

1. With fingers held motionless on the home keys, poise your right thumb about a half inch above the SPACE BAR.
2. Type the characters and then press the SPACE BAR 1 time. Bounce your thumb off.

C. Type each line 1 time, pressing the SPACE BAR where you see a space and pressing the ENTER key at the end of a line.

C. THE ENTER← KEY

The ENTER key moves the insertion point to the beginning of a new line. Reach to the ENTER key with the fourth finger of your right hand. Keep your J finger at home. Lightly press the ENTER key. Practice using the ENTER key until you can do so with confidence and without looking at your hands.

```
asdf jkl; asdf jkl; ↵
asdf jkl; asdf jkl; ↵
```

LEFT HAND

First Finger	F
Second Finger	D
Third Finger	S
Fourth Finger	A

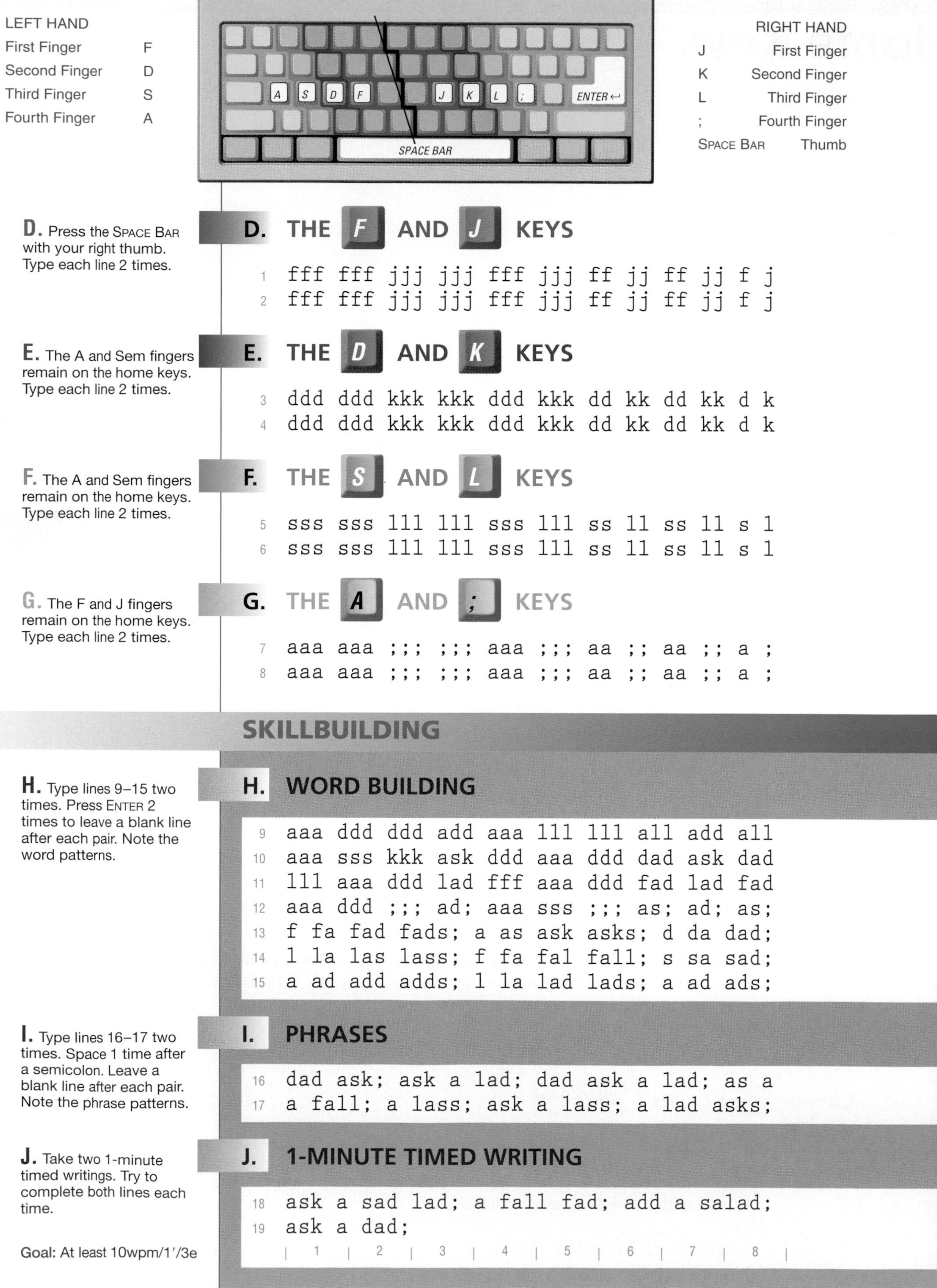

RIGHT HAND

J	First Finger
K	Second Finger
L	Third Finger
;	Fourth Finger
SPACE BAR	Thumb

D. Press the SPACE BAR with your right thumb. Type each line 2 times.

D. THE F AND J KEYS

```
1  fff fff jjj jjj fff jjj ff jj ff jj f j
2  fff fff jjj jjj fff jjj ff jj ff jj f j
```

E. The A and Sem fingers remain on the home keys. Type each line 2 times.

E. THE D AND K KEYS

```
3  ddd ddd kkk kkk ddd kkk dd kk dd kk d k
4  ddd ddd kkk kkk ddd kkk dd kk dd kk d k
```

F. The A and Sem fingers remain on the home keys. Type each line 2 times.

F. THE S AND L KEYS

```
5  sss sss lll lll sss lll ss ll ss ll s l
6  sss sss lll lll sss lll ss ll ss ll s l
```

G. The F and J fingers remain on the home keys. Type each line 2 times.

G. THE A AND ; KEYS

```
7  aaa aaa ;;; ;;; aaa ;;; aa ;; aa ;; a ;
8  aaa aaa ;;; ;;; aaa ;;; aa ;; aa ;; a ;
```

SKILLBUILDING

H. Type lines 9–15 two times. Press ENTER 2 times to leave a blank line after each pair. Note the word patterns.

H. WORD BUILDING

```
9   aaa ddd ddd add aaa lll lll all add all
10  aaa sss kkk ask ddd aaa ddd dad ask dad
11  lll aaa ddd lad fff aaa ddd fad lad fad
12  aaa ddd ;;; ad; aaa sss ;;; as; ad; as;
13  f fa fad fads; a as ask asks; d da dad;
14  l la las lass; f fa fal fall; s sa sad;
15  a ad add adds; l la lad lads; a ad ads;
```

I. Type lines 16–17 two times. Space 1 time after a semicolon. Leave a blank line after each pair. Note the phrase patterns.

I. PHRASES

```
16  dad ask; ask a lad; dad ask a lad; as a
17  a fall; a lass; ask a lass; a lad asks;
```

J. Take two 1-minute timed writings. Try to complete both lines each time.

Goal: At least 10wpm/1′/3e

J. 1-MINUTE TIMED WRITING

```
18  ask a sad lad; a fall fad; add a salad;
19  ask a dad;
    | 1 | 2 | 3 | 4 | 5 | 6 | 7 | 8 |
```

New Keys

Goals

- Touch-type the H, E, O, and R keys
- Type at least 11wpm/1′/3e

Fingers are named for home keys. (Example: The middle finger of the left hand is the D finger.)

A. WARMUP

A. Type 2 times.

```
1 fff jjj ddd kkk sss lll aaa ;;; fff jjj
2 a salad; a lad; alas a fad; ask a lass;
```

NEW KEYS

B. THE H KEY

B. Type each line 2 times. Space 1 time after a semicolon.

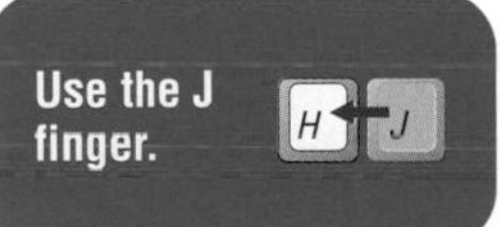

Use the J finger.
H
J


```
3 jjj jhj jhj hjh jjj jhj jhj hjh jjj jhj
4 has has hah hah had had aha aha ash ash
5 hash half sash lash dash hall shad shah
6 as dad had; a lass has half; add a dash
```

C. THE E KEY

C. Type each line 2 times. Keep your eyes on the copy as you type.

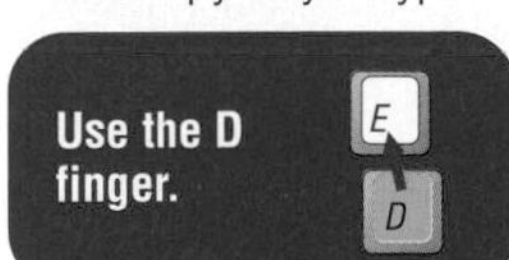

Use the D finger.
E
D


```
7 ddd ded ded ede ddd ded ded ede ddd ded
8 lea led he; he see; eke fed sea lee fee
9 feed keel ease heal held seal lead fake
10 he fed a seal; she held a lease; a keel
```

D. THE O KEY

D. Type each line 2 times. Keep fingers curved.

Use the L finger.
O
L


```
11 lll lol lol olo lll lol lol olo lll lol
12 doe off foe hod oh; oak odd ode old sod
13 shoe look kook joke odes does solo oleo
14 he held a hook; a lass solos; old foes;
```

E. Type each line 2 times. Keep the A finger at home.

E. THE R KEY

```
15 fff frf frf rfr fff frf frf rfr fff frf
16 red ark ore err rah era rod oar her are
17 oars soar dear fare read role rare door
18 a dark red door; he read a rare reader;
```

SKILLBUILDING

F. Type each line 2 times. Do not type the red vertical lines.

F. WORD PATTERNS

```
19 dale kale sale hale|fold sold hold old;
20 feed deed heed seed|dash sash lash ash;
21 lake rake sake fake|dear sear rear ear;
```

G. Take two 1-minute timed writings. Try to complete both lines each time. Press ENTER only at the end of line 23.

Goal: At least 11wpm/1′/3e

G. 1-MINUTE TIMED WRITING

```
22 she asked for a rare old deed; he held
23 a red door ajar;
   | 1 | 2 | 3 | 4 | 5 | 6 | 7 | 8 |
```

Keyboarding Connection

What Is the Internet?

What is the easiest way to go to the library? Try using your fingertips! The Internet creates a "virtual library"—a library with no walls. Nothing can match the Internet as a research device. It is not just one computer but an immense connection of computers talking to one another and organizing and exchanging information.

The Internet is synonymous with cyberspace, a word describing the power and control of information. The Internet has been called "a network of networks" linked together to deliver information to users. The Internet connects more than 200 million people to over 3 million computer networks.

The Internet is considered a wide area network (WAN) because the computers on it span the entire world. Each day the Net increases at about 1000 new users every hour.

YOUR TURN List some ways the Internet, as a virtual library, enhances your research activities.

New Keys

Goals

- Touch-type the M, T, P, and C keys
- Type at least 12wpm/1′/3e

A. Type 2 times.

A. WARMUP

1 aa ;; ss ll dd kk ff jj hh ee oo rr aa;
2 he held a sale for her as she had asked

NEW KEYS

B. Type each line 2 times.

B. THE M KEY

3 jjj jmj jmj mjm jjj jmj jmj mjm jjj jmj
4 mad mom me; am jam; ram dam ham mar ma;
5 arms loam lame roam make fame room same
6 she made more room for some of her ham;

C. Type each line 2 times.

C. THE T KEY

7 fff ftf ftf tft fff ftf ftf tft fff ftf
8 tar tam mat hot jot rat eat lot art sat
9 told take date late mart mate tool fate
10 he told her to set a later date to eat;

D. Type each line 2 times.

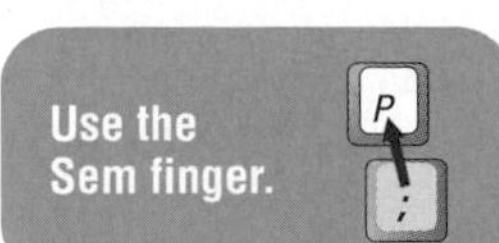

D. THE P KEY

11 ;;; ;p; ;p; p;p ;;; ;p; ;p; p;p ;;; ;p;
12 pat pal sap rap pet par spa lap pad mop
13 pale palm stop drop pelt plea slap trap
14 please park the red jeep past the pool;

E. Type each line 2 times.

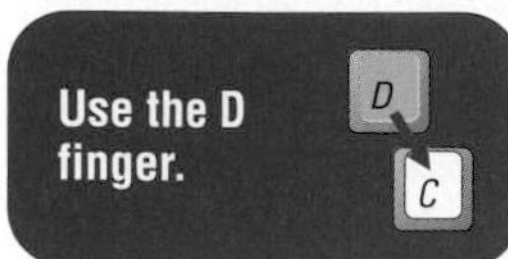

E. THE C KEY

```
15 ddd dcd dcd cdc ddd dcd dcd cdc ddd dcd
16 cot cod sac act car coo arc ace cop cat
17 pack tack chat coat face aces deck cost
18 call her to race cool cars at the track
```

SKILLBUILDING

F. Sit in the correct position as you type these drills. Refer to the illustration in the Introduction. Type each line 2 times. Do not type the red vertical lines.

F. SHORT PHRASES

```
19 as so|she had|has met|let her|fast pace
20 to do|ask her|for the|had pop|look past
21 do as|lap top|her pad|let pat|halt them
22 as he|had for|red cap|she let|fast plot
```

G. Take two 1-minute timed writings. Try to complete both lines each time. Use word wrap. Press ENTER only at the end of line 24.

Goal: At least 12wpm/1′/3e

G. 1-MINUTE TIMED WRITING

```
23 the old store at home had lots of cheap
24 stools for the sale;
   | 1 | 2 | 3 | 4 | 5 | 6 | 7 | 8 |
```

Strategies for Career Success

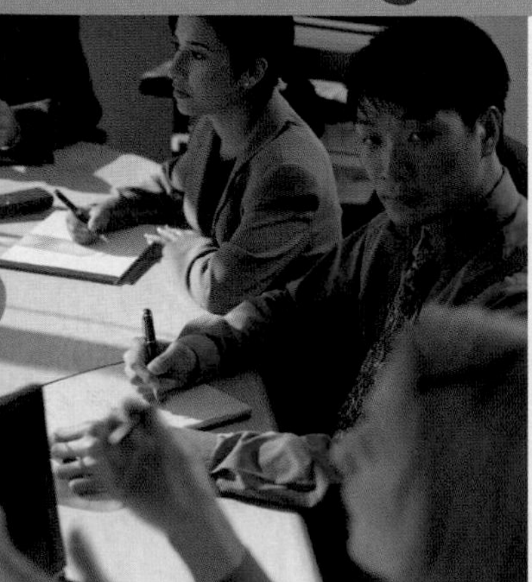

Being a Good Listener

Silence is golden! Listening is essential for learning, getting along, and forming relationships.

Do you tend to forget people's names after being introduced? Do you look away from the speaker instead of making eye contact? Do you interrupt the speaker before he or she finishes talking? Do you misunderstand people? Answering yes can indicate poor listening skills.

To improve your listening skills, follow these steps. *Hear the speaker clearly.* Do not interrupt; let the speaker develop his or her ideas before you speak. *Focus on the message.* At the end of a conversation, identify major items discussed. Mentally ask questions to help you assess the points the speaker is making. *Keep an open mind.* Do not judge. Developing your listening skills benefits everyone.

YOUR TURN Assess your listening behavior. What techniques can you use to improve your listening skills? Practice them the next time you have a conversation with someone.

Lesson 4

New Keys

Goals

- Touch-type the RIGHT SHIFT, V, period, and W keys
- Count errors
- Type at least 13wpm/1′/3e

A. Type 2 times.

A. WARMUP

1 the farmer asked her to feed the mares;
2 the late callers came to mop the floor;

NEW KEYS

B. Type each line 2 times.

Use the Sem finger.
SHIFT

B. THE RIGHT SHIFT KEY

To capitalize letters on the left half of the keyboard:

1. With the J finger at home, press and hold down the RIGHT SHIFT key with the Sem finger.
2. Press the letter key.
3. Release the RIGHT SHIFT key and return fingers to home position.

3 ;;; ;A; ;A; ;;; ;S; ;S; ;;; ;D; ;D; ;;;
4 Art Alf Ada Sal Sam Dee Dot Flo Ted Tom
5 Amos Carl Chet Elsa Fred Sara Todd Elda
6 Carl Amos took Sara Carter to the races

C. Type each line 2 times.

Use the F finger.
F
V

C. THE V KEY

7 fff fvf fvf vfv fff fvf fvf vfv fff fvf
8 Val eve Eva vet Ava vat Eve ova Vel vee
9 have vase Vera ever vast Reva dove vest
10 Dave voted for Vassar; Val voted for me

D. Type each line 2 times. Space 1 time after a period following an abbreviation; do not space after a period within an abbreviation; space 1 time after a period ending a sentence.

Use the L finger.
L

D. THE . KEY

11 lll l.l l.l .l. lll l.l l.l .l. lll l.l
12 dr. dr. ea. ea. sr. sr. Dr. Dr. Sr. Sr.
13 a.m. acct. A.D. p.m. Corp. amt. Dr. Co.
14 Selma left. Dave left. Sarah came home.

E. Type each line 2 times.

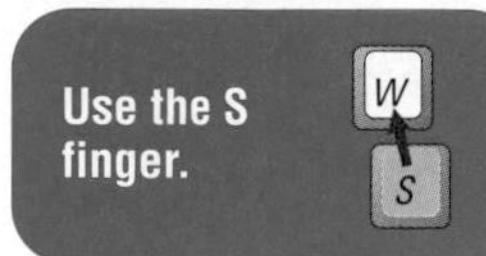

E. THE W KEY

15 sss sws sws wsw sss sws sws wsw sss sws
16 wow sow war owe was mow woe few wee row
17 wake ward wart wave wham whom walk what
18 Wade watched Walt Shaw walk for a week.

SKILLBUILDING

F. Type each line 2 times.

F. BUILD SKILL ON SENTENCES

19 Amos Ford saw Emma Dale feed the mares.
20 Dr. Drake called Sam; he asked for Ted.
21 Vera told a tale to her old classmates.
22 Todd asked Cale to move some old rakes.

G. Type each line 1 time. After typing all the lines, count your errors. Refer to the Introduction if you need help.

G. COUNTING ERRORS IN SENTENCES

23 Ada lost her letter; Dee lost her card.
24 Dave sold some of the food to a market.
25 Alva asked Walt for three more matches.
26 Dale asked Seth to watch the last show.

H. Take two 1-minute timed writings. Try to complete both lines each time.

Goal: At least 13wpm/1′/3e

H. 1-MINUTE TIMED WRITING

27 Val asked them to tell the major to see
28 Carla at that local farm.

| 1 | 2 | 3 | 4 | 5 | 6 | 7 | 8 |

Review

Goals

- Reinforce new-key reaches
- Type at least 14wpm/1′/3e

A. Type 2 times.

A. WARMUP

1 Dave called Drew to ask for a road map.
2 Elsa took three old jars to her mother.

SKILLBUILDING

B. Type each line 2 times. Do not type the red vertical lines.

B. WORD PATTERNS

3 feed seed deed heed|fold cold mold told
4 fame tame lame same|mate late date fate
5 lace face mace race|vast last cast fast
6 park dark hark mark|rare dare fare ware

C. Type each line 2 times.

C. PHRASES

7 at the|he has|her hat|for the|come home
8 or the|he had|her top|ask the|late date
9 to the|he met|her mop|ask her|made more
10 of the|he was|her pop|ask too|fast pace

D. Type each line 2 times.

D. BUILD SKILL ON SENTENCES

11 She asked Dale to share the jar of jam.
12 Cal took the tools from store to store.
13 Darel held a sale to sell some clothes.
14 Seth watched the old cat chase the car.

E. Take a 1-minute timed writing on each line. Review your speed and errors.

E. SENTENCES

Carl loved to talk to the tall teacher.
She dashed to take the jet to her home.
Walt asked her to deed the farm to Ted.
| 1 | 2 | 3 | 4 | 5 | 6 | 7 | 8 | = Number of 5-stroke words

F. Take two 1-minute timed writings on the paragraph. Press ENTER only at the end of the paragraph. Review your speed and errors.

F. PARAGRAPH

CUMULATIVE WORDS

Rachael asked Sal to take her to school 8
for two weeks. She had to meet Freda or 16
Walt at the school to work on the maps. 24
| 1 | 2 | 3 | 4 | 5 | 6 | 7 | 8 |

G. Take two 1-minute timed writings. Review your speed and errors.

Goal: At least 14wpm/1′/3e

G. 1-MINUTE TIMED WRITINGS

Dot Crews asked Al Roper to meet her at 8
the tree to look for a jacket. 14
| 1 | 2 | 3 | 4 | 5 | 6 | 7 | 8 |

Keyboarding Connection

Using Search Engines

How can you most efficiently find information on the Web? Use a search engine! A search engine guides you to the Web's resources. It analyzes the information you request, navigates the Web's many networks, and retrieves a list of relevant documents. Popular search engines include Google, Excite, Alta Vista, and Yahoo.

A search engine examines electronic databases, wire services, journals, article summaries, articles, home pages, and user group lists. It can access material found in millions of Web sites. When you request a specific keyword search, a search engine scans its large database and searches the introductory lines of text, as well as the title, headings, and subheadings of a Web page. The search engine displays the information that most closely matches your request.

YOUR TURN Try different search engines and see which ones you like best. Choose three of your favorite search engines. Then conduct a search using the keywords "touch typing." (Don't forget the quotation marks.) Compare the results for each search engine.

Unit 2

Keyboarding: The Alphabet

LESSON 6
I LEFT SHIFT - G

LESSON 7
U B : X

LESSON 8
Y , Q /

LESSON 9
N Z ? TAB

LESSON 10
Review

New Keys

Goals

- Touch-type the I, LEFT SHIFT, hyphen, and G keys
- Type at least 15wpm/1′/3e

A. Type 2 times.

A. WARMUP

1 The major sold three wool hats at cost.
2 Dale took her cats to the vet at three.

NEW KEYS

B. Type each line 2 times.

B. THE I KEY

3 kkk kik kik iki kkk kik kik iki kkk kik
4 aid did fir him kid lid mid pit sip tip
5 chip dice itch film hide iris kite milk
6 This time he left his tie at the store.

C. Type each line 2 times.

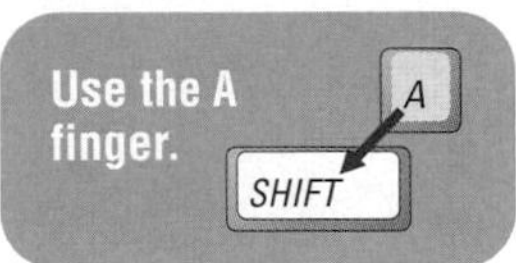

C. THE LEFT SHIFT KEY

To capitalize letters on the right half of the keyboard:

1. With the F finger at home, press and hold down the LEFT SHIFT key with the A finger.
2. Press the letter key.
3. Release the LEFT SHIFT key and return fingers to the home position.

7 aaa Jaa Jaa aaa Kaa Kaa aaa Laa Laa aaa
8 Joe Kip Lee Hal Mat Pat Jim Kim Les Pam
9 Jake Karl Lake Hope Mark Jack Kate Hale
10 Les Lee rode with Pat Mace to the park.

D. Type each line 2 times. Do not space before or after a hyphen; keep the J finger in home position.

D. THE - KEY

11 ;;; ;p; ;-; ;-; -;- ;;; ;-; -;- ;;; ;-;
12 two-thirds two-fifths trade-off tip-off
13 look-alike jack-of-all-trades free-fall
14 I heard that Ms. Lee-Som is well-to-do.

E. Type each line 2 times. Keep wrists low but not resting on the keyboard.

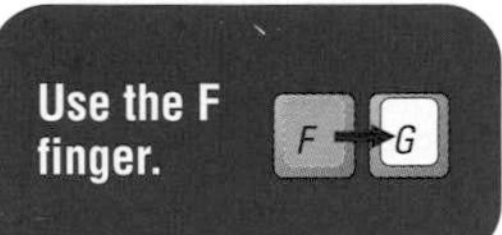

E. THE G KEY

```
15 fff fgf fgf gfg fff fgf fgf gfg fff fgf
16 age cog dig fig hog jog lag peg rag sag
17 gold rage sage grow page cage gate wage
18 Gail G. Grove greeted the great golfer.
```

SKILLBUILDING

F. Type each line 2 times.

F. TECHNIQUE PRACTICE: SPACE BAR

```
19 Vic will meet. Ed is here. Ava is here.
20 See them. Do it. Make these. Hold this.
21 See Lester. See Kate. See Dad. See Mom.
22 Take this car. Make the cakes. Hide it.
```

G. Type each line 2 times.

G. TECHNIQUE PRACTICE: HYPHEN KEY

```
23 Two-thirds were well-to-do look-alikes.
24 Jo Hames-Smith is a jack-of-all-trades.
25 Phil saw the trade-offs at the tip-off.
26 Two-fifths are packed for Jo Mill-Ross.
```

H. Take two 1-minute timed writings. Review your speed and errors.

Goal: At least 15wpm/1′/3e

H. 1-MINUTE TIMED WRITING

```
                                            WORDS
27 Al Hall left the firm two weeks ago. I       8
28 will see him at the office at three.        15
   | 1 | 2 | 3 | 4 | 5 | 6 | 7 | 8 |
```

New Keys

Goals

- Touch-type the U, B, colon, and X keys
- Type at least 16wpm/1′/3e

A. Type 2 times.

A. WARMUP

1 Evette jogged eight miles with Christi.
2 Philip gave Shari the award for spirit.

NEW KEYS

B. Type each line 2 times. Keep your other fingers at home as you reach to U.

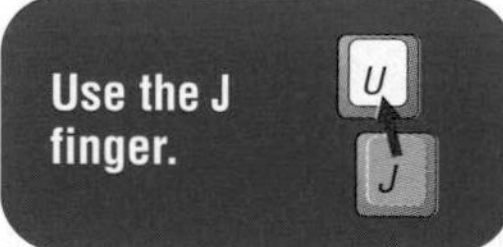

B. THE U KEY

3 jjj juj juj uju jjj juj juj uju jjj juj
4 cue due hue put rut cut dug hut pup rum
5 cult duet fuel hulk just lump mule pull
6 Hugh urged us to put out the hot fires.

C. Type each line 2 times.

C. THE B KEY

7 fff fbf fbf bfb fff fbf fbf bfb fff fbf
8 bag cab bad lab bat rib bar tab beg web
9 bake back bead beef bath bail beam both
10 Bart backed Bill for a big blue bumper.

D. The colon is the shift of the semicolon key. Type each line 2 times. Space 1 time after a period following an abbreviation and 1 time after a colon.

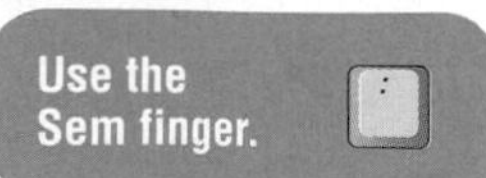

D. THE : KEY

11 ;:; ;:; ;:; :;: ;:; ;:; ;:; :;: ;:; ;:;
12 Dr. Poole: Ms. Shu: Mr. Rose: Mrs. Tam:
13 Dear Ed: Dear Flo: Dear James: Dear Di:
14 Date: To: From: Subject: for the dates:

E. Type each line 2 times.

E. THE X KEY

sss sxs sxs xsx sss sxs sxs xsx sss sxs

box fox hex lax lux mix six tax vex wax

apex axle exam flax flex flux taxi text

Max asked six pals to fix a sixth taxi.

SKILLBUILDING

F. Type each line 2 times.

F. TECHNIQUE PRACTICE: COLON KEY

as follows: these people: this example:

Dear Sirs: Dear Madam: Dear Mrs. Smith:

Dear Di: Dear Bo: Dear Peter: Dear Mom:

for this part: as listed: the projects:

G. Type each line 2 times.

G. WORD PRACTICE

Top row

We were told to take our truck to Hugo.

There were two tired people at the hut.

Please write to their home to tell Tom.

Home row

Jake asked his dad for small red flags.

Sara added a dash of salt to the salad.

Dale said she had a fall sale at Drake.

Bottom row

He came to the mall at five to meet me.

Victoria came to vote with ample vigor.

Mable Baxter visited via the Marta bus.

H. Take two 1-minute timed writings. Review your speed and errors.

Goal: At least 16wpm/1′/3e

H. 1-MINUTE TIMED WRITING

	WORDS
Dear Jack: Fred would like to take Jill	8
Wells to the home game at five tomorrow.	16
1 | 2 | 3 | 4 | 5 | 6 | 7 | 8	

New Keys

Goals

- Touch-type the Y, comma, Q, and slash keys
- Type at least 17wpm/1′/3e

A. Type 2 times.

A. WARMUP

1 Jack asked Philip if Charlie came home.
2 Kim had a short meal with Victor Baker.

NEW KEYS

B. Type each line 2 times.

Use the J finger.
Y
J

B. THE Y KEY

3 jjj jyj jyj yjy jjj jyj jyj yjy jjj jyj
4 boy cry day eye fly guy hay joy key may
5 yard year yelp yoke yolk your yule play
6 Peggy told me that she may try to stay.

C. Type each line 2 times.

Use the K finger.
K

C. THE , KEY

7 kkk k,k k,k ,k, kkk k,k k,k ,k, kkk k,k
8 as, at, do, if, is, it, of, oh, or, so,
9 if so, if it is, what if, what of, too,
10 Dale, Barbra, Sadie, or Edith left too.

D. Type each line 2 times.

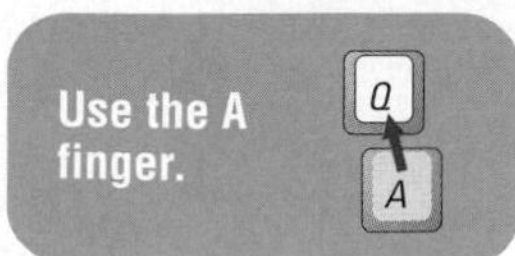

Use the A finger.
Q
A

D. THE Q KEY

11 aaa aqa aqa qaq aaa aqa aqa qaq aaa aqa
12 quip quit quack quail quake quart quash
13 quest quick quilts quotes quaver queasy
14 Four quiet squires quilted aqua quilts.

E. Type each line 2 times. Do not space before or after a slash.

Use the Sem finger.

E. THE / KEY

15 ;;; ;/; ;/; /;/ ;;; ;/; ;/; /;/ ;;; ;/;
16 his/her him/her he/she either/or ad/add
17 do/due/dew hale/hail fir/fur heard/herd
18 Ask him/her if he/she chose true/false.

SKILLBUILDING

F. Type each line 2 times.

F. PHRASES

19 if it is|she will do|will he come|he is
20 he said so|who left them|will she drive
21 after all|he voted|just wait|to ask her
22 some said it|for that firm|did she seem

G. Type each line 2 times.

G. TECHNIQUE PRACTICE: SHIFT KEY

23 Ada, Idaho; Kodiak, Alaska; Lima, Ohio;
24 Lula, Georgia; Sully, Iowa; Alta, Utah;
25 Mr. Ray Tims; Mr. Ed Chu; Mr. Cal York;
26 Ms. Vi Close; Ms. Di Ray; Ms. Sue Ames;

H. Take two 1-minute timed writings. Review your speed and errors.

Goal: At least 17wpm/1′/3e

H. 1-MINUTE TIMED WRITING

27 George predicted that Lu will have five 8
28 boxed quilts. David Quayle was to pack 16
29 a mug. 17

| 1 | 2 | 3 | 4 | 5 | 6 | 7 | 8 |

New Keys

Goals

- Touch-type the N, Z, question mark, and TAB keys
- Type at least 18wpm/1′/3e

A. Type 2 times.

A. WARMUP

```
1  I quit the sales job at Huber, Georgia.
2  Alice packed two boxes of silver disks.
```

NEW KEYS

B. Type each line 2 times.

B. THE N KEY

```
3  jjj jnj jnj njn jjj jnj jnj njn jjj jnj
4  and ban can den end fan nag one pan ran
5  aunt band chin dent find gain hang lawn
6  Al and Dan can enter the main entrance.
```

C. Type each line 2 times. Keep the F finger at home as you reach to the Z.

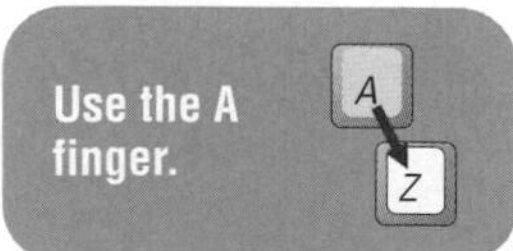

C. THE Z KEY

```
7  aaa aza aza zaz aaa aza aza zaz aaa aza
8  zap zig buzz gaze haze jazz mazes oozes
9  zip zoo zinc zing zone zoom blaze craze
10 The size of the prized pizza amazed us.
```

D. The question mark is the shift of the slash. Space 1 time after a question mark at the end of a sentence. Type each line 2 times.

D. THE ? KEY

```
11 ;;; ;?; ;?; ?;? ;;; ;?; ;?; ?;? ;;; ;?;
12 Can John go? If not Jane, who? Can Ken?
13 Who will see? Can this be? Is that you?
14 Why not quilt? Can they go? Did he ask?
```

E. The word counts in this book credit you with 1 stroke for each paragraph indention in a timed writing. Press the TAB key after the timing starts.

E. THE TAB KEY

The TAB key is used to indent paragraphs. Reach to the TAB key with the A finger. Keep your other fingers on the home keys as you quickly press the TAB key. Pressing the TAB key moves the insertion point 0.5 inch (the default setting) to the right.

F. Type each paragraph 2 times. Press ENTER only at the end of the paragraph.

F. PRACTICE THE TAB KEY

15	Each	Tab→	day	Tab→	set	Tab→	your	Tab→	goal
16	to		type		with		more		speed.
17	You		will		soon		reach		your
18	goal		if		you		work		hard.

SKILLBUILDING

G. Type each line 2 times.

G. TECHNIQUE PRACTICE: QUESTION MARK

```
19 Who? Why? How? When? What? True? False?
20 Is it Mo? Why not? What for? Which one?
21 Did Mary go? Is Clinton ready? Why not?
22 Who competed with me? Dana? James? Kay?
```

H. Type each line 2 times.

H. PHRASES

```
23 and the|for the|she is able|can they go
24 for him|ask him|they still|did they fly
25 of them|with us|can he send|ought to be
26 has been able|they need it|he will call
```

I. Type each paragraph 2 times.

I. TECHNIQUE PRACTICE: HYPHEN

Hyphens are used:

- To show that a word is divided (lines 27 and 31).
- To make a dash using two hyphens with no space before or after (lines 28 and 31).
- To join words in a compound word (lines 29, 30, and 32).

```
     Can Larry go to the next tennis tourna-
ment? I am positive he--like Lane--will find
the event to be a first-class sports event.
If he can go, I will get first-rate seats.
     Larry--like Ella--enjoys going to tourna-
ments that are always first-rate, first-class
sporting events.
```

J. Space 1 time after a semicolon, colon, and comma and 1 time after a period and question mark at the end of a sentence. Type each line 2 times.

J. PUNCTUATION PRACTICE

```
Kate writes; John sings. Are they good?
Send these items: pens, pencils, clips.
Hal left; she stayed. Will they attend?
Wes made these stops: Rome, Bern, Kiev.
```

K. Take two 1-minute timed writings. Review your speed and errors.

Goal: At least 18wpm/1′/3e

K. 1-MINUTE TIMED WRITING

```
     Zelda judged six typing contests          7
that a local firm held in Piqua. Vick         14
Bass was a winner.                            18
| 1 | 2 | 3 | 4 | 5 | 6 | 7 | 8 |
```

Strategies for Career Success

Preparing a Job Interview Portfolio

Don't go empty-handed to that job interview! Take a portfolio of items with you. Definitely include copies of your resume and your list of references, with at least three professional references. Your academic transcript is useful, especially if you are asked to complete a company application form. Appropriate work samples and copies of certificates and licenses are also helpful portfolio items.

The interview process provides you the opportunity to interview the organization. Include a list of questions you want to ask during the interview.

A comprehensive portfolio of materials will benefit you by giving you a measure of control during the interview process.

YOUR TURN Start today to compile items for your interview portfolio. Include copies of your resume, your reference list, and copies of certificates and licenses. Begin developing a list of interview questions. Think about appropriate work samples to include in your portfolio.

Review

Goals

- Reinforce new key reaches
- Type at least 19wpm/1′/3e

A. Type 2 times.

A. WARMUP

1 She expects to work hard at her job.
2 Keith had a very quiet, lazy afternoon.

SKILLBUILDING

B. Take a 1-minute timed writing on each paragraph. Review your speed and errors.

B. SHORT PARAGRAPHS

3 You can utilize your office skills 7
4 to complete tasks. Some types of jobs 15
5 require more skills. 19

6 You will be amazed at how easily 7
7 and quickly you complete your task when 15
8 you can concentrate. 19

| 1 | 2 | 3 | 4 | 5 | 6 | 7 | 8 |

C. Type each line 2 times.

C. WORD PATTERNS

9 banister minister adapter filter master
10 disable disband discern discord discuss
11 embargo emerge embody empty employ emit
12 enforce endure energy engage engine end
13 precept precise predict preside premier
14 subtract subject subsist sublime subdue
15 teamster tearful teaches teak team tear
16 theater theirs theory thefts therm them
17 treason crimson season prison bison son
18 tribune tribute tripod trial tribe trim

D. Type each line 2 times. Keep fingers curved and wrists low but not resting on the keyboard as you practice these lines.

D. ALPHABET REVIEW

19 Alda asked Alma Adams to fly to Alaska.
20 Both Barbara and Bill liked basketball.
21 Carl can accept a classic car in Cairo.
22 David dined in a dark diner in Detroit.
23 Elmo said Eddie edited the entire text.
24 Five friars focused on the four fables.
25 Guy gave a bag of green grapes to Gina.
26 Haughty Hugh hoped Hal had helped Seth.
27 Irene liked to pickle pickles in brine.
28 Jon Jones joined a junior jogging team.
29 Kenny kept a kayak for a trek to Akron.
30 Lowell played a well-planned ball game.
31 Monica made more money on many markups.
32 Ned knew ten men in a main dining room.
33 Opal Orem opened four boxes of oranges.
34 Pat paid to park the plane at the pump.
35 Quincy quickly quit his quarterly quiz.
36 Robin read rare books in their library.
37 Sam signed, sealed, and sent the lease.
38 Todd caught trout in the little stream.
39 Uncle Rubin urged Julie to go to Utica.
40 Viva Vista vetoed the five voice votes.
41 Walt waited while Wilma went to Weston.
42 Xu mixed extra extract exactly as told.
43 Yes, your young sister played a cymbal.
44 Zesty zebras zigzagged in the Ohio zoo.

E. Take two 1-minute timed writings. Review your speed and errors.

Goal: At least 19wpm/1′/3e

E. 1-MINUTE TIMED WRITING

45 Zoe expected a quiet morning to do 7
46 all of her work. Jean Day was to bring 15
47 five of the tablets. 19

| 1 | 2 | 3 | 4 | 5 | 6 | 7 | 8 |

Unit 3

Keyboarding: The Numbers

LESSON 11
5 7 3 9

LESSON 12
Review

LESSON 13
8 2 0

LESSON 14
4 6 1

LESSON 15
Review

Number Keys

Goals

- Touch-type the 5, 7, 3, and 9 keys
- Type at least 19wpm/2′/5e

A. Type 2 times.

A. WARMUP

The law firm of Quayle, Buster, Given, and 9
Rizzo processed all the cases last June and July; 19
however, we will seek a new law firm next summer. 29

| 1 | 2 | 3 | 4 | 5 | 6 | 7 | 8 | 9 | 10 |

NEW KEYS

B. Type each line 2 times.

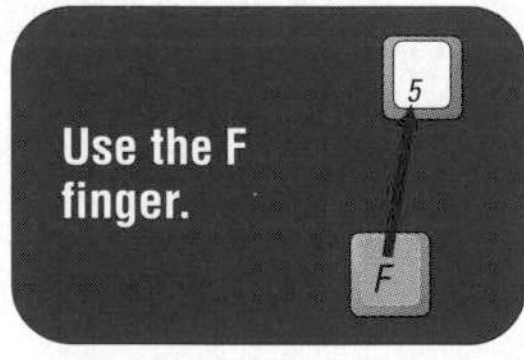

B. THE 5 KEY

fr5f fr5f f55f f55f f5f5 f5f5 5 55 555 5,555 5:55
55 fibs 55 foes 55 fibs 55 fads 55 furs 55 favors
The 55 students read the 555 pages in 55 minutes.
He found Item 55 that weighed 55 pounds 5 ounces.

C. Type each line 2 times.

C. THE 7 KEY

ju7j ju7j j77j j77j j7j7 j7j7 7 77 777 7,777 7:77
77 jigs 77 jobs 77 jugs 77 jets 77 jars 77 jewels
The 77 men bought Items 77 and 777 for their job.
Joe had 57 books and 77 tablets for a 7:57 class.

D. Type each line 2 times.

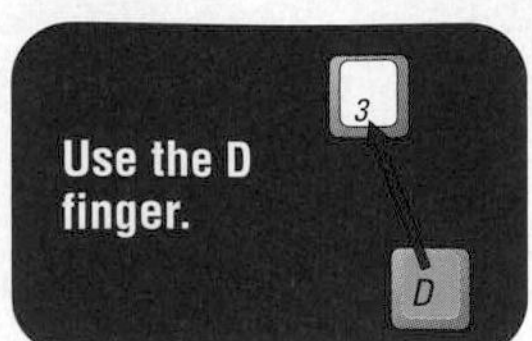

D. THE 3 KEY

de3d de3d d33d d33d d3d3 d3d3 3 33 333 3,333 3:33
33 dots 33 dies 33 dips 33 days 33 dogs 33 drains
The 33 vans moved 73 cases in less than 33 hours.
Add 55 to 753; subtract 73 to get a total of 735.

E. Type each line 2 times.

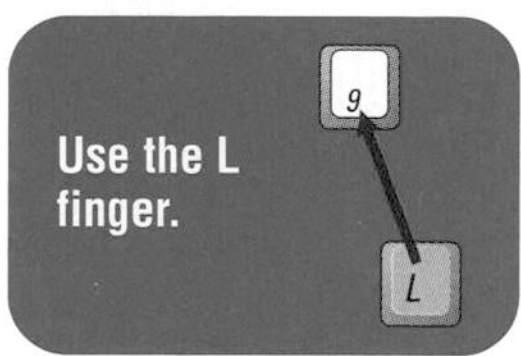

E. THE 9 KEY

16 1o91 1o91 1991 1991 1919 1919 9 99 999 9,999 9:99
17 99 lads 99 lights 99 labs 99 legs 99 lips 99 logs
18 Their 99 cans of No. 99 were sold to 99 managers.
19 He had 39 pens, 59 pads, 97 pencils, and 9 clips.

SKILLBUILDING

F. Type each line 2 times.

F. NUMBER PRACTICE: 5, 7, 3, AND 9

20 The 57 tickets were for the April 3 show at 9:59.
21 Mary was to read pages 33, 57, 95, and 97 to him.
22 Kate planted 53 tulips, 39 mums, and 97 petunias.
23 Only 397 of the 573 coeds could register at 5:39.

G. Type each line 2 times. Keep other fingers at home as you reach to the SHIFT keys.

G. TECHNIQUE PRACTICE: SHIFT KEY

24 Vera Rosa Tao Fay Jae Tab Pat Yuk Sue Ann Sal Joe
25 Andre Fidel Pedro Chong Alice Mike Juan Fern Dick
26 Carlos Caesar Karen Ojars Julie Marta Scott Maria
27 Marge Jerry Joan Mary Bill Ken Bob Ray Ted Mel Al

H. PROGRESSIVE PRACTICE: ALPHABET

If you are not using the GDP software, turn to page SB-7 and follow the directions for this activity.

I. Take two 2-minute timed writings. Review your speed and errors.

Goal: At least 19wpm/2′/5e

I. 2-MINUTE TIMED WRITING

28 Zach paid for six seats and quit because he 9
29 could not get the views he wanted near the middle 19
30 of the field. In August he is thinking of going 29
31 to the ticket office early to purchase tickets. 38

| 1 | 2 | 3 | 4 | 5 | 6 | 7 | 8 | 9 | 10

Review

Goal

- Type at least 20wpm/2′/5e

A. Type 2 times.

A. WARMUP

```
     Rex played a very quiet game of bridge with        9
Zeke. In March they played in competition with         18
39 players; in January they played with 57 more.       28
|  1  |  2  |  3  |  4  |  5  |  6  |  7  |  8  |  9  |  10
```

SKILLBUILDING

B. Take three 12-second timed writings on each line. The scale below the last line shows your wpm speed for a 12-second timed writing.

B. 12-SECOND SPEED SPRINTS

```
A good neighbor paid for these ancient ornaments.
Today I sit by the big lake and count huge rocks.
The four chapels sit by the end of the old field.
The signal means help is on its way to the child.
    5    10    15    20    25    30    35    40    45    50
```

C. Take a 1-minute timed writing on the first paragraph to establish your base speed. Then take four 1-minute timed writings on the remaining paragraphs. As soon as you equal or exceed your base speed on one paragraph, advance to the next, more difficult paragraph.

C. SUSTAINED PRACTICE: SYLLABIC INTENSITY

```
     People continue to rent autos for personal          9
use and for their work, and car rental businesses       19
just keep growing. You may want to try one soon.        29

     It is likely that a great deal of insurance         9
protection is part of the standard rental cost to       19
you. You may, however, make many other choices.         28

     Perhaps this is not necessary, as you might         9
already have the kind of protection you want in a       19
policy that you currently have on the automobile.       29

     Paying separate mileage charges could evolve        9
into a very large bill. This will undoubtedly be        19
true if your trip involves distant destinations.        29
```

D. Type each line 2 times.

D. ALPHABET PRACTICE

```
Packing jam for the dozen boxes was quite lively.
Fay quickly jumped over the two dozen huge boxes.
We vexed Jack by quietly helping a dozen farmers.
The quick lynx from the zoo just waved a big paw.
Lazy brown dogs do not jump over the quick foxes.
```

E. Type each line 2 times.

E. NUMBER PRACTICE

```
Mary was to read pages 37, 59, 75, and 93 to Zoe.
He invited 53 boys and 59 girls to the 7:35 show.
The 9:37 bus did not come to our stop until 9:55.
Purchase Order 53 listed Items 35, 77, 93, and 9.
Flight 375 will be departing Gate 37 at 9:59 p.m.
```

F. Type each sentence on a separate line. Type 2 times.

F. TECHNIQUE PRACTICE: ENTER KEY

```
Can he go? If so, what? We are lost. Jose is ill.
Did she type the memos? Tina is going. Jane lost.
Max will drive. Xenia is in Ohio. She is tallest.
Nate is fine. Ty is not. Who won? Where is Nancy?
No, she cannot go. Was he here? Where is Roberta?
```

G. Type each line 2 times. Space without pausing.

G. TECHNIQUE PRACTICE: SPACE BAR

```
a b c d e f g h i j k l m n o p q r s t u v w x y
an as be by go in is it me no of or to we but for
Do you go to Ada or Ida for work every day or so?
I am sure he can go with you if he has some time.
He is to be at the car by the time you get there.
```

H. Take two 2-minute timed writings. Review your speed and errors.

Goal: At least 20wpm/2′/5e

H. 2-MINUTE TIMED WRITING

```
     Jack and Alex ordered six pizzas at a price      9
that was quite a bit lower than was the one they     19
ordered yesterday. They will order from the same     29
place tomorrow for the parties they are planning     38
to have.                                             40
| 1 | 2 | 3 | 4 | 5 | 6 | 7 | 8 | 9 | 10
```

Number Keys

Goals

- Touch-type the 8, 2, and 0 keys
- Type at least 21wpm/2′/5e

A. Type 2 times.

A. WARMUP

Mary, Jenny, and Quinn packed 79 prizes in 9
53 large boxes for the party. They will take all 19
of the boxes to 3579 North Capitol Avenue today. 29

| 1 | 2 | 3 | 4 | 5 | 6 | 7 | 8 | 9 | 10

NEW KEYS

B. Type each line 2 times.

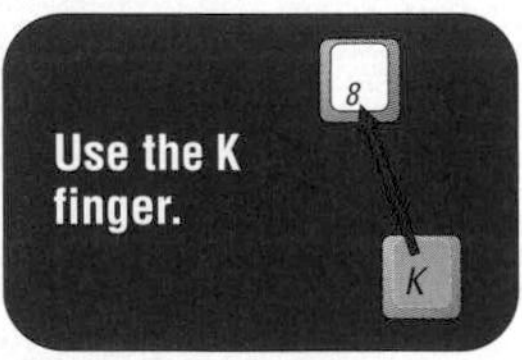

B. THE 8 KEY

ki8k ki8k k88k k88k k8k8 k8k8 8 88 888 8,888 8:88
88 inks 88 inns 88 keys 88 kits 88 kids 88 knives
Bus 38 left at 3:38 and arrived here at 8:37 p.m.
Kenny called Joe at 8:38 at 883-7878 or 585-3878.

C. Type each line 2 times.

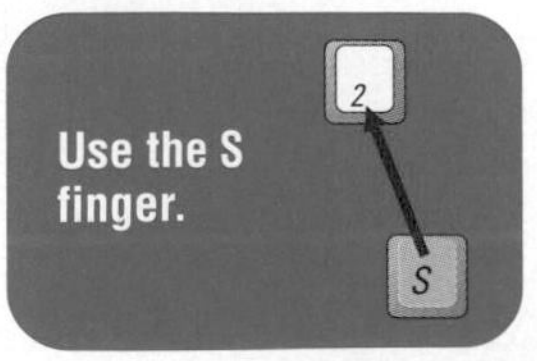

C. THE 2 KEY

sw2s sw2s s22s s22s s2s2 s2s2 2 22 222 2,222 2:22
22 seas 22 sets 22 sons 22 subs 22 suns 22 sports
The 22 seats sold at 2:22 to 22 coeds in Room 22.
He added Items 22, 23, 25, 27, and 28 on Order 2.

D. Type each line 2 times.

D. THE 0 KEY

;p0; ;p0; ;00; ;00; ;0;0 ;0;0 0 00 000 0,000 0:00
20 pads 30 pegs 50 pens 70 pins 80 pits 900 parks
You will get 230 when you add 30, 50, 70, and 80.
The 80 men met at 3:05 with 20 agents in Room 90.

SKILLBUILDING

E. Type each line 2 times.

E. NUMBER PRACTICE

16 Jill bought 55 tickets for the 5:50 or 7:50 show.
17 Maxine called from 777-7370 or 777-7570 for Mary.
18 Sally had 23 cats, 23 dogs, and 22 birds at home.
19 Items 35, 37, 38, and 39 were sent on October 30.
20 Did Flight 2992 leave from Gate 39 at 9:39 today?
21 Sue went from 852 28th Street to 858 28th Street.
22 He sold 20 tires, 30 air filters, and 200 wipers.

F. Type each sentence on a separate line. For each sentence, press TAB, type the sentence, and then press ENTER. After you have typed all 11 sentences, insert a blank line and type them all a second time.

F. TECHNIQUE PRACTICE: TAB KEY

23 Casey left to go home. Where is John? Did
24 Susan go home with them?

25 Isaiah drove my car to work. Sandy parked
26 the car in the lot. They rode together.

27 Pat sold new cars for a new dealer. Dana
28 sold vans for the same dealer.

29 Nick bought the nails to finish the job.
30 Chris has the bolts. Dave has the wood.

G. PACED PRACTICE

If you are not using the GDP software, turn to page SB-14 and follow the directions for this activity.

H. PROGRESSIVE PRACTICE: ALPHABET

If you are not using the GDP software, turn to page SB-7 and follow the directions for this activity.

I. Take two 2-minute timed writings. Review your speed and errors.

Goal: At least 21wpm/2′/5e

I. 2-MINUTE TIMED WRITING

31 Jim told Bev that they must keep the liquid 9
32 oxygen frozen so that it could be used by the new 19
33 plant managers tomorrow. The oxygen will then be 29
34 moved quickly to its new location by transport or 39
35 rail on Tuesday. 42

| 1 | 2 | 3 | 4 | 5 | 6 | 7 | 8 | 9 | 10

Number Keys

Goals

- Touch-type the 4, 6, and 1 keys
- Type at least 22wpm/2′/5e

A. Type 2 times.

A. WARMUP

```
1      We quickly made 30 jars of jam and won a big     9
2 prize for our efforts on March 29. Six of the jam    19
3 jars were taken to 578 Culver Drive on April 28.     29
  |  1  |  2  |  3  |  4  |  5  |  6  |  7  |  8  |  9  |  10
```

NEW KEYS

B. Type each line 2 times.

B. THE 4 KEY

```
4 fr4f fr4f f44f f44f f4f4 f4f4 4 44 444 4,444 4:44
5 44 fans 44 feet 44 figs 44 fins 44 fish 44 flakes
6 The 44 boys had 44 tickets for the games at 4:44.
7 Matthew read 4 books, 54 articles, and 434 lines.
```

C. Type each line 2 times.

C. THE 6 KEY

```
8 jy6j jy6j j66j j66j j6j6 j6j6 6 66 666 6,666 6:66
9 66 jabs 66 jams 66 jobs 66 jars 66 jots 66 jewels
10 Tom Lux left at 6:26 on Train 66 to go 600 miles.
11 There were 56,640 people in Bath; 26,269 in Hale.
```

D. Type each line 2 times.

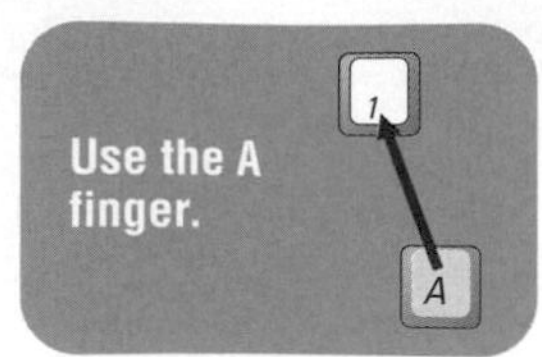

D. THE 1 KEY

```
12 aqla aqla alla alla ala1 ala1 1 11 111 1,111 1:11
13 11 aces 11 arms 11 aims 11 arts 11 axes 11 arenas
14 Sam left here at 1:11, Sue at 6:11, Don at 11:11.
15 Eric moved from 1661 Main Street to 1116 in 1995.
```

E. Type each line 2 times. Focus on accuracy rather than speed as you practice the number drills.

E. NUMBER PRACTICE

Adding 10 and 20 and 30 and 40 and 70 totals 170.
Al selected Nos. 15, 16, 17, 18, and 19 to study.
The test took Sam 10 hours, 8 minutes, 3 seconds.
Did the 39 men drive 567 miles on Route 23 or 27?
The 18 shows were sold out by 8:37 on October 18.
On April 29-30 we will be open from 7:45 to 9:30.

F. PROGRESSIVE PRACTICE: NUMBERS

If you are not using the GDP software, turn to page SB-11 and follow the directions for this activity.

G. Take two 1-minute timed writings. Review your speed and errors.

G. HANDWRITTEN PARAGRAPH

Good writing skills are critical for success 9
in business. Numerous studies have shown 18
that these skills are essential for job advancement. 27

| 1 | 2 | 3 | 4 | 5 | 6 | 7 | 8 | 9 | 10

H. PACED PRACTICE

If you are not using the GDP software, turn to page SB-14 and follow the directions for this activity.

I. Take two 2-minute timed writings. Review your speed and errors.

Goal: At least 22wpm/2′/5e

I. 2-MINUTE TIMED WRITING

James scheduled a science quiz next week for 9
George, but he did not let him know what time the 19
exam was to be taken. George must score well on 29
this exam in order to be admitted to the class 38
at the Mount Garland Academy. 44

| 1 | 2 | 3 | 4 | 5 | 6 | 7 | 8 | 9 | 10

Review

Goal

- Type at least 23wpm/2′/5e

A. Type 2 times.

A. WARMUP

```
     Jeffrey Mendoza quickly plowed six fields so    9
that he could plant 19 rows of beets, 28 rows of    19
corn, 37 rows of grapes, and 45 rows of olives.     28
|  1  |  2  |  3  |  4  |  5  |  6  |  7  |  8  |  9  |  10
```

SKILLBUILDING

B. Take three 12-second timed writings on each line. The scale below the last line shows your wpm speed for a 12-second timed writing.

B. 12-SECOND SPEED SPRINTS

```
The lane to the lake might make the auto go away.
They go to the lake by bus when they work for me.
He just won and lost, won and lost, won and lost.
The man and the girl rush down the paths to town.
    5    10    15    20    25    30    35    40    45    50
```

C. Press Tab 1 time between columns. Type 2 times.

C. TECHNIQUE PRACTICE: TAB KEY

aisle	Tab→	break	Tab→	crank	Tab→	draft	Tab→	earth
Frank		Guinn		Henry		Ivan		Jacob
knack		learn		mason		night		ocean
print		quest		rinse		slide		title
Umberto		Victor		Wally		Xavier		Zenger

D. Type each line 2 times. Try not to slow down for the capital letters.

D. TECHNIQUE PRACTICE: SHIFT KEY

```
Sue, Pat, Ann, and Gail left for Rome on June 10.
The St. Louis Cardinals and New York Mets played.
Dave Herr took Flight 481 for Memphis and Toledo.
An address for Karen Cook is 5 Bar Street, Provo.
Harry Truman was born in Missouri on May 8, 1884.
```

E. Type each line 2 times.

E. PUNCTUATION PRACTICE: HYPHEN

Jan Brooks-Smith was a go-between for the author.
The off-the-record comment led to a free-for-all.
Louis was a jack-of-all-trades as a clerk-typist.
Ask Barbara--who is in Central Data--to find out.
Joanne is too old-fashioned to be that outspoken.

PPP PRETEST → PRACTICE → POSTTEST

PRETEST
Take a 1-minute timed writing. Review your speed and errors.

F. PRETEST: Vertical Reaches

A few of our business managers attribute the 9
success of the bank to a judicious and scientific 19
reserve program. The bank cannot drop its guard. 29

| 1 | 2 | 3 | 4 | 5 | 6 | 7 | 8 | 9 | 10

PRACTICE
Speed Emphasis:
If you made 2 or fewer errors on the Pretest, type each *individual line* 2 times.
Accuracy Emphasis:
If you made 3 or more errors, type each *group* of lines (as though it were a paragraph) 2 times.

G. PRACTICE: Up Reaches

at atlas plate water later batch fatal match late
dr draft drift drums drawn drain drama dress drab
ju jumpy juror junky jumbo julep judge juice just

H. PRACTICE: Down Reaches

ca cable cabin cadet camel cameo candy carve cash
nk trunk drink prank rinks brink drank crank sink
ba batch badge bagel baked banjo barge basis bank

POSTTEST
Repeat the Pretest timed writing and compare performance.

I. POSTTEST: Vertical Reaches

J. PROGRESSIVE PRACTICE: ALPHABET

If you are not using the GDP software, turn to page SB-7 and follow the directions for this activity.

K. Take two 2-minute timed writings. Review your speed and errors.

Goal: At least 23wpm/2′/5e

K. 2-MINUTE TIMED WRITING

Jeff Malvey was quite busy fixing all of the 9
frozen pipes so that his water supply would not 19
be stopped. Last winter Jeff kept the pipes from 29
freezing by wrapping them with an insulated tape 38
that protected them from snow and ice. 46

| 1 | 2 | 3 | 4 | 5 | 6 | 7 | 8 | 9 | 10

Unit 4

Keyboarding: The Symbols

LESSON 16
$ ( ) !

LESSON 17
Review

LESSON 18
*** # '**

LESSON 19
& % " @

LESSON 20
Review

Symbol Keys

Goals

- Touch-type the $ ( ) and ! keys
- Type at least 24wpm/2′/5e

A. Type 2 times.

A. WARMUP

1 Gill was quite vexed by that musician who 9
2 played 5 jazz songs and 13 country songs at the 18
3 fair. He wanted 8 rock songs and 4 blues songs. 28

| 1 | 2 | 3 | 4 | 5 | 6 | 7 | 8 | 9 | 10

NEW KEYS

B. Dollar is the shift of 4. Do not space between the dollar sign and the number. Type each line 2 times.

B. THE $ KEY

4 frf fr4f f4f f4$f f$$f f$$f $44 $444 $4,444 $4.44
5 I quoted $48, $64, and $94 for the set of chairs.
6 Her insurance paid $150; our insurance paid $175.
7 Season concert seats were $25, $30, $55, and $75.

C. Parentheses are the shifts of 9 and 0. Do not space between the parentheses and the text within them. Type each line 2 times.

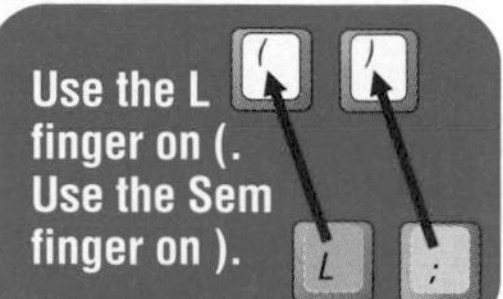

Use the L finger on (.
Use the Sem finger on).

C. THE (AND) KEYS

8 lo91 lo91 lo(1 lo(1 l((l ;p0; ;p0; ;p); ;p); ;));
9 Please ask (1) Al, (2) Pat, (3) Ted, and (4) Dee.
10 Sue has some (1) skis, (2) sleds, and (3) skates.
11 Mary is (1) prompt, (2) speedy, and (3) accurate.

12 Our workers (Lewis, Jerry, and Ty) were rewarded.
13 The owner (Ms. Parks) went on Friday (August 18).
14 The Roxie (a cafe) had fish (salmon) on the menu.
15 The clerk (Ms. Fay Green) will vote yes (not no).

D. EXCLAMATION is the shift of 1. Space 1 time after an exclamation point at the end of a sentence. Type each line 2 times.

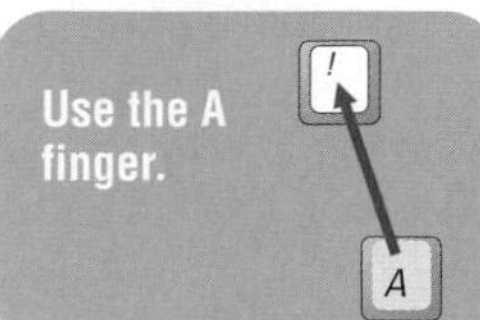

D. THE ! KEY

```
aqa aqla aq!a a!!a a!!a Where! Whose! What! When!
Put those down! Do not move them! Leave it there!
He did say that! Jake cannot take a vacation now!
You cannot leave at this time! Janie will go now!
```

SKILLBUILDING

E. Type the paragraph 2 times.

E. TECHNIQUE PRACTICE: SPACE BAR

```
     We will all go to the race if I win the one
I am going to run today. Do you think I will be
able to run at the front of the pack and win it?
```

F. Take three 12-second timed writings on each line. The scale below the last line shows your wpm speed for a 12-second timed writing.

F. 12-SECOND SPEED SPRINTS

```
Walking can perk you up if you are feeling tired.
Your heart and lungs can work harder as you walk.
It may be that a walk is often better than a nap.
If you walk each day, you may have better health.
    5    10    15    20    25    30    35    40    45    50
```

G. PACED PRACTICE

If you are not using the GDP software, turn to page SB-14 and follow the directions for this activity.

H. Take two 2-minute timed writings. Review your speed and errors.

Goal: At least 24wpm/2′/5e

H. 2-MINUTE TIMED WRITING

```
     Katie quit her zoo job seven days after she       9
learned that she was expected to travel to four       19
different zoos in the first month of employment.      28
After quitting that job, she found an excellent       38
position which did not require her to travel much.    48
 | 1 | 2 | 3 | 4 | 5 | 6 | 7 | 8 | 9 | 10
```

Review

Goal

- Type at least 25wpm/2′/5e

A. Type 2 times.

A. WARMUP

```
1      Yes! We object to the dumping of 25 toxic          9
2 barrels at 4098 Nix Street. A larger number (36)       19
3 were dumped on the 7th, costing us over $10,000.       28
  |  1  |  2  |  3  |  4  |  5  |  6  |  7  |  8  |  9  |  10
```

SKILLBUILDING

B. Type each line 2 times.

B. NUMBER PRACTICE

```
4 we 23 pi 08 you 697 row 492 tire 5843 power 09234
5 or 94 re 43 eye 363 top 590 quit 1785 witty 28556
6 up 70 ye 63 pit 085 per 034 root 4995 wrote 24953
7 it 85 ro 49 rip 480 two 529 tour 5974 quite 17853
8 yi 68 to 59 toy 596 rot 495 tier 5834 queue 17373
9 op 90 qo 19 wet 235 pet 035 rope 4903 quote 17953
```

C. Type each line 2 times.

C. WORD BEGINNINGS

```
10 tri trinkets tribune trifle trick trial trip trim
11 mil million mileage mildew mills milky miles mild
12 spo sponsor sponge sports spore spoon spool spoke
13 for forgiving forbear forward forbid forced force

14 div dividend division divine divide diving divers
15 vic vicinity vicious victory victims victor vices
16 aff affliction affiliates affirms affords affairs
17 tab tablecloth tabulates tableau tabloids tablets
```

D. Type each line 2 times.

D. WORD ENDINGS

```
18 ive repulsive explosive alive drive active strive
19 est nearest invest attest wisest nicest jest test
20 ply supply simply deeply damply apply imply reply
21 ver whenever forever whoever quiver waiver driver
```

tor inventor detector debtor orator doctor factor
lly industrially logically legally ideally really
ert convert dessert expert invert diverts asserts
ink shrink drink think blink clink pink sink rink

E. PROGRESSIVE PRACTICE: ALPHABET

If you are not using the GDP software, turn to page SB-7 and follow the directions for this activity.

F. Take two 1-minute timed writings. Review your speed and errors.

F. HANDWRITTEN PARAGRAPH

In this book you have learned the reaches 9
for all alphabetic and number keys. You have 18
also learned a few of the symbol keys. In the 27
remaining lessons you will learn the other 36
symbol keys. You will also build your speed 45
and accuracy when typing. 50

| 1 | 2 | 3 | 4 | 5 | 6 | 7 | 8 | 9 | 10

G. DIAGNOSTIC PRACTICE: NUMBERS

If you are not using the GDP software, turn to page SB-5 and follow the directions for this activity.

H. Take two 2-minute timed writings. Review your speed and errors.

Goal: At least 25wpm/2′/5e

H. 2-MINUTE TIMED WRITING

From the tower John saw that those six big 9
planes could crash as they zoomed quickly over 18
treetops on their way to the demonstration that 28
was scheduled to begin very soon. We hope there 37
is no accident and that the pilots reach their 47
airports safely. 50

| 1 | 2 | 3 | 4 | 5 | 6 | 7 | 8 | 9 | 10

Strategies for Career Success

Goodwill Messages

Would you like to strengthen your relationship with a customer, coworker, or boss? Send an unexpected goodwill message! Your expression of goodwill has a positive effect on business relationships.

Messages of congratulations or appreciation provide special opportunities to express goodwill. These messages can be quite brief. If your handwriting is good, send a handwritten note on a professional note card. Otherwise, send a letter or e-mail.

A note of congratulations might be "I just heard the news about your (award, promotion, etc.). My very best wishes." An appreciation note could be "Thank you for referring me to. . . . Your confidence and trust are sincerely appreciated."

YOUR TURN Send a goodwill message to someone to express congratulations or appreciation.

Lesson 18

Symbol Keys

Goals

- Touch-type * # and ' keys
- Type at least 26wpm/2′/5e

A. Type 2 times.

A. WARMUP

```
1        Bill Waxmann quickly moved all 35 packs of       9
2   gear for the Amazon trip (worth $987) 26 miles       18
3   into the jungle. The move took 14 days in all.       27
    |  1  |  2  |  3  |  4  |  5  |  6  |  7  |  8  |  9  |  10
```

NEW KEYS

B. ASTERISK is the shift of 8. Type each line 2 times.

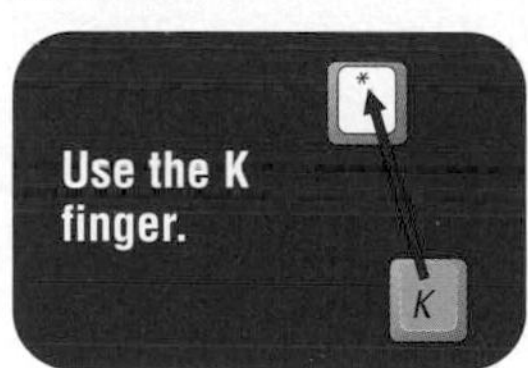

Use the K finger.
K

B. THE * KEY

```
4   kik ki8k k8*k k8*k k**k k**k This book* is great.
5   Use an * to show that a table source is included.
6   Asterisks keyed in a row (*******) make a border.
7   The article quoted Hanson,* Pyle,* and Peterson.*
```

C. NUMBER (if before a figure) or POUNDS (if after a figure) is the shift of 3. Type each line 2 times.

Use the D finger.
D

C. THE # KEY

```
8   de3d de3#d d3#d d3#d d##d d##d #3 #33 #333 #3,333
9   Al wants 33# of #200 and 38# of #400 by Saturday.
10  My favorite seats are #2, #34, #56, #65, and #66.
11  Please order 45# of #245 and 13# of #24 tomorrow.
```

D. Apostrophe is to the right of the semicolon. Type each line 2 times.

D. THE ' KEY

```
;'; ';' ;'; ';' Can't we go in Sue's or Al's car?
It's Bob's job to cover Ted's work when he's out.
What's in Joann's lunch box for Sandra's dessert?
He's gone to Ty's banquet, which is held at Al's.
```

SKILLBUILDING

E. PACED PRACTICE

If you are not using the GDP software, turn to page SB-14 and follow the directions for this activity.

F. PROGRESSIVE PRACTICE: NUMBERS

If you are not using the GDP software, turn to page SB-11 and follow the directions for this activity.

G. Take two 1-minute timed writings. Review your speed and errors.

G. HANDWRITTEN PARAGRAPH

You have completed the first segment of 8
your class. You have learned to type all of 17
the alphabetic keys, the number keys, and some 26
of the symbol keys. Next you will learn the 35
remaining symbol keys on the top row. 42

| 1 | 2 | 3 | 4 | 5 | 6 | 7 | 8 | 9 | 10

H. Take two 2-minute timed writings. Review your speed and errors.

Goal: At least 26wpm/2'/5e

H. 2-MINUTE TIMED WRITING

```
     Max had to make one quick adjustment to his     9
television set before the football game began.      18
The picture during the last game was fuzzy and      28
hard to see. If he cannot fix the picture, he may   38
have to purchase a new television set; and that     47
may be difficult to do.                             52
```

| 1 | 2 | 3 | 4 | 5 | 6 | 7 | 8 | 9 | 10

Symbol Keys

Goals

- Touch-type & % " and @ keys
- Type at least 27wpm/2′/5e

A. Type 2 times.

A. WARMUP

```
1      The teacher (James Quayle) gave us some work   9
2  to do for homework for 11-28-05. Chapters 3 and 4  19
3  from our text* are to be read for a hard quiz.     28
   |  1  |  2  |  3  |  4  |  5  |  6  |  7  |  8  |  9  |  10
```

NEW KEYS

B. AMPERSAND (sign for *and*) is the shift of 7. Space before and after the ampersand. Type each line 2 times.

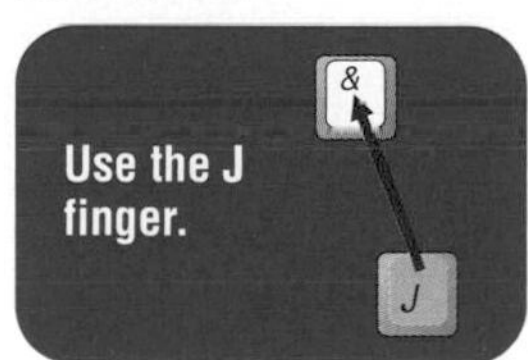

B. THE & KEY

```
4  juj ju7j j7j j7&j j&&j j&&j Max & Dee & Sue & Ken
5  Brown & Sons shipped goods to Crum & Lee Company.
6  Johnson & Loo brought a case against May & Green.
7  Ball & Trump vs. Vens & See is being decided now.
```

C. PERCENT is the shift of 5. Do not space between the number and the percent sign. Type each line 2 times.

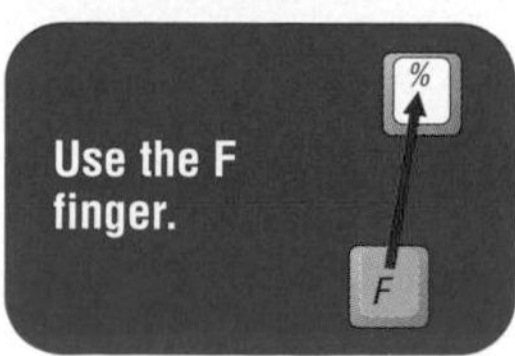

C. THE % KEY

```
8  ft5f ft5%f f5%f f5%f f%%f f%%f 5% 55% 555% 5,555%
9  Robert quoted rates of 8%, 9%, 10%, 11%, and 12%.
10 Pat scored 82%, Jan 89%, and Ken 90% on the test.
11 Only 55% of the students passed 75% of the exams.
```

D. Quotation is the shift of the apostrophe. Do not space between quotation marks and the text they enclose. Type each line 2 times.

D. THE " KEY

```
12 ;'; ";" ;"; ";" "That's a super job," said Mabel.
13 The theme of the meeting is "Improving Your Job."
14 John said, "Those were good." Sharon said, "Yes."
15 Allison said, "I'll take Janice and Ed to Flint."
```

E. At is the shift of 2. Space before and after @ except when used in an e-mail address. Type each line 2 times.

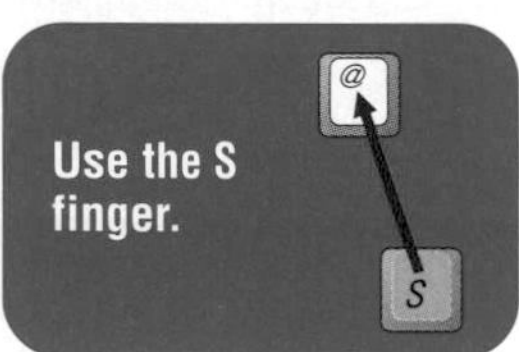

E. THE @ KEY

```
16 sws sw2s s2@s s2@s s@@s s@@s Buy 15 @ $5 in June.
17 He can e-mail us at this address: projec@edu.com.
18 Order 12 items @ $14 and another 185 items @ $16.
19 Lee said, "I'll buy 8 shares @ $6 and 5 @ $7.55."
```

FORMATTING

F. Read these rules about the placement of quotation marks. Then type lines 20-23 two times.

F. PLACEMENT OF QUOTATION MARKS

1. The closing quotation mark is always typed *after* a period or comma but *before* a colon or semicolon.
2. The closing quotation mark is typed *after* a question mark or exclamation point if the quoted material itself is a question or an exclamation; otherwise, the quotation mark is typed *before* the question mark or exclamation point.

```
20 "Hello," I said. "My name is Hal; I am new here."
21 Zack read the article "Can She Succeed Tomorrow?"
22 James said, "I'll mail the check"; but he didn't.
23 Did Amy say, "We lost"? She said, "I don't know."
```

SKILLBUILDING

G. Type each line 2 times.

G. ALPHABET AND SYMBOL PRACTICE

Gaze at views of my jonquil or red phlox in back.
Jan quickly moved the six dozen big pink flowers.
Joe quietly picked six razors from the woven bag.
Packing jam for the dozen boxes was quite lively.

Mail these "Rush": #38, #45, and #67 (software).
No! Joe's note did not carry a rate of under 9%.
Lee read "The Computer Today." It's here Monday.
The book* cost us $48.10, 12% higher than yours.

H. Take a 1-minute timed writing on the first paragraph to establish your base speed. Then take four 1-minute timed writings on the remaining paragraphs. As soon as you equal or exceed your base speed on one paragraph, advance to the next, more difficult paragraph.

H. SUSTAINED PRACTICE: NUMBERS AND SYMBOLS

We purchased several pieces of new computer 9
equipment for our new store in Boston. We were 19
amazed at all the extra work we could get done. 28

For our department, we received 5 printers, 9
12 computers, and 3 fax machines. We heard that 19
the equipment cost us several thousand dollars. 28

Next week 6 computers (Model ZS86), 4 old 9
copiers (drums are broken), and 9 shredders will 18
need to be replaced. Total cost will be high. 28

Last year $150,890 was spent on equipment 9
for Iowa's offices. Breaman & Sims predicted a 18
17% to 20% increase (*over '99); that's amazing. 28

| 1 | 2 | 3 | 4 | 5 | 6 | 7 | 8 | 9 | 10

I. Take two 2-minute timed writings. Review your speed and errors.

Goal: At least 27wpm/2'/5e

I. 2-MINUTE TIMED WRITING

Topaz and onyx rings were for sale at a very 9
reasonable price last week. When Jeanette saw the 19
rings with these stones, she quickly bought them 29
both for her sons. These jewels were difficult to 39
find, and Jeanette was pleased she could purchase 49
those rings when she did. 54

| 1 | 2 | 3 | 4 | 5 | 6 | 7 | 8 | 9 | 10

Review

Goal

- Type at least 28wpm/2′/5e

A. Type 2 times.

A. WARMUP

1 Vin went to see Exhibits #794 and #860. He 9
2 had quickly judged these zany projects that cost 19
3 $321 (parts & labor)--a 5% markup from last year. 29

| 1 | 2 | 3 | 4 | 5 | 6 | 7 | 8 | 9 | 10

SKILLBUILDING

B. Type each line 2 times.

B. PUNCTUATION PRACTICE

period 4 Go to Reno. Drive to Yuma. Call Mary. Get Samuel.
comma 5 We saw Nice, Paris, Bern, Rome, Munich, and Bonn.
semicolon 6 Type the memo; read reports. Get pens; get paper.
colon, hyphen 7 Read the following pages: 1-10, 12-22, and 34-58.
exclamation point 8 No! Stop! Don't look! Watch out! Move over! Jump!

question mark 9 Can you wait? Why not? Can he drive? Where is it?
colon, apostrophe 10 I have these reports: Susan's, Bill's, and Lou's.
dash 11 It's the best--and cheapest! Don't lose it--ever.
quotation marks 12 "I can," she said, "right now." Val said, "Wait!"
parentheses 13 Quint called Rome (GA), Rome (NY), and Rome (WI).

PPP PRETEST → PRACTICE → POSTTEST

PRETEST
Take a 1-minute timed writing. Review your speed and errors.

C. PRETEST: Alternate- and One-Hand Words

14 The chairman should handle the tax problem 9
15 downtown. If they are reversed, pressure tactics 19
16 might have changed the case as it was discussed. 28

| 1 | 2 | 3 | 4 | 5 | 6 | 7 | 8 | 9 | 10

PRACTICE
Speed Emphasis:
If you made 2 or fewer errors on the Pretest, type each *individual* line 2 times.
Accuracy Emphasis:
If you made 3 or fewer errors, type each *group* of lines (as though it were a paragraph) 2 times.

D. PRACTICE: Alternate-Hand Words

the with girl right blame handle antique chairman
for wish town their panel formal problem downtown
pan busy they flair signs thrown signals problems

E. PRACTICE: One-Hand Words

lip fact yolk poplin yummy affect reverse pumpkin
you cast kill uphill jumpy grease wagered opinion
tea cage lump limply hilly served bravest minimum

POSTTEST
Repeat the Pretest timed writing and compare performance.

F. POSTTEST: Alternate- and One-Hand Words

G. Take three 12-second timed writings on each line. The scale below the last line shows your wpm speed for a 12-second timed writing.

G. 12-SECOND SPEED SPRINTS

Paul likes to work for the bank while in college.
They will make a nice profit if the work is done.
The group of friends went to a movie at the mall.
The man sent the forms after she called for them.
5 10 15 20 25 30 35 40 45 50

H. Take two 1-minute timed writings. Review your speed and errors.

H. HANDWRITTEN PARAGRAPH

In your career, you will use the 7
skills you are learning in this course. 15
However, you will soon discover that you 23
must also possess human relations skills. 31

I. MAP

Follow the GDP software directions for this exercise in improving keystroking accuracy.

J. DIAGNOSTIC PRACTICE: NUMBERS

If you are not using the GDP software, turn to page SB-5 and follow the directions for this activity.

K. Take two 2-minute timed writings. Review your speed and errors.

Goal: At least 28wpm/2′/5e

K. 2-MINUTE TIMED WRITING

Jake or Peggy Zale must quickly fix the fax 9
machine so that we can have access to regional 18
reports that we think might be sent within the 28
next few days. Without the fax, we will not be 37
able to complete all our monthly reports by the 47
deadlines. Please let me know of any problems. 56
1 2 3 4 5 6 7 8 9 10

Part 2

Basic Business Documents

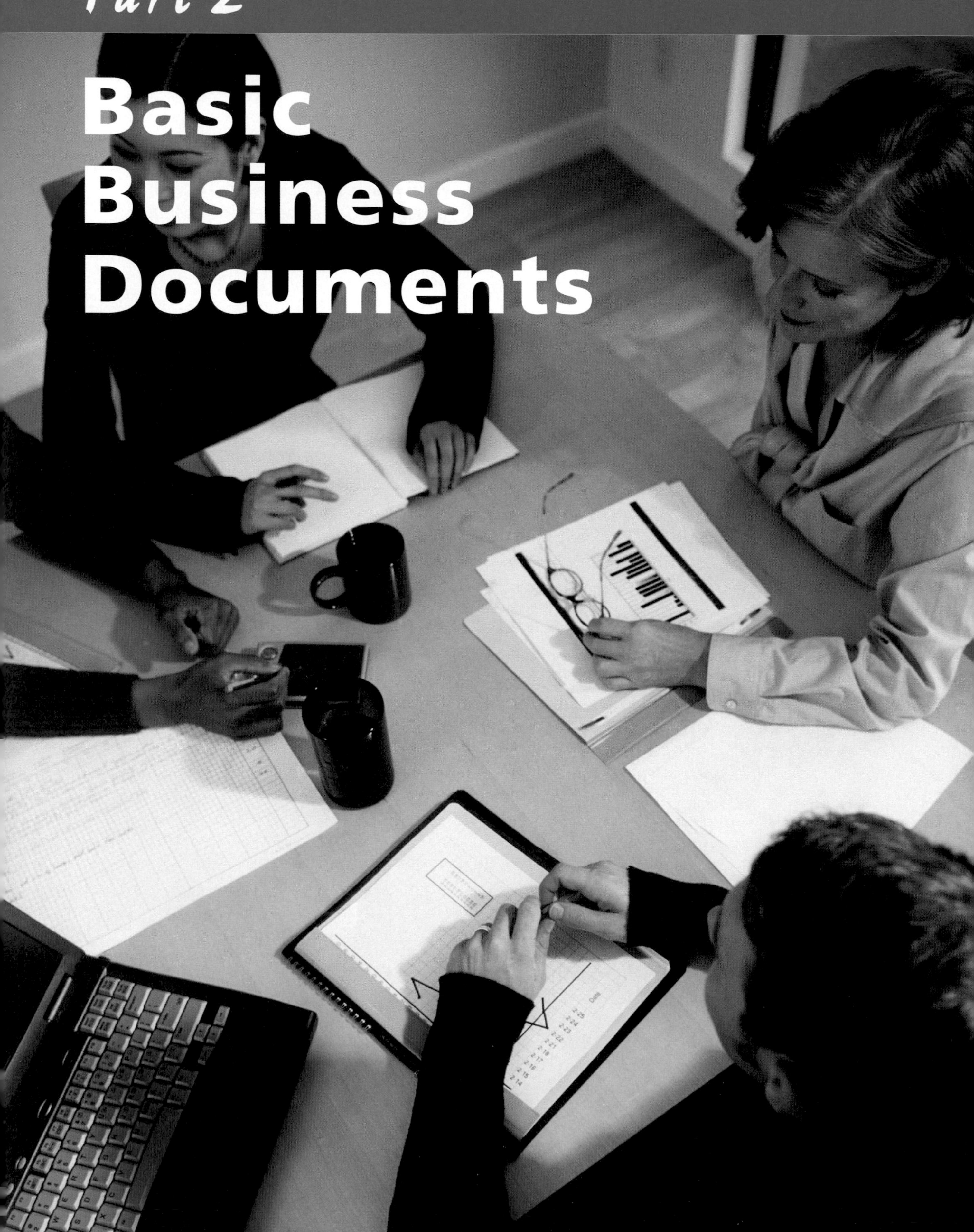

Keyboarding in Business and Administrative Services

Opportunities in Business and Administrative Careers

Occupations in the business and administrative services cluster focus on providing management and support services for various companies. The many positions found in this cluster include receptionist, bookkeeper, administrative professional or assistant, claim examiner, accountant, word processor, office manager, and chief executive officer.

Managers and administrators are in charge of planning, organizing, and controlling businesses. Management support workers gather and analyze data to help company executives make decisions. Administrative support workers perform a variety of tasks, such as recordkeeping, operating office equipment, managing their own projects and assignments, and developing high-level integrated software skills as well as Internet research skills. Ideally, everyone in business should be patient, detail-oriented, and cooperative. Excellent written and oral communication skills are definitely an asset as well.

Many companies have been revolutionized by advances in computer technology. As a result, keyboarding skill provides a definite advantage for those who work in business and administrative services. Now, more than ever, success in the business world is dependent upon adaptability and education.

Objectives

KEYBOARDING

- Operate the keyboard by touch.
- Type at least 36 words per minute on a 3-minute timed writing with no more than 4 errors.

LANGUAGE ARTS

- Develop proofreading skills and correctly use proofreaders' marks.
- Use capitals, commas, and apostrophes correctly.
- Develop composing and spelling skills.

WORD PROCESSING

- Use the word processing commands necessary to complete the document processing activities.

DOCUMENT PROCESSING

- Format e-mail, business and academic reports, business letters in block style, envelopes, memos, and tables.

TECHNICAL

- Answer at least 90 percent of the questions correctly on an objective test.

Unit 5

E-Mail and Word Processing

LESSON 21
Orientation to Word Processing: A

LESSON 22
Orientation to Word Processing: B

LESSON 23
Orientation to Word Processing: C

LESSON 24
Orientation to Word Processing: D

LESSON 25
E-Mail Basics

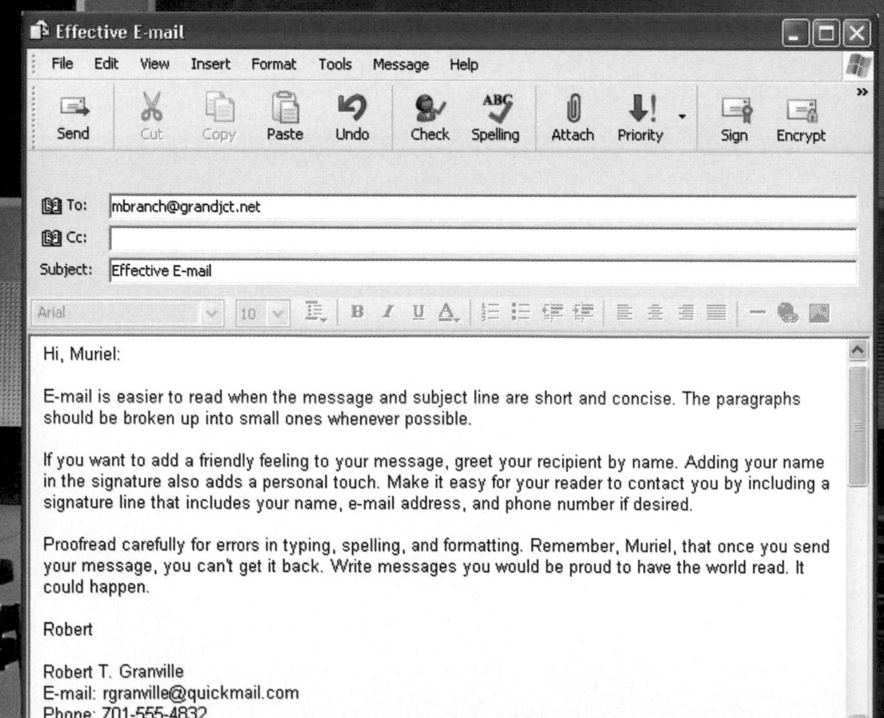
Effective E-mail
File Edit View Insert Format Tools Message Help
Send Cut Copy Paste Undo Check Spelling Attach Priority Sign Encrypt
To: mbranch@grandjct.net
Cc:
Subject: Effective E-mail
Arial 10
Hi, Muriel:
E-mail is easier to read when the message and subject line are short and concise. The paragraphs should be broken up into small ones whenever possible.
If you want to add a friendly feeling to your message, greet your recipient by name. Adding your name in the signature also adds a personal touch. Make it easy for your reader to contact you by including a signature line that includes your name, e-mail address, and phone number if desired.
Proofread carefully for errors in typing, spelling, and formatting. Remember, Muriel, that once you send your message, you can't get it back. Write messages you would be proud to have the world read. It could happen.
Robert
Robert T. Granville
E-mail: rgranville@quickmail.com
Phone: 701-555-4832

Lesson 21

Orientation to Word Processing: A

Goals

- Improve speed and accuracy
- Refine language arts skills in punctuation and grammar
- Practice basic word processing commands

A. Type 2 times.

A. WARMUP

```
     Juan Valdez will lead 10 managers during this sales      10
period; his expert input has always been valuable. Will       22
Quentin earn 8% commission ($534) after order #K76 arrives?  34
| 1 | 2 | 3 | 4 | 5 | 6 | 7 | 8 | 9 | 10 | 11 | 12
```

SKILLBUILDING

B. PROGRESSIVE PRACTICE: NUMBERS

If you are not using the GDP software, turn to page SB-11 and follow the directions for this activity.

C. PACED PRACTICE

If you are not using the GDP software, turn to page SB-14 and follow the directions for this activity.

LANGUAGE ARTS

D. Study the rules at the right.

D. COMMAS AND SENTENCES

Note: The callout signals in the left margin indicate which language arts rule from this lesson has been applied.

RULE ▶ , direct address

Use commas before and after a name used in direct address.

Thank you, John, for responding to my e-mail so quickly.

Ladies and gentlemen, the program has been canceled.

RULE ▶ fragment

Avoid sentence fragments.

Not: She had always wanted to be a financial manager. But had not had the needed education.

But: She had always wanted to be a financial manager but had not had the needed education.

Note: A fragment is a part of a sentence that is incorrectly punctuated as a complete sentence. In the first sentence above, "but had not had the needed education" is not a complete sentence because it does not contain a subject.

RULE ▶ run-on

Avoid run-on sentences.

Not: Mohamed is a competent worker he has even passed the MCSE exam.

Not: Mohamed is a competent worker, he has even passed the MCSE exam.

But: Mohamed is a competent worker; he has even passed the MCSE exam.

Or: Mohamed is a competent worker. He has even passed the MCSE exam.

Note: A run-on sentence is two independent clauses that run together without any punctuation between them or with only a comma between them.

Edit the paragraph to insert any needed punctuation and to correct any errors in grammar.

```
     You must be certain, Sean that every e-mail message is concise. And also complete. In addition, Sean, use a clear subject line the subject line describes briefly the principal content of the e-mail message. You should use a direct style of writing, use short lines and paragraphs. The recipient of your e-mail message will be more likely to read and respond to a short message. Than a long one. Your reader will be grateful for any writing techniques. That save time. Another thing you should do Sean is to include an appropriate closing, your reader should know immediately who wrote the message.
```

FORMATTING

Word Processing Manual

E. WORD PROCESSING

Study Lesson 21 in your word processing manual. Complete all of the shaded steps while at your computer.

Keyboarding Connection

Defining the E-Mail Address

With most e-mail software, a header at the top of each e-mail message contains the sender's address. What is the meaning of the strange configuration of an e-mail address?

An e-mail address contains three parts: anyname@server.com. First is the e-mail user's name (before the @ symbol). Next is the name of the host computer the person uses (before the period). The third part is the zone, or domain, for the type of organization or institution to which the host belongs (e.g., *edu* = education; *gov* = government; *com* = company).

Be careful to include each part of an e-mail address and punctuate the address completely and correctly. Even a small error will prevent your message from reaching the recipient.

YOUR TURN Have you ever sent an e-mail that did not reach its recipient because of an address error? What type of error did you make?

Orientation to Word Processing: B

Goals

- Practice hyphenation
- Type at least 28wpm/3′/5e
- Practice basic word processing commands

A. Type 2 times.

A. WARMUP

1 Zenobia bought 987 reams of 16# bond paper from V & J 11
2 Co. @ $5/ream. Part of this week's order is usable. About 23
3 24 percent is excellent quality; the rest cannot be used. 34
| 1 | 2 | 3 | 4 | 5 | 6 | 7 | 8 | 9 | 10 | 11 | 12

SKILLBUILDING

B. Type each line 2 times.

B. HYPHEN PRACTICE

Hyphens are used:

1. To show that a word is divided (lines 4 and 8).
2. To make a dash by typing two hyphens with no space before or after (lines 5 and 8).
3. To join words in a compound (lines 6, 7, and 9).

4 Can Larry possibly go with us next week to the golf tourna-
5 ment? I am positive that he--like you--would enjoy the game
6 and realize that it is a first-class sporting event. If you
7 think he can go, I will get first-class reservations on the
8 next plane. Larry--just like Tom and me--always likes every-
9 thing to be first-class and first-rate. Money is no object.

Note: In your word processing program, when you type text followed by two hyphens (--) followed by more text and then a space, an em dash (—) will automatically be inserted.

C. PROGRESSIVE PRACTICE: ALPHABET

If you are not using the GDP software, turn to page SB-7 and follow the directions for this activity.

D. Take two 3-minute timed writings. Review your speed and errors.

Goal: At least 28wpm/3′/5e

D. 3-MINUTE TIMED WRITING

Once you learn to use a variety of software programs, 11
you will feel confident and comfortable as you are using a 23
computer. All you have to do is take that first step and 34
decide to strive for excellence. 41
Initially, you might have several questions as you 52
gaze up at a screen that is filled with icons. If you try 62
to learn to use just one or two commands each day, you may 75
soon find that using software is very exciting. 84

| 1 | 2 | 3 | 4 | 5 | 6 | 7 | 8 | 9 | 10 | 11 | 12

FORMATTING

Word Processing Manual

E. WORD PROCESSING

Study Lesson 22 in your word processing manual. Complete all of the shaded steps while at your computer.

Strategies for Career Success

Preparing to Conduct a Meeting

Do you want to conduct a successful meeting? Meetings tend to fail because they last too long and attendees do not stay focused. First, determine the meeting's purpose (e.g., to make a decision or obtain/provide information).

Decide who needs to attend the meeting. Include those who can significantly contribute, as well as decision makers. Prepare an agenda, that is, a list of items to be discussed. Distribute it to attendees a few days before the meeting.

Choose where you will conduct the meeting and schedule the room. Determine if you will be teleconferencing, videoconferencing, or needing audiovisual equipment. If appropriate, arrange for refreshments. Check the room temperature, acoustics, and lighting. Attention to these details will increase your chances for a successful outcome.

YOUR TURN Think about a meeting you attended that was a failure. What could the meeting leader have done to better prepare for the meeting?

Lesson 23

Orientation to Word Processing: C

Goals

- Improve speed and accuracy
- Refine language arts skills in composing
- Practice basic word processing commands

A. Type 2 times.

A. WARMUP

```
     We expect the following sizes to be mailed promptly    11
on January 8: 5, 7, and 9. Send your payment quickly so     22
that the items will be sure to arrive before 2:35* (*p.m.)! 33
| 1 | 2 | 3 | 4 | 5 | 6 | 7 | 8 | 9 | 10 | 11 | 12
```

SKILLBUILDING

B. Take a 1-minute timed writing on the first paragraph to establish your base speed. Then take four 1-minute timed writings on the remaining paragraphs. As soon as you equal or exceed your base speed on one paragraph, advance to the next, more difficult paragraph.

B. SUSTAINED PRACTICE: CAPITALS

```
     The insurance industry will see some changes because   11
of the many natural disasters the United States has seen in 23
the last few years in places like California and Florida.   34

     The major earthquakes in San Francisco, Northridge,    11
and Loma Prieta cost thousands of dollars. Faults like      22
the San Andreas are being watched carefully for activity.   33

     Some tropical storms are spawned in the West Indies    11
and move from the Caribbean Sea into the Atlantic Ocean.    22
They could affect Georgia, Florida, Alabama, and Texas.     33

     Some U.S. cities have VHF-FM radio weather stations.   11
NASA and NOAA are agencies that launch weather satellites   23
to predict the locations, times, and severity of storms.    34
```

C. DIAGNOSTIC PRACTICE: SYMBOLS AND PUNCTUATION

If you are not using the GDP software, turn to page SB-2 and follow the directions for this activity.

LANGUAGE ARTS

D. Answer each question with a complete sentence.

D. COMPOSING SENTENCES

16 Do you prefer Word as a word processing software, or do you prefer something else?
17 What search engine do you prefer when you search for information on the Web?
18 Do you like Internet Explorer, or do you prefer Netscape Navigator as a Web browser?
19 What class are you now taking that is best preparing you for the workplace?
20 If you could work in any foreign country, which one would you choose?
21 What documents do you type most frequently as a student: letters, reports, or tables?

FORMATTING

Word Processing Manual

E. WORD PROCESSING

Study Lesson 23 in your word processing manual. Complete all of the shaded steps while at your computer.

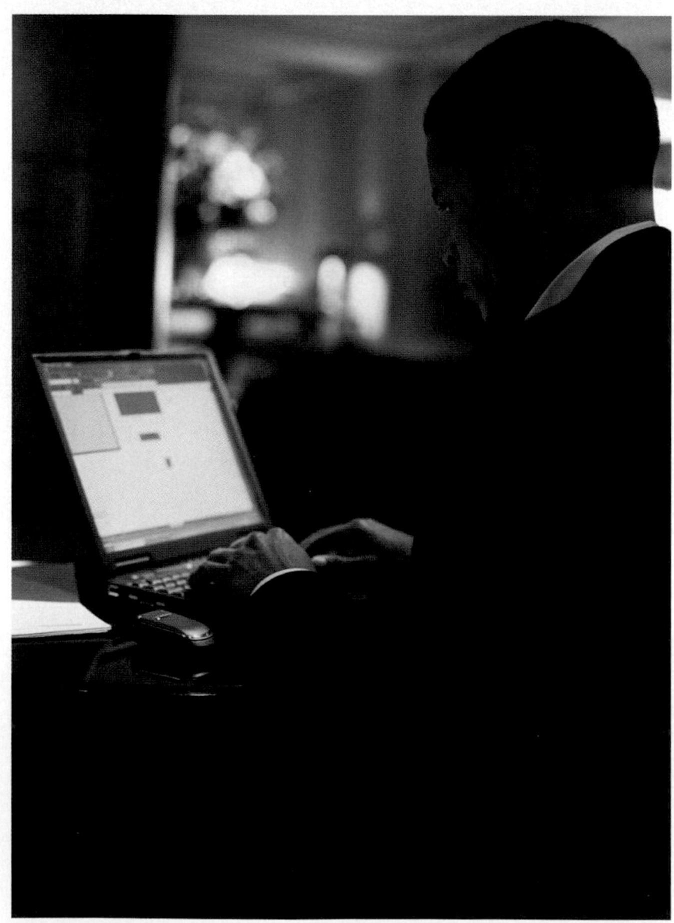

Lesson 24

Orientation to Word Processing: D

Goals

- Type at least 29wpm/3′/5e
- Practice basic word processing commands

A. Type 2 times.

A. WARMUP

```
 1      The experts quickly realized that repairs could cost   11
 2 "$985 million" and might exceed 60% of their budget. Will   22
 3 Valdez & Co. begin work before 12 or just wait until 4:30?  34
   | 1 | 2 | 3 | 4 | 5 | 6 | 7 | 8 | 9 | 10 | 11 | 12
```

SKILLBUILDING

B. Take three 12-second timed writings on each line. The scale below the last line shows your wpm speed for a 12-second timed writing.

B. 12-SECOND SPEED SPRINTS

```
 4 Mary will be able to go home when she can run fast and far.
 5 Sam can come to the store if he is able to stop for a soda.
 6 Suzy knows that she must send the mail out by noon or else.
 7 Only a few good desks will be made by the end of this week.
   5 10 15 20 25 30 35 40 45 50 55 60
```

PRETEST → PRACTICE → POSTTEST

PRETEST
Take a 1-minute timed writing. Review your speed and errors.

C. PRETEST: Common Letter Combinations

```
 8      He tried to explain the delay in a logical way. The    11
 9 man finally agreed to insure the package and demanded to    22
10 know why the postal worker did not record the total amount. 34
   | 1 | 2 | 3 | 4 | 5 | 6 | 7 | 8 | 9 | 10 | 11 | 12
```

PRACTICE
Speed Emphasis:
If you made 2 or fewer errors on the Pretest, type each *individual* line 2 times.
Accuracy Emphasis:
If you made 3 or more errors, type each *group* of lines (as though it were a paragraph) 2 times.

D. PRACTICE: Word Beginnings

```
11 re reuse react relay reply return reason record results red
12 in inset inept incur index indeed intend inning insured ink
13 de dents dealt death delay detest devote derive depicts den
```

E. PRACTICE: Word Endings

```
14 ly lowly dimly apply daily barely unruly deeply finally sly
15 ed cured tamed tried moved amused tasted billed creamed fed
16 al canal total equal local postal plural rental logical pal
```

POSTTEST
Repeat the Pretest timed writing and compare performance.

F. POSTTEST: Common Letter Combinations

G. Take two 3-minute timed writings. Review your speed and errors.

Goal: At least 29wpm/3′/5e

G. 3-MINUTE TIMED WRITING

If you ever feel tired as you are typing, you should 11
take a rest. Question what you are doing that is causing 22
your muscles to be fatigued. You will realize that you 33
can change the fundamental source of your anxiety. 43
Take a deep breath and enjoy the relaxing feeling as 54
you exhale slowly. Check your posture to be sure that 65
you are sitting up straight with your back against the 76
chair. Stretch your neck and back for total relaxation. 87

| 1 | 2 | 3 | 4 | 5 | 6 | 7 | 8 | 9 | 10 | 11 | 12

FORMATTING

Word Processing Manual

H. WORD PROCESSING

Study Lesson 24 in your word processing manual. Complete all of the shaded steps while at your computer.

Keyboarding Connection

Business E-Mail Style Guide

Watch those e-mail p's and q's! Even though e-mail is relatively informal, you need to be succinct and clear. Greet your reader with a formal "Dear . . . ," or an informal "Hi . . . ," etc. Put the most important part of your message first. Watch the length of your paragraphs; four to five lines per paragraph won't put off your reader.

Use asterisks, caps, dashes, etc., for emphasis. Avoid unfamiliar abbreviations, slang, or jargon. Not everyone who receives your business e-mail may know a particular catchword or phrase. Proofread your e-mail. Be concerned about grammar, punctuation, and word choice. Use your e-mail's spell checker.

End your business e-mail politely. Expressions of appreciation (e.g., "Thanks") or goodwill (e.g., "Best wishes") let your reader know you are finishing your message.

YOUR TURN In Lesson 25 you will learn how to format and compose e-mail messages. Create an e-mail message to send to a coworker, colleague, or friend. Review the e-mail for adherence to the guidelines listed above.

E-Mail Basics

Goals

- Improve speed and accuracy
- Refine language arts skills in proofreading
- Format and compose a basic e-mail message

A. Type 2 times.

A. WARMUP

1 Exactly 610 employees have quit smoking! About half 11
2 of them just quit recently. They realized why they can't 22
3 continue to smoke inside the buildings and decided to stop. 34

| 1 | 2 | 3 | 4 | 5 | 6 | 7 | 8 | 9 | 10 | 11 | 12

SKILLBUILDING

B. Tab 1 time between columns. Type 2 times.

B. TECHNIQUE PRACTICE: TAB KEY

4	A. Uyeki	B. Vorton	C. Wetzel	D. Xenios	E. Young
5	F. Zeller	G. Ambrose	H. Brown	I. Carter	J. Denney
6	K. Elmer	L. Fraser	M. Greene	N. Hawkins	O. Irvin
7	P. Jarvis	Q. Krueger	R. Larkin	S. Majors	T. Norris
8	U. Vassar	V. Hagelin	W. Wesley	X. Bernet	Y. Robins

C. MAP

Follow the GDP software directions for this exercise in improving keystroking accuracy.

LANGUAGE ARTS

D. Study the proofreading techniques at the right.

D. PROOFREADING YOUR DOCUMENTS

Proofreading and correcting errors are essential parts of document processing. To become an expert proofreader:

1. Use the spelling feature of your word processing software to check for spelling errors; then read the copy aloud to see if it makes sense.
2. Proofread for all kinds of errors, especially repeated, missing, or transposed words; grammar and punctuation; and numbers and names.
3. Check for formatting errors such as line spacing, tabs, margins, and use of bold.

E. Compare these lines with lines 4–7 in the 12-second speed sprints on page 57. Edit the lines to correct any errors.

E. PROOFREADING

9 Mary will be able to go when she can run fast and far.
10 Sam can come to the store if she is able to stop for soda.
11 Suzy know that she must send the mail out by noon or else.
12 Only a few good disks will be made by the end of this week.

F. BASIC PARTS OF AN E-MAIL MESSAGE

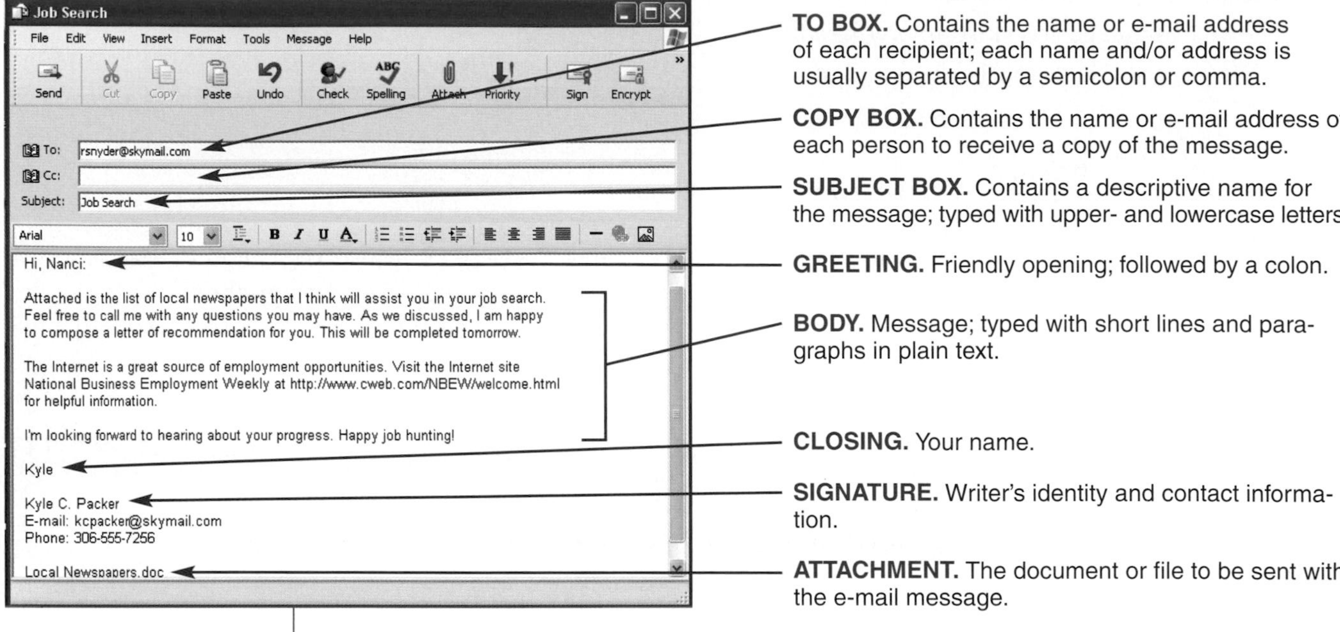
Job Search
File Edit View Insert Format Tools Message Help
Send Cut Copy Paste Undo Check Spelling Attach Priority Sign Encrypt
To: rsnyder@skymail.com
Cc:
Subject: Job Search
Arial 10
Hi, Nanci:
Attached is the list of local newspapers that I think will assist you in your job search. Feel free to call me with any questions you may have. As we discussed, I am happy to compose a letter of recommendation for you. This will be completed tomorrow.
The Internet is a great source of employment opportunities. Visit the Internet site National Business Employment Weekly at http://www.cweb.com/NBEW/welcome.html for helpful information.
I'm looking forward to hearing about your progress. Happy job hunting!
Kyle
Kyle C. Packer
E-mail: kcpacker@skymail.com
Phone: 306-555-7256
Local Newspapers.doc
TO BOX. Contains the name or e-mail address of each recipient; each name and/or address is usually separated by a semicolon or comma.
COPY BOX. Contains the name or e-mail address of each person to receive a copy of the message.
SUBJECT BOX. Contains a descriptive name for the message; typed with upper- and lowercase letters.
GREETING. Friendly opening; followed by a colon.
BODY. Message; typed with short lines and paragraphs in plain text.
CLOSING. Your name.
SIGNATURE. Writer's identity and contact information.
ATTACHMENT. The document or file to be sent with the e-mail message.

G. FORMATTING AND COMPOSING AN E-MAIL MESSAGE

> E-mail formats will vary, depending on your e-mail provider. Most e-mail message screens will allow space for the *To*, *Cc*, and *Subject* entries as well as a separate area for the e-mail message. The attachment feature is often displayed on the toolbar as a paper clip icon.

1. Use the address book feature or type the e-mail address of each recipient in the *To, Cc,* or *Bcc* boxes. A semicolon or comma is usually automatically inserted to separate several names.
2. If you use the reply feature, include the original message if it helps the reader remember the topic(s) more easily.
3. Use a descriptive, concise subject line with upper- and lowercase letters.

   Example: Items for Meeting Agenda
4. Use the attachment feature if you need to attach a file or document.
5. Use a friendly greeting. Follow the greeting with a colon. Use the recipient's first name or a courtesy title and last name for a more businesslike greeting.

   Example: Hi, Jim: or Dear Jim:

   Example: Jim: or Mr. Andrews:
6. Use short lines (about 60 characters) with plain text, or let the lines word wrap if your e-mail program supports word wrap.
7. Keep paragraphs short and type them with normal capitalization and punctuation in plain text. Typing in all-caps is considered shouting.
8. Type paragraphs single-spaced and blocked at the left with 1 blank line between them.
9. A closing is optional. Type your name in the closing, and leave 1 blank line above and below the closing.

   Example: Sandy Hill or Sandy
10. Use a signature line so the recipient clearly knows your identity and contact information.

    Example:
    Sandra R. Hill
    E-mail: srhill@server.com
    Phone: 661-555-1223
11. Revise and proofread your message carefully before sending it. You can't get it back!

Word Processing Manual

H. WORD PROCESSING: E-MAIL A DOCUMENT

Study Lesson 25 in your word processing manual. Complete all of the shaded steps while at your computer. Then format the jobs that follow.

DOCUMENT PROCESSING

Correspondence 25-1

E-Mail Message

1. Type the greeting and body for the e-mail message below.
2. Type the sender's name 1 blank line below the final line of the e-mail message.
3. Type the sender's signature line, including the e-mail address, 1 blank line below the sender's name
4. Type the phone number below the signature line.
5. Proofread your e-mail message for typing, spelling, and formatting errors.

Hi, Muriel: ↓2X

E-mail is easier to read when the message and subject line are short and concise. The paragraphs should be broken up into small ones whenever possible. ↓2X

If you want to add a friendly feeling to your message, greet your recipient by name. Adding your name in the signature also adds a personal touch. Make it easy for your reader to contact you by including a signature line that includes your name, e-mail address, and phone number if desired. ↓2X

Proofread carefully for errors in typing, spelling, and formatting. Remember, Muriel, that once you send your message, you can't get it back. Write messages you would be proud to have the world read. It could happen. ↓2X

Robert ↓2X

Robert T. Granville
E-mail: rgranville@quickmail.com
Phone: 701-555-4832

Correspondence 25-2

E-Mail Message

1. Type an e-mail message to `Ernesto Sanchez`.
2. Type the greeting as: `Hi, Ernesto:`
3. Type the following message: `I now have e-mail access using my new cable modem. You can now send me the photos you took at our annual meeting, because I will be able to access them at a much faster rate.`

   `Thank you, Ernesto, for bringing your digital camera to the meeting so that we could all enjoy the photos you took.`
4. Type the closing as `Karen` and the signature line as `Karen Drake`.
5. Type Karen Drake's e-mail address as `kdrake@brightway.net` and her phone number as `404-555-6823`.
6. Proofread your e-mail message for typing, spelling, and formatting errors.

Unit 6

Reports

LESSON 26
One-Page Business Reports

LESSON 27
Multipage Rough-Draft Business Reports

LESSON 28
Business Reports With Lists

LESSON 29
Academic Reports

LESSON 30
Academic Reports With Displays

AN ANALYSIS OF CORPORATE SICK-LEAVE POLICIES

Recent Trends in the Business World

Linda C. Motonaga

April 5, 20--

Corporate sick-leave policies must be studied carefully in order to maximize employee productivity and minimize excessive absenteeism. The reasons for absences and the responsiveness of employers to the needs of the employees must be examined in order to determine some practical alternatives to current policies.

REASONS FOR ABSENCE

There are many reasons employees are absent from work. Illness and personal emergency are common reasons for absenteeism. However, recent surveys have shown that about 28% of reported sick time isn't due to illness. This percentage is on the rise. Recent studies have also shown that absences due to personal needs and stress are increasing. Also, many workers believe that they are "entitled" to a day off now and then. Perhaps it is time for employers to revamp their sick-leave policies and make these policies more responsive to the needs of the employees.

RESPONSIVENESS OF EMPLOYERS

If employees are finding it necessary to take sick days when they are not ill, it makes sense to conclude that possibly employers are either not aware of why absenteeism exists or have chosen not to respond to their employees' needs. One thing is certain—ignoring the problem will not make it go away.

POSSIBLE SOLUTIONS

Flexible scheduling is one creative way in which employers can respond to the needs of employees. If workers are given the opportunity for a flexible working schedule, stress levels should go down, and personal needs can be handled during the time they are off. Another solution might be to give employees a fixed number of days off each year for reasons other than illness. This gives workers a legitimate reason for a planned absence and gives employers some advance notice so that absences do not hurt productivity.

ENDING PROCRASTINATION

Judy Baca

Everyone at one time or another has put off some task, goal, or important plan at work for any number of reasons. Perhaps you think time is too short or the task isn't really that important. Either way, procrastination can lead to a stalled life and career.

EVALUATE YOUR SITUATION

Joyce Winfrey of Time Management Incorporated has some very good advice that will help you begin to move forward. She says that you should ask yourself two very basic questions about why you are procrastinating:

1. Am I procrastinating because the task at hand is not really what I want?
2. Is there a valid reason for my procrastination?

After you have asked yourself these questions, Ms. Winfrey suggests that you do the following:

> Look deep within yourself. If you are looking for excuses, then the process of asking these questions will be a waste of your time. However, if you answer these questions honestly, you might find answers that surprise you and that will help clarify your situation.

She also recommends several techniques that can help you get back on task and put an end to procrastination.

PRACTICE NEW TECHNIQUES

Identifying and understanding the techniques that follow is the first step. Once you know what to do, you can begin to practice these steps daily.

2

Take Baby Steps. Don't make any task bigger than it really is by looking at the whole thing at once. Break it down into baby steps that are manageable.

Don't Strive for Perfectionism. If you are waiting for the perfect solution or the perfect opportunity, you will be immobilized. Accept the fact that no one and nothing is perfect. Then accept your mistakes and move on.

Enjoy the Task. Enjoy the task at hand and find something in it that is positive and rewarding. Confront your fears with a plan of action.

Remind yourself of all these techniques daily. Post them by your telephone, by your desk, or in your car. You will find that your personal life and career will gain momentum, and success will soon be yours.

One-Page Business Reports

Goals

- Type at least 30wpm/3′/5e
- Format one-page business reports

A. Type 2 times.

A. WARMUP

```
     Mr. G. Yoneji ordered scanners* (*800 dots per inch)    11
in vibrant 24-bit color! He quickly realized that exactly    22
31% of the work could be scanned in order to save money.     34
| 1 | 2 | 3 | 4 | 5 | 6 | 7 | 8 | 9 | 10 | 11 | 12
```

SKILLBUILDING

B. Take three 12-second timed writings on each line. The scale below the last line shows your wpm speed for a 12-second timed writing.

B. 12-SECOND SPEED SPRINTS

```
She went to the same store to find some good books to read.
Frank will coach eight games for his team when he has time.
Laura sent all the mail out today when she left to go home.
These pages can be very hard to read when the light is dim.
5 10 15 20 25 30 35 40 45 50 55 60
```

C. DIAGNOSTIC PRACTICE: SYMBOLS AND PUNCTUATION

If you are not using the GDP software, turn to page SB-2 and follow the directions for this activity.

D. Take two 3-minute timed writings. Review your speed and errors.

Goal: At least 30wpm/3′/5e

D. 3-MINUTE TIMED WRITING

```
     Holding a good business meeting may require a great      11
deal of thought and planning. The meeting must be well        22
organized, and an agenda must be prepared. It may be hard     33
to judge how long a meeting will take or how many people      45
will discuss important issues.                                51
     A good leader is required to execute the agenda. He or   62
she must know when to move on to the next topic or when to    73
continue debate on a topic. After a productive meeting, a     85
leader should be pleased.                                     90
| 1 | 2 | 3 | 4 | 5 | 6 | 7 | 8 | 9 | 10 | 11 | 12
```

Reference Manual

Refer to page R-8C of the Reference Manual for an illustration of a report in academic style.

E. BASIC PARTS OF A REPORT

There are two basic styles of reports: business and academic. The illustration that follows is for a business report.

↓6X

14 pt **AN ANALYSIS OF CORPORATE SICK-LEAVE POLICIES** ↓2X

12 pt↓ **Recent Trends in the Business World**

Linda C. Motonaga ↓2X

April 5, 2003 ↓2X

Corporate sick-leave policies must be studied carefully in order to maximize employee productivity and minimize excessive absenteeism. The reasons for absences and the responsiveness of employers to the needs of the employees must be examined in order to determine some practical alternatives to current policies. ↓2X

REASONS FOR ABSENCE ↓2X

There are many reasons employees are absent from work. Illness and personal emergency are common reasons for absenteeism. ↓2X

Illness. Illness is often caused by all the stress in the workplace. Employees may have to care for parents and children. ↓2X

Personal Needs. Recent studies have also shown that absences due to personal needs are increasing. Two important questions must be addressed. ↓2X

1. Should employers rethink their sick-leave policies? ↓2X

2. How can a newly instituted sick-leave policy be more responsive to the needs of the employee? ↓2X

POSSIBLE SOLUTIONS ↓2X

Flexible scheduling is one creative way in which employers can respond to the needs of employees. If workers are given the opportunity for a flexible working schedule, stress levels should go down and personal needs can be handled during the time they are off. Another solution might be to give employees a fixed number of days off each year for reasons other than illness. This gives workers a legitimate reason for a planned absence and gives employers some advance notice so that absences do not hurt productivity.

TITLE. Subject of the report; centered; typed about 2 inches from the top of the page in bold and all-caps, with a 14-point font size; 2-line titles are single-spaced.

SUBTITLE. Secondary or explanatory title; centered; typed 1 blank line below the title, in bold, with upper- and lowercase letters.

BYLINE. Name of the writer; centered; typed 1 blank line below the previous line, in bold.

DATE. Date of the report; centered; typed 1 blank line below the previous line, in bold.

BODY. Text of the report; typed 1 blank line below the previous line, single-spaced and positioned at the left margin, with 1 blank line between paragraphs.

SIDE HEADING. Major subdivision of the report; typed 1 blank line below the previous line and beginning at the left margin, in bold and all-caps.

PARAGRAPH HEADING. Minor subdivision of the report; typed 1 blank line below the previous line at the left margin, in bold, with upper- and lowercase letters; followed by a period (also in bold).

LIST. Numbered or bulleted items in a report; typed at the left margin, single-spaced, with 1 blank line above and below the list. If the list includes multiline items, insert 1 blank line between the individual items.

F. BUSINESS REPORTS

To format a business report:

- Single-space business reports.
- Press ENTER 6 times to begin the first line of the report approximately 2 inches from the top of the page.
- Change the font size to 14 point, and type the title in all-caps, centered, in bold. Single-space a 2-line title.
- Press ENTER 2 times and change the font size to 12 point.
- If the report includes a subtitle, byline, or date, type each item centered and in bold upper- and lowercase letters.
- Press ENTER 2 times after each line in the heading block.
- Insert 1 blank line after all paragraphs.
- Do not number the first page of a report.

G. REPORTS WITH SIDE HEADINGS

To format side headings:

- Insert 1 blank line before and after side headings.
- Type side headings at the left margin, in bold, and in all-caps.

Word Processing Manual

H. WORD PROCESSING: ALIGNMENT AND FONT SIZE

Study Lesson 26 in your word processing manual. Complete all of the shaded steps while at your computer. Then format the jobs that follow.

DOCUMENT PROCESSING

Report 26-1

Business Report

Type this report in standard format for a business report with side headings.

Type the actual current year in place of 20--.

↓6X

14 pt. **AN ANALYSIS OF CORPORATE SICK-LEAVE POLICIES** ↓1X ↓2X

14 pt.↓ **Recent Trends in the Business World** ↓2X

Linda C. Motonaga ↓2X

April 5, 20-- ↓2X

Corporate sick-leave policies must be studied carefully in order to maximize employee productivity and minimize excessive absenteeism. The reasons for absences and the responsiveness of employers to the needs of the employees must be examined in order to determine some practical alternatives to current policies. ↓2X

REASONS FOR ABSENCE ↓2X

There are many reasons employees are absent from work. Illness and personal emergency are common reasons for absenteeism. However, recent surveys have shown that about 28 percent of reported sick time isn't due to illness. This percentage is on the rise. Recent studies have also shown that absences due to personal needs and stress are increasing. Also, many workers believe that they are "entitled" to a day off now and then. Perhaps it is time for employers to revamp their sick-leave policies and make these policies more responsive to the needs of the employees. ↓2X

In your word processor, when you type text followed by two hyphens (--), followed by more text and then a space, an em dash (—) will automatically be inserted.

RESPONSIVENESS OF EMPLOYERS ↓2X

If employees are finding it necessary to take sick days when they are not ill, it makes sense to conclude that possibly employers either are not aware of why absenteeism exists or have chosen not to respond to their employees' needs. One thing is certain—ignoring the problem will not make it go away. ↓2X

(Continued on next page)

POSSIBLE SOLUTIONS ↓2X

Flexible scheduling is one creative way in which employers can respond to the needs of employees. If workers are given the opportunity for a flexible working schedule, stress levels should go down and personal needs can be handled during the time they are off. Another solution might be to give employees a fixed number of days off each year for reasons other than illness. This gives workers a legitimate reason for a planned absence and gives employers some advance notice so that absences do not hurt productivity.

Report 26-2

Business Report

Open the file for Report 26-1 and make the following changes:

1. Delete the subtitle, and change the byline to `Amy Ho`.
2. Change the date to `October 23`.
3. Change the second side heading to `EMPLOYER RESPONSIVENESS`.
4. Delete the last two sentences in the last paragraph at the end of the report. Add the following sentences to the end of the last paragraph:

```
Employees will not feel the
need to invent elaborate
reasons for their absences.
They will feel as if they are
in control of their schedule
outside of work so that they
can determine the best way to
schedule their time off. When
they return to work, they will
feel relaxed and ready to work.
```

Multipage Rough-Draft Business Reports

Goals

- Improve speed and accuracy
- Refine language arts skills in punctuation
- Identify and apply basic proofreaders' marks
- Format multipage rough-draft business reports

A. Type 2 times.

A. WARMUP

1 On 7/23 the office will convert to a new phone system. 11
2 A freeze on all toll calls is requested for July. Account 23
3 #GK95 has a balance of $68 and isn't expected to "pay up." 35
| 1 | 2 | 3 | 4 | 5 | 6 | 7 | 8 | 9 | 10 | 11 | 12

SKILLBUILDING

B. Take a 1-minute timed writing on the first paragraph to establish your base speed. Then take four 1-minute timed writings on the remaining paragraphs. As soon as you equal or exceed your base speed on one paragraph, advance to the next, more difficult paragraph.

B. SUSTAINED PRACTICE: PUNCTUATION

4 Anyone who is successful in business realizes that the 11
5 needs of the customer must always come first. A satisfied 23
6 consumer is one who will come back to buy again and again. 34

7 Consumers must learn to lodge a complaint in a manner 11
8 that is fair, effective, and efficient. Don't waste time 22
9 talking to the wrong person. Go to the person in charge. 34

10 State your case clearly; be prepared with facts and 11
11 figures to back up any claim--warranties, receipts, bills, 22
12 and checks are all very effective. Don't be intimidated. 34

13 If the company agrees to work with you, you're on the 11
14 right track. Be specific: "I'll expect a check Tuesday," 22
15 or "I'll expect a replacement in the mail by Saturday." 33

C. PROGRESSIVE PRACTICE: ALPHABET

If you are not using the GDP software, turn to page SB-7 and follow the directions for this activity.

D. Study the rules at the right.

D. COMMAS AND SENTENCES

Note: The callout signals in the left margin indicate which language arts rule from this lesson has been applied.

RULE ▶
, independent

The underline calls attention to a point in the sentence where a comma might mistakenly be inserted.

Use a comma between independent clauses joined by a coordinate conjunction (unless both clauses are short).

Ellen left her job with IBM, and she and her sister went to Paris.

But: Ellen left her job with IBM_ and went to Paris with her sister.

But: John drove_ and I navigated.

Note: An independent clause is one that can stand alone as a complete sentence. The most common coordinate conjunctions are *and, but, or,* and *nor.*

RULE ▶
, introductory

Use a comma after an introductory expression (unless it is a short prepositional phrase).

Before we can make a decision, we must have all the facts.

But: In 2000_ our nation elected a new president.

Note: An introductory expression is a group of words that come before the subject and verb of the independent clause. Common prepositions are *to, in, on, of, at, by, for,* and *with.*

Edit the paragraph to insert any needed punctuation and to correct any errors in grammar.

```
     Business reports should be single-spaced and all lines in the heading block should be typed in bold. If the report title has two lines it should be single-spaced and in all caps. Include a subtitle below the title. You should type the subtitle 1 blank line below the title and it should be typed in both upper- and lowercase letters. Most reports include a byline and a date. After the date begin typing the report body. If there is a side heading type it in all caps and bold.
```

FORMATTING

E. BASIC PROOFREADERS' MARKS

Proofreaders' marks are used to indicate changes or corrections to be made in a document (called a *rough draft*) that is being revised for final copy. Study the chart to learn what each proofreaders' mark means.

Proofreaders' Marks	Draft	Final copy
⌒ Omit space	data base	database
∨ or ∧ Insert	if hes going, (not)	if he's not going,
≡ Capitalize	Maple street	Maple Street
Delete	a ~~final~~ draft	a draft
# ∧ Insert space	allready to	all ready to

(Continued on next page)

Proofreaders' Marks	Draft	Final Copy
if (when) Change word	and if (when) you	and when you
/ Use lowercase letter	our /President	our president
∽ Transpose	they all see	they see all
ss Single-space	ss [first line / second line]	first line second line
¶ New paragraph	. . . to use it. ¶ We can	. . . to use it. We can

Note that a new paragraph may be formatted either by inserting a blank line before it in a single-spaced document or by indenting the first line 0.5 inch ( ) in a double-spaced document.

F. MULTIPAGE BUSINESS REPORTS

To format a multipage report:

- Use the same side margins for all pages of the report.
- Leave an approximate 2-inch top margin on page 1.
- Leave an approximate 1-inch bottom margin on all pages.

Note: When you reach the end of a page, your word processing software will automatically insert a soft page break. If a soft page break separates a side heading from the paragraph that follows it, insert a hard page break just above the side heading to keep them together.

- Leave a 1-inch top margin on continuing pages.
- Do not number the first page. However, number all continuing pages at the top right margin.

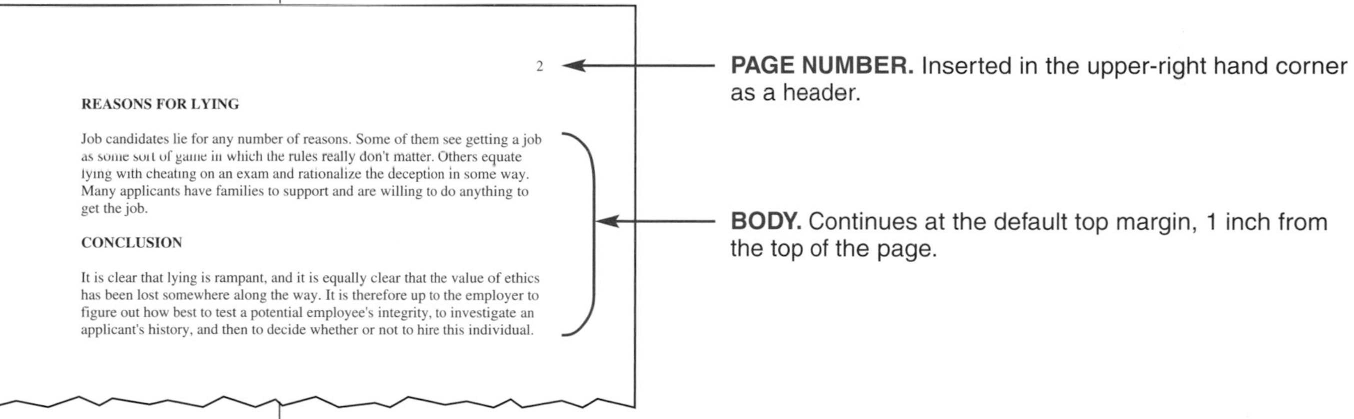
2

REASONS FOR LYING

Job candidates lie for any number of reasons. Some of them see getting a job as some sort of game in which the rules really don't matter. Others equate lying with cheating on an exam and rationalize the deception in some way. Many applicants have families to support and are willing to do anything to get the job.

CONCLUSION

It is clear that lying is rampant, and it is equally clear that the value of ethics has been lost somewhere along the way. It is therefore up to the employer to figure out how best to test a potential employee's integrity, to investigate an applicant's history, and then to decide whether or not to hire this individual.

PAGE NUMBER. Inserted in the upper-right hand corner as a header.
BODY. Continues at the default top margin, 1 inch from the top of the page.

G. BUSINESS REPORTS WITH PARAGRAPH HEADINGS

To format paragraph headings:

- Type paragraph headings at the left margin in bold and in upper- and lowercase letters.
- Follow the paragraph heading by a bold period and 1 space.

Word Processing Manual

H. WORD PROCESSING: PAGE NUMBERING AND PAGE BREAK

Study Lesson 27 in your word processing manual. Complete all of the shaded steps while at your computer. Then format the jobs that follow.

DOCUMENT PROCESSING

Report 27-3

Business Report

Note: The report lines are shown with extra spacing to accommodate the proofreaders' marks. Use standard business report spacing when you type the report.

1. Type the report using standard business report format.
2. Type side headings at the left margin in bold and all-caps.
3. Type any paragraph headings at the left margin in bold and in upper- and lowercase letters, followed by a bold period and 1 space.
4. Insert a page number at the top right, and suppress the page number on the first page.
5. Spell-check, preview, and proofread your document for spelling and formatting errors before printing it.

The ¶ symbol indicates the start of a new paragraph. In a business report, paragraphs are blocked (not indented).

ETHICS

THE INTEGRITY AND MORALS

\#

OFJOB APPLICANTS

By Elizabeth Reddix

April 5, 20--

INTRODUCTION

90 percent of

¶ Some studies have found that about 9 out of 10 job applicants have lied in

\#

someway in order to land a job. The lies range from small exaggerations to

as

blatant and completely fraudulent information such lying about a degree or

perhaps about ones history of earnings. After tallying the results of a survey

, introductory

of a large group of College students, one psychologist found that

about

approximately 90 out of 100 of them were willing to lie in order to land a job

that they really wanted.

¶ One way to help screen out the deceptions from the truth is to identify the

most common deceptions. A nother way is to try to understand why

applicants feel the need to lie. After these factors are identified and

, introductory

\#

understood it will be easier tomake some judgment calls on the ethical

integrity of an applicant.

COMMON DECEPTIONS

¶ There are a great many areas in which job applicants are willing to make

false statements in order to get a job. These could include verbal statements

or written ones.

totally

School activities. Many job applicants are willing to exaggerate or falsify

totally their participation in school activities. In order to prove leader ship

, introductory

ability, an applicant might be willing to say that he or she was president of a

nonexistent club or perhaps organized some type of fund-raising fictional

activity.

(Continued on next page)

, introductory

, introductory

~~Former~~ **Job titles.** Another area rampant with deception is the list of previous /Job /Titles. In order to make a ~~previous~~ former job sound more impressive, a job contender might add a word or two to the title or perhaps rename the title al together.

Computer Experience. Since we live in an age of computer technology, most employers are looking for people with computer experience. Usually the more computer experience a ~~person~~ candidate has, the better off he or she will be in terms of competing with others for the same position.

REASONS FOR LYING

¶ Job /Candidates lie for any number of reasons. Some of them see getting a job as some sort of game in which the rules don't really matter. Others equate lying with cheating on an exam and rationalize the deception in some way. Many applicants have families to support and are willing to do any thing to get the job.

Conclusion

, independent

¶ It is clear that lying is ~~quite~~ rampant, and it is equally clear that the value of ethics has been lost some where along the way. It is therefore up to the employer to figure out how best to test a potential employee's integrity, to investigate an applicant's history, and then to decide whether or not to hire this individual.

Report 27-4

Business Report

Open the file for Report 27-3 and make the following changes:

1. Change the byline to `Diane Jackson.`
2. Change the date to `July 7.`
3. Change the third side heading to `COMMON REASONS FOR LYING.`
4. Add this sentence to the end of the last paragraph:

   `The importance of ethics in a future employee should never be underestimated.`

Lesson 28

Business Reports With Lists

Goals

- Type at least 31wpm/3′/5e
- Format business reports with bulleted and numbered lists

A. Type 2 times.

A. WARMUP

```
     At 8:30, Horowitz & Co. will fax Order #V546 to us for   11
immediate processing! Just how many additional orders they    23
will request isn't known. About 7% of the orders are here.    35
|  1  |  2  |  3  |  4  |  5  |  6  |  7  |  8  |  9  |  10  |  11  |  12
```

SKILLBUILDING

B. Take three 12-second timed writings on each line. The scale below the last line shows your wpm speed for a 12-second timed writing.

B. 12-SECOND SPEED SPRINTS

```
Mary will not be able to meet them at the game later today.
The class is not going to be able to meet if they are gone.
They could not open that old door when the chair fell over.
This very nice piece of paper may be used to print the job.
    5    10    15    20    25    30    35    40    45    50    55    60
```

PPP PRETEST → PRACTICE → POSTTEST

PRETEST
Take a 1-minute timed writing. Review your speed and errors.

C. PRETEST: Close Reaches

```
     The growth in the volume of company assets is due to     11
the astute group of twenty older employees. Their answers     23
were undoubtedly the reason for the increase in net worth.    35
|  1  |  2  |  3  |  4  |  5  |  6  |  7  |  8  |  9  |  10  |  11  |  12
```

PRACTICE
Speed Emphasis:
If you made 2 or fewer errors on the Pretest, type each *individual* line 2 times.
Accuracy Emphasis:
If you made 3 or more errors, type each *group* of lines (as though it were a paragraph) 2 times.

D. PRACTICE: Adjacent Keys

```
as ashes cases class asset astute passes chased creased ask
we weave tweed towed weigh wealth twenty fewest answers wet
rt worth alert party smart artist sorted charts turtles art
```

E. PRACTICE: Consecutive Fingers

```
un undue bunch stung begun united punish outrun untie funny
gr grand agree angry grade growth egress hungry group graph
ol older solid tools spool volume evolve uphold olive scold
```

POSTTEST
Repeat the Pretest timed writing and compare performance.

F. POSTTEST: Close Reaches

G. Take two 3-minute timed writings. Review your speed and errors.

Goal: At least 31wpm/3′/5e

G. 3-MINUTE TIMED WRITING

```
     Credit cards can make shopping very convenient, and    11
they frequently help you record and track your spending.    22
However, many card companies charge high fees for using     33
their credit cards.                                         37
     You must realize that it may be better to pay in cash  48
and not use a credit card. Look at all your options. Some   60
card companies do not charge yearly fees. Some may give     71
you extended warranties on goods you buy with their credit  83
cards. Judge all the details; you may be surprised.         93
|  1  |  2  |  3  |  4  |  5  |  6  |  7  |  8  |  9  |  10  |  11  |  12
```

FORMATTING

H. BULLETED AND NUMBERED LISTS

- Numbers or bullets call attention to items in a list. If the sequence of the items is important, use numbers rather than bullets.
- Numbers and bullets either appear at the left margin or are indented to the same point as the paragraphs in the document.
- The numbers and bullets themselves are followed by an indent, and carry-over lines are indented automatically to align with the text in the previous line, not the bullet or number.

I. BUSINESS REPORTS WITH LISTS

To format a list in a business report:

- Press ENTER 2 times to insert 1 blank line above the list.
- Type the list *unformatted* (without the bullets or numbers) at the left margin.
- If all the items in the list are 1 line long, single-space the entire list.
- If any items in the list are multiline, single-space each item in the list but insert a blank line between the items for readability.
- Press ENTER 2 times to insert 1 blank line below the list.
- Select all lines of the list and apply the number or bullet feature to the selected lines of the list only.

Word Processing Manual

J. WORD PROCESSING: BULLETS AND NUMBERING

Study Lesson 28 in your word processing manual. Complete all of the shaded steps while at your computer. Then format the jobs that follow.

Report 28-5

Business Report

1. Type the report using standard business report format.
2. Use the bullet and numbering feature to add bullets or numbers to the list after typing the list unformatted.

INCREASING YOUR ENERGY
Shannon Wahlberg
August 21, 20--

When your energy level is running high, you are more creative, happier, and more relaxed. Some people believe that we are born with a personality that is innately energetic, lethargic, or somewhere in between. However, we are all capable of generating more energy in our lives at home or at work.

CREATING MORE ENERGY

There are many ways in which you can generate more energy before you leave for work. These two methods are simple and can be practiced without a great deal of planning:

1. Wake up to natural light by opening your curtains before you go to bed. The light coming in signals your body to stop releasing melatonin, a hormone that tells your body to continue sleeping.
2. Play music that is lively and upbeat. This will set the tone for the day.

MAINTAINING MORE ENERGY

Once you have raised your energy level at home, you can also learn to maintain your energy level at work.

- Remain positive throughout the day.
- Avoid people who are negative and have low energy. Instead, seek out those who are cheerful and positive. They will boost your energy level.
- Avoid high-fat foods, sweets, and heavy meals during the working day.
- Accept your periods of low energy as natural rhythms, knowing that they will pass. This will help you relax.

If you practice these methods to create and maintain your energy levels, you will find that these techniques will become a natural part of your daily life. Enjoy the change and experiment with your own techniques!

Report 28-6

Business Report

Open the file for Report 28-5 and make the following changes:

1. Change the first side heading to `HOW TO CREATE MORE ENERGY.`
2. Change the second side heading to `HOW TO MAINTAIN MORE ENERGY.`
3. Change the third bulleted item to this: `Avoid foods with caffeine, such as sodas and coffee.`
4. Change the fourth bulleted item to this: `Monitor your sleep. Sleeping too long can make you just as tired as sleeping too little.`

Lesson 29

Academic Reports

Goals

- Improve speed and accuracy
- Refine language arts skills in proofreading
- Format academic reports

A. Type 2 times.

A. WARMUP

```
     Will the package arrive at 9:45 or 11:29? The exact      11
answer to this question could mean the difference between     23
losing or saving their account; Joyce also realizes this.     34
| 1 | 2 | 3 | 4 | 5 | 6 | 7 | 8 | 9 | 10 | 11 | 12
```

SKILLBUILDING

B. Type each paragraph 1 time. Change every masculine pronoun to a ferminine pronoun. Change every feminine pronoun to a masculine pronoun.

B. TECHNIQUE PRACTICE: CONCENTRATION

```
     She will finish composing the report as soon as he has
given her all the research. Her final draft will be turned in
to her boss; he will submit it to the company president.
     His new job with her company was fascinating. When the
chance to join her firm came up, he jumped at it immediately.
I wonder if she will give him a promotion anytime soon.
```

C. PACED PRACTICE

If you are not using the GDP software, turn to page SB-14 and follow the directions for this activity.

Strategies for Career Success

Turning Negative Messages Positive

Accentuate the positive. When communicating bad news (e.g., layoffs, product recalls, price increases, personnel problems), find the positive.

People respond better to positive rather than negative language, and they are more likely to cooperate if treated fairly and with respect. Avoid insults, accusations, criticism, or words with negative connotations (e.g., *failed*, *delinquent*, *bad*). Focus on what the reader can do rather than on what you won't or can't let the reader do. Instead of "You will not qualify unless . . . ," state "You will qualify if you are . . . ."

Assuage your audience's response by providing an explanation to support your decision and examples of how they might benefit. Analyze your audience and decide whether to give the negative news in the beginning, middle, or end of your message. Regardless of your approach, always maintain goodwill.

YOUR TURN Review some of your written documents and observe if they have a positive tone.

LANGUAGE ARTS

D. Type these frequently misspelled words, paying special attention to any spelling problems in each word.

D. SPELLING

```
10 personnel information its procedures their committee system
11 receive employees which education services opportunity area
12 financial appropriate interest received production contract
13 important through necessary customer employee further there
14 property account approximately general control division our
```

Edit the sentences to correct any misspellings.

```
15 All company personel will receive important information.
16 Are division has some control over there financial account.
17 There comittee has received approximately three contracts.
18 The employe and the customer have an oportunity to attend.
19 We have no farther interest in the property or it's owner.
20 When it is necessary, apropriate proceedures are followed.
```

FORMATTING

E. MORE PROOFREADERS' MARKS

1. Review the most frequently used proofreaders' marks introduced in Lesson 27.

2. Study the additional proofreaders' marks presented here.

Proofreaders' Marks		Draft	Final Copy
ds	Double-space	ds [first line / second line	first line second line
......	Don't delete	a ~~true~~ story	a true story
○	Spell out	the only (1)	the only one
⊐	Move right	[Please send	Please send
⊏	Move left	[May 1	May 1
~~	Bold	Column Heading	**Column Heading**
ital	Italic	ital Time magazine	*Time* magazine
u/l	Underline	u/l Time magazine	Time magazine
↗	Move as shown	(readers) will see	readers will see

Note that a new paragraph may be formatted either by inserting a blank line before it in a single-spaced document or by indenting the first line 0.5 inch (⊐) in a double-spaced document.

F. ACADEMIC REPORTS

To format an academic report:

1. Double-space academic reports.
2. After you have set the line spacing to double, press ENTER 3 times to begin the first line of the academic report about 2 inches from the top of the page.
3. Type the title in all-caps, centered, in bold, and change the font size to 14 point. Double-space a 2-line title.
4. Press ENTER 1 time and change the font size to 12 point.
5. If the report includes a subtitle, byline, or date, type each item centered, in bold and upper- and lowercase letters; press ENTER 1 time after each line in the heading block.
6. Type side headings at the left margin, in bold and all-caps.
7. Press TAB 1 time at the start of paragraphs and paragraph headings to indent them 0.5 inch.
8. Type paragraph headings in bold and in upper- and lowercase letters, and follow the paragraph heading with a bold period and 1 space.
9. Insert an approximate 1-inch bottom margin on all pages, and insert a 1-inch top margin on continuation pages.
10. Do not number the first page. However, number all continuation pages at the top right margin.

Word Processing Manual

G. WORD PROCESSING: LINE SPACING

Study Lesson 29 in your word processing manual. Complete all of the shaded steps while at your computer. Then format the jobs that follow.

DOCUMENT PROCESSING

Report 29-7

Academic Report

1. Type this report in standard format for an academic report.
2. Type the 2-line title double-spaced, and use standard format for the rest of the heading block.
3. Insert a page number at the top right, and suppress the page number on the first page.
4. Spell-check, preview, and proofread your document for spelling and formatting errors before printing it.

Reference Manual

See page R-8C and R-8D of the Reference Manual for an illustration of a multipage report in academic style.

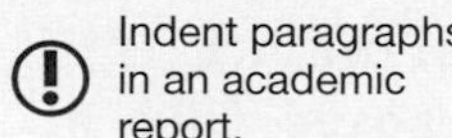

Indent paragraphs in an academic report.

Highlighted words are spelling words from the language arts activities.

ELECTRONIC SAFEGUARDS IN
THE DIGITAL WORLD

Trends in Technology

Kevin Nguyen

July 13, 20--

More and more people are using computers and the Internet for a wide variety of reasons, both personal and professional. Most of the technology requires the use of passwords, user names, pin numbers, and miscellaneous other important codes for users to access their accounts. Unfortunately, at times it seems as if the number of codes that are necessary is increasing in geometric proportions. The problem is how to maintain accurate records of these various security codes and still preserve a secure environment, technologically speaking.

(Continued on next page)

SECURITY CODE OVERLOAD

People need 1 or sometimes 2 security codes just to log on to their computers. Several more are needed to access web sites, trade stocks, and shop and bank online, just to name a few activities. In addition most people need to remember codes for their home phones, work phones, cell phones, and voice mail. Banks require codes to withdraw money and use credit cards and ATMs. With so many security codes proliferating on a daily basis, its no wonder that we are often frustrated and frazzled as we move through our daily lives going about our personal and professional business. To add insult to injury we are often being asked to change our passwords and codes on a regular basis.

MANAGING SECURITY CODES

Several things can be done to help manage this ever-growing list of security codes. Try to choose passwords that are in some way meaningful to you but that cannot be guessed at by an intruder. Use a combination of letters and numbers. An article in the magazine Technology Bytes suggests using using street addresses or names of pets that can be easily remembered but that have no logical association with anything else.

If you decide to keep a list of security codes, make sure to protect the file in an appropriate way. If you must write down your passwords, physically lock them up. You must control and manage these important and necessary security codes to protect your personal and financial information.

Report 29-8

Academic Report

Open the file for Report 29-7 and make the following changes:

1. Change the byline to Nancy Dodson.
2. Add this paragraph below the last paragraph at the end of the report:

   A number of Web sites are available to help you remember your passwords and user names. However, these sites can help you do much more than simply manage your security codes. Some sites can provide instant registration at new sites with just one click. They also offer price comparisons while you shop anywhere on the Web, and they bring together the best search engines all in one place for easier searching. They can also filter e-mail to help you eliminate cluttered e-mail boxes full of junk.

Academic Reports With Displays

Goals

- Type at least 32wpm/3′/5e
- Format rough-draft academic reports with indented lists and displays

A. Type 2 times.

A. WARMUP

```
     Did Zagorsky & Sons charge $876 for the renovation?     11
An invoice wasn't quite right; the exact amount charged in   22
July can be found in an e-mail message to zagsons@post.com.  34
| 1 | 2 | 3 | 4 | 5 | 6 | 7 | 8 | 9 | 10 | 11 | 12
```

SKILLBUILDING

B. MAP

Follow the GDP software directions for this exercise in improving keystroking accuracy.

C. DIAGNOSTIC PRACTICE: NUMBERS

If you are not using the GDP software, turn to page SB-5 and follow the directions for this activity.

D. Take two 3-minute timed writings. Review your speed and errors.

Goal: At least 32wpm/3′/5e

D. 3-MINUTE TIMED WRITING

```
     If you want to work in information processing, you      10
may realize that there are steps that you must take to      21
plan for such an exciting career. First, you must decide    33
whether or not you have the right personality traits.       44
     Then you must be trained in the technical skills you   54
need in such an important field. The technology is changing 66
each day. You must stay focused on keeping up with these    78
changes. Also, you must never quit wanting to learn new     89
skills each day you are on the job.                         96
| 1 | 2 | 3 | 4 | 5 | 6 | 7 | 8 | 9 | 10 | 11 | 12
```

FORMATTING

E. ACADEMIC REPORTS WITH LISTS

To format a list in an academic report:

- Press ENTER 1 time to begin the list.
- Type the list *unformatted* at the left margin, double-spaced.
- Press ENTER 1 time after the last line in the list.
- Select all lines of the list and apply the number or bullet feature to the selected lines of the list only. Do not include the blank lines above and below the list in your selection.
- Increase or decrease the indent of the list as needed so that the list begins at the same point of indention as the paragraphs in the report.

F. ACADEMIC REPORTS WITH INDENTED DISPLAYS

A paragraph having 4 lines or more that are quoted or having lines that need special emphasis should be formatted so that the paragraph stands out from the rest of the report. To format academic reports with indented displays:

- Type the paragraph single-spaced and indented 0.5 inch from both the left and the right margins (instead of enclosing it in quotation marks).
- Use the indent command in your word processing software to format a displayed paragraph.

Word Processing Manual

G. WORD PROCESSING: INCREASE INDENT AND CUT, COPY, AND PASTE

Study Lesson 30 in your word processing manual. Complete all of the shaded steps while at your computer. Then format the jobs that follow.

DOCUMENT PROCESSING

Report 30-9

Academic Report

1. Type the report using standard academic report format.
2. Type the list using standard format for lists in an academic report. Use the number feature to add numbers to the list after you have typed the list unformatted. Use the cut-and-paste feature to move the second numbered item.
3. Type the display using standard format for indented displays in an academic report.
4. Type paragraph headings indented 0.5 inch, in bold, and in upper- and lowercase letters, and follow the paragraph heading with a bold period and 1 space.
5. Insert a page number at the top right margin, and suppress the page number on the first page.

Reference Manual

See page R-8D of the Reference Manual for an illustration of a multipage report in academic style with a displayed paragraph.

ENDING PROCRASTINATION

Judy Baca

Every one at one time or another has put of some task, goal or important plan at work for any number of reasons. perhaps you think time is too short or the task isn't really that important. Either way, procrastination can lead to a stalled life and career.

(Continued on next page)

EVALUATE YOUR SITUATION

Joyce Winfrey of Time Management Incorporated has some very good advice that will help you to begin to move forward. She says that you should ask yourself 2 very basic questions about why you are procrastinating:

1. Is there a valid reason for my procrastination?
2. Am I procrastinating because the task at hand is not really what I want?

After you have asked yourself these questions, ms. Winfrey suggests that you do the following:

Look deep within yourself. If you are looking for excuses, then the process of asking these questions will be a waste of your time. However, if you answer these questions honestly, you might find answers that surprise you and that will help clarify your situation.

She also recommends several techniques can help you get back on task and put an end to procrastination.

PRACTICE NEW TECHNIQUES

Identifying and understanding the techniques which follow is the first step. Once you know what to do you can begin to practice these steps daily.

Take Baby Steps. Don't make any task bigger than it really is by looking at the whole thing at once. Break it down into babysteps that are manageable.

Dont Strive for Perfectionism. If you are waiting for the perfect solution or the perfect opportunity, you will immobilized. Accept the fact that no one and nothing is perfect. Then accept your mistakes and move on.

Enjoy the Task. Enjoy the task at hand and find something in it that is positive and rewarding. Confront your fears with a plan of action.

Remind yourself of all these techniques daily. Post them by your telephone, your desk, or your car. You will find that your personal life and career will gain momentum, and success will soon be yours.

Report 30-10

Academic Report

Progress and Proofreading Check

Documents designated as Proofreading Checks serve as a check of your proofreading skill. Your goal is to have zero typographical errors when the GDP software first scores the document.

1. Type the report using standard academic report format for a multipage academic report with a list.
2. Make all changes as indicated by the proofreaders' marks.

TIPS FOR HELPING YOU
PREPARE FOR YOUR EXAM

Betty Goldberg
June 8, 20--

in school you have taken some exams. Whether you are an excellent exam taker or a novice at the task, you have experienced a degree of stress related to your performance on an exam. There are some steps you can take to reduce the stress of taking an exam, and these suggestions will likely help you throughout your life.

PREPARING FOR THE EXAM

Of course, it's always easier to take an exam from an Instructor whom you have had in previous classes, because you know what to expect. From past experience, you know whether the Instructor likes to use objective or subjective questions, whether the Instructor focuses on the textbook or on class notes, and the difficulty of the questions the Instructor asks.

If you don't know what to expect, however, you need to prepare for all possibilities. Be sure that you review all pertinent materials for the exam—whether they come from classnotes, the textbook, field trips, or class room presentations.

SURVIVING THE DAY BEFORE THE EXAM

Be sure you know where and at what time the exam will be administered. Organize the materials you need to bring with you to the exam. You need pencils, pens, calculators, disks, or paper. Try to get a good night sleep the night before the exam, and don't upset your usual routine.

Taking The Exam

Now that the day of the exam has arrived, there are several actions you should take to ensure that you perform well:

1. Arrive at the test sight early so that you are ready to take the exam when the instructor announces the beginning time. That means that before you have to be sure to get up early enough to have a light breakfast leaving for the exam.
2. Read very carefully the instructions provided to be sure you answer the questions correctly.
3. Keep track of time so that you don't get stuck and spend too much of your time on any one part of the exam.
4. Try to keep a positive attitude.
5. Relax as best you can—a relaxed performance is much more productive than a stressed performance.

Unit 7

Correspondence

LESSON 31
Business Letters

LESSON 32
Business Letters With Enclosure Notations

LESSON 33
Envelopes and Labels

LESSON 34
Memos

LESSON 35
Correspondence Review

April 3, 20--

Ms. Linda Lopez
Account Manager
The Internet Connection
7625 Maple Avenue
Pomona, CA 91765

Dear Ms. Lopez:

Our company is interested in hosting an educational seminar this spring that will focus on meeting the growing need for information industry professionals to keep abreast of emerging new technologies and trends. We are specifically interested in information on high-speed Internet connections.

I understand that The Internet Connection specializes in these seminars and will also help businesses analyze their needs and choose an appropriate solution. I am in the process of contacting several companies similar to yours who might be interested in conducting these seminars. Please contact me by Thursday or Friday at the latest so that we can discuss this matter further.

I appreciate the fine service we have always received from you in the past, Ms. Lopez, and I look forward to hearing from you.

Sincerely,

Ruzanna Petroska
Technology Specialist

urs

MEMO TO: All Salaried Employees

FROM: Amy Vigil, Human Resources

DATE: November 2, 20--

SUBJECT: Health Care Benefit Plan

Effective January 1, Allied Aerospace Industries will contract with MedNet to begin a new health benefits program for all eligible salaried personnel. A brochure outlining important program information will be mailed to you soon.

An open enrollment period will be in effect during the entire month of January. If you and your family are interested in one of the MedNet health plan options, you may transfer yourself and your dependents into any appropriate plan. All applications must be received no later than midnight, January 31. You may also access your plan over the Internet at www.mednet.com if it is more convenient.

If you have any questions or need any help understanding your options, please call me at Ext. 134. I will be happy to help you select the plan that is best for you.

urs

Trend Electronics
2206 31st Street
Minneapolis, MN 55407-1911

Mr. Charles Goldstein
Software Solutions
2981 Canwood Street
Roselle, IL 60172

Business Letters

Goals

- Improve speed and accuracy
- Refine language arts skills in capitalization
- Format a business letter in block style

A. Type 2 times.

A. WARMUP

```
     You can save $1,698 when you buy the 20-part video      10
series! Just ask for Series #MX5265 in the next 7 days;      22
ordering early qualifies you for a sizable discount of 5%.   33
| 1 | 2 | 3 | 4 | 5 | 6 | 7 | 8 | 9 | 10 | 11 | 12
```

SKILLBUILDING

B. Take three 12-second timed writings on each line. The scale below the last line shows your wpm speed for a 12-second timed writing.

B. 12-SECOND SPEED SPRINTS

```
Mary will be able to go home when she can run fast and far.
Sam can come to the store if he is able to stop for a soda.
Suzy knows that she must send the mail out by noon or else.
Only a few good desks will be made by the end of this week.
5 10 15 20 25 30 35 40 45 50 55 60
```

C. PROGRESSIVE PRACTICE: ALPHABET

If you are not using the GDP software, turn to page SB-7 and follow the directions for this activity.

D. PROGRESSIVE PRACTICE: NUMBERS

If you are not using the GDP software, turn to page SB-11 and follow the directions for this activity.

LANGUAGE ARTS

E. Study the rules at the right.

E. CAPITALIZATION

Note: The callout signals in the left margin indicate which language arts rule from this lesson has been applied.

RULE ▶ ≡ sentence

Capitalize the first word of a sentence.
Please prepare a summary of your activities.

RULE ▶ ≡ proper

Capitalize proper nouns and adjectives derived from proper nouns.
Judy Hendrix drove to Albuquerque in her new Pontiac convertible.

Note: A proper noun is the official name of a particular person, place, or thing.

(Continued on next page)

RULE ▶ ≡ time

Capitalize the names of the days of the week, months, holidays, and religious days (but do not capitalize the names of the seasons).

On Thursday, November 25, we will celebrate Thanksgiving, the most popular holiday in the fall.

Edit the paragraph to insert or delete capitalization.

```
The american flag can be seen flying over the White House in Washington. Our Country's flag is often seen flying over Government buildings on holidays like July 4, independence day. Memorial Day signals the end of spring and the start of Summer. Most Americans consider Labor day the beginning of the fall season. In december many people observe christmas and Hanukkah. most government holidays are scheduled to fall on either a Monday or a friday. Sometimes the birthdays of Historical figures are also celebrated.
```

FORMATTING

F. BASIC PARTS OF A BUSINESS LETTER

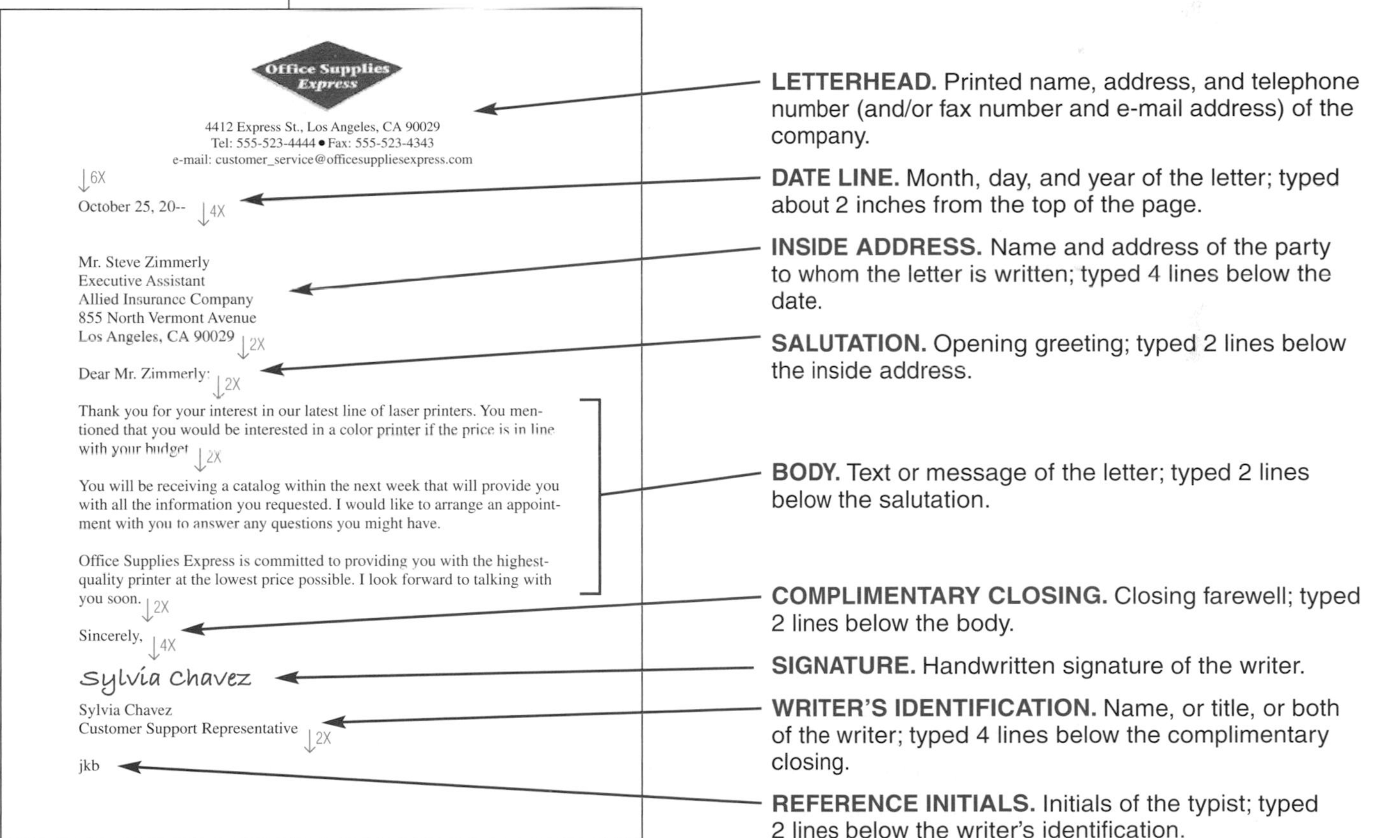
Office Supplies Express

4412 Express St., Los Angeles, CA 90029
Tel: 555-523-4444 • Fax: 555-523-4343
e-mail: customer_service@officesuppliesexpress.com

↓6X

October 25, 20-- ↓4X

Mr. Steve Zimmerly
Executive Assistant
Allied Insurance Company
855 North Vermont Avenue
Los Angeles, CA 90029 ↓2X

Dear Mr. Zimmerly: ↓2X

Thank you for your interest in our latest line of laser printers. You mentioned that you would be interested in a color printer if the price is in line with your budget. ↓2X

You will be receiving a catalog within the next week that will provide you with all the information you requested. I would like to arrange an appointment with you to answer any questions you might have.

Office Supplies Express is committed to providing you with the highest-quality printer at the lowest price possible. I look forward to talking with you soon. ↓2X

Sincerely, ↓4X

Sylvia Chavez

Sylvia Chavez
Customer Support Representative ↓2X

jkb

LETTERHEAD. Printed name, address, and telephone number (and/or fax number and e-mail address) of the company.
DATE LINE. Month, day, and year of the letter; typed about 2 inches from the top of the page.
INSIDE ADDRESS. Name and address of the party to whom the letter is written; typed 4 lines below the date.
SALUTATION. Opening greeting; typed 2 lines below the inside address.
BODY. Text or message of the letter; typed 2 lines below the salutation.
COMPLIMENTARY CLOSING. Closing farewell; typed 2 lines below the body.
SIGNATURE. Handwritten signature of the writer.
WRITER'S IDENTIFICATION. Name, or title, or both of the writer; typed 4 lines below the complimentary closing.
REFERENCE INITIALS. Initials of the typist; typed 2 lines below the writer's identification.

G. BUSINESS LETTERS IN BLOCK STYLE

1. Type all lines beginning at the left margin.
2. Press ENTER 6 times to begin the first line of the letter about 2 inches from the top of the page, and then type the date.
3. After the date, press ENTER 4 times and type the inside address. Leave 1 space between the state and the ZIP Code.

(Continued on next page)

4. After the inside address, press ENTER 2 times and type the salutation. For standard punctuation, type a colon after the salutation. Press ENTER 2 times after the salutation.
5. Single-space the body of the letter, but press ENTER 2 times between paragraphs. Do not indent paragraphs.
6. Press ENTER 2 times after the last paragraph and type the complimentary closing. For standard punctuation, type a comma after the complimentary closing.
7. Press ENTER 4 times after the complimentary closing and type the writer's identification.
8. Press ENTER 2 times after the writer's identification and type your reference initials in lowercase letters with no periods or spaces.

Word Processing Manual

H. WORD PROCESSING: INSERT DATE

Study Lesson 31 in your word processing manual. Complete all of the shaded steps while at your computer. Then format the jobs that follow.

DOCUMENT PROCESSING

Correspondence 31-3

Business Letter in Block Style

1. Type the letter using standard block style.
2. Use standard punctuation: a colon after the salutation and a comma after the complimentary closing.
3. Use word wrap for the paragraphs. Press ENTER only at the end of each paragraph. Your lines may end differently from those shown in the illustration.
4. Type your initials for the reference initials.
5. Spell-check, preview, and proofread your letter for typing, spelling, and formatting errors.

↓6X
March 27, 20-- ↓4X

≡ proper

Ms. Linda Lopez
Account Manager
The Internet Connection
7625 Maple Avenue
Pomona, CA 91765 ↓2X

≡ proper

Dear Ms. Lopez: ↓2X

≡ sentence, ≡ time
≡ proper

Our company is interested in hosting an educational seminar this spring that will focus on meeting the growing need for information industry professionals to keep abreast of emerging new technologies and trends. We are specifically interested in information on high-speed Internet connections. ↓2X

≡ sentence
≡ time

I understand that The Internet Connection specializes in these seminars and will also help businesses analyze their needs and choose an appropriate solution. I am in the process of contacting several companies similar to yours who might be interested in conducting these seminars. Please contact me by Thursday or Friday at the latest so that we can discuss this further. ↓2X

(Continued on next page)

≡ sentence
≡ proper

I appreciate the fine service we have always received from you in the past, Ms. Lopez, and look forward to hearing from you. ↓2X

Sincerely, ↓4X

≡ proper
≡ proper

Ruzanna Petroska
Technology Specialist ↓2X

Remember to type your initials in place of urs.

urs

Correspondence 31-4

Business Letter in Block Style

Open the file for Correspondence 31-3 and make the following changes:

1. Change the date to `May 8`.

2. Change the writer's identification to: `Gail Madison` and her job title to `Technology Engineer`.

Correspondence 31-5

Business Letter in Block Style

Note: The | symbol indicates the end of a line. The ¶ symbol indicates the start of a new paragraph.

1. Type the letter using standard block style.

2. Spell-check, preview, and proofread your letter for typing, spelling, and formatting errors.

≡ time
≡ proper
≡ proper
≡ proper

The ¶ symbol indicates the start of a new paragraph. In a business letter, paragraphs are blocked (not indented).

≡ time

May 25, 20-- | Ms. Linda Lopez | Account Manager | The Internet Connection | 7625 Maple Avenue | Pomona, CA 91765 | Dear Ms. Lopez:
¶ Thank you so much for hosting the educational seminar last Tuesday that focused on the topic of high-speed Internet connections. Our company and our employees are now well prepared to make a decision about the best type of Internet connection for their particular needs.
¶ Because this seminar was so successful, I have been authorized to contract with The Internet Connection for a continuing series of seminars on any topics related to emerging new technologies and trends as they apply to the needs of our company and our employees. I will call you on Monday so that we can arrange for a meeting to finalize some contractual issues.
¶ Once again, thank you for a very successful and productive seminar!
Sincerely, | Ruzanna Petroska | Technology Specialist |
urs

Business Letters With Enclosure Notations

Goals

- Type at least 33wpm/3′/5e
- Format a business letter with an enclosure notation

A. Type 2 times.

A. WARMUP

```
     Sales by two travel agencies (Quill, Virgil, & Johnson  11
and Keef & Zane) exceeded all prior amounts. Total sales     23
for that year were as follows: $1,540,830 and $976,233.      34
|  1  |  2  |  3  |  4  |  5  |  6  |  7  |  8  |  9  |  10  |  11  |  12
```

SKILLBUILDING

B. Type each line 2 times.

Technique Tip: Press the BACKSPACE key with the Sem finger without looking at your keyboard.

B. TECHNIQUE PRACTICE: BACKSPACE KEY

1. Type each letter (or group of letters) as shown.
2. When you reach the backspace sign (←), backspace 1 time to delete the last keystroke.
3. Type the next group of letters. The result will be a new word. For example, if you see "hi← at," you would type "hi," backspace 1 time, and then type "at," resulting in the new word "hat" instead of the original word "hit."

```
p←cat c←tab b←peg p←but p←tie t←pop m←pat f←sit m←but t←cub
t←mop b←fib r←fat w←fin p←tin c←top p←ban f←can y←get m←let
di←ye be←ag ge←um ri←ob mu←ad la←id fi←an bi←ad to←ip ro←id
pa←it ti←on fi←un ra←un pi←an ge←ot ba←it fa←it ma←it sa←it
bin←t any←t new←t was←r sea←t tap←n fan←t lap←d for←x fin←x
pin←t ham←d sod←n rid←p rap←n tap←n dip←n sin←p lip←d put←n
```

PPP PRETEST → PRACTICE → POSTTEST

PRETEST
Take a 1-minute timed writing. Review your speed and errors.

PRACTICE
Speed Emphasis: If you made 2 or fewer errors on the Pretest, type each *individual* line 2 times.
Accuracy Emphasis: If you made 3 or more errors, type each *group* of lines (as though it were a paragraph) 2 times.

C. PRETEST: Discrimination Practice

```
     Steven saw the younger, unruly boy take flight as he    11
threw the coin at the jury. The brave judge stopped the      22
fight. He called out to the youth, who recoiled in fear.     33
|  1  |  2  |  3  |  4  |  5  |  6  |  7  |  8  |  9  |  10  |  11  |  12
```

D. PRACTICE: Left Hand

```
vbv verb bevy vibes bevel brave above verbal bovine behaves
wew west weep threw wedge weave fewer weight sewing dewdrop
fgf gulf gift fight fudge fugue flags flight golfer feigned
```

E. PRACTICE: Right Hand

uyu buys your usury unity youth buoys unruly untidy younger
oio coin lion oiled foils foist prior recoil iodine rejoice
jhj jury huge enjoy three judge habit adjust slight jasmine

POSTTEST
Repeat the Pretest timed writing and compare performance.

F. POSTTEST: Discrimination Practice

G. Take two 3-minute timed writings. Review your speed and errors.

Goal: At least 33wpm/3′/5e

G. 3-MINUTE TIMED WRITING

Be zealous in your efforts when you write business 10
letters. Your business writing must convey clearly what 22
it is you want people to read. All of your letters should 33
be formatted neatly in proper business letter format. 44
Before sending your letters, read them quickly just to 55
make sure that they explain clearly what you want to say. 67
Proofread the letters you write for correct grammar and 78
spelling. Use all of your writing skills to display the 89
best image. Your readers will welcome the effort. 99
| 1 | 2 | 3 | 4 | 5 | 6 | 7 | 8 | 9 | 10 | 11 | 12

FORMATTING

H. ENCLOSURE NOTATION

- To indicate that an item is enclosed with a letter, type the word *Enclosure* on the line below the reference initials.

Example: urs
Enclosure

- If more than one item is being enclosed, type the word *Enclosures*.

DOCUMENT PROCESSING

Correspondence 32-6

Business Letter in Block Style

Reference Manual

See page R-3B and R-3C of the Reference Manual for an illustration of a business letter with an enclosure notation.

The | symbol indicates the end of a line.

1. Type the letter using standard business letter format.
2. Spell-check, preview, and proofread your document for spelling and formatting errors.

October 10, 20-- | Ms. Denise Bradford | Worldwide Travel, Inc. | 1180 Alvarado, SE | Albuquerque, NM 87108 | Dear Ms. Bradford:
¶ Our company has decided to hold its regional sales meeting in Scottsdale, Arizona, during the second week of January. I need information on a suitable conference site.

(Continued on next page)

The ¶ symbol indicates the start of a new paragraph.

¶ We will need a meeting room with the following items: 30 computer workstations with an Internet connection, copy stands, mouse pads, and adjustable chairs; an LCD projector with a large screen; and a microphone and podium. The hotel should have a fax machine and on-site secretarial services. We might also need a messenger service.
¶ A final decision on the conference site must be made within the next two weeks. Please send me any information you have available for a suitable location in Scottsdale immediately. I have enclosed a list of conference attendees and their room preferences. Thank you for your help.
Sincerely yours, | Bill McKay | Marketing Manager | urs | Enclosure

Correspondence 32-7

Business Letter in Block Style

1. Open the file for Correspondence 32-6.
2. Change the inside address to `1032 San Pedro, SE.`
3. Change the first sentence as follows:
   `Our company has decided to hold its annual national sales meeting during the first week of February in Scottsdale, Arizona.`
4. In the first sentence of the second paragraph, change the information after the colon as follows:
   `30 computer workstations, an LCD projector with a large screen, and a microphone and podium.`

Correspondence 32-8

Business Letter in Block Style

October 20, 20-- | Mr. Bill McKay | Marketing Manager | Viatech Communications | 9835 Osuna Road, NE | Albuquerque, NM 87111 | Dear Mr. McKay:
¶ Thank you for your inquiry regarding a conference site in Scottsdale, Arizona, for 35 people during the second week of January.
¶ I have enclosed the following brochures with detailed information on some properties in Scottsdale that provide exclusive service to businesses like yours: Camelback Resorts, Shadow Pines Suites, and Desert Inn Resorts and Golf Club. All these properties have meeting rooms that will accommodate your needs and also offer additional services you might be interested in using.

(Continued on next page)

¶ Please call me when you have reached a decision. I will be happy to make the final arrangements as well as issue any airline tickets you may need. Yours truly, | Ms. Denise Bradford | Travel Agent | urs | Enclosures

Envelopes and Labels

Goals

- Improve speed and accuracy
- Refine language arts skills in composing sentences
- Format envelopes and labels and fold letters

A. Type 2 times.

A. WARMUP

Does Quentin know if half of the January order will be ready on 1/7/05? At 4:20 only 36% of the orders had been mailed! Mr. Gray expects a very sizable loss this month. 11 23 34

| 1 | 2 | 3 | 4 | 5 | 6 | 7 | 8 | 9 | 10 | 11 | 12

SKILLBUILDING

B. Take three 12-second timed writings on each line. The scale below the last line shows your wpm speed for a 12-second timed writing.

B. 12-SECOND SPEED SPRINTS

4 Today we want to find out if our work will be done on time.
5 Doug will be able to drive to the store if the car is here.
6 Jan will sign this paper when she has done all of the work.
7 This time she will be sure to spend two days with her sons.

5 10 15 20 25 30 35 40 45 50 55 60

C. PACED PRACTICE

If you are not using the GDP software, turn to page SB-14 and follow the directions for this activity.

LANGUAGE ARTS

D. Answer each question with a complete sentence.

D. COMPOSING: SENTENCES

8 What are your best traits that you will bring to your job when you graduate?
9 What are the best traits that you will want to see in your new boss?
10 Would you rather work for a large or a small company?
11 How much money do you expect to earn on your first job?
12 Would you like your first job to be in a small town or a large city?
13 What do you see yourself doing in ten years?
14 What types of benefits do you think you would like to have?

E. ENVELOPES

The envelope feature of your word processor simplifies your task of addressing a No. 10 envelope. The standard size for business envelopes is 9½ by 4⅛ inches. A business envelope should include the following:

- **Return Address**. If necessary, type the sender's name and address in upper- and lowercase style in the upper left corner. Business stationery usually has a printed return address. Use the default placement and the default font of your word processor for the return address.
- **Mailing Address**. Type the recipient's name and address in upper- and lowercase style (or in all-capital letters without any punctuation) toward the center of the envelope. Use the default placement and the default font of your word processor for the mailing address.

Note: Postal scanners read addresses more efficiently if they are typed in all-capital letters without any punctuation.

Trend Electronics
2206 31st Street
Minneapolis, MN 55407-1911

Mr. Charles R. Harrison
Reliable Software, Inc.
5613 Brunswick Avenue
Minneapolis, MN 55406

Standard large envelope, No. 10, is 9½ 3 4⅛ inches.

F. FOLDING LETTERS

To fold a letter for a No. 10 envelope:

1. Place the letter face up, and fold up the bottom third of the page.
2. Fold the top third of the page down to about 0.5 inch from the bottom edge of the page.
3. Insert the last crease into the envelope first with the flap facing up.

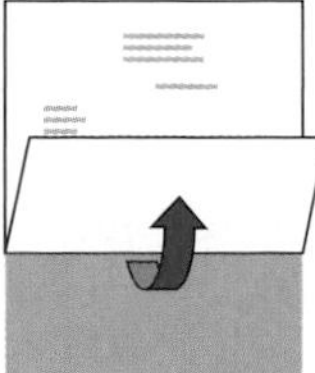

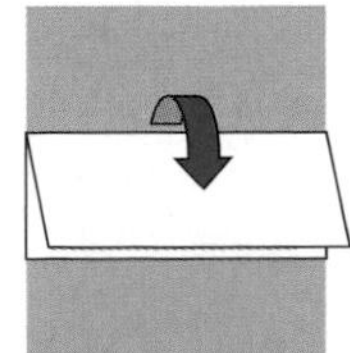

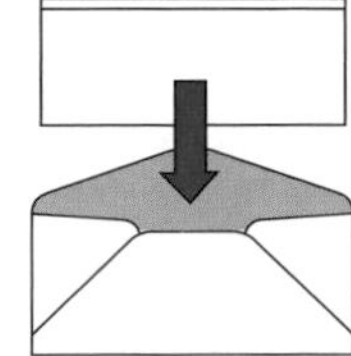

G. LABELS

The label feature of your word processor simplifies the task of preparing various labels. You can use different label settings to print a full sheet of labels or to print a single label. You may want to use a mailing label as an alternative to printing an envelope.

When preparing labels, test the label settings by printing your labels on a blank page before you print them on the actual label form.

Word Processing Manual

H. WORD PROCESSING: ENVELOPES AND LABELS

Study Lesson 33 in your word processing manual. Complete all of the shaded steps while at your computer. Then format the jobs that follow.

DOCUMENT PROCESSING

Correspondence 33-9

Envelope

1. Prepare an envelope with the following mailing address:

   `Mr. Charles Goldstein| Software Solutions|2981 Canwood Street|Roselle, IL 60172`

2. Insert the following return address.

   `Shannon Stone|Data Systems, Inc.|2201 South Street| Racine, WI 53404`

3. Add the envelope to a blank document.

Correspondence 33-10

Envelope

1. Open the file for Correspondence 32-8 and prepare an envelope for the letter.
2. Do not insert a return address.
3. Add the envelope to the letter.

Correspondence 33-11

Mailing Labels

1. Select an address label product about 1 inch deep, large enough to fit a 4-line address. Label choices will vary; however, Avery standard, 5160, Address is a good choice for laser and ink jet printers.
2. Prepare address labels for the names and addresses that follow.
3. Type the addresses in order from left to right as you see them displayed below in the first group.
4. Move to the second group of labels and type them again from left to right.

Purchasing Dept. Abbott Laboratories Abbott Park Chicago, IL 60064	Frank Zimmerly Cartridges, Etc. 1220 Charleston Road Oso Park, CA 90621	John Sanchez Adobe Systems 1585 Charleston Road Los Angeles, CA 90029
Mike Rashid Internet Services 901 Thompson Place Sunnyvale, CA 94088	Jennifer Reagan Aetna Life 151 Farmington Avenue Hartford, CT 06156	Bob Patterson Affiliated Publishing 135 Morrisey Boulevard Boston, MA 02107

Correspondence 33-12

Mailing Labels

1. Select an address label product about 1 inch deep, large enough to fit a 4-line address. Label choices will vary; however, Avery standard, 5160, Address is a good choice for laser and ink jet printers.
2. Prepare a full page of the same label with the following address:

   ```
   Shipping and Receiving|
   E-Office Outlet|1122 North
   Highland Street|Arlington,
   VA 22201
   ```

Correspondence 33-13

Envelope

1. Open the file for Correspondence 32-6 and prepare an envelope for the letter.
2. Insert the following return address:

   ```
   Bill McKay|Viatech
   Communications|9835 Osana
   Road, NE|Albuquerque, NM
   87111
   ```

3. Add the envelope to the letter.

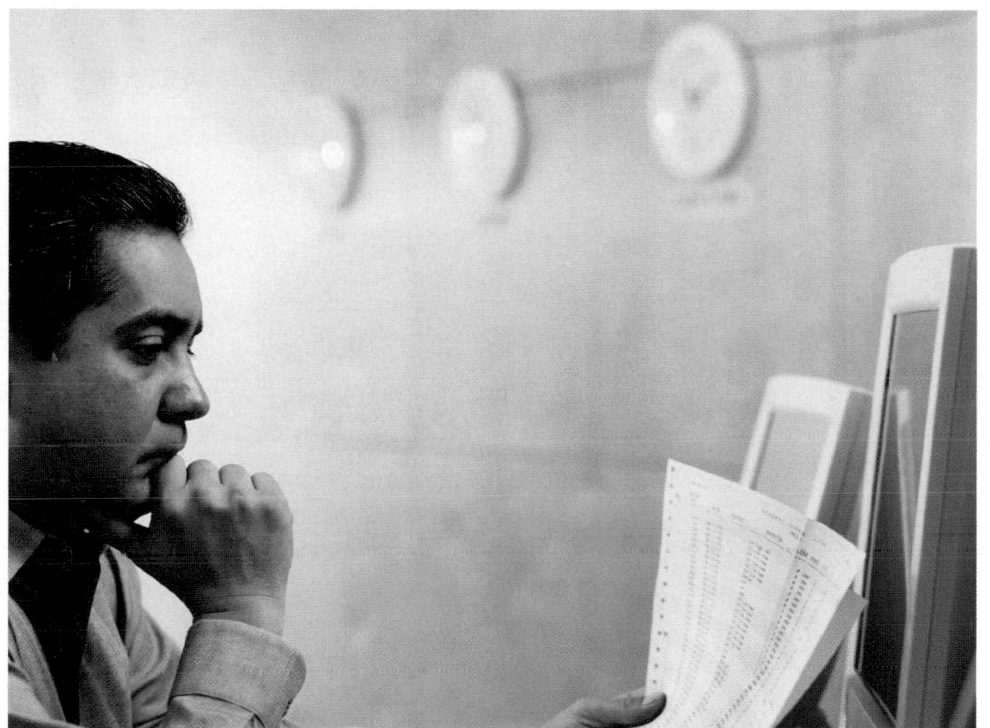

Memos

Goals

- Type at least 34wpm/3′/5e
- Format interoffice memos

A. Type 2 times.

A. WARMUP

The series* (*6 films, 28 minutes) by J. Zeller goes 11
beyond the "basics" of computers. Viewers keep requesting 22
an extension on the following due dates: 3/2, 5/5, and 8/9. 34
| 1 | 2 | 3 | 4 | 5 | 6 | 7 | 8 | 9 | 10 | 11 | 12

SKILLBUILDING

B. DIAGNOSTIC PRACTICE: SYMBOLS AND PUNCTUATION

If you are not using the GDP software, turn to page SB-2 and follow the directions for this activity.

C. PROGRESSIVE PRACTICE: ALPHABET

If you are not using the GDP software, turn to page SB-7 and follow the directions for this activity.

D. Take two 3-minute timed writings. Review your speed and errors.

Goal: At least 34wpm/3′/5e

D. 3-MINUTE TIMED WRITING

Companies that place their ads on the Internet use a 11
process called data mining. They look for patterns in the 22
quantities of data they get from those who visit Web sites. 34
Data mining tracks buying habits of customers and then 46
decides to send ads to them based on their current and past 58
buying patterns. Data mining can also be used to explain 69
buyer behavior and to look at trends. First, a survey is 80
filled out, and then the results are gathered and stored in 92
a file to be analyzed in detail at a later time. 102
| 1 | 2 | 3 | 4 | 5 | 6 | 7 | 8 | 9 | 10 | 11 | 12

FORMATTING

E. MEMOS

A memo is usually sent from one person to another in the same organization. To format a memo on plain paper or on letterhead stationery:

1. Press ENTER 6 times for a top margin of about 2 inches.
2. Type the headings (including the colons) in all-caps and bold: `MEMO TO:`, `FROM:`, `DATE:`, and `SUBJECT:`.
3. Press TAB 1 time after typing the colon to reach the point where the heading entries begin.
4. Insert 1 blank line between the heading lines and between the heading lines and the memo body.
5. Insert 1 blank line between paragraphs. Most memos are typed with blocked paragraphs (no indentions).
6. Insert 1 blank line between the body and the reference initials.

DOCUMENT PROCESSING

Correspondence 34-14

Memo

Refer to page R-7C of the Reference Manual for an illustration of a memo.

1. Type the memo using standard memo format.
2. Spell-check, preview, and proofread your document for spelling and formatting errors before printing it.

↓6X

MEMO TO: All Salaried Employees ↓2X

FROM: Amy Vigil, Human Resources ↓2X

DATE: November 2, 20-- ↓2X

SUBJECT: Health Care Benefit Plan ↓2X

Effective January 1, Allied Aerospace Industries will contract with MedNet to begin a new health benefits program for all eligible salaried personnel. A brochure outlining important program information will be mailed to you soon. ↓2X

An open enrollment period will be in effect during the entire month of January. If you and your family are interested in one of the MedNet health plan options, you may transfer yourself and your dependents into any appropriate plan. All applications must be received no later than midnight, January 31. You may also access your plan over the Internet at www.mednet.com if it is more convenient. ↓2X

If you have any questions or need any help understanding your options, please call me at Ext. 134. I will be happy to help you select the plan that is best for you. ↓2X

urs

Correspondence 34-15

Memo

> The ¶ symbol indicates the start of a new paragraph. In a memo, paragraphs are blocked (not indented).

MEMO TO: Amy Vigil, Human Resources | **FROM:** Dan Westphal | **DATE:** November 23, 20-- | **SUBJECT:** MedNet Benefit Plan

¶ Thank you for the brochure detailing the various options for employees under the MedNet plan. I would like clarification on some of the services included in the plan.

¶ Because both my wife and I are employees of Allied Aerospace Industries, do we have the choice of enrolling separately under different options? In our present plan, I know that this is possible.

¶ We have two dependents. Is it possible to enroll both dependents under different options of the plan, or do they both fall under either one option or the other? I know that in the past you have asked for evidence of dependent status and dates of birth.

¶ If you need any further information, please let me know. Thank you very much for your help.

urs

Correspondence 34-16

Memo

Open the file for Correspondence 34-14 and make the following changes:

1. Send the memo to `All Allied Aerospace Industries Employees.`
2. Change the date to `December 2.`
3. Change the subject line to `Health Care Open Enrollment Period.`

Keyboarding Connection

Searching the Web

Research projects on the World Wide Web! Access up-to-date information from all over the world.

To conduct a search, specify keywords and certain relationships among them. Many search engines use arithmetic operators to symbolize Boolean relationships. A plus sign (+) is used instead of AND, a minus sign (−) instead of NOT, and no sign instead of OR.

Simple document searches match a single keyword (e.g., *cherry*). Advanced searches might match any of the words (e.g., *cherry pie*); all words (e.g., +*cherry* +*pie*); a phrase (e.g., "*cherry pie*"); or some words and not others (e.g., +*cherry* +*pie* −*tree*). There is no space between the plus or minus sign and its word.

YOUR TURN From your Web browser, open a Web search engine site. Type various searches in the entry box of the search engine and start the search. Compare the results.

Lesson 35

Correspondence Review

Goals

- Improve speed and accuracy
- Refine language arts skills in proofreading
- Format various types of correspondence with an attachment notation
- Practice italicizing and underlining

A. Type 2 times.

A. WARMUP

```
     Item #876 won't be ordered until 9/10. Did you gather    11
all requests and input them exactly as they appeared? Zack    23
will never be satisfied until he contacts jack@orders.com.    34
| 1 | 2 | 3 | 4 | 5 | 6 | 7 | 8 | 9 | 10 | 11 | 12
```

SKILLBUILDING

B. MAP

Follow the GDP software directions for this exercise in improving keystroking accuracy.

C. Take a 1-minute timed writing on the first paragraph to establish your base speed. Then take four 1-minute timed writings on the remaining paragraphs. As soon as you equal or exceed your base speed on one paragraph, advance to the next, more difficult paragraph.

C. SUSTAINED PRACTICE: ALTERNATE-HAND WORDS

```
     When eight of them began a formal discussion on some    11
of the major issues, the need for a chair was very evident.  23
A chair would be sure to handle the usual work with ease.    35

     The eight people in that group decided that the work    11
would be done only if they selected one person to be chair   23
of their group. They began to debate all the major issues.   35

     One issue that needed to be settled right up front was  11
the question of how to handle proxy votes. It seemed for a   23
short time that a fight over this very issue would result.   35

     The group worked diligently in attempting to solve the  11
issues that were being discussed. All of the concerns that   23
were brought to the group were reviewed in depth by them.    34
| 1 | 2 | 3 | 4 | 5 | 6 | 7 | 8 | 9 | 10 | 11 | 12
```

LANGUAGE ARTS

D. Edit this paragraph to correct any typing or formatting errors.

D. PROOFREADING

```
     It doesnt matter how fast you can  type or how well you now a software program if you produce documents taht are filled with errors. You must learn to watch for errors in spelling punctuation, and formatting. Look carefully between words and sentences.Make sure that after a period at the end of a sentence, you see one space. Sometime it helps to look at the characters in the sentence justabove the one you are proofreading to ensure accuracy.
```

FORMATTING

E. ATTACHMENT NOTATION

The word *Attachment* (rather than *Enclosure*) is typed below the reference initials when material is physically attached (stapled or clipped) to a memo.

Example: urs
Attachment

Word Processing Manual

F. WORD PROCESSING: ITALIC AND UNDERLINE

Study Lesson 35 in your word processing manual. Complete all of the shaded steps while at your computer. Then format the jobs that follow.

DOCUMENT PROCESSING

Correspondence 35-17

Memo

MEMO TO: All Executive Assistants | **FROM:** Barbara Azar, Staff Development Coordinator | **DATE:** March 25, 20-- | **SUBJECT:** Standardizing Document Formats

¶ Last month we received our final shipment of new laser printers. The installation of these printers in your offices marked the final phase-out of all ink-jet printers.

¶ Because all of us can now use a variety of standardized fonts in our correspondence, please note the following change: <u>From now on, all book and journal titles should be set in Arial Narrow.</u> This new formatting change will help us to standardize our correspondence.

¶ The latest edition of the book *Quick Reference for the Automated Office* has two pages of helpful information on laser printers, which I have attached. Please read these pages carefully, and we will discuss them at our next meeting.

urs | Attachment

Correspondence 35-18

Memo

MEMO TO: Barbara Azar, Staff Development Coordinator | **FROM:** Sharon Hearshen, Executive Assistant | **DATE:** April 3, 20-- | **SUBJECT:** Laser Printer Workshop

¶ The new laser printers we received are <u>fabulous</u>! I know that you worked very hard to get these printers for us, and all of us in the Sales and Marketing Department certainly appreciate your effort.

¶ Several of us would be very interested in seeing the printers demonstrated. Would it be possible to have a workshop with some hands-on training? We are particularly interested in learning about font selection, paper selection, and envelopes and labels.

¶ I have attached an article on laser printers from the latest issue of *Office Technology*. It is very informative, and you might like to include it as a part of the workshop. Please let me know if I can help you in any way.

urs | Attachment

Correspondence 35-19

Business Letter in Block Style

Progress and Proofreading Check

Documents designated as Proofreading Checks serve as a check of your proofreading skill. Your goal is to have zero typographical errors when the GDP software first scores the document.

1. Type the following business letter, and then prepare an envelope for the document.
2. Do not include a return address.
3. Add the envelope to the letter.

October 1, 20-- | Mrs. Elizabeth McGraw | 844 Lincoln Boulevard | Santa Monica, CA 90403 | Dear Mrs. McGraw:

¶ The League of Women Voters is looking for volunteers to work at the various polling places during the upcoming elections. If you think you will be able to volunteer your time, please fill out and mail the following enclosed items: registration form, schedule of availability, and insurance waiver form.

¶ After I receive these items, I will contact you to confirm a location, time, and date.

¶ Your efforts are greatly appreciated, Mrs. McGraw. Concerned citizens like you make it possible for the public to have a convenient place to vote. Thank you for your interest in this very worthy cause!

Sincerely yours, | Ashley Abbott | Public Relations Volunteer | urs | Enclosures

Unit 8

Tables

LESSON 36
Boxed Tables

LESSON 37
Open Tables With Titles

LESSON 38
Open Tables With Column Headings

LESSON 39
Ruled Tables With Number Columns

LESSON 40
Formatting Review

PERSONAL ASSET ACCOUNTS
Wanda Nelson

Account	Amount	Interest Rate
Interest Checking	$ 972.55	3.10%
Money Market	4,500.35	4.90%
	3,250.76	5.07%
sit	550.00	7.41%

GENERAL EQUITY MUTUAL FUNDS

Fund	Current Y
Duncan Insurance	16.3%
Strident Nova	9.3%
First Value	10.7%
Safeguard Policy	11.1%
Vanguard Life	8.5%

CABLE SERVICES AVAILABILITY

Type of Service	Currently Available
Basic	Phoenix
Lifeline	Scottsdale
Expanded	Glendale
Expanded (per channel)	Camelback City

Boxed Tables

Goals

- Type at least 35wpm/3′/4e
- Format boxed tables

A. Type 2 times.

A. WARMUP

```
     A plain paper reader/printer must be ordered; it must   11
accept jackets and have a footprint of 15 x 27* (*inches).   23
Please ask Gary to request Model Z-340 whenever he arrives.  35
| 1 | 2 | 3 | 4 | 5 | 6 | 7 | 8 | 9 | 10 | 11 | 12
```

SKILLBUILDING

B. Take three 12-second timed writings on each line. The scale below the last line shows your wpm speed for a 12-second timed writing.

B. 12-SECOND SPEED SPRINTS

```
The book that is on top of the big desk will be given away.
Bill must pay for the tape or he will have to give it back.
They left the meeting after all of the group had gone away.
The third person to finish all of the work today may leave.
5 10 15 20 25 30 35 40 45 50 55 60
```

C. DIAGNOSTIC PRACTICE: SYMBOLS AND PUNCTUATION

If you are not using the GDP software, turn to page SB-2 and follow the directions for this activity.

D. Take two 3-minute timed writings. Review your speed and errors.

Goal: At least 35wpm/3′/4e

D. 3-MINUTE TIMED WRITING

```
     Technology that tracks eye movements is used by Web       11
designers to judge how people interact with Web pages. It     22
must find out which zone of the page is viewed first, which   34
feature is viewed most often, and how quickly a page comes    46
to the screen.                                                49
     Eye movements are tracked by use of hardware and data    60
analysis software. A camera is employed to find out the eye   72
movements of people who watch a screen. Pupil dilations and   84
scanning patterns of the eyes are measured to document the    96
amount of mental strain that has been exerted.               105
| 1 | 2 | 3 | 4 | 5 | 6 | 7 | 8 | 9 | 10 | 11 | 12
```

FORMATTING

E. BASIC PARTS OF A TABLE

- Tables have vertical columns (identified by a letter in the illustration) and horizontal rows (identified by a number in the illustration).
- A cell, or "box," is created where a column and a row intersect.
- Tables formatted with borders all around (as shown in the illustration) are called boxed tables.
- Tables formatted with no borders are called open tables.
- Center a table vertically when it appears alone on the page.
- Center a table horizontally if the cell widths have been adjusted automatically to fit the contents.

Note: You will learn to center tables vertically and horizontally in Lesson 38.

↓ center page

14 pt **ALASKAN VACATIONS** 12 pt↓**Sailing Dates and Prices** ↓1X				Row 1
↓1X **Northern Departures**	**Interior Stateroom**	**Ocean View Stateroom**	↓1X **Guest**	Row 2
January 12	$599	$699	$ 99	Row 3
February 14	599	699	99	Row 4
March 11	699	799	199	Row 5
April 2	699	799	199	Row 6
May 11	699	799	299	Row 7
June 6	799	899	399	Row 8
July 1	799	899	399	Row 9
August 21	799	899	399	Row 10
Column A	Column B	Column C	Column D	

TITLE. Center and type in all-caps and bold, with a 14-point font. If there is no subtitle, insert 1 blank line after the title.

SUBTITLE. Center on the line below the title, and type in upper- and lowercase letters and bold. Press Enter 1 time to insert a blank line below the subtitle.

HEADING BLOCK. Title and subtitle.

COLUMN HEADINGS. Center or left-align (for text) or right-align (for numbers). Press ENTER to split a 2-line column heading or to move a 1-line column heading down 1 line.

COLUMN ENTRIES. Align text entries at the left; align number entries at the right. Capitalize only the first word and proper nouns. Add spaces after the dollar sign to align with the widest column entry below (add 2 spaces for each digit and 1 space for each comma).

Word Processing Manual

F. WORD PROCESSING: TABLE—INSERT AND AUTOFIT TO CONTENTS

Study Lesson 36 in your word processing manual. Complete all of the shaded steps while at your computer. Then format the jobs that follow.

DOCUMENT PROCESSING

Table 36-1

Boxed Table

Simple tables often do not have titles, subtitles, or column headings.

1. Insert a boxed table with 3 columns and 3 rows.
2. Left-align all column entries.
3. Automatically adjust the column widths for all columns.

Mary Spangler	President	Administration
Joyce Moore	Dean	Jefferson Hall
Thelma Day	Chairperson	Da Vinci Hall

Table 36-2

Boxed Table

1. Insert a boxed table with 2 columns and 4 rows.
2. Left-align all column entries.
3. Automatically adjust the column widths for all columns.

Marie Covey, Executive Editor	Santa Clarita, California
Albert Russell, Associate Editor	Newport, Rhode Island
Bob Harris, Contributing Writer	St. Louis, Missouri
Sylvestra Zimmerly, Art Director	Albuquerque, New Mexico

Table 36-3

Boxed Table

1. Open the file for Table 36-2.
2. Change the name and title in Row 4, Column A, to `Theodore Easton, Film Editor`.
3. Change the city in Row 4, Column B, to `Socorro`.

Table 36-4

Boxed Table

Barbara Azar	Professor	Computer Technologies
Ken Kennedy	Professor	Foreign Languages
Bonnie Marquette	Instructor	Computer Technologies
Kevin Nguyen	Assistant	Social Sciences

Strategies for Career Success

Nonverbal Communication

"It's not what he said, but how he said it." More than 90 percent of your spoken message contains nonverbal communication that expresses your feelings and desires. People respond to this nonverbal language.

Posture can convey your mood. For example, leaning toward a speaker indicates interest. Leaning backward suggests dislike or indifference. Your handshake, an important nonverbal communicator, should be firm but not overpowering.

Your head position provides many nonverbal signals. A lowered head usually expresses shyness or withdrawal. An upright head conveys confidence and interest. A tilted head signifies curiosity or suspicion. Nodding your head shows positive feeling, while left-right head shakes signify negative feeling. Your face strongly expresses your emotions. Narrow, squinting eyes signify caution, reflection, or uncertainty. Wide-open eyes convey interest and attention.

YOUR TURN Turn off the sound on a television program. How much of the plot can you understand just from the nonverbal communication signals?

Lesson 37

Open Tables With Titles

Goals

- Improve speed and accuracy
- Refine language arts skills in punctuation
- Format open tables with titles

A. Type 2 times.

A. WARMUP

```
     The check for $432.65 wasn't mailed on time! Late       10
charges of up to 10% can be expected. To avoid a sizable     22
penalty, just send an e-mail message to quickpay@epay.com.   33
| 1 | 2 | 3 | 4 | 5 | 6 | 7 | 8 | 9 | 10 | 11 | 12
```

SKILLBUILDING

B. Take a 1-minute timed writing on the first paragraph to establish your base speed. Then take four 1-minute timed writings on the remaining paragraphs. As soon as you equal or exceed your base speed on one paragraph, advance to the next, more difficult paragraph.

B. SUSTAINED PRACTICE: ROUGH DRAFT

```
     Various human responses are asymmetrical. This means      11
that we ask more from one side of the body than the other      23
each time we wave, wink, clap our hands, or cross our legs.    35

     Each one of these actions demands a clear desision,       11
usually unconscious and instantaneous, to start the course     23
of moving parts of the body in different directions.           34

All children go though remarkably involved steps as they       12
develop their preferried. As children grows she or he may      23
favor the right hand, the left, or both the same at times.     35

When most kids are eihgt or seven, stability ocurrs,           11
and one hand is permanently dominent over the other. Fore      22
some unnown reason, choose the right hand.                     34
| 1 | 2 | 3 | 4 | 5 | 6 | 7 | 8 | 9 | 10 | 11 | 12
```

C. PACED PRACTICE

If you are not using the GDP software, turn to page SB-14 and follow the directions for this activity.

LANGUAGE ARTS

D. Study the rules at the right.

D. APOSTROPHE

Note: The callout signals in the left margin indicate which language arts rule from this lesson has been applied.

RULE ▶ ' singular

Use *'s* to form the possessive of singular nouns.

The hurricane's force caused major damage to North Carolina's coastline.

RULE ▶ ' plural

Use only an apostrophe to form the possessive of plural nouns that end in *s*.

The investors' goals were outlined in the stockholders' report.

But: The investors outlined their goals in the report to the stockholders.

But: The women's and children's clothing was on sale.

RULE ▶ ' pronoun

Use *'s* to form the possessive of indefinite pronouns (such as *someone's* or *anybody's*); do not use an apostrophe with personal pronouns (such as *hers, his, its, ours, their,* and *yours*).

She could select anybody's paper for a sample.

It's time to put the file back into its cabinet.

Edit the sentences to insert any needed punctuation.

```
16 The womans purse was stolen as she held her childs hand.
17 If the book is yours, please return it to the library now.
18 The girls decided to send both parents donations to school.
19 The childs toy was forgotten by his mothers good friend.
20 The universities presidents submitted the joint statement.
21 The four secretaries salaries were raised just like yours.
22 One boys presents were forgotten when he left the party.
23 If these blue notebooks are not ours, they must be theirs.
24 The plant was designed to recycle its own waste products.
```

FORMATTING

E. TABLE HEADING BLOCK

Note: The title and subtitle (if any) make up the table heading block.

To format a table heading block:

- Type the title centered in all-caps and bold, with a 14-point font in Row 1 of the table. If the table does not have a subtitle, insert 1 blank line after the title.
- Type the subtitle (if any) with a 12-point font centered on the line below the title in upper- and lowercase letters in bold.
- Insert 1 blank line after the subtitle.

Word Processing Manual

F. WORD PROCESSING: TABLE—MERGE CELLS AND BORDERS

Study Lesson 37 in your word processing manual. Complete all of the shaded steps while at your computer. Then format the jobs that follow.

DOCUMENT PROCESSING

Table 37-5

Open Table

1. Insert a table with 2 columns and 5 rows.
2. Merge the cells in Row 1; then center and type the title in bold and all-caps, with a 14-point font.
3. Press ENTER once to insert 1 blank line after the title.
4. Left-align all column entries.
5. Automatically adjust the column widths for all columns.
6. Remove the table borders.

' singular

PC CONNECTION'S LOCATIONS	
Valencia Mall	Santa Clarita, California
Town Center Square	Stevenson Ranch, California
Northridge Mall	Northridge, California
Granary Square	Valencia, California

Table 37-6

Open Table

1. Insert a table with 3 columns and 5 rows.
2. Merge the cells in Row 1; then center and type the title in bold and all-caps, with a 14-point font.
3. Press ENTER 1 time, change to a 12-point font, and type the subtitle centered in bold.
4. Press ENTER 1 time to insert 1 blank line after the subtitle.
5. Left-align all column entries.
6. Automatically adjust the column widths for all columns.
7. Remove the table borders.

' singular

' plural

NEWHALL DISTRICT'S REGISTRATION Seniors' Schedule		
Meadows	Monday, February 14	11 a.m.
Stevenson Ranch	Monday, February 21	10 a.m.
Old Orchard	Monday, February 28	11 a.m.
Wiley Canyon	Monday, March 7	10 a.m.

Table 37-7

Open Table

' singular

1. Insert a table with 2 columns and 6 rows.
2. Use standard table format for an open table with a title and subtitle.

MAR VISTA REALTY'S TOP SELLERS First Quarter	
James Kinkaid	Santa Clarita
Deborah Springer	Northbridge
Patricia Morelli	Woodland Hills
Jan McKay	Malibu
Daniel Aboud	San Luis Obispo

Open Tables With Column Headings

Goals

- Type at least 35wpm/3′/4e
- Format open tables with column headings

A. Type 2 times.

A. WARMUP

```
     Jerry wrote a great article entitled "Interviewing       10
Techniques" on pp. 23 and 78! A&B@bookstore.com expected a    22
sizable number of requests; thus far, 65% have been sold.     33
|  1  |  2  |  3  |  4  |  5  |  6  |  7  |  8  |  9  |  10  |  11  |  12
```

SKILLBUILDING

B. Take three 12-second timed writings on each line. The scale below the last line shows your wpm speed for a 12-second timed writing.

B. 12-SECOND SPEED SPRINTS

```
Blake was paid to fix the handle on the bowls that he made.
Alan led the panel of four men until the work was all done.
Jan will sign this paper when she has done all of the work.
They will focus on their main theme for the last six weeks.
    5    10    15    20    25    30    35    40    45    50    55    60
```

C. PROGRESSIVE PRACTICE: ALPHABET

If you are not using the GDP software, turn to page SB-7 and follow the directions for this activity.

D. Take two 3-minute timed writings. Review your speed and errors.

Goal: At least 35wpm/3′/4e

D. 3-MINUTE TIMED WRITING

```
     Telecommuting is a word you may have heard before but    11
do not quite understand. Very simply, it means working at     23
home instead of driving in to work. Many people like the      34
convenience of working at home. They realize they can save    46
money on expenses like gas, food, and child care.             56
     Most home office workers use a computer in their job.    67
When their work is done, they can just fax or e-mail it to    79
the office. If they must communicate with other workers,      90
they can use the phone, fax, or computer and never have to   102
leave your home.                                             105
|  1  |  2  |  3  |  4  |  5  |  6  |  7  |  8  |  9  |  10  |  11  |  12
```

FORMATTING

Reference Manual

E. COLUMN HEADINGS

Column headings describe the information contained in the column entries. Refer to page R-13A in the Reference Manual for an illustration of column headings.

To format column headings:

- Type the column headings in upper- and lowercase letters and bold.
- If a table has a combination of 1- and 2-line column headings, press ENTER 1 time before typing the 1-line column heading to push the heading down so that it aligns vertically at the bottom of the cell.
- Center column headings in tables with all-text columns.
- Left-align column headings in a column with all text.
- Right-align column headings in a column with all numbers.

Word Processing Manual

F. WORD PROCESSING: TABLE—CENTER HORIZONTALLY AND CENTER PAGE

Study Lesson 38 in your word processing manual. Complete all of the shaded steps while at your computer. Then format the jobs that follow.

DOCUMENT PROCESSING

Table 38-8

Open Table

Note: Center all tables horizontally and vertically from now on.

1. Insert a table with 2 columns and 6 rows.
2. Type the title block in standard table title block format.
3. Type the column headings centered in upper- and lowercase letters and bold.
4. Left-align the column entries.
5. Automatically adjust the column widths for all columns.
6. Remove all table borders.

↓center page

VENDOR LIST
July 1, 20-- ↓1X

Product	**Vendor**
Laser printers	Office Supplies Unlimited
Workstations	PC Junction, Inc.
Cell phones	Satellite Communications
Scanners	Atlantic-Pacific Digital

Table 38-9

Open Table

1. Insert a table with 2 columns and 6 rows.
2. Type the title block in standard table title block format.
3. Type the column headings centered in upper- and lowercase letters and bold.
4. In Column A, press ENTER 1 time to split the column heading into two lines as shown.
5. In Column B, press ENTER 1 time before typing the 1-line column heading to push the heading down so that it aligns vertically at the bottom of the cell.
6. Left-align the column entries.
7. Automatically adjust the column widths for all columns.
8. Remove all table borders.

Press ENTER to create a column heading of 2 lines or to move a single-line heading down 1 line.

COMMITTEE ASSIGNMENTS

Academic Committee Assignments	Professor
Institutional Integrity	Anne McCarthy
Educational Programs	Bill Zimmerman
Student Services	John Yeh
Financial Resources	Steve Williams

Table 38-10

Open Table

1. Open the file for Table 38-8.
2. Change the date to `September 30`.
3. Change the 4 products in Column A as follows:

```
Copiers
Processors
Controller cards
Modems
```

Table 38-11

Open Table

CABLE SERVICES AVAILABILITY ↓1X

Type of Service	Currently Available
Basic	Phoenix
Lifeline	Scottsdale
Expanded	Glendale
Expanded (per channel)	Camelback City

Lesson 39

Ruled Tables With Number Columns

Goals

- Improve speed and accuracy
- Refine language arts skills in spelling
- Format ruled tables with number columns

A. Type 2 times.

A. WARMUP

Does Xavier know that around 8:04 a.m. his July sales 11
quota was realized? Invoice #671 indicates a 9% increase! 23
Several of the employees weren't able to regain their lead. 34
| 1 | 2 | 3 | 4 | 5 | 6 | 7 | 8 | 9 | 10 | 11 | 12

SKILLBUILDING

B. Type the paragraph 2 times. Use the CAPS LOCK key to type a word or series of words in all-caps. Tap the CAPS LOCK key with the A finger.

B. TECHNIQUE PRACTICE: SHIFT KEY AND CAPS LOCK

The new computer has CD-ROM, PCI IDE HDD controller,
and an SVGA card. Mr. J. L. Jones will order one from PC
EXPRESS out of Orem, Utah. IT ARRIVES NO LATER THAN JULY.

PPP PRETEST → PRACTICE → POSTTEST

PRETEST
Take a 1-minute timed writing. Review your speed and errors.

C. PRETEST: Horizontal Reaches

The chief thinks the alarm was a decoy for the armed 11
agent who coyly dashed away. She was dazed as she dodged 22
a blue sedan. He lured her to the edge of the high bluff. 33
| 1 | 2 | 3 | 4 | 5 | 6 | 7 | 8 | 9 | 10 | 11 | 12

PRACTICE
Speed Emphasis:
If you made 2 or fewer errors on the Pretest, type each *individual* line 2 times.
Accuracy Emphasis:
If you made 3 or more errors, type each *group* of lines (as though it were a paragraph) 2 times.

D. PRACTICE: In Reaches

oy foyer loyal buoys enjoy decoy coyly royal cloy ploy toys
ar argue armed cared alarm cedar sugar radar area earn hear
lu lucid lunch lured bluff value blunt fluid luck lush blue

E. PRACTICE: Out Reaches

ge geese genes germs agent edges dodge hinge gear ages page
da daily dazed dance adapt sedan adage panda dash date soda
hi hints hiked hired chief think ethic aphid high ship chip

POSTTEST
Repeat the Pretest timed writing and compare performance.

F. POSTTEST: Horizontal Reaches

LANGUAGE ARTS

G. Type these frequently misspelled words, paying special attention to any spelling problems in each word.

G. SPELLING

```
16 prior activities additional than faculty whether first with
17 subject material equipment receiving completed during basis
18 available please required decision established policy audit
19 section schedule installation insurance possible appreciate
20 benefits requirements business scheduled office immediately
```

Edit the sentences to correct any misspellings.

```
21 We requierd the office to schedule all prior activities.
22 The business scheduled the instalation of the equipment.
23 The decision established the basis of the insurance policy.
24 Please audit any additionl material available to faculty.
25 If possible, they would appreciate recieving them soon.
26 Section requirements to receive benefits were completed.
```

FORMATTING

Review the use of borders in Lesson 37 or in your word processing manual as needed.

H. RULED TABLES WITH NUMBER COLUMNS

To format a ruled table with number columns:

1. Remove all table borders.
2. Apply borders to the top and bottom of Row 2 and to the bottom of the last row.
3. Right-align column headings and column entries with numbers.
4. If the column entry includes a dollar sign, add spaces after the dollar sign to align the dollar sign just to the left of the widest column entry below it as follows: add 2 spaces for each number and 1 space for each comma. In the example below, 3 spaces were added after the dollar sign.

Example:

$ 375
2,150
49

Word Processing Manual

I. WORD PROCESSING: TABLE—ALIGN TEXT IN A COLUMN

Study Lesson 39 in your word processing manual. Complete all of the shaded steps while at your computer. Then format the jobs that follow.

Table 39-12

Ruled Table

1. Insert a ruled table with 3 columns and 5 rows.
2. Type the heading block and table in standard table format.
3. Add spaces after the dollar sign as needed to align the dollar sign just to the left of the widest column entry below it.
4. Remove all table borders and apply borders to the top and bottom of Row 2 and to the bottom of the last row.

Highlighted words are spelling words from the language arts activity.

↓center page

NORTHERN BELL PHONES
Inside Wire Repair Service↓1X

Per-Month Plan	Today's Rates	1995 Rates
Residence	$ .60	$1.00
Business	1.30	1.30
Private Line	3.50	4.50

Table 39-13

Ruled Table

1. Insert a ruled table with 4 columns and 7 rows.
2. Type the heading block and table in standard table format.
3. Add spaces after the dollar sign to align the dollar sign just to the left of the widest column entry below it.
4. Remove all table borders; then apply borders to the top and bottom of Row 2 and to the bottom of the last row.

To align the dollar sign correctly, add 2 spaces for each digit.

↓center page

HOLIDAY RESORT SUITES
Available Rates↓1X

Hotel	Rack Rate	Club Rate	3-Night Savings
Porter Ranch Inn	$ 92.00	$36.00	$ 68.00
Jamaican Inn	119.00	59.50	178.50
Casitas Suites	120.00	60.00	180.00
The Desert Inn Resort	135.00	75.50	178.50
Sannibel Courtyard	150.00	75.00	225.00

Table 39-14

Ruled Table

GENERAL EQUITY MUTUAL FUNDS

Fund	Current Year	Previous Year
Duncan Insurance	16.3%	2.0%
Strident Nova	9.3%	3.5%
First Value	10.7%	12.1%
Safeguard Policy	11.1%	9.7%
Vanguard Life	8.5%	10.1%

Formatting Review

Goals

- Type at least 36wpm/3′/4e
- Format tables with a variety of features
- Format documents with a variety of features

A. Type 2 times.

A. WARMUP

On July 15, a check for exactly $329.86 was mailed to 11
Zak & Quinn, Inc.; they never received Check #104. Does 22
Gary know if the check cleared the company's bank account? 34

| 1 | 2 | 3 | 4 | 5 | 6 | 7 | 8 | 9 | 10 | 11 | 12

SKILLBUILDING

B. MAP

Follow the GDP software directions for this exercise in improving keystroking accuracy.

C. DIAGNOSTIC PRACTICE: NUMBERS

If you are not using the GDP software, turn to page SB-5 and follow the directions for this activity.

D. Take two 3-minute timed writings. Review your speed and errors.

Goal: At least 36wpm/3′/4e

D. 3-MINUTE TIMED WRITING

Employee complaints are often viewed as a negative 10
force in a workplace. In fact, these complaints should be 22
viewed as a chance to communicate with the employee and to 34
improve morale. To ignore the complaint does not make it go 46
away. If you just listen to complaints, you may help to 57
solve small problems before they turn into bigger ones. 68
Often workers expect a chance to be heard by a person 79
who is willing to listen to them quite openly. That person 90
should recognize that the employee has concerns that need 102
to be addressed at this time. 108

| 1 | 2 | 3 | 4 | 5 | 6 | 7 | 8 | 9 | 10 | 11 | 12

Report 40-11

Academic Report

RELATIONSHIPS AT WORK

Jensen Zhao

¶ Do you believe that as long as you get your work done at the end of the day, you have had a successful day on the job? If so, you are badly mistaken. Doing the work is only half the job. The other half is relating to and working with the people around you.

TAKE A TEAM APPROACH

¶ Everything you do and every action you take affects those around you in a close working relationship. Operating as a team means thinking about others and taking actions that will help them reach their goals and achieve the goals of the company.

MAINTAIN A SPIRIT OF COOPERATION

¶ When you work in a spirit of cooperation, those around you will reflect that spirit. Your job will be easier because you will minimize resistance. It takes much more energy to resist one another than it does to cooperate and work together.

VALIDATE THE OPINIONS OF OTHERS

¶ You will find that this simple act of validation will go a long way in helping the spirit of your coworkers. Here are two simple ways to validate the opinions of others:

1. Take time to listen to the issues and accomplishments of those around you.
2. Reflect their opinions in your own words in a spirit of genuine interest.

There is a saying that states, "Your success is my success." Adopt this as your motto, and you will find a great deal of satisfaction at the end of each day.

Correspondence 40-20

Business Letter in Block Style

Note: Omit the return address on the envelope.

December 1, 20--| Mrs. Yvonne Spillotro | 105 North Field Avenue | Edison, NJ 08837 | Dear mrs. Spillotro:

Thank you for choosing Insurance Alliance Of America. Open enrollment for your insurance medical plan is scheduled to begin the first day of January. I hope it was possible for you to review the materials you received last week. Selecting the right benefit plan for you and your family can be an over whelming task. To make ~~this~~ your decision a little easier, I have enclosed a brochure that ~~with this letter~~ summarizing es the key features of each policy.

(Continued on next page)

Please call me if I can help in any way.

HYou might want to browse through our website at www.IAA.com for further details.

Sincerely, | Denise Broers | Customer Support | urs | enclosure

Table 40-15

Three-Column Boxed Table

Progress and Proofreading Check

Documents designated as Proofreading Checks serve as a check of your proofreading skill. Your goal is to have zero typographical errors when the GDP software first scores the document.

PERSONAL ASSET ACCOUNTS Wanda Nelson		
Account	**Amount**	**Interest Rate**
Interest Checking	$ 972.55	3.10%
Money Market	4,500.35	4.90%
Smart Saver	3,250.76	5.07%
Certificate of Deposit	550.00	7.41%

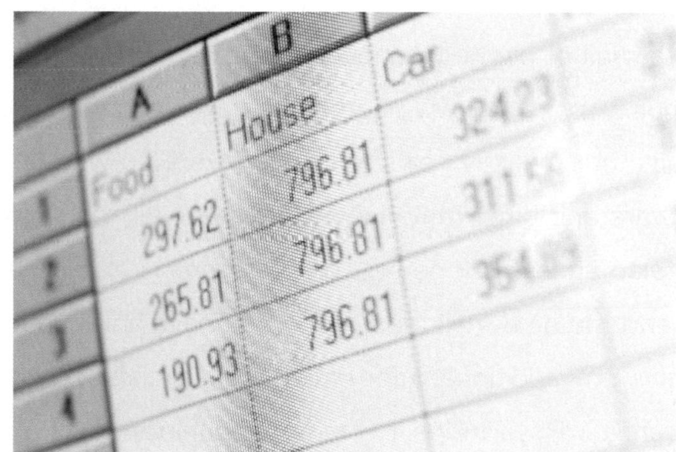

Skills Assessment on Part 2

3-Minute Timed Writing

From the first day of class, you have continuously 10
worked to improve your typing skill. You have worked hard 22
to increase your typing speed and accuracy. You have also 34
learned to format letters, memos, reports, and tables. All 46
of this work is quite an amazing accomplishment. 56
In your lessons, you have worked on learning a wide 66
range of word processing skills. You can expect to make 78
even more progress if you practice your skills regularly. 90
Learn as much as you can each day. Ask questions, and then 102
move toward a new goal each day. 108

| 1 | 2 | 3 | 4 | 5 | 6 | 7 | 8 | 9 | 10 | 11 | 12

Correspondence Test 2-21

Business Letter in Block Style

Note: Omit the return address on the envelope.

March 17 , 20-- | Ms. Dorothy ~~Arlene~~ Turner | Global Moving and Storage | 6830 Via Del Monte | San Jose, CA 95119 | Dear Ms. Turner:

¶ Thank you ~~you~~ for registering your pc Graphics software so promptly. As a registered user, you are entitled to free technical support 24 hours a day. The brochure enclosed will explain in detail how you can reach us ~~either~~ by fax, e-mail or phone whenever you need help. Also, help is always available on our website at www.pcgraphics.com. ¶ All our PC Graphics users will receive our monthly newsletter, which is filled with tips on using your new software and other material we know you will be interested in reading ~~seeing~~. You can also access our newest graphics online at our Web site. ¶ Please call me or send me an e-mail message if you have any questions or would like to receive any additional information. Your satisfaction is our number (1) priority. Sincerely | Roy Phillips | Support Technician | urs | enclosure

Report Test 2-12

Academic Report

TELECOMMUTERS
Visibility at Work
Roy Phillips

¶ Have you ever wondered how to remain "visible" at work when you aren't there for most of the work week? This is a problem many telecommuters are struggling to overcome as

(Continued on next page)

more and more people do their work from home. We all know the advantages of working at home, but it may come with a heavy price unless you work smart. Here are some ways for telecommuters to increase visibility at work.

ATTEND KEY MEETINGS

¶ Make sure that you are notified by e-mail of all key meetings so that you can be sure to be there and make your opinions and your presence known. If meeting agendas or schedules normally are distributed through office mail, make sure there is a procedure in place that distributes these important documents electronically.

COMMUNICATE WITH YOUR SUPERVISOR

¶ Don't think that there is any virtue in keeping quiet about your accomplishments. Make your accomplishments known in an assertive, regular manner. This can be done easily in several different ways.

¶ E-Mail. Use e-mail messages or attachments to e-mail messages to summarize your accomplishments on a project. It would also be a good idea to send your list of work objectives for the week to your supervisor. When a project is finished, send the final documents related to the project. If a picture could help, invest in a digital camera or a scanner and attach a picture.

¶ Answering Machines and Pagers. Make it easy for your boss to contact you. Check your pager and answering machine frequently and return calls promptly. All of these techniques will help ensure your visibility when you aren't there.

Table Test 2-16

Boxed Table

SIENNA VILLA CONDOMINIUMS Association Fees		
Category	**Average Monthly Bill**	**Proposed Increase**
Insurance	$150	$25
Earthquake rider	75	32
Water	65	20
Landscaping	30	5

Part 3

Reports, Correspondence, and Employment Documents

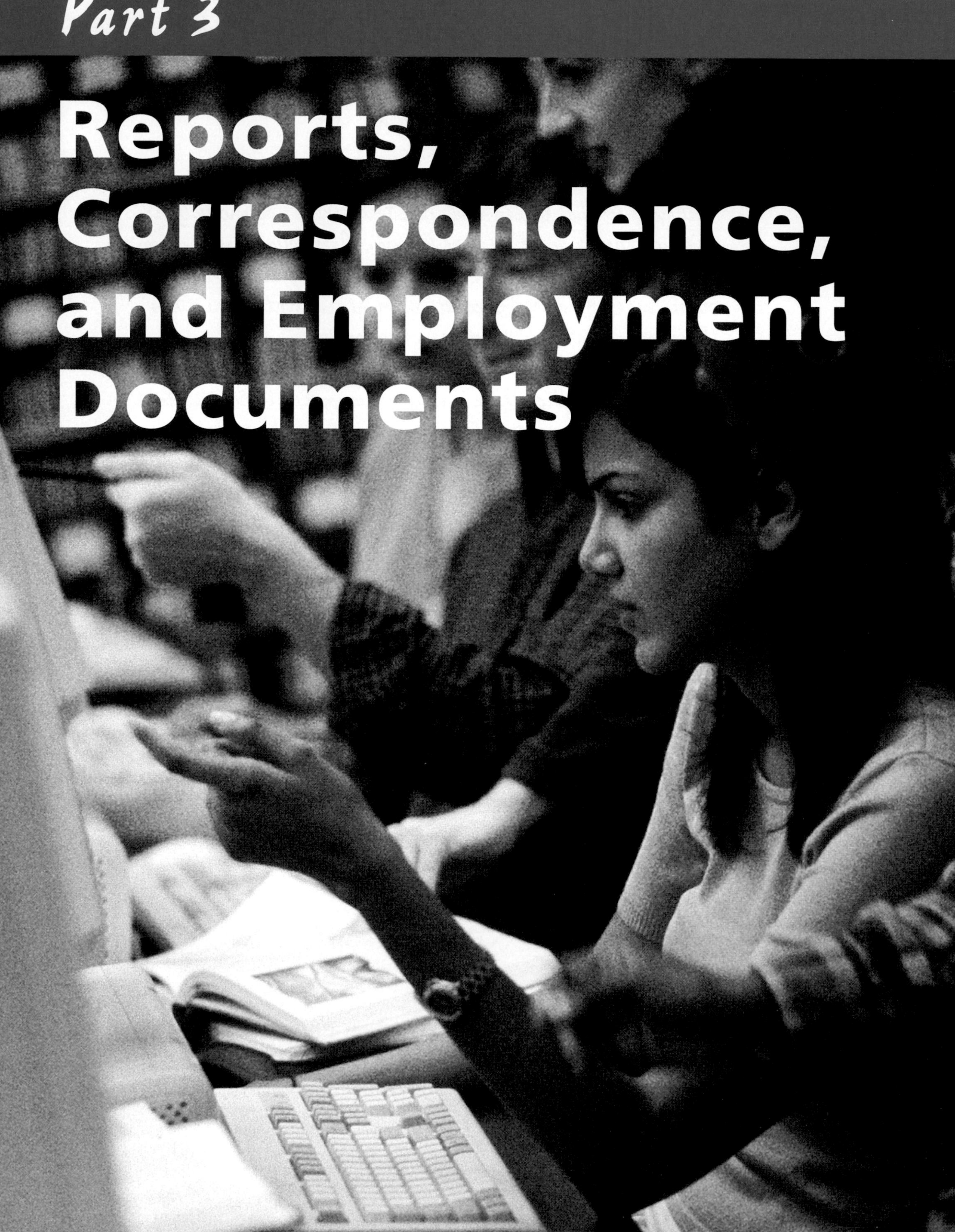

Keyboarding in Education Careers

The education field has many career opportunities, including positions such as teacher, counselor, teacher assistant, administrator, and curriculum designer. Although two of three workers in educational services have professional and related occupations, the education field employs many administrative support, managerial, and service workers.

Teacher assistants provide support for classroom teachers in many ways, allowing instructors more time for lesson planning and actual teaching. Teacher assistants also grade assignments and tests, check homework, keep attendance records, and perform typing, data entry, and filing. Office administration staff perform similar functions for the heads of departments in colleges and universities and for the principals and education boards of elementary and secondary schools.

The use of computer technology in the educational setting is constantly growing. Being proficient with a computer, including keyboarding and formatting skills, is essential for success in the field. The use of the Internet in classrooms has expanded greatly, helping instructors and students to communicate with each other, as well as to perform research for class assignments. Distance learning is growing, too. Increasing numbers of higher education institutions use Internet-based technology to post lessons and coursework electronically. *The Gregg College Keyboarding & Document Processing* text and software are good examples of this development.

Objectives

KEYBOARDING

- Type at least 40 words per minute on a 5-minute timed writing with no more than 5 errors.

LANGUAGE ARTS

- Refine proofreading skills and correctly use proofreaders' marks.
- Use punctuation and grammar correctly.
- Improve composing and spelling skills.

WORD PROCESSING

- Use the word processing commands necessary to complete the document processing activities.

DOCUMENT PROCESSING

- Format business and academic reports, personal-business letters, memos, business letters in modified-block style, and resumes.

TECHNICAL

- Answer at least 90 percent of the questions correctly on an objective test.

Unit 9

Reports

LESSON 41
Business Reports With Footnotes

LESSON 42
Reports in APA Style

LESSON 43
Reports in MLA Style

LESSON 44
Report Citations

LESSON 45
Preliminary Report Pages

Computer Generations 4

Fourth-Generation Computers

This generation is placed in the 1971 to 1999 time category. Again, computers became smaller and faster, and the Intel chip was responsible for most of the changes taking place in this 29-year period.

Enhancements in Speed

Because of the rapid miniaturization that took place with the chip, the CPU, memory, and input/output controls could now be placed on a single chip. Computers were becoming faster and faster, and they were being used in everyday items such as microwave ovens, televisions, and automobiles.

Commercial Applications

Word processing and spreadsheet applications made their debut in this generation, as did home and video game systems. Names such as Pac Man and Atari were very popular with computer users.

Fifth-Generation Computers

According to Allen, the turn of the century marks this generation, and it will be ...en word instructions, and superconductor technology, ...e or no resistance (2005, p. 130).

SHOPPING FOR A HOME

Luisa Rodriguez

Buying a home is a process that many of us will go thr... many other prospective buyers, we will experience this... in our working years. A home is typically the largest p... therefore deserves our careful attention.

"Most people think that the most important criterion i... The site should be on land that is well drained and fre... city zoning plan to determine if you have chosen a site... high water levels. You should also check to see if the g... considerably can cause cracks in foundations and wall...

Moreau suggests that a house survey be undertaken in...

> Key problems are encroachments such as trees, ... the house that overlap the property line or may ... The solution can be as simple as moving or rem...

The buying of a house is a major undertaking with a l... investigated. To ensure that the building is structurally ... use the services of a building inspector.

The walls, ceiling, and floors (if you have a basement)... insulation. "Both the depth and 'R' factor need to be c... addition, cross braces should have been used between ...

Check the roof carefully. Walk around the entire house... all roof lines and angles. Are there any shingles missi...

[1] James Nelson, "A New Home for the Millennium," *Home Pla...*

[2] Eva Bartlett, "Settlement Issues When Buying a New Home," ...

[3] "Home Construction in the 21st Century," *Family Living,* Octo...

[4] Karen Ostrowski, "A Short Course in Buying a Home," *Home...* Company, Boston, 2004, p. 37.

Computer Generations 3

A Brief History of Computer Generations

Joshua T. Reynolds

The invention of the computer did not occur in the past two centuries; in fact, the first computer was probably the abacus, which was used about 5,000 years ago in Asia Minor. As we know them today, computers were first used just after the Second World War, around 1945. Since then, several computer advancements have occurred that make it possible to classify computer power by one of the significant advancements that can be associated with particular time periods or generations. The .following paragraphs summarize the major developments that occurred in each of these generations.

First-Generation Computers

The first generation of computers generally runs from 1945 to 1956. During this time, the first vacuum tube computer, the ENIAC, was invented. The first commercial computer was called the UNIVAC, and it was used by the U.S. Census Bureau. It was also used to predict President Eisenhower's victory in the 1952 presidential election (Baker, 2003).

Second-Generation Computers

During this period, 1956 to 1963, computers were run by transistors. These computers were known for their ability to accept instructions for a specific function that could be stored in the computer's memory. This is also the period when COBOL and FORTRAN were used for computer operations. The entire software industry began in this generation.

Third-Generation Computers

This computer generation ran from 1964 to 1971, and it is characterized by the use of integrated circuits to replace the transistors of the previous generation. As a result of this invention, computers became smaller, faster, and more powerful (Diaz & Moore, 2004).

Business Reports With Footnotes

Goals:

- Improve speed and accuracy
- Refine language arts skills in using quotation marks and italics (or the underline)
- Format reports with footnotes

A. Type 2 times.

A. WARMUP

```
     Tag #743X was attached to a black jug that was 1/3      10
full of a creamy liquid. Tags #914Z and #874V were both      22
attached to beautiful large lamps (crystal and porcelain).   33
|  1  |  2  |  3  |  4  |  5  |  6  |  7  |  8  |  9  |  10  |  11  |  12
```

SKILLBUILDING

B. Take three 12-second timed writings on each line. The scale below the last line shows your wpm speed for a 12-second timed writing.

B. 12-SECOND SPEED SPRINTS

```
Joe must try to type as fast as he can on these four lines.
The screens were very clear, and the print was easy to see.
We will not be able to print the copy until later on today.
The disk will not store any of the data if it is not clean.
5 10 15 20 25 30 35 40 45 50 55 60
```

C. MAP

Follow the GDP software directions for this exercise in improving keystroking accuracy.

LANGUAGE ARTS

D. Study the rules at the right.

D. QUOTATION MARKS AND ITALICS (OR UNDERLINE)

RULE ▶ " direct quotation

Use quotation marks around a direct quotation.

Harrison responded by saying, "Their decision does not affect us."

But: Harrison responded by saying that their decision does not affect us.

RULE ▶ " title

Use quotation marks around the title of a newspaper or magazine article, chapter in a book, report, and similar terms.

The most helpful article I found was "Multimedia for All."

RULE ▶ *title* or title

Italicize (or underline) the titles of books, magazines, newspapers, and other complete published works.

Grisham's *The Brethren* was reviewed in a recent *USA Today* article.

RULE ▶ , direct quotation

Use a comma before and after a direct quotation.

James said, "I shall return," and then left.

(Continued on next page)

Edit the sentences to correct any errors in the use of quotation marks, italics, and commas.

8 The newspaper ad in the March 1 "Tribune" was very effective.
9 *The Power of e-Commerce* is an excellent chapter.
10 Maria answered the question by saying, "I agree."
11 Her title for the report was "The Internet in Action."
12 The magazine cover for "Newsweek" last month was excellent.
13 Karen interrupted by saying, That's exactly right!
14 The realtor replied "The first thing to consider is location."
15 "The margin of error is very small" said Andy.

FORMATTING

Reference Manual

If you want to format a report with endnotes instead of footnotes, study the illustration of endnotes on page R-8C and R-8D of the Reference Manual.

E. REPORTS WITH FOOTNOTES

Footnote references indicate the sources of facts or ideas used in a report. Although footnotes may be formatted in various ways, they have many characteristics in common:

1. Footnote references are indicated in the text by superior figures.
2. Footnotes are numbered consecutively throughout a report.
3. Footnotes appear at the bottom of the page on which the references appear.
4. A footnote should include the name of the author, the title of the book (italicized) or article (in quotation marks), the publisher, the place of publication, the year of publication, and the page number(s).

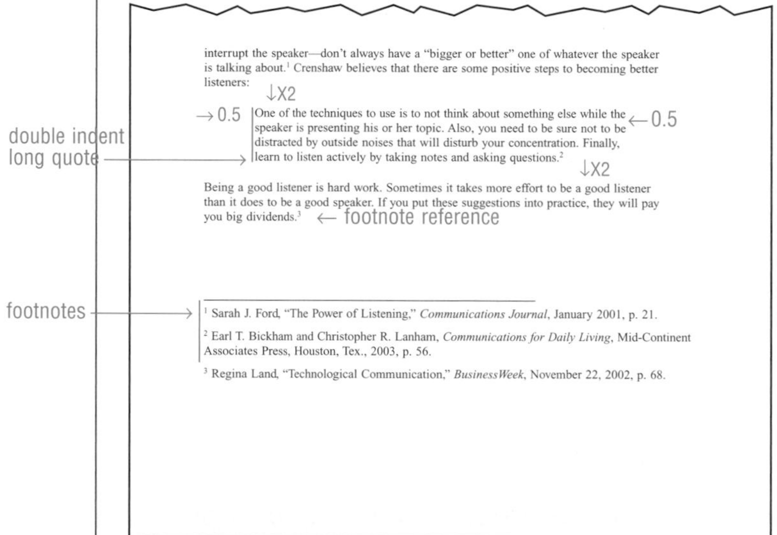

interrupt the speaker—don't always have a "bigger or better" one of whatever the speaker is talking about.[1] Crenshaw believes that there are some positive steps to becoming better listeners:

One of the techniques to use is to not think about something else while the speaker is presenting his or her topic. Also, you need to be sure not to be distracted by outside noises that will disturb your concentration. Finally, learn to listen actively by taking notes and asking questions.[2]

Being a good listener is hard work. Sometimes it takes more effort to be a good listener than it does to be a good speaker. If you put these suggestions into practice, they will pay you big dividends.[3]

[1] Sarah J. Ford, "The Power of Listening," *Communications Journal*, January 2001, p. 21.

[2] Earl T. Bickham and Christopher R. Lanham, *Communications for Daily Living*, Mid-Continent Associates Press, Houston, Tex., 2003, p. 56.

[3] Regina Land, "Technological Communication," *BusinessWeek*, November 22, 2002, p. 68.

F. LONG QUOTATIONS

A paragraph of 4 or more lines that is quoted or considered essential to a report may be highlighted or displayed by using single-spacing and indenting the paragraph 0.5 inch from both the left and the right margins to make it stand out from the rest of the report.

Word Processing Manual

G. WORD PROCESSING: FOOTNOTES

Study Lesson 41 in your word processing manual. Complete all of the shaded steps while at your computer. Then format the jobs that follow.

Report 41-13

Business Report

" direct quotation

SHOPPING FOR A HOME

Luisa Rodriguez

¶ Buying a home is a proces that many of us will go through in our life time. If we are like many prospective buyers, we will experience this decision three or four major times in our working years. A home is typically the largest purchase we will make, and it deserves therefore our careful attention. We must be certain to look carefully at all the information available to us.

¶ "Most people think that the important criteria in shopping for a home is its site,"[1] says John Calendar. The site should be on land that is well drained and free from from flooding that can cause extensive damage. Check the area city zoning plan to determine if you have choosen a site that is free from flooding and highwater levels that can cause extensive damage. You should also check to see if the ground is stable. Ground that shifts can cause cracks in foundations and walls.

¶ Moreau suggests that a home survey be undertaken in the early stages:

> Key problems are encroachments such as tees, buildings, or additions to the house that overlap the property line or may violate zoning regulations. The solution can be as simple as moving or removing trees or bushes from the front or back of your house.[2]

¶ The buying of a house is a major under taking with a long list of items that must be investigated. To ensure that the building is structurally sound, many prospective buyers use the services of a building inspector.

¶ The walls, ceiling, and floors need to be checked for proper insulation. "Both depth and 'r' factor need to be checked for proper levels."[3] In addition, crossbraces should have been used between the beams supporting a floor.

(Continued on next page)

¶ Carefully check the roof. Walk around the entire house so that you have a clear view of all roof lines and angles. Are there any shingles missing or is there water damage?[4]

" title — [1] James Nelson, "A New Home for the Millennium," *home planning magazine*, April 27, 2003, pp. 19-24.

title — [2] Eva Bartlett, "Settlement Issues when Buying a New Home," *Home Finances*, 2002, July, p. 68.

" title — [3] "Home Construction in the 21st Century," *Family Living*, October 9, 2002, p. 75

title — [4] Karen Ostrowski, "A Short Course in Buying a Home," *Homebuilders' Guide*, Kramer Publishing Company, Boston, 2004, p. 37.

Report 41-14

Business Report

Open the file for Report 41-13 and make the following changes:

1. Add these lines to the end of the final paragraph in the report:

    Finally, a thorough check should be made of the heating, cooling, and electrical systems in the home. "These features are as critical as any others to be examined."[5]

    ---

    [5] Maria Gonzalez, *Home Facilities Planning*, Bradshaw Publishing, Salt Lake City, Utah, 2003, p. 64.

2. Insert the footnote as indicated.
3. Remember to italicize book and magazine titles.

Keyboarding Connection

Inedible Cookies

Is that cookie good for you? A cookie is a short text entry stored on your computer that identifies your preferences to the server of the Web site you are viewing.

Certain Web sites use cookies to customize pages for return visitors. Only the information you provide or the selections you make while visiting a Web site are stored in a cookie. You can control how your browser uses cookies.

Use the Help feature in your browser to find out how to control cookies. Try using the keywords "cookie" or "security" when you search the Help index. You will probably find some great tips on how to increase security when working on the Internet.

YOUR TURN Access your browser's cookie policy defaults. Decide if you want to change them.

Lesson 42

Reports in APA Style

Goals

- Type at least 36wpm/3′/3e
- Format reports in APA style
- Format author/year citations

A. Type 2 times.

A. WARMUP

```
     The giant-size trucks, all carrying over 600 bushels,   11
were operating "around the clock"; quite a few of them had   23
dumped their boxes at Joe's during the last 18 to 20 hours.  35
|  1  |  2  |  3  |  4  |  5  |  6  |  7  |  8  |  9  |  10  |  11  |  12
```

SKILLBUILDING

B. PROGRESSIVE PRACTICE: ALPHABET

If you are not using the GDP software, turn to page SB-7 and follow the directions for this activity.

C. Type the paragraph 2 times, using your right thumb to press the SPACE BAR in the center.

C. TECHNIQUE PRACTICE: SPACE BAR

```
     Dale is it. Adam is there. Mark is home. Eve was lost.
Helen can see. Faith can knit. Gayle can fly. Hal can type.
Fly the kite. Swim a mile. Close the door. Lift the weight.
```

D. Take two 3-minute timed writings. Review your speed and errors.

Goal: At least 36wpm/3′/3e

D. 3-MINUTE TIMED WRITING

```
     The size of their first paycheck after they finish        10
college seems quite high to a few young men and women. They    22
rent a place to live that is just too much to pay, or they     34
may buy a car with a huge monthly payment. For some, it        45
takes a while to learn that there are other items in the       57
monthly budget.                                                60
     Some other budget items are food, student loans, car      71
insurance, renters' insurance, credit card debt, health        82
insurance, utilities, and miscellaneous expenses. A good       93
goal is to put a regular amount from each paycheck into a     105
savings account.                                              108
|  1  |  2  |  3  |  4  |  5  |  6  |  7  |  8  |  9  |  10  |  11  |  12
```

Refer to page R-10A of the Reference Manual for additional guidance.

E. REPORTS FORMATTED IN APA STYLE

In addition to the traditional academic style, academic reports may also be formatted in APA (American Psychological Association) style. In the APA style, format the report as follows:

1. Use the default 1-inch top and bottom margins and change the left and right margins to 1 inch.
2. Double-space the entire report.
3. Insert a header for all pages; type a shortened title and insert an automatic page number that continues the page-numbering sequence from the previous page right-aligned inside the header.
4. Center and type the title and byline using upper- and lowercase letters. (Do not bold either the title or the byline.)
5. Indent all paragraphs 0.5 inch.
6. Type main headings centered, using upper- and lowercase letters. Press ENTER 1 time before and after the main heading.
7. Type subheadings at the left margin in italics using upper- and lowercase letters. Press ENTER 1 time before and after the subheading.

Top, bottom, and side margins:
1" Double-space throughout

History of the Internet 3 ← header

A Condensed History of the Internet ← title

Karen Reynolds ← byline

→ tab The Internet has been around for over twenty years in various forms. During the past few years, however, it has experienced phenomenal growth. According to some sources, the Internet began as a military project (Rockwell, 2003). ← author/year citation

How the Internet Is Funded ← main heading

According to Alexander, a great deal of support for the Internet originally came from the U.S. federal government (2004, p. 42). During the late 1980s, however, the use of the Internet expanded so that commercial usage became very popular.

Internet Usage ← subheading

Today, the majority of Internet users are educational and research institutions, business, and government organizations around the globe; however, this user profile will keep changing.

F. AUTHOR/YEAR CITATIONS

Any information based on other sources and used in a report must be documented or cited. The author/year method of citation includes the source information in parentheses at the appropriate point within the text. For more detailed information on APA citations, refer to the illustrations in this book or consult the current APA style guide.

L. 27: Page Numbering

G. WORD PROCESSING: MARGINS, HEADERS, AND FOOTERS

Study Lesson 42 in your word processing manual. Complete all of the shaded steps while at your computer. Then format the jobs that follow.

Report 42-15

Report in APA Style

Remember to add a short title and page number right-aligned in a header.

Computer Generations 3

A Brief History of Computer Generations

Joshua T. Reynolds

¶ The invention of the computer did not occur in the past two centuries; in fact, the first computer was probably the abacus, which was used about 5,000 years ago in Asia Minor. As we know them today, computers were first used just after the Second World War, around 1945. Since then, several computer advancements have occurred that make it possible to classify computer power by one of the significant advancements that can be associated with particular time periods or generations. The following paragraphs summarize the major developments that occurred in each of these generations.

First-Generation Computers

¶ The first generation of computers generally runs from 1945 to 1956. During this time, the first vacuum tube computer, the ENIAC, was invented. The first commercial computer was called the UNIVAC, and it was used by the U.S. Census Bureau. It was also used to predict President Eisenhower's victory in the 1952 presidential election (Baker, 2003).

Second-Generation Computers

¶ During this period, 1956 to 1963, computers were run by transistors. These computers were known for their ability to accept instructions for a specific function that could be stored within the computer's memory. This is also the period when COBOL and FORTRAN were used for computer operations. The entire software industry began in this generation.

Third-Generation Computers

¶ This computer generation ran from 1964 to 1971, and it is characterized by the use of integrated circuits to replace the transistors from the previous generation. As a result of this invention, computers became smaller, faster, and more powerful (Diaz & Moore, 2004).

(Continued on next page)

Fourth-Generation Computers

¶ This generation is placed in the 1971 to 1999 time category. Again, computers became smaller and faster, and the Intel chip was responsible for most of the changes taking place in this 29-year period. Because of the rapid miniaturization that took place with the chip, the CPU, memory, and input/output controls could now be placed on a single chip. Computers were becoming faster and faster; and they were being used in everyday items such as microwave ovens, televisions, and automobiles.

Fifth-Generation Computers

¶ According to Allen, the turn of the century marks this generation, and it will be associated with artificial intelligence, spoken word instructions, and superconductor technology, which allows electricity to flow with little or no resistance (2005, p. 130).

Report 42-16

Report in APA Style

Open the file for Report 42-15 and make the following changes:

1. Place the insertion point at the end of the second sentence in the Fourth-Generation Computers paragraph, and press ENTER 1 time.
2. Type the subheading `Enhancements in Speed` in italics at the left margin; press ENTER 1 time.
3. Press TAB to indent the paragraph.
4. Move the insertion point to the end of the last sentence just above the Fifth-Generation Computers heading; press ENTER 1 time.
5. Type the subheading `Commercial Applications` in italics at the left margin; press ENTER 1 time.
6. Press TAB and type the following text as a paragraph under the new subheading:

```
Word processing and
spreadsheet applications
made their debut in this
generation, as did home
and video game systems.
Names such as Pac-Man and
Atari were very popular
with computer users.
```

Reports in MLA Style

Goals

- Improve speed and accuracy
- Refine language arts skills in composing sentences
- Format reports in MLA style

A. Type 2 times.

A. WARMUP

"Baxter & Heimark, Inc., sold 82 new vehicles (47 cars 11
and 35 trucks) during June," the sales manager reported. 23
This is 16.9% of quarterly sales, an amazing achievement! 34
| 1 | 2 | 3 | 4 | 5 | 6 | 7 | 8 | 9 | 10 | 11 | 12

SKILLBUILDING

B. PROGRESSIVE PRACTICE: NUMBERS

If you are not using the GDP software, turn to page SB-11 and follow the directions for this activity.

C. Take a 1-minute timed writing on the first paragraph to establish your base speed. Then take four 1-minute timed writings on the remaining paragraphs. As soon as you equal or exceed your base speed on one paragraph, advance to the next, more difficult paragraph.

C. SUSTAINED PRACTICE: SYLLABIC INTENSITY

Taking care of aging parents is not a new trend. This 11
issue has arisen more and more, since we are now living 22
longer. Companies are now trying to help out in many ways. 34

Help may come in many ways, ranging from financial aid 12
to sponsoring hospice or in-home respite care. Workers may 24
find it difficult to work and care for aging parents. 35

Why are employers so interested in elder care? Rising 11
interest is the result of a combination of several things. 23
The most notable is a marked increase in life expectancy. 34

Another trend is the increased participation of women, 11
the primary caregivers, in the workforce. Businesses are 22
recognizing that work and family life are intertwined. 33
| 1 | 2 | 3 | 4 | 5 | 6 | 7 | 8 | 9 | 10 | 11 | 12

LANGUAGE ARTS

D. Answer each question with a complete sentence.

D. COMPOSING SENTENCES

16 What are your best traits that you will bring to your job when you graduate?
17 Would you like to work for a small company or a large company?
18 How much money will you expect to earn each month in your first job?
19 Would you like that first job to be in a small town or a large city?
20 As you begin your first job, what career goal will you have in mind?

FORMATTING

Refer to page R-10C of the Reference Manual for additional guidance.

E. REPORTS FORMATTED IN MLA STYLE

In addition to the traditional academic style and APA style, academic reports may also be formatted in MLA (Modern Language Association) style. If citations are used, usually the author's last name and page number are cited inside parentheses. For more detailed information on MLA style, refer to the illustrations in this book or consult the current MLA style guide.

In the MLA style, format the report as follows:

1. Use the default 1-inch top and bottom margins and change the left and right margins to 1 inch.
2. Double-space the entire report.
3. Insert a header for all pages; type the author's last name and the page number right-aligned inside the header and positioned 0.5 inch from the top of the page.
4. Type each element of the heading information (your name, your instructor's name, the class name, and the date) on a separate line at the left margin.
5. Type the date day-month-year style (15 April 20--).
6. Center and type the title using upper- and lowercase letters.
7. Indent all paragraphs 0.5 inch.

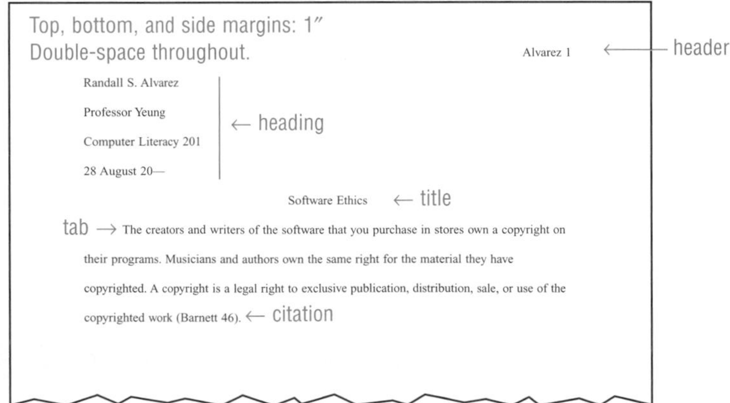

Report 43-17

Report in MLA Style

Remember to type the author's last name and page number right-aligned 0.5 inch from the top as a header. Remember to double-space the entire report.

Lee 1

Youn Suk Lee
Dr. Gloria Hernandez
Telecommunications 315
14 September 20--

Judging a Computer System

¶ Judging the effectiveness of a computer system has taken on a new dimension in the past few years, if for no other reason than the wide range of computer systems from which the user can select. It is, therefore, important that we investigate the criteria that should be considered in making this important decision.

¶ Probably the most obvious criterion to be considered when one purchases a computer system is speed. The value of a computer is directly related to its speed, and a computer's speed is typically measured in gigahertz (GHz). A gigahertz is one billion cycles per second, and many of today's microcomputers run in the range of 2 to 5 GHz (Kramer 173).

¶ Flexibility is especially important because of the rapid turnover of hardware and software in the computer industry. The flexibility of a computer system is important for two general reasons: to accommodate a variety of programs and to permit expandability. Hundreds and possibly thousands of software packages are available today to meet the needs of computer users. The computer you purchase must be able to accommodate this variety of software and be flexible enough to change with the increasing sophistication of software packages. Because of the substantial investment you make in a computer, you do not want to commit your resources to a computer that cannot be expanded to handle (1) newer, more powerful operating systems; (2) "memory-hungry" software packages; (3) network interfaces; and (4) additional users (Hartung and Kallock 239).

¶ A third consideration is convenience. Is it easy to learn how to operate your computer? Does the manufacturer stand by its warranty, and is it difficult to obtain repairs? How convenient is it to buy parts for your computer (such as memory boards and drives) if you want to expand your system? These questions need to be answered, and the answers should be weighed carefully before you purchase a new computer system.

Report 43-18

Report in MLA Style

Espinoza 1

Christina Espinoza

Professor Sakata

Introduction to E-commerce

9 April 20--

¶ The Internet is dramatically changing the way we shop. In years past, our shopping practices consisted of driving to a local mall or department store, walking through the aisles until we found an item we wished to purchase, and then making the purchase and driving home. Today, it is becoming more common to find shoppers doing their shopping via the Internet. Shopping on the Internet brings with it some cautions that we should observe when we shop. Here are some basic rules to follow when shopping on the Internet.

¶ When you are asked to enter information on your order, do not disclose personal information unless it is needed for shipping your order to you. Be sure you know who is collecting this information, why it is needed, and how it is going to be used. Be certain that the information asked for is actually necessary for the purchase. For example, there are few instances when your password should be disclosed.

¶ You should always verify that the company from whom you are purchasing has secured the purchasing procedures. You will often be asked to enter your credit card number to complete the purchase. Be certain that the transfer of this information is made in a secure environment. Also, be certain that you know the exact cost of the item for which you are being charged. The company from which you are purchasing the item should have a built-in calculator so that you know at all times how much your purchase will cost you, including all necessary shipping and handling charges.

¶ Understand exactly what you should do if you encounter a problem with your purchase online. Is there an easy way to contact the company? Does the company have an e-mail address you can use to contact a customer relations representative? Does the company's order page include a telephone number that you can call if you have questions about your order?

Report Citations

Goals

- Type at least 37wpm/3′/3e
- Format bibliographies, references, and works-cited pages

A. Type 2 times.

A. WARMUP

```
1      The prize troops received the following extra gifts:    11
2  $20 from Larson's Bakery; $19 from Calsun, Ltd.;* $50 from  23
3  some judges; and quite a number of $5 gift certificates.    34
   | 1 | 2 | 3 | 4 | 5 | 6 | 7 | 8 | 9 | 10 | 11 | 12
```

SKILLBUILDING

PPP PRETEST → PRACTICE → POSTTEST

PRETEST
Take a 1-minute timed writing. Review your speed and errors.

B. PRETEST: Vertical Reaches

```
4      Kim knew that her skills at the keyboard made her a       11
5  top rival for that job. About six persons had seen her race   23
6  home to see if the mail showed the company was aware of it.   34
   | 1 | 2 | 3 | 4 | 5 | 6 | 7 | 8 | 9 | 10 | 11 | 12
```

PRACTICE
Speed Emphasis:
If you made 2 or fewer errors on the Pretest, type each *individual* line 2 times.
Accuracy Emphasis:
If you made 3 or more errors, type each *group* of lines (as though it were a paragraph) 2 times.

C. PRACTICE: Up Reaches

```
7  se seven reset seams sedan loses eases serve used seed dose
8  ki skids kings kinks skill kitty kites kilts kite kids kick
9  rd board horde wards sword award beard third cord hard lard
```

D. PRACTICE: Down Reaches

```
10 ac races pacer backs ached acute laced facts each acre lace
11 kn knave knack knife knows knoll knots knelt knew knee knit
12 ab about abide label above abode sable abbey drab able cabs
```

POSTTEST
Repeat the Pretest timed writing and compare performance.

E. POSTTEST: Vertical Reaches

F. Take two 3-minute timed writings. Review your speed and errors.

Goal: At least 37wpm/3′/3e

F. 3-MINUTE TIMED WRITING

```
     Every business should have its code of ethics. A code    11
contains rules of conduct and moral guidelines that serve     23
the company and its employees. Some general ethics that may   35
be recognized in the code are equal and fair treatment,       46
truth, and zeal on the job.                                   51
     Companies may include a few rules in the code that       62
relate to their type of work. For example, if some laws       73
govern how they conduct business, an owner just might ask     85
employees to conduct all activities in a just and lawful      96
process. The code of business ethics should be equal for     107
all these workers.                                           111
| 1 | 2 | 3 | 4 | 5 | 6 | 7 | 8 | 9 | 10 | 11 | 12
```

FORMATTING

Refer to page R-9B of the Reference Manual for additional guidance.

G. BIBLIOGRAPHIES

A bibliography is an alphabetic listing of all sources of facts or ideas used or cited in a report. The bibliography is typed on a separate page at the end of a report. In general, titles of major works like books or magazine titles are italicized, and titles of minor works like articles from magazines are typed in quotation marks. For more detailed information on entries in a bibliography, refer to the illustrations in this book or consult a current style guide.

To format a bibliography:

1. Press ENTER 6 times to begin the first line approximately 2 inches from the top of the page.
2. Center and type `BIBLIOGRAPHY` in all-caps, 14-point font, and bold; then press ENTER 2 times.
3. Set a hanging indent and type the first line. Each entry will begin at the left margin, and the carryover lines will automatically be indented 0.5 inch by the hanging indent.
4. Single-space each entry in the bibliography, and press ENTER 2 times between each entry.

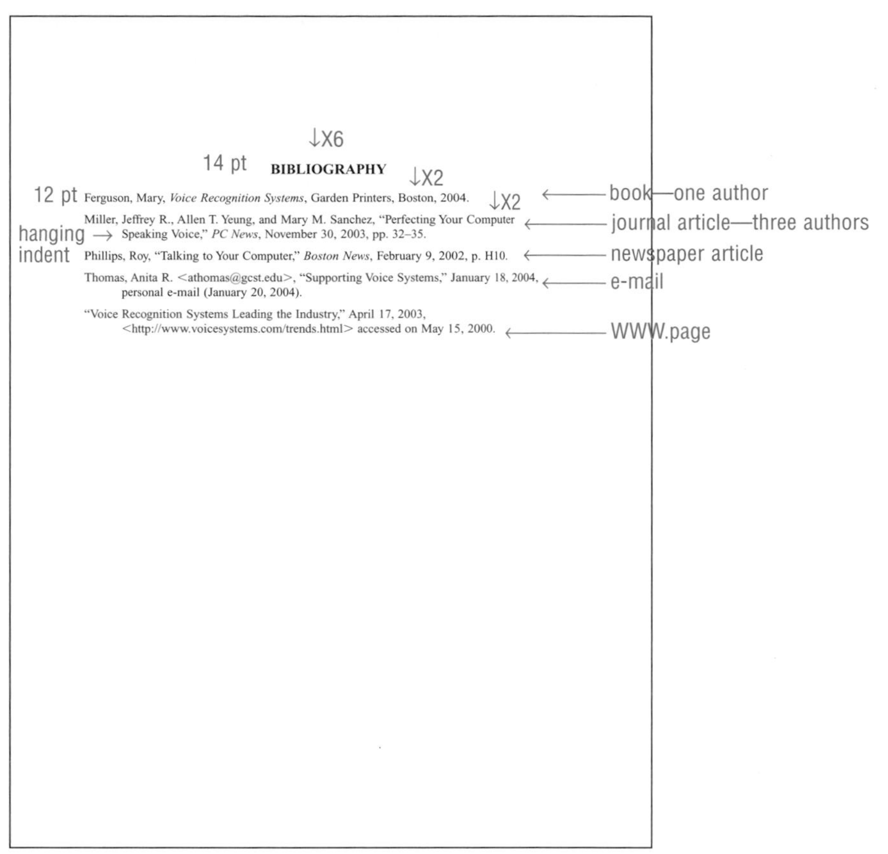

BIBLIOGRAPHY

Ferguson, Mary, *Voice Recognition Systems*, Garden Printers, Boston, 2004.

Miller, Jeffrey R., Allen T. Yeung, and Mary M. Sanchez, "Perfecting Your Computer Speaking Voice," *PC News*, November 30, 2003, pp. 32–35.

Phillips, Roy, "Talking to Your Computer," *Boston News*, February 9, 2002, p. H10.

Thomas, Anita R. <athomas@gcst.edu>, "Supporting Voice Systems," January 18, 2004, personal e-mail (January 20, 2004).

"Voice Recognition Systems Leading the Industry," April 17, 2003, <http://www.voicesystems.com/trends.html> accessed on May 15, 2000.

Refer to page R-10B of the Reference Manual for additional guidance.

H. REFERENCE LIST PAGES IN APA STYLE

A reference list is an alphabetic listing of all sources of facts or ideas used or cited in a report formatted in APA style. The reference list is typed on a separate page at the end of a report. For more detailed information on reference list entries, refer to the illustrations in this book or consult a current APA style guide.

To format an APA reference list page:

1. Use the default 1-inch top and bottom margins and change the left and right margins to 1 inch.
2. Double-space the entire page.
3. Insert a header, type a shortened title, and insert an automatic page number that continues the page-numbering sequence from the previous page right-aligned inside the header.
4. Center and type `References` at the top of the page; then press ENTER 1 time.
5. Set a hanging indent and type the first line. Each reference will begin at the left margin, and the carryover lines will automatically be indented 0.5 inch by the hanging indent.

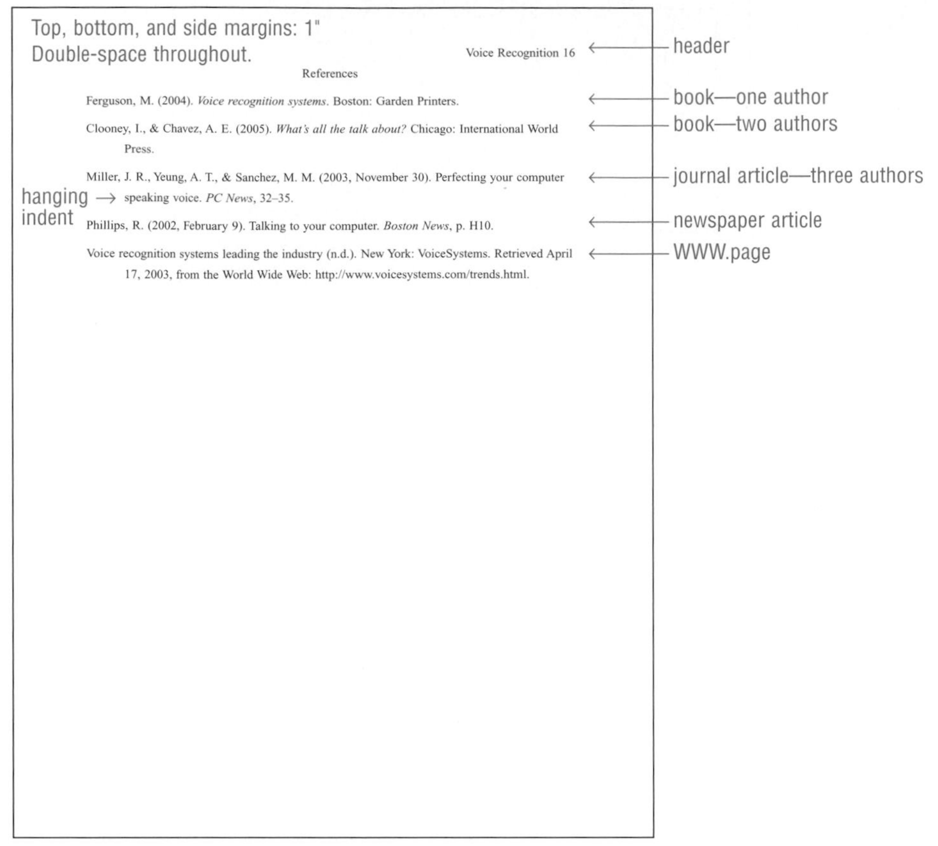
Top, bottom, and side margins: 1"
Double-space throughout.

Voice Recognition 16

References

Ferguson, M. (2004). *Voice recognition systems.* Boston: Garden Printers.

Clooney, I., & Chavez, A. E. (2005). *What's all the talk about?* Chicago: International World Press.

Miller, J. R., Yeung, A. T., & Sanchez, M. M. (2003, November 30). Perfecting your computer speaking voice. *PC News*, 32–35.

Phillips, R. (2002, February 9). Talking to your computer. *Boston News*, p. H10.

Voice recognition systems leading the industry (n.d.). New York: VoiceSystems. Retrieved April 17, 2003, from the World Wide Web: http://www.voicesystems.com/trends.html.

Refer to page R-10D of the Reference Manual for additional guidance.

I. WORKS-CITED PAGES IN MLA STYLE

A works-cited page is an alphabetic listing of all sources of facts or ideas used or cited in a report formatted in MLA style. This reference list is typed on a separate page at the end of a report. For more detailed information on reference list entries, refer to the illustrations in this book or consult a current MLA style guide.

To format a works-cited page:

1. Use the default 1-inch top and bottom margins and change the left and right margins to 1 inch.
2. Double-space the entire page.
3. Insert a header, type the author's last name, insert an automatic page number that continues the page-numbering sequence from the previous page right-aligned inside the header positioned 0.5 inch from the top of the page, and close the header.
4. Type `Works Cited` centered at the top of the page; then press ENTER 1 time.
5. Set a hanging indent and type the first line at the left margin; the carryover lines will automatically be indented 0.5 inch by the hanging indent.

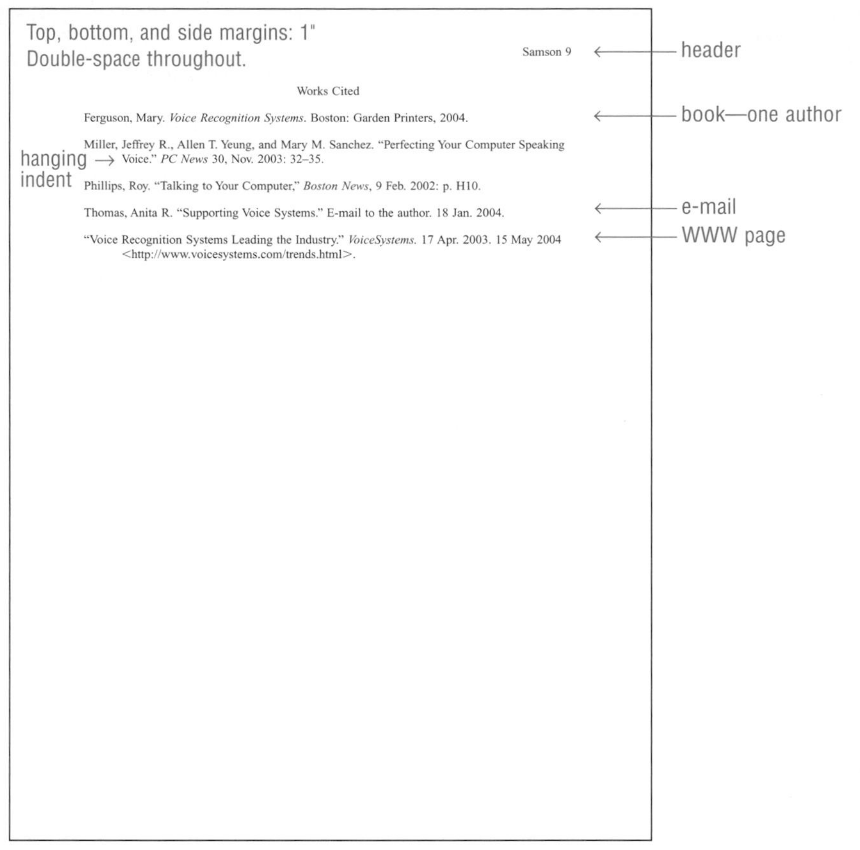

Top, bottom, and side margins: 1"
Double-space throughout.
Samson 9
header
Works Cited
Ferguson, Mary. Voice Recognition Systems. Boston: Garden Printers, 2004.
book—one author
Miller, Jeffrey R., Allen T. Yeung, and Mary M. Sanchez. "Perfecting Your Computer Speaking Voice." PC News 30, Nov. 2003: 32–35.
hanging indent
Phillips, Roy. "Talking to Your Computer," Boston News, 9 Feb. 2002: p. H10.
Thomas, Anita R. "Supporting Voice Systems." E-mail to the author. 18 Jan. 2004.
e-mail
"Voice Recognition Systems Leading the Industry." VoiceSystems. 17 Apr. 2003. 15 May 2004 <http://www.voicesystems.com/trends.html>.
WWW page

Word Processing Manual

J. WORD PROCESSING: HANGING INDENT

Study Lesson 44 in your word processing manual. Complete all the shaded steps while at your computer. Then format the jobs that follow.

DOCUMENT PROCESSING

Report 44-19

Bibliography

Italicize publication titles rather than underlining them.

BIBLIOGRAPHY

Bilanski, Charles R., "Corporate Structures in the New Millennium," Modern Management, Vol. 43, June 2003, pp. 43-46.

Calhoun, Josten C., Stockholders' Guide, Missouri Valley Press, St. Louis, 2003.

Dahlman, Leland, and Joyce C. Mahler, Trends for Boards of Directors, Vineyard Press, Boston, 2003.

Hammersmith Institute, Bold Positions of the New Administration, Hammersmith Institute Press, Baltimore, Md., 1999.

"Investing in the Corporate World," March 27, 2003, <http://www.efinance.com/invest/today'sworld.htm>, accessed on May 18, 2003.

Polaski, James S., "Summary of Investment Guide," e-mail message, October 10, 2003.

Report 44-20

References in APA Style

The Economy of America 16

References

Chandler, R. D., & Thompson, A. S. (2002). *The evolution of America's economy in the late 1800's*. Westerville, OH: Glencoe/ McGraw-Hill. ~~Chapter 24, pp. 130-145.~~

Deming, W. H. (2003). Economists' guide to economic indicators, *The Economic Review, XVI*, 42-44.

Fortenberry, J. E., Kingston, A.E., & Worthington, S. O. (2004). *The environment of business*. Los Angeles: The University Press.

Meier, T. D., & Hovey, D. H. (2002). *economics on the world wide web*. Toronto: The Northern Press.

Tetrault, G. M. (2003). A guide for selecting economic indicators for the business entrepreneur, ~~*The Southern Economic Forecaster*, 23.~~

Zysmanski, R. J. (2004). *American capitalism and its impact on society*. San Francisco: Bay Press Area.

Report 44-21

Works Cited in MLA Style

Cleaves 14

Works Cited

Abernathy, Thomas R. "Welcome to the Internet." E-mail to the author. 19 Mar. 2005.

Benson, Lisa, et al. "E-commerce on the Net." *Online Observer*. Vol. 17. Sept. 2004: 144–146.

Cooper, Stanley. *Trends for the New Millennium*. Denver: Mountain Press, 2003.

Lawrence, Donna, and Becky Silversmith. *Surfer's Guide to the Internet*. Atlanta: Southern Publishers, 2005.

"Starting a Business on the Internet." *Entrepreneur*. 19 Dec. 2003. 12 June 2005 <http://www.entrepreneur.com/startups.htm>.

Tidwell, Joel, and Jean Swanson. "Things You Don't Know About the Internet." *New York Ledger*, 13 May 2004: C2.

Preliminary Report Pages

Goals

- Improve speed and accuracy
- Refine language arts skills in proofreading
- Format title pages and tables of contents

A. Type 2 times.

A. WARMUP

```
     Did Kenny and Hazel see the first Sox ball game? I've    11
heard there were 57,268 people there (a new record). Your     23
home crowd was quiet when the game ended with a 4-9 loss.     34
|  1  |  2  |  3  |  4  |  5  |  6  |  7  |  8  |  9  |  10  |  11  |  12
```

SKILLBUILDING

B. PACED PRACTICE

If you are not using the GDP software, turn to page SB-14 and follow the directions for this activity.

C. DIAGNOSTIC PRACTICE: SYMBOLS AND PUNCTUATION

If you are not using the GDP software, turn to page SB-2 and follow the directions for this activity.

LANGUAGE ARTS

D. Study the proofreading techniques at the right.

D. PROOFREADING YOUR DOCUMENTS

Proofreading and correcting errors are essential parts of document processing. To become an expert proofreader:

1. Use the spelling feature of your word processing software to check for spelling errors; then read the copy aloud to see if it makes sense.
2. Proofread for all kinds of errors, especially repeated, missing, or transposed words; grammar and punctuation; and numbers and names.
3. Use the appropriate software command to see an entire page of your document to check for formatting errors such as line spacing, tabs, margins, and bold.

E. Compare this paragraph with the Pretest on page 137. Edit the paragraph to correct any errors.

E. PROOFREADING

```
     Kim new that her skills at the key board made her a
top rivel for the job. About six persons had scene her race
home to see if the male showd the company was awarre of it.
```

Refer to page R-7B of the Reference Manual for additional guidance.

F. TITLE PAGE

Reports may have a title page, which includes information such as the report title, to whom the report is submitted, the writer's name and identification, and the date. To format a title page, follow these steps:

1. Center the page vertically.
2. Center the title in all caps and bold, using a 14-point font.
3. Press ENTER 2 times; then center the subtitle in upper- and lowercase and bold, using a 12-point font.
4. Press ENTER 12 times; then center the words `Submitted to`.
5. Press ENTER 2 times; then center the recipient's name and identification on separate lines, single-spaced.
6. Press ENTER 12 times; then center `Prepared by`.
7. Press ENTER 2 times; then center the writer's name and identification on separate lines, single-spaced.
8. Press ENTER 2 times; then center the date.

center page↓

14 pt **A TECHNOLOGY ASSESSMENT OF THE**
GRANTLAND CORPORATION ↓2X

12 pt↓ **The Status of Technology in the New Millennium** ↓12X

Submitted to ↓2X

Marcia Abernathy
Regional Manager
Grantland Corporation ↓12X

Prepared by ↓2X

Timothy R. Rassmussen
District V Manager
Grantland Corporation ↓2X

March 20, 20—

Refer to page R-7D of the Reference Manual for additional guidance.

G. TABLE OF CONTENTS

A table of contents is usually included in a long report. The table of contents identifies the major and minor sections of a report and includes page numbers preceded by dot leaders. Dot leaders are a series of periods that guide the reader's eye across the page to the page number at the right. To format a table of contents:

1. Press ENTER 6 times to begin the first line approximately 2 inches from the top of the page.
2. Center and type CONTENTS in all-caps, 14-point font, and bold; then press ENTER 2 times.
3. Set a left tab at 0.5 inch; then set a right tab at 6 inches with dot leaders.
4. Change to 12-point font and type the main heading in all-caps.
5. Press TAB 1 or 2 times as needed to insert dot leaders and to move to the right margin; then type the page number, and press ENTER 2 times.
6. Type the next main heading in a similar fashion. If the next item is a subheading, press TAB 1 time to indent the subheading 0.5 inch.
7. Type the subheading, and then press TAB to insert dot leaders and to move to the right margin; then type the page number, and press ENTER 1 time to type the next subheading or 2 times to type a new main heading.
8. Continue in like fashion until the table of contents is complete.

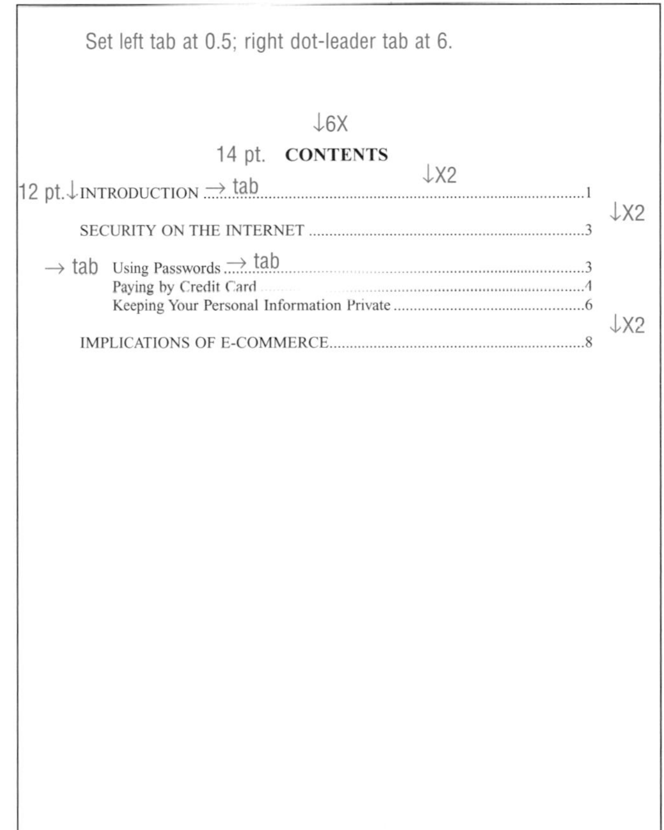
Set left tab at 0.5; right dot-leader tab at 6.

↓6X

14 pt. **CONTENTS**

↓X2

12 pt.↓INTRODUCTION → tab 1

↓X2

SECURITY ON THE INTERNET 3

→ tab Using Passwords → tab 3

Paying by Credit Card 4

Keeping Your Personal Information Private 6

↓X2

IMPLICATIONS OF E-COMMERCE 8

H. WORD PROCESSING: TAB SET—DOT LEADERS

Study Lesson 45 in your word processing manual. Complete all of the shaded steps while at your computer. Then format the jobs that follow.

Report 45-22

Title Page

↓center page

14 pt. **DISTANCE LEARNING CLASSROOMS** ↓2X

12 pt.↓ **Using Technology to Reach Students at a Distance** ↓12X

Prepared by ↓2X

Alicia T. Gonzalez
Technology Coordinator
T-Systems Media, Inc. ↓12X

February 19, 20--

Report 45-23

Table of Contents

Set left tab at 0.5; right dot-leader tab at 6.

↓6X

14 pt. **CONTENTS**

↓X2

Report 45-24

Title Page

Create a title page for the report below entitled LOOKING INTO THE 21ST CENTURY and a subtitle that reads Some Predictions for the New Millennium. The report is to be submitted to Alfredo Sanchez, District Manager, Millennium Concepts, Inc. The report is being prepared by Richard P. Morgan, Computer Consultant, Millennium Concepts, Inc. Use a date of May 18, 20--.

Report 45-25

Table of Contents

CONTENTS

Report 45-26

Business Report

Progress and Proofreading Check

Documents designated as Proofreading Checks serve as a check of your proofreading skill. Your goal is to have zero typographical errors when the GDP software first scores the document.

Do not indent paragraphs in a business report.

LOOKING INTO THE 21ST CENTURY
Some Predictions for the New Millennium
Evelyn Hasagawa

¶ It is predicted that computers will alter almost every activity of our lives in the first ten years of this millennium. There is strong evidence to suggest that this prediction will soon become a reality. This report will summarize the changes we will experience in the areas of artificial intelligence and the Internet.

ARTIFICIAL INTELLIGENCE

¶ Artificial intelligence is generally described as a computer's ability to assume an intelligence similar to that of the human brain—thus, its ability to reason and make decisions based on a preassigned set of facts or data.[1] But many experts predict that the computer's power will not stop there. They predict that the computer will soon become much smarter than humans by a process in which "intelligent" computers create even more intelligent computers. What we learn from these computers will have a far greater impact than the combined discoveries of the microscope, telescope, and X-ray machines.

¶ It is also predicted that the power of computers will double every 18 months through the year 2010.[2] With these enhancements, robots will displace humans from farms and factories; we will travel in cars, planes, and trains that are operated solely by computers; and traveling on the interstate highways will be as safe as watching television at home.

(Continued on next page)

COMPUTERS AND THE INTERNET

¶ The Internet will continue to expand and proliferate around the world. The speed at which information is transmitted on today's Internet will be considered a "snail's pace" on tomorrow's telemetric system. Most computers will transmit information at gigabit speeds and higher.[3] Computer security will be "foolproof," and most business transactions will be conducted on the Net. Fewer people will travel to foreign countries to vacation since "virtual vacations" will be commonplace.

---

[1] Peter F. Boyd, "Artificial Intelligence," *Journal of Computer Trends*, January 2004, pp. 23–24, 36.

[2] Toshida Doi, "Is Computer Intelligence Better Than the Human Brain?" *Power PC Magazine*, April 2003, pp. 14–17.

[3] Melanie T. Reynolds, "Tomorrow's Brainpower," March 17, 2004, <http://www.businessweek.com/2004/brainpower.htm>, accessed on August 19, 2005.

Strategies for Career Success

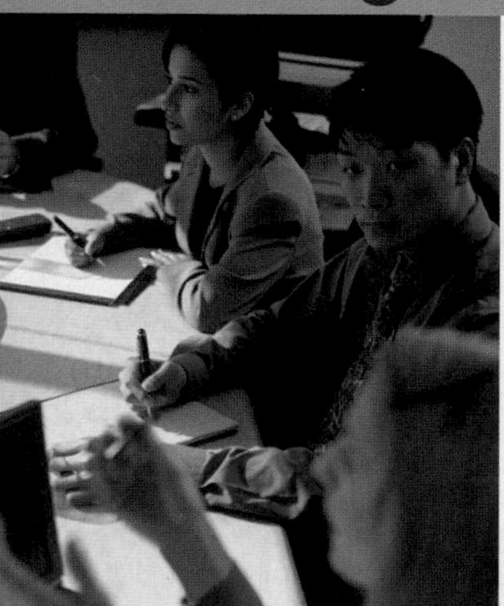

Letter of Transmittal

A letter or memo of transmittal introduces a report or proposal. Such letters provide an overview of the report in an informal, conversational writing style.

Let the recipient know what you are sending; for example, "Enclosed is the proposal you requested." If you're submitting an unsolicited report, explain why you've written the report. Include the report topic and identify the person or persons who authorized the report. Recap the main points. Cite any specific information that would help your audience comprehend the material. Is it a draft?

Conclude with a note of appreciation, a willingness to discuss the report, and intended follow-up action. Will you do something? Do you want feedback? If you want the reader to act, explain what you need and provide a deadline; for example, "Please provide your comments by July 15."

YOUR TURN List some ways that a letter of transmittal can promote goodwill between the sender and recipient.

Unit 10

Correspondence

LESSON 46
Personal Titles and Complimentary Closings in Letters

LESSON 47
Personal-Business Letters

LESSON 48
Memos With Lists

LESSON 49
Letters With Copy Notations

LESSON 50
Letters in Modified-Block Style

January 10, 20--

Mrs. Connie Filstad
4034 Kennedy Lane
Mount Vernon, WA 98274-2340

Dear Mrs. Filstad:

We at Mirror Lake Homes believe that your selection of a SunCity townhouse is just the right choice for you. The SunCity model received three national awards the 12th of last month. You have selected one of the most popular of our six models. As you requested, a brochure of the SunCity model is enclosed. Fifty-four units in the Creekwood site in Mount Vernon, Washington, have been built since December 2000.

I am certain you will agree that the $500 earnest money you put down was a wise decision on your part, and the 6.5 percent loan you received was the best available through our lending agency.

Thank you, Mrs. Filstad, for the opportunity to work with you these past few days. If you have any questions, please let us know.

Sincerely,

(Mrs.) Maria Martinez
Sales Director

urs
Enclosure

November 30, 20--

Sales Manager
Bachmann's Nursery and Landscaping
6823 Oneta Avenue
Youngstown, OH 44500-2175

Dear Sales Manager:

As you requested on the telephone, I am providing the following list of events relating to my tree problem.

1. On April 15, I purchased at your branch in Warren four silver maples for the atrium outside our Riverdale office. We also purchased four Japanese red maples at your branch in Niles later that afternoon.
2. After about six months, one silver maple and one red maple had died. I phoned both the Warren and Niles branches several times on November 1, but no one returned my messages.
3. On November 8, I phoned your nursery in an attempt to have these trees replaced. Again, there was no response.

As these trees were expensive, I expect that you will either replace them or reimburse me for the cost of the trees. I shall look forward to hearing from you.

Sincerely,

Marvin L. Norgaard
Grounds Manager

urs

MEMO TO: Charles A. Cornelius, President

FROM: Alfred A. Long, Convention Director

DATE: September 8, 20--

SUBJECT: Convention Locations

As you know, this year's convention will meet in Jacksonville, Florida. It is the Executive Board's decision to rotate the convention site to each of the districts in our region. Our next three conventions will be held in the following locations:

- Mobile, Alabama
- Atlanta, Georgia
- Myrtle Beach, South Carolina

In May the Board will travel to Mobile to visit the location of our next convention site. When we return, we will draft our convention site proposal for you.

urs

Personal Titles and Complimentary Closings in Letters

Goals

- Type at least 37wpm/3′/3e
- Format personal titles in letters
- Format complimentary closings in letters

A. Type 2 times.

A. WARMUP

B & Z requested 14 boxes at $37/box. The items they 11
wanted were #6 and #17. A discount of 20% would bring the 22
total to approximately $950. Will you verify that order? 33

| 1 | 2 | 3 | 4 | 5 | 6 | 7 | 8 | 9 | 10 | 11 | 12

SKILLBUILDING

B. DIAGNOSTIC PRACTICE: NUMBERS

If you are not using the GDP software, turn to page SB-5 and follow the directions for this activity.

C. Take three 12-second timed writings on each line. The scale below the last line shows your wpm speed for a 12-second timed writing.

C. 12-SECOND SPEED SPRINTS

Nine of those new women were on time for the first session.
She could see that many of those old memos should be filed.
Forty of the men were at the game when that siren went off.
The line at the main hall was so long that I did not go in.

5 | 10 | 15 | 20 | 25 | 30 | 35 | 40 | 45 | 50 | 55 | 60

Keyboarding Connection

Evaluating Internet Sources

Are you sure your Internet source has valid information? Because of the broad availability of the Internet and the lack of careful review stages like the ones built into print publishing, you must be cautious about the dependability of information you find on the Internet. Evaluate information on the Internet by the same standards you use to evaluate other sources of information.

The best way to assure that information is valid is to get it from a reputable source. The Internet versions of established, reputable journals in medicine (for example, *Journal of the American Medical Association*), business (for example, *Harvard Business Review*), engineering, computer science, and so forth, warrant the same level of trust as the printed versions.

When you do not use established, reputable Web sites, use caution. Keep in mind that anyone can publish on the Internet. For many sources, there are no editorial review safeguards in place.

YOUR TURN Search the Web for more assessment methods.

D. Take two 3-minute timed writings. Review your speed and errors.

Goal: At least 37wpm/3′/3e

D. 3-MINUTE TIMED WRITING

```
     Now is a great time for you to look for a job. Most       11
employers look for people who have mastered a few office       22
skills. For example, if you have acquired good computer        33
skills and are capable of working with people around you       45
and are steadfast, you can find a good job. There are some     56
who will pay top dollar to find and keep good workers.         67
     Your first impression on a prospective employer will      78
be a lasting one. Your resume should list your job skills,     90
your experience, and your personal information. Your zeal     102
when you interview for a job must come through.               111
| 1 | 2 | 3 | 4 | 5 | 6 | 7 | 8 | 9 | 10 | 11 | 12
```

FORMATTING

E. PERSONAL TITLES IN CORRESPONDENCE

Inside Addresses
Always use a courtesy title before a person's name in the inside address of a letter; for example, *Mr., Mrs.,* or *Dr.*

Type a person's title on the same line with the name (separated by a comma), if the title is short, or on the line below. The title and business name may be typed on the same line (separated by a comma) if they are both short.

Personal Titles in Inside Addresses
Mr. Frank R. Yashiro, Manager
Landmark Security Systems

Mrs. Joyce Mansfield
Executive Director
Tanner Hospital

Dr. Carlotta Torres
Manager, Duke Oil Co.

Salutations
When possible, use a person's name in the salutation. The correct form for the salutation is the courtesy title and the last name. If you do not know the name of the person, use a job title or *Ladies and Gentlemen*. A colon is used after the salutation in standard punctuation.

Personal Titles in Salutations
Dear Ms. North:
Dear Dr. Chapman:
Dear Mr. Wagner:
Dear Sales Manager:
Ladies and Gentlemen:

F. COMPLIMENTARY CLOSINGS IN CORRESPONDENCE

Every letter should end with a complimentary closing. Some frequently used complimentary closings are *Sincerely, Sincerely yours, Yours truly, Cordially*, and *Respectfully yours.*

In the closing lines, do not use a courtesy title before a man's name. A courtesy title may be included in a woman's typed name or her signature. A comma is used after the complimentary closing in standard punctuation.

Closing Lines

Sincerely yours,

Gretchen Day

Miss Gretchen Day
Account Manager

Cordially,

(Ms.) Juanita Ponce

Juanita Ponce
Marketing Director

Yours truly,

Ben R. Cameron

Ben R. Cameron
Regional Supervisor

DOCUMENT PROCESSING

Correspondence 46-22

Business Letter in Block Style

January 10, 20-- | Mrs. Connie Filstad | 4034 Kennedy Lane | Mount Vernon, WA 98274-2340 | Dear Mrs. Filstad:

¶ We at Mirror Lake Homes believe that your selection of a SunCity townhouse is just the right choice for you. The SunCity model received three national awards last month. You have selected one of the most popular of our six models. As you requested, a brochure of the SunCity model is enclosed. Fifty-four units in the Creekwood site in Mount Vernon, Washington, have been built since December 2002.

¶ I am certain you will agree that the $500 earnest money you put down was a wise decision on your part, and the 6.5 percent loan you received was the best available through our lending agency.

¶ Thank you, Mrs. Filstad, for the opportunity to work with you these past few days. If you have any questions, please let us know.

Sincerely, | (Mrs.) Maria Martinez | Sales Director | urs | Enclosure

Correspondence 46-23

Business Letter in Block Style

May 20, 20-- | Mr. Lawrence S. Alwich | 1800 East Hollywood Avenue | Salt Lake City, UT 84108 | Dear Mr. Alwich:

¶ Our radio station would like you to reply to our editorial about the proposed airport site that aired from Provo, Utah, on May 15. Actually, you are 1 of over 27 listeners who indicated your desire for us to air your rebuttal.

¶ Of the more than 100 request letters for equal time, we selected yours because you touched on most of the relevant points of this topic.

¶ We will contact you further about taping your rebuttal on June 4. Please read the enclosed disclaimer that we would like you to sign before airing the rebuttal.

Yours truly, | Peng T. Lim | General Manager | urs | Enclosure

Personal-Business Letters

Goals

- Improve speed and accuracy
- Refine language arts skills in number expression
- Format personal-business letters

A. Type 2 times.

A. WARMUP

```
     "Rex analyzed the supply," Margie said. Based on the      11
results, a purchase request for 7# @ $140 (23% of what we      22
needed) was issued. Was Jackie surprised by this? Vi was!      34
| 1 | 2 | 3 | 4 | 5 | 6 | 7 | 8 | 9 | 10 | 11 | 12
```

SKILLBUILDING

B. PACED PRACTICE

If you are not using the GDP software, turn to page SB-14 and follow the directions for this activity.

C. PROGRESSIVE PRACTICE: ALPHABET

If you are not using the GDP software, turn to page SB-7 and follow the directions for this activity.

LANGUAGE ARTS

D. Study the rules at the right.

D. NUMBER EXPRESSION

RULE ▶ # general

In general, spell out numbers zero through ten, and use numerals for numbers above ten.

We rented two movies for tonight.
The decision was reached after 27 precincts sent in their results.

RULE ▶ # figures

Use numerals for

- **Dates. (Use *st, d,* or *th* only if the day comes before the month.)**
  The tax report is due on April 15 (*not* April $15^{\underline{th}}$).
  We will drive to the camp on the 23d (or *23rd* or *23rd*) of May.
- **All numbers if two or more *related* numbers both above and below ten are used in the same sentence.**
  Mr. Carter sent in 7 receipts, and Ms. Cantrell sent in 22.
  But: The 13 accountants owned three computers each.
- **Measurements (time, money, distance, weight, and percent).**
  The $500 statue we delivered at 7 a.m. weighed 6 pounds.
- **Mixed numbers.**
  Our sales are up 9½ (or *9 1/2* or *9.5*) percent over last year.

(Continued on next page)

Edit the sentences to correct any errors in number expression.

```
On the 3d of June, when she turns 60, 2 of her annuities
will have earned an average of 10 3/4 percent.
All seven investors were interested in buying 14 condos
if they were located within fifteen miles of each other.
The credit fee is fifteen dollars, and the interest is set
at 8 percent; escrow will close on March 23rd before five p.m.
The parcel weighed two pounds. She also mailed three large
packages and twelve small packages on June 4.
They paid 2.5 points on the loan amount.
```

FORMATTING

E. PERSONAL-BUSINESS LETTERS

Personal-business letters are prepared by individuals to conduct their personal business. To format a personal-business letter:

1. Type the letter on plain paper or personal stationery, not letterhead.
2. Include the writer's address in the letter directly below the writer's name in the closing lines.
3. Since the writer of the letter usually types the letter, reference initials are not used.

DOCUMENT PROCESSING

Correspondence 47-24

Personal-Business Letter in Block Style

Reference Manual

Refer to page R-3D of the Reference Manual for an illustration of a personal-business letter.

↓6X

October 1, 20-- ↓4X

Ms. Valarie Bledsoe, Director
City Parks and Recreation Department
7034 Renwick Avenue
Syracuse, NY 13210-0475 ↓2X

Dear Ms. Bledsoe: ↓2X

\# general
\# figures

Thank you for the excellent manner in which your department accommodated our family last summer. About 120 Turners attended the reunion at Rosedale Park on August 21.

\# general
\# figures

I would like to again request that Shelter 5 be reserved for our next year's family reunion on August 20. A confirmation of the date from your office will be appreciated. ↓2X

Sincerely, ↓4X

Blair R. Turner
2410 Farnham Road
Syracuse, NY 13219

Correspondence 47-25

Personal-Business Letter in Block Style

This personal-business letter is from Roberto G. Trujillo, who lives at 482 22d Street East, Lawrence, KS 66049. Use July 13, 20--, as the date, and supply the appropriate salutation and closing using standard punctuation. The letter is to be sent to Mr. Robert A. Sotherden, Administrator | Glencrest Nursing Home | 2807 Crossgate Circle | Lawrence, KS 66047.

¶ Thanks to you and dozens of other people, the fall crafts sale at Glencrest was highly successful. I am very appreciative of the ways in which you helped. ¶ I particularly wish to thank you for transporting the display tables and chairs to Glencrest and back to the community center. Many people from the community center attended the sale and commented about how nice it was of you and your staff to support such an activity. ¶ Having a parent who is a resident of the home, I am grateful that over 20 people from the Lawrence area volunteer their services to help make life more pleasant for the residents. Please accept my special thanks to you and your staff for supporting the many activities that benefit all Glencrest residents.

general

Correspondence 47-26

Personal-Business Letter in Block Style

June 4, 20-- | Mr. Karl E. Davis | 5270 Rosecrans Avenue | Topeka, KS 67284 | Dear Mr. Davis:

¶ Your presentation at the Sand Hills Country Club was one of the most enjoyable our members have ever observed. It is always a pleasure to have professionals like you speak on ways college graduates can prepare themselves for future employment. I especially enjoyed the question-and-answer session at the conclusion of your ~~wonderful~~ presentation, and I received many favorable comments from other attendees as well.

¶ Our professor has suggested that we take the information you gave us and prepare a web site that focuses on the key points 6 you mentioned in your speech. That way, many of our class mates can take advantage of your excellent advice when preparing for their 1st search job. We have also found at least 20 ~~several~~ other sources to use on the world wide web that we plan to include on ~~in~~ our web site.

general

figure

(Continued on next page)

¶ I believe this is one of the most interesting assignments I have ever been assigned, thank to the excellent information you provided. Members of my project team are excited to see there information on our web site. The project has given other students an incentive to construct their own web sites pertaining to job searches and interviewing techniques.

figure

¶ If you would like to view our Web site, you can do so at the following URL which will be posted by the 10th of the month: www.tamu.edu/comm/abed3600/interview.html. Again, thank you for all your excellent ideas.

Sincerely, | Tamika Yamemoto | 3421 Carlisle Avenue | Topeka, KS 67209

Lesson 48

Memos With Lists

Goals

- Type at least 38 wpm/3′/3e
- Format lists in correspondence

A. Type 2 times.

A. WARMUP

Three travel agencies (Jepster & Vilani, Quin & Bott, 11
and Zeplin & Wexter) sold the most travel tickets for the 23
past 12 months. They sold 785, 834, and 960 total tickets. 34
| 1 | 2 | 3 | 4 | 5 | 6 | 7 | 8 | 9 | 10 | 11 | 12

SKILLBUILDING

B. DIAGNOSTIC PRACTICE: SYMBOLS AND PUNCTUATION

If you are not using the GDP software, turn to page SB-2 and follow the directions for this activity.

C. Type each sentence on a separate line by pressing ENTER after each sentence.

C. TECHNIQUE PRACTICE: ENTER KEY

Debit the accounts. Balance your checkbook. Add the assets.
Take the discount. Send the statements. Compute the ratios.
Review the accounts. Credit the amounts. Figure the totals.
Prepare the statements. Send the catalog. Call the clients.

D. Take two 3-minute timed writings. Review your speed and errors.

Goal: At least 38wpm/3′/3e

D. 3-MINUTE TIMED WRITING

Some of us like to use the Internet for shopping. With 11
just a simple click of the mouse, you can shop for almost 23
any type of product. You can purchase books, cars, food, 34
games, toys, zippers, boxes, and even golf clubs by using 46
the computer to shop online. 52
The advantages of using the Web to shop with such ease 63
are many. First, you can shop from any place that has some 75
access to the Internet. Second, you can compare all prices 86
with other places before you make any purchase. Third, you 98
can have your purchases shipped directly to you. All the 110
savings mount quickly. 114
| 1 | 2 | 3 | 4 | 5 | 6 | 7 | 8 | 9 | 10 | 11 | 12

FORMATTING

Refer to pages R-3B, R-3C, and R-5B of the Reference Manual for examples of lists in correspondence. Refer to page R-12C of the Reference Manual for an overview of formatting lists.

E. LISTS IN CORRESPONDENCE

Numbers or bullets may be used in correspondence to call attention to items in a list. If the sequence of the items is important, use numbers rather than bullets.

1. Begin the number or bullet at the left margin for blocked paragraphs.
2. Press ENTER 2 times to insert 1 blank line before and after the list.
3. Within the list, use single spacing as is used in the rest of the document.
4. If all items require no more than 1 line, single-space between the items in the list. If any item requires more than 1 line, single-space each item but press ENTER 2 times to insert 1 blank line between each item.

To format a list in correspondence:

1. Type the list unformatted. (**Note:** If you apply the number or bullet feature at the start of the list, any paragraphs that might follow will usually be indented incorrectly.)
2. Select the items in the list.
3. Apply the number or bullet feature.
4. Decrease the indent to move the position of bullets or numbers to the left margin.

DOCUMENT PROCESSING

Correspondence 48-27

Memo

Refer to page R-12C of the Reference Manual for an overview of formatting lists.

↓6X →tab

MEMO TO: Charles A. Cornelius, President ↓2X

FROM: Alfred A. Long, Convention Director ↓2X

DATE: September 8, 20-- ↓2X

SUBJECT: Convention Locations ↓2X

As you know, this year's convention will meet in Jacksonville, Florida. It is the Executive Board's decision to rotate the convention site to each of the districts in our region. Our next three conventions will be held in the following locations: ↓2X

- Mobile, Alabama
- Atlanta, Georgia
- Myrtle Beach, South Carolina ↓2X

In May the Board will travel to Mobile to visit the location of our next convention site. When we return, we will draft our convention site proposal for you. ↓2X

urs

Correspondence 48-28

Memo

MEMO TO: Marcia Davis | **FROM:** Alex Pera | **DATE:** April 9, 20-- | **SUBJECT:** Program Descriptions

¶As you requested, I have contacted the speakers for our afternoon session discussions. All three speakers have sent me a brief description of their sessions, and they are listed in the order of presentation as follows:

1. Salon A. This session will discuss the advantages of e-commerce and its influence on the economy of the United States.
2. Salon B. This session will introduce several suggestions for enhancing your Web site.
3. Salon C. This session will discuss changes occurring in Internet access and its impact on entrepreneurial ventures.

¶By next Monday I will send you an introduction for each speaker.
urs

Correspondence 48-29

Memo

Open the file for Correspondence 48–27 and make the following changes:

1. Change the three convention sites to Miami, Florida; Raleigh, North Carolina; and Montgomery, Alabama.
2. Change the final paragraph to indicate that the Board will travel to Miami.

Strategies for Career Success

Reducing Bias in Business Communication

Everything we do in business communication attempts to build goodwill. Bias-free language and visuals help maintain the goodwill we work so hard to create.

Bias-free language does not discriminate against people on the basis of sex, physical condition, race, age, or any other characteristic. Do not emphasize gender-specific words in your business vocabulary. Instead, incorporate gender-neutral words (for example, chairman is chairperson) into your business communication.

Organizations that treat people fairly should also use language that treats people fairly. The law is increasingly intolerant of biased documents and hostile work environments. Practice nondiscriminatory behavior by focusing on individual merits, accomplishments, skills, and what you might share in common rather than illustrating differences. Treating every group with respect and understanding is essential to gaining loyalty and future business while cultivating harmonious relationships.

YOUR TURN Review a document that you have recently written. Is the document bias-free?

Letters With Copy Notations

Goals

- Improve speed and accuracy
- Refine language arts skills in spelling
- Format letters with copy notations

A. Type 2 times.

A. WARMUP

```
     "Look at them! Have you ever seen such large birds?"    11
When questioned later on an exam, about 80% to 90% of the    22
junior girls were amazed to learn that they were ospreys.    34
|  1  |  2  |  3  |  4  |  5  |  6  |  7  |  8  |  9  |  10  |  11  |  12
```

SKILLBUILDING

B. MAP

Follow the GDP software directions for this exercise in improving keystroking accuracy.

C. Take a 1-minute timed writing on the first paragraph to establish your base speed. Then take four 1-minute timed writings on the remaining paragraphs. As soon as you equal or exceed your base speed on one paragraph, advance to the next, more difficult paragraph.

C. SUSTAINED PRACTICE: NUMBERS AND SYMBOLS

```
     The proposed road improvement program was approved      10
by the county commissioners at their last meeting. There     22
were about ten citizens who spoke on behalf of the project.  34

     The plan calls for blacktopping a 14-mile stretch on    11
County Road #2356. This is the road that is commonly called  23
the "roller coaster" because of all the curves and hills.    34

     There will be 116 miles blacktopped by J & J, Inc.      10
(commonly referred to as the Jeremy Brothers*). J & J's      22
office is at 1798 30th Avenue past the 22d Street bridge.    33

     Minor road repair costs range from $10,784 to a high    11
of $163,450 (39% of the total program costs). The "county    23
inspector" is to hold the project costs to 105% of budget!   34
|  1  |  2  |  3  |  4  |  5  |  6  |  7  |  8  |  9  |  10  |  11  |  12
```

LANGUAGE ARTS

D. Type this list of frequently misspelled words, paying special attention to any spelling problems in each word.

D. SPELLING

16 per other receipt present provided commission international
17 service position questions following industrial maintenance
18 well absence support proposal mortgage corporate management
19 upon balance approval experience facilities recommendations
20 paid because premium procedure addition directors currently

Edit the sentences to correct any misspellings.

21 The international comission provided a list of proceedures.
22 That industrial maintainance proposal is curently in place.
23 The directers and management supported the recomendations.
24 Those present raised a question about a corperate morgage.
25 Six of the folowing persons have now given their aproval.
26 In adition, Kris has premium experience at the facilitys.

FORMATTING

E. COPY NOTATIONS

Making file copies of all documents you prepare is a good business practice. At times you may also need copies to send to people other than the addressee of the original document.

A copy notation is typed on a document to indicate that someone else besides the addressee is receiving a copy.

1. Type the copy notation on the line below the reference initials or below the attachment or enclosure notation.
2. At the left margin, type a lowercase *c* followed by a colon.
3. Press the SPACE BAR 1 time and type the name of the person receiving the copy.
4. If more than one person is receiving a copy, type the names on one line separated by a comma and space between each name.

Sincerely, ↓4X

Lester A. Fagerlie
Branch Manager ↓2X

jlt
Enclosure
c: Mrs. Coretta D. Rice, Dr. Thomas Moore

DOCUMENT PROCESSING

Correspondence 49-30

Business Letter in Block Style

Highlighted words are spelling words from the language arts activities.

May 11, 20-- | Mr. and Mrs. Richard Belson | 783 Wellcourt Lane | Mount Vernon, WA 98273-4156 | Dear Mr. and Mrs. Belson:

¶ Marian Dickenson has informed me that you have several questions pertaining to the maintenance proposal that was submitted by the directors and approved by management. It is our position, based upon the procedures we provided following last week's meeting, that the proposal was submitted to corporate headquarters prior to your inquiry. Therefore, your questions should be directed to Alfred A. Long in our Seattle office.

¶ It has been our experience that inquiries such as yours will receive an immediate response because of the support you have demonstrated during other maintenance negotiations. I would recommend that you call me if you have not heard from Mr. Long by the 13th of the month. In the absence of Mr. Long's response, I am sending you a copy of other materials related to your inquiry.

¶ Thank you for your interest in this matter.

Sincerely, | Theodore A. Gardner | Sales Director | urs | c: Marian Dickenson

Correspondence 49-31

Business Letter in Block Style

Open the file for Correspondence 49-30 and make the following changes:

1. Send the letter to Mr. and Mrs. George Tanner | 105 Royal Lane | Commerce, TX 75428
2. Add the following sentence to the end of the second paragraph:

   `These materials are enclosed for your review.`

3. Include an enclosure notation.
4. Send a copy of this letter to Marian Dickenson and also to Carla Orellano.

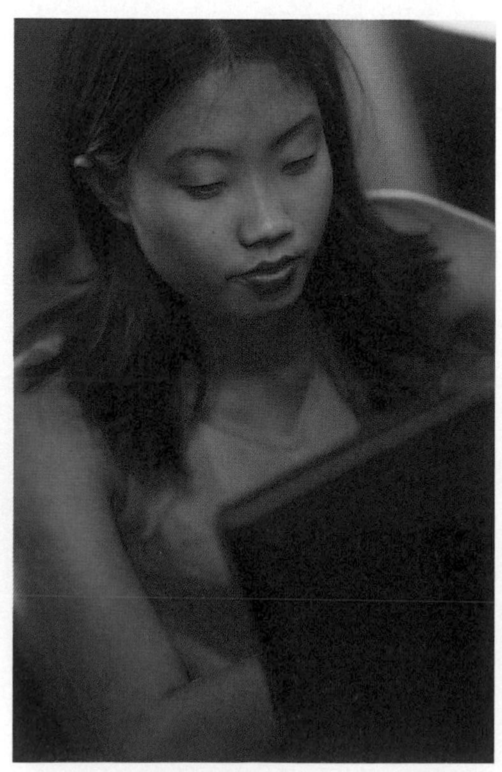

Lesson 50

Letters in Modified-Block Style

Goals

- Type at least 38wpm/3′/3e
- Format letters in modified-block style

A. Type 2 times.

A. WARMUP

Mark Kara's quilts down by 25%: #489, #378, and #460. 11
Leave the prices as they are for the remainder of the sizes 23
in that section. Eleven adjoining sections will be next. 34

| 1 | 2 | 3 | 4 | 5 | 6 | 7 | 8 | 9 | 10 | 11 | 12

SKILLBUILDING

PPP PRETEST → PRACTICE → POSTTEST

PRETEST
Take a 1-minute timed writing. Review your speed and errors.

B. PRETEST: Alternate- and One-Hand Words

The chair of the trade committee served notice that 11
the endowment grant exceeded the budget. A million dollars 23
was the exact amount. The greater part might be deferred. 35

| 1 | 2 | 3 | 4 | 5 | 6 | 7 | 8 | 9 | 10 | 11 | 12

PRACTICE
Speed Emphasis:
If you made 2 or fewer errors on the Pretest, type each *indivdual* line 2 times.
Accuracy Emphasis:
If you made 3 or more errors, type each *group* of lines (as though it were a paragraph) 2 times.

C. PRACTICE: Alternate-Hand Words

amendment turndown visible suspend visual height signs maps
authentic clemency dormant figment island emblem usual snap
shamrocks blandish problem penalty profit thrown chair form

D. PRACTICE: One-Hand Words

pumpkin eastward plumply barrage greater poplin trade holly
minikin cassette opinion seaweed created kimono union exact
minimum attracts reserve million scatter unhook plump defer

POSTTEST
Repeat the Pretest timed writing and compare performance.

E. POSTTEST: Alternate- and One-Hand Words

F. Take two 3-minute timed writings. Review your speed and errors.

Goal: At least 38wpm/3'/3e

F. 3-MINUTE TIMED WRITING

```
     The Web is a vast source of facts and data on many       10
topics. You can view many newspapers, zip through weather     22
reports, find a tax form and learn how to complete it, and    34
search for a job. You can find answers to health questions    46
and learn about world events almost as soon as they occur.    57
     E-mail is another part of the Internet that people are   69
using more often. They use e-mail to keep in touch with       80
friends and family in a quick and efficient way that costs    92
very little. They can write down their thoughts and send     103
messages just as if they were writing a letter or memo.      114
| 1 | 2 | 3 | 4 | 5 | 6 | 7 | 8 | 9 | 10 | 11 | 12
```

FORMATTING

G. MODIFIED-BLOCK STYLE LETTERS

Modified-block style is a commonly used format for business letters. The date, the complimentary closing, and the writer's identification line(s) are typed at the horizontal centerpoint for each of these lines. Begin the document by first setting a left tab at the centerpoint (usually at 3 inches), and then press TAB 1 time to move to the centerpoint before typing each of these lines. (**Note:** These lines are *not* centered horizontally.)

1. Clear all tabs and set a left tab at the centerpoint (usually at 3 inches).
2. Press ENTER 6 times to begin the letter about 2 inches from the top of the page.
3. Press TAB 1 time to move to the centerpoint, and type the date of the letter.
4. Press ENTER 4 times, and type the inside address at the left margin.
5. Press ENTER 2 times, type the salutation at the left margin, and press ENTER 2 times again.
6. Type the paragraphs blocked at the left margin, and press ENTER 2 times after all paragraphs.
7. After typing the final paragraph, press ENTER 2 times and press TAB 1 time to move to the centerpoint.
8. Type the complimentary closing, and then press ENTER 4 times.
9. Press TAB 1 time to move to the centerpoint, and type the writer's identification. If the writer's identification is to be typed on 2 lines, press TAB 1 time again for any additional line.
10. Press ENTER 2 times, and type the reference initials and remaining letter parts at the left margin.

(Continued on next page)

Garner Homes
4782 Eureka Avenue
Bellingham, WA 98452
http://www.garner.com

"Putting a Roof on America"

↓6X

→ tab to centerpoint November 29, 20-- ↓4X

Mr. and Mrs. Arvey Gates
2308 Hannegan Road
Bellingham, WA 98226 ↓2X

Dear Mr. and Mrs. Gates: ↓2X

Val Osugi, who hosted our Ridgeway open house last Saturday, has referred your unanswered questions to me. We are pleased that you are interested in a Garner home.

The usual down payment is 20 percent of the total selling price, but some lending agencies require a smaller amount in certain situations. Garner Homes is not itself involved in home financing, but we work with the financial institutions shown on the enclosed list.

Yes, the lot you prefer can accommodate a walkout basement. Val will be in touch with you soon. We can have your new Ridgeway ready for occupancy within 90 days. ↓2X

→ tab to centerpoint Sincerely, ↓4X

Alfred A. Long

→ tab to centerpoint Alfred A. Long
Sales Director ↓2X

azk
Enclosure
c: Loan Processing Dept.

Go To Word Processing Manual

H. WORD PROCESSING: RULER TABS AND TAB SET

Study Lesson 50 in your word processing manual. Complete all of the shaded steps while at your computer. Then format the jobs that follow.

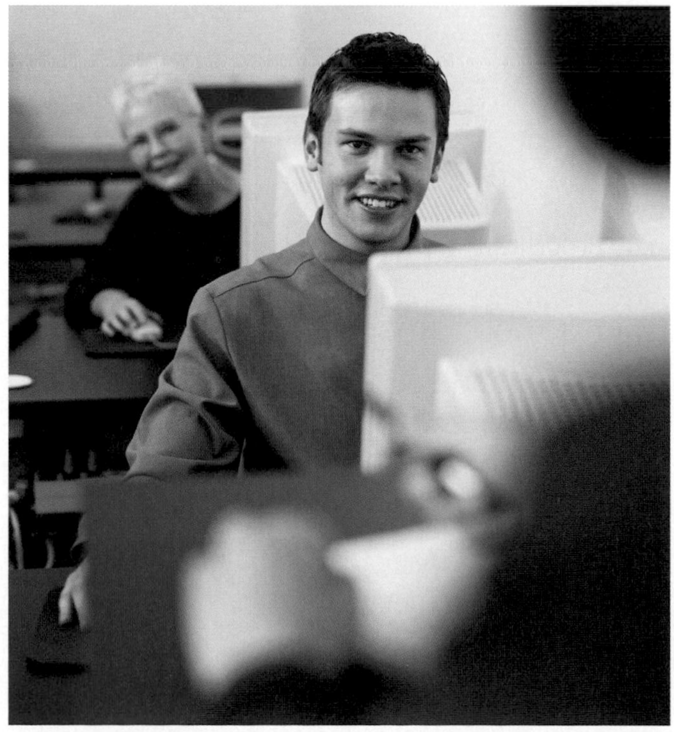

DOCUMENT PROCESSING

Correspondence 50-32

Business Letter in Modified-Block Style

Refer to page R-3B of the Reference Manual for additional guidance.

↓6X

tab to centerpoint November 29, 20-- ↓4X

Mr. and Mrs. Arvey Gates
2308 Hannegan Road
Bellingham, WA 98226 ↓2X

Dear Mr. and Mrs. Gates: ↓2X

Val Osugi, who hosted our Ridgeway open house last Saturday, has referred your unanswered questions to me. We are pleased that you are interested in a Garner home.

The usual down payment is 20 percent of the total selling price, but some lending agencies require a smaller amount in certain situations. Garner Homes is not itself involved in home financing, but we work with the financial institutions shown on the enclosed list.

Yes, the lot you prefer can accommodate a walkout basement. Val will be in touch with you soon. We can have your new Ridgeway ready for occupancy within 90 days. ↓2X

tab to centerpoint Sincerely, ↓4X

Alfred A. Long

tab to centerpoint Alfred A. Long
Sales Director ↓2X

urs
Enclosure
c: Loan Processing Dept.

Correspondence 50-33

Business Letter in Modified-Block Style

Reference Manual

Refer to page R-12C of the Reference Manual for information on formatting lists and an illustration.

Use November 30, 20--, as the date as you format this modified-block style letter to be sent to the sales manager at Bachmann's Nursery and Landscaping | 6823 Oneta Avenue | Youngstown, OH 44500-2175

Dear Sales Manager:

¶ As you requested on the telephone, I am providing the following list of events relating to my tree problem.

1. On April 15, I purchased at your branch in Warren four silver maples for the atrium outside our Riverdale office. We also purchased four Japanese red maples at your branch in Niles later that afternoon.
2. After about six months, one silver maple and one red maple had died. I phoned both the Warren and Niles branches several times on November 1, but no one returned my messages.
3. On November 8, I phoned your nursery in an attempt to have these trees replaced. Again, there was no response.

¶ As these trees were expensive, I expect that you will either replace them or reimburse me for the cost of the trees. I shall look forward to hearing from you.

Sincerely, | Marvin L. Norgaard | Grounds Manager | urs

Correspondence 50-34

Business Letter in Modified-Block Style

December 10, 20-- | Mr. Marvin L. Norgaard | 4782 Saranac Avenue | Youngstown, OH 44505-6207 | Dear Mr. Norgaard:

¶ This is in response to your recent letter.

¶ Your trees will be replaced without cost to you. We will make sure that the replacement trees will match the others you purchased in both size and color. I am enclosing a warranty for these new trees so that you can feel confident that we stand behind our product.

¶ The survival rate for trees cannot be perfect; however, we are indeed sorry that you have had to have this temporary setback.

¶ The communication breakdown with our two branch offices should not have occurred. We will take steps to ensure that this will not happen in the future. You can be confident that the appearance of your atrium will be restored and that the beauty of the new trees will add to your property's value. Thank you for shopping at Bachmann's.

Sincerely, | Mrs. Alice G. Schmidt | Co-owner | urs | Enclosure | c: Mr. Raul Cornejo, Co-owner

Correspondence 50-35

Personal-Business Letter in Modified-Block Style

Progress and Proofreading Check

Documents designated as Proofreading Checks serve as a check of your proofreading skill. Your goal is to have zero typographical errors when the GDP software first scores the document.

March 11, 20-- | Ms. Karen Shalicky | Lincoln Travel Center | 2384 Longdale Avenue | Suite 4113 | Boston, MA 02134-3489 | Dear Ms. Shalicky:
¶ I am interested in taking a cruise in one of the following regions:
- Alaska Inland Passageway
- Caribbean Islands
- Greek Isles

¶ Could you please send me some promotional materials for these cruises? My financial resources are such that I would like to limit my cruise package to $5,000 and would prefer a cruise no longer than ten days in length. I will be accompanied by my friend Bonnie Davis, and I assume that any quotes you give me could apply to both of us.
¶ We would like to do sightseeing in some of these locations. Do you have special excursions available to passengers? I am enclosing a list of the sites we would like to visit in each of these regions.
¶ The best time for us to travel is between June 1 and June 20, and we would like you to schedule our trip around those dates. I hope to hear from you soon.
Yours truly, | Rita Wright | 678 Ardale Avenue | Milton, MA 02186-2190 | Enclosure | c: Bonnie Davis

Keyboarding Connection

Avoid E-Mail Flame Wars

Don't fan the flames! A flame is an offensive e-mail that expresses anger, criticism, or insults. If flames are transmitted to a mailing list, they can produce a long list of flames and counter flames known as flame wars.

You may be tempted to join in, but this is a waste of everyone's time. Often the initial offense was merely a poorly worded e-mail that a reader interpreted as an insult. There are those who intentionally send inflammatory e-mails called flame bait. Resist the urge to send a cutting response, and consider whether the writer's intent was to provoke you.

If your reader misjudges something you wrote and becomes offended, just apologize. A timely apology can thwart a potential fire. Avoid miscommunication by watching how you word your e-mails.

YOUR TURN Have you ever been insulted by an e-mail? What was your response?

Unit 11

Employment Documents

LESSON 51
Traditional Resumes

LESSON 52
Electronic Resumes

LESSON 53
Letters of Application

LESSON 54
Follow-Up Letters

LESSON 55
Integrated Employment Project

PATSY R. ROTHEL

2525 Hickory Ridge Drive, Plant City, FL 33567
Phone: 813-555-0704; e-mail: prothel@netmail.com

OBJECTIVE To continue my career in computer graphics by securing a position related to graphic design.

EDUCATION Central Florida Business College, Valrico, Florida
Two years of related courses in graphic design

Plant City High School, Plant C
Graduated: May 2005

EXPERIENCE *Graphic Designer, NetView, Inc.*
Orlando, Florida
October 2004–Present
Designed Web pages for
central Florida. Edited p
database for Web-based

Copy Editor, The Plant City Pr
Plant City, Florida
May 2000–September 2004
Assisted the news editor
editing copy for daily ne
from local businesses. C
the Week forum.

ACTIVITIES
- Spanish Honor Society, 2001
- Member, Phi Beta Lambda, 2
- Newsletter Editor, *CFBC Ne*
- President, FBLA Chapter, 19
- Treasurer, FBLA Chapter, 19

REFERENCES References available upon requ

August 10, 20--

Personnel Director
Arlington Communications
2403 Sunset Lane
Arlington, TX 76015-3148

Dear Personnel Director:

Please consider me as an applicant for a position with Arlington Communications. My strengths have always been in the communication arts, as you can see on the enclosed resume, which lists a number of courses in English, speech, and communication technology. The two part-time jobs I held during the summer months at your company convinced me that Arlington Communications is the place where I want to work.

If you would like to interview me for any possible openings this summer or fall, please
d to hearing from you.

April 7, 20--

Ms. Kay Brewer, Personnel Director
Blanchard Computer Systems
2189 Dace Avenue
Sioux City, IA 51107

Dear Ms. Brewer:

Thank you for the opportunity of interviewing yesterday with Blanchard Computer Systems. Please express my appreciation to all of those who were involved.

The interview gave me a good feeling about the company. The positive description that you shared with me convinced me that Blanchard is indeed a company at which I would like to work. I was greatly impressed with the summary of social service programs that are sponsored by Blanchard for citizens throughout the community.

You may recall that I have had experience with all of the equipment that is used. It appears to me that my strengths in computer application software and office systems would blend in well with your company profile.

I look forward to hearing from you soon regarding your decision on the position of data records operator.

Sincerely,

Arlene F. Jefferson
1842 Amber Road
Wayne, NE 68787

Lesson 51

Traditional Resumes

Goals

- Improve speed and accuracy
- Refine language arts skills in the use of commas
- Format traditional resumes

A. Type 2 times.

A. WARMUP

```
     Janice had sales of over $23,000; Kathy's sales were   11
only $17,368 for the same quiet period. Craig agreed that   22
some inventory sizes were wrong and should be exchanged.    34
| 1 | 2 | 3 | 4 | 5 | 6 | 7 | 8 | 9 | 10 | 11 | 12
```

SKILLBUILDING

B. MAP

Follow the GDP software directions for this exercise in improving keystroking accuracy.

C. Take a 1-minute timed writing on the first paragraph to establish your base speed. Then take four 1-minute timed writings on the remaining paragraphs. As soon as you equal or exceed your base speed on one paragraph, advance to the next, more difficult paragraph.

C. SUSTAINED PRACTICE: CAPITALIZATION

```
     There are several different approaches that one can   11
take when considering a major purchase. Some people make   22
the mistake of simply going to a store and making a choice. 34

     When one couple decided to buy a chest-type freezer,   11
they looked at a consumer magazine in the library. The      22
Sears, Amana, and General Electric were shown as best buys. 34

     That same issue of their magazine compared electric    11
ranges. Jonathan and Mary Anne found that the Maytag, Magic 23
Chef, Amana, and Gibson were determined to be best buys.    34

     Best buys for full-size microwave ovens were the Sharp 11
Carousel, Panasonic, and GoldStar Multiwave. Good midsize   23
models were the Frigidaire, Panasonic, and Sears Kenmore.   34
| 1 | 2 | 3 | 4 | 5 | 6 | 7 | 8 | 9 | 10 | 11 | 12
```

LANGUAGE ARTS

D. Study the rules at the right.

D. COMMAS

RULE ▶ , date

Use a comma before and after the year in a complete date.

We will arrive on June 2, 2005, for the conference.

But: We will arrive on June 2 for the conference.

But: Work should be submitted between November 2005 and December 2005.

RULE ▶ , place

Use a comma before and after a state or country that follows a city (but not before a ZIP Code).

Joan moved to Vancouver, British Columbia, in May.

Send the package to Douglasville, GA 30135, by Express Mail.

But: Send the package to Georgia by Express Mail

Edit the sentences to correct any errors in the use of commas.

16 The warehouse building will be ready in September, 2004.

17 The attorney told a clerk to use June 30, 2005 as the date.

18 The books were sent to Los Angeles, CA, 90029 on July 13, 2005 and will arrive soon.

19 The move to Toledo, Ohio, was scheduled for November, 2004.

FORMATTING

E. TRADITIONAL RESUMES

When you apply for a job, you may be asked to submit a resume. The purpose of a resume is to convey your qualifications for the position you are seeking. A resume should include the following:

- Personal information (name, address, telephone number, and e-mail address).
- Your career objective (optional).
- A summary of your educational background and special training.
- Previous work experience.
- Any activities or personal achievements that relate to the position for which you are applying.
- References (optional). If an employer requests references, you should have at least three people who can tell a prospective employer what kind of worker you are.

Often, your resume creates the first impression you make on a prospective employer; be sure it is free of errors.

Various styles are acceptable for formatting a resume. Choose a style (or design one) that is attractive and that enables you to get all the needed information on one or two pages. The first page of a resume should start about 2 inches from the top of the page.

To format a traditional resume:

1. Press ENTER 6 times.
2. Insert an open table with 2 columns and 1 row for each section of the resume. **Note:** In the example that follows, you would use 6 rows.
3. Merge the cells in Row 1.
4. Change to center alignment.
5. Type your name in all caps in Arial Bold 14 pt. in Row 1, and press ENTER 2 times.
6. Change to Arial Bold 12 pt; then type your street address followed by a comma and 1 space; type your city followed by a comma and 1 space; then type your state followed by 1 space and your ZIP Code; press ENTER 1 time.

(Continued on next page)

7. Type `Phone:` followed by 1 space; then type your area code and phone number followed by a semicolon and 1 space.
8. Type `e-mail:` followed by 1 space and your e-mail address.
9. Press ENTER 1 time.
10. Apply a bottom border to Row 1.
11. Move to Row 2, Column A; and press ENTER 1 time.
12. Type the entry in Column A in all caps and bold in Times New Roman 12 pt., and press TAB to move to Column B.
13. Press ENTER 1 time, and type the information related to the Column A heading in Column B.
14. Press ENTER as needed in each section to insert 1 blank line between sections. **Note:** Type job titles and business names in italics.
15. Continue typing all entries until you are finished. **Note:** For any job descriptions, increase the indent to reposition the information. For any lists, decrease the indent until the list is positioned at the left of the column.
16. Decrease the width of Column A to about 1.25 inch to accommodate the longest entry and provide a small amount of space after the longest entry.

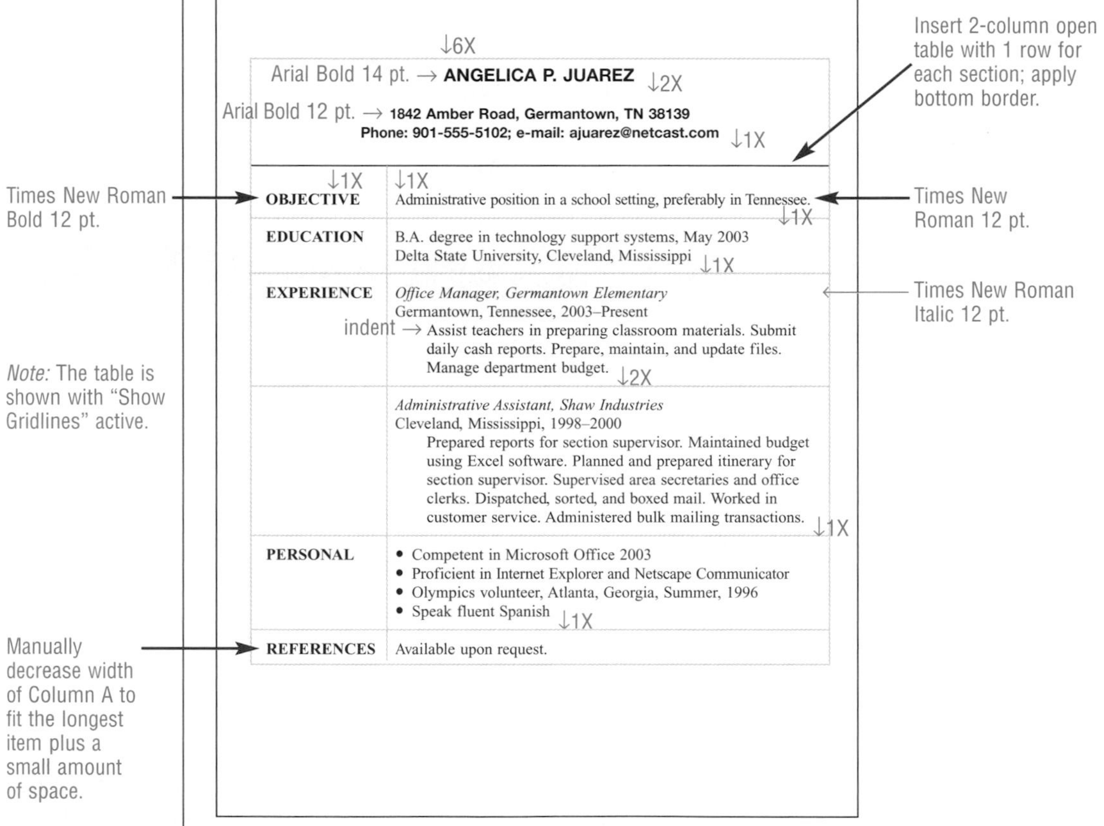

Word Processing Manual

F. WORD PROCESSING: FONTS AND TABLES—CHANGING COLUMN WIDTH

Study Lesson 51 in your word processing manual. Complete all of the shaded steps while at your computer. Then format the jobs that follow.

Report 51-27

Resume in Traditional Style

Insert 2-column open table with 1 row for each section; apply top border.

↓6X

Arial Bold 14 pt. → **PATSY R. ROTHEL** ↓2X

Arial Bold 12 pt. → **2525 Hickory Ridge Drive, Plant City, FL 33567**
Phone: 813-555-0704; e-mail: prothel@netmail.com ↓1X

Times New Roman Bold 12 pt.

Times New Roman 12 pt.

Times New Roman Italic 12 pt.

Note: The table is shown with "Show Gridlines" active.

Manually decrease width of Column A to fit longest item.

↓1X **OBJECTIVE**	↓1X To continue my career in computer graphics by securing a position related to graphic design. ↓1X
EDUCATION	Central Florida Business College, Valrico, Florida A.A. degree in graphics design Graduated: May 2005 ↓2X Plant City High School, Plant City, Florida Graduated: May 2003 ↓1X
EXPERIENCE	*Graphic Designer, NetView, Inc.* Orlando, Florida October 2005–Present indent → Designed Web pages for Internet-connected companies in central Florida. Edited page copy for Web sites. Created a database for Web-based users. ↓2X *Copy Editor, The Plant City Press* Plant City, Florida May 2003–September 2005 Assisted the news editor with typing, proofreading, and editing copy for daily newspaper. Solicited subscriptions from local businesses. Conducted interviews for Citizens of the Week forum. ↓1X
ACTIVITIES	• Member, Phi Beta Lambda, 2004–2005 • Newsletter Editor, *CFBC News*, 2004 • President, FBLA Chapter, 2002 • Treasurer, FBLA Chapter, 2001 ↓1X
REFERENCES	References available upon request.

Report 51-28

Resume in Traditional Style

Open the file for Report 51-27 and make the following changes:

1. Change the name to JOYCE K. LEE.
2. Change the address to 10234 Wood Sorrell Lane, Burke, VA 22015.
3. Change the phone number to 703-555-4902 and the e-mail address to jklee@netlink.net.
4. Replace the OBJECTIVE entry with the following:
   To gain experience in retail sales as a foundation for a retail management position.
5. Replace both of the EDUCATION entries with the following:
   Central High School, Burke, Virginia | Graduated: May 2003.
6. Change the first EXPERIENCE entry to the following:
   Computer Systems Technician, Kramer & Kramer, Inc. | Harrisburg, Virginia | June 2004-Present | Duties include reviewing, installing, and updating software programs used for processing legal documents.
7. Change the second EXPERIENCE entry to the following:
   Salesclerk, Blanchard's Department Store | Richmond, Virginia | May 2002-May 2004 (part-time) | Duties included selling sporting goods and operating Panasonic cash register. Assisted sales manager in completing monthly sales reports.
8. Change the entries for ACTIVITIES to the following:
   Volunteer for Habitat for Humanity, 2000-Present | Member, Computer Technicians Association, 2000-Present | Senior Class President, 2002-2003 | Member, Intramural Soccer Team, 2001-2003 | Member, Beta Club, 2001-2003.

Strategies for Career Success

Formatting Your Resume

The format of your resume communicates important skills—neatness and the ability to organize. Make a good first impression by following these guidelines.

Watch the spacing on your resume. A crowded resume implies that you cannot summarize. Leave adequate white space between the section headings of your resume. Use different font sizes, boldface, and italics to separate and emphasize information. Font sizes should be between 10 and 14.

Print your resume on good-quality 8½" × 11" white or off-white bond paper (for example, 20-pound stock). Colored paper doesn't provide enough contrast when your resume is copied or faxed.

Proofread your resume for spelling errors and consistency of format. Ask a few friends to review it and provide feedback.

YOUR TURN Print one copy of your resume on a dark-colored paper and print one copy on white paper. Photocopy each resume. Which provides the better contrast for readability?

Electronic Resumes

Goals

- Type at least 39wpm/5′/5e
- Format an electronic resume

A. Type 2 times.

A. WARMUP

```
     The new firm, Kulver & Zweidel, will be equipped to      11
handle from 1/6 to 1/4 of Martin's tax needs after they       22
move to the new location at 1970 Gansby, just east of Main.  34
| 1 | 2 | 3 | 4 | 5 | 6 | 7 | 8 | 9 | 10 | 11 | 12
```

SKILLBUILDING

B. Take three 12-second timed writings on each line. The scale below the last line shows your wpm speed for a 12-second timed writing.

B. 12-SECOND SPEED SPRINTS

```
Pat went back to the store where she had seen the red book.
The good girl was sure that she had not seen that old door.
There was a huge change when he walked into the same class.
Pat was met at the door with one red rose and a giant cake.
5 10 15 20 25 30 35 40 45 50 55 60
```

C. PROGRESSIVE PRACTICE: ALPHABET

If you are not using the GDP software, turn to page SB-7 and follow the directions for this activity.

D. Take two 5-minute timed writings. Review your speed and errors.

Goal: At least 39wpm/5'/5e

D. 5-MINUTE TIMED WRITING

     Have you completed your education when you graduate 11
from high school or finish your college work? Most people 22
look forward to reaching milestones, such as graduation or 34
completing a course. Have they learned everything they will 46
need to know to be successful in the real world? The answer 58
is not so simple. 62
     Learning continues to occur long after you leave the 72
classroom. No matter what job or career you pursue, you 84
will learn something new every day. When you investigate 95
new ideas, ask questions, or find a different way to do a 107
job, you are continuing to learn. In the process, you gain 118
additional experience, develop new skills, and become a 130
better worker. 133
     Getting along with your peers, for example, is not 143
something that you learn from studying books. You learn to 155
be a team player when you listen to your coworkers and 166
share your ideas with them. Do not hesitate to acquire new 178
skills or to initiate new ideas. Be zealous in your efforts 190
to continue your education. 195

| 1 | 2 | 3 | 4 | 5 | 6 | 7 | 8 | 9 | 10 | 11 | 12

FORMATTING

E. ELECTRONIC RESUMES

An electronic resume is a resume that has been formatted for display on the Internet and for electronic transmission via e-mail. Format an electronic resume as follows:

1. Use a monospaced font like Courier New, and use the default font size.
2. Use left alignment.
3. Use a line length of 60 characters maximum.
4. Do not hyphenate words at the end of a line.
5. Do not press TAB to indent lines. Instead, space 5 times.
6. If any lines wrap to a second line, press ENTER immediately after the last word of the first line, space 5 times if the turnover line should be indented, and continue typing the lines in this way until all lines for a section are completed.
7. Do not use any special formatting features (bold, italic, or underline) or graphic features (rules, bullets, pictures, boxes, tables, or columns).
8. Use all-caps as a substitute for bold or underline.
9. To create a bulleted list, space 5 times, and type an asterisk; space 1 time and type the line. On the wraparound line, space 7 times and continue typing in this way until all lines for the bulleted list are completed.
10. Save the resume as a text-only file (one that has a .txt extension).

Word Processing Manual

F. WORD PROCESSING: SAVING IN TEXT-ONLY FORMAT

Study Lesson 52 in your word processing manual. Complete all of the shaded steps while at your computer. Then format the jobs that follow.

DOCUMENT PROCESSING

Report 52-29

Resume in Electronic Style

Type the electronic resume as shown in the illustration below according to these guidelines:

- Change to 12 pt. Courier New.
- Press the SPACE BAR 5 times to indent lines.
- Press the SPACE BAR 5 times, type an asterisk, and type a space, as shown, to create a bulleted list.
- If any lines wrap to a second line, press ENTER immediately after the last word of the first line, space 5 times if the turnover line should be indented or 7 times if the turnover line is part of a bulleted list, and continue typing the lines in this way until all lines for a section are completed.
- Save the resume as a text-only file.

```
BRENDA COTTON ↓2X

→ 5 spaces 1611 Amherst Way
     Emporia, KS 66801
     Phone: 316-555-1384
     E-mail: bcotton@plains.net
     Home page: http://www.esc.org/staff/cotton.htm ↓2X

OBJECTIVE

→ 5 spaces Staff-level accounting position in an educational ↓1X
→ 5 spaces institution or public accounting firm.

EDUCATION

→ 5 spaces, *, 1 space * B.B.A. degree in accounting from Emporia State ↓1X
→ 7 spaces               University, Emporia, Kansas, May 2004 ↓2X

     * High school diploma from Central High School,
       Wichita, Kansas, June 2000

EXPERIENCE

     * STAFF ACCOUNTANT, Gateway Properties
       Emporia, Kansas
       December 2003-Present
       Responsible for budget control. Prepare variance
       report and annual business plan. Generate fixed-
       asset inventory. Prepare consolidated monthly
       financials.

     * ACCOUNTS RECEIVABLE CLERK, Aris Corporation
       Salina, Kansas
       January 2002-December 2003
       Posted cash receipts, prepared bank deposits, and
       processed tax requests.

PERSONAL

     *  Proficient in Microsoft Office desktop tools
     *  Member of AICPA
     *  Graduated summa cum laude from Emporia State

REFERENCES

     Available upon request.
```

Report 52-30

Resume in Electronic Style

Type an electronic resume in correct format for ALLEN P. HUNTER, 10234 Wood Sorrell Lane, Burke, VA 22015; Phone: 703-555-4902; E-mail, aphunter@netlink.net.

1. Type this OBJECTIVE entry: `Retail management entry-level position with a midsize | department store.`
2. Type these two EDUCATION entries as a bulleted list:
   `* Central Virginia Business College, Burke, Virginia, | December 2004`
   `* High school diploma from Central High School, Burke, | Virginia, May 2002`
3. Type these EXPERIENCE entries as a bulleted list:
   `* COMPUTER SYSTEMS TECHNICIAN, Kramer & Kramer, Inc. | Harrisburg, Virginia | June 1999-Present | Duties include reviewing, installing, and updating | software programs used for processing legal | documents and monitoring computer network system for | branch offices.`
   `* SALESCLERK, Blanchard's Department Store | Richmond, Virginia | May 2000-May 2002 (part-time) | Duties included selling sporting goods and operating | Panasonic cash register. Assisted sales manager in | completing monthly sales reports generated by Word | and Excel software programs.`
4. Type PERSONAL entries as a bulleted list:
   `* Volunteer for Habitat for Humanity, 2000-Present |`
   `* Senior Class President, 1999 |`
   `* Member, Intramural Soccer Team, 1997-1999`
5. Type this REFERENCES entry: `Available upon request.`
6. Save the resume as a text-only file.

```
ALLEN P. HUNTER

     10234 Wood Sorrell Lane
     Burke, VA 22015
     Phone: 703-555-4902
     E-mail: aphunter@netlink.net

OBJECTIVE

     Retail management entry-level position with a midsize
     department store.

EDUCATION

     * Central Virginia Business College, Burke, Virginia,
       December 2004

     * High school diploma from Central High School, Burke,
       Virginia, May 2002

EXPERIENCE

     * COMPUTER SYSTEMS TECHNICIAN, Kramer & Kramer, Inc.
       Harrisburg, Virginia
       June 1999-Present
       Duties include reviewing, installing, and updating
       software programs used for processing legal
       documents and monitoring computer network system for
       branch offices.

     * SALESCLERK, Blanchard's Department Store
       Richmond, Virginia
       May 2000-May 2002 (part-time)
       Duties included selling sporting goods and operating
       Panasonic cash register. Assisted sales manager in
       completing monthly sales reports generated by Word
       and Excel software programs.

PERSONAL

     * Volunteer for Habitat for Humanity, 2000-Present
     * Senior Class President, 1999
     * Member, Intramural Soccer Team, 1997-1999

REFERENCES

     Available upon request.
```

Letters of Application

Goals

- Improve speed and accuracy
- Refine language arts skills in composing paragraphs
- Format letters of application

A. Type 2 times.

A. WARMUP

```
1      Prices were quickly lowered (some by as much as 50%) @  11
2  Julia's garage sale. She could see that extra sales would   24
3  not be over the 9%* she had projected to finance the prize. 36
   | 1 | 2 | 3 | 4 | 5 | 6 | 7 | 8 | 9 | 10 | 11 | 12
```

SKILLBUILDING

PRETEST → PRACTICE → POSTTEST

PRETEST
Take a 1-minute timed writing. Review your speed and errors.

B. PRETEST: Common Letter Combinations

```
4      They formed an action committee to force a motion for   11
5  a ruling on your contract case. This enabled them to comply 24
6  within the lawful time period and convey a common message.  36
   | 1 | 2 | 3 | 4 | 5 | 6 | 7 | 8 | 9 | 10 | 11 | 12
```

PRACTICE
Speed Emphasis:
If you made 2 or fewer errors on the Pretest, type each *individual* line 2 times.
Accuracy Emphasis:
If you made 3 or more errors, type each *group* of lines (as though it were a paragraph) 2 times.

C. PRACTICE: Word Beginnings

```
7  for forget formal format forces forums forked forest formed
8  per perils period perish permit person peruse perked pertly
9  com combat comedy coming commit common compel comply comets
```

D. PRACTICE: Word Endings

```
10 ing acting aiding boring buying ruling saving hiding dating
11 ble bubble dabble double enable feeble fumble tumble usable
12 ion action vision lesion nation bunion lotion motion legion
```

POSTTEST
Repeat the Pretest timed writing and compare performance.

E. POSTTEST: Common Letter Combinations

F. PROGRESSIVE PRACTICE: NUMBERS

If you are not using the GDP software, turn to page SB-11 and follow the directions for this activity.

LANGUAGE ARTS

G. Choose one of the phrases at the right; then compose a paragraph of three to four sentences on that topic.

G. COMPOSING PARAGRAPHS

13 My computer was working fine until it . . .
14 The Internet has helped me complete my class assignments by . . .
15 Several of us decided to take the cruise because . . .
16 I have several skills, but my best skill is . . . .

FORMATTING

Refer to page R-12B of the Reference Manual for additional guidance.

H. LETTERS OF APPLICATION

A letter of application is sent along with a resume to a prospective employer. Together, the letter and the resume serve to introduce a person to the organization.

The letter of application should be no longer than one page and should include (1) the job you are applying for and how you learned of the job, (2) the highlights of your enclosed resume, and (3) a request for an interview.

DOCUMENT PROCESSING

Correspondence 53-36

Personal-Business Letter in Modified-Block Style

September 15, 20-- | Ms. Kay Brewer, Personel Director | Blanchard Computer Systems | 2189 Dace Ave. | Sioux City, IA 51107 | Dear Ms. Brewer:

¶ Please consider me as an applicant for the position of Data Records Operator advertized in the September 13th edition of the Sioux City Press.

¶ In May I will graduate with an A.A. degree in Systems Office from West Iowa Business College. My enclosed resume shows that I have completed courses in Excel, Access, and Microsoft word. I also have significant experience in working on the internet. The skills I gained using these software packages and accessing the Internet will be extremely useful to your branch office in Sioux City.

¶ The position with your company is appealing to me. If you wish to interview me for the position, please call me at 402-555-7265.

Sincerely, | Arlene Jefferson | 1842 Amber Road | Wayne, Ne 68787 | Enclosure

Correspondence 53-37

Personal-Business Letter in Block Style

August 10, 20-- | Personnel Director | Arlington Communications | 2403 Sunset Lane | Arlington, TX 76015-3148 | Dear Personnel Director:
¶ Please consider me as an applicant for a position with Arlington Communications. My strengths have always been in the communication arts, as you can see on the enclosed resume, which lists a number of courses in English, speech, and communication technology. The two part-time jobs I held during the summer months at your company convinced me that Arlington Communications is the place where I want to work.
¶ If you would like to interview me for any possible openings this summer or fall, please call me at 903-555-2340. I look forward to hearing from you.
Sincerely, | Kenneth R. Diaz | 105 Royal Lane | Commerce, TX 75428 | Enclosure

Strategies for Career Success

Writing a Job Application Letter

What's the goal of the letter that accompanies your resume? The goal is to get the interview. No two letters of application are alike.

In the opening paragraph, state your purpose (for example, the position applied for, how you became aware of it).

In the middle section, sell yourself. Convince the reader that you are the best match for the job. If you respond to a job posting, match your qualifications to the job description. If you send an unsolicited letter, specify how the employer will benefit from your qualifications. Also, refer to your resume.

In the closing paragraph, show confidence in your abilities (for example, "I'm certain I can meet your needs for a . . ."). Then state a specific time you will call to schedule an interview.

YOUR TURN Obtain a job description for which you believe you are qualified. List the job requirements, and then list your qualifications that match.

Follow-Up Letters

Goals

- Type at least 39wpm/5′/5e
- Format follow-up letters

A. Type 2 times.

A. WARMUP

```
     Quite a night! All sixty senior citizens (including      11
the handicapped) really enjoyed that play. Over 3/4 of the   22
tickets were sold; most had been sold by Frank's workers.    34
|  1  |  2  |  3  |  4  |  5  |  6  |  7  |  8  |  9  |  10  |  11  |  12
```

SKILLBUILDING

B. DIAGNOSTIC PRACTICE: SYMBOLS AND PUNCTUATION

If you are not using the GDP software, turn to page SB-2 and follow the directions for this activity.

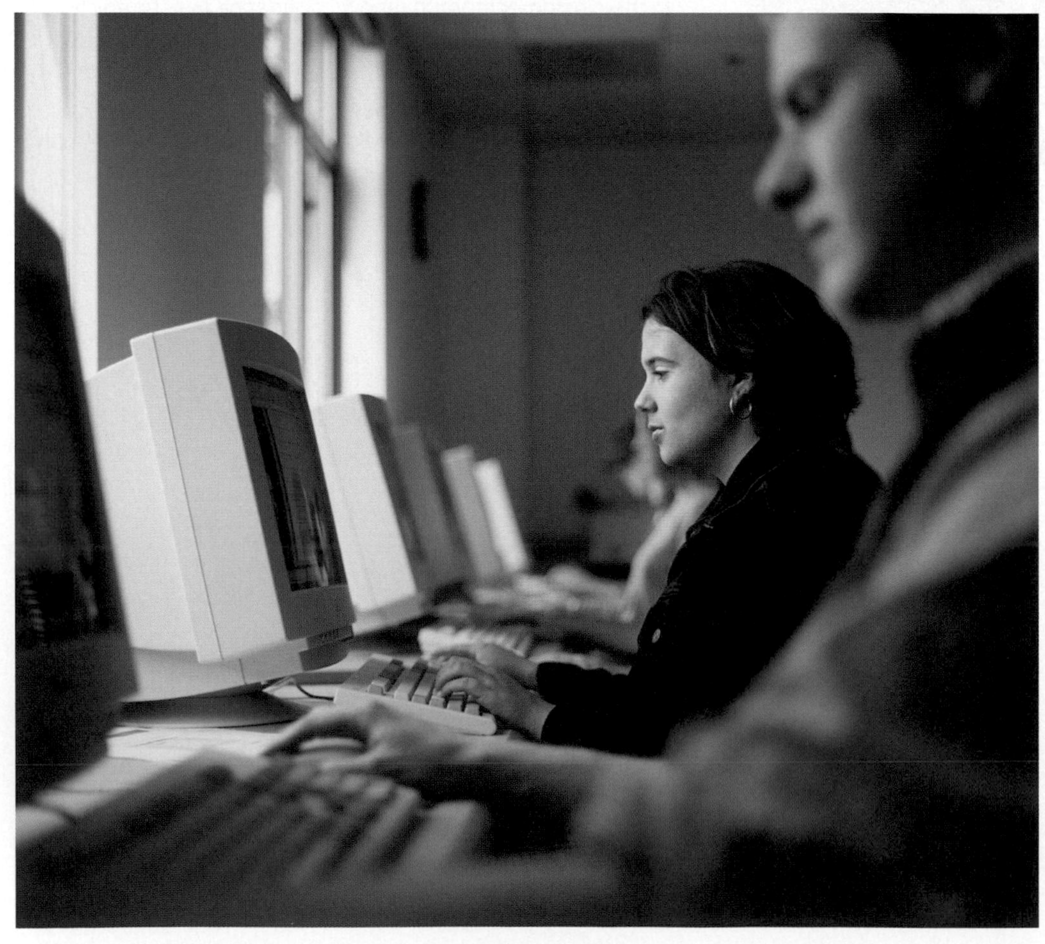

C. Take two 5-minute timed writings. Review your speed and errors.

Goal: At least 39wpm/5'/5e

C. 5-MINUTE TIMED WRITING

```
     In the past, typing was a skill that was used only by     11
those who were secretaries, students, and office workers.      23
High school students who were in school with plans for         34
going on took a typing class so that they could type their     45
work with ease and skill. Often students who wanted to be      57
hired for office jobs would make a plan to take advanced       68
courses in typing.                                              72
     As prices drop and as we have more and more advances      83
in technology of all types, people are recognizing that        94
they need keyboarding skills. From the top executive to the   106
customer service representative, everyone needs to be able    118
to use a computer keyboard. Workers in almost any kind of     130
business use their keyboarding skills to perform their        141
daily tasks.                                                   143
     Employers are looking for skilled workers who type       154
with consistent speed and accuracy. People who can type       165
documents accurately and enter data quickly are needed for    177
many types of careers. Skills in keyboarding are important    188
assets for several types of jobs.                              195
| 1 | 2 | 3 | 4 | 5 | 6 | 7 | 8 | 9 | 10 | 11 | 12
```

FORMATTING

D. FOLLOW-UP LETTERS

As soon as possible after your interview (preferably the next day), you should send a follow-up letter to the person who conducted your interview. In the letter you should:

- Use a positive tone.
- Thank the person who conducted the interview.
- Mention some specific information you learned during the interview.
- Highlight your particular strengths.
- Restate your interest in working for that organization and mention that you look forward to a favorable decision.

DOCUMENT PROCESSING

Correspondence 54-38

Personal-Business Letter in Block Style

September 12, 20-- | Ms. Carole Rothchild | Personnel Director | Arlington Communications | 2403 Sunset Lane | Arlington, TX 76015-3148 | Dear Ms. Rothchild:

¶ It was a real pleasure meeting with you yesterday and learning of the wonderful career opportunities at Arlington Communications. I enjoyed meeting all the people, especially those working in the Publications Division. Thank you for taking the time to tell me about the interesting start-up history of the company and its location in Arlington.

¶ I believe my experience and job skills match nicely with those you are seeking for a desktop publishing individual, and this position is exactly what I have been looking for. You may recall that I have had experience with all of the equipment and software that are used in your office.

¶ Please let me hear from you when you have made your decision on this position. I am very much interested in joining the professional staff at Arlington Communications.

Sincerely yours, | Kenneth R. Diaz | 105 Royal Lane | Commerce, TX 75428

Correspondence 54-39

Personal-Business Letter in Modified-Block Style

April 7, 20-- | Ms. Kay Brewer, Personnel Director | Blanchard Computer Systems | 2189 Dace Avenue | Sioux City, IA 51107 | Dear Ms. Brewer:

¶ Thanks you for the opportunity of interviewing with Blanchard computer Systems yesterday. Please express my appreciation to all of those who were involved.

¶ The interview gave me a very good feeling about the company. The positive description that you shared me with convinced me that blanchard is in deed a company at which I would like to work. I was greatly impressed with the summary of social service programs for citizens throughout the community that are sponsored by Blanchard.

(Continued on next page)

¶ You may recall that I have had experience with all of the equipment that is used. It appears to me that ^my strengths in ~~software~~ ^computer application soft ware ^and office systems would blend in well with your ~~company~~ profile.

¶ I look forward to hearing you from soon regarding you^r decision on the position of data records operator.

Sincerely, | Arlene F. Jefferson | 1842 Amber Road | Wayne, NE 68787

Correspondence 54-40

Personal-Business Letter in Modified-Block Style

Open the file for Correspondence 54-39, and make the following changes:

- Change the date of the letter to `August 7, 20--`.
- Send the letter to `Mr. William E. Takashi | Personnel Director | Hawkeye Computers, Inc. | 5604 Melrose Avenue | Sioux City, IA 51105`.
- Replace "Blanchard Computer Systems" with `Hawkeye Computers` in both the first and the second paragraphs.
- Change "yesterday" in the first paragraph to `August 5`.
- Change the complimentary closing to `Yours truly`.
- Change "data records operator" to `technology support assistant` in the final paragraph.

Strategies for Career Success

Interview Thank-You Letter

Expressing your appreciation is a very important follow-up step in your job search. Send a thank-you letter or e-mail within 24 hours after your interview.

In the opening paragraph, thank the interviewer for taking time to meet with you. Make a positive statement about the company or interview feature (for example, meeting potential coworkers).

In the middle paragraph, close the sale. Address any qualifications you neglected to mention. Turn around an interview weakness (for example, reconsider your statement that you wouldn't travel). Strengthen your relationship with the interviewer (for example, refer the interviewer to a good article on a topic in which he or she expressed interest).

In the closing paragraph, ask to be notified when the decision is made. A thank-you letter ensures that your last impression is a positive one.

YOUR TURN After your next interview, send a thank-you letter that effectively closes the sale.

Lesson 55

Integrated Employment Project

Goals

- Improve speed and accuracy
- Refine language arts skills in proofreading
- Format employment documents

A. Type 2 times.

A. WARMUP

Lex was quite pleased with his travel plans; the trip 11
to Bozeman was on Flight #578 on July 30, and the return is 23
on August 12 on Flight #643. The ticket will cost $1,090. 34
| 1 | 2 | 3 | 4 | 5 | 6 | 7 | 8 | 9 | 10 | 11 | 12

SKILLBUILDING

B. Type the columns 2 times. Press TAB to move from column to column.

B. TECHNIQUE PRACTICE: TAB

J. Barnes	P. Varanth	S. Childers	M. Christenson
F. Gilsrud	J. Benson	D. Bates	M. Jordan
B. Harringer	J. Suksi	J. Lee	P. North
V. Hill	A. Budinger	T. Gonyer	S. Kravolec

C. PACED PRACTICE

If you are not using the GDP software, turn to page SB-14 and follow the directions for this activity.

LANGUAGE ARTS

D. Edit this paragraph to correct any typing or formatting errors.

D. PROOFREADING

The Smith were please to learn from their insurance
agent that the covrage ona $50,000 life insurance policy
policy would be increased by $ 20,000 at no extra cost.

The continued to pay the same premum, not knowing that the
cash value of there original policy was being taped each
month to pay an addition premium for hte new coverage.

In this unit you have learned how to prepare a resume, an application letter, and a follow-up letter—all of which are frequently used by job applicants. You will now use these skills in preparing the documents necessary to apply for the job described in the newspaper ad illustrated below.

Desktop Publisher

NetJobs, a worldwide leader in employment and job searches, has an immediate opening for a desktop publisher. This person will work in the ad production and Web page design office.

This is an entry-level position within the Advertising Department in our San Francisco office. Applicant must have experience in using Word, FrontPage, and PageMaker. Creative ability and typing skills are a must. Candidate must be able to work in a fast-paced team environment and be highly self-motivated.

Excellent company benefits are available, and they include a comprehensive medical and dental program, disability insurance, and a credit union.

If interested, send a letter of application and resume to:

Ms. Danielle E. Rose
HRM Department
NetJobs, Inc.
9350 Kramer Avenue
San Francisco, CA 94101

NetJobs Is an Equal Opportunity Employer

Report 55-31

Resume in Traditional Style

Prepare a resume for yourself as though you are applying for the job described in the ad above. Use actual data in the resume. Assume that you have just graduated from a postsecondary program. Include school-related activities, courses you have completed, and any part-time or full-time work experience you may have acquired. Make the resume as realistic as possible, and provide as much information as you can about your background.

Correspondence 55-41

Personal-Business Letter in Block Style

Prepare an application letter to apply for the position described in the ad. Date your letter March 10. Emphasize the skills you have acquired during your years in school and while working in any part-time or full-time positions. Use Correspondence 53-37 as a guide for your letter.

Correspondence 55-42

Personal-Business Letter in Modified-Block Style

Assume that your interview was held on March 25 and that you would very much like to work for NetJobs. It is now the day after your interview. Prepare a follow-up letter expressing your positive thoughts about working for NetJobs. Use Correspondence 54-39 as a guide for your letter.

Correspondence 55-43

Personal-Business Letter in Block Style

April 15, 20-- | Mr. Blair N. Scarborough | Wyatt Insurance Agency | 2834 International Blvd. | Fort Worth, TX 76390 | Dear Mr. Scarborough:

¶ My adviser, Dr. Bonnie Allworth, mentioned to me that you have an opening for a computer specialist in your Denton office. I would like to be considered as an applicant for that position.

¶ My extensive training and experience in using various software programs are ideal for the position you have open. As a student at Texas State University, I won two national awards in computer programming competition. Also, as my enclosed resume indicates, I have completed several computer courses that uniquely qualify me for the computer specialist position at Wyatt Insurance Agency.

¶ At Texas State University I took an active leadership role as president of the local chapter of Phi Beta Lambda. In my junior year I was treasurer of my campus fraternity, and during my senior year I was elected class president. These activities have provided me with valuable leadership and teamwork skills that I hope to demonstrate at Wyatt.

¶ I am very interested in working for Wyatt Insurance Company. I will telephone your office later this week to arrange an interview with you at your convenience. If you would like to speak to me prior to that time, please telephone me at my home number, 901-555-3203, after 5 p.m. or e-mail me at pmcclean@stu.edu.

Sincerely, | Pat R. McClean | 894 Cremans Avenue | Fort Worth, TX 76384 | Enclosure

Correspondence 55-44

Personal-Business Letter in Modified-Block Style

Assume that you have interviewed for the position mentioned in the previous letter and that you would now like to send a follow-up letter dated June 15, 20--, to Mr. Blair N. Scarborough, thanking him for the interview. Use the inside address, salutation, and closing lines shown in Correspondence 55-43 to create the follow-up letter below:

Progress and Proofreading Check

Documents designated as Proofreading Checks serve as a check of your proofreading skill. Your goal is to have zero typographical errors when the GDP software first scores the document.

¶ Thank you for the time you spent with me yesterday, telling me about the computer specialist position with Wyatt. My interview with you reaffirmed my interest in working for Wyatt.

¶ I was very impressed with work done in your Information Processing Department. The hardware and software you use for writing computer code and the people working in that department are very appealing to me.

¶ I believe my particular background and skills blend perfectly with this position. I hope to hear from you by the end of next week for a positive decision on my employment. Thank you again for bringing me in for the interview.

Strategies for Career Success

Looking for a Job

Don't waste time! Start your job search early. Scan the Help Wanted section in major Sunday newspapers for job descriptions and salaries. The Internet provides electronic access to worldwide job listings. If you are interested in a particular company, access its home page.

Ask a reference librarian for handbooks (for example, *Occupational Outlook Handbook*), government publications (for example, *Federal Career Opportunities*), and journals or magazines in your field. Visit your college placement office. Sign up for interviews with companies that visit your campus.

Talk with people in your field to get advice. Look for an internship or join a professional organization in your field. Attend local chapter meetings to network with people in your chosen profession.

Taking the initiative in your job search will pay off!

YOUR TURN Visit the Internet site for the *National Business Employment Weekly* at http://www.employmentguide.com, which provides more than 45,000 national and international job listings online.

Unit 12

Skillbuilding and In-Basket Review

LESSON 56
In-Basket Review (Insurance)

LESSON 57
In-Basket Review (Hospitality)

LESSON 58
In-Basket Review (Retail)

LESSON 59
In-Basket Review (Nonprofit)

LESSON 60
In-Basket Review (Manufacturing)

MEMO TO: Blanche O. Pruitt

FROM: Kevin Hite

DATE: January 11, 20--

SUBJECT: District Meetings

As you know, each year we rotate the location of our district meetings to one of our regional offices. This year our meeting will be held in your region, preferably in Albuquerque. Would you please contact the hotels in Albuquerque and select a suitable site for this year's meeting, which will be held on March 7 and 8.

...'s meeting that this year's meeting would high... ...ically, we want to focus on the following issues:

...lesign to attract a higher percentage of the mar-...

...e procedures so that our order processing routine ...eb visitor?

...age to encourage visitors to view a greater per-...

...e arrangements for our meeting site. I look for-... ...h.

October 16, 20--

Mr. Brandon T. Wright
District Manager
206 South Rock Road
Wichita, KS 67210

Dear Mr. Wright:

Several of our service representatives have indicate... clients are becoming increasingly interested in the ... evaluating their insurance carriers. All-City has prid... service record with its policyholders, and the servic... shared this record with prospective customers. How... characteristics about All-City are also shared with t...

Please be sure that your representatives share the fo... potential customers:

- Our claims are handled quickly and with a minim...
- Our ratio of number of policies to number of com...
- No disciplinary actions have been taken against A...

Please share this information with your service repr... updated information on our services is provided on ... their policyholders' use.

Sincerely,

Ellen B. Boldt
Executive Vice President

lcm

September 15, 20--

Ms. Rolanda L. Farmer
203 Grand Avenue
Bozeman, MT 59715

Dear Ms. Farmer:

Your order for Internet service has been processed, and you can enjoy surfing the Web immediately! As a customer of Global Communications, a subsidiary of Disk Drives, Etc., you will enjoy several benefits:

1. You will receive 24/7 customer service when using our service hotline at 1-800-555-3888.
2. You will be protected by E-Protect, Global's virus protection software. This software is updated weekly, and you can download weekly updates at www.global.net.
3. You will receive 10 Mbytes of Web page space.
4. You will receive automated credit card billing, as requested.

A complete listing of all our services is enclosed for your perusal.

Thank you for joining Global Communications. Please e-mail us at support@gc.net if you have any questions, or call us on our service hotline. We expect the coming months of providing Internet service to you to be a very enjoyable experience for both of us.

Sincerely,

Nancy Mendez
Sales and Marketing Director

jrt
Enclosure

Lesson 56

In-Basket Review (Insurance)

Goals

- Type at least 40wpm/5′/5e
- Format insurance documents

A. Type 2 times.

A. WARMUP

Kyu Choi jumped at the opportunity to assume 40% of 11
the ownership of your restaurant. Alverox & Choi Chinese 22
Cuisine will be opening quite soon at 1528 Waysata Street. 34

| 1 | 2 | 3 | 4 | 5 | 6 | 7 | 8 | 9 | 10 | 11 | 12

SKILLBUILDING

B. DIAGNOSTIC PRACTICE: NUMBERS

If you are not using the GDP software, turn to page SB-5 and follow the directions for this activity.

C. Take three 12-second timed writings on each line. The scale below the last line shows your wpm speed for a 12-second timed writing.

C. 12-SECOND SPEED SPRINTS

Kay Sue is on her way to that new show to take some photos.
Most of the ones who go may not be able to make it on time.
When they got to their seats, they were glad they had come.
Both men and women might take some of their pets with them.

5 10 15 20 25 30 35 40 45 50 55 60

Keyboarding Connection

Creating an E-Mail Signature File

Creating a signature file saves you time and adds a personal touch to your e-mail messages! A signature file is a tag of information at the end of your e-mail. It may include your signature, a small graphic, your address, your phone number, or a quotation. The signature file appears on every e-mail message you send. Use the following guidelines to create a signature file.

Open your e-mail software. Open the menu item that allows you to create a signature file. Type the information you want to include in your signature file. Close the file.

YOUR TURN Create a signature file. Then address an e-mail to yourself. Type “Test” in the Subject box. In the body, type “This is a test of the signature file.” Send the e-mail. Open the test e-mail and locate your signature file at the bottom of the e-mail message.

D. Take two 5-minute timed writings. Review your speed and errors.

Goal: At least 40wpm/5′/5e

D. 5-MINUTE TIMED WRITING

When you begin to think about a career, you should 10
assess your personal abilities and interests. Do you have a 22
natural aptitude in a certain area? Do you have special 34
interests or hobbies that you would like to develop into a 45
career? Do you enjoy working with other people, or do you 57
like to work on your own? Would you like to work in a large 69
office, or do you prefer to work outdoors? These questions 81
are important to consider when you think about your career. 93
Your quest to find the perfect career will be more 103
successful if you try to maximize the opportunities that 115
are available. For example, you might consider working with 127
an organization that offers you career counseling. A career 139
counselor is trained to help you determine your aptitudes 150
and interests. You may contact people who work in a career 162
that interests you and ask to shadow them on their jobs and 174
ask them questions. You might find an online service to 185
help you find a very interesting career that will meet each 197
of your goals. 200

| 1 | 2 | 3 | 4 | 5 | 6 | 7 | 8 | 9 | 10 | 11 | 12

DOCUMENT PROCESSING

Correspondence 56-45

Business Letter in Block Style

Situation: You are employed in the office of All-City Insurance of Columbia, Missouri. Their offices are located at 17 North Eighth Street, Columbia, MO 65201-7272. All-City handles auto, home, and life insurance coverage in Iowa, Kansas, and Missouri. You work for Ellen B. Boldt, executive vice president. Ms. Boldt prefers the letter in block style and *Sincerely* as the complimentary closing. Add your reference initials as appropriate.

October 16, 20-- | Mr. Brandon T. Wright | District Manager | 206 South Rock Road | Wichita, KS 67210 | Dear Mr. Wright:

¶ Several of our service representatives have indicated on our Web site chat room that new clients are becoming increasingly interested in the criteria to consider when evaluating their insurance carriers. All-City has prided itself in years past on its reputable service record with its policyholders, and the service representatives have undoubtedly shared this record with prospective customers. However, we want to be certain that other characteristics about

(Continued on next page)

All-City are also shared with these potential policyholders.

¶ Please be sure that your representatives share the following service characteristics with potential customers:

- Our claims are handled quickly and with a minimum of "red tape."
- Our ratio of number of policies to number of complaints is the highest in the industry.
- No disciplinary actions have been taken against All-City in the past 50 years.

¶ Please share this information with your service representatives and inform them that updated information on our services is provided on our home page for their use or for their policyholders' use.

Refer to page R-12C of the Reference Manual for information on formatting lists.

Provide suitable closing lines.

Correspondence 56-46

Memo

Ms. Boldt has dictated the following memo for you to transcribe. As you can see, there are several rough-draft changes that you will have to make to the memo.

MEMO TO: Sheila Parsons, Training Director

FROM: Ellen B. Boldt, ^Executive Vice President

DATE: October 17, 20--

SUBJECT: Training seminar

¶ Our new agent training seminar will be held on December ^#10, and we plan ^again ~~this year as we have in the past~~ to conduct separate sessions for auto and life insurance policies. You will be in charge of the ~~auto~~ insurance seminars^, and Victor Samuels will conduct the life insurance seminars.

¶ I expect that this years auto insurance seminars will present our ⑥ basic coverage areas using the latest presentation demo software for the following:

(Continued on next page)

Refer to page R-12C of the Reference Manual for information on formatting lists.

- Bodily injury liability
- Medical payments or personal injury protection
- Property damage liability
- Collision
- Comprehensive
- Uninsured Motorist

We are the market leaders in bodily injury liability and property damage liability coverages. Therefore you should plan to spend at least one-half of your presentation discussing our strengths in these coverages. You might want to include in your presentation the fact that our coverages in these areas have more than surpased those of our competitors for the past 7 years or so.

¶ Use Table 1, which is enclosed, to be sure that we explain the variety of discounts offered for Iowa, Kansas, and missouri.

urs | Enclosure

Table 56-17

Boxed Table

Prepare Table 56-17 on a full sheet of paper in correct table format as an enclosure for the memo to Ms. Parsons. Press ENTER to create the 1- and 2-line column headings, as shown, before automatically adjusting the table width.

DISCOUNT PROGRAMS (For Selected States)	
Available Discounts	**Discount Amount (%)**
Air Bag	Up to 8.5
Antitheft Device	Up to 18
Claims Cost Reduction	Up to 1.8
Driving Course	Up to 4.5
Good Driver	20
Good Student	Up to 16
Mature Driver	Up to 1.8
Multipolicy	2 up to 7
Multivehicle	Up to 25
New Driver	Up to 10
Select Professionals Program	4.5 up to 14

In-Basket Review (Hospitality)

Goals

- Improve speed and accuracy
- Refine language arts skills in number expression and in the use of the hyphen
- Format hospitality documents

A. Type 2 times.

A. WARMUP

```
     Dexter gave an ultimatum: Quit driving on the lawn or   11
I will call the police. A fine of $100 (or even more) may    23
be levied against Kyle, who lives at 2469 Zaine in Joplin.   34
| 1 | 2 | 3 | 4 | 5 | 6 | 7 | 8 | 9 | 10 | 11 | 12
```

SKILLBUILDING

B. PROGRESSIVE PRACTICE: ALPHABET

If you are not using the GDP software, turn to page SB-7 and follow the directions for this activity.

C. PACED PRACTICE

If you are not using the GDP software, turn to page SB-14 and follow the directions for this activity.

LANGUAGE ARTS

D. Study the rules at the right.

D. NUMBER EXPRESSION AND HYPHENATION

RULE ▶ # word

Spell out

- **A number used as the first word of a sentence.**
  Seventy-five people attended the conference in San Diego.
- **The shorter of two adjacent numbers.**
  We have ordered 3 two-pound cakes and one 5-pound cake for the reception.
- **The words *million* and *billion* in round numbers (do not use decimals with round numbers).**
  Not: A $5.00 ticket can win $28,000,000 in this month's lottery.
  But: A $5 ticket can win $28 million in this month's lottery.
- **Fractions.**
  Almost one-half of the audience responded to the question.

Note: When fractions and the numbers twenty-one through ninety-nine are spelled out, they should be hyphenated.

(Continued on next page)

RULE - number

Hyphenate compound numbers between twenty-one and ninety-nine and fractions that are expressed as words.

Twenty-nine recommendations were approved by at least three-fourths of the members.

Edit the sentences to correct any errors in number expression.

4 Seven investors were interested in buying 2 15-unit condos.
5 The purchase price for the buildings will be $3,000,000.00 each, which is 1/2 the total.
6 The computers were mailed in 5 40-pound boxes for 2/3 of the price paid yesterday.
7 Our food chain sold hamburgers for $3.00 each last year.
8 I can sell nearly one-half of all the tickets at the gate on November 13.
9 59 parking spaces are located within 1/2 mile of the city center.
10 We must place our mailing pieces in 8 twenty-pound bags for the mail clerk.
11 I don't believe more than 1/5 of the drivers have insurance.

DOCUMENT PROCESSING

Situation: Today is August 21, and you are employed in the office of Suite Retreat, a group of vacation resorts in Naples, Florida. Your employer, the general manager, is Mr. Aaron Hynes. Mr. Hynes is attending a meeting in Miami and has left the following jobs for you to complete. Press ENTER to create the 1- and 2-line column headings as displayed before automatically adjusting the table width.

Table 57-18

Open Table

SUITE RETREAT PROPERTIES
Selected Beach Rentals

Property	Rooms	Rental Rate In Season	Rental Rate Off Season
Carriage House	4	$3,500	$2,400
Naples Hideaway	5	2,750	2,100
Ocean Breeze	5	3,850	2,700
Princeton Palace	4	3,200	2,550
Seville Landings	6	4,250	3,100
The Vanderbilt	5	3,475	2,575
Westover Estates	6	5,250	4,150

Correspondence 57-47

Business Letter in Modified-Block Style

August 21, 20-- | Mr. Leland Mott | 243 Worth Street | Raleigh, NC 27603 | Dear Mr. Mott:

¶ We were pleased to hear of your interest in renting one of our prime beach units in Naples, Florida. I have enclosed a listing of all our current properties in the Naples area. We have 14 two-bedroom rentals, 15 three-bedroom rentals, and 11 four-bedroom rentals. Five of our three-bedroom units have already been rented for this season; one-half of the other thirty-four units are still available.

word

word

≡ number

¶ Let me review a few of the particulars of each unit with you. Our Carriage House and Naples Hideaway have Gulf Coast views and garage facilities. The Ocean Breeze and Princeton have lake views and tennis courts. The Seville, Vanderbilt, and Westover have a Gulf Coast view and a private golf course.

¶ If you plan to rent one of our units, please be sure to notify us by writing or by calling our toll-free number at 1-800-555-1348.

Sincerely, | Aaron Hynes | General Manager | urs | Enclosure | c: Theresa McDonald, Celeste Binghamton

Keyboarding Connection

Finding Business Information on the Internet

To begin research on a business-related topic, try one of the following sites:

Business Resources on the Web at www.cio.com/bookmark provides links to Cable News Network (CNN) Business News, the Wall Street Journal Money and Investing Update, and other news sources. It includes information about careers, Electronic Data Interchange (EDI) and the Internet, general business sources, training, marketing, and resources for entrepreneurs.

Business Administration Internet Resources at www.acad.sunytccc.edu/library/busman.htm provides links to news and financial market updates, the Securities and Exchange Commission (SEC), Thomas Register, U.S. Census Bureau, U.S. Economic and Labor Statistics, and World Bank reports.

Selected Business Resources on the Web at www.bls.gov provides information about marketing, finance, small business, business law, international business, stock markets, and a link to the Small Business Administration.

YOUR TURN Access one of the business information sites listed above and explore its offerings.

Mr. Hynes has recently purchased a fishing resort on Lake Okeechobee, Florida, and plans to open it on September 1. Type the following report and send it to the *Naples Press* so that it will appear in this Sunday's special *Travel and Tourism* section. Use a standard business format to prepare the report.

Report 57-32

Business Report

FISHING PARADISE SCHEDULED TO OPEN | Suite Retreat | Naples, Florida

¶ Suite Retreat is celebrating the grand opening of its newest fishing resort, Kamp Kellogg, located on the northwest corner of Lake Okeechobee, on the banks of the Kissimmee River.

GENERAL INFORMATION

¶ The following information will give you an overview of our policies and accommodations:

¶ **Reservations**. The reservation desk will open on September 1 to reserve your cabin at our beautiful resort. You can reach reservations via the Internet by logging on to our Web site at http://www.kampkellogg.com.

¶ **Accommodations.** Whether you're looking for deluxe accommodations or rustic surroundings, Kamp Kellogg has it all. You have a choice of rustic cabins nestled in the woods or large chalets overlooking Lake Okeechobee.
If you enjoy an evening of relaxation, each cabin includes a gazebo, out near the water's edge, that is screened in for a perfect evening of comfort.

¶ **Amenities.** Your lodging choice includes full kitchens for those who want to do their own cooking, or you can order a full meal through our catering service. Each unit has a game room with a large-screen television, VCR, videotapes, and computer workstation with Internet connection. Outside the sliding glass door is a covered deck, equipped with a barbecue grill and hot tub.

LAKE OKEECHOBEE

¶ Lake Okeechobee lies geographically in the center of the state of Florida. The name "Okeechobee" was given to the lake by the Seminole Indians, and it means "big water." Lake Okeechobee is the largest freshwater lake in the United States occurring in one state. It is approximately 37 miles long and 30 miles wide, with an average depth of almost 10 feet. The lake produces more bass over 8 pounds than any other lake in the United States. It is famous for bass, crappie, and bluegill fishing. Several species of wildlife also thrive around the lake, such as the bald eagle, blue heron, egret, white ibis, sand hill crane, turkey, vulture, owl, alligator, bobcat, turkey, and panther.

Refer to page R-12C of the Reference Manual for information on formatting lists.

PRICING INFORMATION

¶ We are offering a special introductory rate of $250 through November 1. This rate includes the following:

- Two-night stay for a family of four (# word)
- Two half days of fishing (# word)
- One USCG-licensed fishing guide (# word)
- Tackle and bait

¶ A full refund will be made if the fishing excursion is canceled because of inclement weather or failure of equipment (boat, trailer, or vehicle). If only a partial day of fishing is completed, one-half of the charges will be refunded. (- number)

Lesson 58

In-Basket Review (Retail)

Goals

- Type at least 40wpm/5′/5e
- Format retail documents

A. Type 2 times.

A. WARMUP

```
1      Do you think 1/3 of the contents of the five quart-     11
2  sized boxes would be about right? I do! If not, they can    22
3  adjust the portions by adding 6 or 7 gallons of warm water. 34
   | 1 | 2 | 3 | 4 | 5 | 6 | 7 | 8 | 9 | 10 | 11 | 12
```

SKILLBUILDING

B. DIAGNOSTIC PRACTICE: SYMBOLS AND PUNCTUATION

If you are not using the GDP software, turn to page SB-2 and follow the directions for this activity.

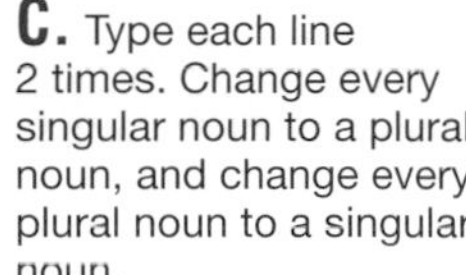

C. Type each line 2 times. Change every singular noun to a plural noun, and change every plural noun to a singular noun.

C. TECHNIQUE PRACTICE: CONCENTRATION

```
4  Debit the accounts. Balance your checkbook. Add the assets.
5  Take the discount. Send the statements. Compute the ratios.
6  Review the accounts. Credit the amounts. Figure the totals.
7  Prepare the statements. Send the catalog. Call the clients.
```

D. Take two 5-minute timed writings. Review your speed and errors.

Goal: At least 40wpm/5'/5e

D. 5-MINUTE TIMED WRITING

Most workers will learn about their success on the job 11
at least once a year. The person in charge will be the one 23
to conduct these reviews. Even though the job review is 34
important, either party might not look forward to such a 46
meeting. Frequently, an employee and a boss can view these 57
meetings as a time to discuss everything that this person 69
has done wrong in the last year. Such a negative approach 81
can add a lot of stress and tension between the employee 92
and management. In the long run, work performance suffers. 104
A good manager must learn a new way to conduct more 114
positive job reviews. Such a meeting might start by sizing 126
up what the employee has done to help improve things in the 138
past year. Positive comments may include coming to work on 150
time, working well with others, and being willing to pitch 162
in whenever needed. Next, the areas for improvement may be 174
discussed. Then the employee should be given the chance to 185
ask questions, write a response to the appraisal, and get 197
other feedback. 200

| 1 | 2 | 3 | 4 | 5 | 6 | 7 | 8 | 9 | 10 | 11 | 12

DOCUMENT PROCESSING

Situation: You are employed as an administrative assistant for Good Sports, a retailer for sports equipment and clothing in Denver, Colorado. Your employer is Mr. Kevin Hite, marketing director for Good Sports. Upon arriving at your office on Monday morning, you notice that Mr. Hite has left several jobs that need to be completed for his signature. He prefers a letter in block style in his correspondence and uses *Sincerely* as the complimentary closing.

Correspondence 58-48

Business Letter in Block Style

January 10, 20-- | Mr. Alex R. Chaney, Principal | Madison Heights High School | 1839 East Colfax Avenue | Denver, CO 80212 | Dear Mr. Chaney:

¶ Thank you for your invitation to advertise on your school's Web site. We were delighted to have the opportunity to sponsor last week's Marathon Mile at Madison Heights High School and hope that all the participants enjoyed the competition and spectator activities.

¶ This week my office staff will be putting together a Web page that we would like to display on the Web space you have so generously provided. It is my understanding that the Web site will remain online throughout this school year. We will be certain to maintain it on a regular basis so that our products and prices always remain current.

(Continued on next page)

Add the closing lines to Mr. Hite's letter. Send copies of this letter to Ardele Stevens, Jennifer Smits, and Randall Campbellton.

¶ The Marathon Mile has certainly become one of the county's most popular school events. We look forward to the opportunity of cosponsoring next year's Marathon Mile at Madison Heights.

Correspondence 58-49

Memo

MEMO TO: Blanche O. Pruitt | **FROM:** Kevin Hite | **DATE:** January 11, 20-- | **SUBJECT:** District Meetings

¶ As you know, each year we rotate the location of our district meetings to one of our regional offices. This year our meeting will be held in your region, preferably in Albuquerque. Would you please contact the hotels in Albuquerque and select a suitable site for this year's meeting, which will be held on March 7 and 8.

¶ We decided at our last regional managers' meeting that this year's meeting would highlight our Internet sales campaign. Specifically, we want to focus on the following issues:

Reference Manual

Refer to page R-12C of the Reference Manual for information on formatting lists.

1. How can we improve our Web page design to attract a higher percentage of the market?
2. How can we improve our e-commerce procedures so that our order-processing routine is easier and faster for the average Web visitor?
3. What links can we add to our home page to encourage visitors to view a greater percentage of our product line?

¶ Please let me know when you have made arrangements for our meeting site. I look forward to meeting with all of you in March. | urs

Table 58-19

Boxed Table

WEEKLY BICYCLE SPECIALS
January 13, 20--

Model	**Price**	**Special Features**
Comanche	$270	15" Y-frame; 18-speed drivetrain; adjustable seat
Cyclone	375	Our lightest bike; preassembled; wired blue color
Duster	480	Front suspension fork; semislick tires; 24-speed
Trail Blazer	725	Titanium frame; aluminum seat post; two bottle mounts

Lesson 59

In-Basket Review (Nonprofit)

Goals

- Improve speed and accuracy
- Refine language arts skills in spelling
- Format government documents

A. Type 2 times.

A. WARMUP

Crowne and Metzner, Inc., employees* joined with 68 11
youngsters to repair the brick homes of 13 elderly persons; 23
several became very well acquainted with six of the owners. 35
| 1 | 2 | 3 | 4 | 5 | 6 | 7 | 8 | 9 | 10 | 11 | 12

SKILLBUILDING

B. MAP

Follow the GDP software directions for this exercise in improving keystroking accuracy.

C. Take a 1-minute timed writing on the first paragraph to establish your base speed. Then take four 1-minute timed writings on the remaining paragraphs. As soon as you equal or exceed your base speed on one paragraph, advance to the next, more difficult paragraph.

C. SUSTAINED PRACTICE: PUNCTUATION

The men in the warehouse were having a very difficult 11
time keeping track of that inventory. Things began to go 22
much more smoothly for them when they got the new computer. 34

Whenever something was shipped out, a computer entry 11
was made to show the changes. They always knew exactly what 23
merchandise was in stock; they also knew what to order. 34

Management was pleased with that improvement. "We 10
should have made the change years ago," said the supervisor 22
to the plant manager, who was in full agreement with him. 34

This is just one example (among many) of how the work 11
areas can be improved. Workers' suggestions are listened 22
to by alert, expert managers. Their jobs are better, too. 34
| 1 | 2 | 3 | 4 | 5 | 6 | 7 | 8 | 9 | 10 | 11 | 12

LANGUAGE ARTS

D. Type this list of frequently misspelled words, paying special attention to any spelling problems in each word.

D. SPELLING

```
development determine enclosed complete members recent site
permanent personal facility medical library however purpose
representative implementation electrical discussed eligible
organization performance minimum discuss expense areas next
professional arrangements separate changes reason field pay
```

Edit the sentences to correct any misspellings.

```
Members of the medicle and profesional group discussed it.
The development of the seperate cite will be completed.
A recent representive said the libary facility may be next.
A perpose of the electricle organization is to get changes.
However, the implimentation of changes will be permenant.
Arrangments for the enclosed eligable expenses are listed.
| 1 | 2 | 3 | 4 | 5 | 6 | 7 | 8 | 9 | 10 | 11 | 12
```

DOCUMENT PROCESSING

Situation: Today is October 10. You work for Quick Trip, a ride-share company located in Windsor, Connecticut.

Your company is a nonprofit commuter company that provides the following services: move people to and from work, conduct parking studies, match people with available rides, and publish a commuter ride-share weekly report.

Your job responsibilities include preparing reports that summarize weekly commuter news, typing correspondence to advertise and promote Quick Trip's services, and communicating with area commuters who subscribe to Quick Trip's services.

Today, you must (1) prepare a report that summarizes services offered by Quick Trip, and (2) create a table that lists new additions to the weekly report.

Report 59-33

Business Report

QUICK TRIP

Windsor's Premier Ride-Share

¶ If you're tired of driving that one- to two-hour commute into Connecticut's busy metropolitan areas, then let us take that burden ~~on for you.~~ off your shoulders. Quick Trip, the metro's premier ride-share company, is a convenient, economical way to get to & from work. All you have to do is get on board!

(Continued on next page)

Costs of Commuting

¶ A recent article showed that commuting just 15 miles each way can cost a minimum of 1,200 per year; sharing the ride with some one else can cut your comuting expenses in half.[1] In addition to the cost of gas, you must also figure in other costs of transportation such as maintenance on your vehicle, insurance premiums, depreciation, and finance charges.[2] When you consider all these costs, ride-sharing takes on a whole new significance. You should also consider how you are helping the trafic congestion and air pollution problems by ride-sharing. And don't forget about the possibility of being involved in an accident. Finally you can reduce stress by ride-sharing because you can choose to leave the driving to someone else.

RESERVATIONS AND BENEFITS

¶ If you want to reserve a seat on a Quick Trip route, just call one of our professional service representatives at 1-800-555-Trip. Our representatives in the field have information on routes, schedules, rides availability, and other benefits. For example, we have an E-ride available for you if there is an emergency that requires you to get home. Here are some special benefits with Quick Trip:

Reference Manual

Refer to page R-12C of the Reference Manual for information on formatting lists.

- A free commute for every 500 comuting miles.
- Separate insurance and medical coverage.
- Flexible payment policies.
- A free commute for every 500 commuting miles.
- Full insurance coverage.
- Flexible payment policies.
- 4 free taxi rides home per year in the event of illness or personal emergency.

SERVICE AREAS

¶ Quick Trip serves the cities of Plainville, Rocky Hill, Manchester, Windsor, New Haven, and Sufield. Next month we open routes to Avon, Glastonbury,

(Continued on next page)

Durham, and Middletown. In all, we have over 300 regular routes state wide, and service is expanding monthly. Easy access is guaranteed with all our routes. To view our entire service area, go to our web site, http://www.qt.com, and link to the Quick Trip regional service map area. The map details all our routes, highlights specific pickup points, and identifies our regional service facilities. Visit our site today and become a ride-share enthusiast!

---

[1] Erica Sommers, "Ride-Sharing for the Environment," *Environmental Planning*, February 21, 2004, p. 18.

[2] Joshua R. Blake, *Cleaning Up America*, New Haven Publishing, Manchester, Connecticut, 2005, p. 138.

Table 59-20

Boxed Table

QUICK TRIP COMMUTER BULLETIN
For October

From	To	Name	Telephone
Manchester	Rocky Hill	S. Baskin	860-555-5581
Manchester	Windsor	E. Lindholm	203-555-4684
Manchester	Suffield	P. Mack	860-555-4322
New Haven	Plainville	T. Thompson	203-555-1249
Rocky Hill	Windsor	J. Kiczuk	860-555-1842
Suffield	Manchester	M. Duprey	203-555-9339
Suffield	New Haven	B. Huehner	203-555-0442
Suffield	New Haven	M. Mac	203-555-1844
Windsor	Manchester	L. Smith	203-555-8893
Windsor	Rocky Hill	R. McCaffrey	203-555-7782

In-Basket Review (Manufacturing)

Goals

- Type at least 40wpm/5′/5e
- Format manufacturing documents

A. Type 2 times.

A. WARMUP

"Fay's #6 report shows 26 pens @ .49 each and 37 pens 11
@ .79 each," the CEO announced. Mrs. Bailey's reaction was 23
quite amazing as 80 jobs were validated with checked boxes. 35
| 1 | 2 | 3 | 4 | 5 | 6 | 7 | 8 | 9 | 10 | 11 | 12

SKILLBUILDING

PPP PRETEST → PRACTICE → POSTTEST

PRETEST
Take a 1-minute timed writing. Review your speed and errors.

B. PRETEST: Close Reaches

Sally took the coins from the pocket of her blouse 10
and traded them for seventy different coins. Anyone could 22
see that Myrtle looked funny when extra coins were traded. 34
| 1 | 2 | 3 | 4 | 5 | 6 | 7 | 8 | 9 | 10 | 11 | 12

PRACTICE
Speed Emphasis:
If you made 2 or fewer errors on the Pretest, type each *individual* line 2 times.
Accuracy Emphasis:
If you made 3 or more errors, type each *group* of lines (as though it were a paragraph) 2 times.

C. PRACTICE: Adjacent Keys

as asked asset based basis class least visas ease fast mass
we weary wedge weigh towel jewel fewer dwell wear weed week
rt birth dirty earth heart north alert worth dart port tort

D. PRACTICE: Consecutive Fingers

sw swamp swift swoop sweet swear swank swirl swap sway swim
gr grade grace angry agree group gross gripe grow gram grab
ol older olive solid extol spool fools stole bolt cold cool

POSTTEST
Repeat the Pretest timed writing and compare performance.

E. POSTTEST: Close Reaches

F. Take two 5-minute timed writings. Review your speed and errors.

Goal: At least 40wpm/5'/5e

F. 5-MINUTE TIMED WRITING

```
     Information technology is among the fastest-growing       11
job fields today and is also one of the fields to change       22
the quickest. The goal of many schools is to try to prepare    34
students to be specialists in a workplace that continues to    46
be challenging and will need to change quickly as advances     58
are made in technology.                                        63
     Those who wish to work in a field that will not stand     74
still need to know all about the systems with which they       85
labor. Network administrators, for example, will often take    97
courses to certify that they have a sound knowledge of any    109
of the new hardware. They must also learn about specific      120
equipment and have an understanding of how new software       131
will function with hardware.                                  137
     Those who wish to pass certification exams must have     148
the zeal, determination, and drive to complete all of the     160
requirements. They know that it will not be long before the   172
current systems will be upgraded or new software will be      183
released. They need to learn the latest systems and review    195
their certification again.                                    200
| 1 | 2 | 3 | 4 | 5 | 6 | 7 | 8 | 9 | 10 | 11 | 12
```

DOCUMENT PROCESSING

Situation: You are an administrative assistant, and you work for Disk Drives, Etc., in Phoenix, Arizona. Your supervisor is Ms. Nancy Mendez, sales and marketing director. Ms. Mendez has asked you to prepare the following documents for her while she is in a staff meeting this morning. The letter is to be prepared for her signature, the table will be enclosed with the letter, and she will initial the memo before sending it out this afternoon.

Correspondence 60-50

Business Letter in Block Style

September 13, 20-- | Ms. Nancy Luo | 1387 Rim Drive | Flagstaff, AZ 86001-3111 | Dear Ms. Luo:

¶ We were pleased to see that you have used our Web site at www.tosabi.com to inquire about our online catalog. We specialize in computer drives of all types: CD-ROM, DVD, Zip, Jaz, floppy, and hard drives. I have enclosed a listing of our most popular CD-ROM writers that will appear online next week in our catalog. As a new customer, you are invited to visit our catalog and place your order at these special prices.

(Continued on next page)

¶ Our online customers receive the same privileges as our hard-copy catalog shoppers. These online privileges include:

- No shipping charges.
- Toll-free customer support line.
- Discounts on 10 or more purchases.
- Ninety-day warranties (parts and labor) on all purchases.

¶ We look forward to many years of doing business with you. Please e-mail me at nmendez@tosabi.net if you have any questions or would like additional information.
Sincerely, | Nancy Mendez | Sales and Marketing Director | urs | Enclosure | c: S. Choi, W. Matson

Table 60-21
Boxed Table

Your finished table will have different line endings for Column D when you resize the column widths to fit the contents.

CD-ROM WRITERS (Effective Dates September 18-23)			
Model No.	**Part No.**	**Price**	**Specifications**
460RW	841120	$199	4x speed write, 16x speed read, CD recording software
2600E	841111	235	4x speed write, 24x speed read, 4x speed rewrite, stores up to 650 MB per disk
9282E	841415	415	Rewritable. 4x speed write, 8x speed read, Direct CD software
8428S	842013	595	Rewritable. 8x speed write, 24x speed read, 2x speed erase, Direct CD software
93422R	841712	658	Rewritable. 4x speed write, 6x speed read, 2x speed rewrite, Direct CD software, CDR-DJ

Correspondence 60-51
Memo

MEMO TO: Claudia Crenshaw | Publications Department | **FROM:** Nancy Mendez | Sales and Marketing Director | **DATE:** September 13, 20-- | **SUBJECT:** Ad in the *Arizona Daily Sun*
¶ Claudia, please include the following criteria in our ad that will run in the *Arizona Daily Sun* this Sunday:

1. Quarter-page ad
2. Run-time: 2 weeks
3. Location: Business Section as well as Classified Section
4. Contact: Include telephone, fax, and e-mail numbers

¶ This is our first ad piece in the *Sun* since we ran that special promotion last March. Let's add some graphics to make this one an "eye-catcher." | urs

Correspondence 60-52

Business Letter in Modified-Block Style

Reference Manual

Refer to page R-12C of the Reference Manual for information on formatting lists.

September 15, 20-- | Ms. Rolanda L. Farmer | 203 Grand Avenue | Bozeman, MT 59715 | Dear Ms. Farmer:

¶ Your order for Internet service has been processed, and you can enjoy surfing the Web immediately! As a customer of Global Communications, a subsidiary of Disk Drives, Etc., you will enjoy several benefits:

1. You will receive 24/7 customer service when using our service hotline at 1-800-555-3888.
2. You will be protected by E-Protect, Global's virus protection software. This software is updated weekly, and you can download weekly updates at www.gc.net.
3. You will receive 10 Mbytes of Web page space.
4. You will receive automated credit card billing, as requested.

¶ A complete listing of all our services is enclosed for your perusal.

¶ Thank you for joining Global Communications. Please e-mail us at support@gc.net if you have any questions, or call us on our service hotline. We expect the coming months of providing Internet service to you to be a very enjoyable experience for both of us.

Sincerely, | Nancy Mendez | Sales and Marketing Director | urs | Enclosure

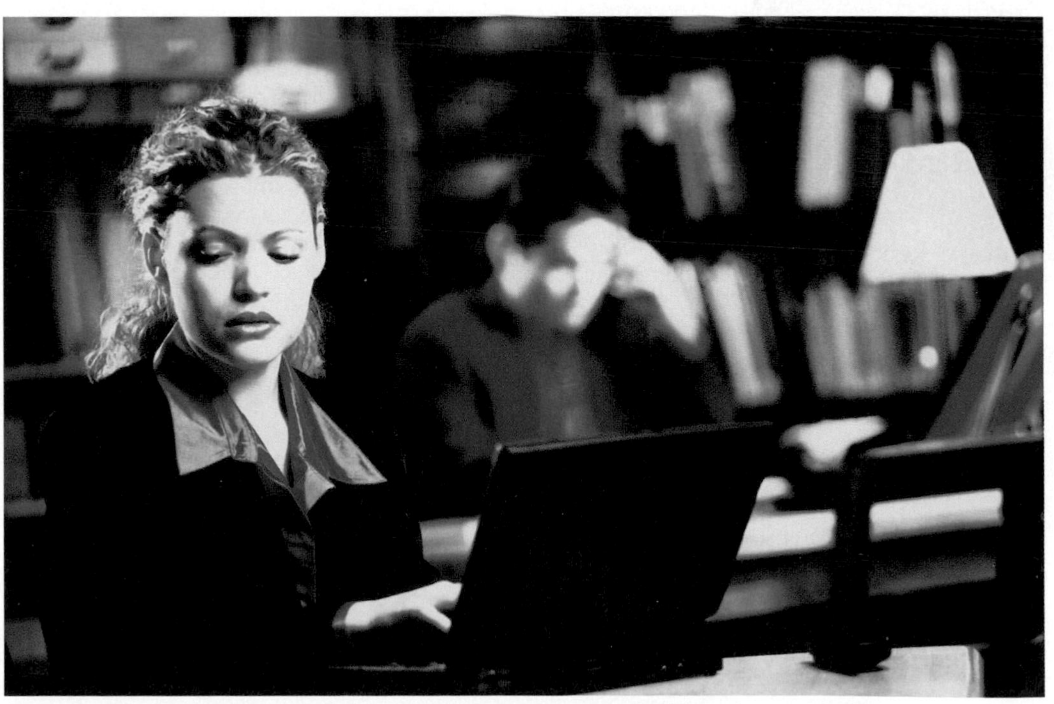

Table 60-22

Boxed Table

Progress and Proofreading Check

Documents designated as Proofreading Checks serve as a check of your proofreading skill. Your goal is to have zero typographical errors when the GDP software first scores the document.

Your finished table will have different line endings for all columns when you resize the column widths to fit the contents.

CUSTOMER SERVICES (Effective October 1, 20--)		
Service	**Description/Comments**	**Representative**
24/7 Service	Call 1-800-555-3888; wait time is usually less than 1 minute.	M. R. Osumi, mrosumi@global.net
Virus-Protection Service	E-Protect software is downloaded automatically to your computer when service is installed.	W. N. Gauthier, wngauth@global.net
Web Space	10 MB of Web page space is standard; an additional 10 MB can be obtained on an as-needed basis.	M. J. Martinez, mjmartinez@global.net
Credit Card Billing	When requested by the customer, we automatically send your monthly bill to a credit card of your choice.	L. T. Matthews, ltmatt@global.net

Strategies for Career Success

Successful Interviewing Techniques

The interview is a useful tool for researching information. Here are some steps to effective interviewing.

Conduct preliminary research so you can ask intelligent questions and make efficient use of the interview time. Prepare a list of questions (for example, an interview script) to use in the interview. Make sure the questions are open-ended, unbiased, and geared toward gathering insights you can't gain through reading. Be prepared to take notes, listen actively, and ask follow-up questions, as needed.

Greet the interviewee by name and thank him or her for taking time to talk with you. Explain why you are interested in interviewing him or her. Stay within the scheduled time limits. In closing the interview, thank the interviewee again, and ask if you can get in touch if other questions come to mind.

YOUR TURN Prepare a list of questions you might use in interviewing someone concerning the current U.S. immigration policies.

Skills Assessment on Part 3

5-Minute Timed Writing

People are often the most prized assets in a business. 11
Excellent firms know that having well-qualified workers is 23
an important step to ensure the success of the company. The 35
people in charge can play a huge part in how much success a 47
firm will have when they provide a workplace that is meant 59
to support teams of people who can work together to achieve 71
a common goal. When people know they are being encouraged 82
to work toward achieving their own goals as well as the 94
goals of the company, they will respond by working to their 106
highest potential with ardor and zeal. 113
Managers need to show that they value the hard work 124
and long hours that employees put in to ensure the success 136
of the business. People thrive on compliments that show 147
their work is appreciated. They like to be rewarded in some 159
way when they have done an exceptional job. When those in 171
charge are successful in motivating the employees to work 182
to their full potential, their company will prosper. The 194
result is that each person wins. 200

| 1 | 2 | 3 | 4 | 5 | 6 | 7 | 8 | 9 | 10 | 11 | 12

Correspondence Test 3-53

Business Letter in Block Style

Add an envelope to the letter, and omit the return address.

July 13, 20-- | Mr. Anthony Gillespie | Goddard Properties | 1808 Augusta Court | Lexington, KY 40505-2838 | Dear Mr. Gillespie:

¶ Let me introduce myself. I am committee chair of a group that monitors development projects in Lexington, Kentucky. It was brought to my attention that your proposal to construct 100 three- and four-bedroom homes was approved by the city council last night. As a resident in a neighboring community, I wish to share with you the stipulations

(Continued on next page)

we would like you to incorporate into your development project:

- The new homes should have no less than 2,700 square feet of living space.
- All structures should have brick frontage.
- No external, unattached buildings should be constructed.

¶ Following these stipulations will ensure that your homes adhere to our community building codes. Sincerely, | Dora H. Hayes | Committee Chair | urs | c: S. Benefield, T. Grace

Correspondence Test 3-54

Memo

MEMO TO: Ana Pacheco
FROM: Liang Quan
DATE: June 26, 20--
SUBJECT: Desktop Publishing Certificate

¶ Our DTP certificate seminar will be held in St. Louis on August 14. Upon request of last year's participants, we want to be sure to include the following topics:

- Integrated Computer Applications
- Advanced Desktop Publishing
- Introduction to Computer Graphics
- Graphic Design A and B

¶ These were the four most popular topics at last year's seminar. Let's use a brochure design similar to the one we used at the Denver meeting last year. A copy of that brochure is attached for you to review. | urs | Attachment

Report Test 3-34

Business Report

AIR POLLUTION

¶ When we hear about pollution, we tend to think of smog, traffic congestion, acid rain, and other pollutant-related terms. However, we also need to consider the air we breathe as we work.

AIR QUALITY AND POLLUTANTS

¶ We need to be concerned about indoor air because it can affect the health, comfort, and productivity of workers.[1]

¶ **Strategies to Improve Air Quality.** The three basic approaches to improving air quality include the use of air pressure to keep the pollutants "at bay," the use of ventilation systems to remove the pollutants, and the use of filters to clean the air. The pollutants can appear in various forms but are typically biological contaminants, chemical pollutants, or particles.

¶ **Pollutant Descriptions.** Biological contaminants can include viruses, molds, bacteria, dust mites, pollen, and water spills. These contaminants cause allergic reactions that trigger asthma attacks for an estimated 16 million Americans.[2] Chemical pollutants include tobacco smoke and accidental chemical spills. Particles include such pollutants as dust and dirt from drywall, carpets, copying machines, and printing operations.[3]

MANAGERS' RESPONSIBILITIES

¶ Office managers should help by reviewing records pertaining to air conditioning and ventilation systems. They should also provide training sessions for employees to learn about maintaining clean air. Finally, they should keep a record of reported health complaints related to polluted air and aid in resolving these complaints.

AIR QUALITY IS A TEAM EFFORT

¶ All workers can have a positive impact on improving the quality of the air they breathe. For example, simply making sure that air vents and grilles are not blocked will help improve the quality of air. People who smoke should do so only in areas designated as smoking areas for employees.

---

[1] Karen Scheid, "Pollution at Work," *Los Angeles Times*, May 4, 2004, p. C8.

[2] "Dirty Air in Today's Offices," March 12, 2004, <http://www.airamerica.com/dirty.htm>, accessed on May 13, 2004.

[3] Carlos Sanchez, *Pollutants in America*, Southwest Press, Albuquerque, 2003.

Part 4

Advanced Formatting

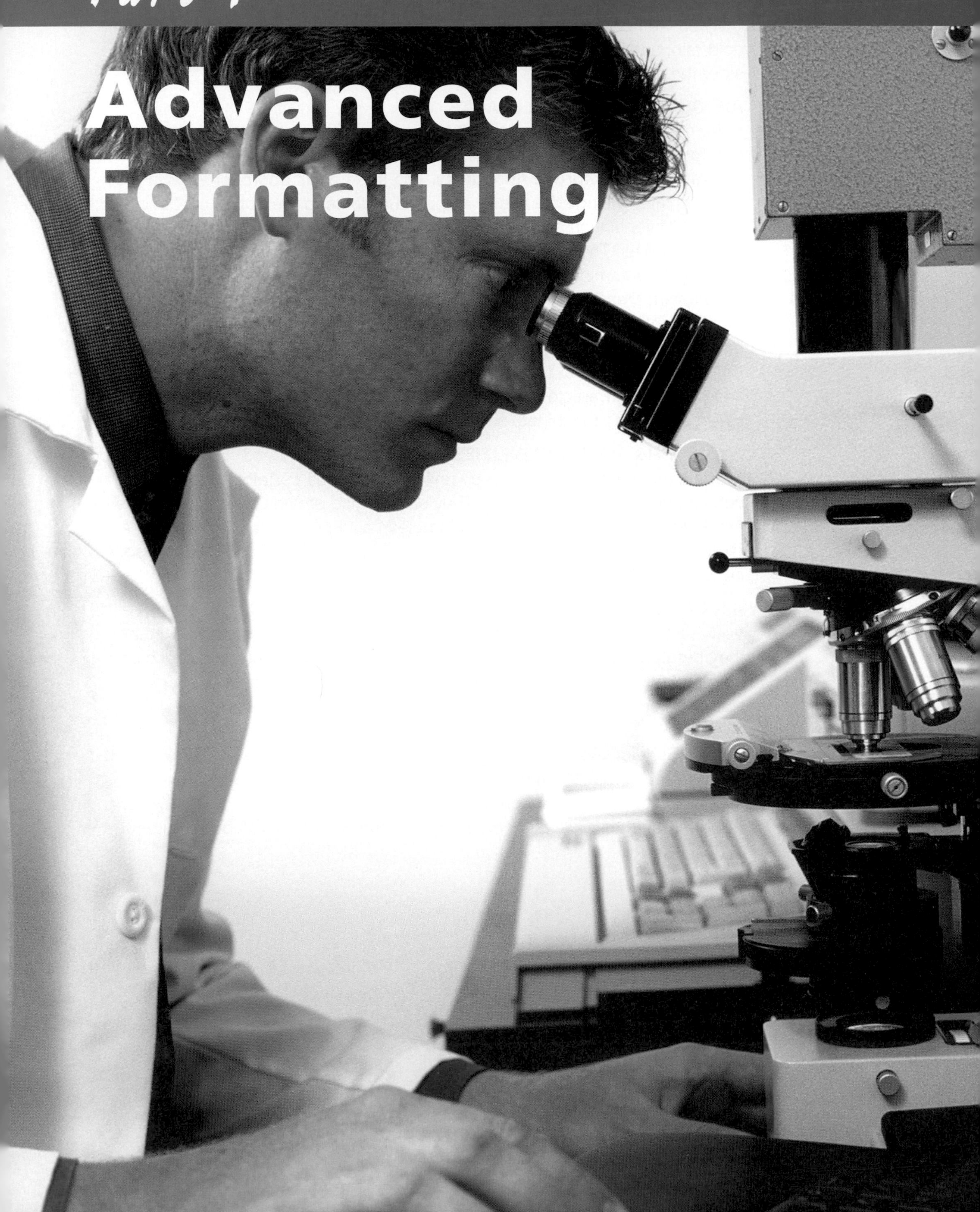

Keyboarding in Health Services

Within the health services job cluster, there is an enormous range of job opportunities in the medical and health care industry. Hundreds of different occupations exist in health care practice, including business-oriented positions. In fact, career opportunities within this cluster are among the fastest growing in the national marketplace. The current job outlook is quite positive because the growth in managed care has significantly increased opportunities for doctors and other health professionals, particularly in the area of preventive care. In addition, the aging population requires more highly skilled medical workers.

Opportunities in Health Careers

Consider health care jobs, medical careers, health care management, and medical management. Various job possibilities exist in these areas, and work as a medical transcriber, clinical technician, nurse, medical analyst, surgical technician or surgeon, physical therapist, orderly, pharmacist, or medical researcher can most likely be easily found. Interestingly, keyboarding skill is important for all of these positions.

Objectives

KEYBOARDING

- Type at least 43 words per minute on a 5-minute timed writing with no more than 5 errors.

LANGUAGE ARTS

- Refine proofreading skills and correctly use proofreaders' marks.
- Use capitals, punctuation, and grammar correctly.
- Improve composing and spelling skills.
- Recognize subject/verb agreement.

WORD PROCESSING

- Use the word processing commands necessary to complete the document processing activities.

DOCUMENT PROCESSING

- Format reports, multipage letters, multipage memos, and tables.

TECHNICAL

- Answer at least 90 percent of the questions correctly on an objective test.

Unit 13

Skill Refinement

LESSON 61
Skillbuilding and Report Review

LESSON 62
Skillbuilding and Letter Review

LESSON 63
Skillbuilding, Memo, and E-Mail Review

LESSON 64
Skillbuilding and Table Review

LESSON 65
Skillbuilding and Employment Document Review

LEADERSHIP SKILLS NEEDED IN BUSINESS

Sally Rodriguez

Leadership skills are needed now more than ever in business and industry if our nation is to maintain a leading role in the business world of tomorrow. With the advent of a common European community without boundaries, the Asian influence throughout the world, and the development of a common North American business community, we must have leaders with vision and the appropriate skills for meeting the challenges of the new, very technical century.

Each of the new skills that a successful leader needs is discussed in the following pages.

LEADERSHIP

Leadership has been defined in a variety of

of an individual when he or she is directing the acti

goal.î[1]

A successful leader is one who is committed

and services, for improving the firmís market positi

her employees. A leader possesses a value system t

Leaders who make decisions affecting the firm, em

beliefs that influence decision making.

[1] Judith R. Gordon, *A Diagnostic Approach to Organizational* 2002, p. 393.

2

SKILLS THAT A LEADER NEEDS

A good leader must have the prerequisite skills if he or she is to be effective in business. Many textbook and business journal writers have used various terms to describe these skills. Zander lists such skills as being critical to success as a leader and identifies them as the ability to delegate responsibilities, to be fair with subordinates, and to be consistent.[2] However, Zander also discusses communications, human relations, and a sense of humor as special skills that a leader *should* possess. These skills are often acquired on the job with the assistance of mentors within the firm.

PROBLEM SOLVING

Dealing with problems is a delicate business. On the one hand, leaders do not want to anger anyone, especially union personnel, by being too harsh. On the other hand, they must confront problems head-on. Leaders should first make a special effort to identify clearly the real problem. Second, they should pinpoint the individual factors that may be causing the problem. Finally, they should take definite steps to correct the problem.

y, 3rd ed., McGraw-Hill/Irwin, New York, 2002, pp. 274-

MEMO TO: Frank Janowicz, Ticket Manager

FROM: Sam Steele, Executive Director

DATE: March 1, 20--

SUBJECT: Ticket Sales Campaign

We tentatively have scheduled 114 concerts for Orchestra Hall for the calendar year beginning September 1, 20--. The attached list shows the new season ticket prices for the main floor, mezzanine, balcony, and gallery.

These prices are grouped in 11 different concert categories, which reflect the varied classical tastes of our patrons. These groupings also consider preferences for day of the week, time of day, and season of the year.

Please see me at 3 p.m. on March 10 so that we can review our ticket sales campaign. Last year's season ticket holders have had ample time to renew their subscriptions; we must now concentrate on attracting new season subscribers. I shall look forward to reviewing your plans on the tenth.

lpu
Attachment

Lesson 61

Skillbuilding and Report Review

Goals

- Improve speed and accuracy
- Refine language arts skills in the use of commas
- Format reports

A. Type 2 times.

A. WARMUP

```
     A queen quickly adjusted 12 blinds as the bright sun      11
blazed down from the sky; she then paced through the 19        22
rooms (all very large) next to the castle for 38 minutes.      33
| 1 | 2 | 3 | 4 | 5 | 6 | 7 | 8 | 9 | 10 | 11 | 12
```

SKILLBUILDING

B. Take three 12-second timed writings on each line. The scale below the last line shows your wpm speed for a 12-second timed writing.

B. 12-SECOND SPEED SPRINTS

```
Most of those autos on the road had only one or two people.
Those boys and girls did the right thing by doing the work.
Some of the men ran to the gym to work out with their kids.
All of the new male workers were given a tour of the plant.
||||5||||10||||15||||20||||25||||30||||35||||40||||45||||50||||55||||60
```

C. DIAGNOSTIC PRACTICE: SYMBOLS AND PUNCTUATION

If you are not using the GDP software, turn to page SB-2 and follow the directions for this activity.

LANGUAGE ARTS

D. Study the rules at the right.

D. COMMAS

Note: The callout signals in the left margin indicate which language arts rule from this lesson has been applied.

RULE ▶ ,series

Use a comma between each item in a series of three or more.

We need to order paper, toner, and font cartridges_for the printer.

They saved their work, exited their program, and turned off their computers_when they finished.

Note: Do not use a comma after the last item in a series.

The underlines call attention to a point in the sentence where a comma might mistakenly be inserted.

RULE ▶ ,transitional expression

Use a comma before and after a transitional expression or independent comment.

It is critical, therefore, that we finish the project on time.

Our present projections, you must admit, are inadequate.

But: You must admit_our present projections are inadequate.

Note: Examples of transitional expressions and independent comments are *in addition to, therefore, however, on the other hand, as a matter of fact*, and *unfortunately*.

Edit the sentences to correct any errors in the use of the comma.

8 The lawyer the bank and the courthouse received copies.
9 The closing was delayed therefore for more than an hour.
10 The abstract deed and contract were all three in order.
11 Ms. Sperry's flight was delayed however for two hours.
12 Happily the drinks snacks and napkins arrived on time.
13 This offer I think will be unacceptable to the board.

DOCUMENT PROCESSING

Report 61-35

Business Report

,transitional expression

The ¶ symbol indicates the start of a new paragraph. In a business report, paragraphs are blocked (not indented).

Word Processing Manual Review:

L. 21–24: *All*
L. 23: Bold
L. 26: Alignment and Font Size

Reference Manual

Review: R-8A: Business Report.

,series

UTI EMPLOYEE TRAINING PROGRAMS

Asako Kudo, Training Coordinator

¶ Various training techniques are used in business and industry to [help] ~~update~~ employees[,] [acquire new] skills ~~and to assist them in acquiring new skills~~. ~~It should be no surprise, therefore, that conscientious employees are eager to participate in training programs.~~ Some ~~of the various~~ [effective] techniques that United Transportation Inc. [(UTI)] uses in its training programs are ~~described below~~ [discussed in this report].

ON-THE-JOB TRAINING AND LECTURES

¶ Two of the most frequently used and [highly effective] training methods are on-th[e]-job training and lectures.

¶ **On-the-Job Training.** on the job training saves time and money by ~~permitting~~ [enabling] individuals [to] train at the workplace. ~~This method lets~~ the trainer use[s] the workstation in place of a classroom. ~~While there are many benefits from this type of experience,~~ on-the-job training does require careful coordination to [e]insure that learning objectives are achieved.

¶ **Lectures.** Lectures are often used because they are a low-cost method of ~~training~~ [instruction]. Lectures[,] which require little action on the part of the trainer, may not be effective when introducing employees to new techniques and work program[s].

CONFERENCES

¶ In ~~the~~ [a] conference, ~~method of instruction,~~ small groups of employees are taught by a ~~conference~~ director, manager, or outside consultant. ~~This method of instruction results in~~ [Conferences provide] considerable give-and-take ~~between the director and the employees.~~ For learning to occur, the ~~director~~ [trainer] must be [skilled] in the use of interactive tech[n]iques.

(Continued on next page)

DISTANCE EDUCATION

¶ A growing segment of UTI's training is now delivered on-line via the internet. Some of these courses, called distance education, are designed and managed by UTI, but an increasing number are designed and managed form independent vendors, such as educational institutions and management-consulting firms. These on-line courses are not only cost-effective but also permit the trainee to complete the course at a time that is convenient for them.

The UTI Training Department estimates that within five years, 80% or more of its training modules will be delivered on-line at a projected annual cost savings of at least 575,000 dollars.

Report 61-36

Academic Report

The ¶ symbol indicates the start of a new paragraph. In an academic report, paragraphs are indented.

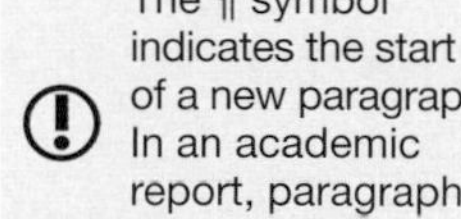

Word Processing Manual Review:

L. 27: Page Numbering and Page Break
L. 29: Line Spacing
L. 35: Italics
L.41: Footnotes

Reference Manual

Review: R-8C and R-8D: Academic Report

,series

,transitional expression

LEADERSHIP SKILLS NEEDED IN BUSINESS

Sally Rodriguez

¶ Leadership skills are needed now more than ever in business and industry if our nation is to maintain a leading role in the business world of tomorrow. With the advent of a common European community without boundaries, the Asian influence throughout the world, and the development of a common North American business community, we must have leaders with vision and the appropriate skills for meeting the challenges of the new, very technical century.

¶ Each of the new skills that a successful leader needs is discussed in the following pages.

LEADERSHIP

¶ Leadership has been defined in a variety of ways. One definition is "the behavior of an individual when he or she is directing the activities of a group toward a shared goal."[1]

¶ A successful leader is one who is committed to ideas—ideas for future products and services, for improving the firm's market position, and for the well-being of his or her employees. A leader possesses a value system that is ethically and morally sound. Leaders who make decisions affecting the firm, employees, and society have a set of beliefs that influence decision making.

SKILLS THAT A LEADER NEEDS

¶ A good leader must have the prerequisite skills if he or she is to be effective in business. Many textbook and business journal writers have used various terms to describe these skills. Zander lists such skills as being critical to success as a leader and identifies them as the ability to delegate responsibilities, to be fair with subordinates, and to be consistent.[2] However, Zander

(Continued on next page)

,series

also discusses communications, human relations, and a sense of humor as special skills that a leader *should* possess. These skills are often acquired on the job with the assistance of mentors within the firm.

PROBLEM SOLVING

,transitional expression

,transitional expression

,transitional expression

¶ Dealing with problems is a delicate business. On the one hand, leaders do not want to anger anyone, especially union personnel, by being too harsh. On the other hand, they must confront problems head-on. Leaders should first make a special effort to identify clearly the *real* problem. Second, they should pinpoint the individual factors that may be causing the problem. Finally, they should take definite steps to correct the problem.

[1] Judith R. Gordon, *A Diagnostic Approach to Organizational Behavior*, 2nd ed., Allyn and Bacon, Boston, 2002, p. 393.
[2] Raymond T. Zander, *Office Management Today*, 3rd ed., McGraw-Hill/Irwin, New York, 2002, pp. 274–275.

Report 61-37

Business Report

Open the file for Report 61-36 and make the following changes.

1. Change the report from academic style to business style.
2. Assume that Aaron Wojak wrote the report, and change the byline accordingly.
3. Delete the third paragraph. Note that this results in the elimination of the first footnote.
4. Add a fourth side heading, THE LEADER AS TEACHER. Then add the following paragraph:

   Those who are in leadership positions often assume that workers learn how to perform a job simply by doing it without guidance. The real leader plans well-structured orientation sessions for new workers and does the same for all workers whenever there is new technology to be learned or when there is a change in policy or procedure.

   (**Note:** If necessary, force a page break to prevent the new side heading from appearing at the bottom of the first page.)
5. Finally, add a footnote at the end of the paragraph you inserted in step 4:

   Ahmed Bazarak, "The Leader as Teacher," *The Manager's Newsletter,* July 18, 2004, pp. 14-17.

Skillbuilding and Letter Review

Goals

- Type at least 40wpm/5′/5e
- Format business letters and personal-business letters

A. Type 2 times.

A. WARMUP

```
     Quist & Zenk's sales were exactly $247,650; but the    10
cost of goods sold was $174,280 (70.37%). The profit made   22
was small after other, extensive expenses were subtracted   34
| 1 | 2 | 3 | 4 | 5 | 6 | 7 | 8 | 9 | 10 | 11 | 12
```

SKILLBUILDING

B. MAP

Follow the GDP software directions for this exercise in improving keystroking accuracy.

Strategies for Career Success

Corrective Feedback

Sometime in your career, you will give someone corrective feedback. You can use positive communication to do this and not appear to criticize the person.

Here are some things you should not do. Do not correct the person in front of others. Avoid giving feedback when you are angry. Stay away from personal comments (for example, "That idea will get us nowhere!"). Do not diminish a person's enthusiasm (for example, "We've never done that before, and we're not starting now.").

Here are some things you should do. Listen to the person's side of the situation. Express yourself in a positive way (for example, "You're getting much closer."). Be specific about what the person can do to correct the situation. Follow up within a short time and identify all progress.

YOUR TURN Think about the last time you received corrective feedback. Did the person giving you feedback use techniques to create a positive outcome?

C. Take two 5-minute timed writings. Review your speed and errors.

Goal: At least 40wpm/5'/5e

C. 5-MINUTE TIMED WRITING

```
     Digital photography has revolutionized the way we take  11
pictures. A digital camera puts our photos in a format that  23
makes them easy to print and share with others. Using a      34
digital camera also has the advantage that we can quickly    46
print out our photos and see the results of our efforts. We  58
can also insert our photos into word processing documents,   70
send them by e-mail to our friends, or post them on the Web  82
where they can be viewed by all. We can even connect our     93
camera to a television set and have our images displayed in 105
a slide show presentation.                                  111
     Another advantage of digital photography is that the   121
expense of developing your own photos is much less because  133
you do not have to buy many rolls of film, nor do you have  145
to have your photos developed by others. Also, your photos  157
can be edited if you do not like what you see. You can crop 169
the photo, adjust its color or contrast, take out red-eye   180
imperfections, and even add or delete elements from the     192
photo or from other photos you have taken.                  200
|  1  |  2  |  3  |  4  |  5  |  6  |  7  |  8  |  9  |  10  |  11  |  12
```

DOCUMENT PROCESSING

Correspondence 62-55

Personal-Business Letter in Modified-Block Style

The ¶ symbol indicates the start of a new paragraph. In a personal-business letter, paragraphs are blocked (not indented).

Reference Manual

Review: R-3D: Personal-Business Letter

October 1, 20-- | Dr. Anthony L. Robbins | 2345 South Main Street | Bowling Green, OH 43402 | Dear Anthony:

¶ Thank you for your letter of September 25, in which you inquired about my trip to New York City. Your letter brought back a lot of memories of those days when I was one of your students.

¶ I plan to leave on October 15 for a two-week business and vacation trip to the city. While at Columbia University, I will be conducting a workshop on the utilization of voice-activated equipment.

¶ My work at Columbia will be completed on October 22, after which I plan to attend a number of plays, visit the Metropolitan Museum of Art, and take one of the sightseeing tours of the city.

¶ If you and your wife would care to join me on October 22, please let me know. I would be most happy to make reservations at the hotel for you and to purchase theater tickets. Why don't you consider joining me in the "Big Apple."

Sincerely, | Bryan Goldberg | 320 South Summit Street | Toledo, OH 43604

Correspondence 62-56

Business Letter in Modified-Block Style

Word Processing Manual Review:

L. 50: Ruler Tabs and Tab Sets

Reference Manual

Review: R-3B: Business Letter in Modified-Block Style

June 3, 20--

Director of Product Development

Hampton Associates, Inc.

830 Market St.

San Francisco, Ca 94103-1925

Dear Director of Product Development:

¶ I recently read an article in Business Week concerning how computer buyers can make standards happen. It was a very interesting article. It indicates that if customers demand products standard when they purchase computers, participate in standard-setting groups, and band together with other customers, they will do better in the long run. Have you had customer groups help you or provide you with information on the adoption of more standards, such as in the areas of industry wide interfaces, a mix and match of computergear and programs, and building the best system for each application utilized?

¶ I would appreciate any data that you might furnish for me with relationship to customers and your firm working together to set past or future standards.

Sincerely yours,

Alice Karns

Vice President

urs

Correspondence 62-57

Business Letter in Block Style

Word Processing Manual Review:

L. 33: Envelopes

Reference Manual

Review pages **R-3A** and **R-6A** of the Reference Manual.

Revise Correspondence 62-56, making the following changes:

1. Change the letter to block style.
2. Change the date to `June 5, 20--`.
3. Send the letter to Ms. Heidi M. Fischer at Gramstad Brothers, Inc., located at 5417 Harbord Drive in Oakland, CA 94618.
4. Change the salutation.
5. Combine the second and third paragraphs into one paragraph.
6. Add the following text as a new third paragraph:

   `Some of my colleagues and I would like to get involved with others in an effort to make desired changes. I am confident that there are others around the Bay area who feel the same way.`

7. Prepare an envelope for the letter.

Skillbuilding, Memo, and E-Mail Review

Goals

- Improve speed and accuracy
- Refine language arts skills in composing paragraphs
- Format memos and an e-mail message

A. Type 2 times.

A. WARMUP

```
     "When is the quarterly jury report due?" asked Glenn.   11
He had faxed forms* to 64 of the 135 prospective jurors.     22
Only about one dozen of 596 citizens could not be located.   34
|  1  |  2  |  3  |  4  |  5  |  6  |  7  |  8  |  9  |  10  |  11  |  12
```

SKILLBUILDING

PRETEST
Take a 1-minute timed writing. Review your speed and errors.

B. PRETEST: Discrimination Practice

```
     The entire trip on a large train was better than we     11
had hoped. Polite police looked out for both the young and   23
old. One unit was outnumbered by herds of frolicking deer.   35
|  1  |  2  |  3  |  4  |  5  |  6  |  7  |  8  |  9  |  10  |  11  |  12
```

PRACTICE
Speed Emphasis:
If you made no more than 1 error on the Pretest, type each *individual* line 2 times.
Accuracy Emphasis:
If you made 2 or more errors, type each *group* of lines (as though it were a paragraph) 2 times.

C. PRACTICE: Left Hand

```
rtr trip trot sport train alert courts assert tragic truest
asa mass salt usage cased cease astute dashed masked castle
rer rear rest overt rerun older before entire surest better
```

D. PRACTICE: Right Hand

```
mnm menu numb hymns unmet manly mental namely manner number
pop post coop opera pools opens polite proper police oppose
iui unit quit fruit suits built medium guided helium podium
```

POSTTEST
Repeat the Pretest timed writing and compare performance.

E. POSTTEST: Discrimination Practice

F. PACED PRACTICE

If you are not using the GDP software, turn to page SB-14 and follow the directions for this activity.

LANGUAGE ARTS

G. COMPOSING: PARAGRAPH

Read through the paragraphs in the 5-minute timed writing in Lesson 62. Compose a paragraph to include the type of operating system, application software, and utility programs loaded on the computers used in your keyboarding class.

DOCUMENT PROCESSING

Correspondence 63-58

Memo

Review: R-4D: Memo

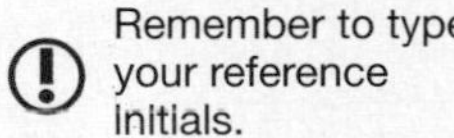

The ¶ symbol indicates the start of a new paragraph. In a memo, paragraphs are blocked (not indented).

Remember to type your reference initials.

MEMO TO: Frank Janowicz, Ticket Manager | **FROM**: Sam Steele, Executive Director | **DATE**: March 1, 20-- | **SUBJECT**: Ticket Sales Campaign

¶We tentatively have scheduled 114 concerts for Orchestra Hall for the calendar year beginning September 1, 20--. The attached list shows the new season ticket prices for the main floor, mezzanine, balcony, and gallery.

¶These prices are grouped in 11 different concert categories, which reflect the varied classical tastes of our patrons. These groupings also consider preferences for day of the week, time of day, and season of the year.

¶Please see me at 3 p.m. on March 10 so that we can review our ticket sales campaign. Last year's season ticket holders have had ample time to renew their subscriptions; we must now concentrate on attracting new season subscribers. I shall look forward to reviewing your plans on the tenth.

urs | Attachment

Correspondence 63-59

E-Mail Message

Review: R-5C: E-mail Message in Internet Explorer, or **R-5D:** E-mail Message in Yahoo!

Type the e-mail greeting, body, closing, and signature below in correct format.

Greeting: Mr. Phillips:

Body: ¶ Please send information and prices on the security software you recently advertised in *PC Magazine*.

¶ We are interested in implementing a new security program for the personal computers in our main office and would like to study the specifications and features your system provides.

¶ Thank you for your assistance.

Closing: Charles

Signature: C. H. Cox

E-mail address: chcox@mailserver.net

Phone: 770-555-2843

Correspondence 63-60

Memo

MEMO TO: Edo Dorati Cabaret pops Conductor

FROM: Sam Steele, Executive Director

DATE: March 2, 20--

Subject: Erving Berlin Concert

Our Patron Advisory Program Committee recommens in its their attached letter that the Erving Berlin concert begin with some pre-World War I hits, followed by music from the '20s and '30s. Favorites from this era are hit songs from Music Box Review, Puttin' on The Ritz, and Follow the the Fleet. After the intermission the committee suggest songs from the '40s and '50s, hits from Annie get Your Gun, Call me Madam, Easter parade. A planning meeting has been scheduled for you, Dolly Carpenter (the Rehearsals Coordinator), and me on Mar. 9 at 10 A.M. at Orchestra Hall. I shall look foreward to seeing you then.

urs

Attachment

c: Dolly Carpenter

Correspondence 63-61

Memo

MEMO TO: Dolly Carpenter, Rehearsals Coordinator

FROM: Sam Steele, Executive Director

DATE: March 3, 20--

SUBJECT: Summer Cabaret Pops Concerts

¶ We are pleased that you will be our rehearsals coordinator for this summer's Cabaret Pops concerts. The five biweekly concerts will run from June 13 through August 8.

¶ As the concert schedule is much lighter during the summer months, I am quite confident that you will be able to use the Orchestra Hall stage for all rehearsals. This is the preference of Edo Dorati, who will be the conductor for this year's Cabaret Pops concerts.

¶ I look forward to seeing you on June 1.

Skillbuilding and Table Review

Goals

- Type at least 40wpm/5′/5e
- Format tables

A. Type 2 times.

A. WARMUP

There were two big questions: (1) Would both have to 11
be present to pick up the license? and (2) Is a blood test 23
required? Jeff and Faye were quite dizzy with excitement. 34
| 1 | 2 | 3 | 4 | 5 | 6 | 7 | 8 | 9 | 10 | 11 | 12

SKILLBUILDING

B. Take a 1-minute timed writing on the first paragraph to establish your base speed. Then take four 1-minute timed writings on the remaining paragraphs. As soon as you equal or exceed your base speed on one paragraph, advance to the next, more difficult paragraph.

B. SUSTAINED PRACTICE: ALTERNATE-HAND WORDS

The town council decided to shape its destiny when a 11
rich landowner lent a hand by proposing to chair the audit 23
committee. He will be a good chairman, and eight civic 34
club members will work to amend some troublesome policies. 46

One problem relates to the change in profit for many 11
of the firms in the city. As giant property taxes do not 22
relate to income, they wish to make those taxes go down. 33
The result means increases in their sales or income taxes. 45

All eight members of the town council now agree that 11
it is time to join with other cities throughout the state 23
in lobbying with the state legislature to bring about the 35
needed change. The right balance in taxes is the goal. 46

The mayor pointed out that it is not only business 10
property owners who would be affected. Homeowners should 22
see a decrease in property taxes, and renters might see 33
lower rents, as taxes on rental property would be lowered. 45
| 1 | 2 | 3 | 4 | 5 | 6 | 7 | 8 | 9 | 10 | 11 | 12

C. Take two 5-minute timed writings. Review your speed and errors.

Goal: At least 40wpm/5'/5e

C. 5-MINUTE TIMED WRITING

The computer has changed the way you do things in the 11
office today. Jobs that used to take many hours to complete 23
now can be done in less time. A quick review of ways in 34
which your computer can help you streamline your work may 46
be in order. 49

Most software programs include helpful wizards that 59
can guide you through any project. You can use a stored 70
template, or you can create your own style. You do not need 82
to write your thoughts in longhand on paper before you type 94
them. Composing and revising documents as you type them 105
will save you lots of time. 111

Your computer is valuable for more than just writing 122
letters. Using different software applications, you can 133
create dazzling presentations for all to see. You can also 145
build databases for sorting and storing all types of data, 156
format spreadsheets, create your own calendar and colorful 168
charts, and perform calculations. You can even publish your 180
own newsletter and make business cards. It is exciting to 192
consider the ways you can use a computer. 200

| 1 | 2 | 3 | 4 | 5 | 6 | 7 | 8 | 9 | 10 | 11 | 12

DOCUMENT PROCESSING

Table 64-23

Boxed Table

Word Processing Manual Review:

L. 36: Table—Create; AutoFit to Contents
L.37: Table—Merge Cells
L.38: Center a Table Horizontally and Center Page
L.39: Table—Align Text in a Column

Reference Manual

Review: R-13A: Boxed Table

$700 COMPOUNDED ANNUALLY FOR 7 YEARS AT 7 PERCENT		
Beginning of Year	**Interest**	**Value**
First	$00.00	$ 700.00
Second	49.00	749.00
Third	52.43	801.43
Fourth	56.10	857.53
Fifth	60.03	917.56
Sixth	64.23	981.79
Seventh	68.72	1,050.51
Eighth	78.68	1,129.19

Table 64-24

Open Table

Word Processing Manual Review:

L. 37: Tables—Borders

Reference Manual

Review: R-13B: Open Table

1. Insert a table with 3 columns and 9 rows.
2. Merge the cells in Row 1, and center the title in all-caps, bold, and 14-point font. Press ENTER 1 time.
3. Center the subtitle in upper- and lowercase, bold, and 12-point font. Press ENTER 1 time.
4. Center and bold the column headings.
5. Type the information in the body of the table.
6. Automatically adjust the column widths.
7. Center the table horizontally and vertically.
8. Spell-check, preview, and proofread your table for spelling and formatting errors before printing it.

SALES CONFERENCES
All Sessions at Regional Offices

Date	**City**	**Leader**
October 7	Boston	D. G. Gorham
October 17	Baltimore	James B. Brunner
October 24	Miami	Becky Taylor
November 3	Dallas	Rodney R. Nordstein
November 10	Minneapolis	Joanne Miles-Tyrell
November 17	Denver	Becky Taylor
November 26	Los Angeles	Rodney R. Nordstein

Table 64-25

Ruled Table

Reference Manual

Review: R-13C: Ruled Table

SECOND HALF-YEAR SALES
Ending December 31, 20--

Month	**Sales Quotas ($)**	**Actual Sales ($)**
July	335,400	350,620
August	370,750	296,230
September	374,510	425,110
October	390,270	390,110
November	375,890	368,290
December	360,470	378,690
TOTAL	2,207,290	2,209,050

Skillbuilding and Employment Document Review

Goals

- Improve speed and accuracy
- Refine language arts skills in proofreading
- Format employment documents

A. Type 2 times.

A. WARMUP

```
     Only 6 of the 18 competitors weighed more than 149#.    11
All Big Five matches were scheduled in Gym #3. Amazingly,    23
about 1/3 of the #1 Jaguars were picked to acquire titles.   35
|  1  |  2  |  3  |  4  |  5  |  6  |  7  |  8  |  9  |  10  |  11  |  12
```

SKILLBUILDING

B. PROGRESSIVE PRACTICE: NUMBERS

If you are not using the GDP software, turn to page SB-11 and follow the directions for this activity.

C. TECHNIQUE PRACTICE: BACKSPACE KEY

Type each word as shown until you reach the backspace sign (←). Then backspace 1 time and replace the previously typed character with the one shown.

First Letter	h←fall s←dash h←lead k←heel p←cage b←rare d←bark l←date t←sold
Middle Letter	has←lf far←te mak←de roo←am do←ive fas←ce war←ve wee←ak yok←lk
Last Letter	sale←t they←m helm←d wall←k pals←e milk←d told←l quip←t main←l

D. PROGRESSIVE PRACTICE: ALPHABET

If you are not using the GDP software, turn to page SB-7 and follow the directions for this activity.

LANGUAGE ARTS

E. Compare this paragraph with the fourth paragraph of Report 61-36 on page 217. Edit the paragraph to correct any errors.

E. PROOFREADING

A successful leader is one who is commited to ideas-ideas for future product and services for improving the firms market position, and for the wellbeing of his or her employes. A leeder possesses a value system that is ethicly and morally sound. leaders who make decisions effecting the firm, employees, and society, have set of beliefs that influence decision making.

DOCUMENT PROCESSING

Report 65-38

Traditional Resume

Word Processing Manual Review:

L. 51: Fonts

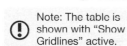

Reference Manual

Review: R-12A: Resume

1. Press ENTER 6 times.
2. Insert an open table with 2 columns and 5 rows.
3. Merge the cells in Row 1.
4. Change to center alignment.
5. Type the individual's name in Arial Bold, all-caps, and 14-point font. Press ENTER 2 times.
6. Change to 12-point Arial Bold, and type the street address, city, state, and ZIP Code. Press ENTER 1 time.
7. Type the phone number and e-mail address. Press ENTER 1 time.
8. Apply a bottom border to Row 1.
9. Move to Row 2, Column A. Press ENTER 1 time; then type the section heading in 12-point Times New Roman Bold, all-caps.
10. Move to Column B, press ENTER 1 time, and type the information pertaining to the section. Press ENTER 1 time after the final line in Row 2, Column B.
11. Move to Row 3, Column A, and type the second section heading. Then move to Column B, and type the corresponding information for this section. Press ENTER 1 time after the final line in Row 3, Column B.
12. Move to Row 4, and repeat steps 9 and 10 until all remaining sections have been completed. (Do not insert a hard return at the end of the references section information.)
13. Manually adjust the column widths as needed.

Note: The table is shown with "Show Gridlines" active.

<table>
<tr><td colspan="2" align="center">TIMOTHY J. ROBINSON

5816 Foxfire Road, Lawton, OK 73501
Phone: 405-555-3039; e-mail: trobinso@lcc.edu</td></tr>
<tr><td>EDUCATION</td><td>Lawton Community College, Lawton, Oklahoma
Associate in Business degree, Office Systems, June 2003 Specialization in computer applications software (Microsoft Word, Excel, Access), business communication, and office systems management.

Frederick High School, Frederick, Oklahoma
Graduated: May 2001</td></tr>
<tr><td>EXPERIENCE</td><td>Computer Systems Technician, September 2001-Present
Selkirk & Associates, Lawton, Oklahoma
Duties include installing and updating computer software programs throughout the firm.

Secretary II, July 1999–August 2001 (part-time)
Kittredge Insurance Agency, Frederick, Oklahoma
Duties included typing and word processing while reporting to the administrative assistant to the owner.</td></tr>
<tr><td>ACTIVITIES</td><td>College Choir, 2001–2003
Business Students Club, 2001–2003 (Secretary, 2002–2003)
Varsity Basketball, 2001–2003
Intramural Soccer, 2001–2003</td></tr>
<tr><td>REFERENCES</td><td>Available upon request.</td></tr>
</table>

Correspondence 65-62

Application Letter in Block Style

Review: R-12B: Application Letter

March 10, 20-- | Mrs. Denise F. Klenzman | Director of Human Resources | Cole Enterprises | 3714 Crestmont Avenue | Norman, OK 73069 | Dear Mrs. Klenzman:

¶ Please consider me an applicant for the position of Computer Systems Coordinator with your firm. I became aware of the new position through a friend who is an employee at Cole Enterprises. I have been employed at Selkirk & Associates since graduating from high school in 2001. During this time I have also earned an assoc. in business degree at Lawton Community College. The resume enclosed shows that I have had several courses in computer application soft ware and office systems. I am confident that my educational experience background and my computer systems experience make me highly qualified for the position with your firm. You may callme for an interview at 405-555-4572 3039.

Sincerely yours, | Timothy J. Robinson | 5816 Foxfire Road | Lawton, OK 73501 | Enclosure

Correspondence 65-63

Follow-Up Letter in Block Style

Progress and Proofreading Check

Documents designated as Proofreading Checks serve as a check of your proofreading skill. Your goal is to have zero typographical errors when the GDP software first scores the document.

March 19, 20-- | Mrs. Denise F. Klenzman | Director of Human Resources | Cole Enterprises | 3714 Crestmont Avenue | Norman, OK 73069

Dear Mrs. Klenzman:

¶ Thank you for the opportunity to meet with you yesterday and to learn of the exciting career opportunities at Cole Enterprises. It was inspiring for me to learn about future plans for your forward-looking company.

¶ I am confident that my education and my experience qualify me in a special way for your position of computer systems coordinator. I am familiar with all of your present equipment and software.

¶ I would very much like to join the professional staff at Cole Enterprises. Please let me know when you have made your decision.

Sincerely yours, | Timothy J. Robinson | 5816 Foxfire Road | Lawton, OK 73501

Unit 14

Reports

LESSON 66
Itineraries

LESSON 67
Agendas and Minutes of Meetings

LESSON 68
Procedures Manual

LESSON 69
Reports Formatted in Columns

LESSON 70
Report Review

Presentation Software Guide Cartwright Services, Page 2

FORMATTING SLIDES

Once you have written your presentation, you can place your key points on slides using presentation software. Follow these steps to prepare your presentation slides.

- Select a template or background that is appropriate for every slide.
- Select a layout such as text copy or bulleted or numbered lists.
- Use the edit, copy, and paste commands to add text to your presentation slides.

FORMATTING THE PRESENTATION

After you finish preparing the slides for your presentation, you may want to change the method by which each slide appears on the screen or the way individual points are displayed on the screen. In presentation software, moving from one slide to another is known as transition. Transition is accomplished by following these steps:

- Select the slides you want to control by the transition method.
- Select a transition method such as Cover Right or Wipe Left.
- Run through the slide show to determine whether or not you are satisfied with the transition.

Slide presentations can also be formatted so that each point you make on an individual slide appears individually on the screen. To structure your slides this way, follow these steps:

y a build effect.
Fly From Left.
ermine whether or not you are satisfied with

f a slide, and it can be added easily to selected
resentation. Several clip art images are included in
of them can be used in slides that you prepare. If
ip are images from other packages. To insert a clip
age, follow these steps:

the clip art to appear.
image.
clip art library.
rect location on the slide.
if it is to appear on all slides.

CALIFORNIA PLANNING MEETING

Itinerary for Nancy Perkins

July 8-10, 20--

MONDAY, JULY 8

2:45 p.m.-4:05 p.m. Flight from Houston to Los Angeles; United Flight 834; seat 10C; nonstop

TUESDAY, JULY 9

10 a.m.-11:15 a.m. Flight from Los Ange
seat 4A; nonstop

WEDNESDAY, JULY 10

7 p.m.-11:15 p.m. Flight from Sacramen
7B; nonstop; dinner

NOTES

1. Adam Broderick, chief engineer for Natural Gas
Los Angeles.
2. At 7 p.m. on July 8, you will have dinner with C
the Hollywood & Vine Restaurant.
3. You will have a 9 a.m. tour of the wastewater tre
Wednesday, July 10.
4. At 12 noon on Wednesday, July 10, you will hav
at J. C. Crawford's. Topic: Senate Bill 4501-68.

PERFORMING SUCCESSFULLY

Ginger Nichols

We have been involved in giving performances since our very early years, when we played a part in a class play or participated in competitive sports events at our school. The most terrifying part of each performance was probably the fear that we would "freeze" when it came our turn to perform. Whenever we find ourselves in this predicament, the best thing to do is to accept that fear and to learn to let it work for us, not against us. We need to recognize that nervousness or fear may set in during our performance. Then, when it does happen (if it does), we will be ready to cope with it and overcome it.

If you forget some of your lines in a recitation, try to remember other lines and recite them. Doing so may help those forgotten lines to "pop back" into your memory so that you put them in at a later time, if possible.

You always want to leave your audience with the idea that you have given them something worthwhile that they can use or apply to their own lives. For maximum impact on your audience and to make sure that they remember what you say, use audiovisual aids to reinforce your message. Remember, however, that audiovisual aids are nothing more than aids. The real message should come in the words you choose when giving your presentation.

Study your speech well; even rehearse it if necessary. However, do not practice it to the extent that it appears that you are merely reading what is written down on the paper in front of you. Much of your personality should be exhibited while you are giving your speech. If you are an enthusiastic, friendly person who converses well with people face-to-face, then that same persona should be evident during your speech. A good piece of advice is to just go out there and be yourself—you will be much more comfortable by doing so, and your audience will relate to you better than if you try to exhibit a different personality when at the podium.

No matter how rapidly you speak in general, slow down when you are in front of a group. The fact that you are nervous can cause your speech rate to increase. The best way to slow down your speaking is to breathe deeply. Doing so also causes your nervous system to relax, allowing you to proceed with your speech calmly.

Finally, possibly the best advice for giving a successful speech is to be prepared. You will be more confident if you are thoroughly prepared. Do your research, rehearse your speech, and make notes about where you want to give emphasis or use an audiovisual aid.

Itineraries

Goals

- Type at least 41wpm/5'/5e
- Format itineraries

A. Type 2 times.

A. WARMUP

```
     Had Phil been given a quiz on a subject that had been   11
reviewed by Max and Kay? Frank scored 89 on that quiz; Sue   23
scored 93 (*math only). Both tests were taken on 10/25/04.   35
| 1 | 2 | 3 | 4 | 5 | 6 | 7 | 8 | 9 | 10 | 11 | 12
```

SKILLBUILDING

B. Take three 12-second timed writings on each line. The scale below the last line shows your wpm speed for a 12-second timed writing.

B. 12-SECOND SPEED SPRINTS

```
This is not the person who is my first choice for this job.
The day was bright as the sun shone on the clear blue lake.
All of you should take a long walk when the sun sets today.
This line has many easy words in it to type your very best.
| | | | 5 | | | | 10 | | | | 15 | | | | 20 | | | | 25 | | | | 30 | | | | 35 | | | | 40 | | | | 45 | | | | 50 | | | | 55 | | | | 60
```

Keyboarding Connection

Observing Netiquette

Netiquette is proper conduct for e-mail users. It shows courtesy and professionalism and conveys a good impression of you and your company. Since e-mail is close to speech, it is the most informal of business documents.

Check your e-mail daily. Try to answer it the same day it arrives. Don't let it accumulate in your mailbox; you risk offending the sender. Use regular capitalization. All-caps indicate SHOUTING; all-lowercase letters convey immaturity. Most readers tolerate an infrequent typo, but if your message is filled with errors, you appear unprofessional. Use your spell-checker, and don't overwhelm people with unnecessary e-mails. Use discretion. Make sure the information is relevant to each e-mail recipient.

Be considerate. Be professional. Anything you write can wind up in your personnel file. E-mail that criticizes another person can be forwarded to him or her without your knowledge.

YOUR TURN Review your next e-mail message for the use of netiquette.

C. PROGRESSIVE PRACTICE: ALPHABET

If you are not using the GDP software, turn to page SB-7 and follow the directions for this activity.

D. Take two 5-minute timed writings. Review your speed and errors.

Goal: At least 41wpm/5′/5e

D. 5-MINUTE TIMED WRITING

Making a successful presentation to an audience is a 11
skill that is absolutely essential in your career. The art 23
of speaking before a group requires planning and hard work. 35
Although different speakers prepare in much different ways, 47
a speaker should try to adhere to certain rules. 56

As the speaker, you are quite visible to people in the 68
audience. Therefore, you should always try to make a good 79
first impression. When you walk to the podium to speak, you 91
give the audience a chance to notice your neat appearance, 103
good posture, and confident manner. You will improve the 114
quality of your voice if you stand up straight and hold 126
your shoulders back and stomach in. 133

As you talk, use your eyes, face, and hands to help 143
you connect with your listeners. Maintain eye contact by 155
just moving your eyes over the group without focusing on 166
any one person. Use hand movements and facial expressions 177
to convey meanings to your audience. By utilizing these 189
techniques, you will improve your speaking skills, and your 201
effort will be noted. 205

| 1 | 2 | 3 | 4 | 5 | 6 | 7 | 8 | 9 | 10 | 11 | 12

FORMATTING

E. ITINERARIES

An itinerary is a proposed outline of a trip that provides a traveler with information such as flight times and numbers, meeting times, travel dates, and room reservations. An itinerary may also include notes of special interest to the traveler.

Report 66-39

Itinerary

Review R-11C: Itinerary

1. Press ENTER 6 times to leave an approximately 2-inch top margin.
2. Insert an open table with 2 columns and 10 rows.
3. Merge the cells in Row 1, and center the title in all-caps, bold, and 14-point font. Press ENTER 2 times.
4. Center the subtitle in upper- and lowercase, bold, and 12-point font. Press ENTER 2 times.
5. Center and bold the date. Press ENTER 1 time.
6. Move to Row 2, Column A, and type the date in all-caps; then press ENTER 1 time. Merge cells.
7. Move to Row 3, Column A, and type the time. Then move to Column B and type the corresponding information for this time. Press ENTER 1 time after the final line in Column B.
8. Move to Row 4 and repeat steps 5 and 6 until all dates, times, and entries have been completed. (Do not insert a hard return at the end of the final itinerary entry.)
9. Manually adjust the column widths as needed.

Note: The table is shown with "Show Gridlines" active.

↓6X

14 pt **PORTLAND SALES MEETING** ↓2X 12 pt **Itinerary for Arlene Gilsdorf** ↓2X **March 12-18, 20--** ↓1X	
THURSDAY, MARCH 12 ↓1X	
5:10 p.m.-5:55 p.m.	Flight from Detroit to Minneapolis; Northwest 83 (Phone: 800-555-1222); e-ticket; Seat 8D; nonstop ↓1X
6:30 p.m.-8:06 p.m.	Flight from Minneapolis to Portland; Northwest 2363; e-ticket; Seat 15C; nonstop; dinner ↓1X
SUNDAY, MARCH 15	
10:35 a.m.-12:22 p.m.	Flight from Portland to Los Angeles; United Airlines 360; e-ticket; Seat 15F; nonstop; breakfast
TUESDAY, MARCH 17	
8 a.m.-9:22 a.m.	Flight from San Francisco to Los Angeles; United Airlines 748; e-ticket; Seat 10D; nonstop; snack
WEDNESDAY, MARCH 18	
3:40 p.m.-5:50 p.m.	Flight from Los Angeles to Detroit; Southwest 327; e-ticket; Seat 17D; nonstop; snack

Report 66-40

Itinerary

INTERCO SEMINAR

Itinerary for Mrs. Helen Kyslowsky

September 25-29, 20--

WEDNESDAY, SEPTEMBER 25

6:50 p.m.–9:10 p.m. Flight from Columbus to Boston; America West 2053; Seat 13F; nonstop

FRIDAY, SEPTEMBER 27

9 a.m.–10:17 a.m. Flight from Boston to New York City; US Airways 454; Seat 10D; nonstop

SUNDAY, SEPTEMBER 29

2:07 p.m.–4:18 p.m. Flight from New York City to Columbus; US Airways 324; Seat 9A; nonstop

Report 66-41

Itinerary

CALIFORNIA PLANNING MEETING | **Itinerary for Nancy Perkins** | **July 8-10, 20--** | **MONDAY, JULY 8** | Leave at 2:45 p.m. and arrive at 4:05 p.m. Houston to Los Angeles; United Flight 834; Seat 10C; nonstop | Marriott (310-555-1014) King-sized bed; nonsmoking room; late arrival guaranteed (Reservation No. 45STX78) | **TUESDAY, JULY 9** | Leave at 10 a.m. and arrive at 11:15 a.m. Los Angeles to Sacramento; American Flight 206; Seat 4A; nonstop | **WEDNESDAY, JULY 10** | Leave at 7 p.m. and arrive at 11:15 p.m. Sacramento to Houston; United Flight 307; Seat 7B; nonstop; dinner

Agendas and Minutes of Meetings

Goals

- Improve speed and accuracy
- Refine language arts skills in the use of hyphens, abbreviations, and agreement
- Format agendas and minutes of meetings

A. Type 2 times.

A. WARMUP

```
     Rex Yantz was calm before quitting his job at the zoo   11
on 7/10/03. On 8/23/03 he applied for a job at Vance &       22
Walton, "specialists" in corporate law and bankruptcies.     33
| 1 | 2 | 3 | 4 | 5 | 6 | 7 | 8 | 9 | 10 | 11 | 12
```

SKILLBUILDING

B. DIAGNOSTIC PRACTICE: SYMBOLS AND PUNCTUATION

If you are not using the GDP software, turn to page SB-2 and follow the directions for this activity.

C. DIAGNOSTIC PRACTICE: NUMBERS

If you are not using the GDP software, turn to page SB-5 and follow the directions for this activity.

D. Type 2 times!

D. TECHNIQUE PRACTICE: SHIFT/CAPS LOCK

```
     RHONDA KORDICH was promoted on APRIL 1 to SENIOR
SECRETARY. The SOLD sign replaced the FOR SALE sign at
1904 ELM DRIVE. The trip to DULUTH was on INTERSTATE 35.
```

LANGUAGE ARTS

E. Study the rules at the right.

E. HYPHENS

Note: The callout signals in the left margin indicate which language arts rule from this lesson has been applied.

RULE ▶ -compound adjective

Hyphenate compound adjectives that come before a noun (unless the first word is an adverb ending in *-ly*).

We reviewed an up-to-date report on Wednesday.

But: The report was up_to_date.

But: We reviewed the highly_rated report.

The underline calls attention to a point in the sentence where a hyphen might mistakenly be inserted.

Note: A compound adjective is two or more words that function as a unit to describe a noun.

F. AGREEMENT

RULE ▶ agreement singular, agreement plural

Use singular verbs and pronouns with singular subjects; use plural verbs and pronouns with plural subjects.

I was happy with my performance.
Janet and Phoenix were happy with their performance.
Among the items discussed were our raises and benefits.

G. ABBREVIATIONS

RULE ▶ abbreviate none

In general business writing, do not abbreviate common words (such as *dept.* or *pkg.*), compass points, units of measure, or the names of months, days of the week, cities, or states (except in addresses).

Almost one-half of the audience indicated they were at least 5 feet 8 inches tall.

Note: Do not insert a comma between the parts of a single measurement.

Edit the sentences to correct any errors in grammar and mechanics.

```
7  The Queens visited Hickory to look at four bedroom homes.
8  Cindy Wallace has a part time job after school.
9  The accountants was extremely busy from March through April.
10 Lydia and Margaret were invited to present their report.
11 The portfolio include several technology stocks.
12 The planning committee will meet on Tue., Sept. 26.
13 Please credit the acct. for the amt. of $55.48.
14 The mgr. said the org. will move its headquarters to NC.
```

FORMATTING

H. AGENDAS

An agenda is a list of topics to be discussed at a meeting. It may also include a formal program of a meeting and consist of times, rooms, speakers, and other related information. Follow these steps to format an agenda:

1. Press ENTER 6 times to leave an approximately 2-inch top margin.
2. Center and type the name of the company or committee in all-caps, bold, and 14-point font.
3. Press ENTER 2 times, and then center and type `Meeting Agenda` in upper- and lowercase, bold, and 12-point font.
4. Press ENTER 2 times, and then center and type the date in upper- and lowercase, bold, and 12-point font.
5. Press ENTER 2 times, change the line spacing to double, and turn off bold.
6. Type all the items in the agenda, and then highlight the items and apply a number format to them.

↓6X

14 pt **ALLIANCE CORPORATION STAFF MEETING** ↓2X

12 pt↓ **Meeting Agenda** ↓2X

November 17, 20-- ↓2X

1. Approval of minutes of October 15 meeting ↓2X
2. Progress reports of new district offices
3. Discussion of attendance at the National Hardware Association's meeting
4. Multimedia installation update: B. Harris
5. Annual fund drive: T. Henderson

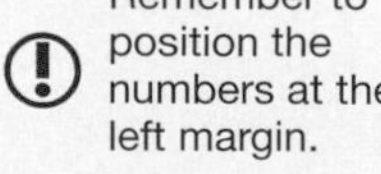

Remember to position the numbers at the left margin.

I. MINUTES OF MEETINGS

Minutes of a meeting are a record of items discussed during a meeting. To format meeting minutes, follow these steps:

1. Press ENTER 6 times to leave an approximately 2-inch top margin.
2. Insert an open table with 2 columns and 6 rows.
3. Merge the cells in Row 1, and center the title in all-caps, bold, and 14-point font. Press ENTER 2 times.
4. Center `Minutes of the Meeting` in upper- and lowercase, bold, and 12-point font. Press ENTER 2 times.
5. Center the date; then press ENTER 1 time.
6. Move to Row 2, Column A; then type the first section heading, `ATTENDANCE`, in bold, all-caps.
7. Move to Column B, and type the information pertaining to the section. Press ENTER 1 time after the final line in all Column B entries.
8. Move to Row 3, Column A, and type the second section heading. Then move to Column B and type the corresponding information for this section. Press ENTER 1 time after the final line in Row 3, Column B.
9. Move to Row 4 and repeat steps 6 and 7 until all remaining sections have been completed.
10. Type the closing and signature lines in Column B of the final row. Remember to press ENTER 4 times to allow room for the signature. Do not press ENTER after typing the signature line.
11. Manually adjust the column widths as needed.

↓6X

14 pt **PLANNING COMMITTEE** ↓2X

12 pt **Minutes of the Meeting** ↓2X

February 10, 20-- ↓1X

ATTENDANCE	The Planning Committee meeting was called to order at 1 p.m. on February 10, 20—, by Michelle North, chairperson. Members present were Cal Anderson, L. T. Braddock, Lisa Samson, Sharon Owens, and J. R. Stern. ↓1X
OLD BUSINESS	The committee reviewed bids for the purchase of a new computer for the Cheyenne office. We will accept the lower of two bids that have been submitted.
NEW BUSINESS	The committee reviewed a proposal for a new complex in Helena. After much discussion, the committee agreed to contact the Helena county clerk's office to get information on zoning ordinances.
ADJOURNMENT	The meeting was adjourned at 2:45 p.m. The next meeting is scheduled for March 22 in Room 16. ↓1X
	Respectfully submitted, ↓4X *L. T. Braddock* L. T. Braddock, Secretary

Note: The table is shown with "Show Gridlines" active.

Word Processing Manual

J. WORD PROCESSING: HYPHENATION

Study Lesson 67 in your word processing manual. Complete all of the shaded steps while at your computer. Then format the jobs that follow.

Report 67-42

Agenda

↓6X

14 pt **ALLIANCE CORPORATION STAFF MEETING** ↓2X

12 pt↓ **Meeting Agenda** ↓2X

November 17, 20-- ↓2X

1. Approval of minutes of October 15 meeting ↓2X
2. Progress reports of new district offices
3. Discussion of attendance at the National Hardware Association's annual meeting
4. Multimedia installation update: B. Harris
5. Annual fund drive: T. Henderson

Word Processing Manual Review:

Review: L. 28: Bullets and Numbering

Reference Manual

Review: R-11A: Meeting Agenda

Report 67-43

Agenda

APEX MULTIMEDIA CORPORATION

Meeting Agenda

October 13, 20--

1. *Call to order*
2. *Approval of minutes of September 10 meeting*
3. *Progress reports on Sherman contract (Julia Adams)*
4. *Upgrading of 8.0 presentation media*
5. CD-ROM *development program (Ray Sanchez)*
6. *Internet configuration (JoAnn Hubbard)*
7. *Adjournment*

Report 67-44

Minutes of a Meeting

Note: The table is shown with "Show Gridlines" active.

↓6X 14 pt **PLANNING COMMITTEE** ↓2X 12 pt↓ **Minutes of the Meeting** ↓2X **February 10, 20--** ↓1X	
ATTENDANCE	The Planning Committee meeting was called to order at 1 p.m. on February 10, 20--, by Michelle North, chairperson. Members present were Cal Anderson, L. T. Braddock, Lisa Samson, Sharon Owens, and J. R. Stern. ↓1X
OLD BUSINESS	The committee reviewed bids for the purchase of a new computer for the Cheyenne office. We will accept the lower of two bids that have been submitted.
NEW BUSINESS	The committee reviewed a proposal for a new complex in Helena. After much discussion, the committee agreed to contact the Helena county clerk's office to get information on zoning ordinances.
ADJOURNMENT	The meeting was adjourned at 2:45 p.m. The next meeting is scheduled for March 22 in Room 16. ↓1X
	Respectfully submitted, ↓4X L. T. Braddock, Secretary

Report 67-45

Minutes of a Meeting

PERSONEL COMMITTEE (N)

Minutes of the Meeting

May 14, 20--

ATTENDENCE (A)

A (special) meeting of the Personnel Committee was held (on May 14, 20--,) in the office of Mr. Cameron. (All) Members present were

(Continued on next page)

except Richard Dixon, who was repre sented by Monica Zick man. The meeting was called to order at 2 p. m.

Old Business A copy of the survey is attached. Eighty-eight employees participated in a survey that had been completed by Andrea Fields. The minutes of the last monthly meeting were read.

NEW BUSINESS Ms. Samuels discussed the need for planning a campaign for job applicants about vacancies occur within the company. Frank Lundquist will draft a flier to be sent to the Park view sentinel. Programs for the N P A convention to be held in Des Moines were distributed to all members. Each committee member were asked to distribute copies to employees in his or her department.

ADJOURN The meeting was adjourned at 3:25 a.m. The next meeting has been scheduled for July 10 in the conference center.

Respectfully submitted,

Brandon Stinson, Secretary

Lesson 68

Procedures Manual

Goals

- Type at least 41wpm/5′/5e
- Format a procedures manual

A. Type 2 times.

A. WARMUP

```
     Zach sharpened the ax for Quinn just to help him win  10
the $100 tree-cutting event to be held in Kildeer on May 8  23
(if it doesn't rain). The prize will be $250--fantastic!   34
| 1 | 2 | 3 | 4 | 5 | 6 | 7 | 8 | 9 | 10 | 11 | 12
```

SKILLBUILDING

B. MAP

Follow the GDP software directions for this exercise in improving keystroking accuracy.

C. Take two 5-minute timed writings. Review your speed and errors.

Goal: At least 41wpm/5′/5e

C. 5-MINUTE TIMED WRITING

```
     Taking photos with a digital camera is a process that  11
is quite unique and very different from taking photos with  23
film. Most digital cameras store images on a device such as  35
a memory card or a memory stick. The number of photos you  46
can store on a card or stick depends on how many megabytes  58
it can hold. Once you reach the limit of the memory device,  70
you can store no new images until you either transfer or  82
delete the old ones to make room for new ones.  91
     The advantages of using a memory device are many. For  102
example, the card or stick can be used over and over; or,  114
when the device is full, just simply remove it and put in a  126
new device. You can also move the images to the computer,  137
where they can reside on your hard drive for as long as you  149
want. If the memory card or stick you have does not have  161
enough memory, you can upgrade the megabyte size. Finally,  172
you can see instantly any images you have taken with the  184
camera. If you decide not to keep an image in the camera,  195
you can delete it to make room for other images.  205
| 1 | 2 | 3 | 4 | 5 | 6 | 7 | 8 | 9 | 10 | 11 | 12
```

FORMATTING

D. PROCEDURES MANUAL

Organizations often prepare procedures manuals to assist employees in identifying the steps or methods they must follow to accomplish particular tasks. To format a procedures manual:

1. Type the manual as a single-spaced report.
2. Place a header on every page except the first page. The header may include such items as the title of the manual (at the left margin) and the company name and page number (at the right margin).
3. Place a footer on every page including the first page. The footer should be in italics and may include the same information as the header, or it may identify the content of that page (for example, "Training Program").

Employees' Manual Chandler Industries, Page 7

The purpose of this procedures manual is to assist managers who are responsible for developing training programs for new employees who have been hired in any of the seven regional branches of Chandler Industries. The basic content of this training program is outlined in the following paragraphs. ↓2X

INTRODUCTION ↓2X

This section identifies specific ways the manual should be used at Chandler Industries as well as the content of the manual. Answers are provided to the following questions: ↓2X

1. Where does the training manual fit within the training program?
2. For whom is the manual designed, and what does it contain?
3. How should the manual be used?
4. Can the manual be used in a classroom setting?
5. Can the manual be used as self-paced instructional material?
6. Can study guides accompany the manual? ↓2X

PROGRAM PHILOSOPHY AND GOALS ↓2X

This section reveals the nature of the training program. The statements below provide the context for all courses within Chandler Industries. The focus of the section is as follows: ↓2X

- Why does this program exist, and who benefits from it?
- What company needs are satisfied by this program?
- What goals, tasks, and competencies are satisfied by this program?
- What specific skills does this training program develop?

Training Program

DOCUMENT PROCESSING

Report 68-46

Procedures Manual

1. Turn on hyphenation.
2. In page numbering, change the page number to start at page 7, and then create a header as follows: Type `Employees' Manual` at the left margin. Type `Chandler Industries, Page 7` aligned at the right margin.
3. Create a footer by typing *`Training Program`* in italic and aligned at the left margin.
4. Type the following portion of a procedures manual.

Word Processing Manual Review:

L. 27: Page Numbering
L. 42: Headers and Footers

Employees' Manual Chandler Industries, Page 7

¶ The purpose of this procedures manual is to assist managers who are responsible for developing training programs for new employees who have been hired in any of the seven regional branches of Chandler Industries. The basic content of this training program is outlined in the following paragraphs.

(Continued on next page)

INTRODUCTION
¶ This section identifies specific ways the manual should be used at Chandler Industries as well as the content of the manual. Answers are provided to the following questions:

Remember to single-space the entire list if all items in the list are 1 line long.

1. Where does the training manual fit within the training program?
2. For whom is the manual designed, and what does it contain?
3. How should the manual be used?
4. Can the manual be used in a classroom setting?
5. Can the manual be used as self-paced instructional material?
6. Can study guides accompany the manual?

PROGRAM PHILOSOPHY AND GOALS
¶ This section describes the nature of the training program. The statements below provide the context for all courses within Chandler Industries. The focus of the section is as follows:

- Why does this program exist, and who benefits from it?
- What company needs are satisfied by this program?
- What goals, tasks, and competencies are satisfied by this program?
- What specific skills does this training program develop?

Training Program

Report 68-47

Procedures Manual

1. In page numbering, change the page number to start at page 2.
2. Create a header as follows:
   Type `Presentation Software Guide` at the left margin. Type `Cartwright Services, Page 2` aligned at the right margin.
3. Type `Formatting` as a footer at the left margin and in italic.

Presentation Software Guide　　Cartwright Services, Page 2

FORMATTING SLIDES
¶ Once you have written your presentation, you can place your key points on slides using presentation software. Follow these steps to prepare your presentation slides.

Remember to insert a blank line between items in a multiline list in a single-spaced document.

- Select a template or background that is appropriate for every slide.
- Select a layout such as text copy or bulleted or numbered lists.
- Use the edit, copy, and paste commands to add text to your presentation slides.

FORMATTING THE PRESENTATION
¶ After you finish preparing the slides for your presentation, you may want to change the method by which each slide appears on the screen or the way individual points are displayed on the screen. In presentation software, moving from one slide to another is known as transition. Transition is accomplished by following these steps:

- Select the slides you want to control by the transition method.
- Select a transition method such as Cover Right or Wipe Left.
- Run through the slide show to determine whether or not you are satisfied with the transition.

(Continued on next page)

¶ Slide presentations can also be formatted so that each point you make on an individual slide appears individually on the screen. To structure your slides this way, follow these steps:

- Select the slides to be controlled by a build effect.
- Select a build effect style such as Fly From Left.
- Run through the slide show again to determine whether or not you are satisfied with the build effect.

Formatting

Report 68-48

Procedures Manual

1. Open the file for Report 68-47.
2. Remove the third bulleted item under the FORMATTING SLIDES heading.
3. Add the following sections to the end of the report.

ADDING CLIP ART

¶ Clipart enhances the appearance of a slide, and it can be easily added to selected slides or to every other slide in your presentation. Several clip art images are included in this presentation package, and any one of them can be used in slides that you prepare. If you choose, however, you can insert clip art images from other packages. To insert a clip art from your presentation package, follow these steps:

- Select the slide on which you want the clip art to appear.
- Click the icon for adding a clip art image. This icon is found on the menu bar.
- Select the image from the software clip art library. The slide can come from the presentation package or you can retrieve it from another clip art package.
- Size and move the image to its correct location on the presentation slide.
- Copy the image to the master slide if it is to appear on all slides.

¶ You can also change the appearance of the clip art image by (1) changing the colors used in the image; (2) flipping the image so that its horizontal or vertical position is reversed (mirror image); (3) changing the contrast or brightness of the image; and (4) cropping the image so that unwanted sections are eliminated from view.

Reports Formatted in Columns

Goals

- Improve speed and accuracy
- Refine language arts skills in spelling
- Format magazine articles

A. Type 2 times.

A. WARMUP

```
     On 12/30/02 Jim gave Alex and Pam a quiz--it was quite  11
difficult! Neither scored higher than 82%; their average     22
was 79. They should retake the quiz by the 4th or 5th.       32
| 1 | 2 | 3 | 4 | 5 | 6 | 7 | 8 | 9 | 10 | 11 | 12
```

SKILLBUILDING

B. PACED PRACTICE

If you are not using the GDP software, turn to page SB-14 and follow the directions for this activity.

PPP PRETEST → PRACTICE → POSTTEST

PRETEST
Take a 1-minute timed writing. Review your speed and errors.

C. PRETEST: Horizontal Reaches

```
     Four famous adults gazed at a wren on our farm gate.    11
A group of gawking writers wrote facts about an additional   23
upward gain in wildlife numbers on their supply of pads.     34
| 1 | 2 | 3 | 4 | 5 | 6 | 7 | 8 | 9 | 10 | 11 | 12
```

PRACTICE
Speed Emphasis:
If you made no more than 1 error on the Pretest, type each *individual* line 2 times.
Accuracy Emphasis:
If you made 2 or more errors, type each *group* of lines (as though it were a paragraph) 2 times.

D. PRACTICE: In Reaches

```
wr wrap wren wreak wrist wrote writer unwrap writhe wreaths
ou pout ours ounce cough fouls output detour ousted coupons
ad adds dead adult ready blade advice fading admits adheres
```

E. PRACTICE: Out Reaches

```
fa fact farm faith sofas fakes faulty unfair famous defames
up upon soup upset group upper upturn supply uplift upsurge
ga gate gave cigar gains legal gazing legacy gawked garbage
```

POSTTEST
Repeat the Pretest timed writing and compare performance.

F. POSTTEST: Horizontal Reaches

LANGUAGE ARTS

G. Type this list of frequently misspelled words, paying special attention to any spelling problems in each word.

G. SPELLING

```
13 personnel information its procedures their committee system
14 receive employees which education services opportunity area
15 financial appropriate interest received production contract
16 important through necessary customer employee further there
17 property account approximately general control division our
```

Edit the sentences to correct any misspellings.

```
18 The revised systom was adopted by the finantial division.
19 Four employes want to serve on the new property commitee.
20 Approximatly ten proceedures were included in the contract.
21 Further informasion will be recieved from the customers.
22 Their was much interest shown by the production personal.
23 The services in that aria are necesary for needed control.
```

FORMATTING

H. MAGAZINE ARTICLES

Magazine articles can be formatted as two-column reports. Follow these steps:

1. Press ENTER 6 times to leave an approximately 2-inch top margin on page 1.
2. Center and type the article title in all-caps, bold, and 14-point.
3. Press ENTER 2 times; then center and type the byline in upper- and lowercase, bold, and 12-point.
4. Press ENTER 2 times and change to left alignment.
5. Turn on hyphenation, if needed.
6. Format the document for a 2-column layout; then change to justified alignment. (Remember to select "This point forward" from the "Apply to" section of the Columns dialog box.)
7. Type the article single-spaced; insert 1 blank line before and after all side headings.
8. Create a header to print on all pages except page 1 to identify the author's name and the page number at the top right of every page. Use only the author's last name and the page number in the header (for example, `Davis 2`).

↓6X
14 pt **MEMBER BUYING SERVICES** ↓2X
12 pt **Brenda T. Mysweski** ↓2X

Policyholders of AICA (and their dependents) are eligible for a wide range of discount services. These services provide you with a variety of items you can purchase, from automobiles to computers to jewelry. Here are some examples of the merchandise and services that are available to all AICA members. ↓2X

AUTO PRICING ↓2X

You can order the most sophisticated auto information guide on the market. The guide will give you information on retail prices, vehicle specifications, safety equipment, and factory-option packages. ↓2X

When you are ready to place your order for an automobile, a team of company experts will work with you and with the prospective dealer to ensure that you are getting the best possible price through a network of nationwide dealers. You are guaranteed to get the best price for the automobile you have chosen.

Once you have purchased your automobile, AICA will provide all your insurance needs. Discounts on policy rates are provided for completion of a driver-training program, for installed antitheft devices, and for installed passive restraint systems such as air bags.

Finally, we can make your purchase decision and easy one by always providing a low-rate finance plan for you. You can be certain that you are getting the most competitive interest rate for the purchase of your automobile when you finance with AICA.

CAR RENTAL DISCOUNTS

When you need to rent an automobile while traveling, special rates are available to you from five of the largest car rental agencies.

Mysweski 2

ROAD AND TRAVEL SERVICES

You can enjoy the security of emergency road service through the AICA Road and Travel Plan. This plan also includes discounts on hotels and motels.

As an AICA traveler, you can take advantage of our exclusive discounts and bonuses on cruises and tours. Our travel plan provides daily and weekend trips to over 100 destinations. Take advantage of this wonderful opportunity to let AICA serve all your travel needs.

MERCHANDISE BUYING

Each quarter a buying services catalog will be sent to you. This catalog includes a variety of items that can be purchased through AICA—and you'll never find better prices! Through the catalog you can purchase jewelry, furniture, sports equipment, electronics, appliances, and computers. To place an order, all you have to do is call AICA toll-free at 1-800-555-3838. Your order will arrive within 10 to 15 days.

Word Processing Manual

I. WORD PROCESSING: COLUMNS

Study Lesson 69 in your word processing manual. Complete all of the shaded steps while at your computer. Then format the jobs that follow.

DOCUMENT PROCESSING

Report 69-49

Magazine Article in Two Columns

MEMBER BUYING SERVICES | Brenda T. Mysweski

¶ Policyholders of AICA (and their dependents) are eligible for a wide range of discount services. These services provide you with a variety of items you can purchase, from automobiles to computers to jewelry. Here are some examples of the merchandise and services that are available to all AICA members.

AUTO PRICING

¶ You can order the most sophisticated auto information guide on the market. The guide will give you information on retail prices, vehicle specifications, safety equipment, and factory-option packages.

¶ When you are ready to place your order for an automobile, a team of company experts will work with you and with the prospective dealer to ensure that you are getting the best possible price through a network of nationwide dealers. You are guaranteed to get the best price for the automobile you have chosen.

(Continued on next page)

¶ Once you have purchased your automobile, AICA will provide all your insurance needs. Discounts on policy rates are provided for completion of a driver-training program, for installed antitheft devices, and for installed passive restraint systems such as air bags.

¶ Finally, we can make your purchase decision an easy one by always providing a low-rate finance plan for you. You can be certain that you are getting the most competitive interest rate for the purchase of your automobile when you finance with AICA.

CAR RENTAL DISCOUNTS

¶ When you need to rent an automobile while traveling, special rates are available to you from five of the largest car rental agencies.

ROAD AND TRAVEL SERVICES

¶ You can enjoy the security of emergency road service through the AICA Road and Travel Plan. This plan also includes discounts on hotels and motels.

¶ As an AICA traveler, you can take advantage of our exclusive discounts and bonuses on cruises and tours. Our travel plan provides daily and weekend trips to over 100 destinations. Take advantage of this wonderful opportunity to let AICA serve all your travel needs.

MERCHANDISE BUYING

¶ Each quarter a buying services catalog will be sent to you. This catalog includes a variety of items that can be purchased through AICA—and you'll never find better prices! Through the catalog you can purchase jewelry, furniture, sports equipment, electronics, appliances, and computers. To place an order, all you have to do is call AICA toll-free at 1-800-555-3838. Your order will arrive within 10 to 15 days.

Report 69-50

Magazine Article in Two Columns

INTERVIEW TECHNIQUES | **By Paul Sanford**

The interview process ~~allows~~ enables a company to gather information about you that ~~has~~ was not ~~been~~ provided on your resume or application form. This information may include~~s~~ ~~such~~ items as you(r) career goals, appearance, personality, poise, attitudes, and ability to express yourself verbally.

APPEARANCE

There are ~~several~~ things you should keep in mind when going ~~for~~ to an interview. You should plan your wardrobe ~~well~~ carefully because first impressions are lasting ones when you walk into the interviewer's office. If you are not quite certain ~~as to~~ about what you should wear, dress conservatively. Whatever you ~~select~~ choose, be sure that your clothing is clean, neat, and comfortable. You should

(Continued on next page)

also pay attention to *important* details such as clean hair, shined shoes, well-groomed nails, and appropriate jewelry and other accessories.

MEETING THE INTERVIEWER

Be sure to arrive at the interview site a few minutes early. Stand when you meet the interviewer ~~for the first time~~. If ~~a handshake is~~ *the interviewer* offer*s*~~ed~~, *to shake hands* shake hands in a confident, firm manner. It is also a good idea not to smoke or chew gum during the interview.

THE INTERVIEW PROCESS

Maintain ~~good~~ *direct* eye contact with the interviewer when you respond to his or her questions. Listen intently to everything that is said. Be aware of ~~the~~ *any* movements you make with your eyes, your hands, and other parts of your body during the interview. Too much movement may be a signal to the interviewer that you are nervous, that you lack confidence, or that you are not certain of your answers.

¶ During the interview ~~process~~, the interviewer will judge not only what you say but also how you say it. As you ~~speak~~ *answer questions*, you will be judged on grammar, articulation, vocabulary, and tone of voice. The nonverbal skills that *the interviewer* may ~~be~~ judge~~d~~ are your attitude, enthusiasm, listening abilit*y*~~ies~~, and promptness in responding to questions.

ENDING THE INTERVIEW

Let the interviewer determine when it is time to close the interview. When this time arrives, ask the interviewer when he or she expects to make a decision on hiring for this position and when you ~~can~~ *may* expect to hear about the job. Thank the interviewer for taking the time to meet with you, and express a ~~positive~~ desire to work for the company.

¶ After the interview, send a follow-up letter to remind the interviewer of your name and your ~~continued~~ interest in the company. Let that person know how to contact you by providing a telephone number where you can be reached, either at home or at your current work location.

Report 69-51

Magazine Article in Two Columns

Word Processing Manual Review:

L. 30: Cut/Copy/Paste

Open the file for Report 69-49 and make the following changes:

1. Make Maria Sanchez the author of the article.
2. Make the MERCHANDISE BUYING section the second paragraph in the article.
3. Add the following section to the end of the article:

MISCELLANEOUS SERVICES | In addition to the above services, AICA provides permanent life insurance, pension plan funding, cash management, and credit card programs. At your request, detailed catalogs will be sent to you that explain each of these services.

Lesson 70

Report Review

Goals

- Type at least 41wpm/5′/5e
- Improve speed and accuracy
- Review report formats

A. Type 2 times.

A. WARMUP

Felix Quayle sat in Seat #14 when he won the jackpot; 11
Van Gill sat in Seat #23 but did not win a prize. Do you 22
think Row 19 (Seats #1560 and #1782) will be lucky for me? 34

| 1 | 2 | 3 | 4 | 5 | 6 | 7 | 8 | 9 | 10 | 11 | 12

SKILLBUILDING

B. Take a 1-minute timed writing on the first paragraph to establish your base speed. Then take four 1-minute timed writings on the remaining paragraphs. As soon as you equal or exceed your base speed on one paragraph, advance to the next, more difficult paragraph.

B. SUSTAINED PRACTICE: ROUGH DRAFT

The possibility of aging and not being able to live as 11
independently as we want to is a prospect that no one wants 23
to recognize. One resource designed to counter some of the 35
negative realities of aging is called the Handyman Project. 47

This type of ~~project~~ program helps support elders and disabled 12
residents in their efforts to maintain the^ir homes. As the 24
name implies, "handy" volunt^ers per for^m minor home repairs 36
such as tight^ening leaky faucets and fixing broken windows. 48

Other type^s of work include: painting, plumbing, yard 11
work, and carpentary. The volunteers are all as divers^ified 23
as the word itself. You may find a retire^e working next too 35
an executive or a student ~~helping~~ assisting a lisensed electrician. 47

(Continued on next page)

o w
Their back grunds may vary, but that they share is the 11

desire find
~~hope~~ to put their ~~cap~~abilities to good use. Volunters ~~take~~ 23

finishing
a high level of personnal satisfaction after ~~doing~~ a job 35

and
~~but~~ spending time with an elder who really needs the help. 47

| 1 | 2 | 3 | 4 | 5 | 6 | 7 | 8 | 9 | 10 | 11 | 12

C. Take two 5-minute timed writings. Review your speed and errors.

Goal: 41wpm/5′/5e

C. 5-MINUTE TIMED WRITING

In most offices, many products that are used each day 11
are made of materials that can now be recycled. Amazingly, 23
items made of glass, steel, aluminum, plastics, and paper 34
can be recycled to make many products that we need. Also, 46
the recycling process can help the environment. 56

Some unique examples of the process of recycling the 66
items we often throw away are listed here. Those old coffee 78
filters can be used to make soles for new shoes. Pieces of 90
paper that are thrown away each day can be used to make 101
tissue paper and paper towels. Most plastics that are used 113
in soda bottles can be recycled for insulation for jackets 125
and car interiors. Used lightbulbs and some glass products 137
can also be used to replace the surface on our streets. 148

Look around the room in which you are working. If you 159
are not already taking part in a recycling program, you may 171
want to recycle some items that you no longer need. Items 183
such as used paper, file folders, and aluminum cans can be 194
collected very quickly. What other items can you add? 205

| 1 | 2 | 3 | 4 | 5 | 6 | 7 | 8 | 9 | 10 | 11 | 12

Report 70-52

Agenda

Crandall First National Bank | Meeting Agenda | May 15, 20--

1. Call to Order
2. Approval of minutes of April 17 meeting (16)
3. Mortgage loans (J. William Hokes)
4. Installment loans (Lorraine Hagen)
5. Series EE bonds (Joni Ellickson)
6. Club memberships (Louise Abbey)
7. Certificates of deposit (~~Louise Abbey~~ Robert Hunt)
8. Closing remarks
9. Adjournment

Report 70-53

Minutes of a Meeting

LITTLETON WATERCOLOUR SOCIETY

Minutes of the Meeting

October 23, 20--

CALL TO ORDER The meeting was called to order by Sandra Garvy at 8 p.m. in the Littleton library confrence room.

OLD BUSINESS susan Firtz furnished each member with a list of artists and the name of the wtercolor paintings each artist is entering in the Fall Arts Fair.

NEW BUSINESS John Cahmpion informed members that a new supply of canvas and oil paint arrived. Members can check out any items ~~they need~~ to begin their winter projects. He reminded everyone that Winter Fair will be held December 14 at the Expo.

ADJOURMENT The meeting was adjourned at 9:45 p.m. The next meeting ~~is~~ will be held November 12.

Respecfully submitted,

Catherine Argetes

Report 70-54

Magazine Article in Two Columns

Type the article in two columns and balance the columns.

Progress and Proofreading Check

Documents designated as Proofreading Checks serve as a check of your proofreading skill. Your goal is to have zero typographical errors when the GDP software first scores the document.

PERFORMING SUCCESSFULLY

Ginger Nichols

¶ We have been involved in giving performances since our very early years, when we played a part in a class play or participated in competitive sports events at our school. The most terrifying part of each performance was probably the fear that we would "freeze" when it came our turn to perform. Whenever we find ourselves in this predicament, the best thing to do is to accept that fear and to learn to let it work for us, not against us. We need to recognize that nervousness or fear may set in during our performance. Then, when it does happen (if it does), we will be ready to cope with it and overcome it.

¶ If you forget some of your lines in a recitation, try to remember other lines and recite them. Doing so may help those forgotten lines to "pop back" into your memory so that you put them in at a later time, if possible.

¶ You always want to leave your audience with the idea that you have given them something worthwhile that they can use or apply to their own lives. For maximum impact on your audience and to make sure that they remember what you say, use audiovisual aids to reinforce your message. Remember, however, that audiovisual aids are nothing more than aids. The real message should come in the words you choose when giving your presentation.

¶ Study your speech well; even rehearse it if necessary. However, do not practice it to the extent that it appears that you are merely reading what is written down on the paper in front of you. Much of your personality should be exhibited while you are giving your speech. If you are an enthusiastic, friendly person who converses well with people face-to-face, then that same persona should be evident during your speech. A good piece of advice is to just go out there and be yourself—you will be much more comfortable by doing so, and your audience will relate to you better than if you try to exhibit a different personality when at the podium.

¶ No matter how rapidly you speak in general, slow down when you are in front of a group. The fact that you are nervous can cause your speech rate to increase. The best way to slow down your speaking is to breathe deeply. Doing so also causes your nervous system to relax, allowing you to proceed with your speech calmly.

¶ Finally, possibly the best advice for giving a successful speech is to be prepared. You will be more confident if you are thoroughly prepared. Do your research, rehearse your speech, and make notes about where you want to give emphasis or use an audiovisual aid.

Unit 15

Correspondence

LESSON 71
Multipage Letters

LESSON 72
Special Letter Features

LESSON 73
More Special Letter Features

LESSON 74
Multipage Memos With Tables

LESSON 75
Memo Reports

March 1, 20--

Mr. Rodney Graae
Thompson Corporation
42 Harris Court
Trenton, NJ 08648

We are indeed interested in designing a new corporate logo and the corresponding stationery for your fine corporation. As I indicated in our recent telephone conversation, we have a design staff that has won many national awards for letterhead form design, and we consider it an honor to be contacted by you.

Within a month, we will submit several basic designs to you and your board of directors. At that time, please feel free to make any comments and suggestions that will help us finalize a design. Here is a modified price list for the printed stationery:

	Cost
)0 sheets)	$ 80.00
s (1,000 cards)	39.50
ıres (1,000 sheets)	219.30
	92.00

can be of further service.

November 8, 20--

CONFIDENTIAL

Mrs. Katie Hollister
11426 Prairie View Road
Kearney, NE 68847

Dear Mrs. Hollister:

Subject: Site for New Elementary School

As you are aware, your 160-acre farm, located in th
Tyro township, is a part of Independent School Dis
schools occupies 2 acres and is adjoined by an 8-ac
planning stages for a fourth elementary school. As
District 17 Board has directed me to initiate discuss
acres of land.

Please call me at your convenience to arrange a me
and me. I look forward to our discussions.

Yours truly,

Irvin J. Hagg
Superintendent

lcv
c: District 17 Board

MEMO TO: All Employees

FROM: Adrienne Barzanov

DATE: March 2, 20--

SUBJECT: New Building Site

We have consulted with several architects and have finalized plans to build a new administrative center at 6400 Easton Plaza. This memo provides general information about plans for the center's exterior and interior development.

EXTERIOR PLANS

Exterior plans will maintain the historical integrity and beauty of the surrounding area and reflect the architecture of other buildings in the office park. Landscaping plans include a parklike area, a picnic area, and a small pond.

INTERIOR PLANS FOR STAFF

Staff will be located within the new facility as follows:

1. Accounting will be located on the first floor in the west wing.
2. Sales and marketing will be located on the first floor in the east wing. All staff will be grouped according to product line.
3. All other staff will be located on the second floor. Exact locations will be determined at a later date.

INTERIOR PLANS FOR SPECIAL FACILITIES

Conference rooms will be located in the center of the building on the first floor to provide easy access for everyone. All rooms will be equipped with state-of-the-art technology.

Our new center will also include a full-service cafeteria, a copy center, a library, an athletic center, and an on-site day care center.

Construction of the new center will begin when we obtain the necessary permits.

mwr

Multipage Letters

Goals

- Improve speed and accuracy
- Refine language arts skills in the use of commas
- Format multipage letters

A. Type 2 times.

A. WARMUP

1 We were quite dazzled when the plumber drove up in a 11
2 C-150 pickup truck! She was joined by 26 young people (all 23
3 students) who gazed intently as she welded six of the rods. 35

| 1 | 2 | 3 | 4 | 5 | 6 | 7 | 8 | 9 | 10 | 11 | 12

SKILLBUILDING

B. Take three 12-second timed writings on each line. The scale below the last line shows your wpm speed for a 12-second timed writing.

B. 12-SECOND SPEED SPRINTS

4 Pam knew that five girls in the other car were on the team.
5 The women drove eight blue autos when they made some trips.
6 All the girls in four other autos may go on the same trips.
7 Spring is the time of the year when they have a lot of pep.

5 10 15 20 25 30 35 40 45 50 55 60

C. DIAGNOSTIC PRACTICE: SYMBOLS AND PUNCTUATION

If you are not using the GDP software, turn to page SB-2 and follow the directions for this activity.

LANGUAGE ARTS

D. Study the rules at the right.

D. COMMAS

Note: The callout signals in the left margin indicate which language arts rule from this lesson has been applied.

RULE ▶ ,nonessential expression

The underline calls attention to a point in the sentence where a comma might mistakenly be inserted.

Use a comma before and after a nonessential expression.

Andre, who was there, can verify the statement.

But: Anyone_ who was there_ can verify the statement.

Van's first book, *Crisis of Management*, was not discussed.

Van's book_ *Crisis of Management*_ was not discussed.

Note: A nonessential expression is a group of words that may be omitted without changing the basic meaning of the sentence. Always examine the noun or pronoun that comes before the expression to determine whether the noun needs the expression to complete its meaning. If it does, the expression is *essential* and does *not* take a comma.

RULE ▶ ,adjacent adjective

Use a comma between two adjacent adjectives that modify the same noun.

We need an intelligent, enthusiastic individual for this job.

But: Please order a new bulletin board for our main conference room.

Note: Do not use a comma after the second adjective. Also, do not use a comma if the first adjective modifies the combined idea of the second adjective and the noun (for example, *bulletin board* and *conference room* in the second example).

Edit the sentences by inserting any needed punctuation.

8 The school president Mr. Roberts will address the students.

9 The fall planning meeting which is held in Charlotte has been canceled.

10 Students planning to take the certification test must register for the orientation class.

11 The sleek luxury car is scheduled for delivery next week.

12 Margaret brought her fast reliable laptop to the meeting.

13 A stamped addressed envelope should be included with the survey.

FORMATTING

E. MULTIPAGE LETTERS

To format a multipage letter:

1. Type the first page on letterhead stationery, and type continuation pages on plain paper that matches the letterhead.
2. Insert a page number at the top right of the second and succeeding pages.

2

A copy of the formal complaint is enclosed for your review. I shall call you in about a week to arrange a time and place for our meeting.

I have never been involved with anything like this before. Any help that you give me will be appreciated.

Sincerely,

Ms. Jeanne M. Hoover
Attorney-at-Law

rmv
Enclosure

DOCUMENT PROCESSING

Correspondence 71-64

Business Letter in Modified-Block Style

Reference Manual

Review: R-5A and R-5B: Multipage Business Letter

October 16, 20-- | Miss Florence B. Glashan | Attorney-at-Law | 2406 Shadows Glade | Dayton, OH 45426-0348 | Dear Miss Glashan: |

¶ It was good to meet you at the convention for trial attorneys in Detroit last week. In addition to the interesting program highlights of the regular sessions, I find that the informal discussions with people like you are an added plus at these meetings. Your contribution to the program was very beneficial to me.

¶ You may recall that I told you I had just been appointed by the court to defend a woman here in Dayton who has been charged with embezzling large sums of money from her previous employer. The defendant had been employed at a large department store for more than 25 years. Because of her valuable years of experience in accounting with the store, she was in charge of accounts receivable at the store. Her previous employer, the plaintiff in the case, claims that she embezzled $18,634 in 2000, $39,072 in 2001, and $27,045 in 2002.

(Continued on next page)

¶ I feel that it is my responsibility to represent my client and to provide the best defense possible. I recall that you mentioned that you had represented defendants in similar cases in previous years. As I prepare for this defense, perhaps you might help me in the following ways:

1. Please send me the appropriate citations for all similar trials in which you participated.
2. Also, please provide me with any other case citations that you think might be helpful to me in this case.
3. Arrange to meet with me soon so that I can benefit from your experience as I prepare for the trial.

¶ A copy of the formal complaint is enclosed for your review. I shall call you in about a week to arrange a time and place for our meeting. Please let me know if there is additional information that would be helpful in preparing for this case.

¶ I have never been involved with anything like this before. Any help that you give me will be appreciated. I shall look forward to working with you.

Sincerely, | Ms. Jeanne M. Hoover | Attorney-at-Law | urs | Enclosure

Use the numbering command for the numbered list.

Remember to insert a blank line before and after the list and between each item in a multiline list.

Correspondence 71-65

Business Letter in Block Style

April 3, 20-- | Mr. Michael Mc Ginty | District Manager | Star & Morgan Company | One DuPont cicle | Washington, DC 2006-2133 |

Dear Mike:

in Reston, Virginia,

¶ It was good to see you at our sales conference last week. Your winning our "golden apple" award for the most sales for the month was well deserved. When you first became part of our sales team, you showed great enthusiasm for you job immediately. There is no doubt that Starr & Morgan is very well represented in the metro Washington area. We particularly want to comment you for otaining the Westminster Account. Acquiing this account has been a major objective for a numbe of years. None of our company's sales represenives have been able to do this feat. Just the idea of a new account of over 500,000 is quite mind-boggling. How did you do it? Did you:

1. sped considerable time with the President Mr. Arch Davis or the Directo of Purchasing, Ms. Betsy Matin?
2. Conduct a series of hands-on workshops for the employees and managers?
3. Develope a special maretking campaign for Westminster it self or use a regular campaign model?
4. Combine various strategies in your efforts to obtain this important account?

(Continued on next page)

¶ Can you let me know what approaches were used to make this sale? Successes of this nature do not happen without a lot of hard work. You are to be commended for putting forth your best efforts to sign the account.

¶ If it can be arranged, a presentation by you at our next sales conference would seem very appropriate. The other sales representatives would benefit much from your success story. Our next meeting will be in late September in Richmond, Virginia. Again, comgratulations on your receipt of this award. All of us here in the home office are pleased greatly with the performance of our entire sales team. Indications are that this will be a year when records are broken and we will be in the media spotlight.

Sincerely yours, | Robert D. Miley Pres | urs | c: R. Olson, Director of Sales

Correspondence 71-66

Business Letter in Modified-Block Style

Open the file for Correspondence 71-64 and make the following changes:

1. Change the addressee to `Ms. Cynthia Barnes, Attorney-at-Law`.
2. Change the office address to:

   ```
   4066 Quarry Estates
   Dayton, OH 45429-1362.
   ```

3. Change the salutation as needed.
4. Add this sentence at the end of the second paragraph:

   ```
   The defendant is also being
   accused of embezzling
   $35,680 in 2003.
   ```

Lesson 72

Special Letter Features

Goals

- Type at least 42wpm/5'/5e
- Format special letter features

A. Type 2 times.

A. WARMUP

Six citizens from 14th Avenue East joined 83 other 10
residents to discuss the #794 proposal* for a new swimming 22
pool. Barry Kelm quoted numbers about current pool usage. 34

| 1 | 2 | 3 | 4 | 5 | 6 | 7 | 8 | 9 | 10 | 11 | 12

SKILLBUILDING

B. MAP

Follow the GDP software directions for this exercise in improving keystroking accuracy.

Strategies for Career Success

Audience Analysis

Knowing your audience is fundamental to the success of any message. Ask the following questions to help identify your audience.

What is your relationship to your audience? Are they familiar—people with whom you work or people unknown to you? The latter will prompt you to conduct some research to better communicate your purpose. What is the attitude of your audience? Are they hostile or receptive to your message? How will your message benefit them? What is your anticipated response? Asking these questions first can help prevent message mishap later.

When writing to a diverse audience, direct your message to the primary audience. These key decision makers will make a decision or act on the basis of your message. Determine the level of detail, organization, formality, and use of technical terms and theory.

YOUR TURN Compose a thank-you e-mail to a friend. How would it differ from an interview thank-you letter?

C. Take two 5-minute timed writings. Review your speed and errors.

Goal: At least 42wpm/5′/5e

C. 5-MINUTE TIMED WRITING

Whether you are searching for your first job or are 11
looking to change jobs, your networking skills may play a 22
crucial role in how successful you are in that endeavor. 34
Networking can be defined in some respects as a group of 45
people who are linked closely together for the purpose of 56
achieving some sort of end result. In this case, the end 68
result will be to establish new contacts who might be able 80
to assist you in your job search. 86

Your network is made up of dozens of people you have 97
met. You can never be sure who has the potential of helping 109
you the most in your job search. Therefore, it is important 121
that you consider all acquaintances. You should certainly 133
network with business associates, and especially those you 145
have met at various meetings and conferences. And don't 156
forget former teachers in whose classes you were enrolled. 168
Former classmates provide an excellent base on which to 179
build your network, and friends and family should also be 190
included. Finally, use the Internet to nurture any online 202
contacts you have made over the years. 210

| 1 | 2 | 3 | 4 | 5 | 6 | 7 | 8 | 9 | 10 | 11 | 12

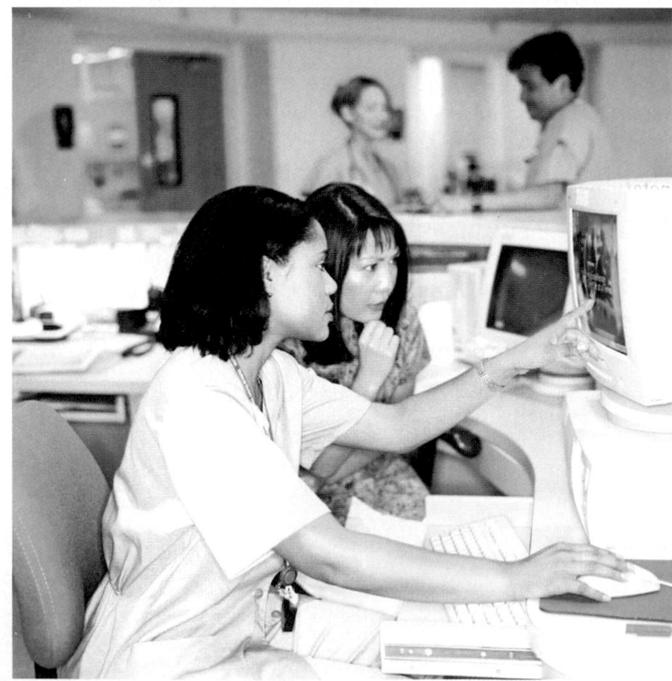

D. MULTIPLE ADDRESSES

Often a letter may be sent to two or more people at the same address or to different addresses:

1. If a letter is addressed to two people at the same address, type each name on a separate line above the same inside address.
2. If a letter is addressed to two people at different addresses, type each name and address, one under the other. Press ENTER 2 times between the addresses.
3. If a letter is addressed to three or more people, type the names and addresses side by side, with one at the left margin and another beginning at the centerpoint. Insert 1 blank line before typing the third name and address at the left margin.

November 19, 20-- ↓4X

Dr. Albert Russell, Professor
Department of English
Appalachian State University
Boone, NC 28608 ↓2X

Dr. Kay Smith, Professor
Director of Business
Grove City College
Grove City, PA 16127 ↓2X

Dear Dr. Russell and Dr. Smith:

E. ON-ARRIVAL NOTATIONS

On-arrival notations (such as *CONFIDENTIAL*) should be typed on the second line below the date, at the left margin. Type the notation in all-caps. Press ENTER 2 times to begin the inside address.

November 19, 20-- ↓2X

CONFIDENTIAL ↓2X

Mr. and Mrs. Earl Walters
3408 Washington Boulevard
New Tripoli, PA 18066 ↓2X

Dear Mr. and Mrs. Walters:

F. SUBJECT LINES

A *subject line* indicates what a letter is about. Type the subject line below the salutation at the left margin, preceded and followed by 1 blank line. (The term *Re* or *In re* may be used in place of *Subject*.)

November 19, 20-- ↓4X

Mr. and Mrs. Earl Walters
3408 Washington Boulevard
New Tripoli, PA 18066 ↓2X

Dear Mr. and Mrs. Walters: ↓2X

Subject: Insurance Enrollment ↓2X

We are pleased to be able to offer you enrollment in our insurance program.

Word Processing Manual

G. WORD PROCESSING: SORT

Study Lesson 72 in your word processing manual. Complete all of the shaded steps while at your computer. Then format the jobs that follow.

DOCUMENT PROCESSING

Correspondence 72-67

Business Letter in Block Style

November 8, 20--

CONFIDENTIAL

Mrs. Katie Hollister
11426 Prairie View Rd.
Kearney, NE 68847

Dear Mrs. Holister:

Subject: Site For New Elementary School

¶ As you are aware, your 160 acre farm, located in the quarter northeast of Section 25 in Tyro township, is a part of independent School District 17. Each of our elementary schools occupies two acres and is adjoined by an 8-acre park. We are now in the early palnning stages for a third elementary school. As you large farm is centrally located, the District 17 Board has directed me to initiate discussions with you for the purchase of 8 acres of land.

(Continued on next page)

¶ I look forward to our discussions. Please call me at your convenience to arrange a meeting with you and/or your attorney and me.

Yours truly,

Irvin J. Hagg

Superintendent

urs

c: District 17 Board

Correspondence 72-68

Business Letter in Block Style

Sort each bulleted list in the letter in ascending order.

October 4, 20-- | Ms. Deborah Campbell Wallace | 7835 Virginia Avenue Northwest | Washington, DC 20037 | Mr. Thomas E. Campbell | 3725 Stevens Road Southeast | Washington, DC 20020 | Dear Ms. Wallace and Mr. Campbell:

¶ We received your letter requesting instructions for transferring stock. The most common stock transfer situations are provided below. Determine which type of transfer you require and select the instructions that apply to your stock transfer.

- Name change
- Transferring shares to another individual(s)
- Transfers involving a deceased shareholder (individual ownership)
- Transfers involving a deceased shareholder (multiple owners)
- Transfers involving a minor
- Transfers involving a power of attorney
- Transfers involving a trust

¶ Every transfer requires a letter of instruction specifying how you want your shares transferred. The following items are required for all types of transfers:

- Name and address of new owner(s)
- Social security number or tax payer identification number
- Preferred form of ownership (that is, joint tenants or tenants in common)
- Indicate total shares that are being transferred
- Sign and date the form

¶ Please be sure to submit all required documentation and note that all documents submitted become part of the permanent record of transfer and will not be returned.

(Continued on next page)

¶ All transfers must have your signature(s) guaranteed by a financial institution participating in the Medallion Signature Guarantee Program.

¶ If you need additional information, you may visit our Web site for step-by-step instructions or you may call one of our customer service representatives at our toll-free number.

Sincerely, | William J. Shawley | Shareholder Services | urs

Correspondence 72-69

Personal-Business Letter in Block Style

(!) Format book titles in italic instead of underlining.

November 17, 20--

Dr. Arif Gureshi
8726 East Ridge Drive
Morehead, KY 40351-7268
Dear Dr. Gureshi:
Subject: The Middle East in the Year 2005 Discussion
¶ Your new book, The Middle East in the Year 2005, has gotten excellent reviews. The citizens of Morehead are pleased that a respected member of one of our local colleges is receiving national attention.
¶ Our book discussion group in Morehead, composed of members of the AAUW (American Association of University Women), has selected your book for discussion at our May meeting. We would very much like you to be a participant; your attendance at the meeting would be a real highlight.
¶ I shall call you next week. Our members are hoping that you will be able to attend and that an acceptable date can be arranged.
Sincerely,

Theresa A. Gorski
2901 Garfield Court
Morehead, KY 40351-2687

More Special Letter Features

Goals

- Improve speed and accuracy
- Refine language arts skills in composing paragraphs
- Format letters with special features

A. Type 2 times.

A. WARMUP

```
     The 83 Lions Club members raised $6,690 (95% of the      11
requested sum) to resurface the tennis courts. Gayle was      22
amazed when sixteen jolly members picked up over 10% more.    34
| 1 | 2 | 3 | 4 | 5 | 6 | 7 | 8 | 9 | 10 | 11 | 12
```

SKILLBUILDING

B. PACED PRACTICE

If you are not using the GDP software, turn to page SB-14 and follow the directions for this activity.

PPP PRETEST → PRACTICE → POSTTEST

PRETEST
Take a 1-minute timed writing. Review your speed and errors.

C. PRETEST: Vertical Reaches

```
     The scents in the trunk scared the rest of the drama     11
class. One judge drank juice and ate pecans as the cranky     23
coach scolded the best junior and bought the pink dresses.    35
| 1 | 2 | 3 | 4 | 5 | 6 | 7 | 8 | 9 | 10 | 11 | 12
```

PRACTICE
Speed Emphasis:
If you made no more than 1 error on the Pretest, type each *individual* line 2 times.
Accuracy Emphasis:
If you made 2 or more errors, type each *group* of lines (as though it were a paragraph) 2 times.

D. PRACTICE: Up Reaches

```
dr draft drank dryer drain drama dread dream drag drew drug
ju judge juice jumpy junks juror julep jumbo judo jump just
es essay nests tests less dress acres makes uses best rest
```

E. PRACTICE: Down Reaches

```
ca cable caddy cargo scare decay yucca pecan cage calm case
nk ankle blank crank blink think trunk brink bank junk sink
sc scale scalp scene scent scold scoop scope scan scar disc
```

POSTTEST
Repeat the Pretest timed writing and compare performance.

F. POSTTEST: Vertical Reaches

LANGUAGE ARTS

G. COMPOSING: PARAGRAPH

Compose a paragraph expressing your opinion on whether or not it is safe to make purchases online. Include precautions and potential dangers.

FORMATTING

H. TABLES WITHIN DOCUMENTS

To format a table that is part of a letter, memo, or report:

1. In a single-spaced document, press ENTER 2 times before and 1 time after the table. Be sure you are outside the table structure before pressing ENTER 1 time.
2. In a double-spaced document, press ENTER 1 time before and after the table.
3. Single-space the body of the table.
4. Adjust the column widths, and center the table within the margins of the document.
5. Never split a table between two pages if it will fit on one page. If a table will not fit at the bottom of the page on which it is first mentioned, place it at the top of the next page.

MEMO TO: Leo Guthrie

FROM: Paul Forester

DATE: January 10, 20--

SUBJECT: Sales Comparison

Listed below are the sales totals for the last two quarters. Please review the information before our staff meeting on Friday. ↓2X

SALES SUMMARY
December 31, 20-- ↓1X

↓1X **Region**	**Third Quarter**	**Fourth Quarter**
Northeast	456,321	512,980
Southeast	335,765	375,112
Northwest	425,666	457,034
Southwest	388,546	410,478

↓1X

Come to the meeting prepared to discuss plans for the upcoming sales promotions that will take place in our district.

I. COMPANY NAME IN CLOSING LINES

Some business firms show the company name in the closing lines of a letter. Type the company name in all-caps on the second line below the complimentary closing. Then press ENTER 4 times and type the writer's name.

Thank you for inviting me to participate in the discussion concerning this issue. ↓2X

Sincerely yours, ↓2X

HENDERSON AND SONS, INC. ↓4X

Mark Henderson, President ↓2X

mjd

J. BLIND COPY NOTATION

A *blind copy (bc:) notation* is used when the addressee is not intended to know that one or more other persons are being sent a copy of the letter. Type the *bc* notation on the file copy at the left margin on the second line after the last item in the letter.

When preparing a letter with a blind copy, print one copy of the letter; then add the blind copy notation and print another.

Thank you for inviting me to participate in the discussion concerning this issue.

Sincerely yours, ↓4X

Mark Henderson
President ↓2X

man ↓2X

bc: Mary Stevenson

K. DELIVERY NOTATION

Type a delivery notation (such as *By fax*) on the line below the enclosure notation (if used) or on the line below the reference initials. A delivery notation comes before a copy notation.

Sincerely yours, ↓4X

Mark Henderson
President ↓2X

opc
Enclosure
By fax
c: Mary Stevenson

L. POSTSCRIPT

If a postscript *(PS)* is added to a letter, it is typed as the last item in the letter, preceded by 1 blank line. If a blind copy notation and postscript are used, the bc: notation follows the postscript.

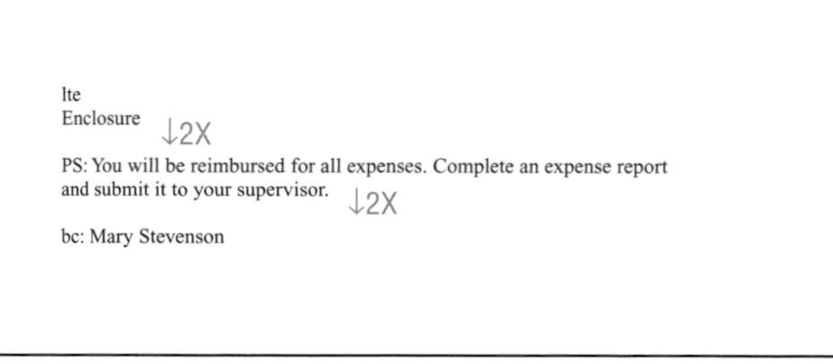

lte
Enclosure ↓2X

PS: You will be reimbursed for all expenses. Complete an expense report and submit it to your supervisor. ↓2X

bc: Mary Stevenson

Word Processing Manual

M. WORD PROCESSING: SHADING

Study Lesson 73 in your word processing manual. Complete all of the shaded steps while at your computer. Then format the jobs that follow.

DOCUMENT PROCESSING

Correspondence 73-70

Business Letter in Block Style

March 1, 20-- | Ms. Maureen Testa | Austin Communications | 37 Pittsburgh Road | Franklin, PA 16323 | Dear Ms. Testa:

¶ We are indeed interested in designing a new corporate logo and the corresponding stationery for your fine company. As I indicated in our recent telephone conversation, we have a design staff that has won many national awards for letterhead form design, and we consider it an honor to be contacted by you.

¶ Within a couple of weeks, we will submit to you and your committee several basic designs. Based on your evaluation and suggestions, we can go from there. Here is a modified price list for the printed stationery:

Automatically adjust the column widths and center the table horizontally.

Stationery	**Cost**
Letterhead (500 sheets)	$ 80.00
Business cards (1,000 cards)	39.50
Coated brochures (1,000 sheets)	219.30
Envelopes	92.00

¶ In the meantime, please call me if we can be of further service.
Sincerely yours, | Samantha A. Steele | General Manager | urs | By fax | bc: Design Department

Correspondence 73-71

Business Letter in Block Style

Open the file for Correspondence 73-70 from Ms. Steele and make the following changes:

1. Send the letter to `Mr. Rodney Graae | Thompson Corporation | 42 Harris Court | Trenton, NJ 08648`
2. Change the word "company" in the first paragraph to `corporation.`
3. Revise the first two sentences of the second paragraph to say:

   `Within a month, we will submit several basic designs to you and your board of directors. At that time, please feel free to make any comments and suggestions that will help us finalize a design.`
4. Change the table to a boxed table.
5. Apply 15 percent shading to the first row of the table.

Correspondence 73-72

Business Letter in Modified-Block Style

November 5, 20-- | Master Gyms, Inc. | 4201 Castine Court | Raleigh, NC 27613-5981 | Ladies and Gentlemen:

¶We have 494 apartments at Fountain Ridge. As the recreation coordinator, I have concerns not only about the leisure-time activities of our residents but also about the health and physical fitness of the more than 1,100 people who call Fountain Ridge home.

(Continued on next page)

¶ Our recreation facilities are excellent. In addition to our two outdoor tennis courts and swimming pool, we have the following indoor facilities: two racquetball courts, swimming pool, whirlpool bath, sauna, steam room, and two billiard tables. However, we have no workout equipment.
¶ During the next few months we will be equipping a new gymnasium. The dimensions of the gym are shown on the enclosed sketch. There will be exercise bicycles, treadmills, and rowing machines. In addition, we would like to install a muscle-toning machine that includes features such as the following: leg press, chest press, shoulder press, arm pull, leg pull, arm lift, leg lift, and sit-up board.
¶ The needs and interests of our residents are varied. Some residents will take full advantage of the equipment we have suggested for the gymnasium. However, many of our residents have expressed interests in an indoor track for walking; others would like to add a track for running. We hope to accommodate as many of the suggestions as we feel are feasible.
¶ The population of the residents in the Fountain Ridge complex consists of a mixture of young and middle-age adult couples as well as single residents. Some of the couples have children who would be old enough to enjoy the facilities. Therefore, safety and durability of the equipment are very important considerations. In addition, we would like to continue to develop our complex in a way that would invite family participation in our recreational activities.
¶ Do you have a sales representative serving this area who could meet with me within a week or ten days? As an alternative, perhaps you have some brochures, including prices, that could be sent to me.
Sincerely yours, | FOUNTAIN RIDGE | Rosa Bailey-Judd | Recreation Coordinator | urs | Enclosure | By fax | PS: Please send a current catalog and price list immediately so that we can prepare for our meeting with the sales representative.

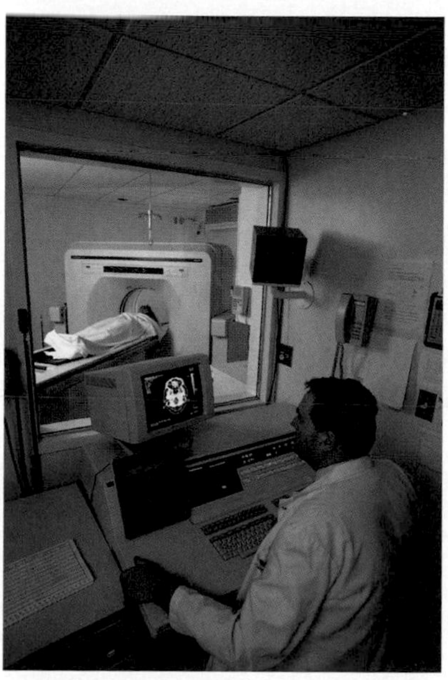

Multipage Memos With Tables

Goals

- Type at least 42wpm/5′/5e
- Format multipage memos with tables

A. Type 2 times.

A. WARMUP

```
     Over 270 cars were backed up near the Baxter & Meintz   11
building after an 18-wheeler jackknifed at an icy junction.  23
About 1/3 to 1/2 of the cars were required to use a detour.  35
|  1  |  2  |  3  |  4  |  5  |  6  |  7  |  8  |  9  |  10  |  11  |  12
```

SKILLBUILDING

B. PROGRESSIVE PRACTICE: ALPHABET

If you are not using the GDP software, turn to page SB-7 and follow the directions for this activity.

C. PROGRESSIVE PRACTICE: NUMBERS

If you are not using the GDP software, turn to page SB-11 and follow the directions for this activity.

Keyboarding Connection

Virus and Spam Prevention

Use caution when opening e-mail attachments or downloading files from the Internet. Download files only from reliable Web sites. Do not open files attached to an e-mail from an unknown source. Also question files attached to a known source. Some viruses replicate themselves and are sent through e-mail without users' knowledge.

Delete any e-mail with an odd subject, a chain e-mail, or electronic junk mail, commonly known as spam. If you're given the opportunity to unsubscribe from a spammer's list, think twice. Your reply will stop the messages on a reputable mailing list but may incite disreputable list marketers.

To protect against lost data, back up your files on a regular basis. Then you will be prepared if a virus infects your computer. New viruses are discovered daily, so update your antivirus software regularly.

YOUR TURN How do you handle junk mail via post? Do you notice similarities when dealing with spam?

D. Take two 5-minute timed writings. Review your speed and errors.

Goal: At least 42wpm/5′/5e

D. 5-MINUTE TIMED WRITING

```
     Have you ever given any thought to starting your own      11
business? Obviously, there is some risk in starting out in     23
a venture such as this. However, if you realize there are      34
some issues to starting up a business, it may not seem to      46
be such a daunting undertaking. Let's quickly look at just     58
some of the issues that are involved in this task.             64
     First of all, you need to think about whether you want    75
to do so badly enough to work long hours without knowing if    87
you will make any money at the end of the month. It would      99
be advantageous if you had worked previously for another      110
company as a manager or have managerial experience.           121
     You have to have some sense for just how much money      131
you will need to start your business. It will take some       143
working capital to get you started. If you have put money     154
aside to invest in the company, there is a good possibility   166
you will succeed. If you don't have enough put aside, can     178
you get credit from a lending institution to assist you       189
through the first few months of operation? And, of course,    201
you'll also need to get credit from suppliers.                210
|  1  |  2  |  3  |  4  |  5  |  6  |  7  |  8  |  9  |  10  |  11  |  12
```

FORMATTING

Word Processing Manual

E. WORD PROCESSING: FIND AND REPLACE

Study Lesson 74 in your word processing manual. Complete all of the shaded steps while at your computer. Then format the jobs that follow.

DOCUMENT PROCESSING

Correspondence 74-73

Memo

MEMO TO: L. B. Chinn, Station Manager | **FROM**: Mitzi Grenell, News Director | **DATE**: May 5, 20-- | **SUBJECT**: FCC European Trip

¶ As you requested, this memo is being sent to you as one in a series to keep you informed about my upcoming trip to Europe. I have been invited by the Federal Communications Commission to participate in a study of television news in European countries. The invitation came from Jill Andrews, FCC vice-chair; and I am, of course, delighted to take part in this challenging project.

(Continued on next page)

¶ One function of this study will be to compare the news in countries that have a long history of free-access broadcasting with the programming in newly democratic countries. I have been assigned to lead a study group to six European countries to gather firsthand information on this topic. We will be visiting England, France, Germany, Poland, Romania, and Latvia from August 24 through September 3. In addition to me, our group will consist of the following members:

Arkady Gromov	Executive Editor *Miami Herald*	Miami, Florida
Manuel Cruz	News Director National Public Radio	Boise, Idaho
Katherine Grant	Station Manager WLBZ-TV	Bangor, Maine
Richard Logan	Operations Manager Cable News System	Provo, Utah

¶ Our initial plans are to spend at least one full day in each of the countries, meeting with the news staff of one or two of the major networks, touring their facilities, viewing recent broadcasts, and becoming familiar with their general operations.

¶ If you need to contact me during my absence, Barbara Brooks, our liaison at the Federal Communications Commission (1919 M Street, NW, Washington, DC 20554; phone: 202-555-3894), will be able to provide a location and phone number.

¶ Arrangements will be made with several different staff members in the News Department to handle my responsibilities here at Channel 5 while I am gone. Dave Gislason will be the contact person for the department. As you can imagine, this is an exciting time for me. Thank you for supporting the project.

| urs | PS: Thanks also for suggesting that this trip be combined with a vacation. My husband and I have discussed the possibility of his joining me for a two-week tour of the Scandinavian countries after the FCC trip has been completed. I shall let you know what our plans are by the end of May.

Correspondence 74-74

Memo

Open the file for Correspondence 74-73 and make the following changes:

1. Jill Andrews has just been promoted to FCC chair.
2. Finland has been added as a seventh country.
3. The trip has been extended through September 5.
4. Each occurrence of the word "news" (lowercase) has to be changed to news programming. (Do not replace News.)
5. Reggie Jordan, Staff Assistant, FCC, Washington, DC, will replace Manuel Cruz on the trip.
6. Gil Friesen will replace Dave Gislason as contact person.

Correspondence 74-75

Memo

MEMO TO: Terri Hackworth, Manager

FROM: Rosa Bailey Judd, Recreation Coordinator

DATE: April 14, 20--

SUBJECT: Fitness room

The new Fitness Room will be ready for use in about 1 month. Your leadership in bringing thsi about is sincerely appreciated. After much investigation (much reading and several interviews), I likely will be requesting approval soon to purchase the equipment:

No.	Type
4	exercise bicycles
1	treadmill
1	muscle-toner machine

Three other types of equipment wer considered seriously, but those listed above enable users to reach objectives with out excessive cost. I am not quite ready to recommend the specific brands or the suppliers for these machines. As we expect that there will be very heavy usage, we are concerned with durbility, warranties, and the available of dependable service personnel. Thanks again for your full support and cooperation with this project.

urs

Strategies for Career Success

Developing Confidence as a Presenter

Public speaking anxiety is quite common. As many as 77 percent of experienced speakers admit to having some anxiety on each speaking occasion. Normally, stage fright decreases with experience.

Even if there are no physical expressions of anxiety, speakers often assume others can see through their smiles to their fears. However, listeners are actually poor judges of the amount of anxiety that speakers experience.

A little anxiety can actually stimulate a better presentation. The best way to control your anxiety is to be well prepared for the presentation. Carefully analyze your audience, research your topic, organize the speech, practice its delivery, and believe in its ideas. Being well prepared puts you in an excellent position to control your anxiety.

YOUR TURN "I'm glad I'm here. I'm glad you're here. I know that I know." What are the benefits of repeating this to yourself before each presentation?

Memo Reports

Goals

- Improve speed and accuracy
- Format memo reports

A. Type 2 times.

A. WARMUP

The sizable judge asked three questions: "What's the 11
best time of the day for you to be in court? Can you leave 23
your job at exactly 4 p.m.? If not, 5 p.m. or 7 p.m.?" 34

| 1 | 2 | 3 | 4 | 5 | 6 | 7 | 8 | 9 | 10 | 11 | 12

SKILLBUILDING

B. Take a 1-minute timed writing on the first paragraph to establish your base speed. Then take four 1-minute timed writings on the remaining paragraphs. As soon as you equal or exceed your base speed on one paragraph, advance to the next, more difficult paragraph.

B. SUSTAINED PRACTICE: SYLLABIC INTENSITY

Each of us has several bills to be paid on a monthly 11
basis. For most of us, a checkbook is the tool that we use 23
to take care of this chore. However, in this electronic 34
age, other ways of doing this have received rave reviews. 45

You will likely be surprised to learn that the most 11
basic way and the cheapest way to pay bills electronically 23
involves the use of a Touch-Tone phone. The time required 35
is approximately a third of that used when writing checks. 47

Several banking institutions offer or plan to offer 11
screen phones as a method for paying bills. It is possible 22
to buy securities, make transfers, and determine account 34
balances. You will save time by using a Touch-Tone phone. 45

A third type of electronic bill processing involves 10
using a microcomputer and a modem. Software programs have 21
on-screen checkbooks linked to bill-paying applications. 34
Other microcomputers use online services through a modem. 46

| 1 | 2 | 3 | 4 | 5 | 6 | 7 | 8 | 9 | 10 | 11 | 12

C. TECHNIQUE PRACTICE: SPACE BAR

We will all go to the race if I win my event today.
Do you think that I will be able to finish the race at the
front of the pack, or do you think there are lots of very
fast runners out there who surely can finish ahead of me?

LANGUAGE ARTS

D. Edit this paragraph to correct any typing or formatting errors.

D. PROOFREADING: EDITING

```
     Many home computer user like the challenge of haveing the latest in both hardware and software technology. Their are those however, who's needs likely can be satisfied at a very low costs. A used 486-chip personnel computer with color monitor and keyboard might be your's for under $ 300. Check out th Yellow Page, or visit a used-computer store.
```

FORMATTING

E. REPORT HEADINGS IN MEMOS

There are times when a memo report is used rather than a cover memo to accompany a report. The memo and the report are combined into one, and headings are formatted as they are in a report.

DOCUMENT PROCESSING

Report 75-55

Memo Report

Review:
R-9C: Memo Report

MEMO TO: All Employees | **FROM:** Franklin Coates, Director | **DATE:** February 24, 20-- | **SUBJECT:** Security System

¶ Beginning March 1, we will install a new security access system. Complete installation should occur by the end of March. The system will include new magnetic card readers at all entrances. It will also provide a more secure working environment, especially in the evenings and on weekends. Entrances will lock and unlock automatically each day during working hours. Please carefully read and follow the detailed instructions for using the new system.

RECEIVING A NEW ACCESS CARD

¶ Once the new system is installed, you will need a new access identification card to enter the building during nonworking hours. Human Resources will begin taking pictures for new cards during the week of March 20. When you are called, report immediately. The cards will be issued as soon as they are ready. To receive your new card, you must turn in your old one.

(Continued on next page)

ENTERING THE BUILDING

¶ Entrances will automatically unlock each working day at 8 a.m and lock at 5 p.m. To enter the building during nonworking hours, slide your access identification card (with the magnetic strip facing left) through the card reader at the right of the entrance door. When the green light comes on, open the door. Do not hold the door open longer than 30 seconds.

¶ Once you enter the building during nonworking hours, please proceed immediately to the front desk and sign in. Record in the logbook your name, department, extension number, and arrival time.

LEAVING THE BUILDING

¶ Before leaving the building, you must sign out. Please record your departure time beside your name. Do not use the special latch handle to open the door, or the alarm will sound. Instead, use the push bar. Once you have opened the door, do not let it remain open longer than 30 seconds, or the alarm will sound. If you accidentally set off the alarm, return to the front desk and call the security company (the telephone number is at the top of the logbook). Be prepared to provide the security personnel with your name, extension number, and access card number.

¶ At times you may need to have the door held open for extended periods of time during nonbusiness hours. In these situations, please make arrangements with Building Maintenance by calling extension 4444.

¶ If you have questions about our new security access system and procedures, please contact me.

urs

Report 75-56

Memo Report

Mr. Coates has asked you to revise Report 75-55 as follows:

1. Use February 25 as the date.
2. Change "nonworking" to `nonbusiness` throughout the report.
3. Add the following sentence at the end of the second paragraph:

   `New employees will be asked for a special form, to be provided by their supervisors.`
4. Change "Building Maintenance" to `Building Security` in the next-to-last paragraph.

Report 75-57

Memo Report

Progress and Proofreading Check

Documents designated as Proofreading Checks serve as a check of your proofreading skill. Your goal is to have zero typographical errors when the GDP software first scores the document.

MEMO TO: All Employees
FROM: Adrienne Barzan
DATE: March 2, 20--
SUBJECT: New Building Site

¶ We have consulted with several architects and have finalized plans to build a new administrative center at 6400 Easton Plaza. This memo provides general information about plans for the center's exterior and interior development.

EXTERIOR PLANS

¶ Exterior plans will maintain the historical integrity and beauty of the surrounding area and reflect the architecture of other buildings in the office park. Landscaping plans include a parklike area, a picnic area, and a small pond.

INTERIOR PLANS FOR STAFF

¶ Staff will be located within the new facility as follows

1. Accounting will be located on the first floor in the west wing.
2. Sales and marketing will be located on the first floor in the east wing. All staff will be grouped according to product line.
3. All other staff will be located on the second floor. Exact locations will be determined at a later date.

INTERIOR PLANS FOR SPECIAL FACILITIES

¶ Conference rooms will be located in the center of the building on the first floor to provide easy access for everyone. All rooms will be equipped with state-of-the-art technology.

¶ Our new center will also include a full-service cafeteria, a copy center, a library, an athletic center, and an on-site day care center.

¶ Construction of the new center will begin when we obtain the necessary permits.

urs

Unit 16

Tables

LESSON 76
Tables With Footnotes or Source Notes

LESSON 77
Tables With Braced Column Headings

LESSON 78
Tables Formatted Sideways

LESSON 79
Multipage Tables

LESSON 80
Using Predesigned Table Formats

CITY BANK Interest Rates Schedule Effective Date: November 11, 2003		
	Rate	**APY**
Value Checking	0.00%	0.00%
City Checking	1.25%	1.27%
Prestige Checking	1.25%	1.27%
Golden Checking	1.50%	1.55%
Regular Savings	1.75%	1.90%
Young Savers	1.75%	1.90%
Christmas Club	1.75%	1.90%
Money Market—Tier I	2.25%	2.30%
Money Market—Tier II	2.50%	2.60%
Money Market—Tier III	2.75%	2.80%
Money Market—Tier IV	3.00%	3.10%
CD—6 month	2.25%	2.50%

CITY BANK Interest Rates Schedule Effective Date: November 11, 2003		
	Rate	**APY***
Value Checking	0.00%	0.00%
City Checking	1.25%	1.27%
Prestige Checking	1.25%	1.27%
Golden Checking	1.50%	1.55%
Regular Savings	1.75%	1.90%
Young Savers	1.75%	1.90%
Christmas Club	1.75%	1.90%
Money Market—Tier I	2.25%	2.30%
Money Market—Tier II	2.50%	2.60%
Money Market—Tier III	2.75%	2.80%
Money Market—Tier IV	3.00%	3.10%
CD—6 month	2.25%	2.50%
CD—1 year	2.35%	2.65%
CD—2 year	2.45%	2.70%
CD—3 year	2.50%	2.75%
*APY=Annual Percentage Yield.		

CUSTOMER DATABASE INFORMATION
(Ohio District)
August 31, 2003

Customer	Address	City	ZIP	Telephone No.	Item	Stock No.
Westphal, Darlene	3309 Aaron Place Street	Kenton	44426	419-555-2384	Pentium Computer	4-138-CW
Roanne, Dennis	20604 Lucille Road South	Columbus	43230	614-555-2074	Laser Printer	3-895-LP
Byrnes, Carl	322 West Lyons Road	Mansfield	44902	216-555-2002	Laser Printer	3-895-LP
Dawson, Cynthia	5914 Bay Oaks Place	Chillicothe	45601	614-555-1399	Color Ink-Jet Printer	2-555-CIJ
Graupmann, Meg	10386 Power Drive	Steubenville	43952	614-555-7821	Pentium Computer	4-238-CW
Neusome, Jo	Box 365	Youngstown	44502	216-555-3885	Pentium Computer	4-238-CW
Shapiro, Tony	6823 Creekwood Drive	Columbus	43085	614-555-2934	Pentium Computer	4-238-CW
Garand, Lisa	26044 Manzano Court	Youngstown	44505	216-555-1777	Flatbed Color Scanner	6-882-CSC
Parker, Tom	936 Eastwind Drive	Cleveland	44121	216-555-2839	Laser Printer	3-895-LP

Tables With Footnotes or Source Notes

Goals

- Type at least 43wpm/5′/5e
- Change text direction
- Insert or delete rows or columns

A. Type 2 times.

A. WARMUP

```
     Order #Z391 must be processed "quickly" and exactly      11
as specified! In January several orders were sent out by      22
mistake; regrettably, one order worth $5,680 was canceled.    34
|  1  |  2  |  3  |  4  |  5  |  6  |  7  |  8  |  9  |  10  |  11  |  12
```

SKILLBUILDING

B. Take three 12-second timed writings on each line. The scale below the last line shows your wpm speed for a 12-second timed writing.

B. 12-SECOND SPEED SPRINTS

```
You paid for the ruby that she owned when he was just five.
Toby wishes to thank all eight of the girls for their time.
Yale is a very fine place to learn about the world of work.
She has a theory that the icy roads will cause a bad wreck.
    5    10    15    20    25    30    35    40    45    50    55    60
```

C. DIAGNOSTIC PRACTICE: SYMBOLS AND PUNCTUATION

If you are not using the GDP software, turn to page SB-2 and follow the directions for this activity.

Strategies for Career Success

Cell Phone Manners Matter

Mind your cell phone manners! Although the cell phone allows you to keep in touch with your boss, coworkers, and clients, it also requires you to consider your communication etiquette. One of the worst violations of etiquette and safety is driving and talking at the same time; and in some states such as New Jersey, cell phone use while driving is restricted to hands free devices. It is much safer to pull off the road to make a call.

Consider others when you use a cell phone in a public place (for example, a restaurant). If you use the phone in public, talk quietly and watch what you say. Cell phones in meetings can distract others; some companies prohibit them in business meetings.

When you call a cell phone user, keep your message brief.

YOUR TURN Observe cell phone users in a public place. Are they mindful of others when they use their phones?

D. Take two 5-minute timed writings. Review your speed and errors.

Goal: At least 43wpm/5'/5e

D. 5-MINUTE TIMED WRITING

```
     Starting up your own business may mean that you are      11
thinking about acquiring an existing business. If so, is      22
that business doing well in the community? If you are going   34
to buy out an established business, you need to know the      45
reason the current owner wishes to sell the company. If       57
there are other businesses in the area, you should first      68
find out what reputation that business has built up in the    80
community. Do other businesses think highly of the company?   92
     You must also consider what type of advertising you     103
plan to use to get your business off to a good start. You    114
might use ads in newspapers, on television, in magazines,    126
or on the Internet. When you start your ad campaign, you     137
should consider hiring an ad agency to put out the best      149
message for your company and its products. You should also   160
consider the types of ads being used by your competitors to  172
determine what has worked well for them.                     181
     Yes, there are major issues that need to be addressed   192
when starting up your own business; and all of the issues    203
should be dealt with before you decide to take such a step.  215
| 1 | 2 | 3 | 4 | 5 | 6 | 7 | 8 | 9 | 10 | 11 | 12
```

FORMATTING

Reference Manual

Refer to pages R-8B and R-13A of the Reference Manual.

E. TABLES WITH FOOTNOTES OR SOURCE NOTES

To format tables with footnotes or source notes:

1. When you insert a table, include an additional row at the bottom of the table for the footnote or source note.
2. Merge the cells in the bottom row.
3. In the bottom row, type the word `Note:` or `Source:` if there is a note or source for the table. Then type the information for the note or source.
4. If there is a footnote, type an asterisk (or another symbol) at the appropriate point within the table. Then type the information for the footnote.

Word Processing Manual

F. WORD PROCESSING: TABLE—TEXT DIRECTION, AND TABLE—INSERT OR DELETE ROWS OR COLUMNS

Study Lesson 76 in your word processing manual. Complete all of the shaded steps while at your computer. Then format the jobs that follow.

DOCUMENT PROCESSING

Table 76-26

Boxed Table

Your completed table will look different from the one shown.

1. Insert a boxed table with 7 columns and 6 rows.
2. Select Row 1, and change the text direction to display vertically bottom to top.
3. Drag down on the bottom border of Row 1 until the column headings display in one continuous line without wrapping.
4. Type the information in the body of the table.

(Continued on next page)

5. Right-align the text in the number columns. **Note:** Do not change the left alignment of the column headings.
6. Merge the cells in the bottom row, and then type the table note.
7. Automatically adjust the column widths.
8. Center the table horizontally and vertically.

Always automatically adjust column widths and center tables horizontally and vertically.

Account Number	Blue Sierra Letterhead	Italian Renaissance Letterhead	Sonoma Desert Letterhead	Watercolor Wash Letterhead	Sandstone Marble Letterhead	Greek Acropolis Letterhead
GV-11	3,500	500	750	1,000	250	1,250
GV-29	2,500	250	250	500	500	250
GV-37	750	1,000	500	2,500	250	2,500
GV-10	250	500	1,000	250	1,500	250
Note: This information is subject to change.						

Table 76-27

Boxed Table

Open the file for Table 76-26 and make the following changes:

1. Delete the table note row.
2. Delete Column G.
3. Insert a column to the left of Column B.
4. Insert a row above Row 3. Type: `GV-72 | 1,250 | 500 | 1,000 | 250 | 750 | 2,000`
5. Type: `French Patina Letterhead | 750 | 1,250 | 250 | 1,000 | 500`
6. Right-align the text in the numbers columns as needed.
7. Apply 10 percent shading to Row 1.

Table 76-28

Boxed Table

Your completed table will look different from the one shown.

1. Insert a boxed table with 5 columns and 6 rows.
2. Select Row 1, and change the text direction to display vertically bottom to top.
3. Drag down on the bottom border of Row 1 until the column headings display in one continuous line without wrapping.
4. Type the information in the body of the table.
5. Right-align the text in the number columns. **Note:** Do not change the left alignment of the column headings.
6. Merge the cells in the bottom row, and then type the source note.
7. Automatically adjust the column widths.
8. Center the table horizontally and vertically.

Office Supply Account	LED Laser Printer	Internal Fax Modem	Cash Management System	Plain-Paper Laser Fax
OE-9	$405	$181	$199	$249
DD-7	395	150	205	234
US-2	410	125	183	252
OB-1	420	167	179	245
Source: March invoices				

Tables With Braced Column Headings

Goals

- Improve speed and accuracy
- Refine language arts skills in capitalization
- Format braced headings in tables

A. Type 2 times.

A. WARMUP

```
1      Six citizens from 14th Avenue East joined 83 other       10
2  residents to discuss the #794 proposal* for a new swimming   22
3  pool. Barry Kelm quoted numbers about current pool usage.    33
   | 1 | 2 | 3 | 4 | 5 | 6 | 7 | 8 | 9 | 10 | 11 | 12
```

SKILLBUILDING

B. DIAGNOSTIC PRACTICE: NUMBERS

If you are not using the GDP software, turn to page SB-5 and follow the directions for this activity.

C. MAP

Follow the GDP software directions for this exercise in improving keystroking accuracy.

LANGUAGE ARTS

D. Study the rules at the right.

D. CAPITALIZATION

RULE ▶ ≡ noun #

Capitalize nouns followed by a number or letter (except for the nouns *line, note, page, paragraph*, and *size*).

Please read Chapter 5, which begins on page 94.

RULE ▶ ≡ compass point

Capitalize compass points (such as *north, south*, or *northeast*) only when they designate definite regions.

From Montana we drove south to reach the Southwest.

Edit the sentences to correct any errors in capitalization.

```
4  The marketing manager had a reservation on flight 505 to Atlanta.
5  Please order two model 6M printers.
6  The desktop publishing seminar will be held in Room 101.
7  Study pages 120-230 for the unit test.
8  Please contact all representatives in the northern states.
9  Have you visited the city of Pittsburgh?
10 The population of the south continues to increase.
```

FORMATTING

E. BRACED COLUMN HEADINGS

A braced column heading is a heading that applies to more than one column (for example, *Retirement Account* in the table shown below):

1. To create a braced column heading, position the insertion point where you want the braced heading to appear.
2. Merge the cells over which the braced heading will appear.
3. Center the braced column heading over the appropriate columns.

DOCUMENT PROCESSING

Table 77-29
Boxed Table

1. Insert a boxed table with 6 columns and 6 rows.
2. Center and type the braced column headings in upper- and lowercase and bold.
3. Type the regular column headings in bold; right-align the number columns.
4. Follow the standard table format.
5. Merge cells as necessary.
6. Center the table horizontally and vertically.

INSURED ACCOUNT DEPOSITS **For Melanie and Frank Bush**					
First World Savings		**Individual Account**		**Retirement Account**	
Month	**Branch**	**M. Bush**	**F. Bush**	**M. Bush**	**F. Bush**
January	Reseda	$5,500	$2,350	$2,000	$10,000
February	Valencia	7,950	5,700	5,500	4,300
March	Van Nuys	2,400	7,300	9,300	2,550

Table 77-30
Boxed Table

1. Insert a boxed table with 4 columns and 6 rows.
2. Center and type the braced column headings in upper- and lowercase and bold.
3. Type the regular column headings in bold; right-align the number columns.
4. Follow the standard table format.
5. Merge cells as necessary.
6. Center the table horizontally and vertically.

CINEPLEX VIDEOS **Sales Trends**			
Western Region		**Total Sales**	
State	**Manager**	**Last Year**	**This Year**
California	George Lucas	$1,956,250	$2,135,433
Nevada	Marjorie Matheson	859,435	1,231,332
Washington	Valerie Harper	737,498	831,352

Table 77-31

Boxed Table

Open the file for Table 77-30 and make the following changes.

1. Change the column heading "Western Region" to `Eastern Region`.
2. Change the state names to `New York | New Jersey | Delaware`.
3. Change the managers' names to `Robert DeLuca | Doris Lynch | Megan Bennett`.
4. Change last year's amounts to `$2,052,659 | 534,958 | 894,211`.
5. Change this year's amounts to `$3,345,312 | 2,311,478 | 925,138`.

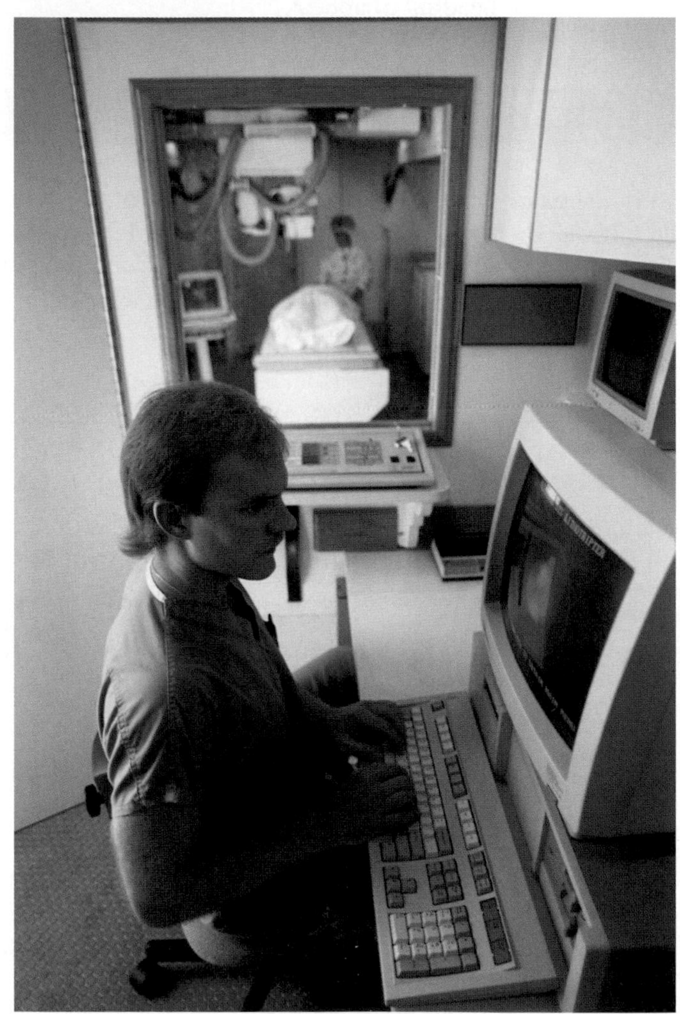

Tables Formatted Sideways

Goals

- Type at least 43wpm/5'/5e
- Format tables in landscape orientation

A. Type 2 times.

A. WARMUP

```
     This week order a monitor with a resolution of 1280 x   11
1024 that supports an optimal refresh rate from V & Q Inc.   23
It will cost $573* (*a 9% savings) if ordered before July!   35
| 1 | 2 | 3 | 4 | 5 | 6 | 7 | 8 | 9 | 10 | 11 | 12
```

SKILLBUILDING

B. PACED PRACTICE

If you are not using the GDP software, turn to page SB-14 and follow the directions for this activity.

Keyboarding Connection

Finding People on the Internet

Remember that long-lost friend from high school? Well, he or she may not be lost for long if you use the Internet's assistance. It is easy to search for a person on the Net by following a few simple steps.

Access a search engine. Click hyperlinks pertaining to finding people such as People Finder or People Search. Enter the information requested about the person, and press the Search button.

Conduct a search for Web sites where you can also find e-mail addresses. Enter the information about the person you are seeking. Click the Search button. Your search should list any names and e-mail addresses that match the name you entered.

YOUR TURN Access a search engine and try to locate the address of a high school friend.

C. Take two 5-minute timed writings. Review your speed and errors.

Goal: At least 43wpm/5'/5e

C. 5-MINUTE TIMED WRITING

```
     This is the third in a series of timed writings on       10
starting up a new business. In this presentation, you will    22
consider some expense and merchandise issues as well as       33
some thoughts on the building you will move into or build.    45
     There are several expenses that you will have to look    57
at for your new business. For example, do you realize how    69
much construction costs will be, or, if you are going to      80
rent a building, how much that expense will amount to? You    92
must also project expenses for insurance on the building     103
and its contents, utilities costs for running the business, 115
interest expense on any loans you secure to purchase or      126
renovate the building, and any advertising expenses.         137
     You must also consider the amount of merchandise you    148
will have on hand when you first open your store. If you     159
have several lines of merchandise, you need to determine     171
how many products and how much of each product you will      182
keep on the shelves and how much you will keep in inventory 194
in your warehouse. To acquire this merchandise, you must     205
locate suppliers who will sell you what you need.            215
| 1 | 2 | 3 | 4 | 5 | 6 | 7 | 8 | 9 | 10 | 11 | 12
```

FORMATTING

Word Processing Manual

D. WORD PROCESSING: PAGE ORIENTATION

Study Lesson 78 in your word processing manual. Complete all of the shaded steps while at your computer. Then format the jobs that follow.

DOCUMENT PROCESSING

Table 78-32

Boxed Table

1. Format the table in landscape orientation.
2. Set 0.5-inch side margins for the page.
3. Insert a boxed table with 7 columns and 11 rows.
4. Type the following column headings in bold:

   `Customer | Address | City | ZIP | Telephone No. | Item | Stock No.`
5. In Column A, type the customer's last name followed by a comma; then type the first name.

(Continued on next page)

CUSTOMER DATABASE INFORMATION

(Ohio District)

August 31, 20---

Darlene
~~Maria~~ Westphal | 3309 aaron Place ~~Avenue~~ Street | Kenton | 44426 | 419-555-2384 | Pentium computer | 4-238-cw

Dennis Roanne | 20604 Lucile Rd. South | Columbus | 43230 | 614-555-2074 | laser printer | 3-895-LP

Carl Byrnes | 322 W. Lyons Road | Mansfield | 44902 | 216-555-2002 | ~~Color~~ Laser Printer | 3-895-LP

Cynthia Dawson | 5914 Bay Oaks Place | Chilicothe | 45610 | 614-555-1399 | Color Ink-Jet Printer | 2-550-cij

Meg Graupmann | 10386 power Dr. | Steubenville | 43952 | 614-555-7821 | Pentium Computer | 4-238-CW

Jo Neusome | Box 365 | Youngtown | 44502 | 216-555-3885 | Pentium computer | 4-238-CW

Tony Shapiro | 6823 Creekwood ~~Lane~~ Drive | Columbus | 43085 | 614-555-2934 | Pentium Computer | ~~5-987-PC~~ 4-238-CW

Lisa Garand | 26044 Manzano Court | Youngstown | 44505 | 216-555-1777 | FlatBed Color Scanner | 6-8820-CSC

Tom Parker | 936 East wind Drive | Cleveland | 44121 | 216-555-2839 | Lasser Printer | 3-895-LP

Table 78-33

Boxed Table

Open the file for Table 78-32, and make the following changes:

1. Change the date to `August 19, 20--`.
2. Sort the table alphabetically by the customers' last names.
3. Change the font for the column headings to Arial Narrow, and shade the headings with a 10 percent fill.

Table 78-34

Boxed Table

1. Change the page orientation to landscape.
2. Insert a boxed table with 7 columns and 6 rows.
3. Use standard table format to type the headings and body of the table.
4. Bold and center-align the column headings.
5. Merge the cells in the bottom row; then type the table footnote.

REGIONAL SALES OFFICES General Information*						
Region	**Street Address**	**City**	**State**	**ZIP**	**Telephone**	**Fax**
East	8787 Orion Place	Columbus	OH	43240	614-555-4951	614-555-4999
Mid-Continent	1415 Elbridge Payne Road	Chesterfield	MO	63017	636-555-9940	636-555-9034
Southeast	3100 Breckinridge Boulevard	Duluth	GA	30096	770-555-7007	770-555-7422
West	21600 Oxnard Street	Woodland Hills	CA	91367	818-555-2675	818-555-2697
*Information on all regional offices is updated each year on July 1.						

Multipage Tables

Goals

- Improve speed and accuracy
- Refine language arts skills in spelling
- Format multipage tables

A. Type 2 times.

A. WARMUP

```
     Please request this key item by June: an XYZ 2000        10
motherboard with 512-MB RAM. I don't expect delivery until    22
7/5; I realize this is a "great" investment for the money!    34
| 1 | 2 | 3 | 4 | 5 | 6 | 7 | 8 | 9 | 10 | 11 | 12
```

SKILLBUILDING

PRETEST → PRACTICE → POSTTEST

PRETEST
Take a 1-minute timed writing. Review your speed and errors.

B. PRETEST: Alternate- and One-Hand Words

```
     They both blame the fight on the visitor. The girl       10
had no right to imply that the proxy was brave enough to      21
draw you into the unholy case. The union will reward you.     32
| 1 | 2 | 3 | 4 | 5 | 6 | 7 | 8 | 9 | 10 | 11 | 12
```

PRACTICE
Speed Emphasis:
If you made no more than 1 error on the Pretest, type each *individual* line 2 times.
Accuracy Emphasis:
If you made 2 or more errors, type each *group* of lines (as though it were a paragraph) 2 times.

C. PRACTICE: Alternate-Hand Words

```
also angle field bushel ancient emblem panel sight fish big
both blame fight formal element handle proxy signs girl and
city chair giant island visitor profit right their laid cut
```

D. PRACTICE: One-Hand Words

```
acts hilly award uphill average poplin refer jolly adds him
area jumpy based homily baggage you'll serve union beat ink
case brave extra limply greater unholy wages imply draw you
```

POSTTEST
Repeat the Pretest timed writing and compare performance.

E. POSTTEST: Alternate- and One-Hand Words

F. PROGRESSIVE PRACTICE: ALPHABET

If you are not using the GDP software, turn to page SB-7 and follow the directions for this activity.

G. Type each sentence on a separate line by pressing ENTER after each sentence.

G. TECHNIQUE PRACTICE: ENTER KEY

13 Start a business. See the banker. Rent a building.
14 Check state codes. Check city codes. Get needed licenses.
15 Contact suppliers. Call utility companies. Buy furniture.
16 Hire the employees. Open the doors. Hope for customers.

LANGUAGE ARTS

H. Type this list of frequently misspelled words, paying special attention to any spelling problems in each word.

H. SPELLING

17 assistance compliance initial limited corporation technical
18 operating sufficient operation incorporated writing current
19 advice together prepared recommend appreciated cannot based
20 benefit completing analysis probably projects before annual
21 issue attention location association participation proposed

Edit the sentences to correct any misspellings.

22 The complience by the corporation was sufficient to pass.
23 I cannot reccomend the project based on the expert advise.
24 The location of the proposed annual meeting was an issue.
25 Your assistance in completeing the project is appreciated.
26 Together we prepared an analysis of their current operation.
27 The writing was incorporated in the initial asociation bid.

FORMATTING

I. MULTIPAGE TABLES

Tables should generally be formatted to fit on one page. However, if a table extends to another page, follow these formatting rules:

1. Repeat the column headings at the top of each new page.
2. Number all pages in the upper right-hand corner.

1

50 LONGEST RIVERS OF THE WORLD
(Miles Rounded To Nearest Ten)

River	Outflow	Miles
Nile	Mediterranean	4,160
Amazon	Atlantic Ocean	4,000
Chang	East China Sea	3,960
Huang	Yellow Sea	3,400
Ob-Irtysh	Gulf of Ob	3,360
Amur	Tatar Strait	2,740
Lena	Laptev Sea	2,730
Congo	Atlantic Ocean	2,720
Mekong	South China Sea	2,600
Niger	Gulf of Guinea	2,590
Yenisey	Kara Sea	2,540
Parana	Rio de la Plata	2,490
Mississippi	Gulf of Mexico	2,340
Missouri	Mississippi River	2,320
Murray-Darling	Indian Ocean	2,310
Volga	Caspian Sea	2,290
Purus	Amazon River	2,100
Medeira	Amazon River	2,010
Sao Francisco	Atlantic Ocean	1,990
Yukon	Bering Sea	1,980
Rio Grande	Gulf of Mexico	1,900
Brahmaputra	Bay of Bengal	1,800
Indus	Arabian Sea	1,800
Danube	Black Sea	1,780
Japura	Amazon River	1,750
Euphrates	Shatt al-Arab	1,700
Zambezi	Indian Ocean	1,700
Tocantins	Para River	1,680
Orinoco	Atlantic Ocean	1,600
Amu	Aral Sea	1,580
Paraguay	Parana River	1,580

2

50 LONGEST RIVERS OF THE WORLD
(Miles Rounded To Nearest Ten)

River	Outflow	Miles
Ural	Caspian Sea	1,580
Ganges	Bay of Bengal	1,560
Salween	Andaman Sea	1,500
Arkansas	Mississippi River	1,460
Colorado	Gulf of California	1,450
Dnieper	Black Sea	1,420
Negro	Amazon	1,400
Syr	Aral Sea	1,370
Irrawaddy	Bay of Bengal	1,340
Orange	Atlantic Ocean	1,300
Red	Atchafalaya River	1,290
Columbia	Pacific Ocean	1,240
Don	Sea of Azov	1,220
Peace	Slave River	1,210
Xi	South China Sea	1,200
Tigris	Shatt al-Arab	1,180
Angara	Yenisey River	1,150
Songhua	Amur River	1,150
Snake	Columbia River	1,040

Word Processing Manual

J. WORD PROCESSING: REPEATING TABLE HEADING ROWS

Study Lesson 79 in your word processing manual. Complete all of the shaded steps while at your computer. Then format the jobs that follow.

DOCUMENT PROCESSING

Table 79-35

Boxed Table

Note: The break in the table may vary.

Follow these steps to create a multipage table:

1. Insert a boxed table with 3 columns and 52 rows.
2. Type the information in the table as shown below.
3. Apply 10 percent shading to the column headings row.
4. Repeat the table heading rows on page 2.
5. Number the pages in the upper right-hand corner.

50 LONGEST RIVERS OF THE WORLD
(Miles rounded to nearest 10)

River	Outflow	Miles
Nile	Mediterranean	4,160
Amazon	Atlantic Ocean	4,000
Chang	East China Sea	3,960
Huang	Yellow Sea	3,400
Ob-Irtysh	Gulf of Ob	3,360
Amur	Tatar Strait	2,740
Lena	Laptev Sea	2,730
Congo	Atlantic Ocean	2,720
Mekong	South China Sea	2,600
Niger	Gulf of Guinea	2,590
Yenisey	Kara Sea	2,540
Parana	Rio de la Plata	2,490
Mississippi	Gulf of Mexico	2,340
Missouri	Mississippi River	2,320
Murray-Darling	Indian Ocean	2,310
Volga	Caspian Sea	2,290
Purus	Amazon River	2,100
Medeira	Amazon River	2,010
Sao Francisco	Atlantic Ocean	1,990
Yukon	Bering Sea	1,980
Rio Grande	Gulf of Mexico	1,900
Brahmaputra	Bay of Bengal	1,800
Indus	Arabian Sea	1,800
Danube	Black Sea	1,780
Japura	Amazon River	1,750
Euphrates	Shatt al Arab	1,700
Zambezi	Indian Ocean	1,700
Tocantins	Para River	1,680
Orinoco	Atlantic Ocean	1,600
Amu	Aral Sea	1,580

50 LONGEST RIVERS OF THE WORLD
(Miles rounded to nearest 10)

River	Outflow	Miles
Paraguay	Parana River	1,580
Ural	Caspian Sea	1,580
Ganges	Bay of Bengal	1,560
Salween	Andaman Sea	1,500
Arkansas	Mississippi River	1,460
Colorado	Gulf of California	1,450
Dnieper	Black Sea	1,420
Negro	Amazon	1,400
Syr	Aral Sea	1,370
Irrawaddy	Bay of Bengal	1,340
Orange	Atlantic Ocean	1,300
Red	Atchafalaya River	1,290
Columbia	Pacific Ocean	1,240
Don	Sea of Azov	1,220
Peace	Slave River	1,210
Xi	South China Sea	1,200
Tigris	Shatt al Arab	1,180
Angara	Yenisey River	1,150
Songhua	Amur River	1,150
Snake	Columbia River	1,040

Table 79-36

Boxed Table

Open the file for Table 79-35, and make the following changes:

1. Sort the table alphabetically by river in ascending order.
2. Apply a double border at the bottom of Row 2.

Table 79-37

Boxed Table

Follow these steps to create a boxed table.

1. Change the page orientation to landscape.
2. Insert a boxed table with 5 columns and 7 rows.
3. Type the table as shown.
4. Apply 100 percent shading (black) to the title row.
5. Apply 10 percent shading to the column heading row.
6. Merge the cells in the bottom row; then type the table footnote.

INVESTMENT SUMMARY				
Limited Partnership	**Date of Issue**	**Initial Cost**	**Dividend***	**Owner**
HS Properties	January 2001	$ 50,000	$ 6,066	Alpha Association
Northern Lumber	May 2001	50,000	4,750	CXT Corporation
ST1	February 2001	50,000	7,500	Smith & Sons, Incorporated
ST2	December 2001	100,000	12,250	Q and S Company
* Annual dividends based on current market analysis.				

Using Predesigned Table Formats

Goals

- Type at least 43wpm/5′/5e
- Format tables using TableAutoFormat

A. Type 2 times.

A. WARMUP

"Just when can we expect to realize a profit of 5% or 11
more?" This kind of question will be important to 2/3 of 22
the shareholders; they own over 89% of the prime holdings. 34

| 1 | 2 | 3 | 4 | 5 | 6 | 7 | 8 | 9 | 10 | 11 | 12

SKILLBUILDING

B. Take a 1-minute timed writing on the first paragraph to establish your base speed. Then take four 1-minute timed writings on the remaining paragraphs. As soon as you equal or exceed your base speed on one paragraph, advance to the next, more difficult paragraph.

B. SUSTAINED PRACTICE: NUMBERS AND SYMBOLS

There is a need at this time to communicate our new 11
pricing guidelines to our franchise outlets. In addition, 23
they must be made aware of inventory implications. They 34
will then be in a position to have a successful operation. 46

Franchise operators could be requested to use either 11
a 20% or a 30% markup. A $50 item would be marked to sell 23
for either $60 or $65. Depending on future prospects for 34
sales, half of the articles would be priced at each level. 46

Ms. Aagard's suggestion is to assign items in Groups 11
#1470, #2830, and #4560 to the 20% category. The Series 77 23
items* would be in the 30% markup category except for the 35
items with a base rate under $100. What is your reaction? 46

Mr. Chavez's recommendation is to assign a 30% markup 11
to Groups #3890, #5290, #6480, and #7180. About 1/4 of the 22
remainder (except for soft goods) would also be in the 30% 34
category. Groups #8340 and #9560 would have a 20% markup. 46

| 1 | 2 | 3 | 4 | 5 | 6 | 7 | 8 | 9 | 10 | 11 | 12

C. Take two 5-minute timed writings. Review your speed and errors.

Goal: At least 43wpm/5′/5e

C. 5-MINUTE TIMED WRITING

```
     Finding a job is a challenge in today's job market,         11
but there are some steps you can take to remain competitive      23
in the job market. First of all, be sure you know something      35
about the company. Do they have offices in a location to         46
which you would move, and is the position in that company        58
one in which you would like to spend the next five to ten        69
years?                                                           71
     To be successful during your interview, you need to         81
know yourself. What are your strengths, and what are your        93
weaknesses, if any? Be sure to emphasize your unique skills     105
both in your resume and during the interview. Let others        116
know what makes you the best candidate for the job. Some        128
excellent traits to emphasize would be enthusiasm, a high       139
motivation level, and an excellent work ethic.                  149
     When you go for your interview, take into account how      160
you dress. Choose your wardrobe as you would for your first     172
day on the job. If you are uncertain as to the particular       183
dress code, always err on the side of conservatism. Also,       195
be watchful of your personal grooming. Make certain your        206
hair is trimmed and your shoes are polished.                    215
| 1 | 2 | 3 | 4 | 5 | 6 | 7 | 8 | 9 | 10 | 11 | 12
```

FORMATTING

Word Processing Manual

D. WORD PROCESSING: TABLE—AUTOFORMAT

Study Lesson 80 in your word processing manual. Complete all the shaded steps while at your computer. Then format the jobs that follow.

Table 80-38

Predesigned Table

1. Use a landscape page orientation.
2. Insert a table with 3 columns and 17 rows.
3. Type the table contents, and then AutoFit to contents.
4. Apply the 3D effects 2 Table AutoFormat.
5. Center the table horizontally and vertically.

CITY BANK Interest Rates Schedule Effective Date: November 11, 2003		
	Rate	**APY**
Value Checking	0.00%	0.00%
City Checking	1.25%	1.27%
Prestige Checking	1.25%	1.27%
Golden Checking	1.50%	1.55%
Regular Savings	1.75%	1.90%
Young Savers	1.75%	1.90%
Christmas Club	1.75%	1.90%
Money Market—Tier I	2.25%	2.30%
Money Market—Tier II	2.50%	2.60%
Money Market—Tier III	2.75%	2.80%
Money Market—Tier IV	3.00%	3.10%
CD—6 month	2.25%	2.50%
CD—1 year	2.35%	2.65%
CD—2 year	2.45%	2.70%
year	2.50%	2.75%

Table 80-39

Predesigned Table

Open the file for Table 80-38 and make the following changes:

1. Use a portrait page orientation.
2. Add 1 blank row between Christmas Club and Money Market—Tier 1.
3. Add 1 blank row between Money Market—Tier IV and CD—6 month.
4. Merge the cells in the inserted rows.
5. Type an asterisk (*) after "APY" in Column C.
6. Insert 1 blank row at the bottom of the table and type `*APY=Annual Percentage Yield.`
7. Apply a Table AutoFormat Table Professional.
8. Center the table horizontally and vertically.

Table 80-40

Predesigned Table

Progress and Proofreading Check

Documents designated as Proofreading Checks serve as a check of your proofreading skill. Your goal is to have zero typographical errors when the GDP software first scores the document.

Follow these steps to insert a table using Table AutoFormat.

1. Insert the following table in default format.
2. Apply the Contemporary Table AutoFormat option.
3. Center the table horizontally and vertically.

BUILDING DIRECTORY Paulding Meeting Facility			
No.	**Room Name**	**Seating**	**Square Feet**
102	Alabama	35	400
104	Colorado	150	1,600
106	Delaware	25	350
108	Georgia	50	600
202	Montana	35	400
204	Nevada	50	600
206	New Jersey	300	3,200
208	Pennsylvania	350	3,600

Skills Assessment on Part 4

5-Minute Timed Writing

Many business firms create their own special documents 11
today by using software packages that are designed to do 23
the job. These packages help people with limited design 34
skills create pages with very little effort. The challenge, 46
though, is for the person to design the pages effectively 57
so that the reader will read them. After all, the reason 69
for putting in all that time and money is to get people to 81
read the articles. 84

Designing pages that are easy to read is not quite as 95
easy as it seems. For example, a reader may be confused if 107
a page has too many headlines. Instead, a reader may want 119
to read fewer headlines that are printed in larger type. 130

Desktop publishers require just a few good tools to 141
interest the reader. A good plan to use is to be sure to 152
put the most important articles at the top of the first page 164
and the less important articles on the inside pages. The 176
use of bullets and side headings are also helpful guides to 188
help a reader zip through pages. A final suggestion is to 199
use pictures and graphics that can make the text much more 211
interesting to read. 215

| 1 | 2 | 3 | 4 | 5 | 6 | 7 | 8 | 9 | 10 | 11 | 12

Correspondence Test 4-76

Memo Report

MEMO

TO: All employees

FROM: Paula Sullivan

Date: January 15, 20--

SUBJECT: Capital Communication Co.

Capital Communication Co. (CCC) operates the fourth-largest network in the U.S. In addition CCC owns 8 television stations, 3 radio stations, and 4 newspapers.

HISTORY

CCC was started in 1962 by a subsidiary of Heartland Publications as a public service network. It began with three radio stations and added both radio and television stations until it went public in 1956. In 1987 it merged with Pacific

(Continued on next page)

Media Company and added 4 newspapers. CCCs largest paper, *The San Antonio Times*, won a pulitzer Prize for writing last year.

EARNINGS With sales of $4.9 billion dollars for the most recent 12-month period and income of $486 million, it continues to lead the "buy" list of most stock brokers. The table shows a break down of its earnings.

CAPITAL COMMUNICATION COMPANY			
Company	Last Year	This Year	Next Year*
Radio	$#1.3	$1.4	$1.4
Television	$1.8	$2.10	$2.2
Newspapers	$1.4	$1.5	$2.0
*Projected			

urs

Correspondence Test 4-77

Business Letter in Block Style

January 10, 20-- | Mr. Owen F. Austin | 1734 Perry Street | Flint, MI 48504 | Dear Mr. Austin:

¶ I am sorry that time constraints shortened our telephone conversation yesterday. Given the circumstances as you presented them, you would be wise to consider drafting a general durable power of attorney as described in Section 495 of the new act.

¶ A power of attorney, under the old law, is effective only up to the time that a person is disabled or incompetent. Now the general durable power of attorney, under the new statute, will remain in effect until a person either revokes it or passes away.

¶ The new law will be very helpful to many elderly and infirm people. Sincerely yours, | C. F. Storden | Attorney-at-Law | urs | PS: You may want to discuss this matter with your children before calling my office for an appointment. | bc: Peggy Austin, Walter Austin

Table Test 4-41

Boxed Table

Add 20 percent shading to the title row and 10 percent shading to column headings and total row.

AMERICAN TRADE (As a Percentage of Total)			
Exports		**Imports**	
Canada	22	Japan	20
Japan	12	Canada	19
Mexico	7	Mexico	6
United Kingdom	6	Germany	5
Germany	5	Taiwan	5
South Korea	4	South Korea	4
Other countries	44	Other countries	41
TOTAL	**100**	**TOTAL**	**100**

Part 5

Specialized Applications

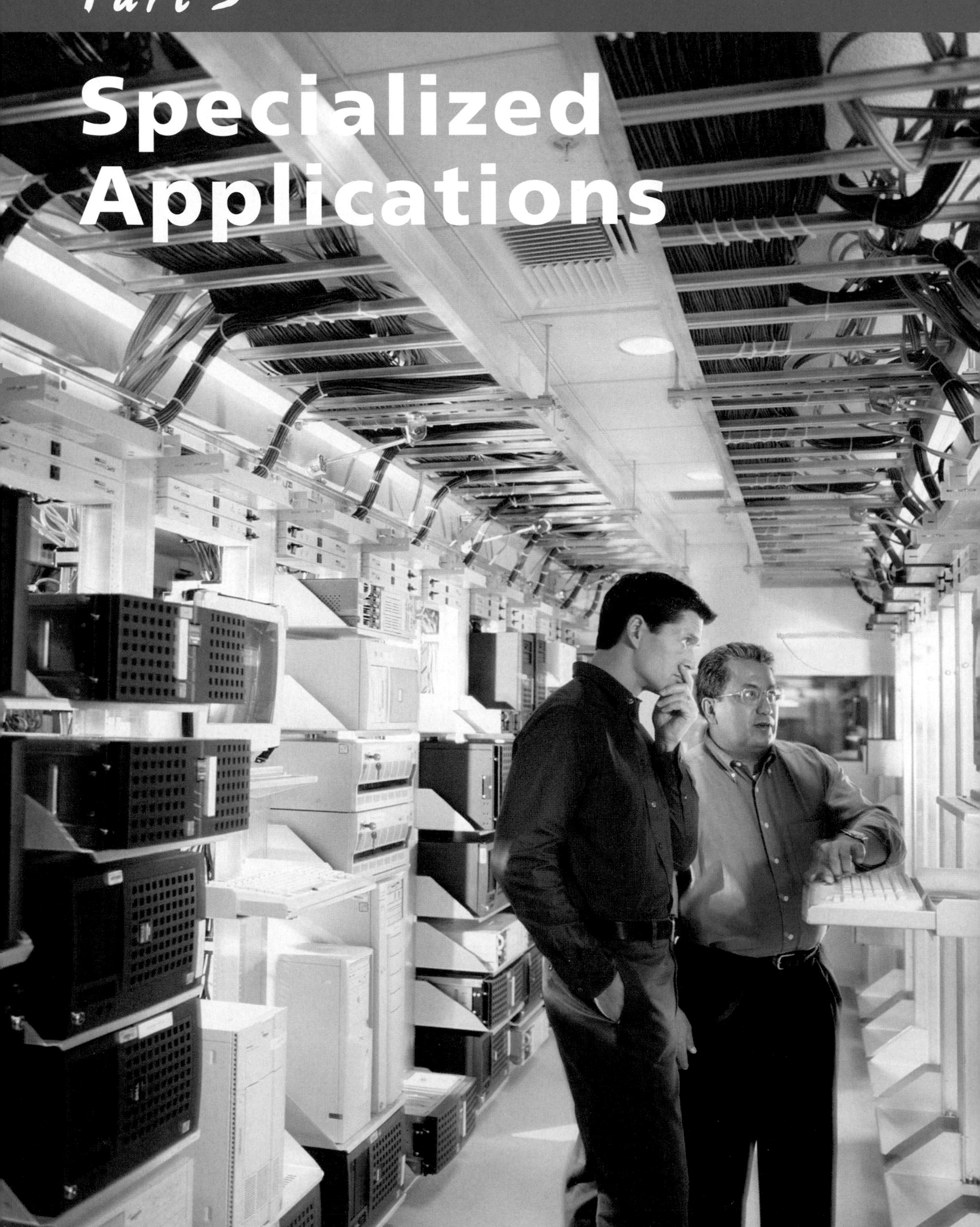

Keyboarding in Information Technology (IT) Services

Work in the IT services cluster involves designing, developing, managing, and operating communication and IT systems, networks, and related hardware and software for telecommunications and computing services.

Opportunities in IT Services

People working in telecommunications design and maintain telephone, satellite, and laser communication systems. Among the numerous IT jobs are programmer, software engineer, technical support representative, information systems operator/analyst, and network administrator. Satellites above the earth receive and send signals, thus speeding up communications. Skilled engineers design systems that enhance the ways by which people communicate.

We are all globally connected by technology, and IT services support those necessary connections. Technology is spreading at an ever-increasing rate and affecting every aspect of our daily lives. This industry is full of opportunity for individuals with superior technical and mathematical skills. The ability to communicate complex ideas clearly, handle many details, and solve problems is an asset. Of course, keyboarding proficiency is critical.

Objectives

KEYBOARDING

- Type at least 47 words per minute on a 5-minute timed writing with no more than 5 errors.

LANGUAGE ARTS

- Refine proofreading skills and correctly use proofreaders' marks.
- Use abbreviations, capitals, and punctuation correctly.
- Improve composing and spelling skills.
- Recognize subject/verb agreement.

WORD PROCESSING

- Use the word processing commands necessary to complete the document processing activities.

DOCUMENT PROCESSING

- Format formal report projects, international business documents, medical office documents, and legal office documents.

TECHNICAL

- Answer at least 90 percent of the questions correctly on an objective test.

Unit 17

Formal Report Project

LESSON 81
Formal Report Project

LESSON 82
Formal Report Project

LESSON 83
Formal Report Project

LESSON 84
Formal Report Project

LESSON 85
Formal Report Project

INTERCULTURAL SEMINARS

Jordan D. Sylvester, Director

Human Resources Department

February 12, 20--

The Marketing Department has been conducting surveys of our worldwide offices, foreign customers, and prospective foreign customers over the last several months. Information received through the use of mailed questionnaires has made us aware of an urgent need to improve our communication skills at the international level.

PROBLEM

Some incidents have been reported to us in which we ha with foreign customers and prospective foreign custome breakdowns in communication. Some of these setbacks conscious negative acts on the part of our employees. H to be lack of awareness of cultural differences and lack that reflect these cultural differences. Indeed, there are misunderstandings, insults, miscues, and avenues for pe miscommunicate.

INTERCULTURAL SEMINARS

Three-day seminars designed to improve intercultural c at regional sites in the United States and in foreign citie

- Beijing
- Hamburg
- Madrid
- Melbourne
- Oslo
- Rio de Janeiro
- Tokyo
- Warsaw

It will be our intent that all employees who have direct c countries will participate in these seminars over a four-

INTERCULTURAL SEMINARS

Submitted to

Jordan D. Sylvester, Director
Human Resources Department

red by

Reyes
Manager
Healthcare

12, 20--

CONTENTS

Formal Report Project

Goals

- Improve speed and accuracy
- Refine language arts skills in grammar
- Format a formal report

A. Type 2 times.

A. WARMUP

```
     The jalopy quivered as it crossed over the 1/5-mile-     11
long bridge on Route 267 about 14 miles south @ Granite       22
Falls. The axle on Richard's truck broke as he whizzed by.    34
| 1 | 2 | 3 | 4 | 5 | 6 | 7 | 8 | 9 | 10 | 11 | 12
```

SKILLBUILDING

B. MAP

Follow the GDP software directions for this exercise in improving keystroking accuracy.

C. Take a 1-minute timed writing on the first paragraph to establish your base speed. Then take four 1-minute timed writings on the remaining paragraphs. As soon as you equal or exceed your base speed on one paragraph, advance to the next, more difficult paragraph.

C. SUSTAINED PRACTICE: CAPITALIZATION

```
     A visit to Europe is a vacation that many people dream  11
of doing. There are many countries to visit and hundreds of  23
sites to see if you can spend at least four weeks on the     34
continent. A trip to Europe is one you will never forget.    46

     If you decide to visit Europe, the months of June and   11
July would probably be the prettiest, but they would also    23
be the busiest. England, France, and Germany are popular     34
countries to visit; Spain is popular for Americans as well.  46

     In England you will want to visit St. Paul's Cathedral  11
and Big Ben. And, of course, when you are in England, you    23
do not want to pass up the opportunity to see Buckingham     34
Palace. Plan on staying a few days to see all the sites.     45

     France certainly is a highlight of any European visit.  11
Paris offers many sites such as the Arc de Triomphe, the     22
Louvre, the Eiffel Tower, and the Gothic Cathedral of Notre  34
Dame. Other cities to visit are Nice, Lyon, and Versailles.  46
| 1 | 2 | 3 | 4 | 5 | 6 | 7 | 8 | 9 | 10 | 11 | 12
```

LANGUAGE ARTS

D. Study the rules at the right.

D. AGREEMENT

RULE ▶ agreement pronouns

Some pronouns *(anybody, each, either, everybody, everyone, much, neither, no one, nobody,* and *one)* are always singular and take a singular verb. Other pronouns *(all, any, more, most, none,* and *some)* may be singular or plural, depending on the noun to which they refer.

Each of the employees has finished his or her task.
Much remains to be done.
Most of the pie was eaten, but most of the cookies were left.

RULE ▶ agreement intervening words

Disregard any intervening words that come between the subject and verb when establishing agreement.

The box containing the books and pencils has not been found.
Alex, accompanied by Tricia, is attending the conference and taking his computer.

Edit the sentences to correct any errors in grammar.

```
20 Everybody who signed up for the trip are to be at Building 16.
21 All the tourists are sending cards to us from their hotels.
22 Everyone on the trip, including spouses, have been having fun.
23 Some of the postcards from their vacations are not arriving.
24 Two of the sales reps from Region 4 were given cash bonuses.
25 The fastest runner from all five teams are receiving a trophy.
```

FORMATTING

Word Processing Manual

E. WORD PROCESSING: STYLES

Study Lesson 81 in your word processing manual. Complete all of the shaded steps while at your computer. Then format the job that follows.

DOCUMENT PROCESSING

Report 81-58 ▶

Business Report

Report 81-58 begins in this lesson and is continued through Lesson 85. You will be applying styles throughout this report that automatically effect formatting changes to fonts, paragraph spacing, bold, and so on. You will therefore notice some differences from standard business report format. Such changes will be called out in directions and illustrations. Use the following guidelines to format the report.

1. First, change to 11-point Arial font; then press ENTER 6 times.
2. Type the title in all-caps, and press ENTER 1 time. **Note**: Do not apply any styles until you have typed the entire report for a given lesson.
3. Type the byline information and the date in upper- and lowercase, and press ENTER 1 time between each line.
4. Press ENTER 2 times after the date and continue typing the remainder of the report in the same way. Press ENTER only 1 time before and after all side headings.
5. Create a header that will display on all pages except the first page. Type the header in 10-point Arial italic. Type `Human Resources Department` at the left margin. Press TAB until you reach the right margin, type `Page` followed by 1 space, and insert an automatic page number. Add a bottom border and close the header.

After you have finished typing the entire document for a particular lesson, go back and make these changes:

Reference Manual

Refer to Reference Manual pages R-8A and R-8B to review the correct format for business reports. Refer to Reference Manual page R-12C for a review of list formatting.

1. Apply the Title style to the report title.
2. Apply the Subtitle style to the subtitle, byline, and date.
3. Apply the Heading 2 style to the side headings. **Note:** The Heading 2 style includes italic.
4. Apply the Heading 3 style to the paragraph headings, including the period at the end.
5. Type the table titles in 13-point Arial Bold. Type the table column headings in 11-point Arial Bold. Type the table body in 11-point Arial.
6. Apply 11-point Arial font to the body of the report as needed.
7. Use the default formatting for the footnotes at the bottom of the page.

Change to 11-point Arial first.

↓6X

INTERCULTURAL SEMINARS ↓1X — Apply the Title style.

Jordan D. Sylvester, Director ↓1X — Apply the Subtitle style.

Human Resources Department ↓1X

February 12, 20-- ↓2X

Arial 11 pt.

agreement intervening words

¶ The marketing department has been doing surveys of our world wide offices, foriegn customers, and prospective foriegn customers over the last several months. Information received through the use of questionnaires has made us aware of an urgent need to improve our communication skills at the international level. ↓1X

Apply the Heading 2 style.

PROBLEM ↓1X

agreement pronouns

¶ Some incidents have been reported to us in which we have failed to negotiate contract with foreign customers and prospective foreign customers because of serious break downs in comunication. Very few of these setbacks have been the result of conscious negative acts on the part of our employees. The main culprit seems to be lack of awareness of cultural differences and a lack of appreciation for the nuances that reflect these cultural differences. Indeed, there almost are unlimited possibilities for misunderstandings, insults, miscues, and avenues for people of good intent to miscommunicate. ↓1X

(Continued on next page)

Apply the Heading 2 style.

INTERCULTURAL SEMINARS

↓1X

agreement intervening words

¶ Three day seminars designed to improve intercultural communication skills will be held at regional sites in the U. S. and in foreign cities where we have offices:

↓1X

Refer to page R-12C of the Reference Manual for a review of list formatting.

- Beijing
- Hamburg
- Madrid
- Melbourne
- Oslo
- Rio de Janeiro
- Tokyo
- Warsaw

↓2X

agreement intervening words

¶ It will be our intend that all employees who have direct contact with people from other countries will participate in these seminars over a four-month period.

¶ It would be unreasonable to assume that a small team of people from our company would have the breadth needed to conduct these seminars in 8 foreign countries. However, Angela Demirchyan, William Hamilton, and Chang Ho Han have agreed to work together as the coordinating team for this effort.

agreement pronouns

¶ Each of these individuals has worked over the past 2 months with the managers of our international offices as well as natives in specific countries to formulate a preliminary plan for these in-service programs. There plan will utilize the expertise of our employees who have had negotiating experience in each country and who have knowledge of customs as demonstrated by natives. We are confident that through this team approach everyone will gain an understanding of problems only not from the position of our company but also from the perspective of those with whom they conduct business.

agreement pronouns

Save this unfinished report. You will resume work on it in Lesson 82.

Lesson 82

Formal Report Project

Goals

- Type at least 44wpm/5'/5e
- Format a formal report

A. Type 2 times.

A. WARMUP

1 The path will be covered by approximately 30 pieces 11
2 of slate from Quarry #19. Schreiner & Zimmer (the general 23
3 contractor) took the joint bid of $638, including delivery. 35

| 1 | 2 | 3 | 4 | 5 | 6 | 7 | 8 | 9 | 10 | 11 | 12

SKILLBUILDING

B. Take three 12-second timed writings on each line. The scale below the last line shows your wpm speed for a 12-second timed writing.

B. 12-SECOND SPEED SPRINTS

4 There are many things to think about if you buy a used car.
5 Two of the main things are its age and the number of miles.
6 Take the car for a test drive in town and on the open road.
7 Pay a fee to an auto expert who will check it over for you.

5 10 15 20 25 30 35 40 45 50 55 60

C. PROGRESSIVE PRACTICE: ALPHABET

If you are not using the GDP software, turn to page SB-7 and follow the directions for this activity.

Strategies for Career Success

Letter of Complaint

Is poor product or bad service getting you down? By writing a concise, rational letter of complaint, you have the possibility of the reader honoring your request.

In the first paragraph, give a precise description of the product or service (for example, model, serial number). Include a general statement of the problem (for example, "It is not working properly."). In the middle section, provide the details of what went wrong (for example, when it happened, what failed). Refer to copies of invoices, checks, and so on. Describe how you were inconvenienced, with details about time and money lost. State what you want (for example, refund, repair, replace). In the closing paragraph, ask for a timely response to the complaint (for example, "Please resolve this problem within the next two weeks.").

YOUR TURN Think about the last time that you experienced poor product or service. Did you write a letter of complaint?

D. Take two 5-minute timed writings. Review your speed and errors.

Goal: At least 44wpm/5'/5e

D. 5-MINUTE TIMED WRITING

Critical thinking is a skill that can be learned and 11
applied to more than a few situations. There are many ways 23
to describe critical thinking skill. The common theme that 34
runs through each of these descriptions is related to the 46
use of cognitive skill. With this skill, the person thinks 58
with a purpose in mind and likely directs some of the focus 70
toward goals. The person looks at a situation and decides 81
rationally what to believe or not to believe. In critical 93
thinking, the goal is to achieve understanding, judge more 105
than one viewpoint, and then solve problems. After a person 117
thinks through all the elements of the problem, a decision 129
is made based on all of the facts and exact findings. Bias, 141
prejudice, and feelings should not sway the final outcome. 152
Critical thinking is useful in reading, listening, 163
speaking, and writing. A critical thinker will ask great 174
questions. He or she listens carefully to others and gives 186
feedback. A critical thinker seeks the truth with zeal and 198
then willingly accepts change when new facts are presented. 210
Critical thinking is important for problem solving. 220

| 1 | 2 | 3 | 4 | 5 | 6 | 7 | 8 | 9 | 10 | 11 | 12

DOCUMENT PROCESSING

Report 81-58 (Continued)

Continue working on Multipage Business Report 81-58.

Refer to Reference Manual

Refer to page R-12C of the Reference Manual for a review of list formatting.

INSTRUCTIONAL APPROACH

¶ Alvarez and Hwang suggest a framework of instruction with the following three components:

1. The cognitive component includes information about communicating with people of other cultures.
2. The effective (affective) component is the area in which attention is given to attitudes, emotions, and resulting behaviors as they are effected (affected) by human interaction in a multi-cultural environment.

(Continued on next page)

3. The experiential component is the "hands-on" element ~~which~~ that suggests different possibilities. Others have found that the use of simulations is a natural for this type of experience. The writing of letters, memos, and reports to persons in other cultures also provides beneficial learning experiences. In addition, the use of tutors can be very helpful to workers unfamiliar with a particular culture.[1]

SEMINAR CONTENT

¶ The cognitive, affective, and experiential ~~frames~~ components would be applied as appropriate for each of the topics included. The coordinating team members have utilized the resources available to them at our ③ local universities.

¶ Most colleges and universities now provide instruction in international communication. While the content at times is integrated into several business administration courses, there has been a trend in recent years to provide a course ~~or courses~~ specifically designed for business interaction in an intercultural setting. The very nature of this type of study makes it very difficult to segment the broad topical areas as all elements are so closely intertwined. However, the tentative seminar plan is to cover the content as described in Table 1.

¶ The seminars must reflect the broad involvement of our international operations. There is a need for many workers in our domestic offices to develop an appreciation of the intercultural chalenge. This is true not only for those in the marketing and sales areas. Those in our Finance Department and our Legal Department are increasingly involved not only with foreign companies but also with huge multinational corporations that at times are as large as or larger than the biggest companies in the ~~entire~~ United States.

¶ Demirchyan, Hamilton, and Han suggest the following list of tentative instructional topics:[2]

---

[1] Ana Maria Alvarez and Allen Hwang, "Communication Across Cultures," *International Business World,* April 2006, pp. 39-42.

[2] Angela Demirchyan, William Hamilton, and Chang Ho Han, *The Dynamics of Intercultural Seminars*, Gateway Publishing, Boston, 2005.

(Continued on next page)

Review the format for placing a table in a report on page R-8B of the Reference Manual.

↓2X

TABLE 1. SEMINAR TOPICS	
Instructional Topic	**Time**
Body Movements	2 hours
Concept of Culture	3 hours
Language	3 hours
Conflict Resolution	2 hours
Intimacy in Relationships	3 hours
Male and female Roles	3 hours
Space and Time	2 hours
Religion, Values, and ethics	4 hours

Arial Bold 13 pt.

Arial Bold 11 pt.

Arial 11 pt.

↓1X

Apply the Heading 3 style.

¶ **Body Positions and Movements.** Body language that is, facial expressions, gestures, and body movements conveys messages about attitude and may be interpreted differently by people in different cultures. For example, firm handshakes are the norm in the U.S.; loose handshakes are the custom in some other countries. The way we stand, sit, and hold our arms may convey different messages in different cultural settings.

Apply the Heading 3 style.

¶ **Concept of culture.** This session will be an over view of the various cultures in which we conduct business, including e-commerce. Clooney identifies the need for varied marketing strategies within the different economic, political, and cultural environments:

Refer to page R-8B for a review of long quotations.

> International Web use and access are growing exponentially, and many businesses are wanting to capitalize on this trend and grab their fair share of this global market. English-speaking audiences are not expected to continue to dominate this market. Certainly, more than a literal translation will be required to reach this culturally diverse audience.[3]

Case studies will be reviewed that are considered classics in the field of international communication. In addition, Summaries of some of our own successes and failures will be reported.

Save this unfinished report. You will resume work on it in Lesson 83.

[3] Arlene D. Clooney, "Cultural Comparisons in E-Commerce," December 19, 2005, <http://www.ecommerce.com/news.htm>, accessed on January 18, 2006.

Formal Report Project

Goals

- Improve speed and accuracy
- Refine language arts skills in composing
- Format a formal report

A. Type 2 times.

A. WARMUP

```
     The 16 young farmers (only 50% over 30 years of age)      11
gathered in Room 209 to begin discussing the earthquake        22
threat; an extra door prize was given as a "joke present."     34
| 1 | 2 | 3 | 4 | 5 | 6 | 7 | 8 | 9 | 10 | 11 | 12
```

SKILLBUILDING

PPP PRETEST → PRACTICE → POSTTEST

PRETEST
Take a 1-minute timed writing. Review your speed and errors.

B. PRETEST: Common Letter Combinations

```
     The insurance agent read the report before giving it      11
to your deputy director. This weekly action showed that        22
the agent really knew the actual input on a daily basis.       33
| 1 | 2 | 3 | 4 | 5 | 6 | 7 | 8 | 9 | 10 | 11 | 12
```

PRACTICE
Speed Emphasis:
If you made no more than 1 error on the Pretest, type each *individual* line 2 times.
Accuracy Emphasis:
If you made 2 or more errors, type each *group* of lines (as though it were a paragraph) 2 times.

C. PRACTICE: Word Beginnings

```
re- repel renew remit relax refer ready react really reveal
in- inept inert inset input infer index incur inches insert
be- bears beams beach below being began befit beauty beside
```

D. PRACTICE: Word Endings

```
-ly truly madly lowly early daily apply hilly simply weekly
-ed sized hired dated cited based acted added opened showed
-nt plant meant giant front event count agent amount fluent
```

POSTTEST
Repeat the Pretest timed writing and compare performance.

E. POSTTEST: Common Letter Combinations

F. PROGRESSIVE PRACTICE: NUMBERS

If you are not using the GDP software, turn to page SB-11 and follow the directions for this activity.

LANGUAGE ARTS

G. COMPOSING A DOCUMENT

Compose a 1-page document in which you describe how you can use the Styles feature in a resume you are preparing for a job search. You might include features such as fonts, font sizes, indentations, and spacing to control the appearance of your resume. Use default margins, double spacing, and two paragraphs in your document. Provide a title, and type your name at the top of the document.

In paragraph 1, you could include information on using styles for those items you want to highlight in your resume such as (1) your name and address at the top of the resume, (2) the section headings that often run down the left side of the resume, and (3) any bullets you want to include for items that contain multiple entries.

In paragraph 2, you could include a brief discussion on (1) the margins to use for your resume, (2) line spacing to use for individual entries, and (3) line spacing to use between entries.

Include a brief summary statement to emphasize the importance of proofreading your document and the need for accuracy in a resume.

FORMATTING

Word Processing Manual

H. WORD PROCESSING: INSERT CLIP ART AND FILES

Study Lesson 83 in your word processing manual. Complete all of the shaded steps while at your computer. Then format the job that follows.

DOCUMENT PROCESSING

Report 81-58

(Continued)

Continue working on Report 81-58.

Insert clip art that is related to communication and similar to this example.

Set the clip art at a size of 1-inch square, and place it at the right margin even with the first line of the Language paragraph.

¶ **Conflict Resolution**. Whether people are involved in negotiating a contract, working together to remedy product quality issues, or resolving contract interpretations, the need for tact and skill is particularly important in the foreign setting. Many of the seminar topics have implications in the area of conflict resolution. While every effort should be made to prevent conflict, there is a need for guidance in resolving disagreements in foreign cultures.
¶ **Intimacy in Relationships**. The degree of physical contact that is acceptable varies considerably. Hugs and kisses are the standard, even in the business office, in some countries. By contrast, the act of touching a person is considered an extreme invasion of privacy in other places. The use of first names may or may not be acceptable. To ask a personal question is extremely offensive in some cultures. While socializing with business clients is to be expected in some countries, it would be highly inappropriate in others. These are only a few of the relationship concerns that will be explored.
¶ **Language**. It is obvious that language differences play a major part in business miscommunication. Whenever there is an interpreter or a written translation involved, the chances for error are increased. There are over 3,000 languages used on the earth. Just as with English, there are not only

(Continued on next page)

grammar rules but also varied meanings as words are both spoken and written. Even with the English language, there are differences in usage between the English used in the United States and that used in England.

¶ Although English is the language usually used in international communication, the topics identified in Table 1 illustrate the complexity of communicating accurately; and the problem continues to grow. For example, literal translations of American advertising and labeling have sometimes resulted in negative feelings toward products. As world trade increases, so does the need for American businesses to understand the complexities of cultural differences. Gregorian offers this example:

> A businessperson must change his or her expectations and assumptions away from what is customary and acceptable in the United States in terms of personal and social conduct to what is customary and acceptable within the culture of the country where they are conducting business. Any other assumption can have serious consequences and undesirable results. In the other person's mind, you are the foreigner and therefore you will be the one who might look out of place or act in a way that is considered socially unacceptable.[4]

¶ A good sense of humor is an asset not only in our personal lives but also in the business environment. However, it probably should be avoided in multicultural settings because the possibilities for misinterpretation are compounded. Do not use humor that makes fun of a particular individual, group, or culture. Remember that what may appear to be humorous to you may have a negative connotation in another culture.

¶ **Male and Female Roles.** There are major contrasts in the ways male and female roles are perceived in different cultures. The right to vote is still withheld from women in countries all over the world. Opportunities for female employment in the business environment vary considerably. Pay differentials for men and women continue to exist even when they are performing the same tasks. Opportunities for advancement for men and women often are not the same.

¶ **Space and Time.** The distance one stands from someone when engaged in conversation is very important. If a person stands farther away than usual, this may signal a feeling of indifference or even a negative feeling. Standing too close is a sign of inappropriate familiarity. However, it should be recognized that different cultures require a variety of space for business exchanges to take place. In the United States, that space is typically from three to five feet, but in the Middle East and in Latin American countries, this distance is considered too far.

¶ There is also the element of time--a meeting that is scheduled for 9 a.m. likely will start on time in the United States, but in some other cultures the meeting may not start until 9:30 or even 10 o'clock. Punctuality and time concepts vary with the customs and practices of each country. Patience really can be a virtue.

Insert clip art that is related to time and similar to this example. The style should be similar to the first clip art you inserted.

Set the clip art at a size of 1-inch square, and place it at the right margin even with the first line in the second paragraph of the Space and Time paragraph.

Save this unfinished report. You will resume work on it in Lesson 84.

---

[4] Gerald Gregorian, *Comparing Cultural Differences*, Dana Publishing Company, Los Angeles, 2003, p. 49.

Lesson 84

Formal Report Project

Goals

- Type at least 44wpm/5′/5e
- Format a formal report

A. Type 2 times.

A. WARMUP

```
     The new schedule* has the Lynx at their home park on   11
July 27 with the zany Waverley Blackhawks. The Lynx scored  23
five fourth-quarter goals in their last game to win 8 to 4! 34
|  1  |  2  |  3  |  4  |  5  |  6  |  7  |  8  |  9  |  10  |  11  |  12
```

SKILLBUILDING

B. DIAGNOSTIC PRACTICE: SYMBOLS AND PUNCTUATION

If you are not using the GDP software, turn to page SB-2 and follow the directions for this activity.

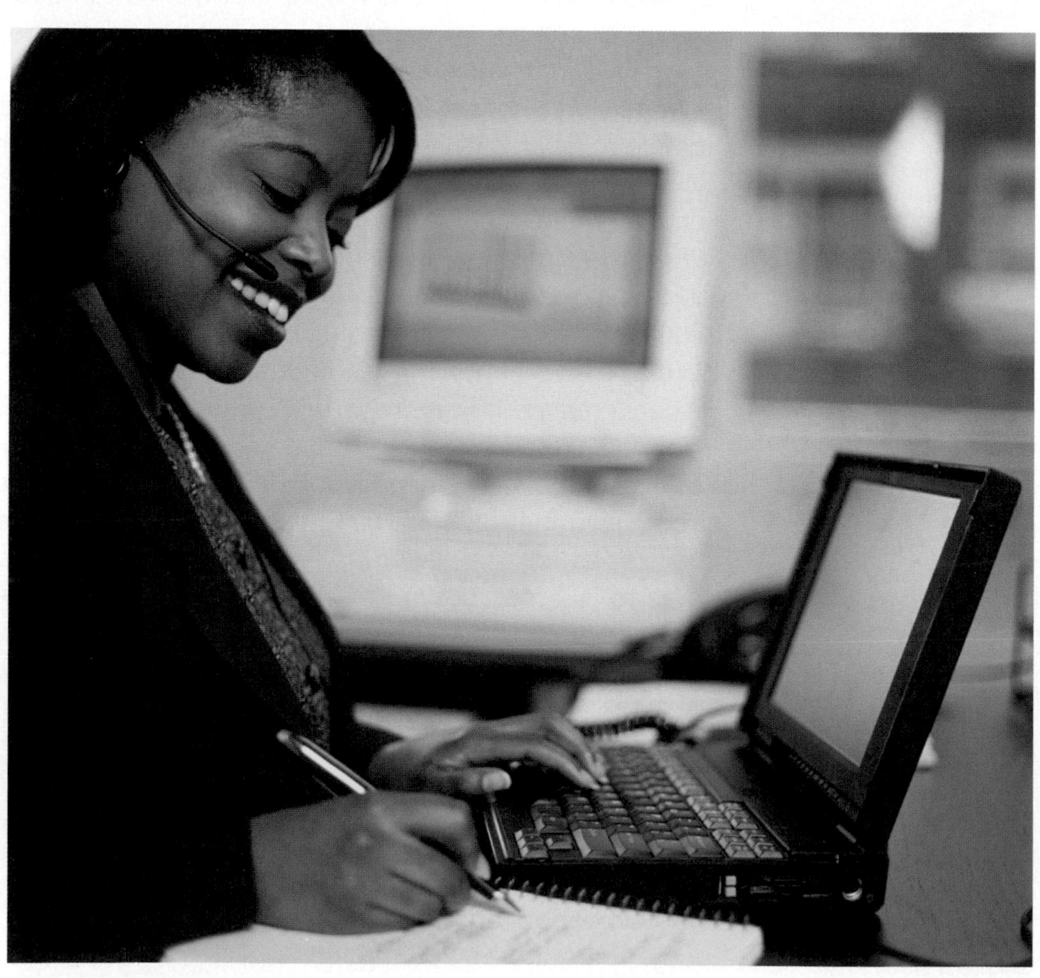

C. Take two 5-minute timed writings. Review your speed and errors.

Goal: At least 44wpm/5'/5e.

C. 5-MINUTE TIMED WRITING

Proofreading skill is developed with practice. You may 11
want to master several techniques that will help develop 23
and improve your proofreading skills. 30
In order to be a successful proofreader, you will want 41
to schedule time to read through the completed job several 53
times. At the first reading, check your work to see if the 65
margins are correct and the page numbers are in the right 77
places. Determine if the spacing and the font styles are 80
correct. With each reading, zoom in on a specific type of 100
error. If possible, read your work out loud and read only 111
one word at a time. You may find that placing a ruler under 123
each line as you read it will give your eyes a manageable 135
amount of text to read. 140
At the next reading, be sure that the content of the 150
document follows a logical order. If any cited works are 162
included, be sure the citations are in the proper format 173
with complete and accurate data. Check to be sure that all 185
the basic rules of grammar, spelling, and punctuation have 197
been followed. Proofread your document when you are fresh 208
and alert. Remember, proofreading takes time and patience. 220

| 1 | 2 | 3 | 4 | 5 | 6 | 7 | 8 | 9 | 10 | 11 | 12

Keyboarding Connection

Sending E-Mail Attachments

Your e-mail program will tell you if an attachment has been sent, but the attachment may arrive in unusable or partially usable form. Often the sender and recipient need to use the same or compatible software to open and use each other's documents, especially if the files contain visuals, records, or spreadsheets.

Send a test e-mail by attaching a test document and ask your receiver to send you one in return. If the test fails with a word processing document, open your word processor, and save the document again as a text file. You may lose some formatting (indents, bold, bullets), but any e-mail program, as well as any word processor, can usually read the file.

YOUR TURN Open a word processing file. Save it as a text file. Open the text file in your word processor. What formatting has changed? Send both files to yourself as e-mail attachments. Open them and note any changes.

Table 84-42

Boxed Table

TABLE 2. FOREIGN-CITY SEMINARS		
City	**First Seminar**	**Second Seminar**
Melbourne	May 2-4	July 5-7
Rio de Janeiro	May 9-11	July 11-13
Beijing	May 16-18	July 18-20
Hamburg	May 23-25	July 25-27
Tokyo	June 6-8	August 1-3
Warsaw	June 13-15	August 8-10
Oslo	June 20-22	August 15-17
Madrid	June 27-29	August 22-24

Arial Bold 13 pt.
Arial Bold 11 pt.
Arial 11 pt.

Report 81-58

(Continued)

Continue working on Report 81-58.

¶ **Religion, Values, and Ethics**. While we can recognize the difficult challenge presented by language differences, this category (religion, values, and ethics) is in some ways the area that can bring about the most serious breakdowns in relations with those from other cultures.

- The very nature of religious beliefs suggests that this is a delicate area for those involved in business transactions in foreign countries. Also, religious beliefs affect the consumption of certain products throughout the world. Examples are tobacco, liquor, pork, and coffee.
- Values are a reflection of religious beliefs for most people. We often hear references to right and wrong as applied to the ideals and customs of a society. Values relate to a range of topics, and they may pertain to areas such as cleanliness, education, health care, and criminal justice. Such values are often very personal and as such can have a variety of interpretations. The more interpretations there are, the more likely it is that miscommunication will occur.
- Ethics can be considered as standards of conduct that reflect moral beliefs as applied to both one's personal life and one's business life.

¶ Huntington suggests that now more than ever, a code of ethics is essential within the business environment. When this code of ethics is missing or if it is not enforced, chaos and financial ruin for everyone associated is often the result.

> A code of ethics is increasingly being recognized as an intrinsic and critical component in any business environment. Newspapers are filled with reports of scandalous, unconscionable, nonethical behavior that has led to the downfall of otherwise successful businesses. The lack of ethics in business conduct has led to disastrous effects for both the businesses in question and the consumers and their investments in these companies.[5]

[5] Marilyn C. Huntington, *Business Ethics and Workplace Compliance*, Horizon Publishing Company, New York, 2005, p. 53.

Insert clip art that is related to world travel and similar to this example. The style should be similar to that of the earlier clip art you inserted.

Set the clip art at a size of 1-inch square, and place it at the right margin even with the first line of the first paragraph.

Save this unfinished report. You will resume work on it in Lesson 85.

TENTATIVE SEMINAR SCHEDULE

¶ As indicated earlier, it is our intent that all employees who have direct contact with people in other cultures will participate in these seminars. For that reason there will be two identical three-day seminars scheduled at each foreign site. Only selected employees in our regional sites in the United States will participate. These people have been tentatively identified on the basis of the extent of their involvement with persons from other countries.
¶ As all employees in our foreign offices will participate, a decision has been made to schedule these seminars through the summer. A tentative schedule for these seminars is shown in Table 2.

↓2X

(Insert Table 84–42 here)

↓1X

The Marketing Department is to be commended for calling our attention to the seriousness of our international communication problem. Angela Demirchyan, William Hamilton, and Chang Ho Han also deserve our sincere thanks for their planning efforts for our intercultural communication seminars. As can be seen, special attention is being given to the seminar topics for these in-service programs. Efforts are also being made to identify instructors and resource persons who will develop instructional strategies that will be effective, interesting, and well received by the participants. These seminars will help significantly in increasing our market share in the international market.

Formal Report Project

Goals

- Improve speed and accuracy
- Refine language arts skills in proofreading
- Format a formal report

A. Type 2 times.

A. WARMUP

Bev ordered the following: 24 #794 napkin boxes, 48 11
#265B quarts of ketchup, and 72 reams of 20-lb white print 22
paper. Did you receive the prize jalapeno peppers we sent? 34
| 1 | 2 | 3 | 4 | 5 | 6 | 7 | 8 | 9 | 10 | 11 | 12

SKILLBUILDING

B. Type the columns 2 times. Press TAB to move from column to column.

B. TECHNIQUE PRACTICE: TAB

M. A. Barnes	Julie Herden	Lynn Masica	Don Trueblood
Nathan Favor	Brett Irvin	Lisa O'Keefe	Matthew Utbert
Lee Chinn	Rick Kenwood	J. E. Perry	Jill Voss-Walin
Xavier Saxon	Lance King	Chad Quinn	Robin Yager

C. PACED PRACTICE

If you are not using the GDP software, turn to page SB-14 and follow the directions for this activity.

LANGUAGE ARTS

D. Compare this paragraph with lines 4-7 on page 305.

D. PROOFREADING

A visitt to Europe is a vacation that many people dreem of doing. There are many countrys to visit and hundreds of sights to see if you can spend at least for weeks on the continnent. A trip too Europe is one you will never forget.

DOCUMENT PROCESSING

Report 85-59

Title Page

Refer to page R-7B of the Reference Manual to format the title page.

Create a title page for Report 81-58 as a separate document using standard format and making these changes:

1. Change to 11-point Arial before typing any part of the title page.
2. Type `INTERCULTURAL SEMINARS` as the title.
3. The report is to be submitted to Jordan D. Sylvester, Director, Human Resources Department. Type `Jordan D. Sylvester, Director` on one line followed by the department name on the next line.
4. The report is being prepared by Lydia Reyes, Marketing Manager, Gold Coast Healthcare.
5. The date is February 12, 20--.
6. When you are finished typing the title page, apply the Title style to the title.

Report 85-60

Table of Contents

Refer to page R-7D of the Reference Manual to format the table of contents.

Create a table of contents for Report 81-58 as a separate document using standard format. The table of contents shown is incomplete. Refer to your report to compose and complete the table of contents. Make these changes:

1. Change to 11-point Arial before typing any part of the table of contents page.
2. Refer to the finished report to compose and type the table of contents. The entries should include all side headings and paragraph headings from the report. Refer to the finished report for the page numbers.
3. Type the side headings in all-caps at the left margin.
4. Type the paragraph headings in upper- and lowercase indented 0.5 inch from the left margin.
5. Do not include the report header.

(Continued on next page)

↓6X

Title style **CONTENTS** ↓X2

Arial 11 pt.

Report 85-61

Bibliography

Refer to page R-9B of the Reference Manual to format the bibliography page.

Arial 11 pt.

Spell-check your report for errors. Proofread it for omitted or repeated words, errors that form a new word, and formatting errors.

Type the bibliography for Report 81-58, shown here as a separate document using standard format. Follow these steps:

1. Change to 11-point Arial.
2. Type the bibliography in standard format.
3. When you are finished with all entries, apply the Title style to "BIBLIOGRAPHY."
4. Do not include the report header.

Title style **BIBLIOGRAPHY**

Alvarez, Ana Maria, and Allen Hwang, "Communication Across Cultures," *International Business World*, April 2006, pp. 39-42.

Clooney, Arlene D., "Cultural Comparisons in E-Commerce," December 19, 2005, <http://www.ecommerce.com/news.htm> accessed on January 18, 2006.

Demirchyan, Angela, William Hamilton, and Chang Ho Han, *The Dynamics of Intercultural Seminars*, Gateway Publishing, Boston, 2005.

Gregorian, Gerald, *Comparing Cultural Differences*, Dana Publishing Company, Los Angeles, 2003.

Huntington, Marilyn C., *Business Ethics and Workplace Compliance*, Horizon Publishing Company, New York, 2005.

Report 81-58

(Continued)

Finalize the report project:

- Proofread all the pages for format and typing errors.
- Assemble the pages in this order: title page, table of contents, body, bibliography, and a blank page for a back cover sheet.
- Staple the report pages together.

Progress and Proofreading Check

Documents designated as Proofreading Checks serve as a check of your proofreading skill. Your goal is to have zero typographical errors when the GDP software first scores the document.

Unit 18

International Formatting

LESSON 86
International Formatting (Canada)

LESSON 87
International Formatting (Mexico)

LESSON 88
International Formatting (France)

LESSON 89
International Formatting (Germany)

LESSON 90
International Formatting (Japan)

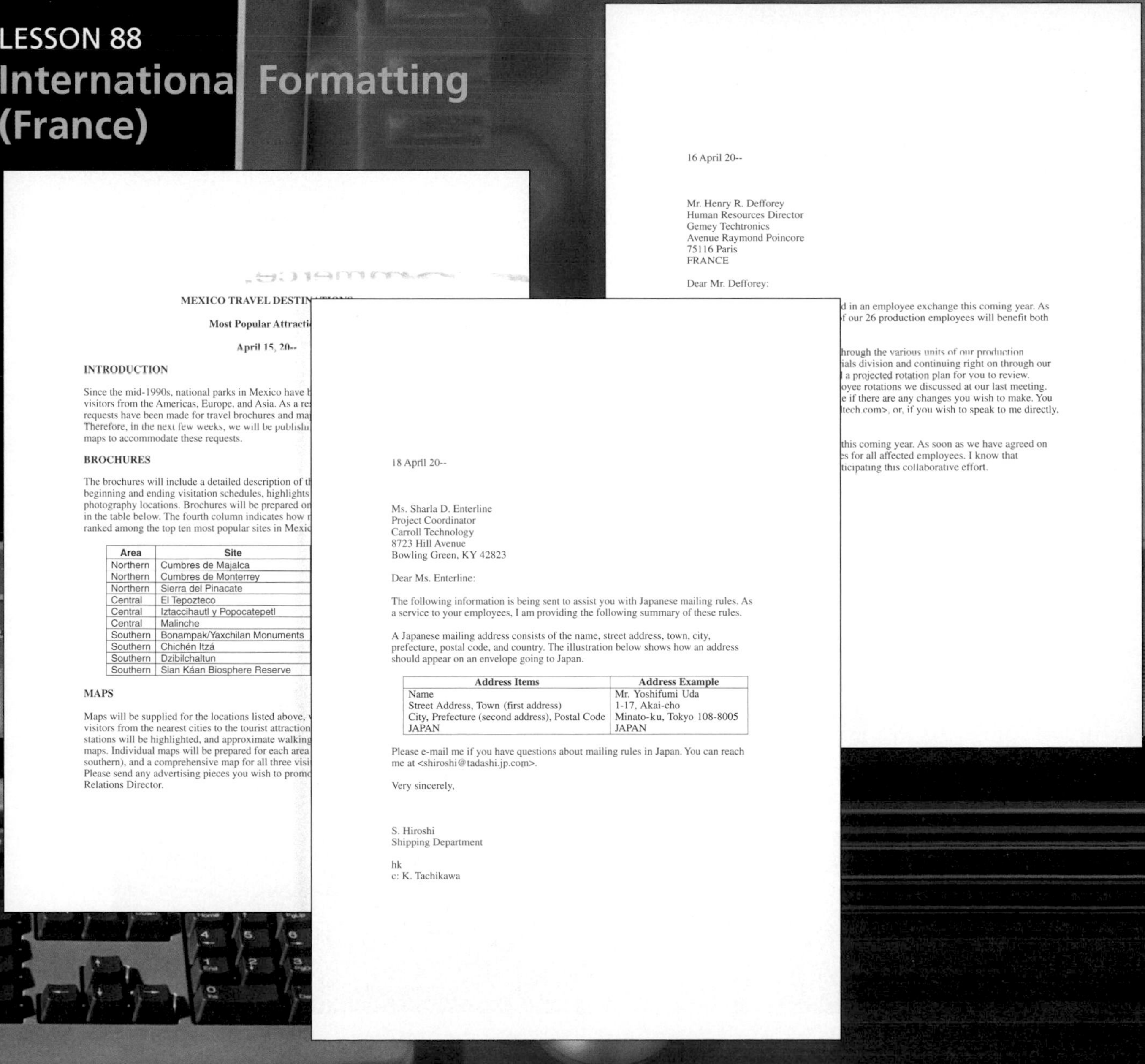

16 April 20--

Mr. Henry R. Defforey
Human Resources Director
Gemey Techtronics
Avenue Raymond Poincore
75116 Paris
FRANCE

Dear Mr. Defforey:

d in an employee exchange this coming year. As f our 26 production employees will benefit both

hrough the various units of our production ials division and continuing right on through our l a projected rotation plan for you to review. oyee rotations we discussed at our last meeting. e if there are any changes you wish to make. You ltech.com>, or, if you wish to speak to me directly,

this coming year. As soon as we have agreed on es for all affected employees. I know that ticipating this collaborative effort.

MEXICO TRAVEL DESTIN

Most Popular Attracti

April 15, 20--

INTRODUCTION

Since the mid-1990s, national parks in Mexico have b visitors from the Americas, Europe, and Asia. As a re requests have been made for travel brochures and ma Therefore, in the next few weeks, we will be publish maps to accommodate these requests.

BROCHURES

The brochures will include a detailed description of th beginning and ending visitation schedules, highlights photography locations. Brochures will be prepared on in the table below. The fourth column indicates how r ranked among the top ten most popular sites in Mexic

Area	Site
Northern	Cumbres de Majalca
Northern	Cumbres de Monterrey
Northern	Sierra del Pinacate
Central	El Tepozteco
Central	Iztaccihautl y Popocatepetl
Central	Malinche
Southern	Bonampak/Yaxchilan Monuments
Southern	Chichén Itzá
Southern	Dzibilchaltun
Southern	Sian Káan Biosphere Reserve

MAPS

Maps will be supplied for the locations listed above, visitors from the nearest cities to the tourist attraction stations will be highlighted, and approximate walking maps. Individual maps will be prepared for each area southern), and a comprehensive map for all three visi Please send any advertising pieces you wish to promo Relations Director.

18 April 20--

Ms. Sharla D. Enterline
Project Coordinator
Carroll Technology
8723 Hill Avenue
Bowling Green, KY 42823

Dear Ms. Enterline:

The following information is being sent to assist you with Japanese mailing rules. As a service to your employees, I am providing the following summary of these rules.

A Japanese mailing address consists of the name, street address, town, city, prefecture, postal code, and country. The illustration below shows how an address should appear on an envelope going to Japan.

Address Items	Address Example
Name	Mr. Yoshifumi Uda
Street Address, Town (first address)	1-17, Akai-cho
City, Prefecture (second address), Postal Code	Minato-ku, Tokyo 108-8005
JAPAN	JAPAN

Please e-mail me if you have questions about mailing rules in Japan. You can reach me at <shiroshi@tadashi.jp.com>.

Very sincerely,

S. Hiroshi
Shipping Department

hk
c: K. Tachikawa

Lesson 86

International Formatting (Canada)

Goals

- Type at least 45wpm/5′/5e
- Format international documents

A. Type 2 times.

A. WARMUP

```
     The lynx at the zoo fought wildly and had to be moved   11
quickly to a new cage (#248-I or #357-II). These adjoining   23
cages place the lynx (all of them) into individual areas.    34
| 1 | 2 | 3 | 4 | 5 | 6 | 7 | 8 | 9 | 10 | 11 | 12
```

SKILLBUILDING

B. DIAGNOSTIC PRACTICE: NUMBERS

If you are not using the GDP software, turn to page SB-5 and follow the directions for this activity.

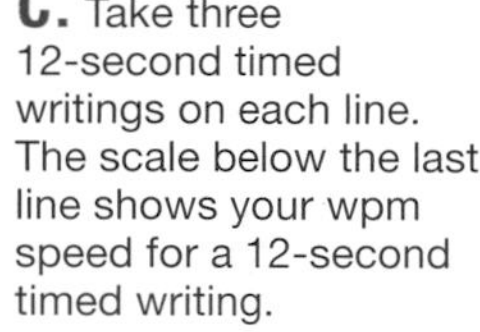

C. Take three 12-second timed writings on each line. The scale below the last line shows your wpm speed for a 12-second timed writing.

C. 12-SECOND SPEED SPRINTS

```
The car will now have to turn off on the lane to the lake.
Mark must type these lines fast and press for a high speed.
We had a lunch at the lake and went for a walk in the park.
Take this disk to have it fixed by the end of your workday.
    5    10    15    20    25    30    35    40    45    50    55    60
```

D. Take two 5-minute timed writings. Review your speed and errors.

Goal: At least 45wpm/5′/5e

D. 5-MINUTE TIMED WRITING

During good economic times, businesses have trouble 11
finding and keeping their skilled workers. As a result, 22
some places may offer great benefits to their workers. This 34
could include such things as sick leave, life insurance, 45
profit sharing, paid time off each year, and flextime. 56
The concept of flextime was introduced to the work 67
force quite a few years ago. Companies adopted the concept 78
for a lot of reasons. Among the top reasons for flexible 90
work schedules at that time were to reduce the number of 101
cars on the road, to help workers to meet their families' 113
needs and demands, and also to attract more women back to 124
the work force. 128
Businesses can manage such a schedule in a few ways. 138
Employees may have a chance to choose when to arrive and 150
leave for the day. This policy allows people who like to 161
work early in the day to start early and end early and vice 173
versa. Other companies may allow their employees to work 185
extended hours for four days and then enjoy three days off. 197
This type of benefit has helped both workers and companies. 209
Companies recognize that their workers are more productive 220
and absences are lower. 225

| 1 | 2 | 3 | 4 | 5 | 6 | 7 | 8 | 9 | 10 | 11 | 12

Keyboarding Connection

Effective Teleconferencing for Meetings

Teleconferencing is a useful way to conduct meetings with businesspersons across the globe. To make the best use of teleconference meetings, follow these guidelines.

Since sound quality varies greatly, use the best equipment available. Allow individual participants enough time to use their technology. Participants should select a conference leader and alternate that leadership. Distribute agendas to everyone in advance, possibly via e-mail.

Be sensitive to time zone differences. Since it is possible someone will experience an inconvenient time, consider rotating the times of the meetings. Assign someone to prepare and e-mail to the participants a brief summary covering the main discussion topics and action items of the teleconference.

YOUR TURN List what you think are the advantages and disadvantages of conducting meetings via teleconference.

E. METRIC PAPER SIZE

Paper size for correspondence in the United States is typically 8.5 × 11 inches. However, correspondence in many foreign countries is often formatted on metric-sized paper. The most popular of these is called A4 paper, and it measures 210 × 297 millimeters—approximately 8.25 × 11.75 inches.

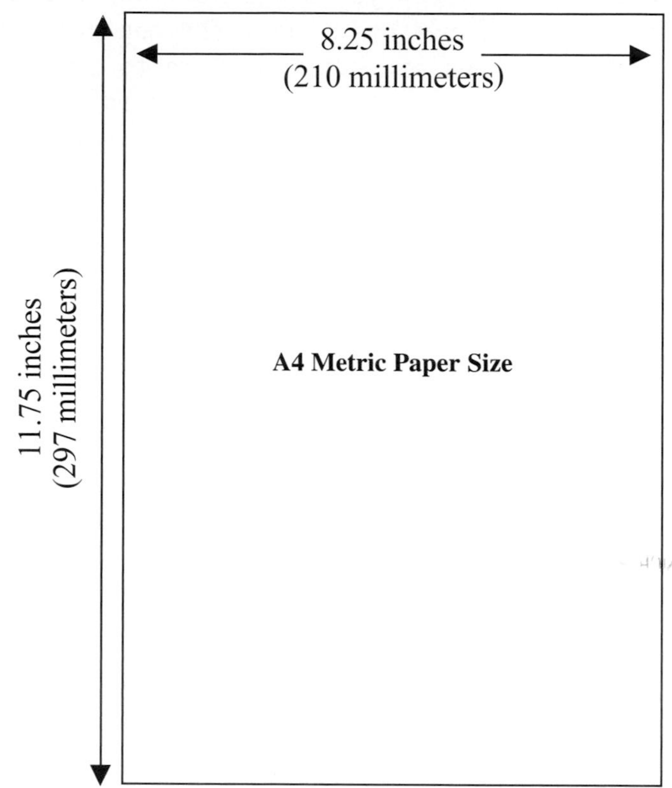

F. METRIC ENVELOPE SIZE

A standard large envelope (No. 10) measures 9.5 × 4.125 inches. A large envelope for metric size paper is called DL, and it measures 110 × 220 millimeters—approximately 4.33 × 8.67 inches. The No. 10 envelope is not as deep as the metric envelope, but it is slightly wider.

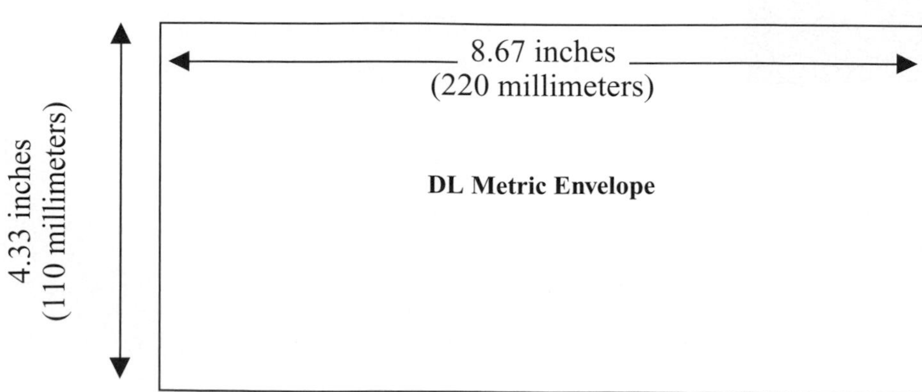

G. INTERNATIONAL ADDRESSES IN LETTERS

International addressing is becoming more common with the increased popularity of the Internet and frequently requires changes to the address lines, such as the addition of special codes, abbreviations, and capitalization. Individual organizational preferences for international address formatting will vary. Therefore, the most technologically efficient formats for international addresses will be used, including the use of all caps and the name of the country spelled out as the last entry of the address, as shown in the examples below.

Canada Address Example:

8437 Dixie Road ← Street Address [street number followed by street name]
Brampton, ON L6T 5P6 ← City/Province/Postal Code [2 spaces after the province; 1 space between first 3 and last 3 characters]
CANADA ← Country Name [typed in all-capitals]

Mexico Address Example:

Av. Chapultepec 28 ← Street Address [street name followed by street number]
06724 Mexico D.F. ← Postal Code/City [postal code and city name; "Mexico D.F." denotes Mexico City]
MEXICO ← Country Name [typed in all-capitals]

France Address Example:

14, Rue Royale ← Street Address [street number followed by a comma and then street name]
75008 Paris ← Postal Code/City
FRANCE ← Country Name [typed in all-capitals]

Germany Address Example:

Mannesmannufer 2 ← Street Address [street name followed by street number]
D-40213 Duesseldorf ← Postal Code/City [international sorting code followed by postal code and city name]
GERMANY ← Country Name [typed in all-capitals]

Japan Address Example:

10-1, Toranomon 2-chome ← Division of the City [lot and building number, followed by neighborhood name, followed by area number]
Minato-ku Tokyo 105-8436 ← City, District/City Name/Postal Code
JAPAN ← Country Name [typed in all-capitals]

H. DAY/MONTH/YEAR FORMAT

In international correspondence, the date line is often formatted in this sequence: day, month, year. Thus, the first line of a letter to a foreign recipient may appear as shown in the illustration.

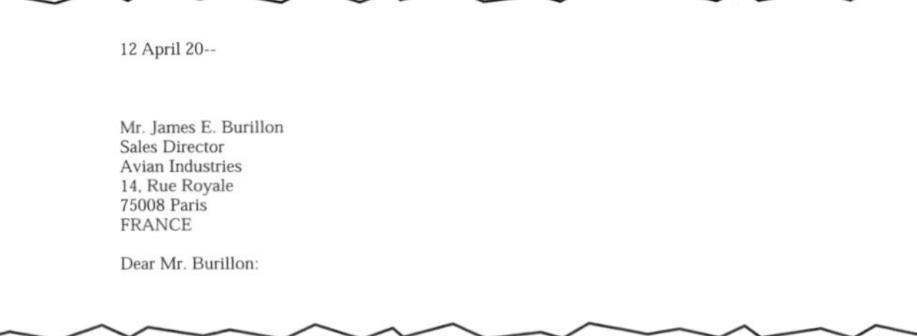
12 April 20--

Mr. James E. Burillon
Sales Director
Avian Industries
14, Rue Royale
75008 Paris
FRANCE

Dear Mr. Burillon:

Word Processing Manual

I. WORD PROCESSING: PAPER SIZE

Study Lesson 86 in your word processing manual. Complete all of the shaded steps while at your computer. Then format the jobs that follow.

DOCUMENT PROCESSING

Situation: You work for World-Tech Industries, an international computer manufacturer located in Vancouver, Canada. World-Tech Industries has a client base in both the United States and Canada. For the purposes of this simulation, your name will be Hiroki Kayano. Your e-mail address is hkayano@worldtech.com and your phone number is +1.702.555.1839.

For the next five days, you will prepare documents for several World-Tech executives. Your firm follows formatting guidelines for metric paper and envelope size and international addresses, dates, phone numbers, and measurements. You will use A4 metric paper and DL metric envelopes for all documents.

Today is April 14, and you will spend your first day preparing documents, which appear in your in-basket. Proofread your work carefully and check for spelling, punctuation, grammar, and formatting errors so that your documents are mailable.

Correspondence 86-78

Business Letter in Modified-Block Style

14 April 20-- | Mr. Alec R. Cousins | Manager, Computer Services | Columbia Enterprises, Ltd. | 338 Dunsmuir Street | Vancouver, BC V4B 5R9 | CANADA | Dear Mr. Cousins:

¶ Thank you for your recent computer order. As you requested, we have added the DVD drives to the 50 computers. There will be no extra charge for exchanging the DVD drives for the ZIP drives that come standard with the C-420 model you ordered.

¶ Your order will be shipped ten business days from the date of your order. Our order processing and shipping departments are online, and you can check the progress of your order by going to <www.worldtech.com> and clicking on Customer Orders.

¶ We look forward to the opportunity to serve your computer needs for many years to come.

Sincerely, | Sharon T. Yates | Sales Manager | hk | c: Terry Mourieux, Pamela Phillips | PS: The special software you ordered with your computers will be installed at our factory, ready for your use when your computers arrive.

Type *hk* as the reference initials for this simulation.

Table 86-43

Boxed Table

Prepare Table 86-43 on A4 paper, in landscape orientation. **Note:** Entries are arranged in ascending order by kilometers from Vancouver, British Columbia.

CUSTOMER SHIPPING ADDRESSES AND DISTANCE				
Name	**Address**	**City/Province**	**Postal Code**	**Kilometers**
Francis Stevens	17820 Attwood Road	Prince George, BC	V2N 653	520
Helene Abrams	269 Acadia Drive, SE	Calgary, AB	T2J 0A6	673
Connie Visocki	39 Blackburn Drive, SW	Edmonton, AB	T6W 1C5	817
Clarence Brewer	157 Caribou Street, E.	Moose Jaw, SK	S6H 0R4	1,266
Christine Osborn	P.O. Box 613	The Pas, MB	R9A 1K7	1,597
Andrew Svenson	14 Island Drive	Flin Flon, MB	R8A 058	1,850
Gary Fitzpatrick	635 Agnes Street	Winnipeg, MB	R3E 1X8	1,869
Lazo Aida	P.O. Box 1016	Churchill, MB	R0B 0E0	2,152
Note: Distance is measured in kilometers from Vancouver.				

Table 86-44

Boxed Table

Open the file for Table 86-43 and make the following changes:

1. Rearrange the entries in Column A so that the last name is given first, followed by a comma, followed by the first name.
2. Rearrange the entries in the table by placing the last names of the customers in alphabetic order.

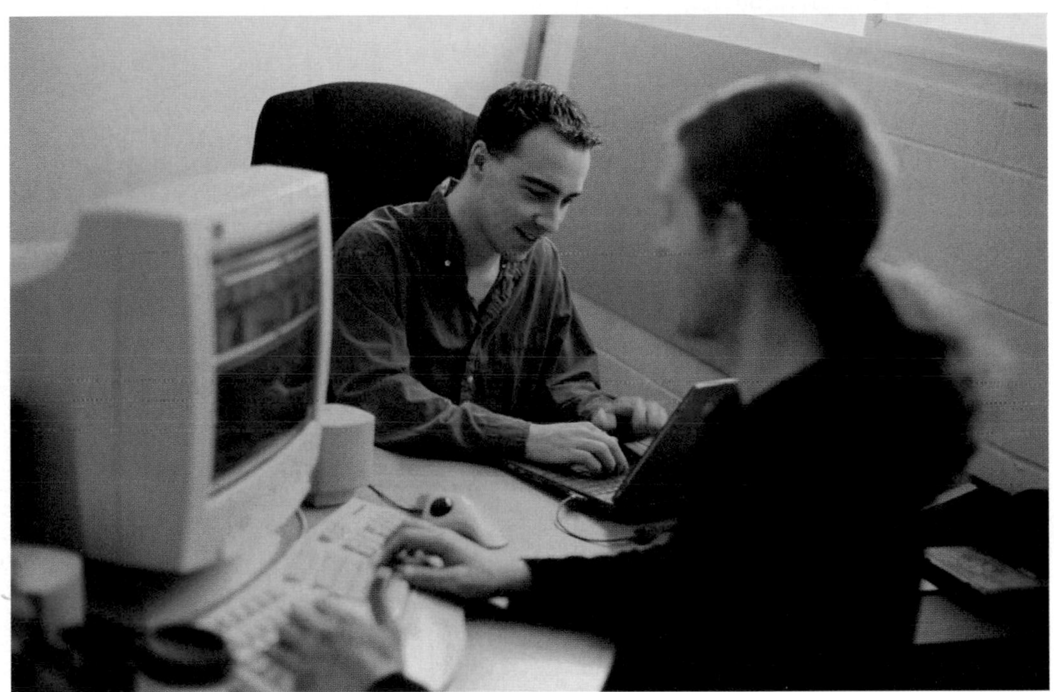

Lesson 87

International Formatting (Mexico)

Goals

- Improve speed and accuracy
- Refine language arts skills in the use of abbreviations
- Format international documents

A. Type 2 times.

A. WARMUP

On 4/25/05 Jamie exercised by "power walking" on the 11
athletic tracks. She also zipped along the city's favorite 23
route (Polk Street & Bell Avenue). It was a quick walk! 34

| 1 | 2 | 3 | 4 | 5 | 6 | 7 | 8 | 9 | 10 | 11 | 12

SKILLBUILDING

B. PROGRESSIVE PRACTICE: ALPHABET

If you are not using the GDP software, turn to page SB-7 and follow the directions for this activity.

C. Type the paragraph 2 times, concentrating on each letter typed.

C. TECHNIQUE PRACTICE: CONCENTRATION

El uso de la bicicleta es muy popular en Barranquilla. Cuando el tiempo es bueno a toda la gente joven le gusta ir a pasear en bicicletas. Me gusta ir a montar en bicicleta, especialmente cuando hace sol y el tiempo es agradable.

LANGUAGE ARTS

D. Study the rules at the right.

D. ABBREVIATIONS

RULE ▶ abbreviate measure

In technical writing, on forms, and in tables, abbreviate units of measure when they occur frequently. Do not use periods.

14 oz 5 ft 10 in 50 mph 2 yrs 10 mo

RULE ▶ abbreviate lowercase

In most lowercase abbreviations made up of single initials, use a period after each initial but no internal spaces.

a.m.	p.m.	i.e.	e.g.	e.o.m.
Exceptions:	mph	mpg	wpm	

RULE ▶ abbreviate ≡

In most all-capital abbreviations made up of single initials, do not use periods or internal spaces.

OSHA	PBS	NBEA	WWW	VCR	MBA
Exceptions:	U.S.A.	A.A.	B.S.	Ph.D.	P.O.
	B.C.	A.D.			

Edit the sentences to correct any errors in the use of abbreviations.

```
A mixture of 25 lb of cement and 100 lb of gravel was used.
The desk height must be reduced from 2 ft. 6 in. to 2 ft 4 in.
The 11 a. m. meeting was changed to 1 p. m. because of a conflict.
The eom statement was published over the Internet on the W.W.W.
She enlisted in the U.S.M.C. after she received her MBA degree.
His Ph. D. dissertation deals with the early history of NATO.
```

FORMATTING

E. INTERNATIONAL URLs

Uniform resource locators (URLs) identify a site on the World Wide Web where specific information can be found. In international URLs, an abbreviation for a country is often included in the URL, as shown in red below.

Country	Uniform Resource Locator (URL)
Canada	http://www.pearlson.animate.chap2.ca
France	http://www.education.grad.up.fr
Germany	http://www.mercedes.de
Japan	http://www.sushi.co.jp
Mexico	http://www.reloj.baja.mx

F. WORD PROCESSING: INSERT SYMBOL

Accents and other marks are used in many languages to indicate how words should be pronounced. Some examples of accents used in Mexico, where Spanish is spoken, are shown below.

Symbol	Spanish Word	English Translation
ñ	Señor, Señorita	Mr., Mrs.
í	el río	river
ó	adiós	good-bye

DOCUMENT PROCESSING

Correspondence 87-79

E-Mail Message

Today is April 15, your second day, and you will prepare an e-mail message and a business report with a table. Begin with the e-mail. Type the e-mail greeting, `Hi, Mr. Noriega:`, and the body shown below in correct format. Type `Hiroki` as the closing, and type this signature: `Hiroki Kayano | E-Mail: hkayano@worldtech.com | Phone: +1.702.555.1839`. Save the e-mail message, but do not send it.

Refer to page R-5C and R-5D: E-Mail Message.

¶ As you know, sales in our international divisions have been accelerating since the advent of our new Jefe automobile. As a result, several new manufacturing plants will open in the next eight years. The first five of these plants will open in France and Germany.

¶ To market our new manufacturing plants and promote the Jefe, our Marketing Division is planning to open new Web sites on the Jefe home page. The following links will be added to advertise our plant expansion:

abbreviate lowercase

- Bordeaux, France: http://www.bordeaux.fr.jefe.new.html
- Toulouse, France: http://www.toulouse.fr.jefe.new.html
- Grenoble, France: http://www.grenoble.fr.jefe.new.html
- Hamburg, Germany: http://www.hamburg.de.jefe.new.html
- Stuttgart, Germany: http://www.stuttgart.de.jefe.new.html

Refer to page R-12C of the Reference Manual for a review of list formatting.

¶ You will be notified when the Web sites go online. Until then, plan to work with your Marketing Division personnel to implement the marketing plan we discussed at our meeting last month (the Henderson Proposal). When the sites go online, we hope to maximize our exposure on the WWW. If they are as successful as we believe they will be, our promotional campaign may also be implemented at our plants in Piedras Negras, Morelia, and Cancún.

abbreviate ≡

Report 87-62

Business Report

Type the report on A4-size paper.

MEXICO TRAVEL DESTINATIONS
Most Popular Attractions
April 15, 20--

¶ Since the mid-1990s, national parks in Mexico have become popular tourist sites for visitors from the Americas, Europe, and Asia. As a result, an increasing number of requests have been made for travel brochures and maps from our Visitors' Bureau. Therefore, in the next few weeks, we will be publishing several new brochures and maps to accommodate these requests.

BROCHURES

¶ The brochures will include a detailed description of the site, providing information on beginning and ending visitation schedules, highlights of the site, and popular photography locations. Brochures will be prepared on the sites and locations shown in the table below.

The fourth column indicates how many years each site has been ranked among the top ten most popular sites in Mexico.

Type the copy at the right in boxed table format, inserting the table into the report.

abbreviate measure

Accent used in Sian Káan

Area	**Site**	**State**	**Top 10**
Northern	Cumbres de Majalca	Chihuahua	2 yrs
Northern	Cumbres de Monterrey	Nuevo Leon	2 yrs
Northern	Sierra del Pinacate	Mexicali	4 yrs
Central	El Tepozteco	Morelos	10 yrs
Central	Iztaccihuatl y Popocatepetl	Morelos	10 yrs
Central	Malinche	Puebla	3 yrs
Southern	Bonampak/Yaxchilan Monuments	Chiapas	7 yrs
Southern	Chichén Itzá	Merida	15 yrs
Southern	Dzibilchaltun	Yucatán	5 yrs
Southern	Sian Káan Biosphere Reserve	Quintana Roo	4 yrs

(Continued on next page)

ñ used in Señor

MAPS

¶ Maps will be supplied for the locations listed above, with detailed insets to guide visitors from the nearest cities to the tourist attractions. Walking trails and resting stations will be highlighted, and approximate walking times will be noted on the maps. Individual maps will be prepared for each area (northern, central, and southern), and a comprehensive map for all three visitor areas will also be available. Please send any advertising pieces you wish to promote to Señor Garcia, Public Relations Director.

International Formatting (France)

Goals

- Type at least 45wpm/5'/5e
- Format international documents

A. Type 2 times.

A. WARMUP

```
     On May 4, 2004, Kaye gave a dazzling talk on graphics;  11
it was quite fantastic! She is also writing an excellent     23
book about graphics with text. It might sell for $23.85.     34
| 1 | 2 | 3 | 4 | 5 | 6 | 7 | 8 | 9 | 10 | 11 | 12
```

SKILLBUILDING

B. DIAGNOSTIC PRACTICE: SYMBOLS AND PUNCTUATION

If you are not using the GDP software, turn to page SB-2 and follow the directions for this activity.

C. PACED PRACTICE

If you are not using the GDP software, turn to page SB-14 and follow the directions for this activity.

Keyboarding Connection

Protecting Your Files With Antivirus Programs

A virus is a computer program intentionally written to contaminate your computer system. Viruses can enter your system from files downloaded from the Internet or can be acquired from infected files sent to you via e-mail, diskette, or other storage media.

You can protect your computer by purchasing an antivirus program. These programs periodically scan your computer system for viruses. They also scan files that you bring into the system. Some antivirus manufacturers allow you to download a trial copy of their software from their Web site. You can try the software for a few days before you decide if you want to buy it.

YOUR TURN If you want to visit antivirus sites to find out what they have to offer, search for *antivirus software* on your search engine.

D. Take two 5-minute timed writings. Review your speed and errors.

Goal: At least 45wpm/5′/5e

D. 5-MINUTE TIMED WRITING

Technology surrounds us. It is everywhere you look. 11
People use cellular phones to speak to one another just 22
about anywhere. They carry their pagers so that they can be 34
reached at any time. Everyone, from the busy executive to 45
the college student, is now quite used to being available 57
at all hours of the day or night. 64
In recent years, busy travelers have become used to 74
using their laptops everywhere. They use computer ports in 86
airports, hotel rooms and lobbies, and even taxis. This 97
technology allows the busy traveler to have access to the 109
Internet while on the go. Using the laptop, the user can 120
access the latest weather report, sports scores, and news, 132
almost as soon as they happen. 138
Using the latest technology, you can keep up with your 150
work and maintain contact with your office. You can even 161
access your bank accounts and pay bills while waiting in 172
traffic. Also, if you are in a new place, you can find a 184
restaurant or call for directions as needed. The technology 196
options that have become available to almost everyone are 207
quite amazing. We are living in a small world that seems to 219
be getting smaller each day. 225

| 1 | 2 | 3 | 4 | 5 | 6 | 7 | 8 | 9 | 10 | 11 | 12

FORMATTING

E. DOT-STYLE TELEPHONE NUMBERS

In the United States, hyphens are used in telephone numbers. A hyphen is used after the 3-digit area code and after the first 3 digits of the telephone number; for example, 701-555-1234. Another format, used in many countries, is to replace the hyphens with periods; for example, 701.555.4832 or 818.555.3424.

F. INTERNATIONAL TELEPHONE ACCESS CODES

Special access codes are needed to make a phone call from one country to another. To make an international call, dial the IDD (International Direct Dialing) code first. Then dial the country code for the country you are calling, next the area code (if any), and finally the phone number. The IDD code in many countries changes periodically.

The United States and Canada have the same IDD (011) and country code (1). When you provide a United States (or Canadian) telephone number in a document being sent to an international address, use a plus sign (+) in front of the area code, instead of the IDD code, followed by 1 (the country code for the United States). For example, if you are writing a letter to an international address and you are giving your own phone number in Los Angeles, you would express your number as +1.323.555.8923. Some of the more common access codes are listed below.

	From U.S. to Foreign Country		From Foreign Country to U.S.	
Country	**IDD Code**	**Country Code**	**IDD Code**	**Country Code**
Canada	011	1	011	1
France	011	33	00	1
Germany	011	49	00	1
Italy	011	39	00	1
Japan	011	81	001	1
Mexico	011	52	98	1
Taiwan	011	886	002	1
United Kingdom	011	44	00	1
Note: The United States and Canada have the same IDD (011) and country code (1).				

DOCUMENT PROCESSING

Today is April 16, your third day, and you will prepare a letter, a table, and an e-mail message. Begin with the letter.

Correspondence 88-80

Business Letter in Block Style

Type the letter on A4-size paper.

16 April 20-- | Mr. Henry R. Defforey | Human Resources Director | Gemey Techtronics | Avenue Raymond Poincore | 75116 Paris | FRANCE | Dear Mr. Defforey:

¶ I am pleased that we will be involved in an employee exchange this coming year. As we discussed earlier, the exchange of our 26 production employees will benefit both companies.

¶ We plan to rotate all 26 employees through the various units of our production process, starting from the raw materials division and continuing right on through our shipping operations. I have enclosed a projected rotation plan for you to review. Included in the plan are all the employee rotations we discussed at our last meeting. Please review the plan and e-mail me if there are any changes you wish to make. You can e-mail me at ssouthern@worldtech.com, or, if you wish to speak to me directly, you can call +1.214.555.9090.

(Continued on next page)

¶ I look forward to working with you this coming year. As soon as we have agreed on the rotation plan, we can make copies for all affected employees. I know that everyone from our end is eagerly anticipating this collaborative effort.

Sincerely, | Sheila T. Southern | Human Resources Manager | hk | Enclosure | c: Ted Lambeer, Shirley Gouet

Table 88-45

Boxed Table

Type the table on A4-size paper.

Apply 20 percent shading to the column headings.

ROTATION PLAN Tech-Group Inc. and Gemey Techtronics		
Department	**Rotation Start Date**	**Rotation End Date**
Raw Materials	3 July 20--	August 11 20--
Board assembly	14 August 20--	22 September 20--
Drive and Assembly	25 Sept. 20--	3 November 20--
Power Unit	6 November 20--	15 December 20--
Testing & Evaluation	18 December 20--	2 Feburary 20--

Correspondence 88-81

E-Mail Message

Type the e-mail greeting, `Hi, Mr. Deforey:`, and the body shown below in correct format. Type `Hiroki` as the closing, and type this signature: `Hiroki Kayano | E-Mail: hkayano@worldtech.com | Phone: +1.702.555.1839`. Save the e-mail message, but do not send it.

¶ I am sending you this e-mail to alert you to a change we must make in the rotation plan I sent you last week. We will have to refit several of our board assembly production unit relay systems during the week of 14 August through 18 August. To avoid significantly altering the remaining rotation plan, I would like to suggest that we use one-half of the drive assembly rotation period to complete the board assembly rotation.

¶ Please respond to my e-mail as soon as possible so that we can make whatever changes are necessary.

International Formatting (Germany)

Goals

- Improve speed and accuracy
- Refine language arts skills in spelling
- Format international documents

A. Type 2 times.

A. WARMUP

Did Jacqueline get 62% of the vote in the election on 11
9/04/00? I think Buzz* (*Kelly) voted for her at 7:35 p.m. 23
that evening, and she was really excited when Jackie won. 34
| 1 | 2 | 3 | 4 | 5 | 6 | 7 | 8 | 9 | 10 | 11 | 12

SKILLBUILDING

B. MAP

Follow the GDP software directions for this exercise in improving keystroking accuracy.

C. Take a 1-minute timed writing on the first paragraph to establish your base speed. Then take four 1-minute timed writings on the remaining paragraphs. As soon as you equal or exceed your base speed on one paragraph, advance to the next, more difficult paragraph.

C. SUSTAINED PRACTICE: PUNCTUATION

One of the strengths you must have if you are going to 11
be a success in business is good writing skills. You must 23
practice your writing skills every day if you want them to 35
improve. Perfection of writing skills takes much practice. 46

You must always strive to write clearly, concisely, 11
and accurately. Remember always that your writing can be 22
examined by more people than just the one to whom you have 34
written. It's often looked at by other readers as well. 45

You want to be sure that your letters always convey a 11
positive, helpful attitude. Don't forget, you represent 22
more than yourself when you write--you also represent your 34
company! This is an important, useful rule to remember. 45

Try to stay away from negative words like "can't" or 11
"won't." Readers also do not like phrases such as "because 23
of company policies" or "due to unforeseen circumstances." 34
Using these words and phrases never helps resolve problems. 46
| 1 | 2 | 3 | 4 | 5 | 6 | 7 | 8 | 9 | 10 | 11 | 12

LANGUAGE ARTS

D. Type this list of frequently misspelled words, paying special attention to any spelling problems in each word.

D. SPELLING

20 means valve entry patient officer similar expenses industry
21 quality judgment academic provisions previously cooperation
22 foreign closing indicated secretary especially construction
23 monitoring assessment continuing registration manufacturing
24 products policies capacity presently accordance implemented

Edit the sentences to correct any misspellings.

25 Every company offiser will have simaler expenses next week.
26 In my judgement, we must insist on co-operation from all.
27 My secretery said that she traveled to a foriegn country.
28 We must continue monitering the progress for assesment.
29 The new policeis must be implimented for all products.

FORMATTING

E. METRIC UNITS OF MEASUREMENT

The metric system of measurement was devised in 1670. It is based on units of 10 and is used by almost every nation in the world. The five common measurements in the metric system are length, area, volume, capacity, and weight and mass. The table below gives the basic units of measure used in the metric and U.S. systems.

Quantity	Metric Units of Measure	U.S. Units of Measure
Length	millimeter, centimeter, meter, kilometer	inch, foot, yard, mile
Area	square centimeter, square meter, hectare	square inch, square foot, square yard
Volume	cubic centimeter, cubic decimeter, cubic meter, liter, hectoliter	cubic inch, cubic foot, fluid ounce, pint, gallon
Weight	milligram, gram, kilogram, tonne	ounce, pound, ton

DOCUMENT PROCESSING

Correspondence 89-82

E-Mail Message

Today is April 17, your fourth day, and you will prepare an e-mail message, a business letter, and a multipage business report with tables. Begin with the e-mail. Type the e-mail greeting, `Hi, Mr. Neubuerger:`, and the body shown below in correct format. Type `Hiroki` as the closing, and type this signature: `Hiroki Kayano | E-Mail: hkayano@worldtech.com | Phone: +1.702.555.1839`. Save the e-mail message, but do not send it.

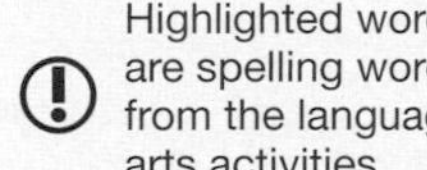
Highlighted words are spelling words from the language arts activities.

¶ The total conversion of our manufacturing plant in Wiesbaden to a metric system, which was discussed previously, is six months away. Ms. Schneider has asked for your continuing support and cooperation as you prepare employees who are presently transferring to the Wiesbaden plant in accordance with the provisions of our policies. Please send me the summary report used when you were monitoring the conversion last year.
¶ The metric system will be quite foreign to many employees, especially the younger ones, who were not involved in the planning stages. The summary report will give them a head start on metrication as indicated in the assessment.
¶ Call Ms. Schneider Thursday morning (+1.702.555.2354) to discuss the Frankfurt plant closing. Plant operations will be transferred to Wiesbaden in July. She has asked that you use your judgment to monitor the quality of the operation closely until the transfer has been fully implemented.

Correspondence 89-83

Business Letter in Block Style

Type the letter on A4-size paper.

17 April 20-- | Ms. Geraldine Sommer | Marketing Department | Deutsch Lebensmittel, Inc. | Mannesmannufer 2 | D-40213 Dusseldorf | GERMANY | Dear Ms. Sommer:
¶ Amalia Rios has asked that I send a copy of the summary report on metrics that we completed last year. As you recall, I sent you that report previously to share with the new employees at our Stuttgart plant.
¶ If you wish, you can e-mail me the copy that accompanied the report, and my secretary will distribute it as needed.
Sincerely, | Klaus Neubuerger | Human Resources Manager | hk

Report 89-63

Business Report

Type the report on A4-size paper.

Insert clip art that is related to measurements and similar to this example.

Set the clip art at a size of about 1-inch square, and place it at the left margin even with the first line of the paragraph.

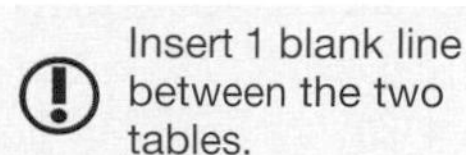

Insert 1 blank line between the two tables.

METRIC SUMMARY REPORT

April 17, 20--

¶ The metric system was devised by Gabriel Mouton, a French man, in 1667. It is a system based on units of 10 and is considered by some to be more accurate and easier to use than the imperial system of measure used in the United States. When it was first defined, a meter was considered to be 1/10,000,000 of the distance from the Pole to the Equator

¶ The most common metric measurements are for length, volume, capacity, and weight and mass. For our wiesbaden plant, the most crucial measurements for new employees from the U.S. will be volume and weight. Comparisons between these two measures appear in Table 1 (comparing volume measures) and Table 2 (comparing weight measures).

Table 1. METRIC/U.S. COMPARISONS FOR VOLUME		
Metric Unit	**Metric Example**	**U.S. Equivalent**
Cubic centimeter	1 cubic centimeter	0.061 cubic inch
Cubic decimeter	1,000 cubic centimeters	0.053 cubic ft
Cubic meter	1,000 cubic decimeters	1.31 cubic yards
Liter	1 cubic decimeter	1.76 pints
Hectoliter	100 Liters	21.99 gal

Table 2. METRIC/U.S. COMPARISONS FOR WEIGHT		
Metric Unit	**Metric Example**	**U.S. Equivalent**
Miligram	1 milligram	0.015 grain
gram	1,000 milligrams	0.035 ounce
Kilogram	1,000 grams	2.205 lbs
Tonne	1,000 kilograms	0.984 ton

(Continued on next page)

¶ Employees will quickly adapt to the metric system when they use it daily. Although we encourage all employees to make calculations in the metric system, it may be helpful for the first few days if they are aware of the conversion factors involved in comparing the 2 measurement systems. The following conversions may therefore be helpful to them:

Refer to page R-12C of the Reference Manual for a review of list formatting.

- Multiply inches by 2.45 to get centimeters
- Multiply feet by 0.305 to get meters
- Multiply miles by 1.6 to get kilometers
- Divide lbs. by 2.2 to get kilograms
- Multiply ounces by 28 to get grams
- Multiply fluid ounces by 30 to get milliliters
- Multiply gallons by 3.8 to get liters

¶ More detailed conversions and metric information can be obtained by visiting the web site for the U.S. metric association at http://lamar.colostate.edu/~hillger/.

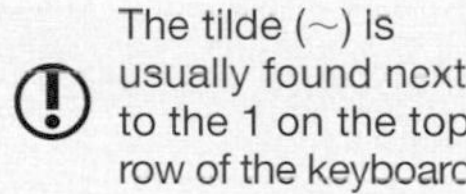

The tilde (~) is usually found next to the 1 on the top row of the keyboard.

International Formatting (Japan)

Goals

- Type at least 45wpm/5′/5e
- Format international documents

A. Type 2 times.

A. WARMUP

```
     James used a dozen of Harold's power trucks to quickly 11
move over 17 large boxes on 11/30/00. I think these trucks 23
(just the diesels) may need maintenance work on 3/24/01.   34
| 1 | 2 | 3 | 4 | 5 | 6 | 7 | 8 | 9 | 10 | 11 | 12
```

SKILLBUILDING

PPP PRETEST → PRACTICE → POSTTEST

PRETEST
Take a 1-minute timed writing. Review your speed and errors.

B. PRETEST: Close Reaches

```
     Uncle Bert chased a fast, weary fox into the weeds of 11
the swamp. He hoped to grab the old gray fox under the    22
bridge with a rope as he darted swiftly from his cold lair. 34
| 1 | 2 | 3 | 4 | 5 | 6 | 7 | 8 | 9 | 10 | 11 | 12
```

PRACTICE
Speed Emphasis:
If you made no more than 1 error on the Pretest, type each *individual* line 2 times.
Accuracy Emphasis:
If you made 2 or more errors, type each *group* of lines (as though it were a paragraph) 2 times.

C. PRACTICE: Adjacent Keys

```
as asked asset based basis class least visas ease fast mass
op opera roped topaz adopt scope troop shops open hope drop
we weary wedge weigh towed jewel fewer dwell wear weed week
```

D. PRACTICE: Consecutive Fingers

```
sw swamp swift swoop sweet swear swank swirl swap sway swim
un uncle under undue unfit bunch begun funny unit aunt junk
gr grade grace angry agree group gross gripe grow gram grab
```

POSTTEST
Repeat the Pretest timed writing and compare performance.

E. POSTTEST: Close Reaches

F. Take two 5-minute timed writings. Review your speed and errors.

Goal: At least 45wpm/5'/5e

F. 5-MINUTE TIMED WRITING

Anyone with a supervisory position will occasionally 11
have to deal with a problem employee. If you learn to deal 23
with this type of worker in a good way, it will benefit 34
everyone within the organization. As a manager, you should 46
address the problem as soon as you are made aware of it. 57
However, if you are extremely upset, it may be best to wait 69
until you calm down and have time to plan what you will 80
say. Avoid using an approach based on reaction, which can 86
often be ineffective and too emotional. Speaking up too 92
quickly might bring you unwanted results. 103

When you talk to an employee, be sure you get to the 111
real issue. Present the facts and tell the employee exactly 122
what he or she is doing wrong on the job. Do not express 134
your own personal opinion. You need to present a positive 146
and mutually fair solution to the employee in question to 157
solve a problem. At the end of the meeting, ask the person 169
to explain his or her problem to you and the changes that 181
are necessary. By following this procedure, you know that 192
everyone understands what is happening. Set up a time to 204
meet in a few days to follow up with this person. 215
225

| 1 | 2 | 3 | 4 | 5 | 6 | 7 | 8 | 9 | 10 | 11 | 12

DOCUMENT PROCESSING

Correspondence 90-84

Business Letter in Block Style

Type the letter on A4-size paper.

Today is April 18, your fifth day, and you will prepare several letters, an e-mail message, and a table. Begin with the letter.

18 April 20-- | Mr. Kouji Tachikawa | Chief Technology Officer | Tadashi Corporation | 7-1, Shiba 5-chome | Minato-ku, Tokyo 108-8001 | JAPAN | Dear Mr. Tachikawa:

¶ It is a distinct pleasure to learn that we will be working together to develop the training manual to be used in our joint venture. Your company has long been known for its excellence in developing instructional materials, and Carroll Technology is pleased to play a collaborative part with you in this venture.

¶ Our development teams have been working with their counterparts in Tadashi over the past several weeks. Your suggestion that we pool our personnel resources was indeed an excellent one that will give us a head start in the development stage.

(Continued on next page)

¶ If I may make one suggestion, I believe it would be helpful for the personnel in our mailing and shipping department to have a better understanding of the labeling procedures used in Japan for distributing the training manuals. Could you please send me some information that might be helpful in this regard? I will do the same for you by sending you the labeling procedures used at Carroll Technology.
Sincerely | Sharla D. Enterline | Project Coordinator | hk | c: Roberta Akiyama, Samuel Hiroshi, Charlene Brandenburger

Correspondence 90-85

E-Mail Message

Type the e-mail greeting, Hi, Ms. Enterline:, and the body shown below in correct format. Type Hiroki as the closing, and type this signature: Hiroki Kayano | E-mail: hkayano@worldtech.com | Phone: +1.702.555.1839. Save the e-mail message, but do not send it.

¶ It is my pleasure to inform you that Samuel Hiroshi will be forwarding to your office a summary of the package labeling procedures used at Tadashi Inc. Employees from many different foreign countries have used these procedures to help them understand mailing requirements in Japan.
¶ After receiving the procedures, feel free to e-mail Mr. Hiroshi with any questions you may have. You can reach him at shiroshi@tadashi.jp.com. If you prefer, you can call Mr. Hiroshi at +81.3.34543113.

Correspondence 90-86

Business Letter in Block Style

Type the letter on A4-size paper.

18 April 20-- | Ms. Sharla D. Enterline | Project Coordinator | Carroll Technology | 8723 Hill Avenue | Bowling Green, KY 42823 | Dear Ms. Enterline:

¶ The following information is being sent to asist [insert: s] you with Japanese mailing rules. As a service to your employees, I am providing the following summary of these rules.

¶ A Japanese mailing address consists ~~mainly~~ of the name, street address, town, city, pre fecture, postal [insert: code], and country. The illustration below shows how [insert: an] address should appear on an envelope going to Japan.

(Continued on next page)

Address Items	Address Example
Name Street ~~St.~~ Address, Town (1st) address) City, Prefecture (2d) address), ^Postal Code JAPAN	Mr. Yoshifumi Uda 1-17, Akai-cho Minato-ku, Tokyo 108-8005 JAPAN

¶ Please ~~E~~-mail me if you have questions about mailing rules in japan. You can reach me at <shiroshi@tadashi.jp.com>.

Very sincerely, | S. Hiroshi | Shipping (Dept.) | hk | c: K. Tachikawa

Table 90-46

Boxed Table

Your line endings will be different from those shown here.

JAPANESE POSTAL CODE REGULATIONS Prepared by Hiroki Kayano	
Postal Code Rule	**Example**
The first line of a Japanese address is used for the addressee's name.	Mr. Takashi Imaizumi Mr. Kazuki Terada
The second line provides a street name or building number.	Kifune 3-402 (this represents building 402 on the 3rd street within the Kifune neighborhood)
The third line gives the city, prefecture (a district within the city), and postal code.	Meito-ku, Nagoya 112-3844 Minato-ku, Tokyo 105-8436
The fourth line gives the name of the country to which the document or package is being mailed.	JAPAN

Correspondence 90-87

Business Letter in Block Style

Type the letter on A4-size paper.

Progress and Proofreading Check

Documents designated as Proofreading Checks serve as a check of your proofreading skill. Your goal is to have zero typographical errors when the GDP software first scores the document.

18 April 20-- | Mr. Fujio Okuda | Sales Manager | Naruto Publishing Company | 7-35, Kitashinagawa 6-chome | Shinagawa-ku, Tokyo 141-0001 | JAPAN | Dear Mr. Okuda:

¶ We are pleased to have this opportunity for two of our computer textbooks to be translated into Japanese and for you to do the same for two of your textbooks in the computer area. As we agreed at our meeting in Takasaki last week, sales for both of our book companies should improve substantially with these translations.

¶ I am enclosing with this letter the first three units of *Computer Essentials* so that your editors can begin the translation process. We will do the same here at Globe Publishing when your first three units from *Global Computers* arrive in Chicago.

¶ Should your editorial staff have any questions during the translation, they can e-mail me at shaddock@worldtech.com or call me at +1.402.555.3848.

Sincerely, | Shannon Haddock | Editorial Director | hk | Enclosure

Unit 19

Medical Office Documents

LESSON 91
Medical Office Documents

LESSON 92
Medical Office Documents

LESSON 93
Medical Office Documents

LESSON 94
Medical Office Documents

LESSON 95
Medical Office Documents

Lesson 91

Medical Office Documents

Goals

- Improve speed and accuracy
- Refine language arts skills in punctuation
- Format medical office documents

A. Type 2 times.

A. WARMUP

```
     The taxes* were quickly adjusted upward by 20 percent   11
because of the improvements to her house (built in 1901).    23
A proposed law might not penalize good homeowners like her.  34
|  1  |  2  |  3  |  4  |  5  |  6  |  7  |  8  |  9  |  10  |  11  |  12
```

SKILLBUILDING

B. MAP

Follow the GDP software directions for this exercise in improving keystroking accuracy.

C. Take a 1-minute timed writing on the first paragraph to establish your base speed. Then take four 1-minute timed writings on the remaining paragraphs. As soon as you equal or exceed your base speed on one paragraph, advance to the next, more difficult paragraph.

C. SUSTAINED PRACTICE: ALTERNATE-HAND WORDS

```
     A downturn in world fuel prices signals a lower profit  11
for giant oil firms. In fact, most downtown firms might      22
see the usual sign of tight credit and other problems. The   34
city must get down to business and make plans in the fall.   46

     The hungry turkeys ate eight bushels of corn that were  11
given to them by our next-door neighbors. They also drank    22
the eight bowls of water that were left in the yard. All in  34
all, the birds caused quite a bit of chaos early that day.   46

     A debate on what to do about that extra acreage in the  11
desert dragged on for four hours. One problem is what the    23
effect may be of moving the ancient ruins to a much safer    34
place. City officials must always protect our environment.   46

     Molly was dressed in a plain pink dress at the annual   11
meeting that was taking place at the hotel in Tempe later    23
that last week in September. The agenda included four very   34
controversial topics that have often generated much debate.  46
|  1  |  2  |  3  |  4  |  5  |  6  |  7  |  8  |  9  |  10  |  11  |  12
```

LANGUAGE ARTS

D. Study the rules at the right.

D. PUNCTUATION

RULE ▶ : explanatory material

Use a colon to introduce explanatory material that follows an independent clause.

The computer satisfies three criteria: speed, cost, and power.
But: The computer satisfies the three criteria of_speed, cost, and power.
Remember this: only one coupon is allowed per customer.

Note: An independent clause can stand alone as a complete sentence. Do not capitalize the word following the colon.

RULE ▶ . polite request

Use a period to end a sentence that is a polite request.

Will you please call me if I can be of further assistance.

Note: Consider a sentence a polite request if you expect the reader to respond by doing as you ask rather than by giving a yes-or-no answer.

Edit the sentences to correct any errors in punctuation.

```
20 We need the following items, pens, pencils, and paper.
21 May I suggest that you send the report by Tuesday?
22 These are some of your colleagues: Bill, Mary, and Ann.
23 Would you please pay my bills when I am on vacation?
24 Our flag is these three colors; red, white, and blue.
25 Would you please start my car to warm it up for me.
```

DOCUMENT PROCESSING

Situation: You work for Lakewood Hospital in Springfield, Oregon. For the purposes of this simulation, your name will be Lucille R. Medford. Your e-mail address is lmedford@lakewood.com.

For the next five days, you will prepare documents for several units within the hospital—Admissions, Billing, Dermatology, Oncology, and Surgery. You will also format various documents including correspondence and medical reports for these units.

Today is November 1. You will spend your first day working in the Admissions Office preparing the documents that appear in your in-basket for today. Proofread your work carefully and check for spelling, punctuation, grammar, and formatting errors so that your documents are mailable.

Correspondence 91-88 ▶

Business Letter in Block Style

November 1, 20-- | Ms. Nancy J. Dodson | 3727 Harris Street | Eugene, OR 97405-4246 | Dear Ms. Dodson:

¶ Thank you for contacting us and considering us as your primary care provider. We are confident that you will be pleased with our services and our patient care, and we look forward to many years of serving your health needs.

¶ Now that you have made your final selection, we would like you to complete the enclosed Patient Information Form and send it back to us at your earliest convenience. As you can see, the form asks mostly for personal information so that we can contact you or your employer if necessary. In addition, the form requests the following information: the name, address, and telephone number of your insurance company and your insurance policy number.

: explanatory material

(Continued on next page)

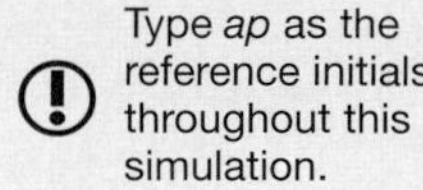
Type *ap* as the reference initials throughout this simulation.

¶ Again, welcome to Lakewood Hospital! If there is any additional information we can provide about our services, do not hesitate to call us at 555-2300 or e-mail me at lmedford@lakewood.com.
Sincerely, | Lucille R. Medford | Office Manager | ap | Enclosure

Table 91-47

Table

Create a patient information form using the illustration below and these steps:

1. Insert a table with 1 column and 15 rows.
2. Split cells as shown to provide room for individual entries.
3. Type the information as shown.
4. Bold the information in Rows 1, 7, and 11.
5. Insert blank lines above and below the centered section headings, and type the headings in 12-point Arial.
6. Insert 5 spaces between the parentheses in Rows 4 and 9.
7. Insert 1 blank line above the information in Rows 2 to 6, 8 to 10, and 12 to 15.
8. Apply 10 percent shading to Rows 1, 7, 11, and 15.

↓1X Arial 12 pt. **PATIENT INFORMATION** ↓1X		
↓1X Date:		
Name: (last, first)		Birth Date:
Street Address:		Phone: ( )
City:	State:	ZIP:
E-Mail		
EMPLOYER INFORMATION		
Employer:		
Street Address:		Phone: ( )
City:	State:	ZIP:
INSURANCE INFORMATION		
Name of Company:		
Address:		
Phone:		Policy Number:
Signature:		Date:

Correspondence 91-89

Memo

MEMO TO: Dr. Abraham Kramer
FROM: Paula Campbell
DATE: November 1, 20--
SUBJECT: Radiology Lab Closing

¶ Next week the Radiology Lab in Building D will be closed for repairs. I realize that this is the week you were going to take a group of interns to see our new equipment.

¶ I have arranged to have the Radiology Lab in Building C open for you to use so that you do not have to postpone the meeting with the interns. I am sending over a passkey for the lab. The passkey will open three doors: main entry, hall entry, lab door.

:explanatory material

¶ Would you please give me a call on Ext. 75 if this lab substitution is not satisfactory with you.

.polite request

ap

c: Dr. Arnold, Dr. Kazinofski

Medical Office Documents

Goals

- Type at least 46wpm/5′/5e
- Format medical office documents

A. Type 2 times.

A. WARMUP

```
     Missy examined these items: the #4261 oil painting, a   11
Bowes & Elkjer porcelain vase, and the 86-piece collection   23
of glazed antique pitchers. There were 337 people present.   34
| 1 | 2 | 3 | 4 | 5 | 6 | 7 | 8 | 9 | 10 | 11 | 12
```

SKILLBUILDING

B. Take three 12-second timed writings on each line. The scale below the last line shows your wpm speed for a 12-second timed writing.

B. 12-SECOND SPEED SPRINTS

```
Their home is on a lake that is right south of the prairie.
They have a boat and motor and spend a lot of time fishing.
Kay caught so many fish that she gave some to the old lady.
She was so pleased that a young girl would do this for her.
5 10 15 20 25 30 35 40 45 50 55 60
```

C. PROGRESSIVE PRACTICE: ALPHABET

If you are not using the GDP software, turn to page SB-7 and follow the directions for this activity.

Strategies for Career Success

Business Communication

There are five components to the communication process, whether written or oral.

The sender is the person who initiates the communication process. The message is the information that needs to be communicated (for example, "There will be a meeting at . . ."). The channel is the method for transmitting the message (for example, e-mail, letter, memo, orally). The audience is the person(s) who receives the message. Feedback is the response given to the sender by the audience that enables the sender to determine if the message was received as intended.

The most effective communication within companies must flow not only downward but also upward.

YOUR TURN Suppose you send a memo to 20 people in your department announcing a meeting to discuss your company's new policy on flextime. Who is the sender? What is the message? What is the channel you use to transmit the message? Who is the audience? What is the ultimate feedback?

D. Take two 5-minute timed writings. Review your speed and errors.

Goal: At least 46wpm/5'/5e

D. 5-MINUTE TIMED WRITING

The first impression you make on a job interview will 11
be a lasting one, and you will want it to be favorable. A 23
safe choice is to dress conservatively. If you have time, 34
find out what people who are currently employed at this 45
company wear to work. You can acquire this information by 57
simply calling the human resources office. Or, you could 68
observe what the current employees are wearing when you 80
pick up a job application from a company. 88
As you plan the details of your appearance before your 99
job interview, be cognizant of all the details. You will 111
want to present a neat and clean appearance. Your clothing 122
should be clean and very neatly pressed. Your hair and your 134
nails should be neatly groomed, and your shoes should be 146
clean and polished. You should use only a small amount of 157
perfume or cologne and wear only basic jewelry. Plan to 169
arrive for the appointment in time to make a final check of 181
your appearance before the interview. 188
Your appearance may not be the sole factor that will 199
secure the job, but it will help you make a positive first 211
impression. Remember to dress for the position you would 222
like rather than the position you have. 230

| 1 | 2 | 3 | 4 | 5 | 6 | 7 | 8 | 9 | 10 | 11 | 12

DOCUMENT PROCESSING

Report 92-64

Business Report

This is November 2, the second day of your assignment at Lakewood Hospital. Today you are assigned to the Billing Office, where you will complete documents related to the activities in that office. Your first assignment is to prepare a report describing the billing process at Lakewood Hospital.

LAKEWOOD BILLING PROCESS

November 2, 20--

¶ The billing process at Lakewood Hospital will be undergoing review soon. This report will explain how fees are determined, how transactions are recorded, how payments are made, and how overdue accounts are collected.

Determining Fees

¶ Fees that a physician charges for services should be fair both to the patients that are under his or her care and to the medical profesion. A doctors' fees should be based on the following critera:

(Continued on next page)

Refer to page R-12C of the Reference Manual for a review of list formatting.

- the amount of time involved in providing the service
- the level of skill required in providing the service
- the degree of expertise required to interpret the results of the service provided

¶ Fees should be identified in a fee schedule that lists procedures performed and the charges assessed for those procedures. The fee schedule should be made available to patients if it's requested. If patients inquire as to amount of the fee an estimate should be given to the patient. In all instances, this estimate should be made available to the patient before treat ment begins.

RECORDING TRANSACTIONS

¶ A record of all patient visits must be maintained. A chargeslip should be used to record procedures. The charge slip includes information such as a check list of all procedures; a checklist of all diagnosis; space for additional information; and an area for all previous charges, payments, As the doctor performs procedures, anotations and changes are made to the charge slip so that it is always kept current. The charge slip should be attached to the patients' chart. When all procedures have been completed, a copy of the charge slip is sent to the patient to indicate the charges incurred during the patient's visit.

MAKING PAYMENT ARRANGEMENTS

¶ A patient's bill can be paid by one of the following methods:

- A patient can pay the bill by cash or check at the conclusion of the visit.
- A patient can pay fixed amounts of the bill at any designated times, weekly or monthly.
- A bill can be sent to the patient at the conclusion of the visit.
- A bill can be sent to the Health Insurance Carrier.

COLLECTING OVERDUE ACCOUNTS

¶ There are a number of reasons why a patient might pay a bill. What ever the reason, however, steps must be taken to collect delinquent accounts. Depending on the number of days the acount has been over due, here are some suggestions for steps that can be taken to collect payment:

(Continued on next page)

1. Attach a reminder when the bill is sent if payment is over ~~thirty~~ 30 days overdue (this is the usual grace period given to accounts).
2. If payment is not received after the reminder is sent, it may be necessary to call the patient to request payment.
3. The next step would be to attach a personal note to a statement that is over due, possibly as long as 60 days.
4. Make one further attempt to telephone the patient for payment.
5. Send a collection letter for payment. The letter should be friendly/ but firm. Remind the patient that the account is overdue. Offer to assist the patient in making payments on a fixed schedule by establishing a payment plan. Leave your telephone number so the patient can call you if there are any questions that need to be answered regarding the bill.
6. The final alternative in collecting an unpaid bill is to turn over the account to a collection agency or go to court for legal action. This is a costly step for both caregivers and patients and it should be used only as a last resort.

Table 92-48

Boxed Table

Press the SPACE BAR 10 times between the phone number and the e-mail address.

STATEMENT

WENDY NEWMAN, M.D.
Lakewood Hospital
970 Kruse Way
Springfield, OR 97477
Phone: 541-555-2300   E-Mail: billing@lakewood.com

Patient: Marion W. Fleming
Address: 1654 Franklin Boulevard
City/State/ZIP: Eugene, OR 97403

Date	Description	Charge	Payment	Balance
3/18/06	EKG	185.00	50.00	135.00
3/18/06	Laboratory work	125.00	25.00	100.00
3/19/06	X-ray	85.00	0.00	85.00
3/21/06	Cholesterol check	75.00	25.00	50.00
3/21/06	Laboratory work	80.00	25.00	55.00
Total Due				**425.00**

Medical Office Documents

Goals

- Improve speed and accuracy
- Refine language arts skills in composing
- Format medical office documents

A. Type 2 times.

A. WARMUP

Did you hear the excellent quartet of junior cadets? 11
Everybody in that crowd (estimated at over 500) applauded 23
"with gusto." The sizable crowd filled the 3/4-acre park. 35
| 1 | 2 | 3 | 4 | 5 | 6 | 7 | 8 | 9 | 10 | 11 | 12

SKILLBUILDING

PPP PRETEST → PRACTICE → POSTTEST

PRETEST
Take a 1-minute timed writing. Review your speed and errors.

B. PRETEST: Discrimination Practice

Did the new clerk join the golf team? James indicated 11
to me that Patricia invited her prior to last Wednesday. He 23
believes she must give you a verbal commitment at once. 34
| 1 | 2 | 3 | 4 | 5 | 6 | 7 | 8 | 9 | 10 | 11 | 12

PRACTICE
Speed Emphasis:
If you made no more than 1 error on the Pretest, type each *individual* line 2 times.
Accuracy Emphasis:
If you made 2 or more errors, type each *group* of lines (as though it were a paragraph) 2 times.

C. PRACTICE: Left Hand

vbv bevy verb bevel vibes breve viable braves verbal beaver
wew went week weans weigh weave wedges thawed weaker beware
ded dent need deals moved ceded heeded debate edging define

D. PRACTICE: Right Hand

klk kale look kilts lakes knoll likely kettle kernel lacked
uyu buys your gummy dusty young unduly tryout uneasy jaunty
oio oils roil toils onion point oriole soiled ration joined

POSTTEST
Repeat the Pretest timed writing and compare performance.

E. POSTTEST: Discrimination Practice

F. PROGRESSIVE PRACTICE: NUMBERS

If you are not using the GDP software, turn to page SB-11 and follow the directions for this activity.

LANGUAGE ARTS

G. COMPOSING AN E-MAIL MESSAGE

Compose an e-mail message to your employer, Dr. Natalie Benson nbenson@lakewood.com, informing Dr. Benson of the appointments you have scheduled for Tuesday, April 17, 20--. The first appointment is with James Mitchell, who is coming for his annual physical—make this appointment at 9 a.m. The second appointment is with Karen McDaniels, who is going to have her blood pressure and cholesterol checked. She will see Dr. Benson at 10 a.m. The final appointment is with Mary Ann Bradley, who will see the doctor about flu symptoms. Be sure you use an appropriate greeting, closing, and signature. Save but do not send this e-mail message.

DOCUMENT PROCESSING

Correspondence 93-90

Business Letter in Modified-Block Style

This is November 3, the third day of your assignment. You will work in a specialty area—the Dermatology Unit. Dermatology is a branch of science dealing with the skin and its structure, functions, and diseases.

November 3, 20-- | Dr. Stanley G. Streisand | Professor of Medical Science | Hillside Medical College | 110 Sunset Drive | Eugene, OR 97403-2120 | Dear Dr. Streisand:

¶ Thank you for the invitation to address the students in your medical science class on the topic of dermatology. As you know, this is my specialty; I am particularly interested in the topic of skin rashes and their causes and treatments.

¶ I recognize that your students are beginning medical school students, so my presentation will focus on a very general talk about dermatology. I am enclosing a copy of a paper I presented at the AMA meeting in San Francisco last week that I think would be appropriate for your students. The audience at my AMA presentation was primarily first-year nursing students who were interested in a general background of the more common types of skin rashes.

¶ Please send me a copy of your program with directions on how to reach your classroom on the day of my presentation. I look forward to meeting with your students.

Sincerely yours, | Angela Miller, M.D. | ap | Enclosure | PS: Please let me know how many students you have in your class so I can prepare an adequate number of handouts for them.

(Continued on next page)

Report 93-65

Business Report

Instead of underlining a word, use italic.

COMMON SKIN RASHES

Their Causes and Cures

Dr. Stanley G. Streisand

¶ Skin rashes are caused by many different things. They are often recognized by symptoms of reddening, itching, blistering, dryness, or scabbing of the skin. Some of the more common ailments that fall into the category of skin rashes are dermatitis, eczema, and psoriasis. This paper will discuss these three common types of skin rashes.

DERMATITIS

¶ Dermatitis is often referred to as contact dermatitis. Some of the more common substances that cause dermatitis are soaps, rubber, jewelry, plants, household and industrial chemicals, cosmetics, and perfumes. Contact dermatitis is further classified as either allergic contact dermatitis or irritant contact dermatitis.

¶ Allergic Contact Dermatitis. This skin rash occurs after contact is made with certain substances, called allergens. The rash occurs as a reaction of the body's immune system to expel the allergen from your skin. Some common allergens are metals in jewelry, cosmetics, and rubber boots.

¶ Irritant Contact Dermatitis. This skin rash does not require exposure to an allergen but can develop when you come in contact with certain substances—skin cleansers, detergents, solvents, and oils.

(Continued on next page)

ECZEMA

¶ Eczema, also known as atopic dermatitis, causes the skin to appear red and blotchy all over. The disease occurs at any age but mainly from infancy to childhood. It affects about 3 percent of the United States population. There are two types of eczema—atopic eczema and hand eczema.

¶ Atopic Eczema. This form of eczema is caused by the house dust mite, by heat, by contact with woolen clothing, by detergents, and by stress.

¶ Hand Eczema. Hand eczema is caused by sensitive skin, too much exposure to wet work, detergents, oils, and greases.

PSORIASIS

¶ Psoriasis is a chronic skin disease characterized by inflammation and skin scaling. This disease affects about 5.5 million people in the United States. It occurs in all age groups and affects both men and women. When psoriasis develops, patches of skin redden and become covered with scales. The skin then cracks and may cause severe irritation in places like the elbows, knees, face, scalp, and lower back.

¶ It is believed that psoriasis is a disorder of the immune system in which there are not enough white blood cells to help protect the body against infection and diseases of this type.

Lesson 94

Medical Office Documents

Goals

- Type at least 46wpm/5′/5e
- Format a formal report

A. Type 2 times.

A. WARMUP

1 Mr. Baxter will move to 1749 Larkin Street; his old 11
2 home is in Gray's Woods, just east of the corner of Parson 22
3 and 167th Avenue. The house sizes are quite different! 33

| 1 | 2 | 3 | 4 | 5 | 6 | 7 | 8 | 9 | 10 | 11 | 12

SKILLBUILDING

B. DIAGNOSTIC PRACTICE: SYMBOLS AND PUNCTUATION

If you are not using the GDP software, turn to page SB-2 and follow the directions for this activity.

C. Take two 5-minute timed writings. Review your speed and errors.

Goal: At least 46wpm/5′/5e

C. 5-MINUTE TIMED WRITING

Innovative technology may bring new problems for our 11
homes and businesses. A rising shift to use a cell phone is 23
causing many people to look at the etiquette of cell phone 35
usage. Are there times and places where a cell phone should 47
not be used? 49

People want to be able to stay in touch, no matter 60
where they are or what they are doing. However, in some 71
places cell phone usage is inappropriate or not allowed. 82
For example, you would not want a ringing cell phone to 93
disrupt an entire production if you are enjoying a concert 105
or play. As a consideration to everyone in the audience, 117
the management may make an announcement asking audience 128
members to turn off their cell phones or pagers before the 140
production begins. Making this request gives everyone the 151
chance to enjoy the show. 156

Often you see someone driving a car while talking on a 168
cell phone. Talking on the phone while you are driving is 179
not a good idea. When you are talking on the phone and not 191
concentrating on driving, you may cause an accident. If you 203
are driving a vehicle in traffic, your full focus should be 215
on the road. Be cognizant of this. Do not use your cell 226
phone when driving. 230

| 1 | 2 | 3 | 4 | 5 | 6 | 7 | 8 | 9 | 10 | 11 | 12

DOCUMENT PROCESSING

Table 94-49

Boxed Table

This is November 4, the fourth day of your assignment. Today you are working in the Oncology Unit. Oncology is a branch of science dealing with the study of tumors.

You will begin by typing this boxed table. Insert 1 blank line after the information in each row.

DESCRIPTIONS AND TREATMENTS OF ADULT BRAIN TUMORS	
Types of Tumors	**Description and Treatment**
Astrocytomas	Tumors that start in brain cells. Treatment includes surgery, chemotherapy, and radiation.
Brain stem gliomas	Tumors located in the bottom part of the brain, which connects to the spinal cord. Treatment includes radiation and biological therapy.

(Continued on next page)

Cerebellar astrocytomas	Tumors that occur in the area of the brain called the cerebellum. Treatment is similar to that for astrocytomas.
Craniopharyngiomas	Tumors that occur near the pituitary gland. Treatment includes surgery and radiation.
Oligodendrogliomas	Tumors that begin in brain cells that provide support and nourishment for the cells that transmit nerve impulses. Treatment includes surgery, chemotherapy, and radiation.

Correspondence 94-91

Business Letter in Block Style

November 4, 20-- | Dr. Samuel Abbott | Sacred Heart Medical Center | 267 Ferry Street | Eugene, OR 97401-2409 | Dear Sam: | Subject: Paul R. Williams.

¶ On September 3 I examined Mr. Williams and discovered a Stage 1A, Cleaved B cell follicular lymphoma in the left inguinal region. I conducted a surgical excision and recommended radiation therapy. Mr. Williams completed his radiation therapy four weeks ago and feels well at this time. He has no complaints, his appetite and energy are normal, and he looks good. His weight is down five pounds upon my recommendation four weeks ago that he lose some excess weight.

¶ There are no abdominal or inguinal lymph nodes to his scrotal sac exam. There are, however, three- to four-millimeter nodes in the right inguinal region that appear totally unchanged from his original exam on September 3. His lungs are clear, his heartbeat is regular, the liver and spleen are not enlarged, and there are no palpable masses.

¶ It appears to me that Mr. Williams has recovered satisfactorily from his radiation therapy. He has requested a second opinion, and I am therefore recommending that he make an appointment with you at his earliest convenience. We will prepare a referral for Mr. Williams and forward it to your office in a day or two.

Sincerely, | Donna Stensland, M.D. | ap

Table 94-50

Boxed Table

Open the file for Table 94-49 and make the following changes:

1. Press ENTER 1 time after the title, change to 12-point Times New Roman, and type the subtitle `November 4, 20--` in bold.
2. Add this entry to the table so that it will appear in alphabetical order:

   ```
   Gliomas
   The general name for
   tumors that come from the
   supportive tissue of the
   brain; for example,
   astrocytomas or
   oligodendrogliomas.
   They may be benign or
   malignant.
   ```
3. Apply a Table AutoFormat of your choice. Select one with distinctive borders and shading that will make the table easier to read.

Lesson 95

Medical Office Documents

Goals

- Improve speed and accuracy
- Refine language arts skills in proofreading
- Format medical office documents

A. Type 2 times.

A. WARMUP

     The extra black vacuum cleaners with the large-sized 11
grips were just lowered to $160 from $240 (a 33 1/3% mark- 23
down). Jay's #57 quilts were marked down to $98 from $108. 34

| 1 | 2 | 3 | 4 | 5 | 6 | 7 | 8 | 9 | 10 | 11 | 12

SKILLBUILDING

B. Type each word as shown until you reach the backspace sign (←). Then backspace 1 time and replace the previously typed character with the character shown. For example, if you see "hi←at," type "hi," backspace 1 time, and then type "at," resulting in the word "hat." *Technique Tip:* Press the BACKSPACE key with the Sem finger, without looking at your keyboard.

B. TECHNIQUE PRACTICE: BACKSPACE KEY

p←cat c←tab b←peg p←but p←tie m←say t←car s←tea s←mad f←
di←ye be←ag ge←um ri←ob mu←ad pa←it ca←rt fa←it fa←in pa←
ham←d any←t new←t was←r sea←t mad←t gag←p tab←r tax←p ant
cheat←p scalp←e charm←t peace←h chart←m trace←k hub←t bib←

C. PACED PRACTICE

If you are not using the GDP software, turn to page SB-14 and follow the directions for this activity.

LANGUAGE ARTS

D. Edit this paragraph to correct any keyboarding or formatting errors.

D. PROOFREADING

     Suprising as it may seem, their has been a good deal
of interest in comunicating with a computer through the
human voice for about fourty years. Researchers haev spent
millions ofdollars in hteir efforts to improve voice input
tecknology. It is likly that in the next decade we will
see many use ful applications in busness and in education.

DOCUMENT PROCESSING

Table 95-51

Boxed Table

This is November 5, the final day of your assignment, and today you are working in the Surgery Unit. The specialty within this unit is knee surgery. Your first assignment is to create a table listing various medical terms and their definitions. Insert 1 blank line after the information in each row.

MEDICAL TERMS AND THEIR DEFINITION s November 5, 20--	
Adenopathy	Swelling or morbid enlargement of the lymph nodes
Ausultation c	The act of listening to sounds made by the various body structures as a diagnostic method
Cholecystectomy	Surgical removal of the gall bladder
Enterostomy	An incision into the intestines that produces a small hole in the abdomen which through the intestines are emptied
Femur	The long bone of the thigh
Fibroperitonal e	Related to the tissue that lines the abdominal cavity which ~~and~~ covers most of the viscera
Laparoscopy	A minimally invasive ~~surgical~~ technique using a fiber - optic instrument
Hemostasis	The arrest of bleeding
Laprаoptomy	incision into the abdominal wall
Trocar	An instrument for withdrawing fluid from a cavity

Report 95-66

Business Report

RECOVERING FROM KNEE SURGERY

Dr. Alec Pera, M.D.

November 5, 20--

¶ Specific procedures should be followed by patients who are recovering from knee surgery. Depending on the particular surgery that was performed, postoperative needs of patients with knee replacements vary greatly. Healthy, young individuals may require only a few therapy sessions to recover from their surgery completely. Older individuals with no family or friends to help them at home may need special assistance or equipment to aid their mobility. Some patients may benefit from a short stay in a rehabilitation facility. To enhance the rate of recovery, patients should identify and address any special needs that may require attention before their operation.

Refer to page R-12C of the Reference Manual for a review of list formatting.

¶ To promote full recovery, Lakewood Hospital has developed a coordinated pathway of physical and occupational therapy for patients' use. Patient Rehabilitation and Therapy Service (PRTS) and Lakewood Hospital have collaborated on recommending a specific sequence of procedures to follow.
¶ Prior to your surgery, we recommend that you:

1. Determine any special equipment that will be required to promote your recovery.
2. Learn correct techniques for performing day-to-day activities such as getting in and out of bed, driving your automobile, taking showers, getting up from a seat, and going up and down stairs.
3. Learn what exercises will help facilitate your recovery.

¶ After surgery, patients must participate in physical therapy to ensure that they can:

- Extend their knee straight or bend it past 90 degrees.
- Place weight on their knee to ensure that they have the strength and stability to hold their weight.
- Use the knee without discomfort (this may take several months).

Correspondence 95-92

E-Mail Message

Prepare this e-mail message. Type the e-mail greeting, `Hi, Dr. Lockhart:`, and the body shown below in correct format. Type `Anna` as the closing, and type this signature: `Anna Padilla | E-Mail: apadilla@lakewood.com | Phone: 541-555-2303`. Save the e-mail message, but do not send it.

Mr. Walden came in today with a crusted lesion in his back. Lesion was removed using 1% Xylocaine with epinephrine loc. Wound was closed with 4.0 nylon sutures. Stitches should be removed in approximately 10 days. Sutures should be kept dry for 3 days. Mr. Walden is to call if he has questions or if problems arise.

Correspondence 95-93

Memo

Dr. Charlene T. Gutierrez, Director of Plastic Surgery, was asked to assist Dr. Alec Pera with surgery on Bryan Owensby. After an office visit with Mr. Owensby, Dr. Gutierrez dictated the following memo to Dr. Pera. Use November 5, 20--, as the date and type the subject `Mr. Owensby's Surgery`. Type Dr. Gutierrez's title on the same line as her name, and use a comma and space between them.

Progress and Proofreading Check

Documents designated as Proofreading Checks serve as a check of your proofreading skill. Your goal is to have zero typographical errors when the GDP software first scores the document.

On Friday I visited with Mr. Bryan Owensby to discuss his options relative to the muscle transfer we plan to complete following radiation treatment. Mr. Owensby is a 53-year-old male who recently had multiple lesions excised. ¶ Mr. Owensby is aware that our goal is to provide healthy tissue that could tolerate the radiation treatment he would need to destroy the malignant cells on his upper thigh. At this time, we plan to complete a skin graft from the contralateral thigh to provide the healthy tissue for radiation treatment. I believe this will give Mr. Owensby the best opportunity for early healing. ¶ A free tissue transfer was also discussed, and this may be an option if the contralateral graft is unsuccessful. Mr. Owensby understands the risks and complications of either method. Scheduling is pending jointly through our offices. Thank you for this opportunity to participate in Mr. Owensby's care. ap | c: Dr. Taiwo Owakoniro, Dr. Lewis Sethna, Dr. Monica Stevens

Unit 20

Legal Office Documents

LESSON 96
Legal Office Documents

LESSON 97
Legal Office Documents

LESSON 98
Legal Office Documents

LESSON 99
Legal Office Documents

LESSON 100
Legal Office Documents

STATE OF KANSAS IN DISTRICT COURT

COUNTY OF DOUGLAS NORTHEAST JUDICIAL DISTRICT

PEOPLE'S BANK)
607 New Hampshire Street) NO. ______
Lawrence, KS 66044-2243)
)
Plaintiff,)
)
vs.) SUMMONS
)
JOHN COUZINS and GLORIA COUZINS,)
)
Defendants.)

THE STATE OF KANSAS TO THE ABOVE-NAMED DEFENDANTS:

You are hereby summoned and required to appear and defend against the Complaint in this action, which is hereby ser... undersigned an Answer or other proper response w... of the Summons and Complaint upon you, exclusiv...

If you fail to do so, judgment by de... relief demanded in the Complaint.

SIGNED this _____ day of Decem...

Ann B...
806 K...
Lawre...
Teleph...
Attorn...

LAST WILL AND TESTAMENT
OF
IRMA J. GOMEZ

I, IRMA J. GOMEZ, residing in Corvallis, Oregon, do hereby make and declare this to be my Last Will and Testament, hereby revoking any and all former Wills and Codicils by me at any time heretofore made.

ARTICLE I

This will is made in Oregon and shall be governed, construed, and administered according to Oregon law, even though subject to probate or administered elsewhere. The Oregon laws applied shall not include any principles or laws relating to conflicts or choice of laws.

ARTICLE II

Whenever used herein, words importing the singular shall include the plural and words importing the masculine shall include the feminine and neuter, and vice versa, unless the context otherwise requires.

ARTICLE III

I am married and my husband's name is Ricardo E. Gomez. All references hereinafter made to "husband" or "spouse" shall refer to him and no other; and if he is not my legal husband at the time of my death, then he shall be deemed for the purpose of this, my last Will and Testament, to have predeceased me. I was formerly married to Henry Woo, who is now deceased. There were three (3) children born of my marriage to Henry Woo. The names of those children are as follows: Judy Parsons, Henry Wayne, and Randy Woo.

ARTICLE IV

If My Spouse Survives. Except as may otherwise be provided hereunder in this Article IV, if my spouse survives me, I devise to my spouse all my interest in household furniture and furnishings, books, apparel, art objects, collections, jewelry, and similar personal effects; sporting and recreational equipment; all other tangible property for personal use; all other like contents of my home and any vacation property that I may own or reside in on the date of my death; all animals; any motor vehicles that I may own on the date of my death; and any unexpired insurance on all such property.

ARTICLE V

If My Spouse Does Not Survive. Except as may be otherwise provided in this Article IV, if my spouse does not survive me, I devise the property described above in this Article (except motor vehicles) to my children who survive me, to be divided

1

among them as they shall agree, or in the absence of such agreement, as my Personal Representative shall determine, which determination shall be conclusive.

ARTICLE VI

If any beneficiary named or described in this Will fails to survive me for 120 hours, all the provisions in this Will for the benefit of such deceased beneficiary shall lapse, and this Will shall be construed as though the fact were that he or she predeceased me.

ARTICLE VII

All estate, inheritance, transfer, succession, and any other taxes plus interest and penalties thereon (death taxes) that become payable by reason of my death upon property passing under this instrument shall be paid out of the residue of my estate without reimbursement from the recipient and without apportionment. All death taxes upon property not passing under this instrument shall be apportioned in the manner provided by law.

IN WITNESS WHEREOF, I have hereunto affixed my hand and seal this _____ day of ____________________, 20--.

____
IRMA J. GOMEZ Testator

The foregoing instrument, consisting of TWO (2) pages (this page included), was on this _____ day of ____________________, 20--, subscribed on each ...Gomez, the above-named Testator and by her ... be her Last Will, in the presence of us, and each ...his presence, and in the presence of each other, ...attesting witnesses thereto.

...esiding at ______________________________

...esiding at ______________________________

2

Legal Office Documents

Goals

- Type at least 47wpm/5′/5e
- Format legal office documents

A. Type 2 times.

A. WARMUP

```
     Marshal bought five chances for the contest. He won       11
six prizes and was given a check for $2,350--these prizes      22
are equal to 1/4th of Jill's winnings for all of last year.    34
| 1 | 2 | 3 | 4 | 5 | 6 | 7 | 8 | 9 | 10 | 11 | 12
```

SKILLBUILDING

B. DIAGNOSTIC PRACTICE: NUMBERS

If you are not using the GDP software, turn to page SB-5 and follow the directions for this activity.

C. Take three 12-second timed writings on each line. The scale below the last line shows your wpm speed for a 12-second timed writing.

C. 12-SECOND SPEED SPRINTS

```
They saw the sun shine through after days and days of rain.
She hopes to get a much higher math score on the next test.
Jo did not study for the math exam she took late last week.
This time he spent at least ten days studying for the test.
    5    10    15    20    25    30    35    40    45    50    55    60
```

Keyboarding Connection

Capturing an Image From the Internet

Would you like to copy an image or graphic from the Internet? It's easy!

Point to the image or graphic and press the right mouse button. When the shortcut menu appears, choose Save Picture As (or Save Image As). The Save Picture dialog box appears. Select the appropriate drive and name the file if necessary. Click Save. The image is usually saved with a .gif, .jpg, or .bmp file extension. To insert the image into a Word document, choose Picture from the Insert menu, and select From File. Locate the file, and click Insert. You could also right-click the image, choose Copy, and then click the Paste button in Word.

YOUR TURN Conduct a Web search and locate an image or graphic to save. Right-click the image, choose Save Picture As, name the file, and save the image. Insert the image into a word processing document.

D. Take two 5-minute timed writings. Review your speed and errors.

Goal: At least 47wpm/5′/5e

D. 5-MINUTE TIMED WRITING

Many businesses across the country are adopting a new 11
dress code called business casual. Depending on the type of 23
place for which you work, business casual can have various 35
meanings. Most places allow their workers to dress down a 46
notch from what was expected in the past. If people wore 58
suits and ties in the past, then the business casual code 69
would allow them to stop wearing ties and suit jackets. It 81
is quite necessary for a business to formulate dress code 93
guidelines for workers to follow when business casual goes 105
into effect. 107

Surveys of various companies show mixed results when 118
employees were given a choice of dressing more casually. 129
Some companies feel business casual is a perk that works 141
for employees. However, other companies report that job 152
productivity rates zoom down when workers are allowed to 163
dress down. More research is needed. 171

When you feel good about the way you look, you will 181
show this attitude in your performance. If your company has 193
adopted a business casual dress code, you must keep in mind 205
that business casual does not mean that you can dress in a 217
sloppy manner. A neat appearance and good grooming always 229
enhance a business casual look. 235

| 1 | 2 | 3 | 4 | 5 | 6 | 7 | 8 | 9 | 10 | 11 | 12

FORMATTING

E. LEGAL DOCUMENTS

Court rules (federal, state, appellate, and so on) and law office preferences determine the format of legal documents including margins, line numbering, line spacing, line lengths, page numbering, indents, alignment, and bolding. Therefore, the legal documents and guidelines in this unit have been designed to serve as simplified examples of acceptable legal formats.

Legal documents are typed on either 8.5- × 14-inch legal paper or 8.5- × 11-inch paper. Court documents often include numbered lines for easy reference in a court of law. *Legal cap* is the name given to the vertical rules that appear at the left and right margins. In legal documents, the *venue* states the name and location of the court and county. The *caption* states the court, the names of the parties, the docket (case) number, the title of the document, and sometimes the name of the judge.

Follow these general formatting guidelines for legal documents in this unit. Refer to the summons shown in the illustration.

- Use default margins all around, single spacing, left alignment, and no bold.
- Set a 1-inch tab, and indent paragraphs 1 inch; press ENTER 2 times between paragraphs.
- Set a 6-inch right tab, and type 20 underscores for the case number.
- Single-space court documents (such as an affidavit of possession, a summons, a complaint, and a judgment), and number all lines. Restart line numbers on each page.

(Continued on next page)

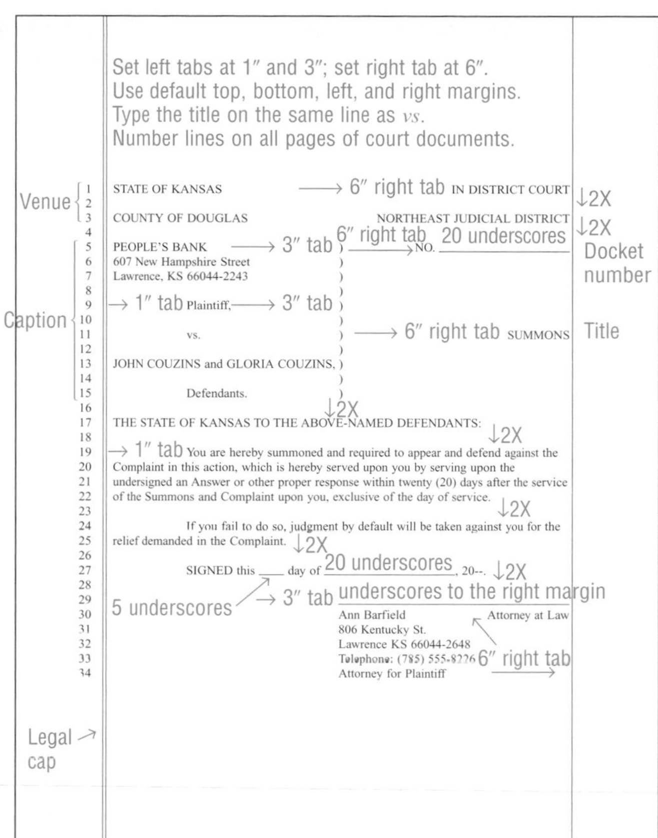

STATE OF KANSAS IN DISTRICT COURT

COUNTY OF DOUGLAS NORTHEAST JUDICIAL DISTRICT

PEOPLE'S BANK)
607 New Hampshire Street) NO. ____________________
Lawrence, KS 66044-2243)
)
Plaintiff,)
)
vs.) SUMMONS
)
JOHN COUZINS and GLORIA COUZINS,)
)
Defendants.)

THE STATE OF KANSAS TO THE ABOVE-NAMED DEFENDANTS:

You are hereby summoned and required to appear and defend against the Complaint in this action, which is hereby served upon you by serving upon the undersigned an Answer or other proper response within twenty (20) days after the service of the Summons and Complaint upon you, exclusive of the day of service.

If you fail to do so, judgment by default will be taken against you for the relief demanded in the Complaint.

SIGNED this _____ day of ____________________, 20--.

____
Ann Barfield Attorney at Law
806 Kentucky St.
Lawrence KS 66044-2648
Telephone: (785) 555-8226
Attorney for Plaintiff

- Single-space noncourt documents (such as a warranty deed and last will and testament), and do not number lines.
- For multipage documents, insert a centered page number at the bottom of each page.
- Set a 3-inch tab, and type the closing parentheses at 3 inches; for signature lines, type continuous underscores from this 3-inch tab setting to the right margin.
- Type 20 underscores for months and case numbers and 5 underscores for dates; insert spaces before and after underscores when the underscores appcar in the middle of a sentence.

Word Processing Manual

F. WORD PROCESSING: LINE NUMBERING

Study Lesson 96 in your word processing manual. Complete all of the shaded steps while at your computer. Then format the jobs that follow.

DOCUMENT PROCESSING

An affidavit is a sworn written statement made under oath.

Report 96-67

Affidavit of Possession

Add line numbering for all lines in this document. When this document is actually typed, the line numbers will vary from those shown here.

AFFIDAVIT OF POSSESSION ↓2X

STATE OF VERMONT ↓2X

COUNTY OF WINDSOR ↓2X

→ 1″ tab Eric Wesley, being first duly sworn, deposes and says: ↓2X

That he is an adult person and is a resident of Windsor County, Vermont, and that his mailing address is P.O. Box 801, Ludlow, VT 05149. ↓2X

(Continued on next page)

That he knows the history, ownership, and occupancy of the following-described property situated in Windsor County, Vermont, to wit:

All that part of the Southeast Quarter of the Northeast Quarter of Section Nine (9), Township Seventy-two (72), further described as follows: Beginning at the Northeast corner of said Southeast Quarter of the Northeast Quarter; thence South along the East line of said quarter 1000.00 feet; thence west 575.00 feet; thence North 200.00 feet; thence West 204.00 feet; thence North 800.00 feet; thence East 979.00 feet.

That the record title holder in fee simple of the above property is Eric Wesley, a single person; that he is presently in possession of the above-described premises;

That ownership of the aforesaid property is based upon an unbroken chain of title through immediate and remote grantors by deed of conveyance which has been recorded for a period of more than twenty-one (21) years, to wit: Since August 21, 1943, at 2 a.m.;

That the purpose of this Affidavit of Possession is to show proof of ownership by providing and recording evidence of possession for marketable title as required by the Marketable Record Title Act of the State of Vermont.

↓2X

5 underscores

Underscore is 5 characters wide.

DATED this _____ day of May, 2006, at Ludlow, Vermont. ↓2X

Underscore starts at 3-inch left tab and ends at the right margin.

Signature title ends at 6-inch right tab.

underscores to the right margin

____

→ 3″ tab Blake Crawford 6″ right tab → Attorney-at-Law

↓2X

Subscribed and sworn to before me this ____ day of May, 2006.

Underscore starts at 3-inch left tab and ends at the right margin.

____

Shirley Blakely Notary Public
Windsor County, Vermont
My Commission Expires July 17, 2012

Correspondence 96-94

Business Letter in Block Style

August 30, 20-- | Mr. Eric Wesley | P.O. Box 801 | Ludlow, VT 05149 | Dear Mr. Wesley:

¶ Enclosed is your copy of the Affidavit of Possession that was filed on your behalf with the Windsor County Courthouse.

¶ As you can see, only the Southeast Quarter of your property was included in the affidavit. We will have to file an additional affidavit if you want to add the Northwest Quarter as well as your Franklin County properties. All affidavits must be completed prior to your property being advertised in the *Windsor News*.

¶ I will be out of the office all of next week. If you have questions, please call my associate, Betty Yu.

Sincerely, | Blake Crawford | urs | Enclosure | c: Marvin Steele, Beverley Perez

Legal Office Documents

Goals

- Improve speed and accuracy
- Refine language arts skills in the use of punctuation
- Format legal office documents

A. Type 2 times.

A. WARMUP

Jacqueline kept prize #2490 instead of #3761 because 11
it was worth 58.5% more value. That was a great prize! Last 23
year the law firm of Adams & Day donated all grand prizes. 34

| 1 | 2 | 3 | 4 | 5 | 6 | 7 | 8 | 9 | 10 | 11 | 12

SKILLBUILDING

B. PROGRESSIVE PRACTICE: ALPHABET

If you are not using the GDP software, turn to page SB-7 and follow the directions for this activity.

C. PACED PRACTICE

If you are not using the GDP software, turn to page SB-14 and follow the directions for this activity.

LANGUAGE ARTS

D. Study the rules at the right.

D. SEMICOLONS

RULE ▶ ; no conjunction

Use a semicolon to separate two closely related independent clauses that are not connected by a conjunction (such as *and, but,* or *nor*).

Management favored the vote; stockholders did not.
But: Management favored the vote, but stockholders did not.

RULE ▶ ; series

Use a semicolon to separate three or more items in a series if any of the items already contain commas.

Staff meetings were held on Thursday, May 7; Monday, June 7; and Friday, June 12.

Note: Be sure to insert the semicolon between (not within) the items in a series.

Edit the sentences to correct any errors in the use of semicolons.

Paul will travel to Madrid, Spain; Lisbon, Portugal, and Nice, France.
Mary's gift arrived yesterday, Margie's did not.
Bring your textbook to class; I'll return it tomorrow.
The best days for the visit are Monday, May 10, Tuesday, May 18, and Wednesday, May 26.
Jan is the president; Peter is the vice president.

Report 97-68

Warranty Deed

A seller who provides a warranty deed warrants (or guarantees) that he or she has full ownership of a property and has the right to sell it. The seller also guarantees all rights of the property to the buyer.

WARRANTY DEED ↓2X

→ 1″ tab THIS INDENTURE, made this _____ (5 underscores) day of October, 2006, between Maria J. Lopez, Grantor, whether one or more, and Barbara Denman, Grantee, whether one or more, whose post office address is 315 Clark Avenue, Ames, IA 50010-3314. ↓2X

WITNESSETH, for and in consideration of the sum of SEVENTY-FIVE THOUSAND and 00/100 DOLLARS ($75,000), Grantor does hereby GRANT to Grantee, all of the following real property lying and being in the County of Story, State of Iowa, and described as follows, to-wit:

Lots Seventeen (17) and Eighteen (18), Block Seventy-three (73), Original Townsite of Ames, Iowa, SUBJECT TO easements, special or improvement taxes and assessments, mineral conveyances, rights-of-way and reservations of record.

(THIS DEED IS IN FULFILLMENT OF THAT CERTAIN CONTRACT FOR DEED ENTERED INTO BY AND BETWEEN THE SAME PARTIES ON THE DATE HEREOF.)

And the said Grantor for herself, her heirs, executors and administrators, does covenant with the Grantee that she is well seized in fee of the land and premises aforesaid and has good right to sell and convey the same in manner and form aforesaid: that the same are free from all encumbrances, except installments of special assessments or assessments for special improvements which have not been certified to the County Treasurer for collection, and the above granted lands and premises in the possession of said Grantee, against all persons lawfully claiming or to claim the whole or any part thereof, the said Grantor will warrant and defend.

WITNESS, the hand of the Grantor.

→ 3″ tab ______________________________ (underscores to the right margin)

Maria J. Lopez

(Continued on next page)

STATE OF IOWA

County of Story

On this ______ day of October, 2006, before me, a notary public within and for said County and State, personally appeared Maria J. Lopez, to me known to be the person described in and who executed the within and foregoing instrument and acknowledged to me that she executed the same as her free act and deed.

____

Boyd H. Fraser 6″ right tab → Notary Public
Story County, Iowa
My Commission Expires June 15, 2012

Table 97-52

Boxed Table

Your finished table will have different line endings for column B when you resize the column widths to fit the contents.

WARRANTY DEED TERMINOLOGY State of Iowa	
Term	Definition
Appurtenance	Something attached to the land
Consideration	The value of the property
Escrow	A system of document transfer in which the document is given to a third party to hold until the conditions of the agreement have been met
Grantee	The person who is buying the property
Grantor	The person who owns the property
Mortgage	The pledge of property as security for a loan
Tenement	Something that can be possessed, such as land or a building
Warranty deed	A deed in which the seller forever guarantees clear title to the land

Correspondence 97-95

E-Mail Message

Reference Manual

Refer to page R-5C and R-5D: E-Mail Message.

Type the e-mail greeting, body, closing, and signature as indicated below in correct format:

1. Type `Hi, David:` as the greeting, type the body shown below, and type `Yen` as the closing.
2. Type this signature: `Yen Nguyen | E-Mail: ynguyen@webmail.net | Phone: 712-555-3435`
3. Save the e-mail message in GDP, but do not send it.

; no conjunction

; series

; no conjunction

¶ You might recall last week that I indicated there might be some fore closure property available and that it would be auctioned at the Story Courthouse. On September 9 3 properties in southern Story county will be auctioned as foreclosures. These properties are located adjacent to the lots you purchased last year I know that you would be interested in expanding your lot size with this purchase. Specifically, they are located in Spring Township, Lot 23; Aiken Township, Lot 17; and Andrews Township, Lot 9.

¶ I expect these properties will sell for around $36,000 each; their excellent location may force the bidding into the $40,000 range. If you cannot be present for the auction but would like to place a bid on the properties, please let me know so that I can act on your behalf as your agent. If you want to do this, send me the bidding range you wish to present for each of the Properties or for all 3 as one combined property. I need confirmation from you no later than September so that I can register your agent to present your bid.

Legal Office Documents

Goals

- Type at least 47wpm/5′/5e
- Format legal office documents

A. Type 2 times.

A. WARMUP

Janet bought dozens of disks (5 or 6) to store her 10
article, "The Internet Sanctions." She quickly sent it to 23
her editor, Max Pavlow, on the 18th or 19th of September. 34

| 1 | 2 | 3 | 4 | 5 | 6 | 7 | 8 | 9 | 10 | 11 | 12

SKILLBUILDING

B. DIAGNOSTIC PRACTICE: SYMBOLS AND PUNCTUATION

If you are not using the GDP software, turn to page SB-2 and follow the directions for this activity.

C. Type the paragraph 2 times, concentrating on each letter typed.

C. TECHNIQUE PRACTICE: SHIFT/CAPS LOCK

Raymond and Karen must travel through TENNESSEE and KENTUCKY on TUESDAY and WEDNESDAY. Raymond will speak in NASHVILLE on the topic of COMPUTER AWARENESS; Karen will speak in LOUISVILLE, and her talk is on INTERNET ACCESS.

Strategies for Career Success

Enhance Your Presentation With Visual Aids

Visual aids capture people's attention while increasing their retention. Use visual aids to present an outline of your presentation, explain detailed technical or numerical information, and summarize your key points.

Be selective. Don't bombard your audience with visuals. Your visual aids should support and clarify your verbal presentation. Consider the size of your audience and the size of the room before selecting your visuals. Audiences have little patience for visuals that are too small to read. Types of visual aids are overhead transparencies, slides, photographs, flip charts, maps, flowcharts, posters, handouts, and computer graphics including tables, graphs, and charts.

Limit the amount of information on a visual. Use simple graphics. Continue displaying the current visual until you are ready to discuss the next one. Always keep the projector or overhead on.

YOUR TURN In what ways would your visual aids differ if your audience had 10 people or 110?

D. Take two 5-minute timed writings. Review your speed and errors.

Goal: At least 47wpm/5′/5e

D. 5-MINUTE TIMED WRITING

From the time you start attending school, you begin to 11
develop new skills in making friends and getting along with 23
people. These skills are used throughout your life journey. 35
If you want to be successful in any business or career, you 47
can't be a loner. You must learn skills for working with 59
people from all cultures. 64

In a corporation, people use their unique skills to 74
work as a team in order to accomplish their goals. Like a 86
finely tuned orchestra or a football team, all members must 98
work together to achieve a desired objective. If a person 110
does not work efficiently within the group, then other team 122
members may have to work harder to compensate so that the 133
effort of the team will not fall short. 141

Working with others allows you the chance to learn 152
from other people. You may also learn some things about 163
yourself. To get along with your coworkers, you may have to 175
overlook the personal faults of others. Everyone has some 186
faults, and your faults may be just as disconcerting to 198
other people as their faults are to you. Your ability to 209
work with people will also enhance your quest for career 220
advancement. You can expect amazing results when you work 232
with your team. 235

| 1 | 2 | 3 | 4 | 5 | 6 | 7 | 8 | 9 | 10 | 11 | 12

DOCUMENT PROCESSING

Report 98-69

Summons

Add line numbers for all lines in this court document. When this document is actually typed, the line numbers will vary from those shown here.

Type the title on the same line as *vs*.

A summons is a document that notifies a defendant that a lawsuit has been filed and an appearance must be made before the court, at a specified time, to answer the charges.

STATE OF KANSAS → 6″ right tab IN DISTRICT COURT ↓2X

COUNTY OF DOUGLAS NORTHEAST JUDICIAL DISTRICT ↓2X

PEOPLE'S BANK → 3″ tab) → 6″ right tab NO. ____________________ (20 underscores)
607 New Hampshire Street)
Lawrence, KS 66044-2243)
→ 3″ tab)
→ 1″ tab Plaintiff, → 3″ tab)
)
→ 1″ tab vs. → 3″ tab) → 6″ right tab SUMMONS
)
JOHN COUZINS and GLORIA)
COUZINS,)
)
Defendants.) ↓2X

THE STATE OF KANSAS TO THE ABOVE-NAMED DEFENDANTS: ↓2X

→ 1″ tab You are hereby summoned and required to appear and defend against the Complaint in this action, which is hereby served upon you by serving upon the undersigned an Answer or other proper response within twenty (20) days after the service of the Summons and Complaint upon you, exclusive of the day of service. ↓2X

If you fail to do so, judgment by default will be taken against you for the relief demanded in the Complaint.

SIGNED this _____ day of December 20--.

5 underscores

→ 3″ tab ______________________________ (underscores to the right margin)
Ann Barfield → 6″ right tab Attorney-at-Law
806 Kentucky Street
Lawrence, KS 66044-2648
Telephone: 785-555-8226
Attorney for Plaintiff

Correspondence 98-96

Memo

MEMO TO: Raymond Ruzi

FROM: Charlotte Libretto

DATE: December 28, 20--

SUBJECT: Client listing

¶ As you requested, I am now enclosing an up-to-date new client list for our Atlanta area clients. This list is cuent as of last week, and it includes clients in the counties of Carroll, Cobb, Douglas, Fulton, and paulding. Please note that the billing hours are shown in this list.

¶ Douglas and Cobb counties represent the greatest number of clients over all, although this list doesn't reveal the total number of clients per county. Just in the past quarter, these two counties represented nearly eighty % of our client base. Cobb County clients do not represent a sizable percentage of our client base, but the opening of three new law offices in that county will most certainly generate considerable business in the coming months.

¶ We will send you an updated list biweekly. The next list will most certainly show substantial gains in Cobb County, and we expect business in Douglas and Fulton counties to continue growing because of the growth in the area West of Atlanta. If you have any questions about any of our new clients please call our main office at 770-555-1843.

urs | Enclosure | c: Blair Kiplan

Table 98-53

Boxed Table

Press ENTER to create the 2-line column heading as displayed before automatically adjusting column widths.

CLIENT LIST
December 28, 20--

Name	Address	County	Billing Hours
Jose Azteca	128 Holly St.	Douglas	25
Carroll Bryan	323 Newnan St.	Carroll	28
Margie Coulon	301 Bradley St.	Paulding	15
Thomas Henry	2900 Shady Grove	Cobb	22
Debra Johnson	215 Griffin Dr.	Cobb	34
Maria Mateo	156 Cypress Circle	Fulton	10
Luther Nicholson	6703 Burns Rd.	Paulding	12
Pearl Nix	106 Alice Lane	Douglas	18
James Presley	622 North Ave.	Carroll	23
Janie Ramey	1202 Park St.	Fulton	32
Heather Sanders	248 Lakeshore Dr.	Cobb	12
Thomas Tarpley	2950 Chapel Hill Rd.	Douglas	29
Vickie Thomas	4821 Hope Rd.	Carroll	9
Kim Wong	111 Pierce St.	Fulton	18
Ray Young	108 Waverly Way	Douglas	30
Tong Zhen	286 Laurel Terrace	Paulding	35

Keyboarding Connection

Coping With Spam

Have you received heaps of unsolicited e-mail, commonly known as spam? Everyone wants to get rid of those irritating online sales pitches. Contrary to popular advice, however, there is not much you can do about them. You can make use of various filters, but they aren't foolproof.

If you end up on a spammer's list and receive a courteous e-mail asking you to reply if you wish to be removed from the list, *do not reply*. The spammer may interpret your reply to mean that you read e-mail, and you may be put on the hot list. The best action is to try to avoid divulging your e-mail address to spammers. Most important, use an alternate account if posting to any kind of online forum.

YOUR TURN How do you deal with postal "junk mail" that you receive? Are there similarities in dealing with spam?

Lesson 99

Legal Office Documents

Goals

- Improve speed and accuracy
- Refine language arts skills in spelling
- Format legal office documents

A. Type 2 times.

A. WARMUP

```
     Zeke sharpened his ax so that he could quite easily    11
saw through 15 very large pine trees. Each load will sell   23
for $175 (to Blake & James Inc.) at next Friday's auction.  35
|  1  |  2  |  3  |  4  |  5  |  6  |  7  |  8  |  9  |  10  |  11  |  12
```

SKILLBUILDING

B. MAP

Follow the GDP software directions for this exercise in improving keystroking accuracy.

C. Take a 1-minute timed writing on the first paragraph to establish your base speed. Then take four 1-minute timed writings on the remaining paragraphs. As soon as you equal or exceed your base speed on one paragraph, advance to the next, more difficult paragraph.

C. SUSTAINED PRACTICE: ROUGH DRAFT

```
     The pattern of employment in our country is undergoing  11
some major changes. Companies are slowly decreasing their    23
permanent staff to just a core group of managers and other   35
high-powered people and are using temporaries for the rest.  47

     This trend is creating an acordion aftermath in many    11
firms: the ability to expand and contract as the time or     23
the balance sheets dictate. Have this range of flexibility   35
would be a key ingredient in the competetive fight to come.  47

     All of these changes would make it tough for all unions 11
to stay a float. They do not have a satisfactery method of   23
organizing such employes. Unions can try to change in to     35
social agenceis, providing aid to members outside of work.   47

     Such services as elder or child care, counseling, debt  11
managment, and even health care maybe of great asistance     23
as employers find it more and more dificult to offer these   35
benfits. Unions may find their niche by filling this gap.    47
|  1  |  2  |  3  |  4  |  5  |  6  |  7  |  8  |  9  |  10  |  11  |  12
```

D. Type this list of frequently misspelled words, paying special attention to any spelling problems in each word.

D. SPELLING

20 distribution executive extension requested specific carried
21 recommended alternative programs access budget issued seize
22 objectives indicated calendar family could these until your
23 administrative accommodate possibility students fiscal past
24 transportation employee's categories summary offered estate

Edit the sentences to correct any misspellings.

25 The execitive requested an extention on spicific programs.
26 I have recomended alternitive programs for early next week.
27 These objectives were indacated for the new calender year.
28 These passed administrative goals will accomodate the team.
29 These categories could be included in the employee summery.

DOCUMENT PROCESSING

Report 99-70

Last Will and Testament

Insert a centered page number at the bottom of each page.

A last will and testament is a legal document stating how a person wants his or her property distributed after death.

LAST WILL AND TESTAMENT
OF
IRMA J. GOMEZ ↓2X

→ Tab I, IRMA J. GOMEZ, residing in Corvallis, Oregon, do hereby make and declare this to be my Last Will and Testament, hereby revoking any and all former Wills and Codicils by me at any time heretofore made. ↓2X

ARTICLE I ↓2X

This will is made in Oregon and shall be governed, construed, and administered according to Oregon law, even though subject to probate or administered elsewhere. The Oregon laws applied shall not include any principles or laws relating to conflicts or choice of laws.

ARTICLE II

Whenever used herein, words importing the singular shall include the plural and words importing the masculine shall include the feminine and neuter, and vice versa, unless the context otherwise requires.

(Continued on next page)

ARTICLE III

I am married and my husband's name is Ricardo E. Gomez. All references hereinafter made to "husband" or "spouse" shall refer to him and no other; and if he is not my legal husband at the time of my death, then he shall be deemed for the purpose of this, my last Will and Testament, to have predeceased me. I was formerly married to Henry Woo, who is now deceased. There were three (3) children born of my marriage to Henry Woo. The names of those children are as follows: Judy Parsons, Henry Wayne, and Randy Woo.

ARTICLE IV

If My Spouse Survives. Except as may otherwise be provided hereunder in this Article IV, if my spouse survives me, I devise to my spouse all my interest in household furniture and furnishings, books, apparel, art objects, collections, jewelry, and similar personal effects; sporting and recreational equipment; all other tangible property for personal use; all other like contents of my home and any vacation property that I may own or reside in on the date of my death; all animals; any motor vehicles that I may own on the date of my death; and any unexpired insurance on all such property.

ARTICLE V

If My Spouse Does Not Survive. Except as may be otherwise provided in this Article IV, if my spouse does not survive me, I devise the property described above in this Article (except motor vehicles) to my children who survive me, to be divided among them as they shall agree, or in the absence of such agreement, as my Personal Representative shall determine, which determination shall be conclusive.

ARTICLE VI

If any beneficiary named or described in this Will fails to survive me for 120 hours, all the provisions in this Will for the benefit of such deceased beneficiary shall lapse, and this Will shall be construed as though the fact were that he or she predeceased me.

ARTICLE VII

All estate, inheritance, transfer, succession, and any other taxes plus interest and penalties thereon (death taxes) that become payable by reason of my death upon property passing under this instrument shall be paid out of the residue of my estate without reimbursement from the recipient and without apportionment. All death taxes upon property not passing under this instrument shall be apportioned in the manner provided by law. ↓2X

(Continued on next page)

IN WITNESS WHEREOF, I have hereunto affixed my hand and seal this ______ day of ____20-character underscore____, 20--. ↓2X
↖5-character underscore

⟶ 3″ tab ______underscores to the right margin______
IRMA J. GOMEZ → 6″ right tab Testator
↓2X

The foregoing instrument, consisting of TWO (2) pages (this page included), was on this ______ day of __________________, 20--, subscribed on each page and at the end thereof by Irma J. Gomez, the above-named Testator and by her signed, sealed, published and declared to be her Last Will, in the presence of us, and each of us, who thereupon, at her request, in her presence, and in the presence of each other, have hereunto subscribed our names as attesting witnesses thereto. ↓2X

Center the last 2 lines.

____30-character underscore____ residing at ____________________________

______________________________ residing at ____________________________

Correspondence 99-97

Business Letter in Block Style

Refer to page R-12C of the Reference Manual for an overview of formatting lists.

July 1, 20-- | Mrs. Irma J. Gomez | 768 Southwest Adams Avenue | Corvallis, OR 97333-4523 | Dear Mrs. Gomez: | Subject: Will Provisions
¶ Your last will and testament has been drafted and is enclosed for your review. Please review it carefully for any specific omissions or deletions.
¶ Although your will has been drafted as you indicated, there are still a couple of alternative inclusions that I would recommend.
• Do you wish to include a fiduciary powers summary in the will?
• What division of estate do you wish to include for your family?
¶ These inclusions could be rather comprehensive. Therefore, could we schedule a meeting for next Tuesday to accommodate these changes? Please call my administrative assistant so she can put you on my calendar.
Sincerely, | Andrea L. Grainger | Attorney-at-Law | urs | Enclosure | c: T. Carter, S. Rohrer, A. Winchester

Lesson 100

Legal Office Documents

Goals

- Type at least 47wpm/5'/5e
- Format legal office documents

A. Type 2 times.

A. WARMUP

Val Lopez and Jack Drew quickly bought six tickets for 11
Sam's $24,600 collector's auto (a 1957 Chevrolet). Over the 23
past month, its value increased by 1.5%. That is fantastic! 35
| 1 | 2 | 3 | 4 | 5 | 6 | 7 | 8 | 9 | 10 | 11 | 12

SKILLBUILDING

PPP PRETEST → PRACTICE → POSTTEST

PRETEST
Take a 1-minute timed writing. Review your speed and errors.

B. PRETEST: Horizontal Reaches

Bart enjoyed his royal blue race car. He bragged about 11
how he learned to push for those speed spurts that helped 23
him win those races. The car had a lot of get-up-and-go. 34
| 1 | 2 | 3 | 4 | 5 | 6 | 7 | 8 | 9 | 10 | 11 | 12

PRACTICE
Speed Emphasis:
If you made no more than 1 error on the Pretest, type each *individual* line 2 times.
Accuracy Emphasis:
If you made 2 or more errors, type each *group* of lines (as though it were a paragraph) 2 times.

C. PRACTICE: In Reaches

oy toy ahoy ploy loyal coyly royal enjoy decoy annoy deploy
ar fare arch mart march farms scars spear barns learn radar
pu pull push puts pulse spurt purge spuds pushy spurs pupil

D. PRACTICE: Out Reaches

ge gear gets ages getup raged geese lunge pages cagey forge
da dare date data dance adage dazed sedan daubs cedar daily
hi high hick hill hinge chief hires ethic hiked chili hitch

POSTTEST
Repeat the Pretest timed writing and compare performance.

E. POSTTEST: Horizontal Reaches

F. Take two 5-minute timed writings. Review your speed and errors.

Goal: At least 47 wpm/5'/5e

F. 5-MINUTE TIMED WRITINGS

Company loyalty may be a thing of the past. A worker 11
who stayed and worked in one place for thirty or more years 23
is rare these days. People are moving to different jobs at 35
a faster pace than in the past. Changing jobs many times 46
over a career no longer carries the stigma of the past. 57
People are looking for new challenges. 65
Those who change jobs are able to market their skills 76
and to get salary increases. Hopping from job to job can 87
pay amazing returns for some careers. Businesses are quite 99
willing to offer higher pay and more perks to attract the 111
best and most skilled people. People who change jobs a lot 123
have the experience and knowledge that other companies are 134
willing to retain. 138
The opportunity to change jobs is there not only for 149
younger workers but also for older workers who are well 160
into their careers. For example, computer technology has 172
been experiencing a boom. The Internet industry has a big 183
demand for computer programmers. People with knowledge in 195
this field can request higher salaries. A company may even 207
offer additional benefits in order to attract experienced 208
workers with great credentials. It is really up to each 229
person to decide what to do. 235

| 1 | 2 | 3 | 4 | 5 | 6 | 7 | 8 | 9 | 10 | 11 | 12

Strategies for Career Success

Letter of Resignation

When you plan to leave a job, you should write a resignation letter, memo, or e-mail to your supervisor and send a copy to Human Resources. Follow these guidelines to write an effective resignation.

Start a resignation letter positively, regardless of why you are leaving. Include how you benefited from working for the company, or compliment your coworkers.

In the middle section, state why you are leaving. Provide an objective, factual explanation and avoid accusations. Your resignation becomes part of your permanent company record. If it is hostile, it could backfire on you when you need references. Stipulate the date your resignation becomes effective (provide at least a two-week notice).

End the letter of resignation with a closing of goodwill (for example, "I wish all of you the best in the future.").

YOUR TURN List the benefits of *not* "burning your bridges" (showing anger or bitterness) in your letter of resignation.

Report 100-71

Complaint

A complaint uses the same format as a summons, as shown in Report 98-69.

Add line numbers for all lines in this court document, and restart line numbers on each page. When this document is typed, the line numbers will vary from those shown here.

Type the title on the same line as *vs.*

Press ENTER 2 times before each Roman numeral.

All Roman numerals are centered between the margins.

A complaint is the initial document filed with a court by a plaintiff to begin an adversarial or action at law proceeding. A judgment is the decision of the court.

STATE OF NORTH DAKOTA — IN DISTRICT COURT

COUNTY OF WALSH — NORTHEAST JUDICIAL DISTRICT

WALSH COUNTY BANK) NO ______
170 Main Street)
Adams, ND 58210)
)
Plaintiff,)
)
vs.) COMPLAINT
)
KENNEDY FARMERS, INC.)
JAMES D. KENNEDY and)
CAROL KENNEDY,)
)
Defendants)

PLAINTIFF FOR ITS CAUSE OF ACTION AND COMPLAINT AGAINST THE DEFENDANTS, COMPLAINS, ALLEGES AND SHOWS TO THE COURT:

I.

That defendants owe plaintiff $5,685.00, plus interest and charges, under the terms of a promissory note executed April 10, 20--, a copy of which is attached hereto and incorporated by reference as "Exhibit A."

II.

That defendants have not, upon due demand, satisfied their obligation under the terms of the promissory note.

III.

That Kennedy Farmers, Inc., is a North Dakota for-profit corporation duly organized under the corporate laws of the State of North Dakota.

IV.

That the registered agent of Kennedy Farmers, Inc., is James D. Kennedy.

(Continued on next page)

V.

That James D. Kennedy executed a Commercial Guaranty for the note dated April 10, 20--, a copy of which is attached hereto and incorporated herein by reference as "Exhibit B."

VI.

That Carol Kennedy executed a Commercial Guaranty on the prior promissory note No. 7249, and the Commercial Guaranty provides that the guaranty extends to ". . . all renewals of, extensions of, modifications of, refinancings of, consolidations of, and substitutions for the promissory note or agreement." A copy of that Commercial Guaranty is attached hereto and incorporated hereby by reference as "Exhibit D."

VII.

That the indebtedness was the renewal of a prior promissory note executed by Kennedy Farmers, Inc., to Walsh County Bank on June 17, 20--, which was in the original principal amount of $6,685.00, a copy of which is attached hereto and incorporated by reference as "Exhibit C."

VIII.

That James D. Kennedy and Carol Kennedy are personally liable for the amount of the debt, as is the corporation, Kennedy Farmers, Inc.

WHEREFORE, PLAINTIFF DEMANDS JUDGMENT AGAINST THE DEFENDANTS, AND EACH OF THEM, AS FOLLOWS:

Refer to page R-12C of the Reference Manual for an overview of formatting lists.

1. For the amount of $3,585.00, plus interest on that amount from and after April 10, 20--, at the rate of 10.75% per annum; and for its costs, late charges, and disbursements in this action;

2. For such other and further relief as the Court may deem appropriate.

SIGNED this ______ day of December, 20--.

____
Harold E. Jensen Attorney-at-Law
405 1st Street
Adams, ND 58210
Telephone: (701)555-4832
Attorney for Plaintiff

Report 100-72

Judgment

A judgment uses the same format as a summons, as shown in Report 98-69.

Add line numbers in this court document.

STATE OF ARIZONA — IN DISTRICT COURT

COUNTY OF MARICOPA — CENTRAL JUDICIAL DISTRICT

Timothy Barnes d/b/a Barnes Computers) 1651 West Baseline Road) Tempe, AZ 85283)) Plaintiff,)) vs.)) Maricopa Hospital Association) d/b/a Maricopa Nursing Care)) Defendant)	CIVIL NO. 43-89-D-00145 JUDGMENT

¶ The defendant, Maricopa Hospital Association, d/b/a Maricopa Nursing Care, having been regularly served with process, and having failed to appear and answer the plaintiff's Complaint filed herein, and the default of said defendant having been duly entered, and it appearing that said defendant is not an infant or an incompetent person, and an affidavit of nonmilitary service having been filed herein, and it appearing by the affidavits of plaintiff that plaintiff is entitled to judgment herein,

¶ IT IS THEREFORE ORDERED AND ADJUDGED, that the plaintiff have and recover from the defendant, Maricopa Hospital Association d/b/a Maricopa Nursing Care, the sum of $8,000.00 plus interest thereon from and after August 10, 20--, until paid, together with costs in the sum of $252.75.

¶ SIGNED this _____ day of __________, 20-- .

____

Clerk of the District Court

Report 100-73

Affidavit

Use the same format as in the affidavit shown in Report 96-67.

Add line numbers for all lines in this court document.

Progress and Proofreading Check

Documents designated as Proofreading Checks serve as a check of your proofreading skill. Your goal is to have zero typographical errors when the GDP software first scores the document.

AFFIDAVIT OF POSSESSION

STATE OF OREGON

COUNTY OF LINN

I, MARILYN T. HUGGINS, being first duly sworn, depose and say:

That I am the petitioner in the above-entitled suit.

That the respondent, RICHARD M. HUGGINS, and I are the parents of BENJAMIN T. HUGGINS. That BENJAMIN T. HUGGINS is currently residing exclusively with me. Respondent is currently residing away from the home at 1529 South Oak Street, Albany, Oregon. That I am a fit and proper person to have immediate and temporary custody of BENJAMIN T. HUGGINS.

I believe that these pending dissolution proceedings will aggravate this situation; therefore, I believe that it is necessary and appropriate for the Court to issue an Order restraining and enjoining respondent from physically or verbally abusing or harassing me or our child in any way.

____

Subscribed and sworn to before me this ______ day of ________________, 20--.

____

Notary Public for Oregon
My commission expires January 7, 2012

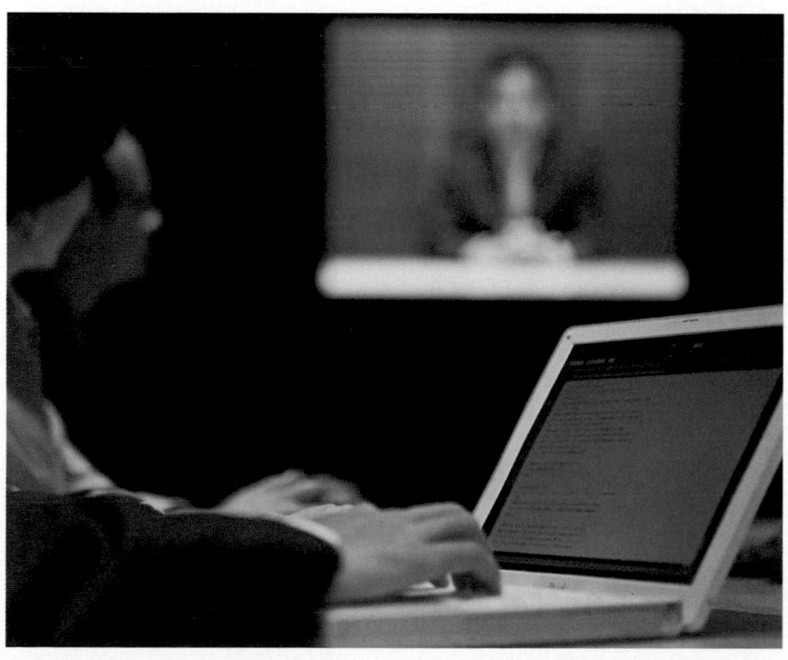

Skills Assessment on Part 5

5-Minute Timed Writing

When you submit your resume to apply for a job, you 11
want your resume to be noticed. Here are some things you 22
might do to make certain your resume receives the time and 34
focus it deserves. 38

First, be neat. Review each page to make sure that it 49
is free of typos and spelling errors. Check each page for 60
correct grammar. Remember that this document will make the 72
first impression with a potential employer. You want the 83
document to represent you in the best way. Use white paper 95
of good quality to print your resume. 103

Second, try to be creative. Make your resume unique. A 114
future employer may be looking for specific things when he 126
or she scans the pages of your resume. Be sure to provide 137
facts that explain exactly what skills you have acquired in 149
positions you have held in the past. Avoid using the same 161
buzzwords that everyone else uses. 168

Finally, state a career objective on your resume. Some 179
experts suggest that by stating a career objective, you are 191
showing a career path. Others think that stating a career 203
objective may limit many job possibilities. If you state a 215
career objective, make sure the objective is in line with 226
the specific job for which you are applying. 235

| 1 | 2 | 3 | 4 | 5 | 6 | 7 | 8 | 9 | 10 | 11 | 12

Correspondence Test 5-98

Business Letter in Block Style

13 July 20-- | Mr. Antoine Lauvergeon | Marketing Director | Alatel Inc. | 54, Rue la Boetie | 75382 Paris | France | Dear Mr. Lauvergeon:

¶ As we predicted, our jefe effort marketing was a tremendous success in the 5 new plants opened last Spring in France and Germany. In fact, sales at those two plants have surpassed our Switzerland and Italy sales over the same period. Much of this sucess is due to your timely marketing campaign that was conducted during the first quarter. Congratulations to you and your staff on this fine effort.

Because of this positive experience, we have decided to expand our promotional campaign at our plants in Negras Piedras, Morelia, and Puebla. Would you please put together a proposal for these plants and send it to me by the end of next week. We are excited about this oportunity and look forward to recieving your proposal.

¶ Again, nice work on the France and Germany effort.

Sincerely, | Harold Deforey | V.P., Marketing | c: Mari Lynn Somnolet, James Lafforgue

Table Test 5-54

Boxed Table

HEMATOLOGY REPORT			
Patient Name:		**Date:**	
	WBC		Glucose
	Hemoglobin		Cholesterol
	PMN		BUN
	Bands		Calcium
	Lymphs		Phosphorous
	Mono		Bilirubin
	Eos		Uric acid
	Baso		Alkaline phosphate
	Platelets		Albumin
	Thyroid		Protein, total

Report Test 5-74

Summons

When this document is typed, the line numbers will vary from those shown here.

STATE OF NEBRASKA — IN DISTRICT COURT

COUNTY OF WAYNE — NORTHEAST JUDICIAL DISTRICT

PAUL C. CREWS 601 Thorman Street Wayne, NE 66787-2243 Plaintiff, vs. ANGELINA WASHINGTON Defendant.	)))))))))))	NO. ______________ SUMMONS

THE STATE OF NEBRASKA TO THE ABOVE-NAMED DEFENDANTS:

You are hereby summoned and required to appear and defend against the Complaint in this action, which is hereby served upon you by serving upon the undersigned an Answer or other proper response within twenty (20) days after the service of the Summons and Complaint upon you, exclusive of the day of service.

If you fail to do so, judgment by default will be taken against you for the relief demanded in the Complaint.

SIGNED this ______ day of May, 20--.

____

Jeremy Richfield Attorney-at-Law
Box 148
Wayne, NE 67878-2648
Telephone: 402-555-1205
Attorney for Plaintiff

Part 6

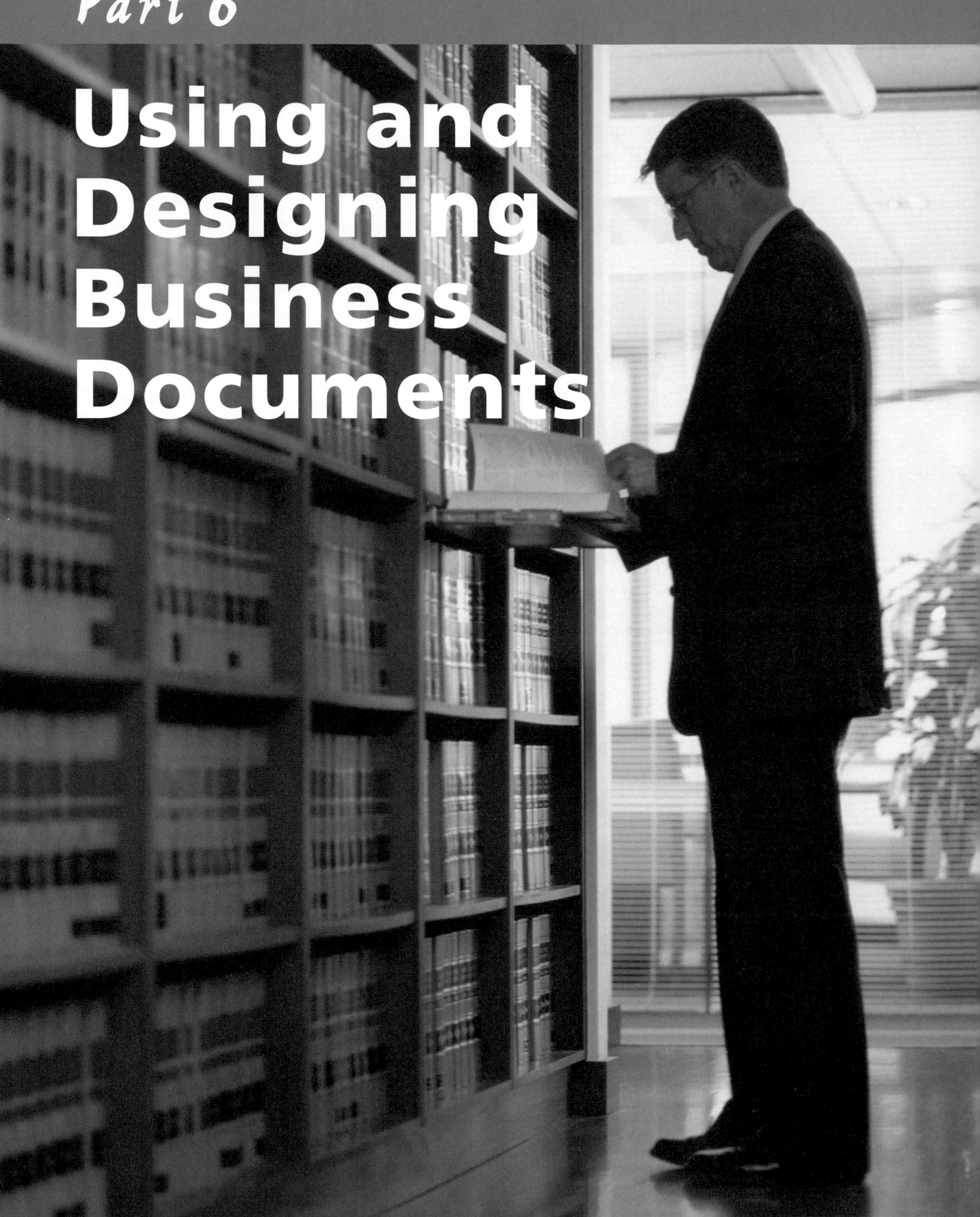

Using and Designing Business Documents

Keyboarding in Legal Services Careers

A career in legal services can take many forms. Lawyers, of course, are responsible for legal work, but a number of other positions in the legal services field are available. Often, lawyers assign tasks to paralegals. Paralegals—also referred to as legal assistants—have taken on a larger percentage of responsibilities in recent years. Another profession in the law field, that of court reporter, requires excellent communication skills. Court reporters are responsible for taking exact notes in court, in meetings, and at any other event where an accurate account of the proceedings is needed. Keyboarding skills are important for many job functions in legal services careers, and they can prove to give a job candidate an advantage.

Paralegals can work in many different business settings, but they are found most commonly in law firms and government offices. Court reporters are responsible for providing an accurate and detailed legal record of any proceeding. For individuals working in the legal services field, strong communication skills, written and spoken, are very important, but being able to convey ideas in a typed report in a timely manner is even more important.

Objectives

KEYBOARDING

- Type at least 50 words per minute on a 5-minute timed writing with no more than 5 errors.

LANGUAGE ARTS

- Refine proofreading skills and correctly use proofreaders' marks.
- Use capitals, punctuation, and grammar correctly.
- Improve composing and spelling skills.
- Recognize subject/verb agreement.

WORD PROCESSING

- Use the word processing commands necessary to complete the document processing activities.

DOCUMENT PROCESSING

- Design office forms, office publications, and Web pages.

TECHNICAL

- Answer at least 90 percent of the questions correctly on an objective test.

Unit 21

Using and Designing Office Forms

LESSON 101
Using Correspondence Templates

LESSON 102
Using Report Templates

LESSON 103
Designing Letterheads

LESSON 104
Designing Notepads

LESSON 105
Designing Miscellaneous Office Forms

From the Desk of Amber Bristol

From the Desk of Amber Bristol

❑ *Urgent*
❑ *Do Today*
❑ *Follow-Up*

❑ *Urgent*
❑ *Do Today*
❑ *Follow-Up*

From the Desk of Amber Bristol

From the Desk of Amber Bristol

❑ *Urgent*
❑ *Do Today*
❑ *Follow-Up*

❑ *Urgent*
❑ *Do Today*
❑ *Follow-Up*

Memorandum

To: Naoe Okubo, Senior Graphics Artist

CC: Roy Phillips, Marketing Manager

From: Gloria Hernandez, Vice President

Date: June 17, 20--

Re: Web Site Redesign

Our Web site needs a complete reorganization and redesign. I know this assignment will be a major challenge, and I have full confidence in your experience and ability. Within the next week, please contact five Web design firms and make arrangements for a formal presentation to you and your staff. Invite Roy Phillips and his staff in marketing as well. When you have chosen the two best candidates, submit your findings to our key executives in a formal presentation. The better of the two will then be chosen.

Because our Web site is critical to our sales and marketing efforts, you must make this assignment a top priority. If you need temporary help to support you in your efforts, let me know.

Thank you for your continued good work, Naoe. I look forward to the presentation and your recommendations.

wn

WINTER SPORTS

2820 Cerillos Road • Santa Fe, NM 87505 • 505-555-3496 • www.wintersports.com

Using Correspondence Templates

Goals

- Improve speed and accuracy
- Refine language arts skills in grammar
- Format correspondence using a template

A. Type 2 times.

A. WARMUP

```
1      The secretary made a reservation on Flight #847; it     11
2  departs at exactly 3:05 on July 6. A sizable number of      22
3  key executives (about 1/2) requested seats in Rows G to M.  33
   | 1 | 2 | 3 | 4 | 5 | 6 | 7 | 8 | 9 | 10 | 11 | 12
```

SKILLBUILDING

B. Take three 12-second timed writings on each line. The scale below the last line shows your wpm speed for a 12-second timed writing.

B. 12-SECOND SPEED SPRINTS

```
4  Bob will lend all the keys to you if you will fix the leak.
5  Ruth wanted to thank you for all of the work you did today.
6  Both of the books will have to be sent to her by next week.
7  Dick paid her half of the money when she signed the papers.
   5  10  15  20  25  30  35  40  45  50  55  60
```

C. PROGRESSIVE PRACTICE: ALPHABET

If you are not using the GDP software, turn to page SB-7 and follow the directions for this activity.

D. PROGRESSIVE PRACTICE: NUMBERS

If you are not using the GDP software, turn to page SB-11 and follow the directions for this activity.

LANGUAGE ARTS

E. Study the rules at the right.

E. ADJECTIVES AND ADVERBS AND AGREEMENT

RULE ▶ adjective/adverb

Use comparative adjectives and adverbs (*-er, more*, and *less*) when referring to two nouns or pronouns; use superlative adjectives and adverbs (*-est, most*, and *least*) when referring to more than two.

The shorter of the two training sessions is the more helpful one.

The longest of the three training sessions is the least helpful one.

RULE ▶ agreement nearer noun

If two subjects are joined by *or, either/or, neither/nor,* or *not only/but also,* make the verb agree with the subject nearer to the verb.

Neither the coach nor the players are at home.

Not only the coach but also the referee is at home.

But: Both the coach and the referee are at home.

Edit the sentences to correct any errors in grammar.

```
8  Of the three printers, the faster one was the most expensive.
9  Of the two phones purchased, the first one is the better model.
10 The quietest of the five printers is also the less expensive.
11 Not only the manager but also the employees wants to attend.
12 Neither the printer nor the monitors is in working order.
13 Either Mr. Cortez or his assistants have to sign the order.
14 Coffee or soft drinks is available for the afternoon session.
15 Not only the manual but also the software were mailed.
```

FORMATTING

F. FILLING IN FORMS

Many business forms can be created by using templates that are provided within word processing software. When a template is opened, a generic form is displayed on the screen. Specific information that is appropriate for that form may then be added.

Template forms contain data fields that correspond to blank sections on printed forms. For example, a memo template may include the guide words *To:, CC:, From:, Date:*, and *Re*: for the subject. Templates are usually designed so that you can replace data in fields easily by clicking in the field and typing or by selecting the information you want to replace and typing. Built-in styles are also readily available.

You can customize a generic template by filling in repetitive information (such as the company name and telephone number) and save it as a new template. Then each time you open that newly created template, the customized information appears automatically.

Word Processing Manual

G. WORD PROCESSING: CORRESPONDENCE TEMPLATES

Study Lesson 101 in your word processing manual. Complete all of the shaded steps while at your computer. Then format the jobs that follow.

DOCUMENT PROCESSING

Form 101-1 ▶

Memo Template

Note: You may want to read and print the information in the template before deleting it.

1. Select the first memo template listed in your word processing software.
2. Follow the directions on the template to type the information for this memo, using the built-in styles as needed.
3. Use the month/day/year format for the date.
4. Type the information for the memo from the copy shown on the next page.

Note 1: In the body of the memo, the cursor will automatically drop down 1 blank line below a paragraph when you press the ENTER key.

Note 2: Remove any extra text boxes that may appear on the page as part of the default memo template.

To: Naoe Okubo Senior Graphic Artist

CC: Mr. Roy Phillips, Marketing Manager

From: Gloria Hernandez, Vice President

Date: June 17, 20--

Re: Website Redesign

¶ Our web site needs a complete redesign and reorganization. I know this assignment is a major challenge, and I have full confidence in your skill and ability. Within the next week, you should contact 5 web design firms and make arrangements for a formal presentation to you and your staff. Please invite Roy Phillips and his staff in Marketing as well. When you have chosen the two best candidates, submit your findings to key executives in a presentation. The better of the two will then be chosen.

adjective/adverb

adjective/adverb

¶ Because our web site is crucial to our sales and marketing efforts you must make this assignment a top priority. If you need temporary help to support you in your efforts, let me know. Thank you for your continued good work, Naoe. I look forward to your presentation and your recomendations.

urs

Form 101-2

Letter Template

1. Select the first letter template listed in your word processing software.
2. Follow the template directions to type the information for this letter using the built-in styles as needed.
   Note: Delete the company slogan text box at the bottom of the template.
3. The company name is `Global Web Resources`.
4. Type each line of the return address on a separate line. (The setup of the return address should be similar to the arrangement you use for the inside address.)

   The return address is as follows:
   `575 Eighth Avenue, Suite 1104`
   `New York, NY 10018`
   `212-555-3495`
   `www.globalwebresources.com`
5. Use the default spacing provided by the template between the date and the inside address.
6. Type the rest of the information into the template, as indicated in the copy below, using standard business letter format for a block-style letter.
   Note: Save this job as FORM 101-2.

June 23, 20-- | Naoe Okubo | Contempo Fashions | 22802 Soledad Canyon | Santa Clarita, CA 91355 | Dear Ms. Okubo:

¶ Thank you for your request for more information on Web page design, layout, and graphics. I have enclosed some brochures that address some of your questions.

agreement nearer noun

¶ Ms. Ina Phillips is our senior account manager in your area. Either her staff members or Ms. Phillips is going to schedule an appointment with you and your staff for a formal presentation of our design portfolios this week. The best way to answer your questions and to help you reach a decision is to

(Continued on next page)

have you see examples of some of the Web sites we have developed for other clients in the fashion industry. I know you will be impressed by the creativity and innovative concepts that Global Web Resources is known for in this business.

¶If you would like a preview now, please go to www.globalwebresources.com and click the link entitled Professional Images to see some of our best designs. Again, thank you for your interest in our services.

Sincerely, | Linda Vigil | Vice President | urs | Enclosures

adjective/adverb

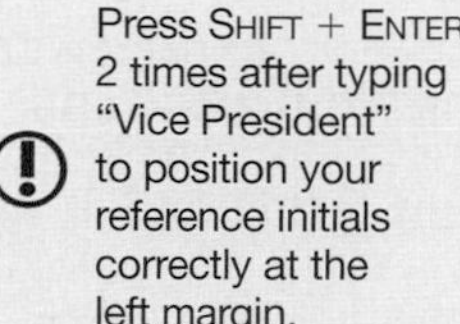

Press SHIFT + ENTER 2 times after typing "Vice President" to position your reference initials correctly at the left margin.

Form 101-3

Memo Template

Select the first memo template listed in your word processing software.

To: Roy Phillips, Marketing Manager | **CC:** Gloria Hernandez, Vice President | **From:** Naoe Okubo, Senior Graphics Artist | **Date:** August 7, 20-- | **Re:** Web Site Redesign

¶I have contacted five Web design firms for formal presentations in our executive boardroom. A schedule of the meeting dates and times is attached. Because Ms. Hernandez has indicated that this assignment is to take top priority, not only current projects but also future work is to be put on hold. If you need any temporary help with any projects in progress, let me know.

agreement nearer noun

¶The Web design firms that have been scheduled are very innovative and creative. The presentations should be exciting. Ask your staff to prepare for the meeting by visiting the Web sites and doing some research on each company. Please forward this memo to the members of your staff.

urs | Attachment

Keyboarding Connection

Transferring Text From a Web Page

Have you ever wished you could copy the text from a Web page? You can!

To select the desired text to copy, click in front of the text and drag to the end of it. (If the text won't highlight, try to click at the end of the desired text and drag backward.) To copy the Web text, from the Edit menu, select Copy. Open your word processing document. Position the cursor where you want to paste the text. From the Edit menu of the word processor, select Paste. The text will appear in the word processing document.

When you copy text information from the Web, you must cite the source in your word processing document by giving the URL (Web page address), Web page name, and author, if given.

YOUR TURN Open a Web page. Copy some text and paste it in a word processing document.

Lesson 102

Using Report Templates

Goals

- Type at least 48wpm/5′/5e
- Format reports using a template

A. Type 2 times.

A. WARMUP

     I am glad the office measures just 15 × 23* (*feet) 11
because the carpet is quite expensive! At $64/yard, we 22
can't afford any mistakes; contact v&zcarpets@mail.com. 33
| 1 | 2 | 3 | 4 | 5 | 6 | 7 | 8 | 9 | 10 | 11 | 12

SKILLBUILDING

B. PACED PRACTICE

If you are not using the GDP software, turn to page SB-14 and follow the directions for this activity.

C. Take two 5-minute timed writings. Review your speed and errors.

Goal: At least 48wpm/5′/5e

C. 5-MINUTE TIMED WRITING

Job stress is not that uncommon in today's workplace. 11
There may be many causes of job stress; but the most likely 23
reasons it occurs are overwork, possible layoffs, conflicts 35
with people at work, or just simply working in a job that 47
is no longer to your liking. 52
Symptoms of job stress are common to many people, and 63
they include changes in sleeping patterns, short temper, 75
upset stomach, headache, and low morale. Although many of 86
us suffer from one or more of the above symptoms, we should 98
take them seriously if the symptoms continue or if we tend 110
to experience three or four of the symptoms at the same 121
time continuously. 125
Sometimes it is possible to reduce the stress in your 136
work by taking a commonsense approach to the situation. If 148
you think that you are being overworked, take a vacation or 160
avoid taking work home with you. If you are concerned about 172
layoffs, then be certain that you are prepared to make a 183
career change if it is required. If you have conflicts with 195
your boss or with others at the office, try to work them 207
out by discussing the issues with the people involved to be 219
certain they understand all aspects of the conflict. Then, 231
work together to minimize any future conflicts. 240

| 1 | 2 | 3 | 4 | 5 | 6 | 7 | 8 | 9 | 10 | 11 | 12

FORMATTING

Word Processing Manual

D. WORD PROCESSING: REPORT TEMPLATES

Study Lesson 102 in your word processing manual. Complete all of the shaded steps while at your computer. Then format the jobs that follow.

DOCUMENT PROCESSING

Form 102-4

Report Template

Note: You may want to read and print the information in the template before deleting it.

1. Select the first report template listed in your word processing software.
2. Type the information for this report using the built-in template styles as needed.
3. On the title page, type the following address:

   575 Eighth Avenue, Suite 1104
   New York, NY 10018
   212-555-3495
   www.globalwebresources.com.

4. The company name is Global Web Resources.
5. The title is Web Design Proposal.
6. The subtitle is Strategies for the Online Presence of Contempo Fashions.
7. Use the same title and subtitle on the second page of the report.
8. Type the rest of the information into the template, as indicated in the copy below.

Introduction

¶ Two major issues need to be addressing ed in terms of the web # site design for Contempo Fashions. The sites most obvious weakness is a its lack of unity. The content seems to be out of sync with the design. The This division is definitely noticeable to the casual observe r.

¶ Often those in charge of content don't have any background in html or coding of any kind, and fell feel locked into the current design because they simply don't know what there their options are. Those in charge of the design can get caught up in trying to create an attractive page that doesn't really effectively work with the content. Global Web Resources is in it the business of providing workable solutions that will to address both of these needs.

Content Issues

¶ The content is by far the first and most important element in a web site. If the content is not effective, it doesnt matter how attractive the design is because noone will bother to read beyond the first page or even the first line. Spelling and grammar must be checked with meticulous care. The credibility of your company is at stake. The readability of the web site can be improved dramatically. Headings, subheadings, bullets and numbers are critical in making your pages readable. Visitors to your site scan for major headings and want to move quickly and efficiently to any items of interest. Visual separation between paragraphs is also critical for readability. The use of

(Continued on next page)

whitespace created by inserting blank lines between paragraphs is generally more effective than indenting paragraphs. Short lines and short pages make readers want to look at your pages rather than avoid them.

Design Issues

¶ The design of the web site is done well overall. Appropriate fonts, colors, and art were used in a manner that complements the image of Contempo Fashions. The site navigation is intuitive and easy to use. However, the design is dated and needs a new look.

¶ The 2 groups that are now managing the site must be given guidance in working together to produce a unified site that is both attractive and effective. The goals of the design group and those in charge of content must be brought into alignment in order to make the content work within the context of the current design. Global Web Resources has a web design solution that will bring the needs of these groups into alignment. Your redesigned site will be visually appealing, informative, and intuitive to the visitor. I look forward to our detailed presentation this week.

Form 102-5

Report Template

Open the file for Form 102-4 and make the following changes:

1. On the title page, change the address as follows:
   `8502 North Ashley Street`
   `Tampa, FL 33604`
   `813-555-1205`
   `www.CTI.com.`
2. The company name is `CompuTek International.`
3. Change the report title both on the title page and on the first page of the report to `Web Site Proposal.`
4. Change the report subtitle both on the title page and on the first page of the report to `Content and Design Recommendations for Contempo Fashions.`
5. Delete the second paragraph under the heading "Introduction."
6. Delete the second paragraph under the heading "Content Issues."
7. Delete the last paragraph of the report.
8. Move the insertion point to the end of the first paragraph under the heading "Design Issues," and press ENTER 1 time.
9. Use the Heading 1 style to add the heading `Solutions.`
10. Move to the end of the report, and add the following paragraphs.
    Paragraph 1:
    `Your Web site should always have new and updated content so that your visitors will have good reason to return. If you continue with your current Web site plan, the maintenance of your site will become a major responsibility. Hundreds of files will need to be maintained whenever you want to make a fundamental change to your site.`

(Continued on next page)

The best approach is to let your writers post new content themselves without having to worry about design issues. This is accomplished through a database-driven Web site.

Paragraph 2:

Building a database-driven Web site requires a great deal of technical expertise and tools such as scripting languages and relational database software. Your operating system must be compatible with these languages and databases. Server-side programming is also critical here. CompuTek International would build a database-driven site design and host the site to minimize technical troubleshooting issues. We look forward to our meeting this week.

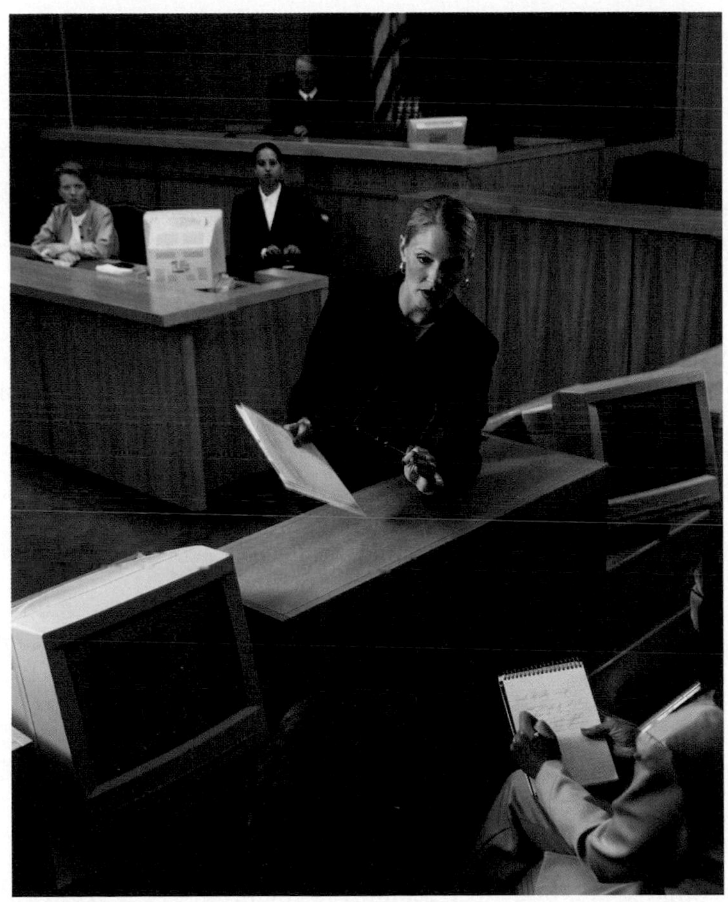

Designing Letterheads

Goals

- Improve speed and accuracy
- Refine language arts skills in composing
- Design letterheads

A. Type 2 times.

A. WARMUP

```
     Does Quentin know if 1/2 of the January order will be   11
ready? At 5:30 about 46% of the orders still hadn't been     22
mailed! Mr. Gray expects a very sizable loss this month.     34
| 1 | 2 | 3 | 4 | 5 | 6 | 7 | 8 | 9 | 10 | 11 | 12
```

SKILLBUILDING

B. DIAGNOSTIC PRACTICE: SYMBOLS AND PUNCTUATION

If you are not using the GDP software, turn to page SB-2 and follow the directions for this activity.

C. These paragraphs are made up of very short words, requiring the frequent use of the SPACE BAR. Do not pause before or after pressing the SPACE BAR. Type the paragraph 2 times.

C. TECHNIQUE PRACTICE: SPACE BAR

```
     He had the car in the shop and knew that the cost for
the work might be high. If the bill for the work was to be
more than he could pay, he knew that he would skip it. It
did not make any sense to put more money into the old car.
     If you are near the old shop, come in to see if you can
pay the bill at that time. If you are not able to pay it at
that time, you can come back to see us when you are able.
```

LANGUAGE ARTS

D. COMPOSING A MEMO

Compose the body of a memo to explain basic design guidelines. Refer to page 411—Section E, Designing a Form—frequently. Use the following suggestions for composing each paragraph:

Paragraph 1. Explain that a simple, balanced design is essential and that typefaces (fonts), attributes, and sizes should be limited.

Paragraph 2. Explain that white space should be used to make text easier to read and graphics easier to see.

Paragraph 3. Explain that word processing software is a powerful tool that makes experimenting easy.

FORMATTING

E. DESIGNING A FORM

Use the following guidelines to design an attractive, effective form:

1. Keep all elements of your design simple and balanced.
2. Limit the number of typefaces, attributes (bold, italics, and so on), and sizes. Using two typefaces is a good rule of thumb.
3. Use white space liberally to separate and open up text and graphics.
4. Use different alignments (left, center, right, and full) to add interest and emphasis.
5. Experiment and change—word processing software makes both easy to do.

Word Processing Manual

F. WORD PROCESSING: SMALL CAPS AND TEXT BOXES

Study Lesson 103 in your word processing manual. Complete all of the shaded steps while at your computer. Then format the jobs that follow.

DOCUMENT PROCESSING

Form 103-6

Letterhead Form

Note: When creating, sizing, or positioning a text box, switch to a whole-page view. When typing text, switch to a page-width view or larger as desired. As you add information to the text box, adjust the size of the text box as needed.

1. Change the left and right margins to 0.25 inch, and press ENTER 2 times.
2. Apply a border to the bottom of the second blank line.
3. Insert a picture of an elementary school or kindergarten.
4. Drag and size the picture so that it looks like the one in the illustration at the left and on page 410.
5. Create a text box next to the school, about the size and in the same position as the one in the illustration, to hold the business name.
6. Remove the line around the text box, and change the fill to none.
7. Change to Arial 18-point small caps, and center and type `Tutor Time`.
8. Change the font color as desired to coordinate with the picture.
9. Create a text box, about the size and in the same position as the one in the illustration, to hold the address of the business.
10. Remove the line around the text box, and change the fill to none.
11. Change the font to Arial 10 point, and right-align and type the lines of the address:

```
4219 Richmond Avenue,
Suite 205
Houston, TX 77027
713-555-7337
www.tutortime.com
```

(Continued on next page)

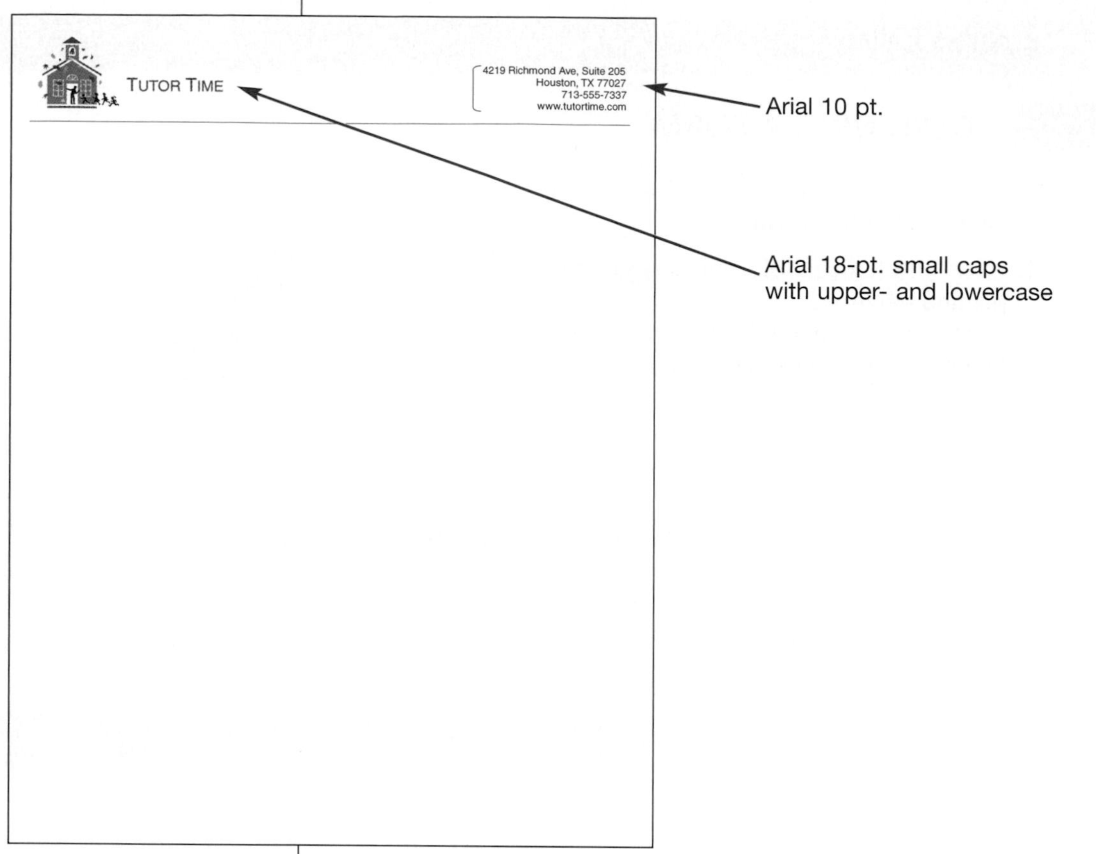

Form 103-7

Letterhead Form

1. Press ENTER 2 times, and insert a picture of your favorite winter sport.
2. Drag and size the picture so that it looks like the one in the illustration on the left and on page 411.
3. Create a text box, about the size and in the same position as the one in the illustration, to hold the name of the business.
4. Remove the line around the text box, and change the fill to none.
5. Change to Times New Roman Italic 24-point small caps, and type `Winter Sports` with upper- and lowercase.
6. Change the font color of the business name to coordinate with one of the colors in the picture.
7. Create a text box, about the size and in the same position as the one in the illustration, to hold the address of the business.
8. Change the font to Times New Roman 10 point and center and type the lines of the address, all on one continuous line.

   ```
   2820 Cerillos Road
   Santa Fe, NM 87505
   505-555-3496
   www.wintersports.com
   ```
9. Insert a diamond-shaped symbol between each item in the address block as shown in the illustration. Insert 1 space before and after the symbol.
10. Add a fill to the text box to coordinate with one of the colors in the picture.

(Continued on next page)

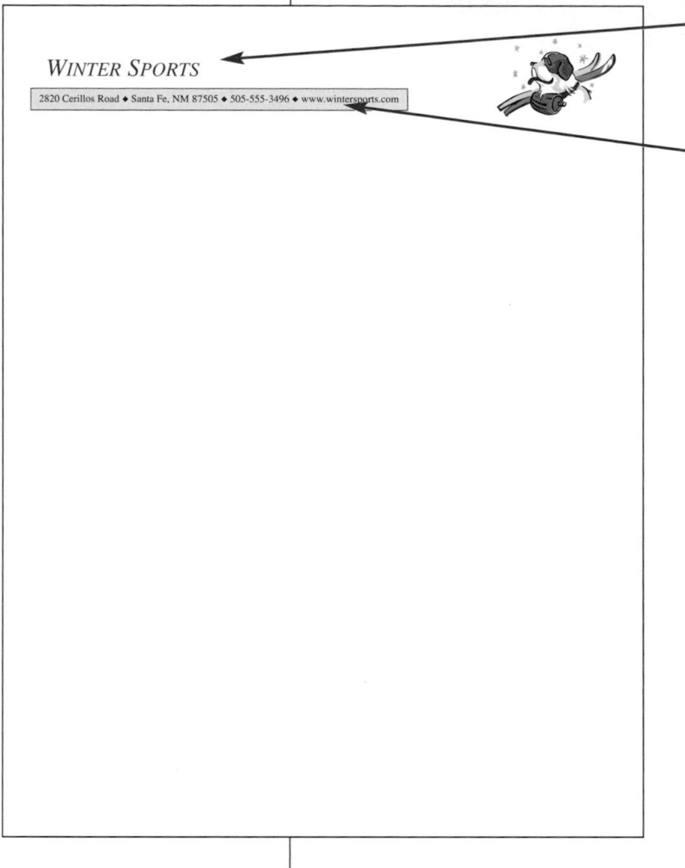

Times New Roman Italic 24-pt. small caps with upper- and lowercase

Times New Roman 10 pt.

Form 103-8

Letterhead Form

1. Create a letterhead design of your own—for you personally, for your school, or for a business.
2. Insert at least one picture that enhances the theme of the letterhead.
3. Remember to include complete information in the address block.
4. Try using fonts that you have not yet applied—experiment with point sizes and attributes.

Strategies for Career Success

Designing the Page for Readability

A well-designed document is appealing to the eye, is easy to read, and shows you are professional and competent. Follow these simple guidelines to increase the readability of your documents.

Use white space (that is, empty space) to make material easier to read by separating it from other text. Side margins should be equal. Create white space by varying paragraph length. The first and last paragraphs should be short—three to five typed lines.

Use bulleted or numbered lists to emphasize material. Lists are normally indented on the left. Make sure all the items in the list are grammatically parallel in structure. Use headings to introduce new material. Use full caps sparingly. Consider desktop publishing software to visually enhance your document. Remember to balance graphics, lists, and text.

YOUR TURN Review a document you have recently written. What page design and format techniques did you use to make the document more readable?

Designing Notepads

Goals

- Type at least 48wpm/5′/5e
- Design notepads

A. Type 2 times.

A. WARMUP

```
     This series* (*2 films, 9 minutes) by J. Zeller goes     11
beyond the "basics" of computers. Viewers keep requesting     22
an extension on the dates; this includes 3/2, 5/5, and 8/9.   34
| 1 | 2 | 3 | 4 | 5 | 6 | 7 | 8 | 9 | 10 | 11 | 12
```

SKILLBUILDING

B. MAP

Follow the GDP software directions for this exercise in improving keystroking accuracy.

C. Take two 5-minute timed writings. Review your speed and errors.

Goal: At least 48wpm/5′/5e

C. 5-MINUTE TIMED WRITING

Employers are always searching for people who have 10
salable skills. Having salable skills makes you unique and 22
desirable as an employee. Developing skills and qualities 34
such as a pleasing personality, a good sense of humor, a 45
positive attitude, an ability to get along with people, and 57
the ability to manage your time and prioritize your work 69
may help you find a job. 74
A tenacious person is persistent and maintains strong 85
work habits. He or she does not give up on a task easily 96
and always expects to finish the assigned task. 106
A good sense of humor and a positive attitude are two 117
traits that can help a person advance on the job. Although 128
there are times to be serious at work, sometimes you have 140
to look at things humorously. If you maintain a positive 151
attitude, other workers will like to work with you. 162
When you acquire the skills to manage your time and 172
prioritize your work, you will be successful in anything 184
you try to do. When you are given an assignment, ask for 195
guidelines so that you will know what needs to be done and 207
in what order. Then try to complete the assignment in a 218
timely fashion. The skills may be difficult to learn, but 230
you will be glad you can manage your time and work. 240

| 1 | 2 | 3 | 4 | 5 | 6 | 7 | 8 | 9 | 10 | 11 | 12

FORMATTING

Word Processing Manual

D. WORD PROCESSING: PRINT OPTIONS

Study Lesson 104 in your word processing manual. Complete all of the shaded steps while at your computer. Then format the jobs that follow.

Form 104-9

Notepad Form

Many ink-jet printers do not print beyond the bottom half inch on a sheet of paper. Keep this in mind when positioning objects at the bottom of a page.

1. Press ENTER 2 times, and insert a picture of an office desk or a picture related to an office notepad.
2. Drag and size the picture so that it looks similar to the one in the illustration on this page.
3. Create a text box, about the size and in the same position as the one in the illustration, to hold the words "From the Desk of Amber Bristol."
4. Remove the line around the text box, and change the fill to none.
5. Change to Arial Bold 18 point, and center and type `From the Desk of Amber Bristol` inside the text box.
6. Create a text box, about the size and in the same position as the one in the illustration, to hold the check box list at the bottom of the notepad.
7. Remove the line around the text box, and change the fill to none.
8. Insert a check box using Wingdings Italic 18 point. Space 1 time.
9. Change to Arial Italic 28 point, type `Urgent` inside the text box, and press ENTER 1 time.
10. Repeat steps 8 and 9 for the remaining lines in the check box list, adding the words `Do Today` and `Follow-Up`.
11. Change to a whole-page view, and select and copy the entire document.
12. Move to the end of the document and insert three hard page breaks to create three additional blank pages.
13. Paste the copied document into each of the three newly created pages.
14. Use the print option to print four pages per sheet on 8.5- × 11-inch paper.

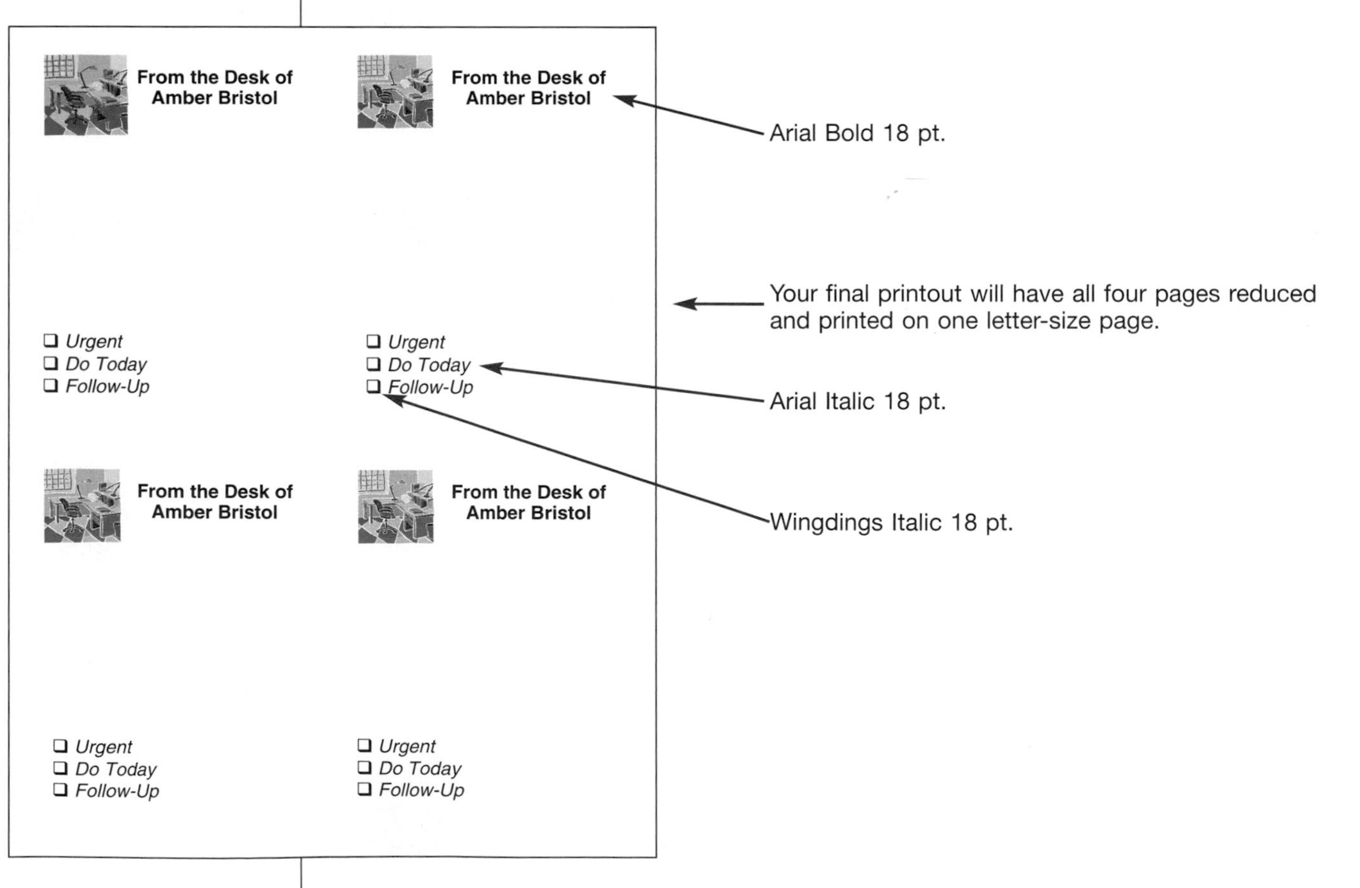

Form 104-10

Notepad Form

1. Press ENTER 2 times, and insert a picture of an office desk or a picture related to a musical note or a personalized office note.
2. Drag and size the picture so that it looks similar to the one in the illustration on this page.
3. Create a text box, about the size and in the same position as the one in the illustration, to hold the words "Just a Note to Say . . ."
4. Remove the line around the text box, and change the fill to none.
5. Change to a script font of your choice in 20-point bold and italic.
6. Center and type `Just a Note to Say` followed by 1 space and 3 periods with 1 space after each period.
7. Create a text box, about the size and in the same position as the one in the illustration, to hold the words at the bottom of the notepad.
8. Change to the same script font used in the first text box, also in 20-point size, and center and type `From the Desk of Darin Diaz` inside the text box.
9. Change to a whole-page view, and select and copy the entire document.
10. Move to the end of the document, and insert three hard page breaks to create three additional blank pages.
11. Paste the copied document into each of the three newly created pages.
12. Use the print option to print four pages per sheet on 8.5- × 11-inch paper.

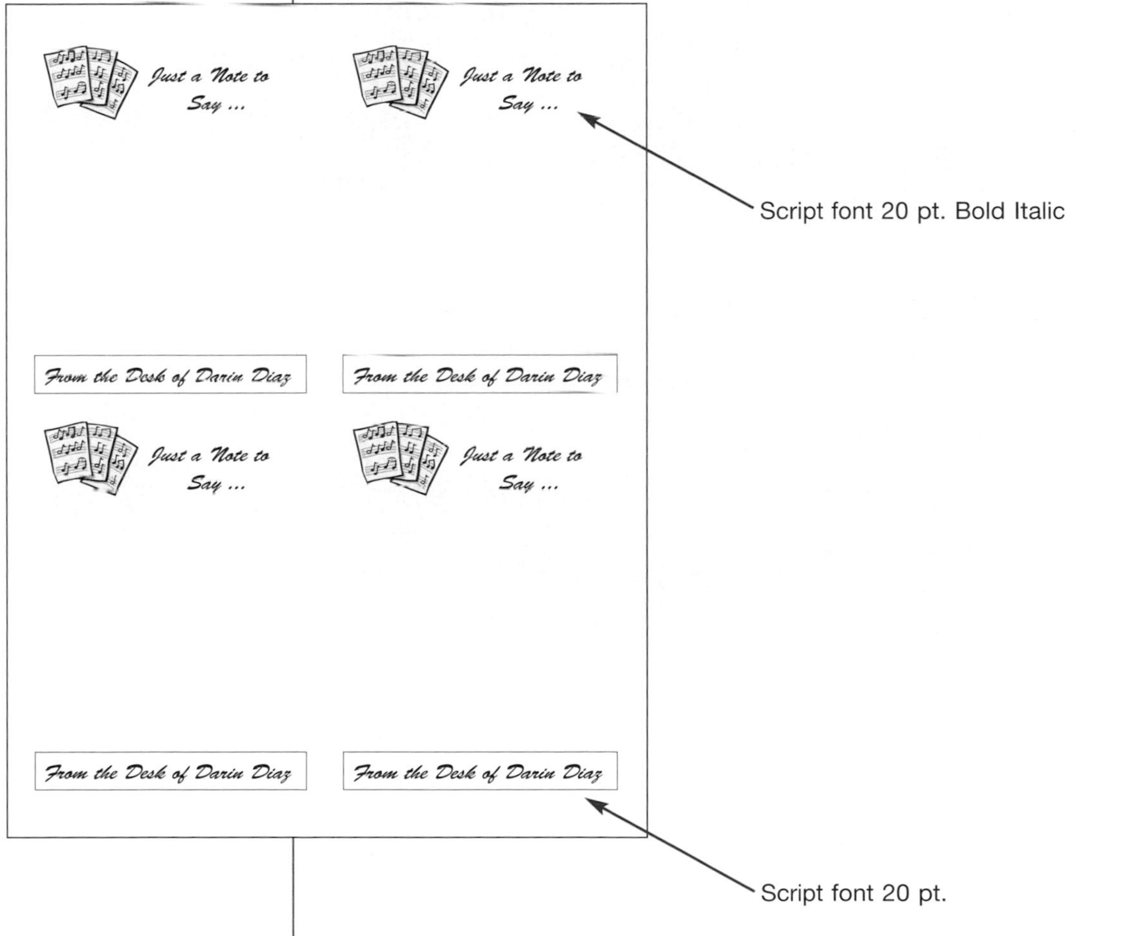

Form 104-11

Notepad Form

1. Create a notepad design of your own—for you personally, for your school, or for a business.
2. Insert at least one picture that enhances the theme of the notepad.
3. Insert at least one text box with a fill.
4. Try using fonts that you have not yet applied. Experiment with point sizes and attributes.

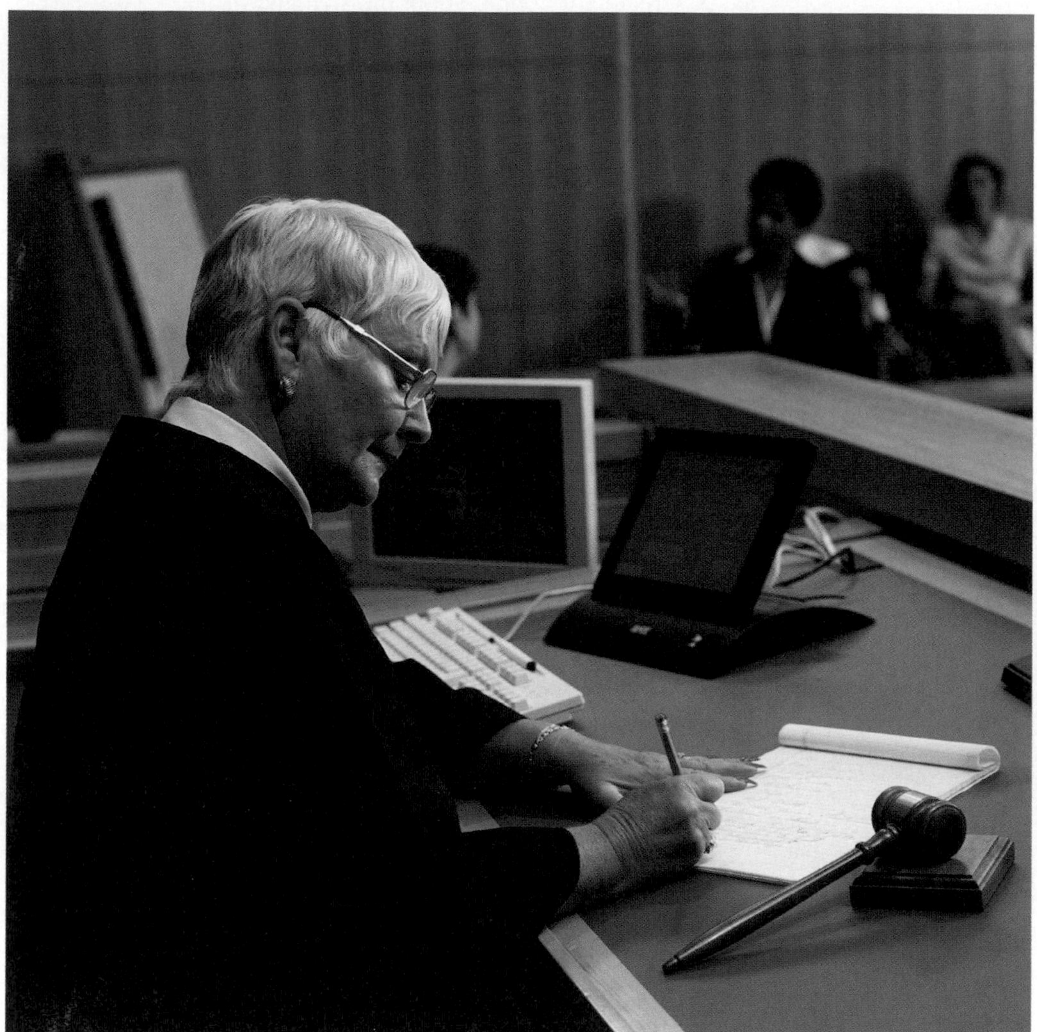

Designing Miscellaneous Office Forms

Goals

- Improve speed and accuracy
- Refine language arts skills in proofreading
- Design miscellaneous office forms

A. Type 2 times.

A. WARMUP

```
1      Item #876 won't be ordered until 9/10. Did you gather   11
2  all requests and input them exactly as they appeared? Zack  23
3  will never be satisfied until he contacts jack@orders.com.  34
   | 1 | 2 | 3 | 4 | 5 | 6 | 7 | 8 | 9 | 10 | 11 | 12
```

SKILLBUILDING

PPP PRETEST → PRACTICE → POSTTEST

PRETEST
Take a 1-minute timed writing. Review your speed and errors.

B. PRETEST: Vertical Reaches

```
4      The man knelt on the lawn and used a knife with skill   11
5  to raise the valve away from the brace. His back ached in   23
6  vain as he crawled over the knoll to fix the flawed valve.  34
   | 1 | 2 | 3 | 4 | 5 | 6 | 7 | 8 | 9 | 10 | 11 | 12
```

PRACTICE
Speed Emphasis:
If you made no more than 1 error on the Pretest, type each *individual* line 2 times.
Accuracy Emphasis:
If you made 2 or more errors, type each *group* of lines (as though it were a paragraph) 2 times.

C. PRACTICE: Up Reaches

```
7  aw away award crawl straw drawn sawed drawl await flaw lawn
8  se self sense raise these prose abuse users serve send seem
9  ki kind kites skill skier skims skips skits kilts king skid
```

D. PRACTICE: Down Reaches

```
10 ac ache track paced brace races facts crack acute back aces
11 kn knob knife kneel knows knack knelt known knoll knot knew
12 va vain vague value valve evade naval rival avail vats vase
```

POSTTEST
Repeat the Pretest timed writing and compare performance.

E. POSTTEST: Discrimination Practice

F. Take a 1-minute timed writing on the first paragraph to establish your base speed. Then take four 1-minute timed writings on the remaining paragraphs. As soon as you equal or exceed your base speed on one paragraph, advance to the next, more difficult paragraph.

F. SUSTAINED PRACTICE: SYLLABIC INTENSITY

13 People continue to rent autos for personal use or for 11
14 their work, and the car-rental business continues to grow. 23
15 When you rent a car, look carefully at the insurance cost. 35
16 You might also have to pay a mileage charge for the car. 46

17 It is likely that a good deal of insurance coverage is 11
18 part of the standard rental cost. But you might be urged 23
19 to procure extra medical, property, and collision coverage. 35
20 If you accept, be ready to see your rental charge increase. 46

21 Perhaps this is not necessary, as you may already have 11
22 the kind of protection you want in a policy that you have 23
23 at the present time. By reviewing your own auto insurance 34
24 policy, you may easily save a significant amount of money. 46

25 Paying mileage charges could result in a really large 11
26 bill. This is especially evident when the trips planned 22
27 involve destinations that are many miles apart. Complete a 34
28 total review of traveling plans before making a decision. 43

LANGUAGE ARTS

G. Compare these lines with lines 25-28 in the Sustained Practice drill above. Edit the lines to correct any errors.

G. PROOFREADING

29 Paying milage charges could result in a very large
30 bill. This is especially evident when the trips planned
31 involve destinations that are manymiles apart. complete a
32 total review of traveling plans before making a decsion.

DOCUMENT PROCESSING

Form 105-12

Directory Form

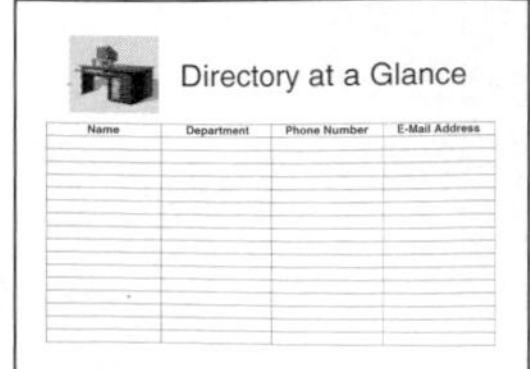

1. Change the page orientation to landscape.
2. Change the top margin to 2.3 inches, and the other margins to 0.75 inch.
3. Press ENTER 1 time.
4. Create a boxed table with 4 columns and 17 rows.
5. Select the entire table and change the font to Arial Bold 18 point.
6. Type these column headings in Row 1: `Name | Department | Phone Number | E-Mail Address`. Change the alignment in the row to center.
7. Move to the top of the document, and insert a picture, associated with a directory, in the same position as the one in the illustration on the left and on page 419.
8. Insert a text box, about the size and in the same position as the one in the illustration, to hold the heading.
9. Change to Arial 48 point, and center and type `Directory at a Glance` inside the text box.
10. Remove the line around the text box, and change the fill to none.
11. Add shading to the cells in Row 1 of the boxed table, using a color that complements the picture.

(Continued on next page)

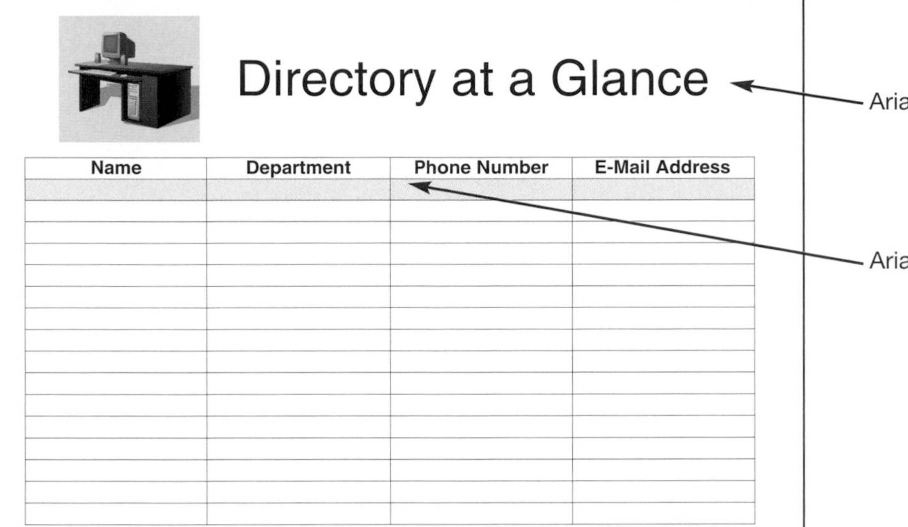

Form 105-13

Sign-In Form

1. Change the top margin to 2 inches and the other margins to 0.75 inch.
2. Create a boxed table with 4 columns and 30 rows.
3. Select Row 1 and change the font to Arial Bold 18 point.
4. Type these column headings in Row 1: `Name | Time In | Doctor's Name | Purpose`. Change the alignment in the row to center.
5. Adjust the column widths manually so they appear similar to the column widths in the illustration on the left and on page 420.
6. Select Rows 2-29 and change the font to Arial Bold 16 point.
7. Insert a picture of an office desk or clip art related to an office notepad.
8. Move the insertion point outside the table, then insert a text box, about the size and in the same position as the one in the illustration, to hold the name of the medical group.
9. Change to Times New Roman 48 point, and center and type `Facey Medical Group`.
10. Remove the line around the text box, and change the fill to none.
11. Create a text box, about the size and in the same position as the one in the illustration, to hold the date line.
12. Change to Arial Bold 12 point, and type `Date:` followed by a series of underlines to form a date line similar to the one in the illustration.
13. Remove the fill and the lines around the text box.
14. Create a text box, about the size and in the same position as the one in the illustration, to hold the names of the doctors.
15. Change to Times New Roman Italic 12 point, and type the following doctors' names in a bulleted list:

    ```
    Dr. Mary Chavez
    Dr. Irving K. Levine
    Dr. Evelyn Jones
    ```
16. Remove the line around the text box, and change the fill to none.
17. Change the font color of the words on the form as desired to coordinate with the picture.

(Continued on next page)

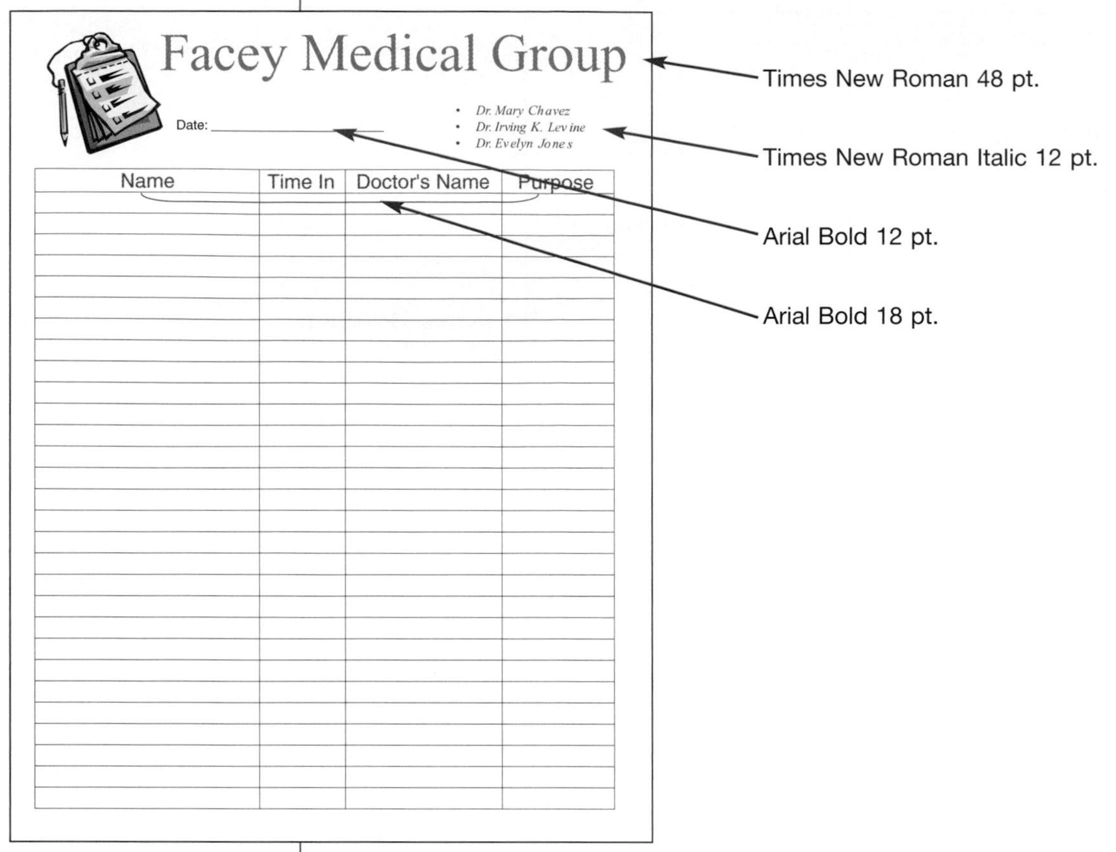

Form 105-14

Memo Template

Select the first memo template listed in your word processing software.

Progress and Proofreading Check

Documents designated as Proofreading Checks serve as a check of your proofreading skill. Your goal is to have zero typographical errors when the GDP software first scores the document.

To: Gloria Hernandez, Vice President | **CC:** Roy Phillips, Marketing Manager | **From:** Naoe Okubo, Senior Graphics Artist | **Date:** September 3, 20-- | **Re:** Web Site Redesign

¶ I have finished evaluating the five Web design firms that made formal presentations to our Web site team last week. The two finalists are Global Web Resources and CompuTek International. Their portfolios and presentations were very impressive. I believe either firm would be an excellent choice. Mr. Phillips agrees with this assessment.

¶ I have arranged for a formal presentation to our key executives for Wednesday afternoon of next week in our corporate dining room. We will have a luncheon first followed by the presentations. I have attached key information from the portfolios of both firms as well as details of Wednesday's meeting. Please let me know if you need any further information.

urs | Attachment

Unit 22

Designing Office Publications

Save hours of time and lots of money by using the Internet wisely when you plan your travel. You can shop for the best airline rates and even name your own price if you are flexible in your travel plans.

Several good books are available to help you use the Internet for your travel plans. Please check our web site at www.TTC.com for suggested books.

Focus on Dallas-Fort Worth

Although this is the world's second busiest airport, it is surprisingly easy to use. However, the transportation between terminals is slow.

LOVE FIELD

Love Field is a $10 to $15 taxi ride from downtown Dallas. The phone number is 214-555-6073.

Love Field is the hub of Western Airlines, which offers service within Texas, to many cities in the surrounding states, and, with stops, to destinations as far away as Chicago.

BETWEEN THE AIRPORT AND TOWN

It costs around $30 to get

Texas Tidbits

- To receive mail while traveling in Dallas, have it sent c/o General Delivery at the city's main post office.
- Most businesses open between 8 a.m. and 10 a.m. and close around 6 p.m. Many are also open on weekends.
- Banks operate weekdays from 9 a.m. until 2 or 3 p.m., and some are also open on Saturday mornings.
- Post offices are open weekdays from 8 a.m. to 5 p.m. and Saturday mornings.

The Traveler's Connection

A Newsletter From E-Travel.com

Volume 9, Issue No. 5 Spring 20--

In This Issue:
A Few Tips for the Smart Traveler, Page 1
Planning Your Travel Online, Page 1
Focus on Dallas-Fort Worth, Page 2
Texas Tidbits, Page 2
Thistle Hill, Page 2

A Few Tips for the Smart Traveler

We all have visions of the perfect vacation. They usually include a beautiful hotel, a comfortable room, great food, and wonderful entertainment. Unfortunately, sometimes our vision doesn't exactly align itself with reality, and our dream has suddenly turned into a nightmare. You can avoid this situation if you will do some smart advance planning.

Here are some smart travel tips that can turn your dream vacation into a reality:

- Do your homework. Your best bet is to find out all you can about your destination before you do anything else. Find a good travel agent, do your own research on the Internet, and buy some good travel books on your destination in your favorite bookstore.

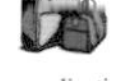

- Carry medications and other essentials with you. To avoid a disaster, carry everything you can't function without in the event that your luggage is lost. This would include medications, money, tickets, toiletries, visas, passports, eyeglasses, and anything else you can think of that is irreplaceable in the course of a day or two.

- Buy travel insurance. If you are taking an expensive vacation and are not completely sure you can make it, buying travel insurance is a wise expenditure. Many people today have children and aging parents whose needs are unpredictable.
- Confirm all reservations. Be sure that all your reservations including hotels, cars, and entertainment are confirmed and that you have the different confirmation numbers and phone numbers written down. Nothing can ruin a trip faster than finding out that you don't have a place to sleep or suitable transportation.

You will find that if you take these tips to heart, your vacation will be just as wonderful as you imagined!

Planning Your Travel Online

The Internet has opened up a wealth of information that used to be the domain of individual travel agencies. If you have a computer and Internet access, you can make reservations, buy tickets, book entertainment packages, and do any number of other things.

Page 1

Global Savings & Loan

Your Guide to Online Banking

Account	ATM Card	Check Writing	Monthly Fee
Regular Checking	None	Unlimited	$ 9.00
Interest Checking	Express Card	Unlimited	10.00
Basic Checking	Express Card	Unlimited	4.50
Student Checking	Express Card	Unlimited	3.00

Note: Fees may apply to telephone banking calls and the use of the ATM Express Card.

Designing Cover Pages

Goals

- Type at least 49wpm/5′/5e
- Design cover pages

A. Type 2 times.

A. WARMUP

```
     Buzz told us that Flight #7864 got into Phoenix just     11
3 minutes before Vick's! This is quite remarkable when        22
you realize that we never planned for such a "coincidence."   34
|  1  |  2  |  3  |  4  |  5  |  6  |  7  |  8  |  9  |  10  |  11  |  12
```

SKILLBUILDING

B. PROGRESSIVE PRACTICE: ALPHABET

If you are not using the GDP software, turn to page SB-7 and follow the directions for this activity.

C. DIAGNOSTIC PRACTICE: NUMBERS

If you are not using the GDP software, turn to page SB-5 and follow the directions for this activity.

Keyboarding Connection

Searching the Yellow Pages

Do you find the Yellow Pages of your phone directory handy? Try the Internet as an alternate source. Many of the Web's search engines have a Yellow Pages feature that is quite useful.

You can use the Yellow Pages feature to search for mailing addresses and phone numbers of businesses and organizations. The Yellow Pages link appears in most leading Internet search engines. These search engines may also provide a map of the location of the business or organization.

The Yellow Pages feature of a search engine is like having all the phone directories in the United States at your fingertips.

YOUR TURN Click the Yellow Pages feature on one of your favorite search engines. Search for a business in your city by name and then by category. Did you retrieve the address and phone number of the business using both search methods?

D. Take two 5-minute timed writings. Review your speed and errors.

Goal: At least 49wpm/5′/5e

D. 5-MINUTE TIMED WRITING

Why do people choose a particular career? Your first 11
instinct might likely be to say that people work to make 22
money. That may be true, but extensive research has shown 34
that many other factors are considered just as important 45
and that these factors should be carefully considered when 57
you are about to accept a new position. 65
There are many rewards that a job can provide such as 76
a chance to be creative, or the chance to spend time with 88
people whose company you enjoy, or the feeling that you are 100
doing something useful for yourself or for your employer. 111
The quality of the work environment is also an important 123
consideration in choosing a career, as is the chance to 134
work closely with people on a daily basis. 142
Obviously, your career should allow you to advance in 153
your field and to be competitive for promotions. You should 165
be able to see a clear line for advancement in your job and 177
be given a chance to demonstrate your abilities so that 189
your coworkers and supervisors recognize your strengths. 200
Parallel to these factors is the need for your job to give 212
you adequate challenges on a daily, continuing basis. If 223
your work is not challenging, boredom will set in, and you 235
might soon be looking for a change in your career. 245

| 1 | 2 | 3 | 4 | 5 | 6 | 7 | 8 | 9 | 10 | 11 | 12

FORMATTING

Word Processing Manual

E. WORD PROCESSING: WORD ART

Study Lesson 106 in your word processing manual. Complete all of the shaded steps while at your computer. Then format the jobs that follow.

DOCUMENT PROCESSING

Report 106-75

Cover Page

To ensure that your document is scored properly, insert 2 spaces at the beginning of the document.

1. Press the SPACE BAR 2 times and insert a picture related to vision or reading.
2. Drag and size the picture so that it looks similar to the one in the illustration on page 424.
3. Insert word art, about the size and in the same position as the one at the top of the illustration, with the words `Preferred Optical Vision Plan` in 2 lines as shown. Use the default font.

(Continued on next page)

Many ink-jet printers do not print beyond the bottom half inch on a sheet of paper. Keep this in mind when positioning objects at the bottom of a page.

4. Choose a style and color to coordinate with the picture.
5. Create a text box, about the size and in the same position as the one at the bottom of the illustration, to hold the directory information.
6. Remove the line around the text box, and change the fill to none.
7. Change to Arial Bold 20 point, center and type `Directory of Participating Vision Care Specialists` in 2 lines as shown in the illustration, and press ENTER 2 times.
8. Change to Arial 16 point, center, and type `for all salaried employees of the San Francisco Community College District` in 2 lines as shown in the illustration, and press ENTER 2 times.
9. Change to Arial 18 point, center, and type `September 20--`.
10. Change any of the font colors to coordinate with the picture as desired.

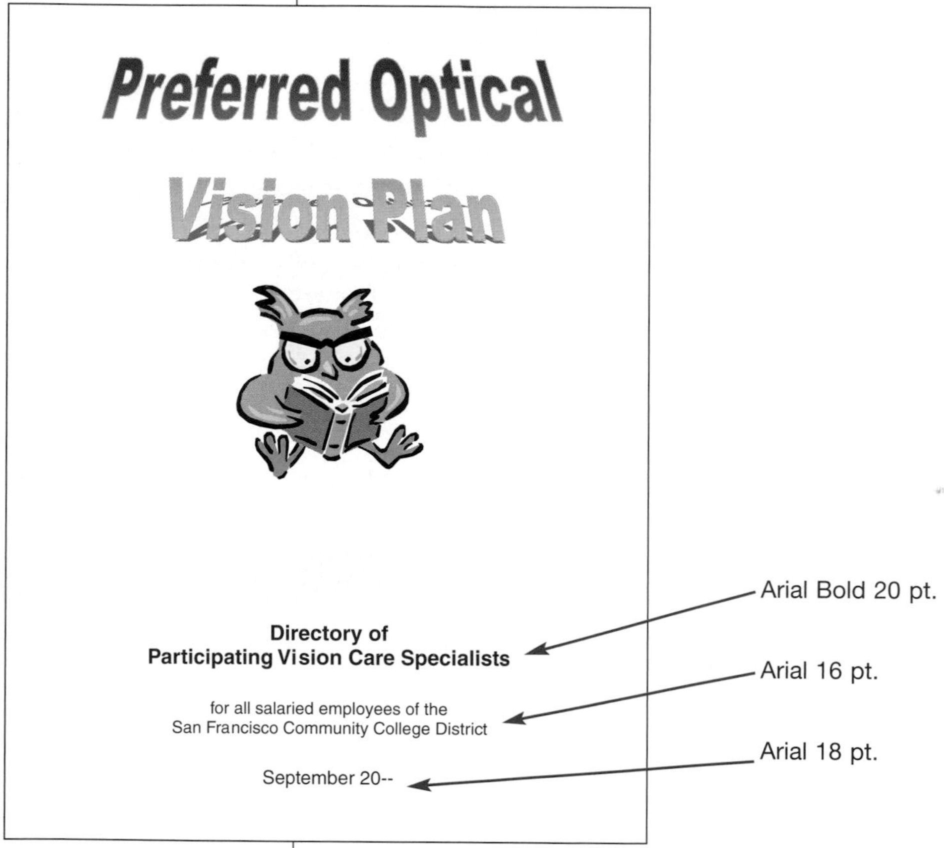

Preferred Optical

Vision Plan

Directory of
Participating Vision Care Specialists

for all salaried employees of the
San Francisco Community College District

September 20--

Arial Bold 20 pt.

Arial 16 pt.

Arial 18 pt.

Report 106-76

Cover Page

1. Press the SPACE BAR 2 times, and insert a picture related to dining.
2. Drag and size the picture so that it looks similar to the one in the illustration on page 425.
3. Insert word art, about the size and in the same position as the one at the top of the illustration, with the words `Sonoma County's Dining Guide` in 2 lines as shown.
4. Choose a style and color for the word art to coordinate with the picture, and use the default font.
5. Create a text box, about the size and in the same position as the one at the bottom of the illustration, to hold the bulleted list.
6. Remove the line around the text box, and change the fill to none.
7. Change to Arial Bold 24 point, and type the following list unformatted (without bullets):
   `Fine Dining`
   `Midrange`
   `Bargain`
8. Apply bullets to the list.

(Continued on next page)

9. Create a text box, about the size and in the same position as the one at the bottom of the illustration, to hold the date.
10. Add a line around the text box, and change the fill to a color that coordinates with the picture.
11. Change to Arial Bold Italic 26 point, and type `Summer 20--`.
12. Change any of the font colors to coordinate with the picture as desired.

Sonoma County's

Dining Guide

- **Fine Dining**
- **Midrange**
- **Bargain**

Summer 20--

Arial Bold 24 pt.

Arial Bold Italic 26 pt.

Report 106-77

Cover Page

1. Create a cover page design of your own to be used as the insert for a view binder that holds information for one of your courses.
2. Insert at least one picture related to the subject of the course.
3. Insert at least one text box with a fill.
4. Insert some word art.
5. Change any of the font colors to coordinate with the picture or word art as desired.

Lesson 107

Designing Announcements and Flyers

Goals

- Improve speed and accuracy
- Refine language arts skills in grammar
- Design announcements and flyers

A. Type 2 times.

A. WARMUP

```
     Does Quentin know if 1/2 of the January order will be    11
ready? At 5:30 about 46% of the orders still hadn't been      22
mailed! Mr. Gray expects a very sizable loss this month.      34
|  1  |  2  |  3  |  4  |  5  |  6  |  7  |  8  |  9  |  10  |  11  |  12
```

SKILLBUILDING

B. Take three 12-second timed writings on each line. The scale below the last line shows your wpm speed for a 12-second timed writing.

B. 12-SECOND SPEED SPRINTS

```
Rico will rush to tidy the big room that held the supplies.
Yale is a very fine school that has some very strict rules.
Helen will audit the books of one civic leader in the city.
The man had a name that was hard for the small girl to say.
||||5||||10||||15||||20||||25||||30||||35||||40||||45||||50||||55||||60
```

C. Type each sentence on a separate line by pressing ENTER after each sentence. Type 2 times.

C. TECHNIQUE PRACTICE: ENTER

```
Decorate the room. Attend the seminar. Go to the theater.
Watch the inauguration. Go to the rally. See the recital.
Run in the marathon. Bake the bread. Vacuum the bedrooms.
Visit the nursing home. Sell the ticket. Drive the truck.
```

D. DIAGNOSTIC PRACTICE: SYMBOLS AND PUNCTUATION

If you are not using the GDP software, turn to page SB-2 and follow the directions for this activity.

LANGUAGE ARTS

E. Study the rules at the right.

E. PRONOUNS

RULE ▶ nominative pronoun

Use nominative pronouns (such as *I, he, she, we, they,* and who) as subjects of a sentence or clause.

The programmer and <u>he</u> are reviewing the code.

Barb is a person <u>who</u> can do the job.

(Continued on next page)

RULE ▶ objective pronoun

Use objective pronouns (such as *me, him, her, us, them,* and *whom*) as objects of a verb, preposition, or infinitive.

The code was reviewed by the programmer and him.
Barb is the type of person whom we can trust.

Edit the sentences to correct any errors in the use of pronouns.

12 `We hope they will take all of them to the concert tomorrow.`
13 `John gave the gift to she on Monday; her was very pleased.`
14 `If them do not hurry, Mary will not finish her work on time.`
15 `The book was proofread by her; the changes were made by he.`
16 `It is up to them to give us all the pages they read today.`
17 `Me cannot assure they that it will not rain for the picnic.`

FORMATTING

Word Processing Manual

F. WORD PROCESSING: TABLE—MOVE

Study Lesson 107 in your word processing manual. Complete all of the shaded steps while at your computer. Then format the jobs that follow.

DOCUMENT PROCESSING

Report 107-78

Announcement

The Hotel
Cosmopolitan
welcomes

NBEA Conference Attendees

Event	Time	Location
President's Welcome	8:30-9:30 a.m.	Mezzanine Ballroom B
Internet Training	10-11:30 a.m.	First Floor Cityscape Room
NBEA Luncheon	12-1 p.m.	Mezzanine Grand Ballroom
Computer Workshops	1-3 p.m.	First Floor Rooms A, B, and D
Research Sessions*	3-5:30 p.m.	Third Floor Rooms 1, 3, and 5
*President's Note: I encourage anyone who is interested to attend our research sessions this afternoon. Dr. Roy Phillips, who will be the facilitator, is excellent. Both of us are available to answer group questions during the session, or you may direct individual questions to either him or me after the session.		

1. Change the left and right margins to 0.5 inch.
2. Press the SPACE BAR 2 times, and insert a picture associated with a large city.
3. Drag and size the picture so that it looks similar to the one in the illustration at the left and on page 428.
4. Create a text box, about the size and in the same position as the one at the top of the illustration, to hold the welcoming message.
5. Remove the line around the text box, and change the fill to none.
6. Change to Arial 28 point, center, and type `The Hotel Cosmopolitan` in 2 lines as shown in the illustration, and press ENTER 1 time.
7. Change to Arial 22 point, and center and type `welcomes`.
8. Insert word art, about the size and in the same position as the one at the top of the illustration, with the words `NBEA Conference Attendees`.
9. Drag and size the word art so that it looks similar to the word art shown in the illustration.
10. Change the word art font for readability if desired.
11. Choose a style and color for the word art to coordinate with the picture.
12. Insert a boxed table with 3 columns and 7 rows, and drag it into position as shown in the illustration.
13. Change to Times New Roman Bold 20 point, and type the centered column headings.
14. Change to Times New Roman 20 point, and type the left-aligned column entries.
15. Type the information in Column C in 2 lines as shown.
16. Merge the cells in Row 7, change to Times New Roman 16 point, and type the information as shown.
17. Automatically adjust the column width for all entries, and drag the table into position again.
18. Add a shading color to the first and last row to coordinate with the word art and picture.

(Continued on next page)

Event	Time	Location
President's Welcome	8:30-9:30 a.m.	Mezzanine Ballroom B
Internet Training	10-11:30 a.m.	First Floor Cityscape Room
NBEA Luncheon	12-1 p.m.	Mezzanine Grand Ballroom
Computer Workshops	1-3 p.m.	First Floor Rooms A, B, and D
Research Sessions*	3-5:30 p.m.	Third Floor Rooms 1, 3, and 5

nominative pronoun
nominative pronoun
objective pronoun
nominative and objective pronouns

*President's Note: I encourage anyone who is interested to attend our research sessions this afternoon. Dr. Roy Phillips, who will be the facilitator, is excellent. Both of us are available to answer group questions during the session, or you may direct individual questions to either him or me after the session.

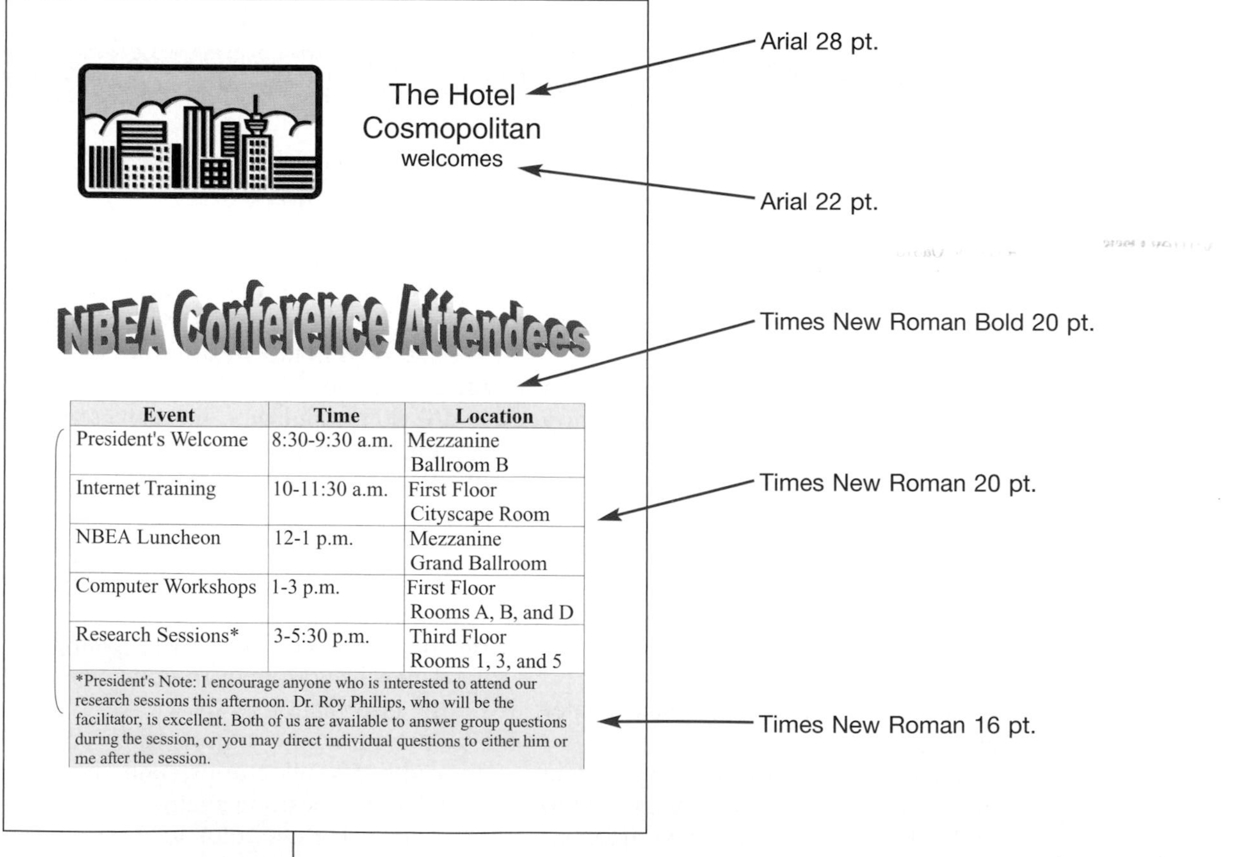

Event	Time	Location
President's Welcome	8:30-9:30 a.m.	Mezzanine Ballroom B
Internet Training	10-11:30 a.m.	First Floor Cityscape Room
NBEA Luncheon	12-1 p.m.	Mezzanine Grand Ballroom
Computer Workshops	1-3 p.m.	First Floor Rooms A, B, and D
Research Sessions*	3-5:30 p.m.	Third Floor Rooms 1, 3, and 5
*President's Note: I encourage anyone who is interested to attend our research sessions this afternoon. Dr. Roy Phillips, who will be the facilitator, is excellent. Both of us are available to answer group questions during the session, or you may direct individual questions to either him or me after the session.		

Report 107-79

Flyer

1. Press the SPACE BAR 2 times, and insert a picture associated with the summer season.
2. Drag and size the picture so that it looks similar to the one shown in the illustration on page 429.
3. Insert word art, about the size and in the same position as the one at the top of the illustration, with the words `Summerset Homes`.
4. Choose a style and color for the word art to coordinate with the picture.

(Continued on next page)

5. Create a text box, about the size and in the same position as the one in the middle of the illustration, to hold the message.
6. Remove the line around the text box, and change the fill to none.
7. Change to Arial 28 point; center and type `Summerset Homes proudly invites you to the grand opening of our newest group of single-family homes!` as shown in the illustration.
8. Create a text box, about the size and in the same position as the one at the bottom of the illustration, to hold the address information.
9. Remove the line around the text box, and add a fill using a color to coordinate with the word art and the fill.
10. Change to Arial 12 point; center and type as shown in the illustration:

    ```
    Summerset Homes
    520 Southwest Harbor Way
    Portland, OR 97201
    800-555-2649
    www.Summerset.com
    ```
11. Insert a star-shaped symbol between each item in the address block as shown in the illustration.
12. Insert 2 spaces before and after the star-shaped symbol.
13. Insert a boxed table with 3 columns and 5 rows, and drag it into position as shown in the illustration.
14. Change to Times New Roman 22 point, and type the column entries.
15. Automatically adjust the column width for all entries, and drag the table into position again.

Shadow Pines	1,235 sq. ft.	$209,990
Ocean View	1,495 sq. ft.	223,990
Country Meadow	1,759 sq. ft.	265,990
Desert Breeze	2,042 sq. ft.	295,990
Valley Oasis	2,537 sq. ft.	322,990

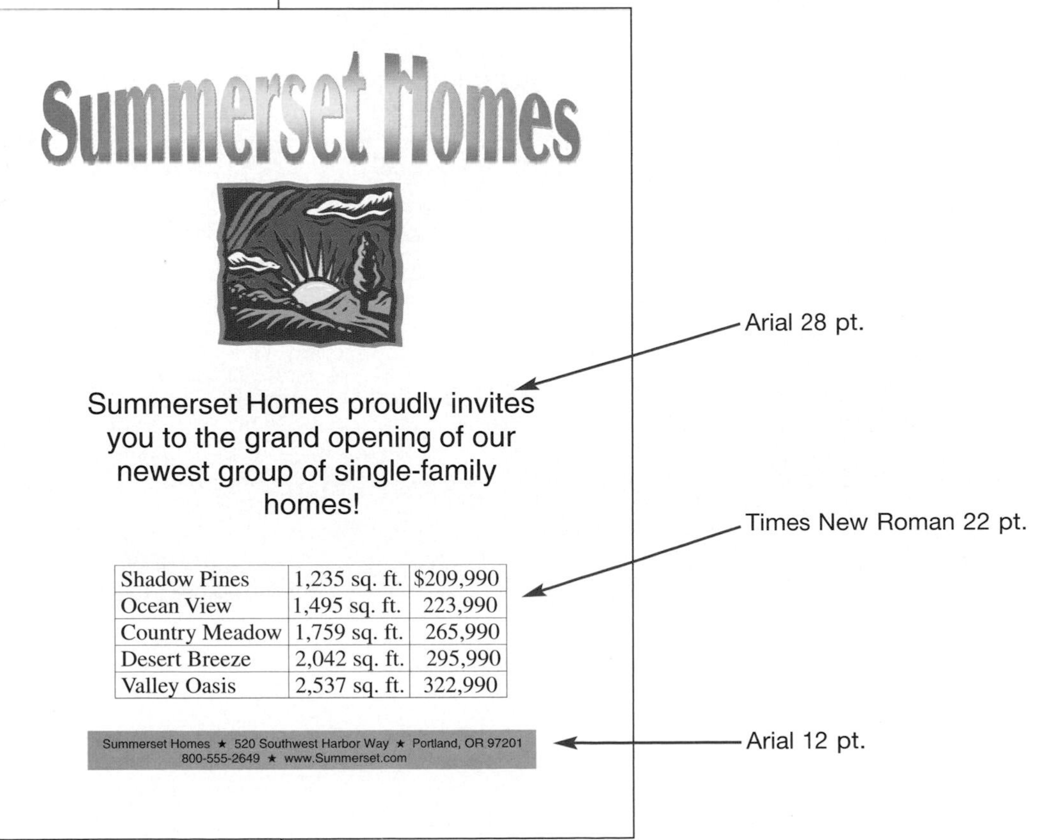

Report 107-80

Announcement or Flyer

1. Create an announcement or flyer design of your own for an upcoming event at work or on campus.
2. Press the SPACE BAR 2 times and insert at least one picture related to the topic of the announcement or flyer.
3. Insert at least one text box with a fill.
4. Insert some word art.
5. Apply color to your fonts to coordinate with the picture or word art.
6. Insert a table that contains information related to the topic of the flyer or announcement.

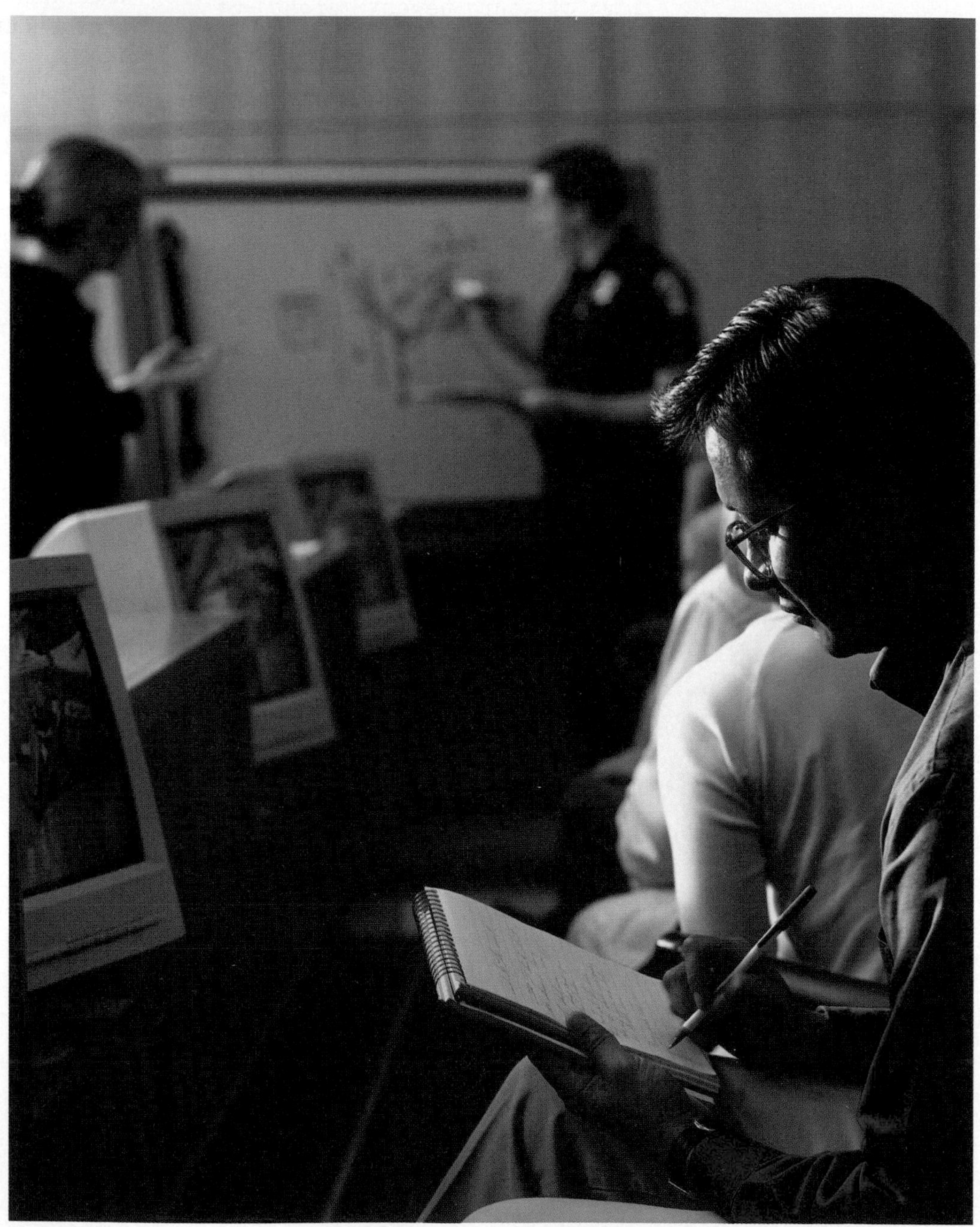

Designing Newsletters: A

Goals

- Type at least 49wpm/5′/5e
- Design newsletters

A. Type 2 times.

A. WARMUP

```
     Does Pamela know if Region 29* (*Ventura) has met the   11
sales quota? Their exact target zone is just not clear;      22
they don't have to submit their totals until 4:30 on 5/7.    34
|  1  |  2  |  3  |  4  |  5  |  6  |  7  |  8  |  9  |  10  |  11  |  12
```

SKILLBUILDING

B. PACED PRACTICE

If you are not using the GDP software, turn to page SB-14 and follow the directions for this activity.

Strategies for Career Success

Managing Business Phone Time

The average American spends an hour a day on the phone. Phone calls can be extremely distracting. Time is spent taking the call and following up after the call. You can take steps to reduce wasted time on the phone.

When you make an outgoing call, organize the topics you want to discuss. Have all the materials you need: pencils, paper, order forms, and so on. When you take an incoming call, answer it promptly. Identify yourself. It is common to answer the phone with your first and last name (for example, "Mary Smith speaking" or "Mary Smith").

Limit social conversation; it wastes time. Give concise answers to questions. At the end of the call, summarize the points made. End the conversation politely.

YOUR TURN Keep a log of your time on the phone for one day. What is your average conversation time? What can you do to reduce your average phone conversation time?

C. Take two 5-minute timed writings. Review your speed and errors.

Goal: At least 49wpm/5'/5e

C. 5-MINUTE TIMED WRITING

```
     Purchasing a home is probably one of the most critical  11
financial decisions you will make in your lifetime. Dozens   23
of questions need to be answered when buying a home. For     34
example, how much of a down payment will you make and how    46
much of a monthly payment on your mortgage will you be able  58
to afford?                                                   60
     In addition to your mortgage payment, there are other   71
costs associated with buying a new home. The mortgage will   83
cover the principal and interest for your loan, but you      94
will also have homeowner's insurance and utilities to pay    106
such as water, sewer, electricity, and gas.                  115
     You may want to purchase a home through a real estate   126
agent, and it is important that you find out how much of a   137
commission will be charged for that service. When working    149
with a real estate agent, you need to let that person know   161
about the kind of community in which you would prefer to     172
live. Do you want to be close to schools, shopping centers,  184
and restaurants, or would you rather purchase a home in a    195
secluded neighborhood away from the noise and congestion of  207
a metropolitan city?                                         211
     When you find a home that you like, look at it very     222
carefully to see if it is structurally well built, if you    234
like the floor plan, and if it is large enough for you.      245
| 1 | 2 | 3 | 4 | 5 | 6 | 7 | 8 | 9 | 10 | 11 | 12
```

FORMATTING

D. NEWSLETTER DESIGN

Newsletters are an excellent forum for communicating information on a wide range of subjects. A well-planned newsletter will employ all the basic principles of good design. However, because newsletters usually include information on a wide variety of topics, they are generally complex in their layout.

Most newsletters have the following elements in common: mastheads, main headings and subheadings, text arranged in flowing newspaper-column format using various column widths to add interest, text boxes to emphasize and summarize, pictures to draw readers' attention and interest to a topic, and a variety of borders and fills.

The design of a multipage newsletter must look consistent from one page to the next. This consistency provides unity to the newsletter design and is often achieved through the use of headers and footers.

Report 108-81

Newsletter

Reminder: You will finish the newsletter in Lessons 109 and 110.

Follow these steps to create the masthead and footer for the first page of the newsletter shown below.

1. Set all margins at 0.75 inch.
2. Create an open table with 2 columns and 2 rows. Drag the middle column border to the left so the first column is about 1.75 inches wide.
3. Right-align Column B.
4. In Column B, Row 1, change to Times New Roman Bold 48 point, and type `The Traveler's Connection` on two lines.
5. Press ENTER 1 time, change to Arial Bold 14 point, and type `A Newsletter From E-Travel.com`.
6. Move to Column A, Row 2, and type `Volume 9, Issue No. 5`.
7. Move to Column B, Row 2, and type `Spring 20--`.
8. Apply borders to the top and bottom of Row 2.
9. In Column A, Row 1, insert a picture associated with world travel.
10. Drag and size the picture so that it looks similar to the one shown in the illustration.
11. Insert a footer, and center and type `Page` followed by 1 space.
12. Insert a page number field and close the footer.

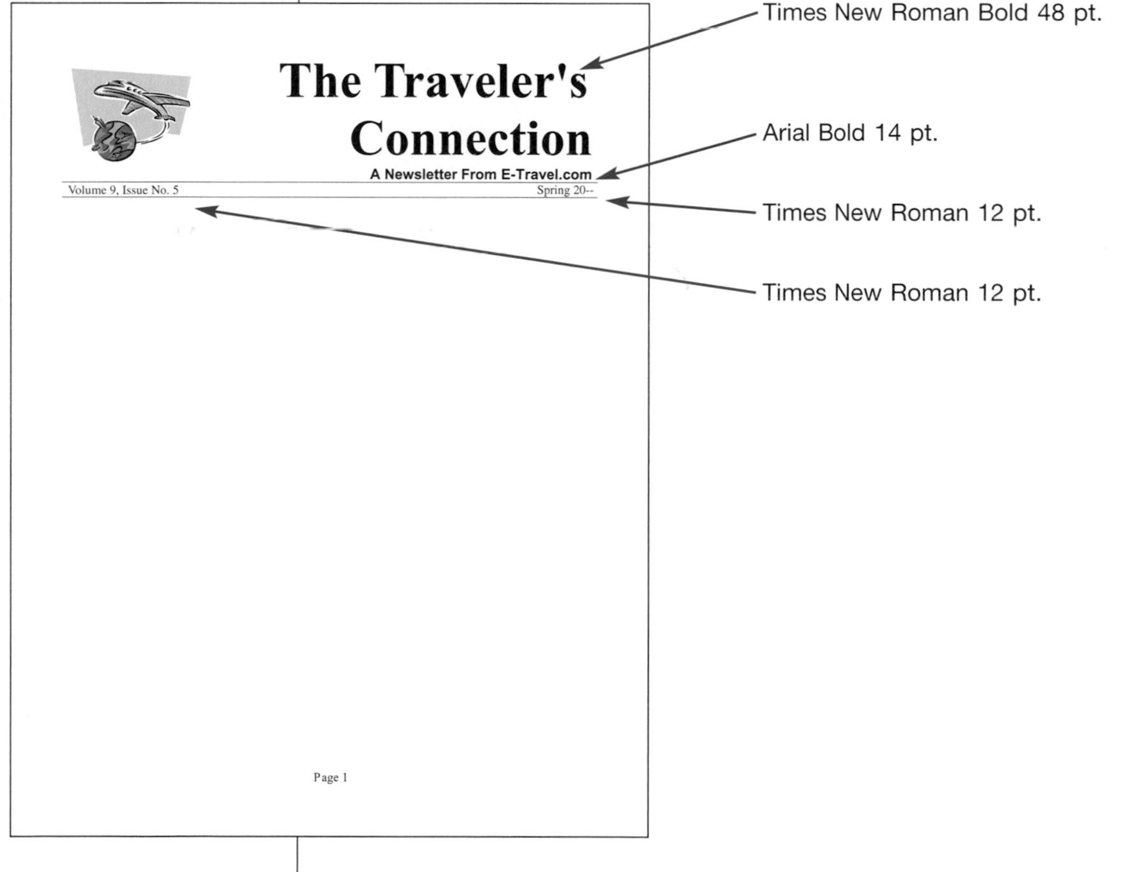

Report 108-82

Newsletter

1. Create a newsletter masthead of your own related to travel and similar to the one in Report 108-81.
2. Use any picture that enhances the purpose of your travel newsletter.

Designing Newsletters: B

Goals

- Improve speed and accuracy
- Refine language arts skills in spelling
- Design newsletters

A. Type 2 times.

A. WARMUP

Approximately 90% of the weekly budget was just used 11
to buy equipment. A very sizable amount totaling $12,654 22
was spent on "necessities" as requested by the department! 34
| 1 | 2 | 3 | 4 | 5 | 6 | 7 | 8 | 9 | 10 | 11 | 12

SKILLBUILDING

PPP PRETEST → PRACTICE → POSTTEST

PRETEST
Take a 1-minute timed writing. Review your speed and errors.

B. PRETEST: Alternate- and One-Hand Words

A great auditor is eager to spend a minimum of eighty 11
hours to amend a problem. If he assessed a penalty that 22
exceeded the usual fee, I reserve the right to correct it. 34
| 1 | 2 | 3 | 4 | 5 | 6 | 7 | 8 | 9 | 10 | 11 | 12

PRACTICE
Speed Emphasis:
If you made no more than 1 error on the Pretest, type each *individual* line 2 times.
Accuracy Emphasis:
If you made 2 or more errors, type each *group* of lines (as though it were a paragraph) 2 times.

C. PRACTICE: Alternate-Hand Words

also amend maps thrown blame city problem panel formal down
snap rigid lens social visit with penalty right height half
chap usual such enrich shape dish auditor spend eighty kept

D. PRACTICE: One-Hand Words

was only great pupil regret uphill scatter homonym assessed
bed join water nylon target pompon savages minimum exceeded
age hook eager union teased limply reserve opinion attracts

POSTTEST
Repeat the Pretest timed writing and compare performance.

E. POSTTEST: Alternate- and One-Hand Words

F. Take a 1-minute timed writing on the first paragraph to establish your base speed. Then take four 1-minute timed writings on the remaining paragraphs. As soon as you equal or exceed your base speed on one paragraph, advance to the next, more difficult paragraph.

F. SUSTAINED PRACTICE: NUMBERS AND SYMBOLS

Shopping in the comfort and convenience of your own 11
living room has never been more popular than it is right 22
now. Shopping clubs abound on cable channels. You could 33
buy anything from exotic pets to computers by mail order. 45

Sometimes you can find discounts as high as 20% off 11
the retail price; for example, a printer that sells for 22
$565 might be discounted 20% and be sold for $452. You 33
should always investigate quality before buying anything. 44

Sometimes hidden charges are involved; for example, 11
a printer costing $475.50 that promises a discount of 12% 22
($57.06) has a net price of $418.44. However, if charges 34
for shipping range from 12% to 15%, you did not save money. 45

You must also check for errors. Several errors have 11
been noted so far: Invoice #223, #789, #273, and #904 had 22
errors totaling $21.35, $43.44, $79.23, and $91.23 for a 34
grand total of $235.25. As always, let the buyer beware. 45

LANGUAGE ARTS

G. Type these frequently misspelled words, paying special attention to any spelling problems in each word.

G. SPELLING

operations health individual considered expenditures vendor
beginning internal pursuant president union written develop
hours enclosing situation function including standard shown
engineering payable suggested participants providing orders
toward nays total without paragraph meetings different vice

Edit the sentences to correct any misspellings.

The participents in the different meetings voted for hours.
The presdent of the union is working toward a resolution.
The health of each individal must be seriously considered.
Engineering has suggested providing orders for the vendor.
One expanditure has been written off as part of oparations.
He is inclosing the accounts payible record as shown today.

Report 109-83

Newsletter (continued)

Reminder: You will finish the newsletter in Lesson 110.

Open the file for Report 108-81 shown on page 433. Follow these steps to continue the newsletter as shown on page 437.

1. Move outside the table below Column A and press ENTER 2 times.
2. Insert File 109, and turn on automatic hyphenation.
3. Carefully place your insertion point in front of the second blank line under the masthead, and select all the newly inserted text including 1 blank line below the last line of text.
4. Create 3 columns with a line between columns.
5. Select the following headings in the newsletter, and change the font to Arial 24 point:
   `A Few Tips for the Smart Traveler`
   `Planning Your Travel Online`
   `Focus on Dallas-Fort Worth`
6. Select the following subheadings in the newsletter and bold them:
   `THE AIRPORT`
   `LOVE FIELD`
   `BETWEEN THE AIRPORT AND TOWN`
7. Place your insertion point in front of the second blank line under the masthead.
8. Insert a table with 1 column and 1 row.
9. Change to Arial 12 point, and type `In This Issue:`. Press ENTER 1 time.
10. Change to Times New Roman Italic 12 point, and type the following lines:
    `A Few Tips for the Smart Traveler, Page 1`
    `Planning Your Travel Online, Page 1`
    `Focus on Dallas-Fort Worth, Page 2`
    `Texas Tidbits, Page 2`
    `Thistle Hill, Page 2`
11. Add a shading color to the table to coordinate with the picture in the masthead.
12. Insert a picture in the space above each of the bulleted items in the first article on the first page of the newsletter. The pictures should be associated in some way with the topic in each of the bulleted items.
13. Drag and size the pictures so that they look similar to the ones shown in the illustration.
14. Place your insertion point in the blank line above the heading "Planning Your Online Travel," and apply a top border.
15. Place your insertion point in the blank line above the heading "Focus on Dallas-Fort Worth," and apply a top border.

(Continued on next page)

The Traveler's Connection

A Newsletter From E-Travel.com

Volume 9, Issue No. 5 Spring 20--

In This Issue:

A Few Tips for the Smart Traveler

We all have visions of the perfect vacation. They usually include a beautiful hotel, a comfortable room, great food, and wonderful entertainment. Unfortunately, sometimes our vision doesn't exactly align itself with reality, and our dream has suddenly turned into a nightmare. You can avoid this situation if you will do some smart advance planning.

Here are some smart travel tips that can turn your dream vacation into a reality:

- Do your homework. Your best bet is to find out all you can about your destination before you do anything else. Find a good travel agent, do your own research on the Internet, and buy some good travel books on your destination in your favorite bookstore.

- Carry medications and other essentials with you. To avoid a disaster, carry everything you can't function without in the event that your luggage is lost. This would include medications, money, tickets, toiletries, visas, passports, eyeglasses, and anything else you can think of that is irreplaceable in the course of a day or two.

- Buy travel insurance. If you are taking an expensive vacation and are not completely sure you can make it, buying travel insurance is a wise expenditure. Many people today have children and aging parents whose needs are unpredictable.

- Confirm all reservations. Be sure that all your reservations including hotels, cars, and entertainment are confirmed and that you have the different confirmation numbers and phone numbers written down. Nothing can ruin a trip faster than finding out that you don't have a place to sleep or suitable transportation. You will find that if you take these tips to heart, your vacation will be just as wonderful as you imagined!

Planning Your Travel Online

The Internet has opened up a wealth of information that used to be the domain of individual travel agencies. If you have a computer and Internet access, you can make reservations, buy tickets, book entertainment packages, and do any number of other things.

Page 1

Arial 12 pt.

Times New Roman Italic 12 pt.

Arial 24 pt.

Arial 24 pt.

Save hours of time and lots of money by using the Internet wisely when you plan your travel. You can shop for the best airline rates and even name your own price if you are flexible in your travel plans.

Several good books are available to help you use the Internet for your travel plans. Please check our Web site at www.TTC.com for suggested books.

Focus on Dallas-Fort Worth

This month's focus is on the Dallas-Fort Worth area.

THE AIRPORT

The Dallas-Fort Worth International Airport is 17 miles from the business districts of each town. The phone number is 214-555-8888.

Although this is the world's second busiest airport, it is surprisingly easy to use. However, the transportation between terminals is slow.

LOVE FIELD

Love Field is a $10 to $15 taxi ride from downtown Dallas. The phone number is 214-555-6073.

Love Field is the hub of Western Airlines, which offers service within Texas, to many cities in the surrounding states, and, with stops, to destinations as far away as Chicago.

BETWEEN THE AIRPORT AND TOWN

It costs around $30 to get to downtown Dallas by taxi from the Dallas-Fort Worth International Airport. It is about $25 to downtown Fort Worth.

Cheaper bus and van service is also available. Please check our Web site at www.TTC.com. for details.

Page 2

Arial 24 pt.

Report 109-84

Newsletter (continued)

1. Open the file for Report 108-81 with the newsletter masthead you created.
2. Follow the steps for Report 109-83, and then delete everything on the second page of the newsletter.
3. Change the information in the contents text box at the top of the first column, insert a picture at the end of the last column of the newsletter to balance the page, and move any pictures around as needed.

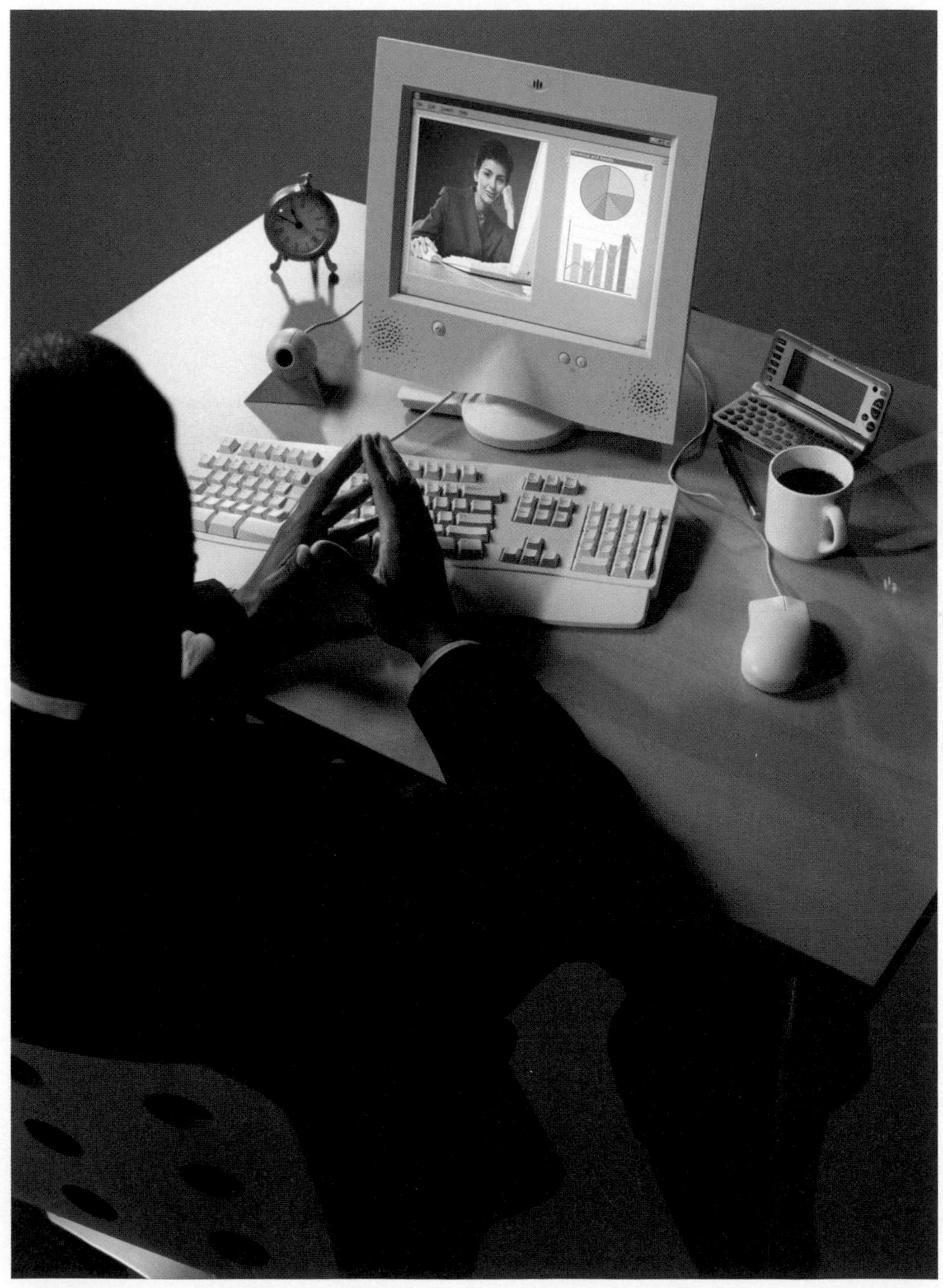

Designing Newsletters: C

Goals

- Type at least 49wpm/5′/5e
- Design newsletters

A. Type 2 times.

A. WARMUP

```
     At exactly 8:30 a.m., Quigley & Co. will host a wide     11
variety of chat room meetings; send e-mail to chat@QC.com.    23
Organizational skills will be the topics in Rooms K5 or J6.   34
| 1 | 2 | 3 | 4 | 5 | 6 | 7 | 8 | 9 | 10 | 11 | 12
```

SKILLBUILDING

B. MAP

Follow the GDP software directions for this exercise in improving keystroking accuracy.

Keyboarding Connection

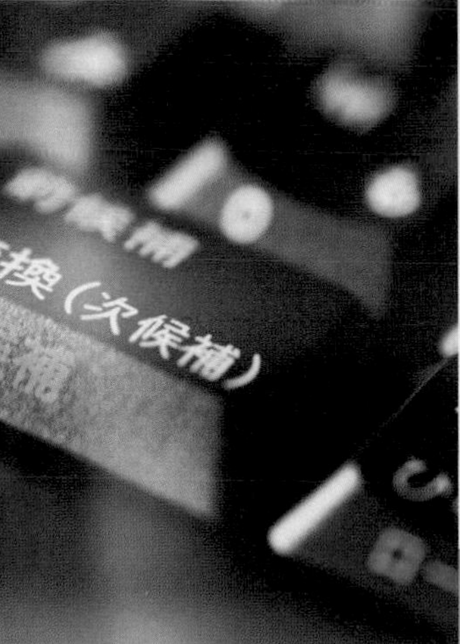

Effective E-Mail Management

Are you bombarded with e-mail? Take a few simple steps to manage e-mail more efficiently and reduce wasted time.

Create separate accounts for receiving messages that require your direct attention. Keep your mailbox clean by deleting messages you no longer need. Create folders to organize messages you need to keep (for example, set up folders for separate projects).

If you receive numerous e-mail messages, consider purchasing an e-mail manager. E-mail manager programs help you manage multiple e-mail accounts, find messages using powerful search functions, and notify you when you receive a message from a specified person.

Keep backups of important files. Be cautious of e-mail from people you do not know. Check your e-mail on a regular basis to avoid buildup of messages.

YOUR TURN Review the current organization of your e-mail. List ways you can improve the management of your e-mail.

C. Take two 5-minute timed writings. Review your speed and errors.

Goal: At least 49wpm/5′/5e

C. 5-MINUTE TIMED WRITINGS

```
     When the rate of unemployment is very low, jobs are        11
easier to find. Although you may find a job easily, what        22
can you do to make sure your job is one you will enjoy?         33
Here are some suggestions to assist you.                        41
     First, be certain you receive a job description when       52
you are hired. The job description should list all of the       64
requirements of the job and the details of what you will be     76
expected to do.                                                 79
     Second, you should receive some type of orientation to     90
your job and the company. During orientation, you will fill    102
out various tax forms, benefit forms, and insurance papers.    114
You may view a video that will help you learn more about       126
the company and available benefits.                            133
     Third, when you start your training, you should take      144
notes, pay attention, and ask questions. You should also       155
have your trainer check your work for a period of time to      167
be sure you are performing your duties correctly. If your      178
tasks are complex, you can break them down into smaller        189
parts so you can remember all aspects of your job.             200
     Finally, when you know your job requirements, chart       210
your work each day. Concentrate on being part of the team.     222
Be zealous in striving to work beyond the expectations of      234
your supervisor. Then, you will achieve job satisfaction.      245
| 1 | 2 | 3 | 4 | 5 | 6 | 7 | 8 | 9 | 10 | 11 | 12
```

DOCUMENT PROCESSING

Report 110-85

Newsletter (continued)

Open the file for Report 109-83, shown on page 437. Follow these steps to finish creating the newsletter shown on pages 441 and 442.

1. Place your insertion point directly in front of the first blank line underneath the last line of text in the newsletter.
2. Insert File 110A.
3. Insert a picture in the space to the right of the heading "Focus on Dallas-Fort Worth" on the second page of the newsletter. The pictures should be associated with the concept of focusing on a subject or associated with Texas.
4. Drag and size the picture so that it looks similar to the one shown in the illustration on page 442.
5. Insert word art, about the size and in the same position as the word art at the top of the bulleted list on the second page of the newsletter, with the words `Texas Tidbits`.
6. Choose a style and color for the word art to coordinate with the newsletter.
7. Insert a picture at the bottom of the second page in the space to the left of the information on "Thistle Hill." The picture should be associated with the

(Continued on next page)

If your printer or computer memory is limited, try previewing the document before you print, and then print only 1 page at a time.

information about Thistle Hill or with Texas.

8. Drag and size the picture so that it looks similar to the one shown in the illustration.
9. Create a text box, about the size and in the same position as the one at the bottom of the newsletter, to hold the information about Thistle Hill.
10. Insert File 110B and adjust the size of the text box as needed.
11. Add a fill color or fill effect to the text box to coordinate with the picture to the left of the text box.
12. Create a text box, about the size and in the same position as the one at the bottom of the newsletter, to hold the information about tours.
13. Change to Times New Roman Bold 12 point, and center and type `For tour information, call 817-555-2663.`
14. Remove the lines around the text box, and change the fill to none.
15. The first page of the newsletter should look like the illustration below.
16. The second page of the newsletter should look like the illustration on page 442.

The Traveler's Connection

A Newsletter From E-Travel.com

Volume 9, Issue No. 5 | Spring 20--

In This Issue:
A Few Tips for the Smart Traveler, Page 1
Planning Your Travel Online, Page 1
Focus on Dallas-Fort Worth, Page 2
Texas Tidbits, Page 2
Thistle Hill, Page 2

A Few Tips for the Smart Traveler

We all have visions of the perfect vacation. They usually include a beautiful hotel, a comfortable room, great food, and wonderful entertainment. Unfortunately, sometimes our vision doesn't exactly align itself with reality, and our dream has suddenly turned into a nightmare. You can avoid this situation if you will do some smart advance planning.

Here are some smart travel tips that can turn your dream vacation into a reality:

- Do your homework. Your best bet is to find out all you can about your destination before you do anything else. Find a good travel agent, do your own research on the Internet, and buy some good travel books on your destination in your favorite bookstore.

- Carry medications and other essentials with you. To avoid a disaster, carry everything you can't function without in the event that your luggage is lost. This would include medications, money, tickets, toiletries, visas, passports, eyeglasses, and anything else you can think of that is irreplaceable in the course of a day or two.

- Buy travel insurance. If you are taking an expensive vacation and are not completely sure you can make it, buying travel insurance is a wise expenditure. Many people today have children and aging parents whose needs are unpredictable.

- Confirm all reservations. Be sure that all your reservations including hotels, cars, and entertainment are confirmed and that you have the different confirmation numbers and phone numbers written down. Nothing can ruin a trip faster than finding out that you don't have a place to sleep or suitable transportation. You will find that if you take these tips to heart, your vacation will be just as wonderful as you imagined!

Planning Your Travel Online

The Internet has opened up a wealth of information that used to be the domain of individual travel agencies. If you have a computer and Internet access, you can make reservations, buy tickets, book entertainment packages, and do any number of other things.

Page 1

(Continued on next page)

Save hours of time and lots of money by using the Internet wisely when you plan your travel. You can shop for the best airline rates and even name your own price if you are flexible in your travel plans.

Several good books are available to help you use the Internet for your travel plans. Please check our web site at www.TTC.com for suggested books.

Focus on Dallas-Fort Worth

This month's focus is on the Dallas-Fort Worth area.

THE AIRPORT

The Dallas-Fort Worth International Airport is 17 miles from the business districts of each town. The phone number is 214-555-8888.

Although this is the world's second busiest airport, it is surprisingly easy to use. However, the transportation between terminals is slow.

LOVE FIELD

Love Field is a $10 to $15 taxi ride from downtown Dallas. The phone number is 214-555-6073.

Love Field is the hub of Western Airlines, which offers service within Texas, to many cities in the surrounding states, and, with stops, to destinations as far away as Chicago.

BETWEEN THE AIRPORT AND TOWN

It costs around $30 to get to downtown Dallas by taxi from the Dallas-Fort Worth International Airport. It is about $25 to downtown Fort Worth.

Cheaper bus and van service is also available. Please check our Web site at www.TTC.com. for details.

Texas Tidbits

- To receive mail while traveling in Dallas, have it sent c/o General Delivery at the city's main post office.
- Most businesses open between 8 a.m. and 10 a.m. and close around 6 p.m. Many are also open on weekends.
- Banks operate weekdays from 9 a.m. until 2 or 3 p.m., and some are also open on Saturday mornings.
- Post offices are open weekdays from 8 a.m. to 5 p.m. and Saturday mornings.
- At traffic lights, it's legal to make a right turn on a red light except when there is a sign at the intersection stating that such a turn is *not* permitted. Of course, come to a full stop first and make sure no traffic is coming.

For tour information, call 817-555-2663

Thistle Hill

In 1903, cattle baron William T. Waggoner built his daughter this three-story mansion as a wedding present. The house was built in a wealthy neighborhood known as Quality Hill. This Georgian Revival-style mansion has been restored to its 1912 condition and is listed in the National Register.

It is located today on Pennsylvania Avenue near the hospital district. It cost about $38,000 when the nearly 11,000-square-foot, red brick structure was built back in 1903. The house was used for lavish dinners and parties to entertain many of Fort Worth's powerful and elite. It was often referred to as the "honeymoon cottage" and was restored in the 1970s.

Page 2

Times New Roman Bold 12 pt.

Report 110-86

Flyer

Progress and Proofreading Check

Documents designated as Proofreading Checks serve as a check of your proofreading skill. Your goal is to have zero typographical errors when the GDP software first scores the document.

1. Press the SPACE BAR 2 times, and insert a picture related to a globe.
2. Drag and size the picture so that it looks similar to the one shown in the illustration on page 443.
3. Insert word art, about the size and in the same position as the one at the top of the illustration, with the words `Global Savings & Loan`.
4. Choose a style and color for the word art to coordinate with the picture.
5. Create a text box with no lines or fill and about the size and in the same position as the one shown at the middle of the illustration.
6. Change to Times New Roman 48 point, and center and type `Your Guide to Online Banking` in 2 lines as shown.
7. Insert a boxed table with 4 columns and 6 rows, and drag it into position as shown in the illustration.
8. Change to Arial Bold 18 point, and type the one- and two-column headings in Row 1 aligned as shown.
9. Move to Row 2, change to Times New Roman 20 point, and type the left-aligned column entries as shown.
10. Right-align the information in Column D, and add spaces after the dollar sign to align the dollar sign just to the left of the widest entry below it.
11. Merge the cells in Row 6, change to Times New Roman 14 point, and type the information as shown.
12. Adjust the column widths manually as shown.
13. Add a shading color to the first and last row to coordinate with the word art and picture.

(Continued on next page)

↓1X **Account**	↓1X **ATM Card**	**Check Writing**	**Monthly Fee**
Regular Checking	None	Unlimited	$ 9.00
Interest Checking	Express Card	Unlimited	10.00
Basic Checking	Express Card	Unlimited	4.50
Student Checking	Express Card	Unlimited	3.00
Note: Fees may apply to telephone banking calls and the use of the ATM Express Card.			

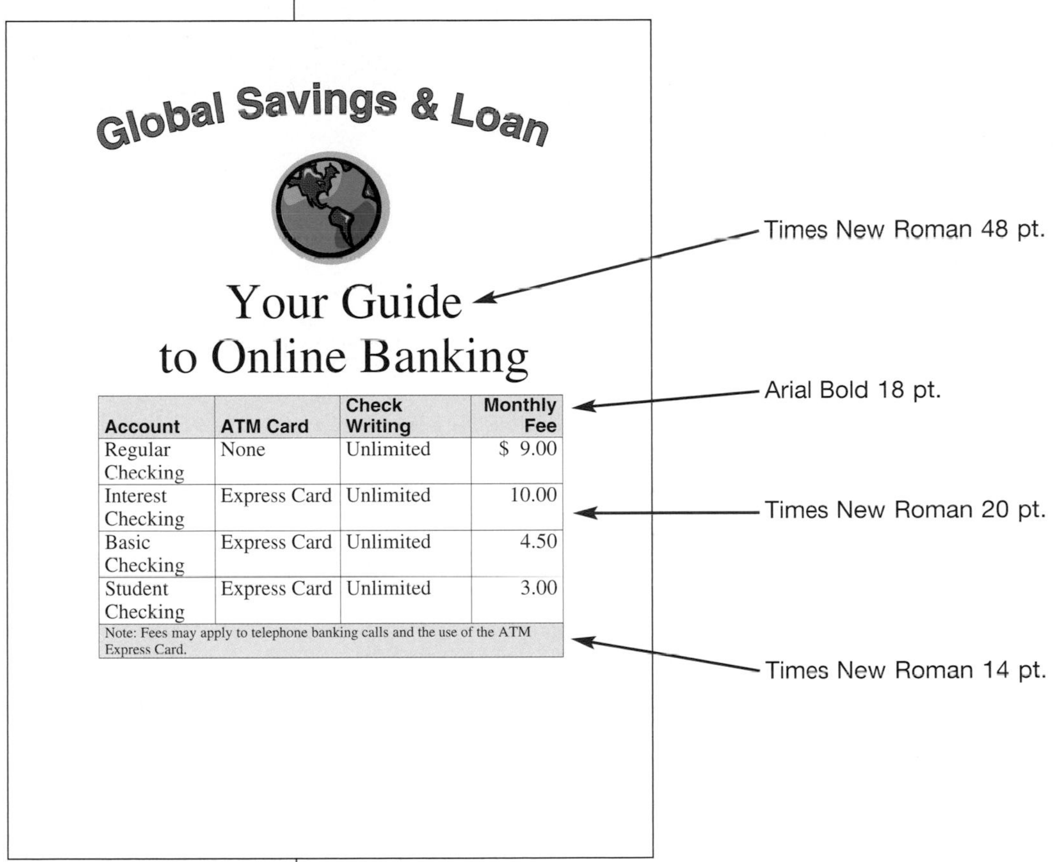

Unit 23

Designing Web Pages

LESSON 111
Creating, Saving, and Viewing Web Pages

LESSON 112
Creating More Web Pages

LESSON 113
Creating Web Pages With Hyperlinks

LESSON 114
Creating More Web Pages With Hyperlinks

LESSON 115
Formatting Web Pages

In The Game
5779 Del Monte Drive
Santa Rosa, CA 95409
888-555-7897
email@InTheGame.com

Home | Contact Us

If there is any sporting good item or apparel item related to baseball and softball, soccer, track and field, or gymnastics that you can't find on our site, we want to hear from you.

E-Mail
Send us an e-mail message now at email@InTheGame.com

Call Us
Call us toll-free at 888-555-7897.

Snail Mail
..., write to us at the address below:
... the Game
...el Monte Drive
...osa, CA 95409

In The Game
5779 Del Monte Drive
Santa Rosa, CA 95409
888-555-7897
email@InTheGame.com

Home | Contact Us

Welcome to In The Game, your online supplier specializing in sporting goods for baseball and softball, soccer, track and field, and gymnastics. We can offer you quality p... to you fast!

Baseball and Softball
If you can't wait to play ball, you'll lov... Our line of gear includes automated ba... machines, batting tees, and radar guns... jerseys, and T-shirts.

Soccer
If scoring goals is on the top of your li... place. We have all types of soccer equ...

Track and Field
Is running your game? We have batons... puts, starting blocks, starting pistols, ...

Gymnastics
You'll flip for our line of clothing, fan w... and training aids are first quality.

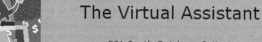

The Virtual Assistant
901 South Rainbow, Suite 1
Las Vegas, Nevada 89145
888-555-3499
email@TVA.com

Home | Services | Fees | References

Do you need a skilled assistant who works tirelessly on your documents, doesn't need any office space, and gives your work that personal touch? The Virtual Assistant is a professional document processing and design service that will help create the professional image your business demands.

You don't get a second chance at a first impression. The graphics experts in our word processing and desktop publishing departments will make sure your documents look gorgeous. Our editors, who have completed a series of rigorous courses in business English and business communications, will make sure they are letter-perfect. Please browse around our site for details.

Word Processing
- Correspondence
- Reports
- Proposals
- Manuals

Desktop Publishing
- Newsletters
- Brochures
- Letterheads
- Resumes

Layout Editing
- In-House Styles
- Custom Styles
- Master Documents
- Table of Contents
- Indexes

Copy Editing
- Proofreading
- Technical Editing
- Grammar Checking
- Writing Style

Creating, Saving, and Viewing Web Pages

Goals

- Improve speed and accuracy
- Refine language arts skills in capitalization
- Create, save, and view Web pages

A. Type 2 times.

A. WARMUP

```
     The taxes* were quickly adjusted upward by 20 percent   11
because of the improvements to her house (built in 1901).   23
A proposed law will not penalize good homeowners like this.  34
|  1  |  2  |  3  |  4  |  5  |  6  |  7  |  8  |  9  |  10  |  11  |  12
```

SKILLBUILDING

B. Take three 12-second timed writings on each line. The scale below the last line shows your wpm speed for a 12-second timed writing.

B. 12-SECOND SPEED SPRINTS

```
Their home is on a lake that is just east of her old house.
He has an old boat that is in bad need of a good paint job.
He got so many fish that she gave some to the nice old man.
She was so nice that it was easy for him to help her drive.
||||5||||10||||15||||20||||25||||30||||35||||40||||45||||50||||55||||60
```

C. PROGRESSIVE PRACTICE: ALPHABET

If you are not using the GDP software, turn to page SB-7 and follow the directions for this activity.

D. PACED PRACTICE

If you are not using the GDP software, turn to page SB-14 and follow the directions for this activity.

E. BASIC PARTS OF A WEB PAGE

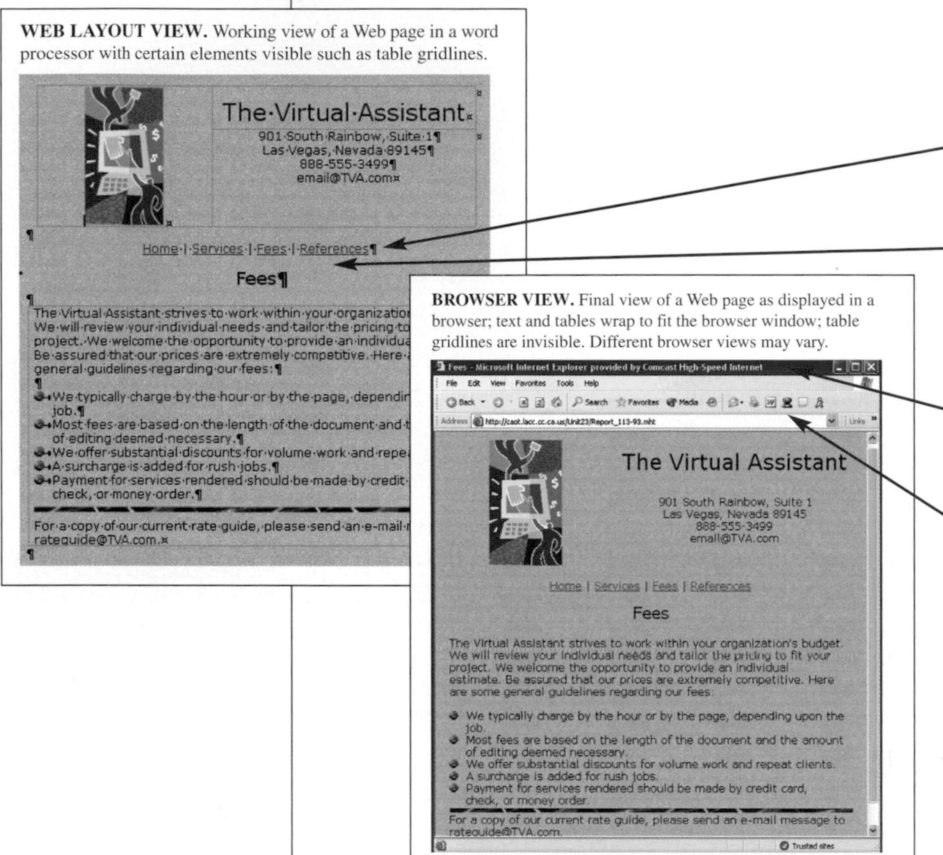

LINK BAR. A group of hyperlinks used to navigate from one Web page to another in a Web site.

HYPERLINKS. These are clicked to move from one Web page to another or to move from one place on a page to another place.

TITLE BAR. Displays the title assigned to the Web page.

ADDRESS BAR. Displays the URL address for the Web page.

F. WEB SITE DESIGN GUIDELINES

Follow these guidelines to design effective Web sites:

- Plan appropriate, specific content first. Define the purpose of the site, and make a list of what visitors need to know.
- Organize the content into logical groups and subgroups, the way you would set up an outline in a report.
- Plan the main page (usually called a home page), which should identify the business and its services.
- Plan and test the site navigation. Hyperlinks help visitors jump from one spot or page to another.
- Plan the content and design details of specific pages, and use tables to position information.
- Design an appropriate, attractive visual theme with consistent design elements on each page to unify your site. Many programs come with a gallery of attractive themes with unified design elements and eye-catching color schemes.
- Use graphics to enhance your page, but use them sparingly because they increase download times.
- Use color to create a mood, attract attention, and categorize information.

Word Processing Manual

G. WEB PAGE—CREATING, SAVING, AND VIEWING

Study Lesson 111 in your word processing manual. Complete all of the shaded steps while at your computer. Then format the jobs that follow.

DOCUMENT PROCESSING

Report 111-87

Web Site

The projects in this unit must be completed in sequence in order for the steps to work correctly!

The file names assigned to the Web pages in this text are not typical. Most home pages are named either index.htm or default.html. The commercial server hosting a Web site should be contacted for any specific requirements for file names and extensions.

The Virtual Assistant Web site that starts in this lesson is continued through Lesson 115. Because each Web page builds upon a previous one, make certain that each Web page is correct before continuing to the next one. Follow these steps to create Report 111-87.htm, the home page of the Web site. Refer to the Web layout view of the home page on page 448 as needed. Note that hyphens are used in place of spaces in Web page file names so that the pages will display properly in a browser.

1. Save Report-111-87.doc as a Web page named Report-111-87.htm, and change the title to `The Virtual Assistant.`
2. Insert a centered, open table with 2 columns and 2 rows.
3. In Column B, Row 1, center and type `The Virtual Assistant.`
4. In Column B, Row 2, center and type these lines:

```
901 South Rainbow, Suite 1
Las Vegas, Nevada 89145
888-555-3499
email@TVA.com
```

5. Merge the cells in Column A, and insert a picture related to an office or business.
6. Resize the picture proportionally until it is about 2 inches wide, and center the picture.
7. Move the insertion point under the table, and press ENTER 1 time,
8. Type the following line centered, using the pipe symbol with 1 space before and after it as shown here. This line will be referred to as the link bar from now on.

   `Home | Services | Fees | References`

   Note: The pipe symbol is above the backslash symbol on most keyboards.
9. Press ENTER 2 times, and insert a centered, open table with 2 columns and 7 rows.
10. Merge the cells in Row 1, and type the information shown on page 448 in Row 1.
11. Move to Row 3, and continue typing the rest of the table as arranged on page 448, leaving Row 2 and Row 5 empty.
12. Save the page, view the Web page in a browser, and compare the browser view with the layout view in your word processor.

Do you need a skilled assistant who works tirelessly on your documents, doesn't need any office space, and gives your work that personal touch? The Virtual Assistant is a professional document processing and design service that will help create the professional image your business demands.

You don't get a second chance at a first impression. The graphics experts in our word processing and desktop publishing departments will make sure your documents look gorgeous. Our editors, who have completed a series of rigorous courses in business English and business communications, will make sure your documents are letter-perfect. Please browse around our site for details.

≡ organization

≡ course

Word Processing	Desktop Publishing
Correspondence	Newsletters
Reports	Brochures
Proposals	Letterheads
Manuals	Resumes
Layout Editing	Copy Editing
In-House Styles	Proofreading
Custom Styles	Technical Editing
Master Documents	Grammar Checking
Table of Contents	Writing Style
Indexes	

Reminder: You will finish building the Web site in Lessons 112 through 115.

(Continued on next page)

	The Virtual Assistant
	901 South Rainbow, Suite 1 Las Vegas, Nevada 89145 888-555-3499 email@TVA.com

Home | Services | Fees | References

Do you need a skilled assistant who works tirelessly on your documents, doesn't need any office space, and gives your work that personal touch? The Virtual Assistant is a professional document processing and design service that will help create the professional image your business demands. You don't get a second chance at a first impression. The graphics experts in our word processing and desktop publishing departments will make sure your documents look gorgeous. Our editors, who have completed a series of rigorous courses in business English and business communications, will make sure they are letter-perfect. Please browse around our site for details.	
Word Processing	Desktop Publishing
Correspondence Reports Proposals Manuals	Newsletters Brochures Letterheads Resumes
Layout Editing	Copy Editing
In-House Styles Custom Styles Master Documents Table of Contents Indexes	Proofreading Technical Editing Grammar Checking Writing Style

Web layout view of home page.

Report 111-88

Your Web Site

Plan and write the content for a Web site for a business of your own to include a home page and three related pages very similar to the Web pages in this unit. You may want to look ahead to the finished Web site on pages 465–466 for ideas. The Web site that starts in this lesson is continued through Lesson 114.

1. Save Report-111-88.doc as a Web page named Report-111-88.htm, and change the title to the name of the business.
2. Insert a centered, open table with 2 rows and 2 columns.
3. In Column B, Row 1, center and type the name of the Web site.
4. In Column B, Row 2, center and type the mailing address and e-mail address of the business.
5. Merge the cells in Column A, and insert a picture related to the business.
6. Resize and align the picture proportionally as needed.
7. Move the insertion point under the table, and press Enter 1 time.
8. Type the following line centered using the pipe symbol with 1 space before and after it as shown here. This line will be referred to as the link bar from now on.

   `Home | Services | Fees | References`

   Note: The pipe symbol is above the backslash symbol on most keyboards.
9. Press Enter 2 times, and insert a centered, open table with 2 columns and 7 rows.
10. Merge the cells in Row 1, and type the desired introductory information in the first row.
11. Move to Row 3, and continue typing the rest of the headings and information, as is done in Report 111-87, leaving Row 2 and Row 5 empty.
12. Save the page, view the Web page in a browser, and compare the browser view with the layout view in your word processor.

Creating More Web Pages

Goals

- Type at least 50wpm/5′/5e
- Create more Web pages

A. Type 2 times.

A. WARMUP

Missy examined these items: the #426 oil painting, a 11
Bowes & Elkjer porcelain vase, and the 86-piece collection 23
of glazed antique pitchers. There were 337 people present. 34
| 1 | 2 | 3 | 4 | 5 | 6 | 7 | 8 | 9 | 10 | 11 | 12

SKILLBUILDING

B. PROGRESSIVE PRACTICE: NUMBERS

If you are not using the GDP software, turn to page SB-11 and follow the directions for this activity.

LANGUAGE ARTS

C. Study the rules at the right.

C. CAPITALIZATION

RULE ▶ ≡ organization

Capitalize common organizational terms (such as *advertising department* and *finance committee*) only when they are the actual names of the units in the writer's own organization and when they are preceded by the word *the*.

The report from the Advertising Department is due today.
But: Our advertising department will submit its report today.

RULE ▶ ≡ course

Capitalize the names of specific course titles but not the names of subjects or areas of study.

I have enrolled in Accounting 201 and will also take the marketing course.

Edit the sentences to correct any errors in capitalization.

8 The advertising department at their firm is excellent.
9 The Finance Committee here at Irwin will meet today.
10 I think I am going to pass keyboarding 1 with flying colors.
11 Their marketing department must approve the proposal first.
12 A class in Business Communications would be very helpful.
13 To take Math 102, you must have taken a beginning math course.

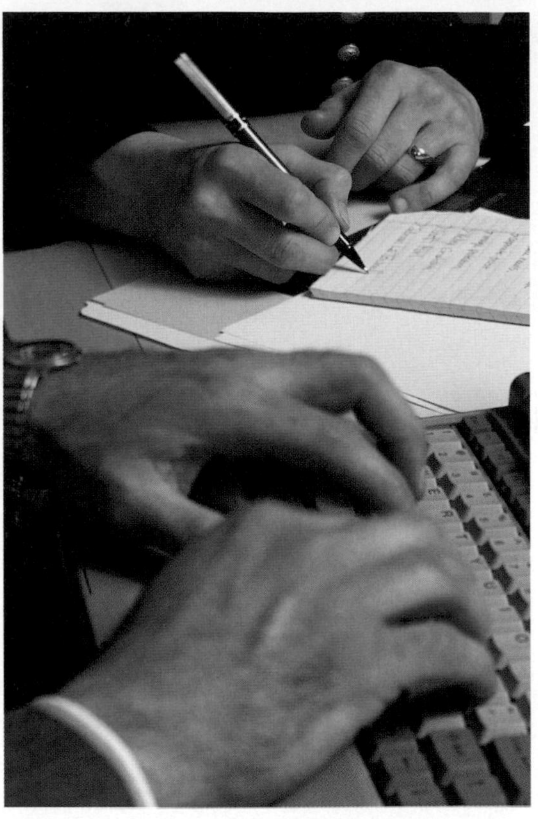

D. Take two 5-minute timed writings. Review your speed and errors.

Goal: At least 50wpm/5′/5e

D. 5-MINUTE TIMED WRITING

Employers want the people who work for them to have 11
many qualities of good character. Character is defined as a 23
distinctive feature of a person or thing. Character may be 34
what you are known for and may be why you remember someone 46
else. What are some of the traits you think of that are 57
linked with good character? A few traits might be respect, 69
honesty, trust, caring, leadership, attitude, tolerance, 81
fairness, and patience. 85

All people should have respect for themselves and for 96
others. If you respect people, you have a high regard for 108
the way they conduct themselves in all aspects of life. 119
However, before you can respect others, you need to have 131
respect for yourself. 135

Honesty and trustworthiness are similar traits. In 145
business dealings, people expect honesty and will admire 157
people who have this quality. They like to build business 168
relationships with companies whose employees are honest, 180
just, and trustworthy. 184

Your attitude is reflected in the way you act toward 195
other people or in the way you speak to them. You can make 207
great strides in advancing your career by taking a look at 219
the way you interact with people. You may want to take a 230
closer look at some character traits you want to improve. 242
Such improvements in life will amaze you. 250

| 1 | 2 | 3 | 4 | 5 | 6 | 7 | 8 | 9 | 10 | 11 | 12

DOCUMENT PROCESSING

Report 112-89

Web Site (continued)

Follow these steps to create a new services page for the Web site named Report-112-89.htm. Refer to the Web layout view of the services page on page 452 as needed. Make the following changes to this report:

1. Change the title to `Services.`
2. Select and delete the table below the link bar.
3. Type `Services` centered on the second blank line below the link bar, and press ENTER 2 times.
4. Insert a centered open table with 1 cell.
5. Type the information below inside the table as shown in the Web layout view of the services page.
6. Save the page, and view the Web page in a browser.

Word Processing¶

We prepare documents with a professional look for correspondence of all types as well as reports, proposals, manuals, and so on.¶

Desktop Publishing¶

Our professional design specialists will create newsletters, brochures, letterheads, and other documents that are sure to capture your imagination.¶

Layout Editing¶

Our layout editors will transform your documents using in-house styles or custom styles. For your longer projects, they are experts at building master documents that include a cover page, table of contents, and index.¶

Copy Editing¶

Our copy editors will make sure that your document content is perfect. Proofreading, grammar, and writing style will all be checked so that your ideas are expressed clearly and effectively.

(Continued on next page)

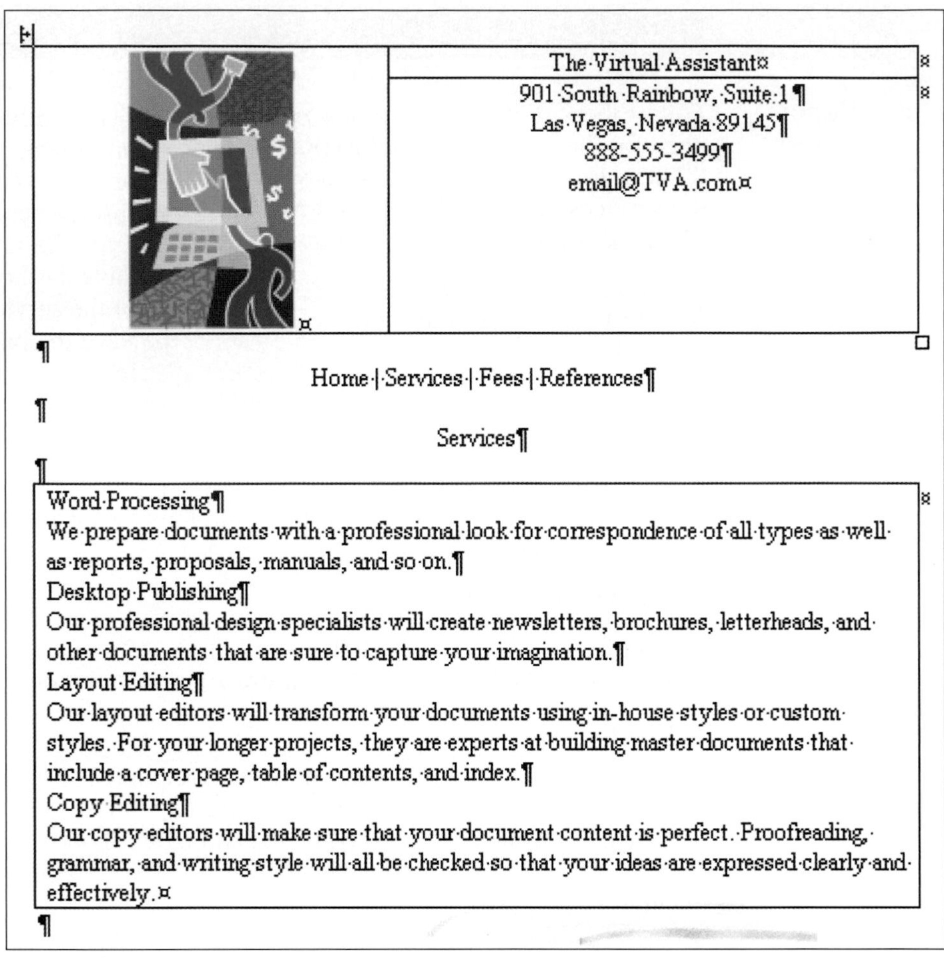

The·Virtual·Assistant¤

901·South·Rainbow,·Suite·1¶
Las·Vegas,·Nevada·89145¶
888-555-3499¶
email@TVA.com¤

¶

Home·|·Services·|·Fees·|·References¶

¶

Services¶

¶

Word·Processing¶
We·prepare·documents·with·a·professional·look·for·correspondence·of·all·types·as·well·as·reports,·proposals,·manuals,·and·so·on.¶
Desktop·Publishing¶
Our·professional·design·specialists·will·create·newsletters,·brochures,·letterheads,·and·other·documents·that·are·sure·to·capture·your·imagination.¶
Layout·Editing¶
Our·layout·editors·will·transform·your·documents·using·in-house·styles·or·custom·styles.·For·your·longer·projects,·they·are·experts·at·building·master·documents·that·include·a·cover·page,·table·of·contents,·and·index.¶
Copy·Editing¶
Our·copy·editors·will·make·sure·that·your·document·content·is·perfect.·Proofreading,·grammar,·and·writing·style·will·all·be·checked·so·that·your·ideas·are·expressed·clearly·and·effectively.¤

¶

Web layout view of services page.

Report 112-90

Your Web Site (continued)

Follow these steps to create a new services page for your Web site named Report 112-90.htm similar to the Web layout view of the services page on this page. Make the following changes to this report:

1. Change the title to `Services`.
2. Select and delete the table below the link bar.
3. Type `Services` centered on the second blank line below the link bar, and press ENTER 2 times.
4. Create a centered open table with 1 cell.
5. Inside the table, type four headings followed by one or two sentences, each describing the services of your business.
6. Save the page, and view the Web page in a browser.

Creating Web Pages With Hyperlinks

Goals

- Improve speed and accuracy
- Refine language arts skills in composing
- Create Web pages with hyperlinks

A. Type 2 times.

A. WARMUP

```
     Did you hear the excellent quartet of junior cadets?    11
Everybody in the crowd (estimated at over 500) applauded     22
"with gusto." The sizable crowd filled the 3/4-acre park.    34
| 1 | 2 | 3 | 4 | 5 | 6 | 7 | 8 | 9 | 10 | 11 | 12
```

SKILLBUILDING

B. DIAGNOSTIC PRACTICE: SYMBOLS AND PUNCTUATION

If you are not using the GDP software, turn to page SB-2 and follow the directions for this activity.

C. Type the columns 2 times. Press TAB to move from column to column.

C. TECHNIQUE PRACTICE: TAB KEY

T. Waters	L. Vigil	S. Zimmerly	D. Colwell	C. Foster
M. Goldbach	R. Hempker	G. Beckert	M. Kinsey	A. Lucero
C. Maclean	J. Nichols	I. Ohlsen	R. Parlee	S. Quale
J. Rondeau	G. Snowden	Y. Tokita	C. Upton	C. Vaughn

LANGUAGE ARTS

D. COMPOSING A PERSONAL-BUSINESS LETTER

Compose a two-paragraph personal-business letter that summarizes the content of the Web site design guidelines on page 446. Address the letter to your instructor; provide a suitable inside address and salutation for your letter. Also, provide a complimentary closing and sign the letter yourself.

In the letter, discuss the following:
Paragraph 1. Describe how to plan an effective Web site.
Paragraph 2. Describe how to design an effective Web site.

FORMATTING

E. HYPERLINKS

Hyperlinks are powerful navigational tools that are critical to the overall plan and design of a Web site. When clicked, they move a visitor from one page or one location on a page to another.

When you create a hyperlink, you must indicate the target. The hyperlink can point to the same page, to a different page, to another site, or perhaps to an e-mail address. You can assign a hyperlink to a word, a group of words, or a picture.

The presence of a text hyperlink is usually indicated by text that is underlined in a color different from that used on the rest of the words on the page. Also, the mouse pointer changes to a hand shape when hovering over a hyperlink.

Word Processing Manual

F. WEB PAGE—HYPERLINKS

Study Lesson 113 in your word processing manual. Complete all of the shaded steps while at your computer. Then format the jobs that follow.

DOCUMENT PROCESSING

Report 113-91

Web Site (continued)

Follow these steps to create a new fees page for the Web site named Report-113-91.htm. Refer to the Web layout view of the fees page on page 455 as needed. Make the following changes to this report:

1. Change the title to `Fees.`
2. Change `Services` to `Fees` on the second blank line below the link bar.
3. Move inside the table below "Services," and select and delete the information inside the table.
4. Type the information below inside the table as shown in the Web layout view of the Fees page.
5. Save the page, and view the Web page in a browser.

The Virtual Assistant strives to work within your organization's budget. We will review your individual needs and tailor the pricing to fit your project. We welcome the opportunity to provide an individual estimate. Be assured that our prices are extremely competitive. Here are some general guidelines regarding our fees:
¶
We typically charge by the hour or by the page, depending upon the job. ¶
Most fees are based on the length of the document and the amount of editing deemed necessary. ¶
We offer substantial discounts for volume work and repeat clients. ¶
A surcharge is added for rush jobs. ¶
Payment for services rendered should be made by credit card, check, or money order. ¶
¶
For a copy of our current rate guide, please send an e-mail message to rateguide@TVA.com. ¶

(Continued on next page)

The·Virtual·Assistant¤
901·South·Rainbow,·Suite·1¶
Las·Vegas,·Nevada·89145¶
888-555-3499¶
email@TVA.com¤

¶

Home·|·Services·|·Fees·|·References¶

¶

Fees¶

¶

The·Virtual·Assistant·strives·to·work·within·your·organization's·budget.·We·will·review·your·individual·needs·and·tailor·the·pricing·to·fit·your·project.·We·welcome·the·opportunity·to·provide·an·individual·estimate.·Be·assured·that·our·prices·are·extremely·competitive.·Here·are·some·general·guidelines·regarding·our·fees:¶
¶
We·typically·charge·by·the·hour·or·by·the·page,·depending·upon·the·job.¶
Most·fees·are·based·on·the·length·of·the·document·and·the·amount·of·editing·deemed·necessary.¶
We·offer·substantial·discounts·for·volume·work·and·repeat·clients.¶
A·surcharge·is·added·for·rush·jobs.¶
Payment·for·services·rendered·should·be·made·by·credit·card,·check,·or·money·order.¶
¶
For·a·copy·of·our·current·rate·guide,·please·send·an·e-mail·message·to·rateguide@TVA.com.¤

¶

Web layout view of fees page.

Report 113-92

Web Site (continued)

Follow these steps to insert hyperlinks on the link bar for the fees page. Make the following changes to this report:

1. Insert three text hyperlinks for the first three words on the link bar as follows:

   Home links to Report-111-87.htm
   Services links to Report-112-89.htm
   Fees links to Report-113-92.htm

2. Manually open Report-111-87.htm (the home page) and Report-112-89.htm (the services page).
3. Insert three text hyperlinks for the first three words on the link bar for each page just as you did in step 1.
4. On Report-111-87.htm (the home page), insert four more text hyperlinks for each of the four headings on the home page ("Word Processing," "Desktop Publishing," "Layout Editing," and "Copy Editing") to link to the services page, Report-112-89.htm.
5. Save all pages, test all the hyperlinks, and edit any hyperlinks as needed.

(Continued on next page)

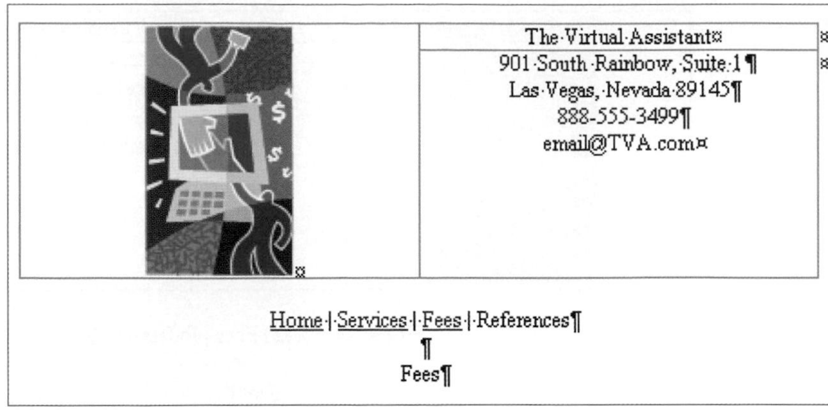

Web layout view of fees page with hyperlinks.

English and business communications, will make sure they are letter-perfect. Please browse around our site for details.	
Word Processing	Desktop Publishing
Correspondence Reports Proposals Manuals	Newsletters Brochures Letterheads Resumes
Layout Editing	Copy Editing
In-House Styles Custom Styles Master Documents Table of Contents Indexes	Proofreading Technical Editing Grammar Checking Writing Style

Web layout view of home page with hyperlinks.

Report 113-93

Your Web Site (continued)

Follow these steps to create a new page for your Web site named Report-113-93.htm similar to the Web layout view of the fees page on this page. Make the following changes to this report:

1. Change the title to `Fees.`
2. Change `Services` to `Fees` on the second blank line below the link bar.
3. Move inside the table below "Services," and select and delete the information inside the table.
4. Type content similar to the fees page on page 455.
5. Save the page, and view the Web page in a browser.

Report 113-94

Your Web Site (continued)

Follow these steps to insert hyperlinks on the link bar for the fees page. Make the following changes to this report:

1. Insert three text hyperlinks for the first three words on the link bar as follows:

   Home links to Report-111-88.htm
   Services links to Report-112-90.htm
   Fees links to Report-113-94.htm

2. Manually open Report-111-88.htm (the home page) and Report-112-90.htm (the services page).
3. Insert three text hyperlinks for the first three words on the link bar for each page just as you did in step 2.
4. On Report-111-88.htm (the home page), insert four more text hyperlinks for each of the four headings on your home page to link to the services page, Report-112-90.htm.
5. Save all pages, test all the hyperlinks, and edit any hyperlinks as needed.

Creating More Web Pages With Hyperlinks

Goals

- Type at least 50wpm/5′/5e
- Create more Web pages with hyperlinks

A. Type 2 times.

A. WARMUP

```
     This series* (*6 films, 28 minutes) by J. Zeller goes    11
beyond the "basics" of computers. Viewers keep requesting     23
an extension on the dates; this includes 3/2, 5/5, and 8/9.   34
| 1 | 2 | 3 | 4 | 5 | 6 | 7 | 8 | 9 | 10 | 11 | 12
```

SKILLBUILDING

B. MAP

Follow the GDP software directions for this exercise in improving keystroking accuracy.

Keyboarding Connection

Using Hypertext

Do you know how to surf the Web? It's easy! The Web contains pages, which are blocks of text, visuals, sound, or animation. Hypertext is a format in which certain words in the text of a Web page are highlighted, underlined, or colored differently from the other words. These colored or highlighted words link to other pages on the Web.

When you point to a hyperlink and click the mouse button, the page connected to that word is displayed. Therefore, one page on the Web can link to many other pages. Hypertext pages do not have to be read in any specific order.

Hypertext enables you to connect and retrieve Web pages from computer networks worldwide. With hypertext, you can point and click or surf your way all over the Web.

YOUR TURN Open a page on the Web. Surf the Web using the hyperlinks displayed on the page.

C. Take two 5-minute timed writings. Review your speed and errors

Goal: At least 50wpm/5′/5e

C. 5-MINUTE TIMED WRITING

Before you apply for jobs, you will want to do some 11
detective work. First, choose a business for which you want 23
to work and then use the Internet to find out about the 34
company. If you find a Web site for the business, then you 46
can learn all about the company, its hiring policies, the 57
job listings, and how to apply for a job opening. 67

When you are researching a company, you want to learn 78
about the history of the company. You may be able to find 90
out how stock analysts expect the company stock to perform 102
in the coming months if the company is publicly held. 112

When you find a job opening for which you know that 123
you want to apply, read carefully to see what type of work 135
experience and education the company requires for the job. 147
When you prepare your resume, emphasize your qualifications 159
based on the requirements listed for the job. If the person 171
who should receive job inquiries is not listed, contact the 183
company by phone or e-mail to get a name. Personalize your 194
cover letter and resume, if possible, for the company. 205

The information you find in your research will be 217
very helpful during the interview with a representative of 228
the company. Ask good questions and speak confidently about 240
the job. Emphasize how your skills would be valuable. 250

| 1 | 2 | 3 | 4 | 5 | 6 | 7 | 8 | 9 | 10 | 11 | 12

Report 114-95

Web Site (continued)

Follow these steps to create a new references page for the Web site named Report-114-95.htm. Refer the Web layout view of the references page on page 460 as needed. Make the following changes to this report:

1. Change the title to `References`.
2. Change `Fees` to `References` on the second blank line below the link bar.
3. Move inside the table below "References," and select and delete the information inside the table.
4. Type the information below inside the table as shown in the Web layout view of the references page.
5. Save the page, and view the Web page in a browser.

↓2X

I've been in a highly successful business for over 10 years and attribute much of that success to the skilled professionals at The Virtual Assistant. I am always confident that my work will go out error-free. They are top-notch professionals and can work for my team anytime! ↓2X

Mike Rashid
Network Engineer
Denver, Colorado ↓4X

The documents produced by The Virtual Assistant are impeccable! I can count on professional, reliable, competent, and efficient service without question. It is so easy to send documents back and forth via the Internet, and we all know that time is money. I highly recommend TVA for any of your word processing needs. ↓2X

Nancy Shipley
Attorney-at-Law
Chicago, Illinois ↓2X

(Continued on next page)

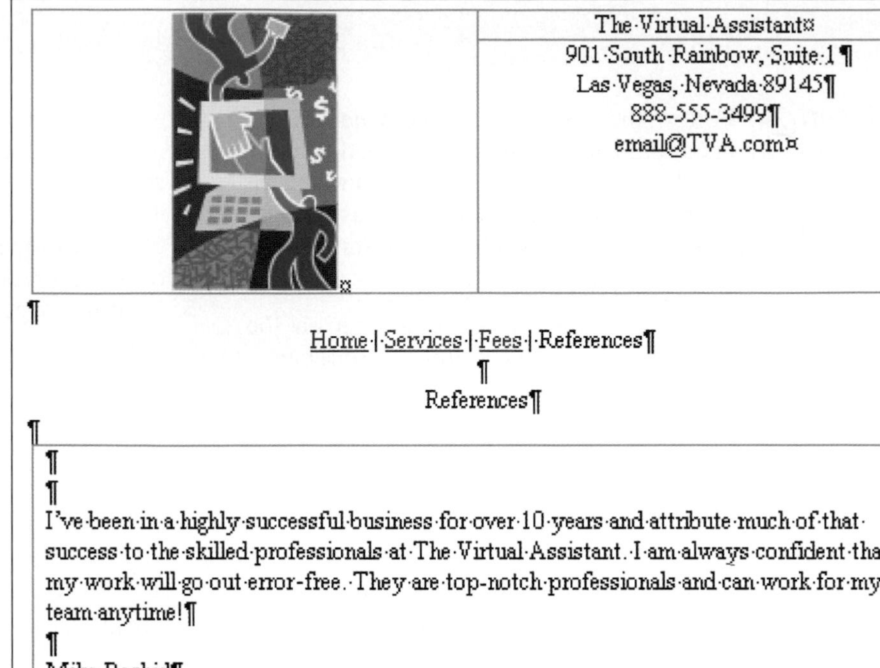

The Virtual Assistant

901 South Rainbow, Suite 1
Las Vegas, Nevada 89145
888-555-3499
email@TVA.com

Home | Services | Fees | References

References

I've been in a highly successful business for over 10 years and attribute much of that success to the skilled professionals at The Virtual Assistant. I am always confident that my work will go out error-free. They are top-notch professionals and can work for my team anytime!

Mike Rashid
Network Engineer
Denver, Colorado

The documents produced by The Virtual Assistant are impeccable! I can count on professional, reliable, competent, and efficient service without question. It is so easy to send documents back and forth via the Internet, and we all know that time is money. I highly recommend TVA for any of your word processing needs.

Nancy Shipley
Attorney-at-Law
Chicago, Illinois

Web layout view of references page.

Report 114-96

Web Site (continued)

Follow these steps to insert any missing hyperlinks on the link bar for all pages. Make the following changes to this report:

1. Insert a text hyperlink for the last word on the link bar as follows:
   References links to Report-114-96.htm.
2. Manually open Report-111-87.htm (the home page), Report-112-89.htm (the services page), and Report-113-92.htm (the fees page).
3. Insert any missing text hyperlinks on the link bar for each page as needed.
4. Save all pages, test all the hyperlinks, and edit any hyperlinks as needed.

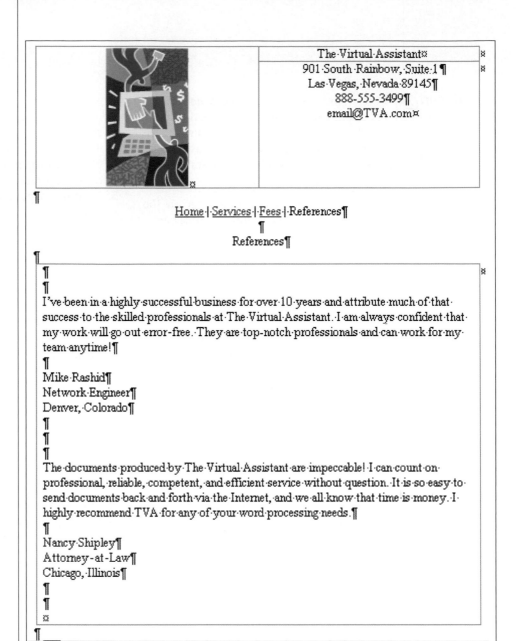

Report 114-97

Your Web Site (continued)

Follow these steps to create a new references page for your Web site named Report-114-97.htm similar to the Web layout view of the references page on page 460. Make the following changes to this report:

1. Change the title to `References`.
2. Change `Fees` to `References` on the second blank line below the link bar.
3. Move inside the table below "References," and select and delete the information inside the table.
4. Type the information for two references; follow the setup for the references page on page 460.
5. Save the page, and view the Web page in a browser.

Report 114-98

Your Web Site (continued)

Follow these steps to insert any missing hyperlinks on the link bar for all pages of your Web site. Make the following changes to this report:

1. Insert a text hyperlink for the last word on the link bar as follows:

   References links to Report-114-98.htm.
2. Manually open Report-111-88.htm (the home page), Report-112-90.htm (the services page), and Report-113-94.htm (the fees page).
3. Insert any missing text hyperlinks on the link bar for each page as needed.
4. Save all pages, test all the hyperlinks, and edit any hyperlinks as needed.

Lesson 115

Formatting Web Pages

Goals

- Improve speed and accuracy
- Refine language arts skills in proofreading
- Format Web pages

A. Type 2 times.

A. WARMUP

```
     Contact bxvacuum@clean.com to order the large-sized      11
grips. They were just lowered to $160 from $240 (a 33 1/3%    22
markdown). Jay's #55 quilts were reduced to $88 from $99.     34
|  1  |  2  |  3  |  4  |  5  |  6  |  7  |  8  |  9  |  10  |  11  |  12
```

SKILLBUILDING

PPP PRETEST → PRACTICE → POSTTEST

PRETEST
Take a 1-minute timed writing. Review your speed and errors.

B. PRETEST: Common Letter Combinations

```
     He did mention that they are sending a lawful taping     11
of the comedy format to a performing combo. A motion to       22
commit a useful option forced a fusion of forty persons.      33
|  1  |  2  |  3  |  4  |  5  |  6  |  7  |  8  |  9  |  10  |  11  |  12
```

PRACTICE
Speed Emphasis:
If you made no more than 1 error on the Pretest, type each *individual* line twice.
Accuracy Emphasis:
If you made 3 or more errors, type each *group* of lines (as though it were a paragraph) 2 times.

C. PRACTICE: Word Beginnings

```
for forty forth format former forget forest forearm forbear
per peril perky period permit person peruse perform persist
com combo comic combat commit common combed compose complex
```

D. PRACTICE: Word Endings

```
ing doing mixing living filing taping sending biking hiding
ion onion nation lotion motion option mention fusion legion
ful awful useful joyful earful lawful helpful sinful armful
```

POSTTEST
Repeat the Pretest timed writing and compare performance.

E. POSTTEST: Common Letter Combinations

F. Take a 1-minute timed writing on the first paragraph to establish your base speed. Then take four 1-minute timed writings on the remaining paragraphs. As soon as you equal or exceed your base speed on one paragraph, advance to the next, more difficult paragraph.

F. SUSTAINED PRACTICE: CAPITALIZATION

Even though he was only about thirty years old, Jason 11
knew that it was not too soon to begin thinking about his 23
retirement. He soon found out that there were many things 34
involved in his plans for an early and long retirement. 45

Even without considering the uncertainty of social 10
security, Jason knew that he should plan his career moves 22
so that he would have a strong company retirement plan. He 34
realized that he should have an Individual Retirement Plan. 45

When he became aware that The Longman Company, the 10
firm that employed him, would match his contributions to a 22
supplemental retirement account, he began saving even more. 34
He used the Payroll Department funds from the Goplin Group. 46

He also learned that The Longman Company retirement 11
plan, his Individual Retirement Plan, and his supplemental 22
retirement account are all deferred savings. With those 33
tax-dollar savings, Jason bought New Venture Group mutuals. 45

LANGUAGE ARTS

G. Edit this paragraph to correct any typing or formatting errors.

G. PROOFREADING

The idea and practise of sharing risk originated in antiquetry. Many years ago, Chinese merchants deviced an injenious way of protecting themselves against the chance of a financialy ruinous accadent in the dangerous river along the trade routtes when they were delivring goods.

FORMATTING

H. MORE WEB SITE DESIGN GUIDELINES

Follow these guidelines to design effective Web sites:

- Experiment with the themes that come with most programs.
- If you use a theme, experiment with the embedded styles that can be applied to titles, headings, subheadings, and so on, for design consistency.
- Choose a consistent look for headings and subheadings, including font size, color, and alignment, for design unity.
- Use color to establish moods: black is somber; white is clean, organized, or sterile; bright colors are energetic but may be hard to read. Experiment and use your judgment.

Word Processing Manual

I. WEB PAGE—DESIGN THEMES

Study Lesson 115 in your word processing manual. Complete all of the shaded steps while at your computer. Then format the jobs that follow.

DOCUMENT PROCESSING

Report 115-99

Web Site (continued)

Follow these steps to format the Web site.

1. Manually open Report-111-87.htm (the home page), Report-112-89.htm (the services page), Report-113-92.htm (the fees page), and Report-114-96.htm (the references page).
2. Apply a design theme to each page that coordinates with the picture at the top of each page. Remove any table borders as needed or if desired.
3. Move to each page, and apply a Heading 1 style to "The Virtual Assistant." Align the text and adjust the table as needed to position the picture and text attractively. Copy and paste the table from one page to the next if desired.
4. Move to the home page, and add a bullet to each item under each heading beginning with the heading "Word Processing."
5. Apply a Heading 3 style to each heading beginning with the heading "Word Processing."
6. Move to the services page, apply a Heading 2 style to "Services," center the line, and delete the blank line below the link bar.
7. Add a bullet to each sentence under each heading.
8. Apply a Heading 3 style to each heading beginning with "Word Processing."
9. Move to the fees page, apply a Heading 2 style to "Fees," center the line, and delete the blank line below the link bar.
10. Add a bullet to each sentence under the first paragraph except for the last sentence on the page.
11. Insert a horizontal line in the blank line after the last bulleted item.
12. Move to the references page, apply a Heading 2 style to "References," center the line, and delete the blank line below the link bar.
13. Place the insertion point in front of the first blank line in the table, and insert a horizontal line.
14. Place the insertion point in front of the second blank line between the references, and insert a horizontal line.
15. Place the insertion point in front of the second blank line under the last reference, and insert a horizontal line.
16. Change any styles, fonts, borders, or colors as desired.
17. Test all the hyperlinks, edit any hyperlinks as needed, and save all pages.
18. View your finished Web site in a browser.

Note: If you would like to format the Web site you created for your own business in Lessons 111–114, follow steps similar to those in Report 115-99.

Keyboarding Connection

Choosing a Different Home Page

You don't have to start at the same home page every time you use your browser. You can change the browser's home page to start at one of your favorite Web pages. Here's how to do it.

In Netscape, go to the chosen page and select Preferences from the Edit menu. Click the Navigator category in the Preferences dialog box. Click the Use Current Page button in the "home page" area. Choose Home Page in the "Navigator starts with" area. Click OK.

In Internet Explorer, from the chosen page select Internet Options from the Tools menu. Click the General tab, and then click the Use Current button in the "home page" area. Click OK.

YOUR TURN Using your browser, access a favorite Web page. Make it your browser's home page.

(Continued on next page)

The Virtual Assistant

901 South Rainbow, Suite 1
Las Vegas, Nevada 89145
888-555-3499
email@TVA.com

Home | Services | Fees | References

Do you need a skilled assistant who works tirelessly on your documents, doesn't need any office space, and gives your work that personal touch? The Virtual Assistant is a professional document processing and design service that will help create the professional image your business demands.

You don't get a second chance at a first impression. The graphics experts in our word processing and desktop publishing departments will make sure your documents look gorgeous. Our editors, who have completed a series of rigorous courses in business English and business communications, will make sure they are letter-perfect. Please browse around our site for details.

Word Processing

- Correspondence
- Reports
- Proposals
- Manuals

Desktop Publishing

- Newsletters
- Brochures
- Letterheads
- Resumes

Layout Editing

- In-House Styles
- Custom Styles
- Master Documents
- Table of Contents
- Indexes

The Virtual Assistant

901 South Rainbow, Suite 1
Las Vegas, Nevada 89145
888-555-3499
email@TVA.com

Home | Services | Fees | References

Services

Word Processing

- We prepare documents with a professional look for correspondence of all types as well as reports, proposals, manuals, and so on.

Desktop Publishing

- Our professional design specialists will create newsletters, brochures, letterheads, and other documents that are sure to capture your imagination.

Layout Editing

- Our layout editors will transform your documents using in-house styles or custom styles. For your longer projects, they are experts at building master documents that include a cover page, table of contents, and index.

Copy Editing

- Our copy editors will make sure that your document content is perfect. Proofreading, grammar, and writing style will all be checked so that your ideas are expressed clearly and effectively.

(Continued on next page)

The Virtual Assistant

901 South Rainbow, Suite 1
Las Vegas, Nevada 89145
888-555-3499
email@TVA.com

Home | Services | Fees | References

Fees

The Virtual Assistant strives to work within your organization's budget. We will review your individual needs and tailor the pricing to fit your project. We welcome the opportunity to provide an individual estimate. Be assured that our prices are extremely competitive. Here are some general guidelines regarding our fees:

- We typically charge by the hour or by the page, depending upon the job.
- Most fees are based on the length of the document and the amount of editing deemed necessary.
- We offer substantial discounts for volume work and repeat clients.
- A surcharge is added for rush jobs.
- Payment for services rendered should be made by credit card, check, or money order.

For a copy of our current rate guide, please send an e-mail message to rateguide@TVA.com.

The Virtual Assistant

901 South Rainbow, Suite 1
Las Vegas, Nevada 89145
888-555-3499
email@TVA.com

Home | Services | Fees | References

References

I've been in a highly successful business for over 10 years and attribute much of that success to the skilled professionals at The Virtual Assistant. I am always confident that my work will go out error-free. They are top-notch professionals and can work for my team anytime!

Mike Rashid
Network Engineer
Denver, Colorado

The documents produced by The Virtual Assistant are impeccable! I can count on professional, reliable, competent, and efficient service without question. It is so easy to send documents back and forth via the Internet, and we all know that time is money. I highly recommend TVA for any of your word processing needs.

Nancy Shipley
Attorney-at-Law
Chicago, Illinois

Report 115-100

Web Site

Progress Check

Your goal is to have zero typographical errors when the GDP software first scores the document.

Follow these steps to create the home page and Contact Us page for this Web site:

1. Change the title of Report-115-100A.htm to `In The Game, Home.`
2. Insert Home-115A.htm into the home page (Report-115-100A.htm).
3. Leave Report-115-100A.htm open, and create an additional new Web page named Report-115-100B; change the title to `In The Game, Contact Us.`
4. Insert the file Contact Us-115B.htm into Report-115-100B.htm.
5. Insert a picture related to sports in the open cell in Column A on the Contact Us page (Report-115-100B.htm).
6. Resize the picture proportionally until it is about 1 inch wide, and center the picture in the open cell in Column A on the Contact Us page.
7. Apply a design theme to the Contact Us page that coordinates with the picture.
8. Apply a Heading 1 style to "In The Game," and center the line on the Contact Us page.
9. Apply a Heading 3 style to the headings "E-Mail," "Call Us," and "Snail Mail" on the Contact Us page.
10. Select the table and the link bar at the top of the Contact Us page, copy it, move to the top of the home page, and paste it.
11. Apply the same design theme to the home page that you used on the Contact Us page.
12. Apply a Heading 3 style to the headings "Baseball and Softball," "Soccer, Track and Field," and "Gymnatics" on the home page.
13. Change any styles, fonts, borders, or colors as desired on both pages.
14. Insert text hyperlinks on the link bar of each page as follows:
    Home links to Report-115-100A.htm
    Contact Us links to Report-115-100B.htm
15. Test all the hyperlinks, edit any hyperlinks as needed, and save all pages.
16. View your finished Web site in a browser.

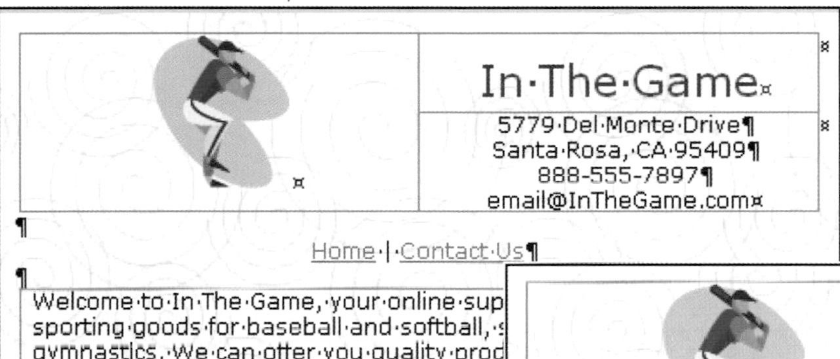

Web layout view of home page.

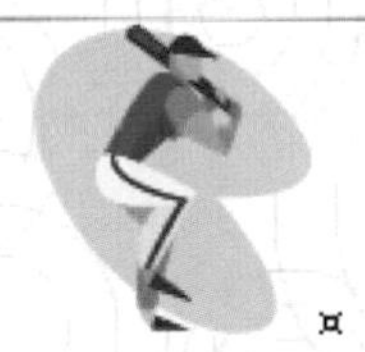

Web layout view of contact us page.

Unit 24

Skillbuilding and In-Basket Review

In-Basket Review (Insurance)

Goals

- Type at least 50wpm/5′/5e
- Format documents used in the insurance industry

A. Type 2 times.

A. WARMUP

```
     He realized that exactly 10% of the budget ($62,475)    11
was questionable. Several key people reviewed it; most of    22
them wanted to reject about 1/3 of the proposed line items!  34
| 1 | 2 | 3 | 4 | 5 | 6 | 7 | 8 | 9 | 10 | 11 | 12
```

SKILLBUILDING

B. PROGRESSIVE PRACTICE: ALPHABET

If you are not using the GDP software, turn to page SB-7 and follow the directions for this activity.

Strategies for Career Success

Managing Group Conflict

Not all team members have the same opinion or approach to solving a problem. Before a group can reach an agreement, conflicts must be addressed and expressed openly. Follow these steps to manage group conflict.

Take everyone's feelings and opinions seriously. Don't be afraid to disagree. Offer and accept constructive criticism. Find points of agreement. When the group makes a decision, support it fully.

Be a good listener. Take notes, maintain eye contact, restate what you hear, and listen for the emotions behind the words. Try to view the situation through the other person's eyes. Don't jump to conclusions. Ask nonthreatening questions to clarify meaning, and listen without interrupting. Most group conflicts don't get resolved until everyone feels he or she has had a chance to be heard.

YOUR TURN When is the last time you had a conflict with a coworker? What did you do about it? What was the result?

C. Take two 5-minute timed writings. Review your speed and errors.

Goal: At least 50wpm/5′/5e

C. 5-MINUTE TIMED WRITING

```
     Several factors should be considered before you buy a   11
new printer for your computer. First, decide how you will    23
use the new printer. If you plan to use the printer for      34
composing letters or reports, you may want to shop for an    45
ink jet printer that is reasonably priced and capable of     57
doing general tasks. If you are purchasing the printer for   69
office use, you may wish to shop for a printer that prints   80
documents more quickly and of exceptional quality. Finally,  92
if you plan to use a digital camera with the printer, you   104
will want a printer that is designed to print documents of  116
photo quality.                                              119
     Resolution, speed, and paper handling are some other   130
factors you should consider when you purchase a printer.    141
Resolution refers to how sharp the image appears on the     152
paper. With printers producing a higher resolution, the     163
imaging gives you higher-quality output. You will see this  175
amazing difference in imaging when you compare some samples 187
of print from the other kinds of printers.                  196
     If you expect to print long documents, then you will   207
want to look for a reliable printer with a feed tray that   218
holds large amounts of paper. The more expensive printers   230
are usually faster printers. After assessing your printer   241
needs, you are ready to make your purchase.                 250
|  1  |  2  |  3  |  4  |  5  |  6  |  7  |  8  |  9  |  10  |  11  |  12
```

DOCUMENT PROCESSING

Form 116-15

Letter Template

Use the first letter template in your word processing software.

Situation: Today is December 27, 20--. You are employed in the office of All-City, Inc., an insurance company in Columbia, Missouri. Offices are located at 17 North Eighth Street, Columbia, MO 65201, and their phone number is 800-555-9981. All City, Inc., handles auto, home, and life insurance coverage. The Web site address is www.ACI.com.

Mr. Greg Scher, executive vice president, has written the letter shown on page 471. You are to type it using a correspondence template. He prefers block-style letters with *Sincerely* as his complimentary closing and uses his title in the writer's identification. The letter should be addressed to Ms. Rosa Nunez, 731 Broad Street, Newark, NJ 07102, and you should use standard punctuation. This letter includes two enclosures. The company slogan is "Insuring you at home and around the world."

¶ Your recent letter was filled with excellent questions, Ms. Nunez, and I am more than happy to answer them for you.
¶ All City, Inc., handles auto, home, and life insurance coverage for you and your family. However, since you are primarily interested in auto insurance, I have enclosed a brochure with the details and a table with required minimum coverage for the states you mentioned.
¶ ACI's automobile policy combines both mandatory and optional coverages in one package. This policy can be tailored to meet your individual needs so that you end up with a policy that provides comprehensive protection. However, the best way for you to understand fully what we can offer you is to schedule a meeting at your convenience.
¶ Ms. Elena Ortega will be calling you in the next day or two to arrange an appointment after you have had a chance to review the enclosed materials. We also have an excellent Web site at ACI.com filled with helpful information. Again, thank you for your inquiry, Ms. Nunez.

Table 116-55
Boxed Table

The boxed table below is to be enclosed with the letter when it is sent to Ms. Nunez.

STATE MINIMUM COVERAGE REQUIREMENTS		
Minimum Limits	**State**	**Required Coverage**
25/50/10	NY	Bodily Injury and Property Damage Liability, Personal Injury Protection, Uninsured Motorist
15/30/5	NJ	Bodily Injury and Property Damage Liability, Personal Injury Protection, Uninsured Motorist
15/30/5	PA	Bodily Injury and Property Damage Liability, Medical Payments
20/40/10	CT	Bodily Injury and Property Damage Liability, Uninsured and Underinsured Motorist

Form 116-16

Letterhead Form

Mr. Scher has sketched out a letterhead form, and he would like you to design the finished letterhead for All-City, Inc.

Insert a decorative image.

Identify our company, including our Web site.

Insert our company slogan with a border above it.

In-Basket Review (Hospitality)

Goals

- Improve speed and accuracy
- Refine language arts skills in word usage
- Format documents used in the hospitality industry

A. Type 2 times.

A. WARMUP

1 The executive meeting won't begin until 8:15; please 11
2 contact just the key people at zfnet@mail.com. Did Kay say 23
3 that quite a group* (*234) is expected by 9 o'clock today? 34

| 1 | 2 | 3 | 4 | 5 | 6 | 7 | 8 | 9 | 10 | 11 | 12

SKILLBUILDING

B. Take three 12-second timed writings on each line. The scale below the last line shows your wpm speed for a 12-second timed writing.

B. 12-SECOND SPEED SPRINTS

4 Half of the space was going to be used for seven new desks.
5 She will soon know if all their goals have been met or not.
6 You must learn to focus on each one of your jobs every day.
7 The group will meet in the new suite that is down the hall.

5 10 15 20 25 30 35 40 45 50 55 60

C. Type line 8. Then type lines 9–11 (as a paragraph), reading the words from right to left. Type 2 times.

C. TECHNIQUE PRACTICE: CONCENTRATION

8 When typing, always strive for complete concentration.
9 concentration. complete for strive always typing, When
10 errors. your on down cut may rate typing your in decrease A
11 errors. of number the reduce to rate reading your down Slow

D. DIAGNOSTIC PRACTICE: SYMBOLS AND PUNCTUATION

If you are not using the GDP software, turn to page SB-2 and follow the directions for this activity.

LANGUAGE ARTS

E. Study the rules at the right.

E. WORD USAGE

RULE ▶ accept/except

***Accept* means "to agree to"; *except* means "to leave out."**

All employees except the maintenance staff should accept the agreement.

RULE ▶ affect/effect

***Affect* is most often used as a verb meaning "to influence"; *effect* is most often used as a noun meaning "result."**

The ruling will affect our domestic operations but will have no effect on Asian operations.

RULE ▶ farther/further

***Farther* refers to distance; *further* refers to extent or degree.**

The farther we drove, the further agitated he became.

RULE ▶ personal/personnel

***Personal* means "private"; *personnel* means "employees."**

All personnel agreed not to use e-mail for personal business.

RULE ▶ principal/principle

***Principal* means "primary"; *principle* means "rule."**

The principle of fairness is our principal means of dealing with customers.

Edit the sentences to correct any errors in word usage.

```
12 The company cannot accept any collect calls, except for his.
13 The affect of the speech was dramatic; everyone was affected.
14 Further discussion by office personal was not appropriate.
15 Comments made during any meeting should never be personal.
16 If the meeting is held any further away, no one will attend.
17 The principle reason for the decision was to save money.
18 Office ethics is a basic principle that should be practiced.
19 He cannot except the fact that the job was delegated to Jack.
20 Any further effects on office personnel will be evaluated.
```

DOCUMENT PROCESSING

Situation: You are employed at the office of Suite Retreat, a group of vacation cottage-style suites in Sanibel, Florida. The office and suites are located at 3539 Shell Basket Lane, Sanibel Island, FL 33957. The phone number is 941-555-3422, and the e-mail address is email@SuiteRetreat.com.

Ms. Maxwell, your boss, has asked you to redesign the Web site for Suite Retreat. She has written a description of Suite Retreat that she wants you to use in the home page. You should also include identifying information and a picture that will capture the feeling of a carefree beach vacation spot. The theme and styles you choose for the Web site should reflect the same image.

Begin by creating the home page as shown on page 476. Add the title `Suite Retreat Home`.

Report 117-101

Web Site

personal/personnel

¶ Are you ready to experience a private beach retreat with warm waters, endless white sand, and blue skies? The personnel at Suite Retreat are at your service and will make sure your stay is a pleasurable one.

¶ Suite Retreat is hidden away on a private beach on the Gulf of Mexico at the end of a secluded country road. You will feel the soothing

affect/effect

effects of our lush, tropical surroundings and charming cottage suites the moment you enter our winding drive. Each suite is beautifully decorated and appointed with marble baths and

personal/personnel

private whirlpools for your personal use. Click

farther/further

here for further details on our suites.

¶ If you are interested in a little recreation during your stay, we have a variety of activities available on the property:

Reference Manual

Refer to page R-12C of the Reference Manual for a review of list formatting.

- Shuffleboard courts and tennis courts
- Bicycles and kayaks
- Swimming and shelling

¶ If you enjoy golf and fine dining, you will find a small golf course and excellent seafood within easy walking distance about a half mile

farther/further

farther down the beach.

Strategies for Career Success

What to Exclude From Your Resume

What items should you omit from your resume? Don't list salary demands. If the job posting requires a salary history, create a separate page listing the salaries for each position you've held. If the job posting wants your salary requirements, in the application letter state, "Salary expectation is in the range . . . ," and provide a range (usually a $5,000 range).

Exclude personal information such as race, gender, health status, age, marital status, religious preference, political preference, national origin, and physical characteristics (for example, height, weight). Do not provide your Social Security number or your photograph.

Exceptions to listing personal information do exist. For example, if you are applying for a job at a political party's headquarters and you are a member of that party, listing your party affiliation might be important to your potential employer.

YOUR TURN Review your resume. Have you included any personal information? If your answer is yes, does it serve a purpose for being in your resume?

Report 117-102

Web Site (continued)

Ms. Maxwell has asked you to continue building the Web site by making the following changes: Change the title to "Suite Retreat Rates." Add two hyperlinks on the rates page to the link bar on both pages. The Home hyperlink should point to Report-117-101.htm, and the Rates hyperlink should point to Report-117-102.htm. Also add a hyperlink on the home page to the word *here* in the last sentence of the second paragraph to link to the Rates page. Apply the same theme and styles as used on the home page to the Rates page, and type the information as shown in the illustration below.

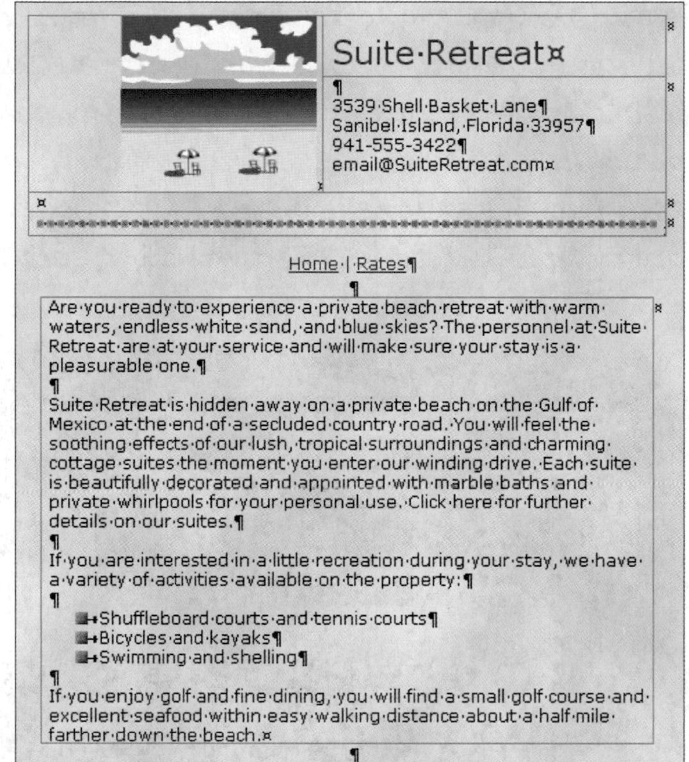

Suite Retreat

3539 Shell Basket Lane
Sanibel Island, Florida 33957
941-555-3422
email@SuiteRetreat.com

Home | Rates

Are you ready to experience a private beach retreat with warm waters, endless white sand, and blue skies? The personnel at Suite Retreat are at your service and will make sure your stay is a pleasurable one.

Suite Retreat is hidden away on a private beach on the Gulf of Mexico at the end of a secluded country road. You will feel the soothing effects of our lush, tropical surroundings and charming cottage suites the moment you enter our winding drive. Each suite is beautifully decorated and appointed with marble baths and private whirlpools for your personal use. Click here for further details on our suites.

If you are interested in a little recreation during your stay, we have a variety of activities available on the property:

- Shuffleboard courts and tennis courts
- Bicycles and kayaks
- Swimming and shelling

If you enjoy golf and fine dining, you will find a small golf course and excellent seafood within easy walking distance about a half mile farther down the beach.

Home page.

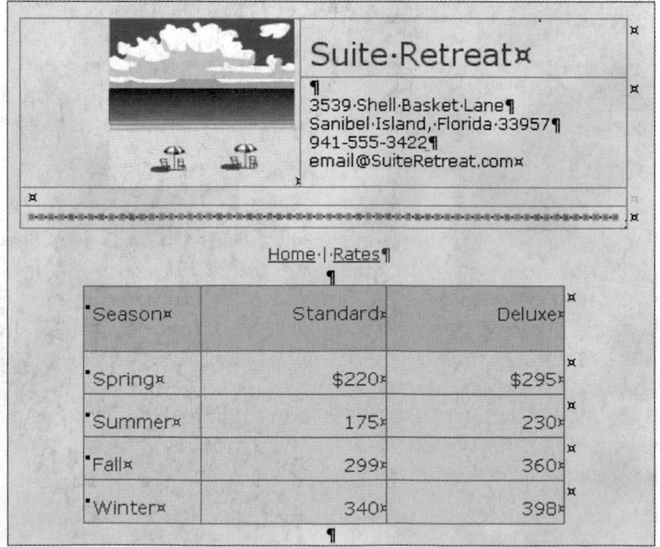

Suite Retreat

3539 Shell Basket Lane
Sanibel Island, Florida 33957
941-555-3422
email@SuiteRetreat.com

Home | Rates

Season	Standard	Deluxe
Spring	$220	$295
Summer	175	230
Fall	299	360
Winter	340	398

Rates page.

In-Basket Review (Retail)

Goals

- Type at least 50wpm/5′/5e
- To format documents used in the retail industry

A. Type 2 times.

A. WARMUP

```
     Does Pamela know if Region 29* (*Ventura) has met the   11
sales quota? Their exact target zone is just not clear;      22
they don't have to submit their totals until 4:30 on 5/7.    34
| 1 | 2 | 3 | 4 | 5 | 6 | 7 | 8 | 9 | 10 | 11 | 12
```

SKILLBUILDING

B. PACED PRACTICE

If you are not using the GDP software, turn to page SB-14 and follow the directions for this activity.

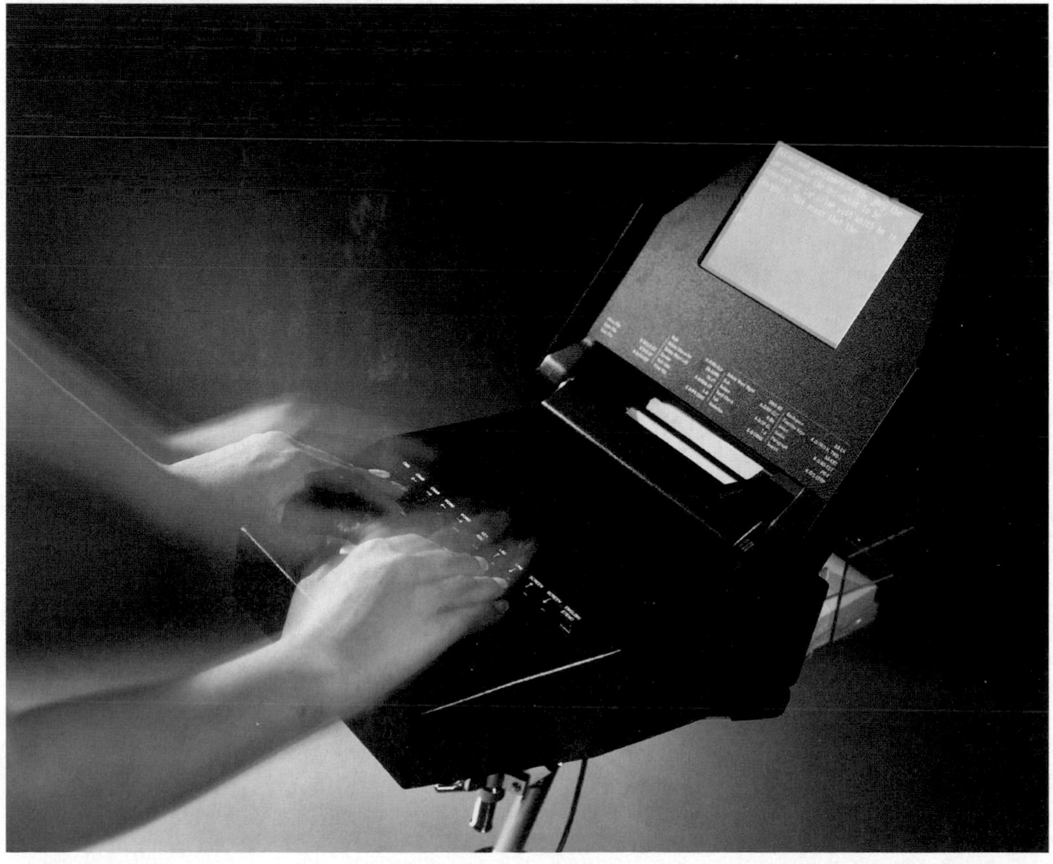

C. Take two 5-minute timed writings. Review your speed and errors.

Goal: At least 50wpm/5′/5e

C. 5-MINUTE TIMED WRITING

```
     Job sharing is a current concept that many places are      11
using to keep valued workers. People are finding a wide         22
range of reasons for not wanting to work full time. Here        34
are some tips on how to approach your boss if you would         45
like to try job sharing.                                        50
     First, check your company handbook for an authorized       61
policy regarding this concept. If there is no rule that         72
prohibits the concept, then try to enlist a coworker who        83
would like to job share and help you in writing a proposal      95
for job sharing where you work.                                101
     Next, define your needs and your goals. Develop a work    113
schedule that will meet all of your personal and monetary      124
needs. Be sure that you include enough time to get the work    136
done. If you want to work at your home on occasion, be sure    148
to state your desires. You might find it is often quite        159
helpful to maintain a journal of your job duties, noting       171
how much time is devoted to each task. Your plan should        182
also include details about the logistics of your proposal.     194
Decide how to cope with unexpected crisis situations.          205
     Finally, time your presentation so there will be no       215
unnecessary interruptions. Be organized, persistent, and       227
professional in your presentation. Prepare to be successful    239
by compiling clearly defined ideas to support your plans.      250
|  1  |  2  |  3  |  4  |  5  |  6  |  7  |  8  |  9  |  10  |  11  |  12
```

DOCUMENT PROCESSING

Form 118-17

Memo Template

Use the first memo template in your word processing software.

Situation: Today is January 5, 20--. You are employed as an administrative assistant to Kelley O'Brian. Ms. O'Brian is vice president of marketing for Sports 'R Us, a retailer for sports equipment and clothing in San Diego, California, at 3939 Townsgate Drive, San Diego, CA 92130. The Web site is www.SRU.com.

The company is in the midst of launching a brand-new line of women's sportswear for the beach. Ms. O'Brian has written the memo below to Hitochi Morimoto, president of Sports 'R Us, with a copy to Barbara Warrick, vice president of sales. You are to type the memo, using a memo template. The subject of the memo is SRU Sunwear Ad Campaign.

(Continued on next page)

¶ I am pleased to tell you that we are in the final stages of our ad campaign to launch our newest line of women's beach sportswear named SRU Sunwear. We are just about to sign Cindy Bloom to serve as our spokesperson and featured model in our magazine ad campaign.

¶ I have scheduled a meeting for next week so that you can meet Cindy and see a representative sampling of our exciting new sportswear line. My staff members will also be ready with a presentation for our ad campaign, which will focus on the practicality and smart good looks of our newest beachwear. I have attached an agenda for your review.

¶ Our company has always been known for the value and quality of our sportswear. This line is based on a smaller emerging brand that will save our customers money while still maintaining the high quality they have come to expect. I look forward to our meeting next week.

Report 118-103

Agenda

Prepare the meeting agenda shown below. The agenda should be attached to the memo when it is sent to Mr. Morimoto. It should be titled SRU SUNWEAR AD CAMPAIGN. The meeting will be held on January 12, 20--, at 11 a.m.

Call to order
Approval of minutes of December 20 meeting
Introduction of Cindy Bloom
Progress report on the status of the ad campaign
Presentation of the ad campaign
Presentation of some samples from the new sportswear line
Announcements
Miscellaneous
Adjournment

Report 118-104

Cover Page

Ms. O'Brian has sketched out a cover page for the ad campaign report and would like you to design the finished cover page for the SRU Sunwear line of beach apparel. The report will be distributed at the meeting.

Insert some word art with the name of our sportswear line.

Insert a picture related to our new line of beach sportswear.

Identify our company and our address, including our Web site.

In-Basket Review (Government)

Goals

- Improve speed and accuracy
- Refine language arts skills in spelling
- Format documents used in government work

A. Type 2 times.

A. WARMUP

```
1      Turner & Finch will charge us $10,234 to complete the   11
2  job. Do they realize that they quoted us an initial fee of  23
3  exactly $9,876? Kelly will call them very soon to verify.   34
   | 1 | 2 | 3 | 4 | 5 | 6 | 7 | 8 | 9 | 10 | 11 | 12
```

SKILLBUILDING

PRETEST → PRACTICE → POSTTEST

PRETEST
Take a 1-minute timed writing. Review your speed and errors.

B. PRETEST: Close Reaches

```
4      Sadly, the same essay was used to oppose and deny the   11
5  phony felony charge. After the weapon was located in his    22
6  pocket, the jury was left to cast the joint ballot anyway.  34
   | 1 | 2 | 3 | 4 | 5 | 6 | 7 | 8 | 9 | 10 | 11 | 12
```

PRACTICE
Speed Emphasis: If you made no more than 1 error on the Pretest, type each *individual* line 2 times.
Accuracy Emphasis: If you made 2 or more errors, type each *group* of lines (as though it were a paragraph) 2 times.

C. PRACTICE: Adjacent Keys

```
7  po post spot pours vapor poker powder oppose weapon pockets
8  sa sash same usage essay sadly safety dosage sample sailing
9  oi oily join point voice doing choice boiled egoist loiters
```

D. PRACTICE: Conscecutive Fingers

```
10 ft left soft often after shift gifted crafts thrift uplifts
11 ny onyx deny nylon vinyl phony anyway skinny felony canyons
12 lo loss solo loser flood color locate floral ballot loaders
```

POSTTEST
Repeat the Pretest timed writing and compare performance.

E. POSTTEST: Close Reaches

F. Take a 1-minute timed writing on the first paragraph to establish your base speed. Then take four 1-minute timed writings on the remaining paragraphs. As soon as you equal or exceed your base speed on one paragraph, advance to the next, more difficult paragraph.

F. SUSTAINED PRACTICE: PUNCTUATION

13 Have you ever noticed that a good laugh every now and 11
14 then really makes you feel better? Research has shown that 23
15 laughter can have a very healing effect on our bodies. It 34
16 is an excellent way to relieve tension and stress all over. 46

17 When you laugh, your heart beats faster, you breathe 11
18 deeper, and you exercise your lungs. When you laugh, your 22
19 body produces endorphins--a natural painkiller that gives 34
20 you a sense of euphoria that is very powerful and pleasant. 46

21 Someone said, "Laugh in the face of adversity." As it 11
22 happens, this is first-rate advice. It's a great way to 22
23 cope with life's trials and tribulations; it's also a good 34
24 way to raise other people's spirits and relieve tension. 45

25 Finding "humor" in any situation takes practice--try 11
26 to make it a full-time habit. We're all looking for ways 22
27 to relieve stress. Any exercise--jogging, tennis, biking, 34
28 swimming, or golfing--is a proven remedy for "the blues." 45

LANGUAGE ARTS

G. Type these frequently misspelled words, paying special attention to any spelling problems in each word.

G. SPELLING

29 practice continue regular entitled course resolution assist
30 weeks preparation purposes referred communication potential
31 environmental specifications original contractor associated
32 principal systems client excellent estimated administration
33 responsibility mentioned utilized materials criteria campus

Edit the sentences to correct any misspellings.

34 It is the responsability of the administration to assist.
35 The principle client prepared the excellent specifications.
36 He mentioned that the critiria for the decision were clear.
37 The contractor associated with the project referred them.
38 He estamated that the potential for resolution was great.
39 I was told that weeks of reguler practice were required.

DOCUMENT PROCESSING

Correspondence 119-99

Business Letter in Block Style

Situation: Today is November 4, 20--. Use this date in all documents as needed. You work as an administrative assistant for Ruth McBride. She is research director for Ride Share, a free government-funded commuter service in Chicago that informs people about commuting alternatives. For the purposes of this simulation, your name will be Roberto Duran. Your e-mail address is rduran@rideshare.net.

Ms. McBride has left the letter below in your in-basket to be sent to Mr. Jason Davis, executive director for Canadian CarShare, which is located at 1233 West Third Avenue, Vancouver, BC V6J 1K1 in Canada. When communicating with Canadian firms, use A4 metric-size paper and adhere to Canadian mailing guidelines.

Ms. McBride prefers a block-style letter with standard punctuation, uses *Sincerely* as the complimentary close, and likes her business title typed below her name in a letter closing. Add this postscript notation at the end of the letter:

```
Any statistics you might
choose to include on the
environmental impact
associated with car sharing
in your Web site at
http://www.carshare.ca
would be very helpful.
```

Highlighted words are spelling words from the language arts activities.

¶ Ride Share is a government-funded commuter service whose mission is to inform our citizens about commuting alternatives in the Chicago area. My responsibility is to gather as many facts as possible regarding the regular practice of car sharing in Canada.

¶ As I understand this concept, a car share client could conceivably mix and match alternative modes of transportation and also have exclusive use of a reserved car for a fixed period of time. For example, a commuter could arrive at work on a train, pick up a reserved car at a nearby parking lot to run errands at lunch, return the car an hour later, and then continue home perhaps using a van pool or bus. The commuter would pay about 20 to 40 cents a kilometer along with some monthly membership fees.

¶ If you can tell me which cities have successfully utilized car sharing in Canada since it was first introduced and why, I can begin preparation for a proposal for a car sharing pilot project as a potential commuter alternative here in the Chicago area.

Correspondence 119-100

Business Letter in Block Style

Open the file for Correspondence 119-99. Ms. McBride would like you to send the same letter to Mr. Frans Zimmerly, executive director of Europa CarShare at Siesmayerstrasse 23, 60323 Frankfurt, GERMANY. When communicating with German firms, use A4 metric-size paper and adhere to German mailing guidelines.

Find and replace all instances of "Canada" with "Germany." Add this postscript at the end of the letter:

`Any statistics you might choose to fax to me at +1.800.555.5553 regarding the environmental impact associated with car sharing in Germany would be very helpful.`

Correspondence 119-101

E-Mail Message

Prepare this e-mail message to be sent to Ms. McBride. Type the e-mail greeting, `Hi, Ms. McBride:`, and the body shown below in correct format. Type `Roberto` as the closing and type this signature: `Roberto Duran | E-Mail: rduran@rideshare.net | Phone: 773-555-0107`. Save the e-mail message, but do not send it.

¶ I sent the two letters to the executive directors of CarShare as you requested. I will follow up in a week with phone calls and e-mail messages as follows:
¶ Mr. Jason Davis
+1.604.877.5555
jdavis@carshare.ubc.ca
¶ Mr. Frans Zimmerly
+49.30.20304-0
fzimmerly@carshare.de
¶ I found some statistics about car sharing that might be useful. Car sharing was first introduced in Quebec City in 1994 and now has about 1,200 users in six Canadian cities. About 90,000 car share commuters are located worldwide, with about half of them in Europe.

Keyboarding Connection

E-Mail Privacy

How private are your e-mail messages? Although there has been a lot of discussion about hacking and Internet security, e-mail may be more secure than your phone or postal mail. In fact, most new-generation e-mail programs have some kind of encryption built in.

It is not hackers who are the most likely to read your e-mail. It is anyone with access to your incoming mail server or your computer. If your computer and incoming server are at work, then you can assume that your supervisor can read your e-mail. In some companies, it is a normal practice to monitor employees' e-mail. Therefore, you should not send e-mail from work that you wouldn't want anyone there to read.

If you are serious about e-mail privacy, you may want to examine other encryption methods. Different products are available to ensure that your e-mail is read only by the intended recipient(s).

YOUR TURN Perform a keyword search, using a search engine (for example, www.altavista.com), for information on different products that are available to protect your e-mail privacy.

Lesson 120

In-Basket Review (Manufacturing)

Goals

- Type at least 50wpm/5′/5e
- Format documents used in the manufacturing industry

A. Type 2 times.

A. WARMUP

```
     Order extra color cartridges very soon! G & K Supply    11
just announced a 15% discount on orders for the following    22
cartridges: QB728 and ZM 436* (*for the ink-jet printers).   34
| 1 | 2 | 3 | 4 | 5 | 6 | 7 | 8 | 9 | 10 | 11 | 12
```

SKILLBUILDING

B. DIAGNOSTIC PRACTICE: NUMBERS

If you are not using the GDP software, turn to page SB-5 and follow the directions for this activity.

C. MAP

Follow the GDP software directions for this exercise in improving keystroking accuracy.

D. Take two 5-minute timed writings. Review your speed and errors.

Goal: At least 50wpm/5′/5e

D. 5-MINUTE TIMED WRITING

```
     With modern technology, it is possible to work at a       11
job full time and never leave your house. You can set up a     22
home office with a phone line, a facsimile, and a computer     34
system. Before choosing to work at home, however, you will     46
want to examine carefully your reasons for working at home.    58
     Some people think about working at home so they can       69
have more time to spend with their families. Other people      80
like to have more flexibility in their work schedule. They     92
are looking for the opportunity to enjoy a better quality     104
of life or to participate in other activities.                113
     There are some factors to consider before you make       124
the decision to work at home. You will want to consider the   135
ultimate cost of benefits that you could give up if you       147
change your place of work. You will want to check with your   159
employer to see if you are entitled to paid vacation days     170
and health insurance or if you can make contributions to      182
your retirement plan. Another factor to consider is the       193
limited contact with peers.                                   198
     Before making the ultimate decision to work at home,     209
develop some realistic expectations of how you will spend     221
each day. Although you can organize your work to fit your     232
schedule, you will find the real challenge is to determine    244
a routine that works for you.                                 250
| 1 | 2 | 3 | 4 | 5 | 6 | 7 | 8 | 9 | 10 | 11 | 12
```

DOCUMENT PROCESSING

Situation: Today is November 5, 20--. Use this date on all documents as needed. You work as an administrative assistant for Melanie Stone at MedPro Manufacturing, one of the largest medical diagnostic equipment manufacturers in the world. The home office is located in Arden, North Carolina, with branch offices located worldwide.

Your boss has left a business report in your in-basket for you to format and type. The title of the report is `MedPro Manufacturing`. The subtitle of the report is `Vision, Innovation, and Partnership`. Use the date after the subtitle.

(Continued on next page)

Report 120-105

Business Report

¶ Med Pro Manufacturing is 1 of the largest medical diagnostic equipment manufacturers in the world. We have been in business for almost eighty 80 years and our company has a solid reputation for quality and reliability in all our manufacturing processes. We take great pride in our current state-of-the-art manufacturing facilitise because we realize that doctors' reputations and patients' lives depend on the quality and reliability of our products and medical supplies.

VISION

¶ MedPro's vision for the New Millennium is to continue the manufacturing of circuit boards, light sources, fiber-optic light guides, and scanning engines.We have in place a stringent quality management process so that our customers are guaranteed a superior product at a competitive price. Because of these high standards, we have our company has attained the most current ISO Certification. We have reduced consistently our manufacturing cycles without sacrificing quality.

INNOVATION

¶ Everyone at MedPro from those on the manufacturing floor to those in the presidents office are is committed to the continuation of the research and development of innovative products and state-of-the-art high-tech manufacturing processes.

Products. Our electronic stethoscope system combined a revolutionary acoustic technology and teamed it with the power of a computer to produce extraordinary results in doctors offices. We specialize in innovative products for kids children. Our autorefractor has allowed optome-trists and ophthalmologists to perform objective refraction on children that is more quickly and easily than ever before. We are committed to the continuous development of innovative products like these.

Manufacturing processes. Our fiber-optic light guides and scanning engines are 2 more examples of how MedPro is committed to innovation in the manufacturing process as well. Our computercontrolled manufacturing

(Continued on next page)

and CAD/ECAD equipment helps us to control precisely the manufacturing of all our medical equipment. These same innovative processes have helped us reduce our costs and reduce our manufacturing cycle.

PARTNERSHIP

¶ One of the most effective ways to ensure success is to develop partnerships with other innovative business es that have the same commitment to high standards and are leaders in ~~there~~ their respective fields. Our team work and collaboration with our partners have helped us to establish an international presence and reputation. ¶ Our website ~~is~~ can be found at http://medpro.com, and it is filled with a wealth of ~~excellent~~ information. All details of our products, services, employees, contact information, and so on, can be foundthere. We look forward to your business.

Correspondence 120-102

Business Letter in Block Style

Progress and Proofreading Check

Documents designated as Proofreading Checks serve as a check of your proofreading skill. Your goal is to have zero typographical errors when the GDP software first scores the document.

A letter that includes a table has also been left in your in-basket to be typed. The letter is to be sent to Mrs. Carmen Tamashiro, associate director for Medical Relief International, which is located at 3-5-1 Kanda Jinbo-cho, Chiyoda-ku Tokyo 101, JAPAN. The subject line is `Relief Medical Supplies`. When communicating with Japanese firms, use A4 metric-size paper and adhere to Japanese mailing guidelines.

Ms. Stone, public relations director, prefers a block-style letter with standard punctuation and likes to use a predesigned format for tables. She prefers *Sincerely* as the complimentary close, uses the company name in the closing, and likes her business title typed below her name in the closing. She does not use a courtesy title.

¶ MedPro Manufacturing is happy to send our tenth shipment of relief medical supplies to be distributed as needed to the people of Japan who have been devastated by recent earthquakes and other natural disasters.

(Continued on next page)

¶ MedPro Manufacturing is happy to send our tenth shipment of relief medical supplies to be distributed as needed to the people of Japan who have been devastated by recent earthquakes and other natural disasters.

¶ Our previous shipments to Japan have amounted to well over $1 million worth of medical supplies such as antibiotics, surgical supplies, catheters, packs, crutches, splints, braces, and slings. MedPro Manufacturing usually sends medical goods and equipment exclusively; however, some of the earlier shipments have also included basic survival supplies. Our employees have helped us in our efforts to gather hundreds of tents, sleeping bags, blankets, flashlights, coats, socks, gloves, and all-weather apparel.

¶ Several international branches of our company would also like to offer their help if you need it. The table below includes all the pertinent information:

Address	E-Mail	Telephone
Marie Desaulnier 27, rue Pasteur 14390 Cabaurg FRANCE	medpro.com@email.fr	+33.1.64531515
Frank Liberman Mittlerer Pfad 9 D-70499 Stuttgart GERMANY	medpro.com@email.de	+49.711.8871624
Manny Yamamoto 16-13, 2-chome Hongo Tokyo 113-0033 JAPAN	medpro.com@email.jp	+81.3.38138841

Note: The table is shown with "Show Gridlines" active.

¶ If I can offer you any further assistance or information, please don't hesitate to contact me at +1.704.555.8945.

Skills Assessment on Part 6

5-Minute Timed Writing

The potential to reach your career goals has never 10
been better. The person who will move forward in a career 22
is the one who will make the bold moves to follow his or 33
her dreams. He or she will have the required attributes of 45
initiative and motivation to put forth maximum efforts in 57
order to realize a fulfilling career. 64
If you want to get ahead in the highly competitive 75
business world today, you need a personal coach or mentor 86
who is experienced in motivating people who want to reach 98
their potential. You may be afraid to go after your dream 110
career because you are afraid of failure. Your personal 121
mentor will help you to minimize any problems you incur. He 133
or she will encourage you to strive for more. 142
When you decide to work with a qualified coach, you 153
are investing in yourself. You can trust your coach to help 165
you through this joyful process of expanding your horizons 176
until you reach your goal. When you think you have reached 188
your limit, your coach will make suggestions for additional 200
improvement. He or she will present the strategies you can 212
use to be successful. Your coach will guide you in making 224
the critical decisions for advancing your career. The final 236
decision to improve your skills and become successful is 247
yours, however. 250

| 1 | 2 | 3 | 4 | 5 | 6 | 7 | 8 | 9 | 10 | 11 | 12 |

Form Test 6-18

Memo Template

Select the first memo template listed in your word processing software.

To: Michael Lani, Human Resources Director | **CC:** Armando Lopez, President | **From:** Charlene Morimoto, Committee Chairperson | **Date:** October 18, 20-- | **Re:** Turkey Trot Fun Run Fund-Raiser

¶ It's time once again for our annual Turkey Trot Fun Run, in which all proceeds are donated to the Read-2-Learn literacy program for inner-city youth. Since 1980, our Read-2-Learn Committee has donated over $200,000 to this very worthy cause, and we have every intention of raising at least $8,000 in this Fun Run on Thanksgiving Day, but we need your help.

¶ As our director of human resources, you are in a unique position to help us raise funds. If you could encourage each of our employees to donate $20 to sponsor one runner in this event, we would easily meet our goals this year. Last year we had over 400 sponsored runners.

(Continued on next page)

¶ The Read-2-Learn program is specifically targeted at the inner-city elementary students in our neighborhood in their quest for basic literacy skills. Our business is located in a rich, multicultural urban neighborhood that is in desperate need of this type of program. I have attached a brochure that explains all details of this reading program and an event flyer. If you need additional copies, please let me know. Also, please visit our Web site at http://www.turkeytrot.org for further details.
¶ urs | Attachments

Report Test 6-106

Web Page

1. Change the title of Report-Test-6-106.htm to `Read-2-Learn.`
2. Insert a centered, boxed table with 2 columns and 4 rows.
3. Type the information on page 494 and arrange it as shown below.
4. Insert a picture related to reading and size it approximately as shown. Apply a coordinated design theme.
5. Insert horizontal lines in Rows 2 and 4. Change any styles, fonts, or colors as desired.

	Read-2-Learn *A Youth Literacy Program of the Los Angeles Public Library*
• • • • • • • • • •	
Our mission is to provide instruction in the basic literacy skills of reading and writing for elementary school children. Read-2-Learn offers participants free tutoring and a variety of other support services. Our volunteer tutors have been trained and will be matched with students to provide optimal conditions for learning and practicing basic reading and writing skills. The learner's interests and needs are always considered first. This literacy program is funded by the Los Angeles Public Library; government grants; special events; and contributions from corporations, foundations and individuals. Our services include the following: • Free individualized tutoring • A resource library including books, tapes, games, and manuals • Basic computer literacy instruction • Small group or one-on-one instruction for learners • Ongoing evaluation and instructional support with a reading specialist • Referrals to other literacy programs	
• • • • • • • • • •	

(Continued on next page)

Read-2-Learn

A Youth Literacy Program of the Los Angeles Public Library

Our mission is to provide instruction in the basic literacy skills of reading and writing for elementary school children. Read-2-Learn offers participants free tutoring and a variety of other support services. Our volunteer tutors have been trained and will be matched with students to provide optimal conditions for learning and practicing basic reading and writing skills. The learner's interests and needs are always considered first.

This literacy program is funded by the Los Angeles Public Library; government grants; special events; and contributions from corporations, foundations, and individuals. Our services include the following:

- Free individualized tutoring
- A resource library including books, tapes, games, and manuals
- Basic computer literacy instruction
- Small group or one-on-one instruction for learners
- Ongoing evaluation and instructional support with a reading specialist
- Referrals to other literacy programs

Report Test 6-107

Flyer

Press the SPACE BAR 2 times, and create the flyer as shown in the illustration.

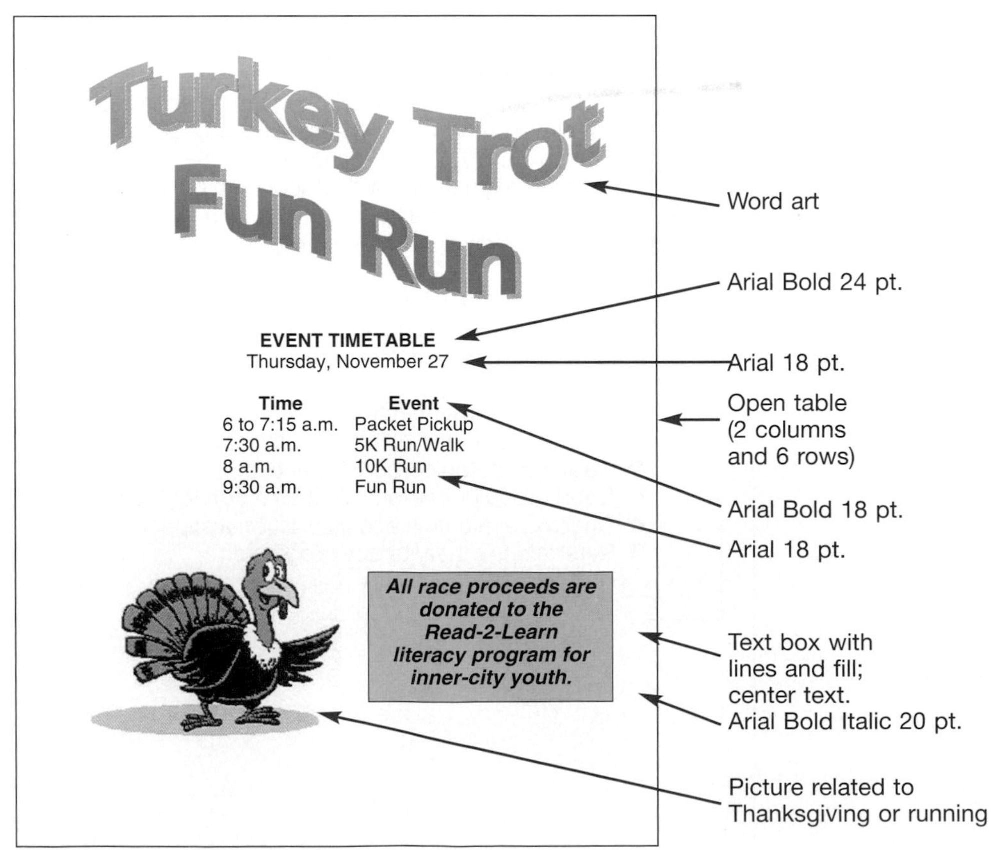

Turkey Trot
Fun Run
EVENT TIMETABLE
Thursday, November 27
Time
Event
6 to 7:15 a.m.
Packet Pickup
7:30 a.m.
5K Run/Walk
8 a.m.
10K Run
9:30 a.m.
Fun Run
All race proceeds are donated to the Read-2-Learn literacy program for inner-city youth.
Word art
Arial Bold 24 pt.
Arial 18 pt.
Open table (2 columns and 6 rows)
Arial Bold 18 pt.
Arial 18 pt.
Text box with lines and fill; center text.
Arial Bold Italic 20 pt.
Picture related to Thanksgiving or running

(Continued on next page)

Type this information in the open table and text box as shown in the flyer illustration on page 494.

EVENT TIMETABLE

Thursday, November 27

Time	**Event**
6 to 7:15 a.m.	Packet Pickup
7:30 a.m.	5K Run/Walk
8 a.m.	10K Run
9:30 a.m.	Fun Run

All race proceeds are donated to the Read-2-Learn literacy program for inner-city youth.

SKILLBUILDING

Diagnostic Practice: Symbols and Punctuation

The Diagnostic Practice: Symbols and Punctuation program is designed to diagnose and then correct your keystroking errors. You may use this program at any time throughout the course after completing Lesson 19.

Directions

1. Type one of the three Pretest/Posttest paragraphs 1 time, pushing *moderately* for speed. Review your errors.
2. Note your results—the number of errors you made on each symbol or punctuation key. For example, if you typed *75&* for *75%*, you would count 1 error on the % key.
3. For any symbol or punctuation key on which you made 2 or more errors, type the corresponding drill lines 2 times. If you made only 1 error, type the drill line 1 time.
4. If you made no errors on the Pretest/Posttest paragraph, type one set of the Practice: Symbols and Punctuation lines on page SB-4.
5. Finally, retype the same Pretest/Posttest, and compare your performance with your Pretest.

PRETEST/POSTTEST

Paragraph 1

```
Price & Joy stock closed @ 5 1/8 yesterday; it was up 13%
from yesterday. If we had sold our "high-demand" shares*
(*300 of them) before 3:30 p.m., we'd have made $15,000,
wouldn't we? Oh, well! I'll be in my office (#13C) crying.
```

Paragraph 2

```
The Time/CNN poll had the slate of Myers & Bassey ahead by
just 5%. Weren't you surprised? I was; after all, "they"*
(*meaning the crew) had ordered 60# of food @ $9.50 a pound
for a victory party at 3:30 p.m. today. What a sad mix-up!
```

Paragraph 3

```
Didn't my colleague* (*Elsa Jones-Salizar) send in $50 as a
10% deposit for reserving Room #5B on Friday and/or Monday?
Attached to her deposit was a note that said, "Call Tibby,
& me @ 10:30 a.m."; I was surprised. She sounded desperate!
```

PRACTICE: Individual Reaches

Ampersand

```
juj ju7j j7j j7&j j&&j j&&j juj ju7j j7j j7&j j&&j j&&j &&&
Alma & Bill & Carr & Dern & Epps & Farr & Gary & Horn & Ing
Jack & Kyle & Mann & Nash & Okum & Parr & Rand & Star & Tua
Uber & Vern & Will & Xang & Year & Zack & Sons & Bros & Inc
```

Apostrophe

```
;;; ;'; ;'; ';' ';' ''' Al's Bo's Di's it's Jo's Li's Moe's
you'd he'll she'd it'll she'll they'd aren't you're they're
we're we've we'll can't you've you'll hasn't didn't they've
she's don't isn't won't hadn't wasn't here's that's what'll
```

Asterisk

```
kik ki8k k8*k k8*k k**k k**k ki8k k8*k k8*k k**k k**k Note*
Ames* Beck* Carr* Dern* Epps* Farr* Gary* Horn* Iago* Jack*
Kyle* Mann* Nash* Okum* Parr* Rand* Star* Teri* Uber* Vern*
Will* Xang* Year* Zack* Note* Star* Also* List* Text* Cite*
```

At Sign

```
sws sw2s s2@s s2@s s@s s@@s and sws sw2s s2@s s2@s s@s s@@s
138 @ 34 and 89 @ 104 and 18 @ 458 and 89 @ 10 and 18 @ 340
162 & 31 and 48 & 606 and 81 @ 923 and 69 @ 42 and 54 @ 128
277 @ 89 and 57 & 369 and 70 @ 434 and 50 @ 15 and 37 @ 512
```

Colon

```
;:; ;:; ;:; ;:; ::: and :/: and :?: and :p: and :-: and :::
From: Name: City: Madam: 4:30 Bill to: Address: To: cc: PS:
Date: Rank: Time: Dept.: 27:1 Subject: Time in: Hi: Re: Cf:
Sirs: Ext.: Apt.: State: 1:00 Ship to: Acts 4:2 FY: ID: OS:
```

Comma

```
kkk k,k k,k and ,k, and ,i, and ,8, and I,I and K,K and ,,,
Ava, ebb, lac, had, foe, elf, hug, ugh, poi, raj, ink, gal,
bum, Ben, ago, cop, req, far, has, dot, tau, env, wow, sax,
I am, you are, he is, we are, they are, Al, Ty, Hy, Jo, Ann
```

Diagonal

```
;:; ;/; /// and p/p and /p/ and 0/0 ;:; ;/; /// and p/p ///
a/c c/o B/L ft/s ac/dc and/or he/she cad/cam due/dew 1/2005
I/O n/a B/S n/30 AM/FM ob/gyn on/off lay/lie fir/fur 2/2006
p/e m/f w/o km/h d/b/a ad/add to/too set/sit him/her 3/2007
```

Dollar Sign

```
frf fr4 f4f f$f f$f f$f $40 $44 $44 f$f f4f $ff $45 $54 $$$
$40 and $82 and $90 and $13 and $33 and $56 and $86 and $25
$214 plus $882 plus $900 plus $718 plus $910 plus $112 plus
$1,937.53 plus $337.89 tax $3,985.43 minus $150.75 discount
```

Exclamation Mark

```
aqa aqla aq!a a!!a a!!a aqa aqla aq!a a!!a a!!a Go! Hi! Lo!
Oh! Wow! Gas! Dig! Yes! Sit! Rats! Darn! Well! Drat! Shoot!
So! Eat! Air! Out! Not! Aim! Whoa! Wait! Whee! Oops! Yahoo!
No! Yea! Eek! Run! Boo! Buy! Look! Help! Duck! Alas! There!
```

Hyphen

```
;:; ;p; ;-; -;- --- and -;- and -;- and -/- and -:- and -P-
add-on be-all F-stop H-bomb A-frame age-old all-day boo-boo
how-to in-out jam-up log-in come-on cop-out end-all fade-in
mix-up no-win say-so tie-up one-act pig-out rip-off T-shirt
```

Number/Pound

```
de3d de3#d d3#d d3#d d##d d##d #33 #33 #333 de3d de3#d d3#d
45# of #245 and 837# of #013 and 31# of #981 and 2# of #013
12# of #883 and 345# of #328 and 67# of #112 and 8# of #109
54# of #542 and 378# of #310 and 13# of #189 and 6# of #657
```

Parentheses

```
lo91 lo91 lo(l lo(l l((l l((l ;p0; ;p0; ;p); ;p); ;)); ;));
(a) (b) (c) (d) (e) (f) (g) (h) (i) (j) (k) (l) (m) (n) (o)
(p) (q) (r) (s) (t) (u) (v) (w) (x) (y) (z) (1) (2) (3) (4)
(5) (6) (7) (8) (9) (0) (@) (#) ($) (&) (*) (-) (;) (,) (:)
```

Percent

```
ftf ft5f f5f f5%f f%%f f%%f ftf ft5f f5f f5%f f%%f f%%f %%%
40% and 82% and 90% and 13% and 33% and 56% and 86% and 25%
21% and 48% and 82% and 90% and 70% and 18% and 91% and 10%
34.5% off 89% increase 12% credit 67% finished 10% discount
```

Period

```
1.1 ... and .1. and .o. and .9. and .(. and .O. and L.L ...
Jan. Feb. Mar. Apr. Jun. Jul. Aug. Sep. Oct. Nov. Dec. a.m.
Sun. Mon. Tue. Wed. Thu. Fri. Sat. Mrs. Esq. Mex. Can. D.C.
I am. I see. We do. He is. I can. Do not. Help me. Go slow.
```

Question Mark

```
;;; ;/; ;?; ??? ?;? and p?p and ?0? and ?)? and ?-? and ???
So? Who? What? Can I? Why not? Who does? Stop here? Is she?
Me? How? When? May I? Who, me? Says who? Do it now? For me?
Oh? Why? Am I? Do we? Am I up? How much? Who knows? Will I?
```

Quotation Mark

```
;'; ;"; ;"; ";" """ and ;'; ;"; ;"; ";" """ and ;"; ";" """
"Eat" "Sit" "Rest" "Stay" "Roll" "Hello" "Look" "Pet" "Dry"
"Yes" "Lie" "Halt" "Next" "Move" "Write" "Type" "Ink" "Sew"
"Beg" "See" "Walk" "Wave" "Stop" "Speak" "File" "Run" "Cry"
```

Semicolon

```
;;; ;:; and ;'; and ;"; and ;p; and ;-; and ;/; and ;?; ;;;
tea; ebb; Mac; mid; lie; arf; hug; nth; obi; Taj; ark; Hal;
dim; man; bio; hop; seq; our; Gus; let; you; Bev; row; lax;
do not cry; that is Liz; see to it; I am sad; we do; I can;
```

PRACTICE: SYMBOLS AND PUNCTUATION

```
Doe & Fry sued May & Ito; Ho & Fox sued Doe & Lee for M&Ms.
Ann's dad said he's happy she's out of school; she'd agree.
Yesterday* (*April 9), the rock star said **** right on TV.
E-mail them at glyden@sales.com to buy 3 @ $89 or 9 @ $250.

Hi, Ross: Place odds of 3:1 on the game at 10:30 and 11:15.
Tom gave Ava, Jo, Al, and Tyson a red, white, and blue car.
On 3/1/2008, he will receive a pension and/or a big buyout.
The $80 skirt was cut to $70 and then $55 for a $25 saving.

What! No ice! I'm mortified! Run, order some more. Quickly!
Jones-Lynch built an all-season add-on to her A-frame home.
Please order 500# of #684, 100# of #133, and 200# of #1341.
The answer is (a) 1, (b) 4, (c) 7, or (d) all of the above.

The car was cut 15% and then 25% for a final saving of 40%.
Mr. R. J. Dix ordered from L. L. Bean on Dec. 23 at 11 a.m.
Who? Me? Why me? Because I can type? Is that a good reason?
"Look," he said, "see that sign?" It says, "Beware of Dog."
Stop here; get out of your car; walk a foot; begin digging.
```

Diagnostic Practice: Numbers

The Diagnostic Practice: Numbers program is designed to diagnose and then correct your keystroking errors. You may use this program at any time throughout the course after completing Lesson 14.

Directions

1. Type one of the three Pretest/Posttest paragraphs 1 time, pushing *moderately* for speed. Review your errors.
2. Note your results—the number of errors you made on each key and your total number of errors. For example, if you type *24* for *25*, you would count 1 error on the number *5*.
3. For any number on which you made 2 or more errors, select the corresponding drill lines and type the drills 2 times. If you made only 1 error, type the drill 1 time.
4. If you made no errors on the Pretest/Posttest paragraph, type 1 set of the drills that contain all numbers on page SB-6.
5. Finally, retype the same Pretest/Posttest, and compare your performance with your Pretest.

PRETEST/POSTTEST

Paragraph 1

```
     The statement dated May 24, 2004, listed 56 clamps; 15
batteries; 169 hammers; 358 screwdrivers; 1,298 pliers; and
1,475 files. The invoice numbered 379 showed 387 hoes, 406
rakes, 92 lawn mowers, 63 tillers, and 807 more lawn items.
```

Paragraph 2

```
     My inventory records dated May 31, 2004, revealed that
we had 458 pints; 1,069 quarts; and 8,774 gallons of paint.
We had 2,953 brushes; 568 scrapers; 12,963 wallpaper rolls;
897 knives; 5,692 mixers; 480 ladders; and 371 step stools.
```

Paragraph 3

```
     Almost 179 hot meals were delivered to the 35 shut-ins
in April, 169 in May, and 389 in June. Several workers had
volunteered 7,564 hours in 2004; 9,348 hours in 2003; 5,468
in 2002; and 6,577 in 2001. About 80 people were involved.
```

PRACTICE: INDIVIDUAL REACHES

```
1 aq aq1 aq1qa 111 ants 101 aunts 131 apples 171 animals a1
They got 11 answers correct for the 11 questions in BE 121.
Those 11 adults loaded the 711 animals between 1 and 2 p.m.
All 111 agreed that 21 of those 31 are worthy of the honor.

2 sw sw2 sw2ws 222 sets 242 steps 226 salads 252 saddles s2
The 272 summer tourists saw the 22 soldiers and 32 sailors.
Your September 2 date was all right for 292 of 322 persons.
The 22 surgeons said 221 of those 225 operations went well.

3 de de3 de3ed 333 dots 303 drops 313 demons 393 dollars d3
Bus 333 departed at 3 p.m. with the 43 dentists and 5 boys.
She left 33 dolls and 73 decoys at 353 West Addison Street.
The 13 doctors helped some of the 33 druggists in Room 336.
```

```
4 fr fr4 fr4rf 444 fans 844 farms 444 fishes 644 fiddles f4
My 44 friends bought 84 farms and sold over 144 franchises.
She sold 44 fish and 440 beef dinners for $9.40 per dinner.
The 1954 Ford had only 40,434 fairly smooth miles by May 4.

5 fr fr5 fr5rf 555 furs 655 foxes 555 flares 455 fingers f5
They now own 155 restaurants, 45 food stores, and 55 farms.
They ordered 45, 55, 65, and 75 yards of that new material.
Flight 855 flew over Farmington at 5:50 p.m. on December 5.

6 jy jy6 jy6yj 666 jets 266 jeeps 666 jewels 866 jaguars j6
Purchase orders numbered 6667 and 6668 were sent yesterday.
Those 66 jazz players played for 46 juveniles in Room 6966.
The 6 judges reviewed the 66 journals on November 16 or 26.

7 ju ju7 ju7uj 777 jays 377 jokes 777 joists 577 juniors j7
The 17 jets carried 977 jocular passengers above 77 cities.
Those 277 jumping beans went to 77 junior scouts on May 17.
The 7 jockeys rode 77 jumpy horses between March 17 and 27.

8 ki ki8 ki8ik 888 keys 488 kites 888 knives 788 kittens k8
My 8 kennels housed 83 dogs, 28 kids, and 88 other animals.
The 18 kind ladies tied 88 knots in the 880 pieces of rope.
The 8 men saw 88 kelp bass, 38 kingfish, and 98 king crabs.

9 lo lo9 lo9ol 999 lads 599 larks 999 ladies 699 leaders l9
All 999 leaves fell from the 9 large oaks at 389 Largemont.
The 99 linemen put 399 large rolls of tape on for 19 games.
Those 99 lawyers put 899 legal-size sheets in the 19 limos.

0 ;p ;p0 ;p0p; 100 pens 900 pages 200 pandas 800 pencils ;0
There were 1,000 people who lived in the 300 private homes.
The 10 party stores are open from 1:00 p.m. until 9:00 p.m.
They edited 500 pages in 1 book and 1,000 pages in 2 books.
```

All numbers

```
a1a s2s d3d f4f f5f j6j j7j k8k l9l ;0; Add 6 and 8 and 29.
That 349-page script called for 10 actors and 18 actresses.
The check for $50 was sent to 705 Garfield Street, not 507.
The 14 researchers asked the 469 Californians 23 questions.
```

All numbers

```
a1a s2s d3d f4f f5f j6j j7j k8k l9l ;0; Add 3 and 4 and 70.
They built 1,299 houses on the 345-acre site by the canyon.
Her research showed that gold was at 397 in September 2004.
For $868 extra, they bought 15 new books and 61 used books.
```

All numbers

```
a1a s2s d3d f4f f5f j6j j7j k8k l9l ;0; Add 5 and 7 and 68.
A bank auditor arrived on May 26, 2004, and left on May 27.
The 4 owners open the stores from 9:30 a.m. until 6:00 p.m.
After 1,374 miles on the bus, she must then drive 185 more.
```

Progressive Practice: Alphabet

This skillbuilding routine contains a series of 30-second timed writings that range from 16wpm to 104wpm. The first time you use these timed writings, take a 1-minute timed writing on the Entry Timed Writing paragraph. Note your speed.

Select a passage that is 2wpm higher than your current speed. Then take six 30-second timed writings on the passage.

Your goal each time is to complete the passage within 30 seconds with no errors. When you have achieved your goal, move on to the next passage and repeat the procedure.

Entry Timed Writing

```
     Bev was very lucky when she found extra quality in the     11
home she was buying. She quietly told the builder that she     23
was extremely satisfied with the work done on her new home.    35
The builder said she can move into her new house next week.    47
| 1 | 2 | 3 | 4 | 5 | 6 | 7 | 8 | 9 | 10 | 11 | 12
```

16wpm

The author is the creator of a document.

18wpm

Open means to access a previously saved file.

20wpm

A byte represents one character to every computer.

22wpm

A mouse may be used when running Windows on a computer.

24wpm

Soft copy is text that is displayed on your computer screen.

26wpm

Memory is the part of the word processor that stores information.

28wpm

A menu is a list of choices to direct the operator through a function.

30wpm

A sheet feeder is a device that will insert sheets of paper into a printer.

32wpm

An icon is a small picture that illustrates a function or an object in software.

34wpm

A window is a rectangular area with borders that displays the contents of open files.

36wpm

To execute means to perform an action specified by an operator or by the computer program.

38wpm

Output is the result of a word processing operation. It can be either printed or magnetic form.

40wpm

Format refers to the physical features which affect the appearance and arrangement of your document.

42wpm A font is a style of type of one size or kind which includes all letters, numbers, and punctuation marks.

44wpm Ergonomics is the science of adapting working conditions or equipment to meet the physical needs of employees.

46wpm Home position is the starting position of a document; it is typically the upper left corner of the display monitor.

48wpm The mouse may be used to change the size of a window and to move a window to a different location on the display screen.

50wpm An optical scanner is a device that can read text and enter it into a word processor without the need to type the data again.

52wpm Hardware refers to the physical equipment used, such as the central processing unit, display screen, keyboard, printer, or drives.

54wpm A peripheral device is any piece of equipment that will extend the capabilities of a computer system but is not required for operation.

56wpm A split screen displays two or more different images at the same time; it can, for example, display two different pages of a legal document.

58wpm When using Windows, it's possible to place several programs on a screen and to change the size of a window or to change its position on a screen.

60wpm With the click of a mouse, one can use a button bar or a toolbar for fast access to features that are frequently applied when using a Windows program.

62wpm An active window can be reduced to an icon when you use Windows, enabling you to double-click another icon to open a new window for formatting and editing.

64wpm Turnaround time is the length of time needed for a document to be keyboarded, edited, proofread, corrected if required, printed, and returned to the originator.

66wpm A local area network is a system that uses cable or another means to allow high-speed communication among many kinds of electronic equipment within particular areas.

68wpm To search and replace means to direct the word processor to locate a character, word, or group of words wherever it occurs in the document and replace it with newer text.

SKILLBUILDING

70wpm Indexing is the ability of a word processor to accumulate a list of words that appear in a document, including page numbers, and then print a revised list in alphabetic order.

72wpm When a program needs information from you, a dialog box will appear on the desktop. Once the dialog box appears, you must identify the option you desire and then choose that option.

74wpm A facsimile is an exact copy of a document, and it is also a process by which images, such as typed letters, graphs, and signatures, are scanned, transmitted, and then printed on paper.

76wpm Compatibility refers to the ability of a computer to share information with another computer or to communicate with some other apparatus. It can be accomplished by using hardware or software.

78wpm Some operators like to personalize their desktops when they use Windows by making various changes. For example, they can change their screen colors and the pointer so that they will have more fun.

80wpm Wraparound is the ability of a word processor to move words from one line to another line and from one page to the next page as a result of inserting and deleting text or changing the size of margins.

82wpm It is possible when using Windows to evaluate the contents of different directories on the screen at the very same time. You can then choose to copy or move a particular file from one directory to another.

84wpm List processing is a capability of a word processor to keep lists of data that can be updated and sorted in alphabetic or numeric order. A list can also be added to any document that is stored in one's computer.

86wpm A computer is a wondrous device, which accepts data that are input and then processes the data and produces output. The computer performs its work by using one or more stored programs, which provide the instructions.

88wpm The configuration is the components that make up your word processing system. Most systems include the keyboard that is used for entering data, a central processing unit, at least one disk drive, a monitor, and a printer.

90wpm Help for Windows can be used whenever you see a Help button in a dialog box or on a menu bar. Once you finish reading about a topic that you have selected, you will see a list of some related topics from which you can choose.

92wpm When you want to look at the contents of two windows when using Windows, you will want to reduce the window size. Do this by pointing to a border or a corner of a window and dragging it until the window is the size that you want.

94wpm Scrolling means to display a large quantity of text by rolling it horizontally or vertically past the display screen. As the text disappears from the top section of the monitor, new text will appear at the bottom section of the monitor.

96wpm The Windows Print Manager is used to install and configure printers, join network printers, and monitor the printing of documents. Windows requires that a default printer be identified, but you can change the designation of it at any point.

98wpm A stop code is a command that makes a printer pause while it is printing to permit an operator to insert text, change the font style, or change the kind of paper in the printer. To resume printing, the operator must use a special key or command.

100wpm A computerized message system is a class of electronic mail that enables any operator to key a message on any computer terminal and have the message stored for later retrieval by the recipient, who can then display the message on his or her terminal.

102wpm Many different graphics software programs have been brought on the market in recent years. These programs can be very powerful in helping with a business presentation. If there is any need to share data, using one of these programs could be quite helpful.

104wpm Voice mail has become an essential service that many people in the business world use. This enables anyone who places a call to your phone to leave a message if you cannot answer it at that time. This special feature helps lots of workers to be more productive.

Progressive Practice: Numbers

This skillbuilding routine contains a series of 30-second timed writings that range from 16wpm to 80wpm. The first time you use these timed writings, take a 1-minute timed writing on the Entry Timed Writing paragraph. Note your speed.

Select a passage that is 4 to 6wpm *lower* than your current alphabetic speed. (The reason for selecting a lower speed goal is that sentences with numbers are more difficult to type.) Take six 30-second timed writings on the passage.

Your goal each time is to complete the passage within 30 seconds with no errors. When you have achieved your goal, move on to the next passage and repeat the procedure.

Entry Timed Writing

Their bags were filled with 10 sets of jars, 23 cookie 11
cutters, 4 baking pans, 6 coffee mugs, 25 plates, 9 dessert 23
plates, 7 soup bowls, 125 recipe cards, and 8 recipe boxes. 35
They delivered these 217 items to 20487 Mountain Boulevard. 47
| 1 | 2 | 3 | 4 | 5 | 6 | 7 | 8 | 9 | 10 | 11 | 12

16wpm There were now 21 children in Room 2110.

18wpm Fewer than 12 of the 121 boxes arrived today.

20wpm Maybe 12 of the 21 applicants met all 15 criteria.

22wpm There were 34 letters addressed to 434 West Cranbrooke.

24wpm Jane reported that there were 434 freshmen and 43 transfers.

26wpm The principal assigned 3 of those 4 students to Room 343 at noon.

28wpm Only 1 or 2 of the 34 latest invoices were more than 1 page in length.

30wpm They met 11 of the 12 players who received awards from 3 of the 4 trainers.

32wpm Those 5 vans carried 46 passengers on the first trip and 65 on the next 3 trips.

34wpm We first saw 3 and then 4 beautiful eagles on Route 65 at 5 a.m. on Tuesday, June 12.

36wpm The 16 companies produced 51 of the 62 records that received awards for 3 of 4 categories.

38wpm The 12 trucks hauled the 87 cows and 65 horses to the farm, which was about 21 miles northeast.

40wpm She moved from 87 Bayview Drive to 657 Cole Street and then 3 blocks south to 412 Gulbranson Avenue.

42wpm My 7 or 8 buyers ordered 7 dozen in sizes 5 and 6 after the 14 to 32 percent discounts had been bestowed.

44wpm There were 34 men and 121 women waiting in line at the gates for the 65 to 87 tickets to the Cape Cod concert.

46wpm Steve had listed 5 or 6 items on Purchase Order 241 when he saw that Purchase Requisition 87 contained 3 or 4 more.

48wpm Your items numbered 278 will sell for about 90 percent of the value of the 16 items that have code numbers shown as 435.

50wpm The managers stated that 98 of those 750 randomly selected new valves had about 264 defects, far exceeding the usual 31 norm.

52wpm Half of the 625 volunteers received over 90 percent of the charity pledges. Approximately 83 of the 147 agencies will have funds.

54wpm Merico hired 94 part-time workers to help the 378 full-time employees during the 62-day period when sales go up by 150 percent or more.

56wpm Kaye only hit 1 for 4 in the first 29 games after an 8-game streak in which she batted 3 for 4. She then hit at a .570 average for 6 games.

58wpm The mail carrier delivered 98 letters during the week to 734 Oak Street and also took 52 letters to 610 Faulkner Road as he returned on Route 58.

60wpm Pat said that about 1 in 5 of the 379 swimmers had a chance of being among the top 20. The best 6 of those 48 divers will receive the 16 best awards.

62wpm It rained from 3 to 6 inches, and 18 of those 20 farmers were fearful that 4 to 7 inches more would flood about 95 acres along 3 miles of the new Route 78.

64wpm Those 7 sacks weighed 48 pounds, more than the 30 pounds that I had thought. All 24 believe the 92-pound bag is at least 15 or 16 pounds above its true weight.

66wpm They bought 7 of the 8 options for 54 of the 63 vehicles last month. They now own over 120 dump trucks for use in 9 of the 15 new regions in the big 20-county area.

68wpm Andy was 8 or 9 years old when they moved to 632 Glendale Street away from the 1700 block of Horseshoe Lane, which is about 45 miles directly west of Boca Raton, FL 33434.

70wpm Doug had read 575 pages in the 760-page book by March 30; Darlene had read only 468 pages. Darlene has read 29 of those optional books since October 19, and Doug has read 18.

72wpm That school district has 985 elementary students, 507 middle school students, and 463 high school students; the total of 1,955 is 54, or 2.84 percent, over last year's grand total.

74wpm Attendance at last year's meeting was 10,835. The goal for this year is to have 11,764 people. This will enable us to plan for an increase of 929 participants, a rise of 8.57 percent.

76wpm John's firm has 158 stores, located in 109 cities in the West. The company employs 3,540 males and 2,624 females, a total of 6,164 employees. About 4,750 of those employees work part-time.

78wpm Memberships were as follows: 98 members in the Drama Guild, 90 members in Zeta Tau, 82 members in Theta Phi, 75 in the Bowling Club, and 136 in the Ski Club. This meant that 481 joined a group.

80wpm The association had 684 members from the South, 830 members from the North, 1,023 members from the East, and 751 from the West. The total membership was 3,288; these numbers increased by 9.8 percent.

Paced Practice

The Paced Practice skillbuilding routine builds speed and accuracy in short, easy steps by using individualized goals and immediate feedback. You may use this program at any time after completing Lesson 9.

This section contains a series of 2-minute timed writings for speeds ranging from 16wpm to 96wpm. The first time you use these timed writings, take the 1-minute Entry Timed Writing.

Select a passage that is 2wpm higher than your current typing speed. Then use this two-stage practice pattern to achieve each speed goal: (1) concentrate on speed, and (2) work on accuracy.

Speed Goal. To determine your speed goal, take three 2-minute timed writings in total. Your goal each time is to complete the passage in 2 minutes without regard to errors. When you have achieved your speed goal, work on accuracy.

Accuracy Goal. To type accurately, you need to slow down—just a bit. Therefore, to reach your accuracy goal, drop back 2wpm from the previous passage. Take consecutive timed writings on this passage until you can complete the passage in 2 minutes with no more than 2 errors.

For example, if you achieved a speed goal of 54wpm, you should then work on an accuracy goal of 52wpm. When you have achieved 52wpm for accuracy, move up 4wpm (for example, to the 56-wpm passage) and work for speed again.

Entry Timed Writing

If you can dream it, you can live it. Follow your 10
heart. There are many careers, from the mundane to the 21
exotic to the sublime. Start your career planning now. 32
Prepare for the future by exploring your talents, skills, 44
and interests. 47

| 1 | 2 | 3 | 4 | 5 | 6 | 7 | 8 | 9 | 10 | 11 | 12

16wpm

Your future is now.[1] Seize each day. After[2] you have explored[3] your personal interests,[4] study the sixteen[5] career clusters[6] for a broad range of[7] job possibilities.[8]

18wpm

While exploring various[1] job options, think about[2] what a job means[3] to you. A job can mean[4] something you do simply[5] to earn money or something[6] you find more rewarding[7] and challenging.[8]

20wpm

If you have a job you enjoy,[1] work means more than[2] just receiving wages.[3] It means using your talents,[4] being among people[5] with like interests, making a[6] contribution, and gaining[7] a sense of satisfaction.[8]

22wpm

What is the difference between a job and a career? Think carefully. A job is work that people do for money. A career is a sequence of related jobs built on a foundation of interests, knowledge, training, and experiences.

24wpm

Learn more about the world of work by looking at the sixteen career clusters. Most jobs are included in one of the clusters that have been organized by the government. During your exploration of careers, list the clusters that interest you.

26wpm

Once you identify your career clusters of interest, look at the jobs within each cluster. Find out what skills and aptitudes are needed, what education and training are required, what the work environment is like, and what is the possibility for advancements.

28wpm

Use your career center and school or public libraries to research career choices. Search the Internet. Consult with professionals for another perspective of a specific career. As you gather information about career options, you may discover other interesting career possibilities.

30wpm

Gain insights into a career by becoming a volunteer, participating in an internship, or working a part-time or temporary job within a chosen field. You will become more familiar with a specific job while developing your skills. You'll gain valuable experience, whether you choose that career or not.

32wpm

Whichever path you choose, strive for a high level of pride in yourself and your work. Your image is affected by what you believe other people think of you as well as by how you view yourself. Evaluate your level of confidence in yourself. If you have self-doubts, begin to build up your self-confidence and self-esteem.

34wpm

Self-esteem is essential for a positive attitude, and a positive attitude is essential for success in the world of work. While you cannot control everything that happens at work, you can control how you react. Your attitude matters. Becoming more confident and cultivating positive thoughts can bring you power in your life and on the job.

36wpm

Several factors lead to success on the job. People who have studied the factors say that it is the personal traits that often determine who is promoted or who is not. One of the finest traits a person can possess is the trait of being likable. Being likable means a person is honest, courteous, loyal, thoughtful, pleasant, kind, and most assuredly, positive.

38wpm

If you are likable, probably you relate well with others. Your kindness serves you well in the workplace. Developing good interpersonal relationships with coworkers will make work more enjoyable. After all, think of all the hours you will spend together. By showing that you are willing to collaborate with your coworkers, most likely you will receive their cooperation in return.

40wpm

Cooperation begins on the first day of your new job. When you work for a company, you become part of the team. Meeting people and learning new skills can be exciting. For some people, however, any new situation can trigger anxiety. The best advice is to remain calm, do your job to the best of your ability, learn the workplace policies, be flexible, avoid being too critical, and always be positive.

42wpm

When you begin a new job, even if you have recently received your college diploma, chances are you will start at the bottom of the organizational chart. Each of us has to start somewhere. But don't despair. With hard work and determination, soon you will be climbing up the corporate ladder. If you are clever, you will embrace even the most tedious tasks, take everything in stride, and use every opportunity to learn.

44wpm

If you think learning is restricted to the confines of an academic institution, think again. You have plenty to learn on the job, even if it is a job for which you have been trained. As a new worker, you won't be expected to know everything. When necessary, do not hesitate to ask your employer questions. Learn all you can about your job and the company. Use the new information to enhance your job performance and to prepare for success.

46wpm

Begin every valuable workday by prioritizing all your tasks. Decide which tasks must be done immediately and which can wait. List the most important tasks first; then determine the order in which each task must be done. After you complete a task, triumphantly cross it off your priority list. Do not procrastinate; that is, don't put off work you should do. If a task needs to be done, do it. You will be on top of your task list if you use your time wisely.

48wpm

Prevent the telephone from controlling your time by learning to manage your business phone calls. Phone calls can be extremely distracting from necessary tasks. When making an outgoing call, organize the topics you want to discuss. Gather needed materials such as pencils, papers, and files. Set a time limit, and stick to business. Give concise answers, summarize the points discussed, and end the conversation politely. Efficient telephone usage will help you manage your time.

50wpm

As with anything, practice makes perfect, but along the way, we all make mistakes. The difference between the successful people and those who are less successful is not that the successful people make fewer mistakes. It's that they don't give up. Instead of letting mistakes bring them down, they use their mistakes as opportunities to grow. If you make a mistake, be patient with yourself. You might be able to fix your mistake. Look for more opportunities for success to be just around the corner.

52wpm

Be patient with yourself when handling problems and accepting criticism. Handling criticism gracefully and maturely may be a challenge. Still, it is vital in the workplace. Criticism presented in a way that can help you learn and grow is constructive criticism . When you see criticism as helpful, it's easier to handle. Believe it or not, there are some employees who welcome criticism. It teaches them better ways to succeed on the job. Strive to improve how you accept constructive criticism, and embrace your growth.

54wpm

People experience continuous growth during a career. Goal setting is a helpful tool along any career path. Some people believe that goals provide the motivation needed to get to the place they want to be. Setting goals encourages greater achievements. The higher we set our goals, the greater the effort we will need to reach these goals. Each time we reach a target or come closer to a goal, we see an increase in our confidence and our performance, leading to greater accomplishments. And the cycle continues to spiral onward and upward.

56wpm

One goal we should all strive for is punctuality. When employees are tardy or absent from the workplace, it costs the company money. If you are frequently tardy or absent, others have to do their own work and cover for you. If you are absent often, your peers will begin to resent you, causing everyone stress in the department. Being late and missing work can damage the relationship with your manager and have a negative effect on your career. To avoid these potential problems, develop a personal plan to assure that you arrive every day on time or early.

58wpm

Holding a job is a major part of being an adult. Some people begin their work careers as adolescents. From the beginning, various work habits are developed that are as crucial to success as the actual job skills and knowledge that a person brings to the job. What traits are expected of workers? What do employers look for when they evaluate their employees? Important personal traits include being confident, cooperative, positive, and dependable. If you are organized, enthusiastic, and understanding, you have many of the qualities that employers value most in their employees.

60wpm

Being dependable is a desirable trait. When a project must be completed by a specific time, a manager will be reassured to know that reliable workers are going to meet the deadline. Workers who are dependable learn to utilize their time to achieve maximum results. Dependable workers can always be counted on, have good attendance records, are well prepared, and arrive on time ready to work. If a company wants to meet its goals, it must have a team of responsible and dependable workers. You, your coworkers, your supervisors, and your managers are all team members, working to reach common goals.

62wpm

The ability to organize is an important quality for the employee who wishes to display good work habits. The worker should have the ability to plan the work that needs to be completed and then be able to execute the plan in a timely manner. An employer requires a competent worker to be well organized. If an office worker is efficient, he or she handles requests swiftly and deals with correspondence without delay. The organized worker does not allow work to accumulate on the desk. Also, the organized office worker returns all phone calls immediately and makes lists of the activities that need to be done each day.

64wpm

Efficiency is another work habit that is desired. An efficient worker completes a task quickly and begins work on the next project eagerly. He or she thinks about ways to save steps and time. For example, an efficient worker may plan a single trip to the copier with several copying jobs rather than multiple trips to do each separate job. Being efficient also means having the required supplies to successfully complete each job. An efficient employee zips along on each project, uses time wisely, and stays focused on the present task. With careful and thorough planning, a worker who is efficient can accomplish more tasks in less time.

66wpm

Cooperation is another ideal work habit. As previously mentioned, cooperation begins on the first day on the job. Cooperation is thinking of all team members when making a decision. A person who cooperates is willing to do what is necessary for the good of the whole group. For you to be a team player, it is essential that you take extra steps to cooperate. Cooperation may mean being a good sport if you are asked to do something you would rather not do. It may mean you have to correct a mistake made by another person in the office. If every employee has the interests of the company at heart and works well as a team player, then cooperation is at work.

68wpm

Enthusiasm is still another work trait that is eagerly sought after by employers. Being enthusiastic means that a person has lots of positive energy. This is reflected in actions toward your work, coworkers, and employer. It has been noted that eagerness can be catching. If workers show they are eager to attempt any project, they will not only achieve the highest praise but will also be considered for career advancement. How much enthusiasm do you show at the workplace? Do you encourage people or complain to people? There will always be plenty of good jobs for employees who are known to have a wealth of zeal and a positive approach to the projects that they are assigned.

70wpm

Understanding is also a preferred work habit for every excellent worker. In today's world, virtually all business includes both men and women of different religions, races, cultures, work ethic, abilities, aptitudes, and attitudes. You'll interact with various types of people as customers, coworkers, and owners. Treat everyone fairly, openly, and honestly. Any type of prejudice is hurtful, offensive, and unacceptable. Prejudice cannot be tolerated in the office. Each employee must try to understand and accept everyone's differences. Because so many diverse groups of people work side by side in the workplace, it is essential that all coworkers maintain a high degree of mutual understanding.

72wpm

It can be concluded that certain work habits or traits can play a major role in determining the success of an employee. Most managers would be quick to agree on the importance of these traits. It is most probable that these habits would be evaluated on performance appraisal forms. Promotions, pay increases, new responsibilities, and your future with the company may be based on these evaluations. You should request regular job performance evaluations even if your company does not conduct them. This feedback will improve your job performance and career development by helping you grow. If you continually look for ways to improve your work habits and skills, then you will enjoy success in the workplace and beyond.

74wpm

You can be certain that no matter where you work, you will use some form of computer technology. Almost every business is dependent upon computers. Companies use such devices as voice mail, fax machines, cellular phones, and electronic schedules. Technology helps to accomplish work quickly and efficiently. A result of this rapidly changing technology is globalization, which is the establishment of worldwide communication links between people. Our world is becoming a smaller, global village. We must expand our thinking beyond the office walls. We must become aware of what happens in other parts of the world. Those events may directly affect you and your workplace. The more you know, the more valuable you will become to the company.

76wpm

Technological advancements are affecting every aspect of our lives. For example, the advent of the Internet has changed how we receive and send information. It is the world's largest information network. The Internet is often called the information superhighway because it is a vast network of computers that connect people and resources worldwide. It is an exciting medium to help you access the latest information. You can even learn about companies by visiting their Web sites. Without any doubt, we are all globally connected, and information technology services support those necessary connections. This industry offers many different employment opportunities. Keep in mind that proficiency in keyboarding is beneficial in this field and in other fields.

78wpm

It is amazing to discover the many careers in which keyboarding skill is necessary today, and the[1] use of the computer keyboard by executive chefs is a prime example. The chefs in major restaurants[2] must prepare parts or all of the meals served while directing the work of a staff of chefs, cooks,[3] and other kitchen staff. The computer has become a necessary tool for a variety of tasks, including[4] tracking inventories of food supplies. By observing which items[5] are favorites and which items are not requested, the chef can calculate food requirements, order food, and supervise the food[6] purchases. Additionally, the computer has proven to be a very practical tool for such tasks as[7] planning budgets, preparing purchase orders for vendors, creating menus, and printing out reports.[8]

80wpm

Advanced technology has opened the doors to a wider variety of amazing new products and services to[1] sell. It seems the more complex the products, the higher the price of the products, or the greater[2] the sales commission, the stiffer the competition. Selling these technical products requires detailed[3] product knowledge, good verbal skills, smooth sales rapport, and proficient keyboarding skills. Business[4] favors people with special training. For example, a pharmacy company may prefer a person with[5] knowledge in chemistry to sell its products. Selling is for people who thrive on challenges and changes[6] in products and services. Sales is appealing to people who enjoy using their powers of persuasion[7] to make the sales. The potential for good earnings is very high for the well-trained salesperson.[8]

82wpm

As you travel about in your sales job or type a report at the office or create Friday night's pasta special[1] for your five-star restaurant, always remember to put safety first. Accidents happen, but they don't[2] have to happen regularly or to have such serious consequences. Accidents cost businesses billions[3] of dollars annually in medical expenses, lost wages, and insurance claims. A part of your job is to make[4] certain you're not one of the millions of people injured on the job every year. You may believe you[5] work in a safe place, but accidents occur in all types of businesses. A few careless people cause most[6] accidents, so ensure your safety on the job. Safety doesn't just happen. Safety is the[7] careful awareness of many people who plan and put into action a safety program that benefits everyone.[8]

84wpm

In today's market, you need more than the necessary skill or the personal qualities described above to[1] succeed in the workplace. Employers also expect their employees to have ethics. Ethics are the principles[2] of conduct governing an individual or a group. Employees who work ethically do not lie, cheat, or steal.[3] They are honest and fair in their dealings with others. Employees who act ethically build a good reputation[4] for themselves and their company. They are known to be dependable and trustworthy. Unethical behavior[5] can have a spiraling effect. A single act can do a lot of damage. Even if you haven't held a job yet, you[6] have had experience with ethical problems. Life is full of many opportunities to behave ethically. Do the[7] right thing when faced with a decision. The ethics you practice today will carry over to your workplace.[8]

86wpm

Now that you know what is expected of you on the job, how do you make sure you will get the job? Almost everyone has experienced the interview process for a job. For some, the interview is a traumatic event, but it doesn't have to be stressful. Preparation is the key. Research the company with whom you are seeking employment. Formulate a list of questions. Your interview provides you the opportunity to interview the organization. Don't go empty-handed. Take a portfolio of items with you. Include copies of your resume with a list of three or more professional references, your academic transcript, and your certificates and licenses. Be sure to wear appropriate business attire. The outcome of the interview will be positive if you have enthusiasm for the job, match your qualifications to the company's needs, ask relevant questions, and listen clearly.

88wpm

How can you be the strongest candidate for the job? Be sure that your skills in reading, writing, mathematics, speaking, and listening are solid. These basic skills will help you listen well and communicate clearly, not only during a job interview, but also at your workplace. The exchange of information between senders and receivers is called communication. It doesn't matter which occupation you choose; you will spend most of your career using these basic skills to communicate with others. You will use the basic skills as tools to gain information, solve problems, and share ideas. You will use these skills to meet the needs of your customers. The majority of jobs available during the next decades will be in the industries that will require direct customer contacts. Your success will be based upon your ability to communicate effectively with customers and coworkers.

90wpm

Writing effectively can help you gain a competitive edge in your job search and throughout your career. Most of us have had occasion to write business letters whether to apply for a job, to comment on a product or service, or to place an order. Often it seems easy to sit and let our thoughts flow freely. In other cases, we seem to struggle to find the proper wording while trying to express our thoughts in exactly the right way. Writing skill can improve with practice. Implement the following principles to develop your writing skill. Try to use language that you would be comfortable using in person. Use words that are simple, direct, kind, confident, and professional. When possible, use words that emphasize the positive side. Remember to proofread your work. Well-organized thoughts and proper grammar, spelling, and punctuation show the reader that you care about the quality of your work.

92wpm

Listening is an essential skill of the communication process. It is crucial for learning, getting along, and forming relationships. Do you think you are an active or passive listener? Listening is not a passive activity. Conversely, active listening is hearing what is being said and interpreting its meaning. Active listening makes you a more effective communicator because you react to what you have heard. Study the following steps to increase your listening skills. Do not cut people off; let them develop their ideas before you speak. If a message is vague, write down your questions or comments, and wait for the entire presentation or discussion to be finished. Reduce personal and environmental distractions by focusing on the message. Keep an open mind. Be attentive and maintain eye contact whenever possible. By developing these basic communication skills, you will become more confident and more effective.

94wpm

Speaking is also a form of communication. In the world of work, speaking is an important way in which to share information. Regardless of whether you are speaking to an audience of one or one hundred, you will want to make sure that your listeners get your message. Be clear about your purpose, your audience, and your subject. A purpose is the overall goal or reason for speaking. An audience is anyone who receives information. The subject is the main topic or key idea. Research your subject. Using specific facts and examples will give you credibility. As you speak, be brief and direct. Progress logically from point to point. Speak slowly and pronounce clearly all your words. Do people understand what you say or ask you to repeat what you've said? Is the sound of your voice friendly and pleasant or shrill and off-putting? These factors influence how your message is received. A good idea is worthless if you can't communicate it.

96wpm

Developing a career is a process. You have looked at your interests, values, skills, aptitudes, and attitudes. Your exploration into the world of work has begun. The journey doesn't stop here, for the present is the perfect place to start thinking about the future. It's where you begin to take steps toward your goals. It's where you can really make a difference. As you set personal and career goals, remember the importance of small steps. Each step toward a personal goal or career goal is a small victory. That feeling of success encourages you to take other small steps. Each step builds onto the next. Continue exploring your personal world as well as the world you share with others. Expect the best as you go forward. Expect a happy life. Expect loving relationships. Expect success in life. Expect fulfilling and satisfying work in a job you truly love. Last but not least, expect that you have something special to offer the world, because you do.

Supplementary Timed Writings

Supplementary Timed Writing 1

All problem solving, whether personal or academic, 10
involves decision making. You make decisions in order to 21
solve problems. On occasion, problems occur as a result of 33
decisions you have made. For example, you may decide to 44
smoke, but later in life, you face the problem of nicotine 56
addiction. You may decide not to study mathematics and 67
science because you think that they are too difficult. 78
Because of this choice, many career opportunities will be 90
closed to you. There is a consequence for every action. Do 102
you see that events in your life do not just happen, but 113
that they are the result of your choices and decisions? 124

How can you prepare your mind for problem solving? A 135
positive attitude is a great start. Indeed, your attitude 147
affects the way in which you solve a problem or make a 158
decision. Approach your studies, such as science and math 170
courses, with a positive and inquisitive attitude. Try to 182
perceive academic problems as puzzles to solve rather than 192
homework to avoid. 198

Critical thinking is a method of problem solving that 209
involves decoding, analyzing, reasoning, evaluating, and 220
processing information. It is fundamental for successful 231
problem solving. Critical thinking is a willingness to 242
explore, probe, question, and search for answers. Problems 254
may not always be solved on the first try. Don't give up. 266
Try, try again. Finding a solution takes sustained effort. 278
Use critical thinking skills to achieve success in today's 290
fast-paced and highly competitive world of business. 300

| 1 | 2 | 3 | 4 | 5 | 6 | 7 | 8 | 9 | 10 | 11 | 12

Supplementary Timed Writing 2

For many, the Internet is an important resource in 10
their private and professional lives. The Internet provides 22
quick access to countless Web sites that contain news, 33
products, games, entertainment, and many other types of 44
information. The Web pages on these sites can be designed, 56
authored, and posted by anyone, anywhere around the world. 68
Utilize critical thinking when reviewing all Web sites. 79

Just because something is stated on the radio, printed 90
in the newspaper, or shown on television doesn't mean that 102
it's true, real, accurate, or correct. This applies to 113
information found on the Internet as well. Don't fall into 125
the trap of believing that if it's on the Net, it must be 137
true. A wise user of the Internet thinks critically about 149
data found on the Net and evaluates this material before 160
using it. 162

When evaluating a new Web site, think about who, what, 173
how, when, and where. Who refers to the author of the Web 185
site. The author may be a business, an organization, or a 197
person. What refers to the validity of the data. Can this 209
data be verified by a reputable source? How refers to the 221
viewpoint of the author. Is the data presented without 232
prejudice? When refers to the time frame of the data. Is 244
this recent data? Where refers to the source of the data. 256
Is this data from an accurate source? By answering these 267
critical questions, you will learn more about the accuracy 279
and dependability of a Web site. As you surf the Net, be 290
very cautious. Anyone can publish on the Internet. 300

| 1 | 2 | 3 | 4 | 5 | 6 | 7 | 8 | 9 | 10 | 11 | 12

Supplementary Timed Writing 3

Office employees perform a variety of tasks during 10
their workday. These tasks vary from handling telephone 21
calls to forwarding personal messages, from sending short 33
e-mail messages to compiling complex office reports, and 44
from writing simple letters to assembling detailed letters 56
with tables, graphics, and imported data. Office workers 67
are a fundamental part of a company's structure. 77

The office worker uses critical thinking in order to 88
accomplish a wide array of daily tasks. Some of the tasks 100
are more urgent than other tasks and should be completed 111
first. Some tasks take only a short time, while others take 123
a lot more time. Some tasks demand a quick response, while 135
others may be taken up as time permits or even postponed 147
until the future. Some of the tasks require input from 158
coworkers or managers. Whether a job is simple or complex, 170
big or small, the office worker must decide what is to be 182
tackled first by determining the priority of each task. 193

When setting priorities, critical thinking skills are 204
essential. The office worker evaluates each aspect of the 216
task. It is a good idea to identify the size of the task, 228
determine its complexity, estimate its effort, judge its 239
importance, and set its deadline. Once the office worker 250
assesses each task that is to be finished within a certain 262
period of time, then the priority for completing all tasks 274
can be set. Critical thinking skills, if applied well, 285
can save the employer money or, if executed poorly, can 296
cost the employer. 300

| 1 | 2 | 3 | 4 | 5 | 6 | 7 | 8 | 9 | 10 | 11 | 12

Supplementary Timed Writing 4

Each day business managers make choices that keep 10
businesses running smoothly, skillfully, and profitably. 21
Each decision regarding staff, finances, operations, and 32
resources often needs to be quick and precise. To develop 44
sound decisions, managers must use critical thinking. They 56
gather all the essential facts so that they can make good, 68
well-informed choices. After making a decision, skilled 79
managers review their thinking process. Over time, they 90
refine their critical thinking skills. When they encounter 102
similar problems, they use their prior experiences to help 114
them solve problems with ease and in less time. 124

What type of decisions do you think managers make that 135
involve critical thinking? Human resources managers decide 147
whom to employ, what to pay a new employee, and where to 158
place a new worker. In addition, human resources managers 170
should be unbiased negotiators, resolving conflict between 182
other employees. Office managers purchase copy machines, 194
computers, software, and office supplies. Finance officers 206
prepare precise, timely financial statements. Top managers 218
control business policies, appoint mid-level managers, and 230
assess the success of the business. Plant supervisors set 242
schedules, gauge work quality, and evaluate workers. Sales 254
managers study all of the new sales trends, as well as 265
provide sales training and promotion materials. 275

Most managers use critical thinking to make wise, well- 286
thought-out decisions. They carefully check their facts, 297
analyze these facts, and make a final judgment based upon 309
these facts. They should also be able to clearly discern 320
fact from fiction. Through trial and error, managers learn 332
their own ways of solving problems and finding the most 343
effective and creative solutions. 350

| 1 | 2 | 3 | 4 | 5 | 6 | 7 | 8 | 9 | 10 | 11 | 12

Supplementary Timed Writing 5

In most classes, teachers want students to analyze 10
situations, draw conclusions, and solve problems. Each 21
of these tasks requires students to use thinking skills. 32
How do students acquire these skills? What is the process 44
students follow to develop thinking skills? 53

During the early years of life, children learn words 63
and then combine these words into sentences. From there, 74
they learn to declare ideas, share thoughts, and express 85
feelings. Students learn numbers and simple math concepts. 97
They may learn to read musical notes, to keep rhythm, to 108
sing songs, and to recognize many popular and classical 119
pieces of music. Students learn colors, identify shapes, 130
and begin drawing. During the early years, students learn 142
the basic problem-solving models. 149

One way to solve problems and apply thinking skills 159
is to use the scientific approach. This approach requires 171
the student to state the problem to be solved, gather all 183
the facts about the problem, analyze the problem, and pose 195
viable solutions. Throughout this process, teachers ask 206
questions that force students to expand their thinking 217
skills. Teachers may ask questions such as these: Did you 229
clearly state the problem? Did you get all the facts? Did 241
you get the facts from the right place? Did you assume 252
anything? Did you pose other possible solutions? Did you 263
keep an open mind to all solutions? Did you let your bias 275
come into play? Did you listen to others who might have 286
insights? Did you dig deep enough? Does the solution make 298
sense to you? 301

This simple four-step process for solving problems 311
gives students a model to use for school, for work, and 322
for life. While the process may not be used to solve every 334
problem, it does provide a starting point to begin using 345
critical thinking skills. 350

| 1 | 2 | 3 | 4 | 5 | 6 | 7 | 8 | 9 | 10 | 11 | 12

Supplementary Timed Writing 6

A major goal for nearly all educators is to teach 10
critical thinking skills to a class. Critical thinking, 21
which is the process of reasonably or logically deciding 32
what to do or believe, involves the ability to compare and 44
contrast, resolve problems, make decisions, analyze and 55
evaluate, and combine and transfer knowledge. These skills 67
benefit the student who eventually becomes a part of the 78
workforce. Whether someone is in a corporate setting, is 89
in a small business, or is self-employed, the environment 101
of today is highly competitive and skilled employees are in 113
great demand. 116

One factor in achieving success in the workforce is 127
having the ability to deal with the varied demands of the 139
fast-paced business world. Required skills are insightful 150
decision making, creative problem solving, and earnest 162
communication among diverse groups. These groups could be 174
employees, management, employers, investors, customers, 185
or clients. 187

In school, we learn the details of critical thinking. 198
This knowledge extends far beyond the boundaries of the 209
classroom. It lasts a lifetime. We use critical thinking 220
throughout our daily lives. We constantly analyze and 231
evaluate music, movies, conversations, fashion, magazine 242
or newspaper articles, and television programs. We all had 254
experience using critical thinking skills before we even 265
knew what they were. So keep on learning, growing, and 276
experimenting. The classroom is the perfect setting for 287
exploration. Take this opportunity to see how others solve 299
problems, give each other feedback, and try out new ideas 311
in a safe environment. 316

A person who has learned critical thinking skills is 327
equipped with the essential skills for achieving success 338
in today's workforce. There are always new goals to reach. 350

| 1 | 2 | 3 | 4 | 5 | 6 | 7 | 8 | 9 | 10 | 11 | 12

Supplementary Timed Writing 7

Use your unique creativity when applying critical 10
thinking skills. One of the first steps in unlocking your 22
creativity is to realize that you have control over your 33
thinking; it doesn't control you. Creativity is using new 45
or different methods to solve problems. Many inventions 56
involved a breakthrough in traditional thinking, and the 67
result was an amazing experience. For example, Einstein 78
broke with tradition by trying lots of obscure formulas 89
that changed scientific thought. Your attitude can form 100
mental blocks that keep you from being creative. When you 112
free your mind, the rest will follow. 120

Do your best to unleash your mind's innate creativity. 131
Turn problems into puzzles. When you think of a task as a 143
puzzle, a challenge, or a game instead of a difficult 154
problem, you open your mind and encourage your creative 165
side to operate. Creative ideas often come when you are 176
having fun and are involved in an unrelated activity. 187
You will find that when your defenses are down, your brain 199
is relaxed and your subconscious is alive; then creative 210
thoughts can flow. 214

Habit often restricts you from trying new approaches 225
to problem solving. Remember, there is usually more than 237
one solution. Empty your mind of the idea of only one way 249
of looking at a problem and strive to see situations in a 261
fresh, new way. How many times have you told yourself that 273
you must follow the rules and perform tasks in a certain 284
way? If you want to be creative, look at things in a new 295
way, break the pattern, explore new options, and challenge 307
the rules. If you are facing a difficult problem and can't 319
seem to find a solution, take a quick walk or relax for 330
a few minutes; then go back to the problem renewed. When 341
working on homework or taking a test, always work the 352
easiest problems first. Success builds success. 362

A sense of humor is key to being creative. Silly and 373
irrelevant ideas can lead to inventive solutions. Humor 384
generates ideas, puts you in a creative state of mind, 395
and makes work exciting! 400

| 1 | 2 | 3 | 4 | 5 | 6 | 7 | 8 | 9 | 10 | 11 | 12

Supplementary Timed Writing 8

Keyboarding is a popular business course for many 10
students. The major objectives of a keyboarding course are 22
to develop touch control of the keyboard and proper typing 34
techniques, build basic speed and accuracy, and provide 45
practice in applying those basic skills to the formatting 57
of letters, reports, tables, memos, and other kinds of 68
personal and business communications. In the early part of 80
a keyboarding course, students learn to stroke by touch 91
using specific techniques. They learn to hit the keys in a 103
quick and accurate way. After the keys are learned and 114
practiced, students move into producing documents of all 125
sizes and types for personal and vocational use. 135

When you first learn keyboarding, there are certain 145
parameters, guidelines, and exercises to follow. There are 157
rules intended to help you learn and eventually master the 169
keyboard. Creating documents requires students to apply 180
critical thinking. What format or layout should be used? 191
What font and font size would be best? Are all the words 202
spelled correctly? Does the document look neat? Are the 213
figures accurate? Are punctuation and grammar correct? 224

There is a lot to learn in the world of keyboarding. 235
Be persistent, patient, and gentle with yourself. Allow 246
failure in class and on the job; that's how we learn. It's 258
okay to admit mistakes. Mistakes are stepping-stones for 269
growth and creativity. Being creative has a lot to do with 281
risk taking and courage. It takes courage to explore new 292
ways of thinking and to risk looking different, being 303
silly and impractical, and even being wrong. Your path to 315
creativity is such a vital component of your critical 326
thinking skills. Allow your creative thoughts to flow 337
freely when producing each of your keyboarding tasks. 348

Keyboarding skill and personal creativity are valuable 359
attributes for life and on the job. The worker who can see 371
situations and problems in a fresh way, reason logically, 383
explore options, and come up with inventive ideas is sure 395
to be a valuable employee. 400

| 1 | 2 | 3 | 4 | 5 | 6 | 7 | 8 | 9 | 10 | 11 | 12

Supplementary Timed Writing 9

One of the most important decisions we all have to 10
face is choosing a career. The possibilities can appear 21
overwhelming. Fear not! Your critical thinking skills will 33
save you! Start your career planning today. Begin with 44
self-assessment. What are your interests? Do you enjoy 55
working indoors or outdoors? Do you prefer working with 66
numbers or with words? Are you the independent type or 77
would you rather work with a group? What are your favorite 89
academic studies? Think about these questions and then 100
create a list of your interests, skills, aptitudes, and 111
values. What you discover about yourself will help you in 123
finding the career that is right for you. 131

After you have explored your personal interests, look 142
at the sixteen career clusters for a wide range of job 153
prospects. Most jobs are included in one of these clusters 165
that have been organized by the government. During your 176
exploration, make a note of the clusters that interest you 188
and investigate these clusters. 194

Gather as much information as possible by using all 205
available resources. Scan the Help Wanted section in the 216
major Sunday newspapers for job descriptions and salaries. 228
Search the Net. The Internet provides electronic access to 240
worldwide job listings. If you want to know more about a 251
specific company, access its home page. Go to your college 263
placement office. Sign up for interviews with companies 274
that visit your campus. Visit your local school or county 286
library and ask the reference librarian for occupational 297
handbooks. Talk with people in your field of interest to 308
ask questions and get advice. Attend chapter meetings of 319
professional organizations to network with people working 331
in your chosen profession. Volunteer, intern, or work a 342
part-time or temporary job within your career choice for 353
valuable, first-hand insight. Taking an initiative in your 365
job search will pay off. 370

A career search requires the use of critical thinking 381
skills. These skills will help you to choose the career 392
that will match your skills and talents. 400

| 1 | 2 | 3 | 4 | 5 | 6 | 7 | 8 | 9 | 10 | 11 | 12

Ten-Key Numeric Keypad

Goal

- To control the ten-key numeric keypad keys.

Some computer keyboards have a separate ten-key numeric keypad located to the right of the alphanumeric keyboard. The arrangement of the keypad enables you to type numbers more rapidly than you can when using the top row of the alphanumeric keyboard.

To input numbers using the ten-key numeric keypad, you must activate the Num Lock (Numeric Lock) key. Usually, an indicator light signals that the Num Lock is activated.

On the keypad, 4, 5, and 6 are the home keys. Place your fingers on the keypad home row as follows:

- First finger (J finger) on 4
- Second finger (K finger) on 5
- Third finger (L finger) on 6

The keypad keys are controlled as follows:

- First finger controls 1, 4, and 7
- Second finger controls 2, 5, and 8
- Third finger controls 3, 6, 9, and decimal point
- Right thumb controls 0
- Fourth finger controls ENTER

Since different computers have different arrangements of ten-key numeric keypads, study the arrangement of your keypad. The illustration shows the most common arrangement. If your keypad is arranged differently from the one shown in the illustration, check with your instructor for the correct placement of your fingers on the keypad.

NEW KEYS

A. Use the first finger to control the 4 key, the second finger to control the 5 key, and the third finger to control the 6 key.

Keep your eyes on the copy.

Before beginning, check to be sure the Num Lock key is activated.

Type the first column from top to bottom. Next, type the second column; then type the third column. Press ENTER after typing the final digit of each number.

A. THE 4, 5, AND 6 KEYS

444	456	454
555	654	464
666	445	546
455	446	564
466	554	654
544	556	645
566	664	666
644	665	555
655	456	444
456	654	456

B. Use the 4 finger to control the 7 key, the 5 finger to control the 8 key, and the 6 finger to control the 9 key.

Keep your eyes on the copy.

Press ENTER after typing the final digit of each number.

B. THE 7, 8, AND 9 KEYS

474	585	696
747	858	969
774	885	996
447	558	669
744	855	966
477	588	699
444	555	666
747	858	969
774	885	996
747	858	969

C. Use the 4 finger to control the 1 key, the 5 finger to control the 2 key, and the 6 finger to control the 3 key.

Keep your eyes on the copy.

Press ENTER after typing the final digit of each number.

C. THE 1, 2, AND 3 KEYS

444	555	666
111	222	333
144	225	336
441	552	663
144	255	366
411	522	633
444	555	666
414	525	636
141	252	363
411	525	636

D. Use the right thumb to control the 0 key.

Keep your eyes on the copy.

Press ENTER after typing the final digit of each number.

D. THE 0 KEY

404	470	502
505	580	603
606	690	140
707	410	250
808	520	360
909	630	701
101	407	802
202	508	903
303	609	405
505	401	506

E. Use the 6 finger to control the decimal key.

Keep your eyes on the copy.

Press ENTER after typing the final digit of each number.

E. THE . KEY

4.5	7.8	1.2
6.5	9.8	3.2
4.4	7.7	1.1
4.4	7.7	1.1
5.5	8.8	2.2
5.5	8.8	2.2
6.6	9.9	3.3
6.5	9.9	3.3
4.5	7.8	1.2
6.5	8.9	1.3

INDEX

NOTE: Page numbers preceded by A- indicate material in Appendix; page numbers preceded by R- indicate material in Reference Manual; page numbers preceded by SB- indicate material in Skillbuilding supplement.

B

C

D

E

N

O

P

Q

R

S

T